Boo Capone
The Untold Story
of a Former LA Gang Leader
& The Original
Five Deuce Hoover Gangsta Crips

Written by
Marcus Samuel Diggs

Editor & Illustrator
Anthony "Rico" Rolle

Co-Editor & Publicist
Richard "Joker" Jason
Special Thanks for Historical Contributions & Shared Memories
Anthony "Insane Fish" Evans | Richard "Lovely" Nevel
Calvin "Spookee" Carter | Brian "ScHool Boy" Harris | Kennedy "Ken Dogg" Evans |
Ray "Big Fat Rat" Simmons | Ravele "Coke Dogg" Douglas | Big Mike Evans
Kimanthi "KiKi" Douglass | Thadron "Ten Speed" Beal
Trent "T-Dogg" Childs | Virgil "Chim-Chim" Meakins | Mark "Sniper" McNabb Leonard
"Lil Dre Dogg" Webb | Jerome "Boscoe" Oates |
Tim "Madman" Davis | Roland "Lil Bandit" Nevel | "Baby Loon" | "Big Face" | Terrell
"Boom-Boom" Hill | Ricky "Ric Roc" Brown | "La Giggles" |
Hoover Kim Brown | Dalonte "Coconut" James | Marcus "Blue Ragg" Baugh | "Chino" |
Marquis " Lil CeeCee" Lofton | Naomi Suehiro | "T-Baby" |
Perkeysha "KeytaBoo" Brewer | "Jaystone2" | Tony "Silent" Washington
oG Tony Stacy | Travis "Big Bub" Washington | Antoine "Pretty Tony" Reed |
Ray "Dhanifu Bey" Cook | Charles "Q-Bone" Rachel

Media contact:
bigboocapone@gmail.com
Write Mr. Marcus Diggs via GTL.
Send commissary via JPAY:
Booking # D13033
California State Prison Solano

I dedicate this book to my Mother & Father, thank you for everything you have done for me. My children Janaye, Tori, Joshua & Jeremiah, My granddaughters Amora & Imani, and my grandson Lil Tori. My nieces & nephews, Lil Tray ball, Lil Pebbles(P2), Baby Pebbles (P3), Kesh Dogg, Lady Dre Dogg, Lil Tiny Dre Dogg, Dun-Dun (Runna), Young Dre Dogg (FiggFace), Boca, D-Mack, Marlisha, Marquita & Lil James. Finally, the Queens of the Fifties, my big sister Linda Gill, Naomi, Mama Mary & Brenda Lee. Thank you for sheltering us, nurturing us, and your unwavering love & commitment.

Based on a True Story.
Some scenarios in this book are fictitious & for entertainment purposes.
Any similarity to actual persons, living or dead, is coincidental. I have
changed some names to protect individuals' privacy.
To maintain the anonymity of the individuals involved,
I have changed some details. Some stories are based on news articles & court
documents & not firsthand knowledge.
These are my memories, from my perspective, and I have tried to represent
events as faithfully as possible.

INTRODUCTION: 6

CHAPTER 1: "I'M BIG BOO CAPONE FROM FIVE-DEUCE HOOVER   12

CHAPTER 2: "FROM THE BAYOU TO THE BAY"   22

CHAPTER 3: SON OF THE REVOLUTION 26

CHAPTER 4: "UNCLE JAMES RAY & THE GLADIATORS" 32

CHAPTER 5: "THE GANGSTA MIDGETS & A GIANT"   36

CHAPTER 6:" THE 52ND STREET SCHOOL OF HARD KNOCKS   46

CHAPTER 7: THE KIWÉ- OG HERBERT GATES & THE FIVE-DEUCE UNDERGROUND 61

CHAPTER 8: "KING CURT & THE ART OF THE HUSTLE" 73

CHAPTER 9: "GOD & GANGSTA"   76

CHAPTER 10: "THE ONE THAT FLEW OVER THE PIGEON COOP-   82

CHAPTER 11: "TOO HARD TOO CRY, TOO YOUNG TO DIE 94

CHAPTER 12: "UNDER THE HOOVER INFLUENCE"   110

CHAPTER 13: "UNCLE ROY: HOT GIRLS & HOT WHEELS 119

CHAPTER 14: "ONCE YOU FIGHT, YOU ALRIGHT"   125

CHAPTER 15: "HOOVER GANGSTA CRIPPIN' AIN'T EASY"   133

CHAPTER 16: THE BATTLE OF THE FIVE-DEUCES   144

CHAPTER 17: NOTHING BIGGER THAN THE PROGRAM   152

CHAPTER 18: "CRIMEY'S & BACK STABBERS"   161

CHAPTER 19: TOUGH HOOVER LOVE   173

CHAPTER 20: "NOTORIETY- A RISING GANGSTAR"   186

CHAPTER 21: "BOO VS COCO: TRIPPIN OFF WATER"   194

CHAPTER 22: "THE ODD COUPLE: BOO & SPOOKEE"   202

CHAPTER 23: "ONE NATION UNDER A GROOVE" 210

CHAPTER 24: "GRAND THEFT AUTO 5.2" 228

CHAPTER 25: "HEAT WAVE, BABES, AND FADES" 248

CHAPTER 26: PITY & PAYBACK 261

CHAPTER 27: JOY & PAIN   274

CHAPTER 28: "LOVE & WAR"   281

CHAPTER 29: PARTY & BULLSHIT   293

CHAPTER 30: "GET IT BACK IN BLOOD"   304

CHAPTER 31: " GOD FORGIVES HOOVER'S DON'T"   312

CHAPTER 32: "BECOMING BOO CAPONE"   321

CHAPTER 33: "THIN LINE BETWEEN LOCS & FOES"   338

CHAPTER 34: "LOVE & WAR PT. 2"   349

CHAPTER 35: "HOOVER BUSINESS"   356

CHAPTER 36: "FIGHT OR PIPE"   371

CHAPTER 37:"CRIP OR CRIP, RIDE OR DIE   376

CHAPTER 38: "NAKED BOOTIES & ROCK HOUSES"   382

CHAPTER 39: "SEPTEMBER TO REMEMBER"   390

CHAPTER 40: "WHEN IT RAINS, IT POURS"   400

CHAPTER 41: "DAYTONS & M-16'S   411

CHAPTER 42: "BAD BUSINESS & UGLY BITCHES"   416

CHAPTER 43: "LOVE & WAR PT.3"   424

CHAPTER 44: "TREASON SEASON"   438

CHAPTER 45: FIVE HUNDRED CRIPS   450

CHAPTER 46: "AMERICA'S MOST WANTED"   460

CHAPTER 47: CREATING MONSTERS   479

CHAPTER 48: "LIVING NIGHTMARES"   494

CHAPTER 49: MADMAN CHRISTMAS   510

CHAPTER 50: "CRAZY EIGHTY-EIGHT"   518

CHAPTER 51: " LOVE AFTER LOCK-UP"   543

CHAPTER 52: "FIVE-DEUCE VERSUS FIVE-O"   550

EPILOGUE: "THE REDEEMED"   580

INTRODUCTION:

There's a certain mystique & fascination with gangs that seems almost inevitable when considering the tangled web of crime, loyalty, and survival that is woven throughout the streets of America. This fascination often breeds misunderstanding, prejudice, and misconceptions, preventing the raw truth from being recognized. For over half a century, the Crips have been the subject of fascination & distortion, projected onto various platforms shaping the minds of a global audience.

I believe that a story is most authentic when told by its original author. So let me introduce myself. My name is Marcus Diggs, and in the streets of South Central I was known as Boo Capone. I was born to Crip, a straight-up, stomp-down Loc that's reputedly known as the Pioneer of Five-Deuce Hoover Gangsta Crip. This is my story, our story, the Fabulous Fifty Boys, the Original FDHGC, whom I'd Like to call the Hriginals & although our reputation precedes us, our true story has yet to be told in the raw & honest form I will share with you.

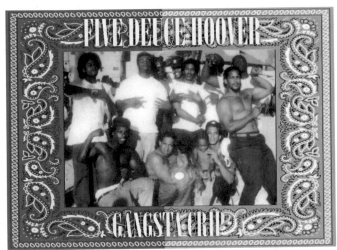

I've always believed in the collective, and that's what I'm always going to represent. Growing up in South Central, our loyalty, courage, and survival instincts were tested daily. As a child, I quickly learned how to fend for myself & stick by those you can trust.

We were born into this cold world, but we will not allow that to define who we are. We are complex, talented, and resourceful beings, with stories of pain, love, and sacrifice that go beyond the lens of newspaper headlines, Gangsta Rap lyrics, or Hollywood movies. We are the Hriginals, and we've earned the right to tell our story.

Our dedication to each other led to the formation of one of the most infamous & world-renowned Crip sets, Five-Deuce Hoover Gangsta Crip. We've seen it all—the rise & fall of our homies & enemies, the desperation to survive & ultimately, the sweet taste of triumph when we rose above it all. I will take you on a journey, a journey of our streets, our struggles, our choices, and the hidden potential that lies beneath.

Let me make one thing clear—this book is not an ode to crime, gang violence, or negativity. Through these words, I will share my triumphs & defeats, my hopes & fears, my pain & my strength. Some stories may shock & disturb you, but they reflect our reality, our lived experiences. In the unforgiving world of Crips & Bloods, some tales will never know the light of day beyond the confines of the streets & prisons they lived & died on.

Our story is told to acknowledge, inform, inspire, and encourage change. It is my hope that by sharing the Hriginals tale, I can help save lives in our global community, while also challenging my homies & the youth who aspire to pursue the life of a gangbanger. I challenge you to leverage your skills, talents, and passions to build something more lasting & purposeful. As the Hriginals, we have a duty to ourselves & our community to rewrite the narrative that third parties have painted of us.

I invite you on this journey to uncover & reveal the truth behind the Five-Deuce Hoover Gangsta Crip. Our tale is one of survival, love, loyalty, and most importantly, hope. The possibilities are endless, but it begins with understanding & embracing the nature of a Hoover Gangsta. We have the power to rise above & become leaders, entrepreneurs, and advocates for justice. Undoubtedly, our story is a testament to the perseverance & resilience of the human spirit. So, let's give them something more to talk about— **THE HRIGINALS**.

Every day I am struck by awe & bewilderment at the incredible excursion that life has taken me on. A voyage that, despite its rugged roads, has led me on a path forged in unity, passion, and brotherhood. From our humble start as kids in the Fifties, my comrades & I have watched, with both amazement & pride, as our creation spread its wings & made its mark on the world.

We never foresaw this remarkable phenomenon unfolding before our eyes. We now bear witness to how something we thought to be entirely ordinary has grown into something extraordinary. To understand the astonishing expansion that has followed our once seemingly inconsequential endeavors, one must first take a look back at the past.

It was in these early years when my homeboys & I simply banded together, united under a common purpose known as Crippin'. We were committed & devoted to each other. Little did we know that our deep bond would soon ignite a raging Canadian wildfire, coursing through the veins of society as if driven by an unstoppable force.

As the years went on & passed us by, the reach of FDHGC became both wider & stronger. The undeniable influence of our united front began to captivate ghettos across the nation, as if firm tendrils were branching out to touch every corner of America. From sea to shining sea, the reach of the Hoover Gangstas knew no bounds. Our presence has since come to be recognized by many.

We can be found in the farthest reaches of the country, from the South—across the warm shores of the Gulf of Mexico in Houston, Texas, Hattiesburg, Mississippi & Shreveport, Louisiana—to the North—from the bustling streets of Hempstead & New York City, to the toughest neighborhoods of New Jersey & Eastern Pennsylvania. Our indomitable spirit has stretched down along the East Coast, from the DMV to the Carolinas, across Georgia to Memphis & down to Florida.

The reach of the Five-Deuces does not simply end within the borders of the United States. Our impact has crossed oceans, transcending cultural barriers & international borders alike. FDHGC is represented beyond North America by individuals who embrace our message of unity & loyalty. The Hoovers have found their way into the hearts & minds of peoples from diverse backgrounds. Our banner flies proudly in countries such as Belize, Brazil, Dominican Republic, Mexico, Puerto Rico, throughout the West Indies & even Africa, Australia & Europe.

For a half century the Hoovers have held a significant position within popular Black culture, inspiring numerous elements of film, television, and music that pay homage to their legacy. The notable Hollywood productions *"South Central," "Baby Boy,"* & *"100 Kilos"* have all been heavily influenced by the lifestyle & experiences of the Hoovers, offering audiences an authentic portrayal of this storied group. Within the realm of black cinema, one character stands out as a tribute to the Hoovers – the legendary *"Doughboy,"* played by renowned rapper & actor Ice Cube in the classic film *"Boyz N the Hood."*

Doughboy was directly inspired by Michael *"Fatbacc"* Winters (H.I.P), a One-oh-Seven Hoover Crip, a well-known & respected figure among the Hoovers. The term *"H.I.P."* signifies Rest in Peace for a Hoover. Winters' impact on the life of acclaimed director John Singleton was immeasurable, as the two were lifelong friends who often shared their real-life experiences to bring authenticity to the stories Singleton immortalized on the silver screen.

Singleton's close relationship with Fatbacc ultimately formed the basis of many of his blockbuster films, reflecting the unyielding bond between these two remarkable individuals. Through Singleton, the world became privy to the culture & lifestyle of the Hoovers, giving the world an authentic insight into what life was truly like for us. In addition to his film work, the iconic director also created the popular television series *"Snowfall"* & was a driving force behind the show *"All American,"* two productions that honored the legacy of the Hoovers &/or continued to highlight our influence within popular culture.

The Hoovers' impact extends beyond the realm of film & television. We have also left an unforgettable mark on the music industry, cultivating, and inspiring a new generation of talented artists who have risen to prominence. Grammy-nominated artists ScHoolBoy

Q & Tyga, as well as rising stars Maxo Kream & Young Costamado, can all trace their roots back to the Hoovers. These artists have helped to bring the culture & spirit of the Hoovers to mainstream audiences, showcasing their undeniable passion for music & the powerful influence they wield.

The Hoovers can also count among their successes the accomplishments of Grammy-winning producer Tateko Bang, who has worked with some of the most respected names in the music industry. Like the aforementioned artists, Bang's connection to the Hoovers has played a pivotal role in shaping his career & creative direction. Moreover, hundreds of undiscovered talents have dedicated their efforts to representing Five-Deuce Hoover Gangsta Crip, the Crip's most renowned & revered faction. These young artists continue to pay tribute to the Groove & work diligently to uphold the Hoovers' esteemed position within popular culture.

What is it about the Hoovers that makes us so appealing to the masses? Our allure lies in our authenticity; our dedication to preserving the values & culture we hold dear while simultaneously striving to forge our own paths & establish a new narrative that is both powerful & at times, heart-wrenching. Audiences are captivated by this unabashed portrayal of a group that is so deeply rooted in struggle yet remains defiantly strong & steadfast in our pursuit of success.

Furthermore, it is our ability to inspire & uplift those around us, fostering a sense of unity & camaraderie. Through our experiences, we have created a bond that is unshakable, a connection that has transcended the test of time & solidified our place within the chronicles of Black culture.

In essence, the Hoovers represent the triumph of the human spirit, as a testament of those willing to fight for a better life. Our legacy is etched within the narratives of film, television, and music, ensuring the world will never forget the monumental impact we've had on the lives of countless people. The Hoovers will undoubtedly continue to shape our culture for generations to come, leaving behind a legacy that will stand the test of time.

CHAPTER ONE: "I'M BIG BOO CAPONE FROM FIVE-DEUCE HOOVER"

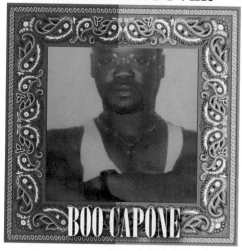

BOO CAPONE

    I promise you everyone will have a moment with me. They will have a story to tell you, some wild episode they will never forget fuckin' with Boo. Maybe a high-speed chase, a shootout, a robbery, one of them Seven Deadly Sins getting committed. Our story begins on 52nd street between Hoover & Figueroa Street in Los Angeles, where we initially took root.

    It was in this concrete jungle, characterized by its hardship & strife, where we first banded together on a quest for camaraderie & security. In time, we discovered that our bonds transcended those of mere friendship, but rather had started to resemble a powerful tribe. As young, ambitious individuals pursuing the same objectives, we simply aspired to follow our own path, bearing no expectations of what might come.

    You may be familiar with the story of original Crips like oG Raymond Lee Washington & Tookie Williams. I am one of their successors. A new breed emerged during the late 1970s & early 1980s, by the late 1980s we gained international infamy.

    Unfortunately, we created an entirely new culture & to some a cancer that was defined as Gangbangin', a term associated with countless deaths & the rise & spread of Ready Rock (Crack Cocaine) throughout the United States.

I'm a 5-foot 2 giant, what I lack in stature I made up for it with a spirit that was immeasurable, the confidence of Priest in *"Superfly"* & reputation as a *"Boss Nigga"* like Fred Williamson. Everyone in the Fifties admired me for my strength & leadership, including my older siblings. I received a lot of love from the homies, a lot of love from my hood & it was mutual, I returned the love with all my being & dedicated my life to the set.

The homegirls used to tell me, they were intimidated by my mean ice-cold Crip demeanor, it struck fear in their hearts until we got acquainted. As soon as they got to know the man behind the attitude, their anxiety melted away, and a feeling of safety washed over them like holy water at a baptism. They were relieved to be riding with a real one. The moments we shared were unpredictable & unforgettable.

We bonded over impressive heists & strong-arm robberies, the spoils of which brought shared joy & awe to my homeboys, regardless of the inherent dangers in our actions. Every escapade, each seemingly more extraordinary than the last, added to the arsenal of stories my circle would pass down for generations. People in our hood spoke with animated eyes as they recounted tales of narrow escapes, brushes with the law, and the sheer bravado it took to perform these daring feats.

The streets of South Central were treacherous & dangerous, I felt I had to protect the Fifties from all outsiders that wanted to victimize us. Very quickly becoming equally as treacherous & dangerous as the surrounding madness to survive. A relentless battle to protect our loved ones transformed us from some bad ass kids into a formidable force, instilling fear in the hearts of adversaries & authorities. Achieving such heightened infamy came at a price - we became the target of both & even a few Crip tribes.

Sometimes it felt as if my reputation preceded me to such an extent that people were under the false presumption that they knew me, simply because they had heard of my get down. Despite my relatively smaller frame, my heart pounded with the might of a lion, leaving a trail of demolished foes everywhere I went. My prowess in squabbling increased my reputation in the Crips. As I continuously left opponents at the receiving end of a brutal beatdown for underestimating me.

Reputations were built on fear & violence. A slight hesitation in showing dominance could have been the only thing separating a survivor from a dead homie. This unspoken rule of the streets was embedded in me, and I strived to live up to those ruthless expectations to gratify my comrades & conceal my vulnerabilities.

I would be a wealthy man if I had 52 cents for every time someone outside of the set met me for the first time & was surprised by my size. On many occasions people have told me upon initial meeting about my reputation.

"I heard so much about you, I thought you were some big ass muthafucka like 7 feet tall, but you all itty bitty."

As my reputation grew, so did my arsenal of abilities, eventually crossing the realm of bare-knuckled brawls to the brutality of urban warfare with the agility & precision of a seasoned 5-star General.

"Crippin'" was like an addiction, a fix I needed daily. The burning urge for a better living, for more money, and desire for temporary vices & pleasures kept me entrenched in the underworld. I didn't know any other way – I only had my homies, FDHGC was my family. In our world, when one of us succeeded, we all did, as we shared the joys of our debauchery together. We were fiercely loyal, protective & steadfast in our belief when it came to success, pussy & paper.

"It ain't no fun if the homies can't have none."-
Nate Dogg

It's hard to imagine now, looking back, how reckless we were when it came to our own health & well-being but for many of us death was a welcome escape & to die in combat or at the hands of an enemy was deemed honorable & heroic. We also had an intoxicating polygamous lifestyle. When one of us fucked, we all fucked, unless she was claimed as wifey.

I was sexing hoes like Magic Johnson at the climax of his career. By some miraculous stroke of luck, I managed to escape that time unscathed, so I praise God, I made it out without catching the monster, AIDS. It's wise to believe that we simply couldn't afford condoms, struggling as we were to make ends meet, but the harsh truth was that we were young, dumb, and full of cum, we chose to not use a rubber.

"Oooo baby, I like it raw." - Ol Dirty Bastard

My life as a young man was marked by the pursuit of power, money, respect & sexual conquests. Los Angeles was a jungle full of predators ready to devour its prey, anybody could have become a victim of its tyranny. It was a dangerous world where predators & prey were constantly shifting roles. We had to live & die by the G code.

As the sun set darkness blanketed Hoover Street, we prowled seeking the next opportunity, the next chance to claim victory in our pursuit of a dollar. It was a rat race against time & the law, fueled by the intoxicating adrenaline that pulsed through our veins. It is important to acknowledge that while our values & actions were misguided, the underlying hunger for success was not entirely misplaced.

Our dreams of achieving greatness were whispers but valid, even if they were pursued through the wrong means. Far too often, black & brown boys like me get caught up in this whirlwind of crime & debauchery, which in turn unleashes a cycle of devastating consequences. We must question why there aren't more opportunities for our youth to pursue their dreams & aspirations legally & safely.

We were locked in a battle against the norms & the expectations of society, forging a path paved with destructive intentions & misguided dreams. We are still human, striving for something greater than ourselves, desperate for a glimpse of a future beyond the shadows of our murky past.

I have since broken free from the shackles of that frenzied existence & pray, I will soon be freed from the physical shackles that bind me. I am a changed man driven by inner strength & determination to carve out a better life for myself. I am grateful for the experiences that molded me into who I am today, and for the opportunity to share my story, in the hopes that it will open the eyes of others to the struggles faced by individuals from disadvantaged backgrounds.

Through education, understanding, and support, we can empower the future generations, allowing them to sculpt their destinies & follow a path that truly leads towards success & fulfillment.

Despite the chaos that played in the great theater of the gangbang capital, there remained quiet moments of clairvoyance where I considered the possibility of an alternative life. Time slowed to a grinding halt, allowing me to catch a glimpse of ordinary moments that I could only dream of experiencing – playing basketball with friends at 48th street park, laughing & cracking jokes joyfully at a family barbecue, even attending school without the looming threat of my rival's seeking retribution for a past offense.

Reality had a habit of shattering these illusions, dragging me back to the alleys & corners where I was destined to fight another day for honor, pride, and respect. Each transition from an oasis of optimism to the ruthless streets of South Central echoed the duality that existed within me - the quintessential conflict between the person I could have been & the person I had become.

"The battles that count aren't the ones for gold medals. The struggles within yourself--the invisible, inevitable battles inside all of us--that's where it's at."- Jesse Owens

By 1980, the noble principles of CRIPS as Community Revolutionary Inner Party Servants had deteriorated into an entangled web of deceit, violence, and tribalism. Our reality transformed from Cuzz Love into a Crip Dogg eat Crip Dogg world. Rob, Steal, Kill became the Five-Deuce Hoover get down.

In the ruthless world of Crips & Bloods, my role as a protector evolved further into a force that even my closest confidants would have to respect or fear, depending on their perspective. Eventually, I mastered the art of channeling the fear & dread that permeated the air & released it in a concentrated form upon anyone foolish enough to cross us.

Some of my memories are lost in PCP clouds. They're fragmented, distant, and, at times, entirely inaccessible. Every now & then, a memory - clear as day - cuts through the haze like a blazing sun.

Golf hat & blue rag upon my head like a crown, Jheri curl dripping, dressed in my signature Levi 501 jeans, Pendleton shirt, and navy blue Chuck Taylors. Walk with me as I swagger down Figueroa, watching dogs chasing cars, biting the tires for no reason.

Accompanied by a loyal, powerful regime & my trusty pocket rocket. One thing's for certain & two things for sure, Hoover got my back.

Our presence was strongly felt by everyone we met. The streets were alive with our energy; little kids viewed us with a mixture of fear, respect, and admiration, knowing full well that being down with the Crips meant entering a thrilling, volatile, and sometimes downright perilous universe.

We ditched school daily to gang-hang because truancy was our specialty. Today was a day like any other, Me & the Locs, Gangsta Dee, Willbone, Too Sweet, Coke Dogg, Joker & Bandit, miscreants looking for mischief & bitches. Desperate for action, we got ourselves into a couple of petty thieveries to prepare for the main event of the evening. With an itch in our trigger fingers, we engaged in heated debates over who we should hit. Six-Deuce Brims or Blood Stone Villains? In the end, the decision was unanimous!

"We gonna hit 'em both!" I roared enthusiastically.

We had to come up with a more creative way to catch fools slipping & prevent a counterattack because the last thing you want to do is go on a mission & come back with a dead homie. Eureka! I had a bright idea.

I turned to Joker, *"Ay, cuH let's jack a school bus."*

We decided to make our way over to the local bus depot. The crew snuck into the parking lot with ease, the security was a lax bunch of space cadets, oblivious to our infiltration.

The Buses were left unlocked, with the keys in the ignition. We successfully creeped the bus off the lot with ease. We rode through the hood drinking 8 balls & Silver Satin, smoking lovely joints blasting *"Friends"* by Whodini.

It's a beautiful day in South Central Los Angeles. The aroma of steak asada & adobo chicken from the taco truck filled the air.

Bandit hollers for me to stop *"Hold on, blue, I'm hungry as muthafucka!"*

Bandit jumps out & returns a couple minutes later with 2 dozen tacos & the street vendor's cashbox. We continue to cruise the ghetto looking for some pretty hoodrats that want to cut class & give us some ass. We planned to do some dirt in this muthafucka, maybe run a train on some hoes, catch a robbery, or a body, if we get lucky, we will accomplish all three.

The sun had set, and dusk settled over the ghetto, it was time to end the dice game & put in some work, each of us armed & dangerous strapped with four revolvers & a sawed off pump. It is time for our mission; Objective: Vanquish Every Rival.

"Time to G-Ride my niggas!" I hollered at the homies.

We loaded up the bus, it was a ritual to get our mind right before putting in work, so we hot boxed the bus with angel dust while we vibed to the sounds of Curtis Mayfield's *"Ghetto Child."*

Our search for the Brims began in earnest, we rode up Vermont towards John Muir. We turned down every backstreet off Budlong, two or three times, it's a ghost town. We go by Harvard Park, no red anywhere.

Too Sweet yells *"Double back, double back, I think I saw a Blood!"*

I make a sharp U-turn, and the bus goes up in 3-wheel motion, my elite driving skills prevent the vehicle from tipping over. We scoured the streets, our eagle-eyed gaze never missing a beat in hopes of spotting our targets.

It seemed luck wasn't on our side - the Brims evaded us like ghosts in the night. Feeling the adrenaline surging through us, losing our patience, and desperate for some action, we shifted course & headed into the Eastside.

"Fuck this! Nobody out here, cuH!" I yelled back at Too Sweet, *"We going to the Eastside."*

There would be no escape this time. We would not be denied. We had all the windows down as low as possible for two reasons, one to let the smoke out before we arrived & secondly to point the guns out. We pulled up on the block the Villains hung out & hustled on, and it was our lucky day.

We found them. Whether it was by chance, fate or even karma, it didn't matter. What did matter, in that moment, was the overpowering rush of excitement, tension, and fear that engulfed us, leaving no room for second thoughts or rational thinking.

I shouted *"Aye y'all got some smoke?"*

"Yeah, Blood we got the best shit in LA!" one of them replied.

The ambush was working. The fools began walking towards their grim fate. When the smoke cleared, we were gone without a trace. The mission was a success, this called for a celebration. We turned this thing into a Bang Bros Bus. We partied until sunrise, we got wasted out of our minds & had psychedelic orgy with some big booty cuties from around the way.

We needed some new artillery to replace the ones we discarded. We decided to crash the bus into a pawn shop to steal a new arsenal of weapons. We stole some sheets off somebody's clothesline & used them to help us carry the merchandise to the turf.

Welcome to a day in the life of a Hoover Gangsta. Crippin' ain't Easy but somebody's gotta do it, and that somebody was me, Big Boo Capone from Five-Deuce Hoover Gangsta Crip!

This was an example of my disillusioned, corrupt train of thought, viewing young men that could have been my friends or relatives, young men that looked just like me as my enemies. I no longer view the world in this grim monochrome perspective.

I push to change the narrative with Baby Loon's concept of Forward Development. As we promote progression through small business ownership, entrepreneurship, education, and forward thinking. We wish to leave a legacy of generational blessings & break the curse of death & incarceration.

"We may encounter many defeats, but we must not be defeated."- Maya Angelou

I sit within these four walls of a small prison cell, haunted by the deep, gnawing pain of another rejected parole hearing & the crushing knowledge that five more years of my existence may be mercilessly snatched away from me. The iron grip of regret & loss grips my heart, tearing it with a bittersweet pain.

I have been shackled by the cold, heartless chains of the California Department of Corrections since the tender age of 29, deemed by society as a menace, a product of its cruel, unforgiving system. The year was 1994 when I was the second person condemned to a lifetime of imprisonment, a wretched existence within these high-security walls, forever doomed as a statistic of the dreaded *'Three Strikes.'*

I dedicate this narrative to my fallen stars who perished in the heat of battle, and our brethren held captive as political prisoners. Together, we offered the ultimate sacrifice of our lives & our freedom for Five-Deuce Hoover Gangsta Crip, never pausing for even the briefest of moments to question our commitment & loyalty.

> *"Go to work in the morn of a new creation...until you have...reached the height of self-progress, and from that pinnacle bestow upon the world a civilization of your own." -Marcus Garvey*

I recall when we started FDHGC. The Fifty Boys, a band of brothers that committed our life to a muddled canvas of survival painted with violence & drugs, bleeding lines between right & wrong. The G Code, we lived by & died by. The rules of our society were clear cut. Loyalty & vengeance were our guidelines. Any trespass against us were to be met with swift & brutal revenge. We were a force to be reckoned with, a combination of strength & ruthlessness striking fear into the hearts of our enemies.

My life as a member of the Crips was far from perfect, but it was mine to live, choices mingling with consequences. The bitter sting of nostalgia assaults me mercilessly as I remember our fallen stars, those who paid the ultimate price in the endless battle for power & respect. The blood of our enemies paints the streets a dark, morbid shade of crimson. A gruesome tribute to our tribesman, whose lives were snuffed out far too soon.

In my heart, I know that I will never truly be free until I atone for my past mistakes. From the hellfire I emerge a stronger, more compassionate man, ready to make a positive impact on the world beyond these cold, desolate walls. I cannot help but envision a world where the Three Strikes program is merely a cruel, long-forgotten vestige of our history. A world where individuals are given the opportunity to right their past wrongs & establish a more just society that cherishes righteousness & redemption over punishment & prejudice.

This narrative is but a small offering, a humble token of my commitment to change, to the fallen tribesmen I consider my family, and to those seeking redemption along this strenuous road. I pray that the lessons of our lives may serve as guiding lights for those who follow in our footsteps, illuminating the path towards hope, healing, and everlasting freedom.

CHAPTER TWO:
"FROM THE BAYOU TO THE BAY"

The silent coil of the Ouachita River, snaking through the heart of Monroe, Louisiana, is a symbol of my family's beginnings amongst the cicadas & magnolias. A modest town, fraught with history, absorbed in mangroves, shrimp boats, and humidity. Its landscape was studded with cypress swamps interspersed with cotton fields as far as the eye could see. My family's move was merely a fragment of the larger mass movement coined the Second Great Migration, where millions of Blacks uprooted from the rural South to urban areas of the North, Midwest, and West.

My grandparents, resilient pillars of a self-affirming Black community, decided to sever their roots from the familiar Louisiana clay. They packed up their dreams & stories wrapping them carefully in memories of the thick bayou, the sultry scent of the marshlands, and the southern rhapsody of Jazz & Creole cuisine that rendered a bitter-sweet charm to Monroe. My family's years in Monroe had eroded their souls & weighed them down with hatred & discrimination.

They envisioned a life where they would be free from the yoke of segregation, a life where their dreams wouldn't be smothered beneath the implacable shadow of the Jim Crow laws. Education, perhaps, was a front-facing reflection of this racial disparity. White flight, ignited by the Brown vs. Board of Education ruling in May 1954, led to the consequent underfunding of Black schools. Thus, my parents & my older siblings—often grappled with limited resources, underpaid teachers, and oversized classes.

It seemed natural for my mother to follow suit so she could have a village to support her growing family. My parents pursued the American dream, a dream rendered achievable by the social & political changes spearheaded by the likes of Martin Luther King Jr, Malcolm X, John Lewis, and countless others who dared to challenge the status quo.

Los Angeles & Oakland, the industrial hubs of the West Coast, were far from a utopia, but they represented an escape from Jim Crow south. The big cities were said to bloom with industries that offered better paying jobs & a promise of improved access to education. Factories that include the manufacturing of automotive parts, paint, chemicals, paper & plastic, furniture production & storage as well as logistics, food processing, lumber & woodworking operations. These jobs created opportunities that were seen as a steppingstone toward achieving the ever-elusive American Dream.

In the light of that flicker of hope, my parents made the bold decision to pack their dreams, hopes into a suitcase of faith – bidding goodbye to their small-town life. In early 1965, my parents made the decision to leave the bayou for the bay. My mama was pregnant with me at the time, and she was determined to make a better life for our family. Despite the adversities, a glimmer of hope sparked when the whispers of greater opportunities nestled in the heart of the Bay reached them.

We made our first home in Oakland, California. Where they found a comfort that Monroe had denied. Access to property rights, improved social services, and educational opportunities, despite the hurdles of redlining & racist pigs. My parents became a part of a flourishing Black community that was gaining momentum in its fight against the institutional atrocities waged upon them. Their journey to Oakland was a move towards empowerment, towards a dream fueled with strength, resilience, and the burning desire to forge a better legacy for their heirs.

I was born on July 19, 1965, at Richmond Medical Center, in Richmond, California. A child of promise & hope in a world of raging racial injustice. While the employment opportunities offered a silver lining, it had its clouds. Yet, they persevered, nurturing their dreams with the same vigor they had in Monroe to give better opportunities to their children.

Our journey from the Bayou to the Bay was a voyage through the raging waters of racism, a trek across the challenging terrains of hope & promise, and an odyssey towards the promised land of the American Dream. My family's story, like that of many other black families, was as much about survival as it was about aspiration.

Armed with ambition, my mother enrolled in the nursing program at Merritt College. She was gifted with the healing touch, and found her passion in offering warmth, and comfort, reminiscent of the Southern hospitality in her DNA.

She often said, *"Nursing isn't just a profession; it's an embodiment of compassion & care."*

By the time I was a year old, our family was thrust into a harsh reality as my father was drafted into the Vietnam War, leaving my mother alone to take care of my 5 siblings & me. Yet, amidst the turmoil, one good thing came out of that dark chapter. My father's time in the military transformed him into a helicopter pilot & mechanic, honing skills that would serve as his bread & butter to provide for our family while leaving him scarred with haunting memories.

I was a baby, so I don't remember much about the person he was prior to the war, but my family told me that the war changed him in many ways, and he was never the same after that experience. Growing up I always felt a sense of distance between my Pops & me. While my older siblings had memories of a loving & caring father, I was left with a shell of that man, a strict & emotionally detached veteran of war.

It wasn't until I was older that I learned about my father's service. He had seen things that nobody should ever have to see, and it had changed him forever. He came back a different man, struggling to adjust to civilian life. Today's doctors probably would have diagnosed him with PTSD, Post Traumatic Stress Disorder, that's a common trend among a lot of Veterans in the armed services.

As I grew up, life followed its course, barreling through our life's ups & downs. The troubled path that I ultimately went down would later conjure up striking parallels to my father's life. Indeed, I would later draw comparisons between PTSD & the Survivor's guilt of a tormented war veteran & the traumatizing effects of life as a South Central gang banger & unjust imprisonment. It is intriguing how the two mirrored each other. The gut-wrenching fear, the horrific violence, and the crushing uncertainty - the echoes of my father's war-ridden past were strikingly similar in my own turbulent journey.

Looking back, I realize my pops had been carrying around this emotional burden for years, trying to cope with it in his own way. I knew then that I had to be there for him, the way he had always been there for us. My father has always been a hero. He had sacrificed so much for his country & his family, and he had done it all without seeking recognition or praise. He was just an ordinary man who had done extraordinary things, and I am proud to be his son.

As it remains today, my tale continues along the difficult path carved out so many years ago, each chapter bound by a shared legacy of draft cards & doing hard time, the American dream & living nightmares. It mirrors the never-ending battles both within & outside us. It is a tale of yesterday's trials & today's tribulation.

CHAPTER THREE:
"SON OF THE REVOLUTION"

The vibrant Black community in Oakland was a celebration of resilience & a continuous pursuit of empowerment. The echoes of the Civil Rights Movement shaped my mind & inscribing a quest for justice & equality upon my heart. Enrolling in Merritt College to achieve her dream of becoming a nurse, she found herself crossing paths with legendary figures.

During my mother's tenure at Merritt College, she became immersed in the Civil Rights Movement & quickly became friends with two young brothers who would go on to start a political group called the Black Panther Party for Self Defense. Huey P. Newton & Bobby Seale, the spirited & passionate founders of the Black Panther Party in 1966, would soon become a part of our lives. They saw my mother's passion & dedication to the cause & invited her to become one of the first female members of the BPP.

My mother's deep empathy & fierce determination made her a kindred spirit to the Black Panthers. She embraced their audacious mission to challenge systemic oppression & protect the black community from the indignities & brutalities it suffered daily. As one of their first female members, she devoted herself to a cause greater than any individual life – the dream of a world where every person was treated with dignity & respect.

The Black Panthers were college aged educated Black men & women that were motivated by the violent assassination of Malcolm X. They were sick & tired of the bullshit & came up with a new spin on fighting for their rights. My mother worked tirelessly to support the Black Panther Party's mission of promoting self-defense, social justice, and equality for all.

The Black Panthers aimed to develop a Black ethnicity united in the struggle for racial equality & social justice. The BPP's philosophy was deeply rooted in Malcolm X's teachings (which advocated Black self-reliance) & the ideas of Frantz Fanon (an Afro-Caribbean psychiatrist, philosopher, and revolutionary). Prowess for self-defense was another cornerstone of the BPP, as emphasized in their Ten-Point Program that rejected pacifism in favor of equipping Black communities with the means for self-defense against racial violence & police brutality.

"You don't have to be a man to fight for freedom. All you have to do is to be an intelligent human being."- Malcolm X

The Panthers policed the pigs. They followed their patrol cars armed with loaded firearms when they patrolled the ghetto. If approached about their weapons, they would recite the law back to them. If they witnessed anyone Black get arrested, they would follow them to the police station & bail them out, whether they were a Panther or not!

My momma was the epitome of a strong Black woman, devoted to her family & a fierce promoter of Back unity. As a Black Panther, my mother was devoted to uplifting & empower our people. She helped to establish their most popular program, the Free Breakfast for School Children, and served as an early model for free student meal programs nationwide. She also provided support for those incarcerated & volunteered her nursing skills to their healthcare clinics that offered free medical care to everyone.

In 2 years', time she graduated from Merritt College with her nursing credentials, a testament to her unwavering commitment to her education & her community. After she graduated, she got a job offer from Good Samaritan Hospital on Wilshire Blvd in Los Angeles, so we relocated when I was two years old. When our family arrived in LA, her newfound purpose resonated within her. She dedicated herself to Good Samaritan for 40 years.

Los Angeles was a city that still bore the scars of the Watts Rebellion, an uprising in response to years of racism & discrimination. It needed hearts like hers, hearts that bled for justice & ached for change. My mother stayed connected to her family & friends in the Bay area & remained an active member of the Oakland chapter. I vaguely remember those long ass road trips back & forth with my mother, and my siblings to visit my aunt & attend Panther meetings.

We settled in the Pueblo projects on the eastside of LA, and I made the acquaintance of a man who would forever alter my understanding of what it meant to be Black in America. My Uncle James Ray, founder of a Pro-Black social club known as the Gladiators, inspired deep pride in Black excellence & unity. As a child, I couldn't have known that my connection to this powerful figure would pave the way for my ascendancy in the Crips.

"The first lesson a revolutionary must learn is that he is a doomed man."-Huey P. Newton

Echoing cries demanding racial equality & social justice, the Watts Rebellion indeed sparked pivotal changes, chief among them was the birth of influential Black political organizations that rose like the phoenix from the ashes of the rebellion, propelling the fight against racial inequality to greater heights.

The Black Congress emerged in response to the dire need for unity within the Black community, primarily in the Los Angeles area. They orchestrated the Watts Summer Festival, an annual multi-dimensional event that celebrated Black culture & heritage in commemoration of the Watts Rebellion. They also formed the Malcolm X Liberation University in North Carolina, providing an African-centered education to young Blacks.

Additionally, there was US (meaning 'us' & not 'U.S.'), a cultural, social, and political group, played a significant role in promoting the concept of Black Power & Afrocentrism. Originating from Los Angeles, California in 1965. US restructured the cultural identity & redefining the values of the African American community. US created Kwanzaa, a week-long celebration of African heritage & African American culture.

Another critical organization spawned from the aftermath of the Watts Rebellion was the Congress of Racial Equality (CORE). Although originating before the Rebellion, CORE underwent radical reformation post-1965, transitioning from a pacifist group to an organization passionately advocating Black Power. CORE emphasized Black autonomy, adopted Black nationalistic ideologies, and dropped its commitment to non-violence, aligning its methods more with the broader Black Power movement & the spirit of the post-Watts rebellion.

In a mere calendar flip a momentous change was overtaking the Black political scene in America. The Black Panther Party (BPP) emerged as arguably the strongest black political organization of all time. There was something about the Panthers that resonated with the times, echoing the call for equality. As the strength of the Black Power movement soared, so too did the scrutiny & opposition.

November 1968, the leaves continued to fall from the trees & America prepared to give thanks, J. Edgar Hoover, the fearsome & controversial director of the Federal Bureau of Investigation (FBI), called his field agents into action. Their task?

In Hoover's words, to *"exploit all avenues of creating dissension within the ranks of the BPP"*.

A monologue of suspicion towards the BPP had evolved into a dialogue of destruction, and the late 60s & early 70s would see one of the most relentless campaigns against a political organization in American history.

The foundation of Hoover's strategy rested upon an FBI program known as the   Program, or COINTELPRO. This misleading benign term disguised a collection of covert & illegal operations aimed to infiltrate, disrupt, and destabilize political organizations that the United States deemed subversive. The Panthers were public enemy #1.

COINTELPRO tactics were divided into four realms: creation of dissent within groups, promotion of rival factions, erosion of public image, and direct harassment or violation. The FBI employed similar tactics with the leadership of the Crips which led to our infamy & notoriety as well as the Crip Civil War.

The aim was to divide & conquer, to weaken & render ineffective. These tactics were not new. They had been employed during the 1940s & 50s against the Socialist Workers Party (SWP) & the Communist Party (CPUSA). What lay unique in the war against the Panthers was its unprecedented scale & relentlessness.

In a one-sided war stretching from 1968 to 1971, these tactics were used to control & neutralize what the government perceived as a dangerous black political group. The Feds spotlight fell on the Panthers, bringing unflinching & predatory attention. What sounded like a plot out of a political crime novel was a reality that millions were blind to - a shadow war fought not only with bullets but with manipulation, subterfuge, and deceit.

A barrage of falsehoods was crafted to smear their public image, often with mainstream media unwittingly complicit in this propaganda. Rival factions were courted & manipulated, fostering dissent that would rip through the heart of the Panthers like a bullet. Behind closed doors, inside the organization, the Feds planted infiltrators & agitators to stir discord.

The FBI's silent assault on the BPP was a parallel shadow to the public struggle for civil rights. In a fierce battle for the future of Black America, the government's silenced artillery of deception was fired with relentless, punishing succession. It targeted the Panthers with physical, and ideological ammunition, seeking to wound bodies & destabilize the mind, to challenge belief, and to break unity.

These operations included a range of tactics from discrediting key members to misdirecting resources & sowing discord to assassinations & wrongful incarcerations. The assassination of notable figures such as Fred Hampton & Bunchy Carter, in conjunction with the character assassination of Stokely Carmichael, showed the world the extreme lengths that the FBI was willing to go to destroy the movement.

A strikingly similar approach was deployed against the Crips, with an overemphasis on punitive measures, wiretapping, and restrictive legislation. Considering that the Crips were categorized as a menace to society rather than a political threat, the heavy-handed tactics seem excessively brutal.

The Street Terrorism Enforcement & Prevention (STEP) Act of the 1980s was enforced amidst rising gang violence, enabling the criminal justice system to impose additional penalties on gang members & affiliates. This selective & discriminatory application bypassed white criminal organizations, suggesting a racially biased implementation of the COINTELPRO tactics.

The media & government claims the Crips lacked a unifying political agenda of the Black Panthers, yet the FBI adopted the 'divide & conquer' strategy. This instigated frequent skirmishes within the Crips' ranks. The incarceration of significant Crip figures under questionable circumstances further escalated internal disputes, leading to the fragmentation & ultimate weakening of the Crip movement.

The operations were profoundly political, aimed at preventing the rise of a *'Black Messiah'* as per J. Edgar Hoover's fears. The FBI's use of COINTELPRO operations against both the Black Panthers & the Crips exposed the systemic racial prejudices embedded in federal operations. The similar techniques applied to both groups - sabotage, incarceration of influential figures, sowing discord, and the adoption of restrictive legislation - reveal a strategy of racial control rather than one purely focused on national security & crime reduction.

As we flip the pages of history, we must remember the shadow of the Black Panther, the silhouette of an organization that dared to challenge the system, and the covert war that sought to mute its roar. The revolutionary fever that surrounded me, the resilience & determination of the Black community, and the powerful examples set by the Black Panthers & the Gladiators formed the crucible that forged my identity.

I straddled the fence of political activism & the Gangsta – dualities that would come to define my life. As a pioneer of FDHGC, the lessons of my upbringing were never lost on me. The echoes of my mother's fearless devotion to the Black Panthers. My father's patriotism & resilience.

The grit of my parents & grandparents weathering the storm of racism in Louisiana & finding the courage to leave their comfort zone. The passion of my Uncle James Ray to preserve Black unity carried deep within the roots of my family tree. These elements cultivated within me, a survivor against unspeakable oppression with the spirit of my ancestors that demanded respect & screamed Black power.

CHAPTER FOUR:
"UNCLE JAMES RAY & THE GLADIATORS"

In the rugged, sun-scorched cityscape of Los Angeles BC—Before Crip—the streets echoed with a different kind of uprising. What *"the man"* now categorizes as gangs, back then solidified as Pro-Black Social Clubs (PBSC). An era not defined by the unified hues of gang loyalties, but rebellious voices against racial violence, these organizations emerged as protective armor for the Black communities. The first PBSC was called the LA Romans from the Eastside.

My Uncle James Ray conjured up long lost tales from the late Fifties, shared stories of these forgotten bastions of resilience. He spoke of the Gladiators, the Businessmen, the Slausons & Blood Alley; each moniker, a tribute to the grit & audacity that coursed through their veins.

My Uncle James Ray was not just an ordinary witness to this tableau of urban struggle & rebellion. He was more than that - he was a pot-stirrer, an instigator, a pioneering force who, in the late 1950s, circa 1957, started the Gladiators. Some notable Gladiators include Big Sand & Big Luigi (Coke Dogg's parents), Big Leo (Coke Dogg's Uncle) Freddy Brooks, Willy Dee, Big Cee (Lil Coke Dogg's Uncle), Wildflower (Dre Dogg's older brother) Al Greene (The CeeCee's uncle), Mama Louise (Ric Roc Mama), Big Ferocious, Luigi & Crazy Kev. Few people know that they started on the Eastside in the area near the old Temple Theatre on S. Vermont Ave & w 58th place, my grandparents later relocated to the Westside where the Gladiators would grow to prominence & become the largest PBSC in South Central.

The Gladiators headquarters was the Fifties, primarily 54th street & Vermont. The stance of defiance & the whisper of rebellion held by the Gladiators were not confined to the narrow alleyways of Vermont & 54th Street alone. They resonated throughout the horizons of Los Angeles, from Exposition Blvd to W Florence Avenue.

These were not lining demarcating territory, but boundaries safeguarding an absolute ideal, an unflinching resistance against systemic racial oppression. Now, the Gladiators' turf pulses with a different beat. It had become the shared haven for twelve tribes of Crips & Bloods.

The Gladiators' turf was only a part of the broader spectrum. East of the Gladiators' turf lay the home ground of the infamous Businessmen. This was once strewn with ambitious young blood, the air tangy with dreams, and servitude to the struggle. The South Park area, as it was known, has since been partitioned into 5-Tray Avalon Gangsta Crip & Five-Deuce Broadway Gangsta Crip territories.

To the southeast, the territories of the Slausons became the 6-pacc East Coast Crips. The generational metamorphosis of these domains passed down an unspoken code of honor & fidelity lingered. Blood Alley bore a similar mark of change & is now the home of Rollin' 20's Neighborhood, Outlaw & Hoover Family Bloods. Regardless, lay the same solid footing of collective identity & the spirit of survival.

Nevertheless, historical allies like the Businessmen & Gladiators still shared an unspoken bond like the United States & United Kingdom that was passed down to the original Five-Deuce Hoovers & Broadways. Our alliance, once as stable as the Great Wall of China, serves as the subtle reminders of the transcending bond of unity & brotherhood.

The clubs preferred to use their fists, knives or bumper jacks, and they were funded by hustling Marijuana & Red Devils, a little red sleeping pill. These clubs preferred hand to hand combat as opposed to guns, the closest thing they had were zip guns, which were homemade firearms that were usually good for one shot.

The Gladiators were a group of young Black men known for their machismo & courage to stand up for what was right. The Black Social Clubs had a common adversary, the Spook Hunters, an anti-negro gang from South Gate that started back in the 1940's. *"Spook"* was a derogatory term for a Black person with a black ass complexion.

The Spook Hunters were notorious for their violent tactics. They targeted Black communities in Los Angeles, spreading hate & violence wherever they could. Their resume included bombing homes, vandalism, and assault. They were known for riding through the hood intimidating, threatening, and inflicting brutal assaults to express their hatred.

When the Gladiators heard about the Spook Hunters vandalizing Black owned businesses & homes around the way they knew they had to act. The Gladiators refused to stand by & watch their community be terrorized. Uncle James Ray taught me the importance of the collective that when we stand together, we can overcome even the most daunting of challenges. That defined being Fifty Strong & that strength transcended to my generation & the generations that followed us!

The Spook Hunters were the complexion for protection & were able to operate without repercussions because they were given a *"get out of jail free card"* by the racist judicial system, so they were never prosecuted for their Hate crimes & deemed a to be nothing but a rumor by the media as no news of their terror was ever reported.

Anti-Negro Gang

(Continued from Page 2)

able to find a single eye-witness to testify to having seen any such jackets or insignia. It is always the friend of a friend who told those who are s, reading the rumors.

In conducting its investigations, the commission staff contacted law enforcement officials, social workers, probation officers, and educators. Many had heard rumors, and several law enforcement agencies have assigned men to the specific task of uncovering the gang. All reported that there is no such group.

One law enforcement official said there might be such a gang, but if so, it is nowhere near as large and powerful as rumor alleges. Another said that a gang with this name existed four years ago, but has not been heard of since.

The Spook Hunters were known to wear bomber jackets with an animation of a black man face with a noose around his neck on the back; they were active until the White Flight. *"White Flight"* is described as a period when whites began relocating out of the Southside in the early 1960's. After the threat of the Spook hunters faded.

The Gladiators & the Slausons would then become archrivals, as PBSC's would start beefing over Eastside versus Westside, Football games & women of course. After the Watts Rebellion of 1965, the PBSC's including the Gladiators & Slausons became more black power orientated & squashed their trivial beefs & formed an alliance.

Bunchy Carter, leader of the Slauson Renegades would establish the Los Angeles chapter of the Black Panther Party in 1967. This civil rights movement helped create a sense of black unity & black power within our communities nationwide. Bunchy was beloved & admired in South Central & called the Mayor of the Ghetto. He was assassinated at UCLA on January 17, 1969.

I spent a lot more time with my Uncle James Ray & the Gladiators after I moved to the Fifties. I went to school with all their kids, cousins, nieces, and nephews. The love & unity of the Gladiators was instilled in us. We became lifelong friends, we became family just like the Gladiators, from the Cradle to the Grave.

CHAPTER FIVE:
"THE GANGSTA MIDGETS & A GIANT"

In 1969, my Pops returned from the war, now that we had two streams of income, my parents had saved enough money to move out of the Pueblos. My parents achieved what seemed an impossible feat for a Black family caught in the struggle & a system designed to put them at a disadvantage. They bought a humble abode. Our new home was a testimony to my parents' spirit. A symbol of their determination to make something out of nothing.

Despite the glossy image of homeownership, we were nothing more than poor black folks in America, bred on a diet of sacrifice & humility. Money was a scarce entity, as elusive as the leprechaun's pot of gold at the end of a rainbow. My father was the patriarch of our home & custodian of our finances. With his business ventures & six children at the back of his mind, my Pops stretched each penny until it screamed for mercy.

Regardless of our struggles we were moving on up like George & Weezy to the Westside of the Fifties, South Hoover Street & W. 52nd place to be exact. My father's return also brought hostility, due to my mother's ties to the BPP. My father didn't like the Black Panthers at all. He didn't like anything that involved socializing & groups of people.

My father was always a man of few words, and he was socially awkward. Sometimes I felt like he didn't love me or understand me, and he looked down on me for being a socialite. My Pops was a man molded by experiences most people wouldn't endure in their worst nightmares.

Similar to many Vietnam veterans he struggled every day with the invisible wounds of PTSD. This facet of his life infused a bitterness in his behavior. He was a prisoner of war to his memories, and often, we became collateral damage. Yet, through the mind fog, flashbacks, and trigger warnings, he tore himself out of bed each morning, reminding us of our lineage & the dignity of hard work.

He was a man's man, he lived to provide, to put food on the table & a roof over our heads. Pops was a genius at survival & sacrifice. My father was a jack of all trades & a master at every single one of them. A mechanic who fixed cars with a genuine touch, a helicopter pilot who kissed the blue skies, and a landscaping maestro who sculpted lawns & trees as if they were works of art.

He was the raw & uncut American dream. My pops was no stranger to blood, sweat & tears. He built our lives around the bits & pennies that he earned & saved, devising ingenious ways to stretch a dollar & still make ends meet.

With a full house of six kids & my baby brother on the way, my father's drastic cost-cutting meant we learned to respect, honor, and value everything we possessed. His eccentric measures might seem harsh to many, but to us, they were a strange sense of comfort, a token of his care & concern for the family.

No matter his struggles, he never failed to provide, to protect, or to guide us, even if his methods occasionally strayed from conventional norms. Now that I look back, I smile at his severe approach, especially when it came to preserving resources like food & bath water.

Bath time was always a source of squabbles between my siblings & me. The heated disputes over who got the first bath, who used the most soap, and who stayed in the tub the longest were part of the daily routine.

He grew frustrated with the oceans we were pouring into the porcelain tub, Pops exploded, *"I'm tired of you muthafuccas making all this bathwater filling up the tub 5-6 times a day! I tell ya what, nobody gonna take a bath til I get home!"*

True to his words, he returned home from a hard day of work, fatigue carving lines of weariness onto his face. He herded us into the backyard with our towels & wash rags, under the pink shadows of the setting sun, soap bars distributed like rationed food during war times.

With a garden hose in hand like an M16, he sprayed us down with icy cold jets of frigid water on full blast, not only scrubbing away the grime of the day but also instilling in our minds the virtue of conservation. The ice-cold water stung like a whip's lash, searing into the innocence of my young heart. A makeshift shower under the moonlight, an unconventional parenting choice, was one of the rawest experiences of hardship & survival I had at such a young age.

Pops hosed us down tirelessly, one after another, his eyes gleaming with a strange satisfaction. The feeling of chilled water biting into my flesh, coupled with the mental shock of such a bizarre ritual, fermented a potent cocktail of resentment within me. My childish mind twisted & turned, only arriving at the conclusion - I despised him. Was this a calculated maneuver to ready us for life? Or was it a twisted methodology born from a troubled past?

It was like he was conditioning us for a life reminiscent of the wartime horrors, he'd survived – a twisted replication of Vietnam's foxhole makeshift baths. It felt like a training regime for the next Watts riots, making us resilient & ready to withstand the social & economic torment of being black in America. A rite of passage into his school of hard knocks. After we were thoroughly soaked & scrubbed, Pops led us back inside. Mama warmed us up with hot tea & had a hot dinner ready to follow our strange bath, and then we were sent to bed.

Pops' survivalist spirit did not only save on water consumption; it also taught us some profound lessons of grit, frugality, and contentment. His unusual methods were not an emblem of deprivation, but a clear message of resilience. They were glimpses into his inner strength & unyielding resolve to take life head-on, no matter what it throws at him.

The dislike I held for him in those trying moments slowly faded into respect over the years. Through that bitter-cold experience, I now realize, he was preparing us for the harsh realities of life, morphing us into hardened steel. He was preparing us for a world where fingers would be pointed at us, stereotypes labeled us, and barriers confronted us because of the color of our skin. He was preparing us for the battleground beyond our backyard. The rebellious youth in me defied this rationale, instinctively directing the hatred towards the man who dared put his offspring under such dire conditions - my very own pops.

My pops was by no means perfect, but he was a fighter who never cowered in the face of life's trials. Struggle, endurance, discipline, and above all, survival- all rendered by an unsung hero. His saga was our legacy - A testament that resonated with his teachings, his sacrifice, and his indomitable spirit, woven with love, sprinkled with hardship, and bound by resilience.

A man who was more than just a father. He was a teacher, a mentor, a disciplinarian, but most importantly, he prepared us for the real world. He taught us that surviving isn't merely about existing; it's about sacrificing to live.

The first kid I met was my boy Brian Harris, he lived around the corner on 53rd street. We were the same age. It didn't take long before we did everything together. Brian probably knows me better than I know myself. I remember when we were around 7 years old, we used to take grass shavings, put it in some bamboo paper & smoke it, you couldn't tell us anything. I think back & laugh my ass off because we literally smoked grass.

One day my brother James' best friend, King Curtis, caught us smoking in Brian's clubhouse. We called it Brian's Ghetto Safari because it was covered with bushes & other vegetation. King Curtis introduced us to our first marijuana joint.

"Watch & learn, little man," he said, his words steadily paced with an air of fluidity as he showed me the proper technique of making a perfectly rolled Zigzag. I couldn't have known it then, but this joint represented a new chapter in my young life, one that would forever remind me of King Curtis. The smell of that first joint was intense as the smoke filled my virgin lungs. We watched the sun set in a swirling haze of red & orange, my body & mind sunk into harmony with the atmosphere itself.

Our older brothers & their friends had a fight club, starring us, they would have us brawl in the backyard to make us tough & for their entertainment also. They would place their bets, and we would fight like cats & dogs. I used to send Brian ass home lumped up every time, so his Momma couldn't stand me, but she loved me because she knew I was RIDE or DIE for her son.

Brian is my first friend & my best friend; we were like 2 peas in a pod. He was my everyday nigga; we were always getting into some shit. As the warm autumn breezes rustled through the trees outside my window, little did I know that the events we shared would create unforgettable adventures & solidify the unbreakable bond between us.

It was the fall of 1974, and I was in the fifth grade at the 52nd Street School. Brian had attended Catholic school up until today when he was expelled after we went up there with Dwayne looking for the kid he fought. Quite proud of his triumph, Brian wasted no time relaying the details to me.

Upon arriving at his house, Dwayne & I found our friend pacing back & forth furiously in his living room, visibly upset.

"What's up, Brian? Why are you so mad, bro?" I asked with concern.

"This punk ass nigga got me suspended & grounded!" Brian recounted the event, his anger rising as he recounted the story.

Apparently, some kids from the eastside were trying to punk him in front of some cuties & he wasn't going to put up with embarrassment or disrespect. Fueled with righteous anger, Brian attacked the ringleader & easily whooped his ass, but it came at a cost. Brian's challenger turned out to be a snitch & told the teacher about their scuffle.

"I need some get back!" he exclaimed; frustration evident in his voice as he recalled the series of injustices he'd endured.

I watched his eyes burn with barely contained fury as he planned his revenge on the snitch.

"What you wanna do, bro?" I asked, ready to follow him to the end of the world.

From the swirling depths of his schemes, Brian determined the perfect payback, that's where Momma Harris' knives came in. We had seen them in the kitchen drawer, and we knew they would be perfect for our little mission. He rummaged through his kitchen drawers & grabbed a few of the sharpest & biggest old hickory knives out of her collection & we concealed them in our pockets.

"We gonna get this nigga!" he declared with a crazed gleam in his eye.

Clutching the knives tightly, he jumped on the handlebars of my beach cruiser & feeling like a couple of real badasses, we made our way to Nativity Catholic School, we chased the kid & his friends, but they escaped. Brian knew where one of them lived, so we made our way there. As we arrived on the snitch's block, we spotted him working on his fancy Schwinn. An idea sprung into our heads, a plan that would serve as payback. Instead of simply beating his ass, we decided we'd beat his ass & steal his bike, causing the rat the same distress that he'd inflicted on my comrade.

The snitch was preoccupied shining the chrome ape handlebars on his brand new 20 inch Schwinn, w/ the 16 inch front wheel. It was perfect. We snuck up behind him, brandishing our stolen knives. The boy slowly backs away from us into his driveway, I see he wants to make this difficult.

I rushed him, Brian & Dwayne were 1 step behind me. I grab the handlebars, he pulls, I pull, tug of war. Brian socks him in the eye with the butt of his knife. Dwayne swung his knife at the kid. He jumps back & loses his grip on the bike to avoid his attack. The boy screams for help, while retreating towards a neighbor's yard. Brian jumps on the bike, Dwayne & I bust a move towards ours & we flee the scene.

Suddenly, the kid's older brother showed up with his homeboys, some West Town Crips! They were bigger than us & didn't take kindly to us threatening & strong arm robbing their homeboy's little brother. I could see the malice in their eyes! The Crips chased us back across the freeway hot on our heels.

We rode those bikes as fast as we could. Our hearts raced but it wasn't beating faster than we peddled! Skrrrt, a Cadillac, came to a screeching stop to avoid hitting us as we came out of the overpass on Flower Street. We lost our pursuers by escaping through 52nd street school & hiding out in my backyard. My brothers Don, James & Calvin were on the block with Thadron & Curt, they ran into the dudes chasing us, the Crips asked them about us, but they didn't confess to knowing us or our whereabouts.

We overheard a heated exchange of words ensued, and for a moment, it seemed as though a full-blown fight would break out. OG Gates, a reputable figure of the Westside Crips, overheard the commotion, so he came over to see what was going on. The respect commanded by oG Gates proved powerful enough to end the confrontation peacefully.

The pursuers left, and we managed to get away with the stolen bike. My brothers come into the backyard & find us all shaken up. They quickly put 2 & 2 together. They told us they had a hunch but now they were certain we were the little fools the Crips were hunting.

They roasted us, making fun of how hard we were breathing & the stupid look of fear on our faces. We told them what happened, and they gave us our props! I learned that crime pays if you get away. After that incident my brothers nicknamed us the Gangsta Midgets.

Brian & Dwayne would become the infamous ScHool Boy & Bow Dee from Five-Deuce Hoover Gangsta Crip. We called him ScHool Boy cause his little ass always went to school, he weighed about 100 pounds soaking wet & still does. He grew up to be a cold playa about his paper.

ScHool Boy was always down for the go get him, he was sneaky, cunning & conniving, setting up an enemy for his demise in a heartbeat was one of his specialties. A little pissed colored, shit talkin' scandalous muthafucka who couldn't fight worth a lick but would put a knife or a hot one in you without hesitation.

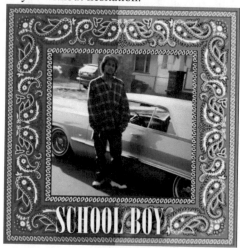

Bow Dee always had my back. A fearless leader who never turned any challenge down. Whether it was a fist fight or a shootout, he stood tall, ten toes down, solid as a rock for FDHGC. He was a great squabbler, a bare-knuckle brawler that became notorious as the hardest-hitting member of the Hriginal Hoover Gangstas. His fierceness along with his unwavering loyalty made him one of the most respected & feared figures in the set. Bow Dee represented the heart of Hoover Gangsta, a man the hood could always count on, especially in the direst circumstances.

My family's move to the westside introduced me to my honorary big brother, Thadron. He lived a couple houses away from us, born seven years apart, Thad & I were thrust together by fate & circumstance. It didn't take long for our bond to form, and before I knew it, I was taking part in the exhilarating world of 52nd street go-kart racing.

Our parents became well acquainted, often getting together for impromptu barbecues & evening chats on the porch. Thad taught me a lot growing up, how to fight, how to weld, and he taught me a lot about crime. He was a prodigy with his hands, we would spend our free time building wooden go-karts with scraps he had salvaged from construction sites around the way. His creations were a thing of beauty, embodying the rough & tumble, do it yourself spirit that defined South Central.

From the beginning, it was clear that my job was to drive these magnificent machines, honing the skills that would make me an undefeated champion on the makeshift tracks of 52nd street. With Thad at the helm, and me in the driver's seat, we quickly became the envy of every kid on the block.

Every weekend was dedicated to racing, we spent hours crafting new karts designed to outpace & outlast the competition. The thrill of hearing the wooden wheels creak & rattle as we tore down 52nd street, a need for speed that still brings a smile to my face. Unknowingly sculpting me into an A-1 wheelman for my future criminal endeavors.

When we weren't racing, he would teach me about the mechanics of our karts. He was a patient teacher, who always made sure I understood what he was doing, and why, before he let me try it on my own. It was during these moments that I began to truly appreciate the genius & talent of my big brother.

As the years went by, his skills only grew, with his knowledge eventually extending to the art of welding. Slowly, we began to see the integration of steel into our karts, making them stronger & faster than ever before.

Thadron, the giant of 52nd street, an imposing figure, standing at an impressive 6'7", with a confident aura & reputation as a knockout artist that demands respect. He was a Westside Hustler with a chiseled physique & unruly, sun-bleached afro were only a few aspects of his unique brilliance. His natural charisma & intelligence were unmatched, and before long, we were more than friends; we were family.

Thad's exceptional talent with his hands that could build anything from wood or steel became instruments of brutal efficiency, beating down fools with precision. He became well-known for his impressive abilities in a squabble & on the basketball court. He dominated at Manual Arts High School & earned recognition as a rising star.

After high school, he was fortunate enough to play college ball & pro ball overseas. However, when he returned to 52nd Street, his athletic prowess took a back seat to his growing reputation as a criminal mastermind & enforcer. He would become known as Big Ten Speed from Five-Deuce Hoover Gangsta Crip. He was nicknamed Ten Speed due to his love of bicycles.

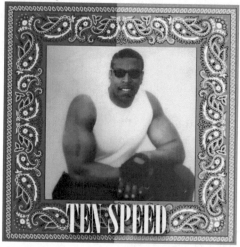

Speed was an instrumental member & leader; he was our protector. If we had a problem with some older cats or some really big dudes Speed would handle it, no questions asked, nobody could beat Speed. He could single-handedly disarm tense situations with a single, intimidating gaze or use his powerful fists to solve problems.

Ten Speed taught me how to defend myself. Every time we crossed paths, we would engage in impromptu sparring sessions, allowing me to hone my skills as a fighter under his watchful eye. He instructed me on a variation of striking techniques & the importance of footwork in the art of squabbling. More significantly, he instilled in me the confidence & mental fortitude necessary to thrive in our harsh surroundings.

Speed wasn't just tough; he was also smart. He knew how to make money & he wasn't afraid to break the law to do it. Ten Speed's greatest lesson to me, however, was the knowledge of crime. His resourcefulness in illegal ventures seemed limitless, and he was always eager to teach me his skill set. From lock picking to hotwiring cars, Ten Speed showed me how to navigate the illicit side of life.

It was through these lessons that we bonded most profoundly. Ten Speed operated with the mind of a strategist, always planning his next criminal endeavor. Ten Speed always ensured that I knew the stakes & rewards, instilling the importance of opportunity risk. I would often accompany him on these exploits, becoming an eager accomplice in his various hustles.

CHAPTER SIX:
"THE 52ND STREET SCHOOL
OF HARD KNOCKS"

In the heart of Los Angeles lies a small but notorious school, affectionately known as 52nd Street Elementary School. While most may pass by this school in the City of Angels without giving it so much as a second glance, for me, it holds more than just memories; it holds the foundation for a bond that has defined my life.

It was here, on these simple school grounds, that I met my lifelong friends—the Hriginal members of our close-knit group that became known as Five-Deuce Hoover Gangsta Crip. The halls & playground of our humble elementary school were home to the birth of our brotherhood & future generations.

As much as I can recall, it all began with the rush of excitement & nerves that filled me on my first day of kindergarten in September of 1970. On my first day of school, I met lifelong friends, Andre & his older brother Tony. Dre & I were the same age, and our brothers were also.

I love these guys because they swore they were the hardest muthafuckas out, and my brothers & I felt the same way. They were my day ones, for real, they stayed 2 blocks away from us on 54th street. The Lee's, my nigga Andre & his brothers Tony & Johnny who became known as notorious Dre Dogg, Gangsta T & Wildflower from Five-Deuce Hoover Gangsta Crip.

The Lee family have been an instrumental element of Five-Deuce Hoover since day one. They are one of the families that would produce generations of leaders in our set. We started as friends & became family, literally & figuratively. My Uncle James Ray is the father of their nephew, my cousin, Timothy Lee Thomas, who became known as the infamous Lil Twindogg (Blind Twin) of Five-Deuce Hoover Gangsta Crip.

DRE DOGG

As my backpack weighed my small frame down, I stepped onto the bustling schoolyard. The raucous laughing children, grumbling teachers, fluttering pigeons, and parents exchanging goodbyes echoed across the soundscape. Despite the overall atmosphere of enthusiasm & anticipation for a new beginning, the source of my anxiety would come at recess that first day.

In the schoolyard, amidst the tumble of torn-up sneakers & worn-out basketballs sat the ultimate prize, one that held an allure even greater than the tallest slide or freshest pack of candy: twenty gleaming tricycles, putting forth promises of speed & exhilaration. To the collective group of kindergartners, the allure of those bright tricycles ruled over all other earthly possessions.

Unfortunately, the mathematics of the situation were not in our favor. With twenty tricycles for twenty-three eager youth, our introductions to these sacred machines would each begin with a race—determined by speed, luck, and sheer determination.

As my fellow classmates & I lined up at the ever-closing door that separated us from the schoolyard & the looming tricycles. I knew I had no intention of being left standing on the sideline like someone stole my puppy watching my classmates race around the lot. We began the mad dash across the playground to claim a tricycle.

I was fixated on my prize, I sprinted towards the trike like Jesse Owens – a sleek blue tricycle with a silver bell that seemed to shimmer with my name on it. Little did I know at that moment, I had competition eyeing the same prize. As my small but powerful legs raced towards my holy grail, the blue tricycle. I soon realized that another child stood in a duel for ownership. We reached the tricycle at the same time, and this unfamiliar challenger really had the balls to try & claim my Tricycle!

It was at this moment I summoned an inner strength somewhere deep within me—a dormant talent & ability for standing up for what was mine. I whooped his ass & I never had to run out there to claim one again. There I was, perched upon my prize, and as I surveyed the playground, it became clear that in the crucible of battle, I had learned the power of the squabble.

I learned an important life lesson, that handling things in this manner not only brought respect among my classmates but also taught me the role that power plays in the eyes of others. All you have to do is let people see you whoop someone's ass, and they won't get out of line with you EVER! Around my way, that's how you earned respect, and I have been earning mine since kindergarten.

My Pops had etched out a reputation for himself as a strict, practical man that left no room for silliness or disobedience. He was colossal cornbread-fed southern man. He towered over everyone in the house, his burly 6-foot 2 physique a perfect representation of the raw strength he had developed growing up in the sharecropper fields of the South. He was a good man, but his interpretations of right & wrong were black & white.

He was a strict disciplinarian who adopted a no-nonsense approach to parenting, but his specialty was mental & verbal abuse, that's how I learned to talk shit so well. This belief had its roots in the unjust southern practices rooted in slavery when masters punished slaves for misconduct. This form of punishment had found its way into my household via my father's disciplinary methods, shaping his parenting philosophy & significantly influencing my upbringing.

Growing up, I had always been smaller than my peers, having inherited my mother's petite frame as opposed to my father's overwhelming largeness. This disparity in size did nothing to ease my anxiety around my father, and let's not forget the oak paddle he mercilessly used when I messed up.

Before long, the gossip surrounding my playground victory had reached the ears of a gang of scrappy boys who would later form the nucleus of Hoover Gangsta. The feeling of power & dominance that ricocheted around me after my first fight intoxicated me. The fear & respect in the eyes of my peers, and the wild fascination I received from the girls added fuel to the fire of my arrogance. I enjoyed this newfound sense of authority.

My newfound talent in fighting had gained the attention & admiration of the young & impressionable schoolgirls in my class. It was nice, I discovered my talent & began to show out with my elite fighting skills. However, this victory was short-lived when I found myself sitting in the principal's office. My joy transitioned swiftly into an overwhelming dread as I awaited the arrival of my parents. The impending doom was nothing compared to the wave of terror that washed over me when I finally laid eyes on my father's towering figure in the doorway of the principal's office.

Upon reaching home I was given an unforgettable beating. The reality of my actions finally sunk in, and I realized the gravity of my misconduct. Like a helpless ragdoll, I was hoisted into mid-air, hanging upside down by my ankles in a vise-like grip of my father's powerful left hand while his right hand wielding the dreaded oak paddle slapping my ass repeatedly in rhythmic swings, each blow followed by a blast of raw pain.

The sharp sting of the oak cutting across my small, trembling body was a bitter lesson in power & disobedience that I still remember to this day. My father's annoyance was not so much about the incident at school itself as it was about the lost earnings due to my misbehavior. *"Yo bad ass makin' me leave work for yo bullshit,"* he growled between strikes.

Each blow I received from that oak paddle on my petite frame was more than just a physical torment; it also marked the imprint of a troubling ideology. It was that brutally cold lesson that taught me how violence was used to promote order. It planted the seed of a terrible truth in my young heart. What I took from the experience was inherently flawed, yet it was seared into my young impressionable mind.

Though shrouded in the raw emotion of a painful past, I learned that while violence can intimidate, it can never teach respect or empathy. The real test of strength & character lies not in physical dominance but in showing discretion & fairness — traits that I now know truly define the mettle of a person. Times have changed, and thankfully, attitudes have evolved. It's true that we are products of our upbringing, but it's also true that we have the power to change the narrative & do better.

As the school bells rang & recesses came & went, I made more lifelong friendships, Michael Tucker, and his big bro Jerry. During our shared time at 52nd Street School, our mischievous activities coupled with our mutual understanding, ignited a bond as spontaneous & unpredictable as the streets we called home. The Tuckers were different. Unlike the rest of us, they had skin pigment so light that it could fool anyone, we called them *"passing."* They had the complexion for protection, the result of being born from a white mother, making them *"White Boyz N the Hood."*

I'll never forget the days when I was the class clown always showing my ass & *"White Mike"* always found himself the butt of my jokes. The Tuckers had reddish-brown hair & green eyes, back in the day we had a term of endearment for them, *"redbones"* or *"mulattos,"* even though some circles frown upon these terms like the word *"nigga."*

In the rich tapestry of Black American history, the terms *"passing," "mulatto,"* & *"red bone"* have held significant cultural & social importance within Black America. These terms trace their origins back to a complex history intertwined with racial identity, societal discrimination, and evolving perceptions of race in America.

The concept of *"passing"* has its roots in the era of slavery & the Jim Crow South. During these times, individuals of mixed racial heritage faced a unique set of challenges in a society sharply divided along racial lines. To *"pass"* meant that a black person could successfully present themselves as white.

Blacks that were passing gained access to privilege, opportunity, and freedom from the systemic oppression faced by blacks in these times. Passing was a double-edged sword. It was a tool for survival in a society where racial identity dictated every aspect of life, from legal rights to social acceptance. While being looked down upon by their peers in the black community that had no way to hide their melanin during a time it was demonized.

The term *"mulatto"* originated during the era of slavery in the United States & was used to describe people of mixed African &

European ancestry. Derived from the Spanish & Portuguese word for mule (mulato), the term reflected the societal view of jungle fever babies, individuals born from a mix of black & white, much like mules were the offspring of donkeys & horses.

Similarly, the term *"red bone"* also emerged as a description for blacks with a lighter complexion & often possessing distinctive physical features such as red or reddish-brown undertones in their skin. The term *"redbone"* carried a complex set of overtones, at times implying attractiveness, desirability, or even social status, while also reflecting the lingering impact of colorism & status within the black community.

As the Civil Rights Movement gained momentum & social perceptions of race began to shift, these terms came under scrutiny. The quest for racial equality & the recognition of the diversity within the black community led to a reevaluation of these terms & the attitudes they embodied. The traditional significance of passing, mulatto, and red bone within the black community underwent a transformation as new generations challenged the limitations & stigmas associated with them.

Well, I used to tease & pick on Mike every day I called him *"white mike," "white boy"* or *"whitey"* & my personal favorite *"light bright."* Today, Mike had had enough of my shit. He reached his boiling point. His face turned a devilish shade of red, he snapped, his cloudy green eyes flipped a switch, and they mirrored the rage inside him. Mike spazzed out in the full glare of the class.

He threw a fit, literally, the tantrum of all tantrums was unleashed like a flood breaking through the levees. He flipped tables over like coins, screaming his lungs out & throwing whatever little his hands could grasp, displaying an erratic show of rebellion. For everyone witnessing this explosion of fury, it was an unforgettable spectacle of sheer hilarity. It was as if Mike had been infected with a sudden surge of madness, unfiltered comedic insanity that converted the classroom into a mini theater of shits & giggles.

I couldn't help but burst out laughing, White Mike had gone completely out of his mind, Psycho Norman Bates. That very moment, we witnessed the birth of the infamous nickname I fittingly awarded him that stuck to him like his light skin, a badge he'd wear forever, marked for my jokes.

My day one homeboys, the Tucker brothers, the infamous Cyko Mike & Evil Red, Hriginal Five-Deuce Hoover Gangsta Crip. It's amazing how our childhood antics could foreshadow the paths we would eventually take. I guess you never know where life's journey will take you.

Later I learned that Cyko Mike's mother wasn't white at all but Creole a mix of French, African, and native American, but French was the most prominent in their design so to us ignorant lil niggas in the hood, they were white. Now I understood why he went crazy when I teased him & called him White Mike, because he was black, and did not identify as white at all.

From an early age, I was made aware of my 'blackness' & what it meant. It was undeniable, the melanin of our skin, the rhythm of our language, the courage in our laughter, our shared experiences. It was a stronghold forged by our history & our struggle.

When I met Cyko Mike, my young mind struggled to fit him into the black-&-white definitions of race. He was the same complexion as those we saw as the oppressors. Yet, he lived amongst us, walked & talked like us, laughed like us. He was one of us. Each time I called him White Mike, he scowled at the moniker, adamantly asserting his black pride & heritage, which was more profound than the color of his skin.

From Cyko Mike, I learned that blackness was a broad spectrum, each bearing its own unique history. I learned that every hue, from the palest white chocolate to the darkest purpliest black, had its place in our community. I understood his frustration when I teased him for his color because he was Black & proud.

No one in the Tucker family identified as white. Their skin tone could fool anyone, but their hearts beat Black Power. They stuck out like a sore thumb in the ghetto. Hence, why I still count Cyko Mike & Evil Red, as the first white Hoover Gangsta Crips based on their complexion for protection, which we would learn to use to our advantage.

They were like Jackie Robinson breaking into the baseball world, nudging the status quo, redefining stereotypes about light skin niggas being soft, and teaching me that judging book by its cover was foolish. As a wiser older man, I see they were fearless revolutionaries, like Huey P. Newton, the leader of the Black Power movement & King of the Light skins charging against the notion that being black was a singular color or identity.

52nd street school, gifted me with so many memories & life lessons. During one of those bright, sunshine-filled Cali days, punctuated by the laughter & energy of children set free from the confines of their classrooms for recess, I was having my usual good times on the monkey bars.

I loved the thrilling feeling of going airborne flipping & flopping, the sensation of defying gravity when I suspended myself in the air briefly before my hands once again found the bars. Through relentless practice & a flair for daredevil stunts, I had mastered a style all my own.

As my peers watched in awe. Among these fascinated spectators, a tall kid appeared captivated by my theatrics. He stepped forward & introduced himself *"What's up! It's pretty dope how you do all those tricks on the monkey bars, my name is Kennedy, but everybody calls me Kenny."*

At first glance, Kenny was an enigma. He was a grade above me, visibly towering over the rest of us. His feet were long as hell like stretched limousines. Yet this physical attribute wasn't what intrigued me most about Kenny. It was his hands & the extraordinary way he used them when he spoke.

His fingers were long as hell as if designed for a purpose beyond the norms of mere mortals. To me, they reminded me of the alluring alien fingers of ET: fascinating & outlandish. As he spoke, it was like witnessing Beethoven orchestrating a symphony before a grand ensemble. But instead of one wand, Kenny had ten – weaving a visual tapestry of vibrant sound waves & emotions with each sentence he spoke.

Our bond was as instantaneous as it was seamless, we were homeboys at first sight. Kenny was my kind of crazy. We got really tight, existing in our own exciting world of playground antics & mischievous escapades. Through Kenny, I met his brothers, each an individual character with their diverse personalities.

Mike the wise big bro, Greg the playa, and Anthony, the fearless adrenaline junkie. I used to think Anthony had mental health issues, but he was just crazy & so was I because I went along with all the crazy shit. The Evans boys soon became my everyday niggas. We were the young lords of the Fifties- riding bikes, playing sports, chasing girls, and building childhood memories meant to last through the unending eclipse of time.

I adopted a funny nickname for Kenny, a homage to his unique physical characteristics. I jokingly called him *"Foots & Fingers."* The nickname stuck, and although it was born out of my endless shit-talking, it encapsulated a camaraderie that was thick as thieves. We walked through the seasons & weathered many storms, threading every memory into the fabric of our brotherly love. However, one particular incident involving Kenny stands out.

One fateful day, as Kenny was walking down the alley by his house, he side-swiped his hand along a gate, enjoying the rhythmic buzz from the rusty metal. Out of the shadows, a vicious dog lunged, attacking Kenny's hand, and grievously snatched half of one of his fingers.

The dog attack was a shocking incident, but Kenny, with his relentless spirit, approached the situation with surprising courage. After undergoing a skin graft, the incident eventually became a tale we narrated with shits & giggles. From that day forward, we changed Kenny's nickname. He became the man, the myth & the legendary Ken Dogg & his brothers Big Mike, Sham Rock & Insane Fish, the notorious Evans clan of Five-Deuce Hoover Gangsta Crip.

Childhood is a canvas of memories painted with numerous experiences & vivid relationships. One of the most meaningful relationships in everyone's life is the unique bond they share with their cousins. This bond is forged by the unbreakable connection, an impenetrable tether of blood & love. Growing up, my bond with my cousin Ravele was similar, he was not just my cousin but my first friend, my confidant, who shared with me the mystery of growing up in our family.

My father & his brother sat on opposite sides of the social spectrum. While my pops preferred solitude & relished in his personal space, his brother - James Ray was a social butterfly, pioneer of the renowned Gladiators. The ironies of life are sometimes humorous, and such was the case with them. As dissimilar as they were, both sides of the family did share a common denominator - the strength & resiliency of our family ties.

This emotional connection led us to move together to California, then the Pueblos & later to the Fifties. Through these transitions, we maintained a bond that transcended the conventional sibling rivalries & despite our contrasting residences, the family ties remained resilient & sturdy. Through my Uncle James Ray, I met his nephew, my cousin Ravele.

Ravele's mother, Big Sand, had a peculiar fondness for Coca-Cola. While she was pregnant with Ravele, her craving for the fizzy drink was so immense that the affectionate nickname 'Coco' was coined. Alas, as fitting as it may seem, my poor cousin Ravele never really liked the nickname. To him, it came off as girly, and he yearned for something more masculine.

So, he shaped & molded it, kneaded it like dough until he was satisfied. A gradual evolution saw 'Coco' becoming 'Coke', a more macho variation of Coca-Cola. This marks Ravele's first assertion of his identity, a subtle yet profound defiance of his predestined path, mirrored in his transformation from Coco to Coke.

Ravele found his unique place. His moniker evolved as he grew older, imitating the changes in his life & personality. We began calling him Coke Dogg, inspired by his constant canine companion. He was barely a teen then, swaggering around the hood with an infectious enthusiasm that endeared him to everyone around the way.

OG COKE DOGG

Coke Dogg has always been a good dude, a man of few words, but when he spoke everyone listened. He is a no-nonsense type of cat; some people would label him a bully because he preferred to let his fist do the talking. He's a big guy, about 6'2" with fists like bricks.

In the 80's his innocent childhood nickname would become more sinister & synonymous with his favorite drug, cocaine. Ravele slowly slipped into the underbelly of narcotics. He indulged & peddled a whole lot of coke back in the day. He embodied the quintessential paradox: a family man who loved his roots but also strived in a dangerous world of Crips, drugs & crime. My big cuH, my loved one, Ravele, the notorious hard hitting knockout artist Big Coke Dogg from Five-Deuce Hoover Gangsta Crip!

I remember around my 10th birthday in the summer of 1975, my cousin, Coke Dogg, welcomed a new kid to our crew. It all started a couple days before, my cousin caught a kid, full of gall & mischief, hurling rocks at his beloved dog from the alley behind his crib. Coke Dogg caught this reckless troublemaker, red handed, alongside his homeboy, Mann from New Orleans, that was in town visiting for the summer.

The kid realized he was caught & outnumbered, so he hit the mad dash. This provoked them to engage in a frantic chase down the narrow alleyway. A puff of dust arose as they bolted down the paths like the roadrunner, the sun casting long, spectral shadows that danced alongside. They cornered the kid, who was remarkably big for a 11 year old.

"You gotta fight me, fool! You violated my crib & my dog!" Coke Dogg growls with his dukes up.

Coke Dogg & the rock-thrower locked eyes & squared up, but some odd reason neither one of them really wanted to squabble, instead of a fight, the tension in the air was replaced with unexpected camaraderie. Both Coke Dogg & the kid, named Robert, locked into an intense debate about who's mama was more gangsta! As you know my auntie Big Sand was one of the big homegirls of the Gladiators & turns out Robert's mom is a reputable Sherm dealer.

Similar Coke Dogg & I, Robert family moved to 54th street from the Pueblos & was now renting the apartment in the same duplex as Willbone. Robert's family occupied the upstairs, while Willbone's family resided on the first floor. This confrontation, could have taken an ugly turn, instead, led to a long-lasting friendship between Coke Dogg & Robert. Robert was introduced to our crew, and he was immediately embraced. A bond of camaraderie formed over familiar surroundings & shared experiences. Coke Dogg would often refer to his new friend as his baby brother – a testament to the deep connection they had developed.

In a show of brotherhood, Coke Dogg passed down his old nickname to Robert, CoCo. However, it was initially spelled with K's instead of C's, signifying 'Knockout.' Robert would become the infamous squabbler & 54th street bully, Big CoCo of Five-Deuce Hoover Gangsta Crip.

Flickering away on the big screen of my precious childhood memories, is my stint as a Drummer boy. My love of music led me to join the 52nd street school Cougars Band & Drill team in 5th & 6th grade. I had the privilege of associating with a brilliant ensemble. I was able to touch lives & transform dreams into reality to the rhythm of my bass & snare.

Mama Mary, was not related to me by blood but by love she was my family & a key figure in my life. She was my friends Michael & Robert's mother & the manager of the band. We shared an inseparable bond built over staccato & legato & her delicious home cooking. Her food was so good, she sold plates as a side hustle at her home on 54th street. Her son Michael was my classmate & I would also get close with his older brother Robert. They would become known as the notorious Lil Fat Rat & Cadillac Bobby of Five-Deuce Hoover Gangsta Crip.

The enthusiasm, energy, and ingenuity that Mama Mary brought to our rehearsals overflowed into our performance & most importantly our lives. She urged us to pour our hearts into our craft, to paint our artistic canvas with the colors of dedication, and perseverance.

Now, let me tell you about a night I will never forget! The spotlight was on us. We were on the stage, facing hundreds of eyes glued to our every move, our every beat at the LA Unified School District competition. Under the able guidance of Mama Mary & driven by the collective ambitions of vivid & eager young musicians, we set the stage on fire with our mesmerizing performance.

Our parade was a vivid palette of meticulous coordination & ebullient spirit. Led by my drum performance, propelled by the cadence of my determination, and embellished by my youthful zest, the spectators were treated to a delightful spectacle. It was not a mere act; it transcended into an unforgettable experience for everyone in attendance.

The repercussions of that success echoed for a long time. We didn't just win the competition—we won hearts. I became the heart throb drummer boy who drummed up a storm of admiration & accolades. School girls praised our performance; their screams of excitement & lavish praises brought a new kind of joy & purpose to my life.

The girls in the crowd were in awe of the music we created & the passion we radiated on stage. The encouragement & attention I received from them shot arrows of delightful pride & desire into my heart. I ain't lying when I say we were the shit! This experience taught me a lot, it imparted the value of teamwork, dedication, and the beautiful art of pleasure in work.

From the very beginning, many of the Hriginal & First Generation members of FDHGC stood by my side, loyal & unwavering. To think it all began with these innocent childhood adventures, where the seeds of our tribe would sprout & grow into a mighty tree, deeply rooted in the concrete of Los Angeles. As the years went by, our brotherhood grew & dominated, asserting our presence in Los Angeles.

One day I was hanging out on 54th street with the whole crew. Crazy Kev from the Gladiators walked by, he looked at us like *"Damn, you lil niggas is deep, I'ma call y'all the Fifty Boys cause y'all represent every street in the Fifties!"*

On 52nd street (The Deuce), We had Myself, Killa Dee, The Nevels - which included Hoova Luv, Bandit & their baby bro Lil Bandit never hesitated to face confrontation head-on. Baby Crazy, a boy with a rambunctious spirit who grew into a formidable gang member, fiercely defending his own.

My next door neighbor Jamaican Mike aka British Mike, who got his name due to his thick accent but wasn't neither British nor Jamaican, he is actually Belizean. These brave souls fought without fear, guided by the burning passion within their hearts.

Just a street away, on the block we dubbed the Tray, there was School Boy, Romel & WisH Dogg (Lil Spookee), residents of 53rd Street. Their addition to our generational members only made us stronger, for it was in the diversity of our collective that our camaraderie blossomed.

54th & 56th street had so many homies they could have easily been their own sets. The ferocious pack of homies on 54th Street (The Foe). Their ranks boasted the likes of Green-Eyed Kev & Dre Dogg. We had several families on the Foe, the Flores brothers- Willbone & Too Sweet, the Allens - Blacc Charles (Egghead), his brother Bobee &

60 | P a g e

his uncle Steve-O, Crip Crazy & his cousin Jaystone - were integral to our brotherhood, as were the Harris brothers, Cadillac Bobby, and Lil Fat Rat.

The Evans, a family of stalwart protectors of the Fifties consisting of Ken Dogg, and Insane Fish, with every additional soul, our bond only tightened, knowing that we had one another's back in times of struggle & strife. On 55th street (The Fifth) we had IncH HigH, his best friend Mouse & his sister Tee Dub, the sole homegirl & lastly my cousin, Coke Dogg. While we may have belonged to different streets, we were, first & foremost, a unified community, we became a family, one big happy gang.

56th Street (The Six) offered its own unique cast of characters, including the likes of Ant Capone, JoJo, Crazy DeDe & Ric Roc. The Six had several sets of brothers the Dailys (Bow Dee & C-Note), and the Miles brothers (Lil Live, Hoppin' Rod, and Slic Ric). Each of these souls not only brought strength but also richness to our brotherhood, fostering a sense of camaraderie that could never be severed.

On 57th Street (The Seven), we had the homie Cyko Mike & the enigmatic Parker brothers, Mad Dogg, and Bel-Aire. Armed with a tenacious spirit & ironclad loyalty, these individuals willingly battled any adversaries of the Groove in the name of honor, respect, and loyalty.

Finally, we had the formidable Big Fat Rat, a man whose very presence struck fear into the hearts of mere mortals. My main man Ray, the Boogeyman of 58th Street embodied the strength & unity that defined our tribe. The Fifty Boys.

Together, we fought, persevered, and triumphed over countless challenges that sought to keep us down. Despite adversities, our spirits remained unbroken, and our loyalty to one another never wavered. Through thick & thin, we stood side by side, fiercely devoted to each other from cradle to the grave.

> *"I believe in the brotherhood of all men, but I don't believe in wasting brotherhood on anyone who doesn't want to practice it with me. Brotherhood is a two-way street."* -Malcolm X

60 | P a g e

CHAPTER SEVEN:
"THE KIWÉ-OG HERBERT GATES
& FIVE-DEUCE UNDERGROUND"

The late '50s & early '60s were remembered as the glory days when the Gladiators claimed an undisputed reign over the blocks from Slauson Avenue to Martin Luther King Boulevard. With an iron fist in a velvet glove, Uncle James Ray had a subtle yet persuasive knack for maintaining order within chaos.

As time pressed on, however, the world continued to evolve. The Gladiators was slowly fading into history's pages. With their departure, the Brims rose to prominence in 1969, seizing the opportunity to claim supremacy over the Gladiators territory & rapidly becoming the largest gang on the west side.

History seemed to be marching forward, leaving behind the legend of the Gladiators. The year 1969 would also introduce oG Raymond Washington & the Cribs at Bethune middle school & Fremont High School, who would eventually become the notorious Crips & the Brims bitter rivals. Around 1971, on the school yard of 52nd Street School, a band of brothers was emerging. It was a time when we were all eager to be a part of something. A group of the fiercest young fighters in 52nd street school emerged known as the Suicide Gang.

Their ranks included Spookee, Blac Dee-Dee, and Big Red Jr, imposing figures with a fiery spirit. The ensemble was completed by Madman, Shithead Ted, Monkey Man, RP, Big Mike, Tony the Tiger, Evil Red & Stillbill, amongst a host of others. Their camaraderie, bravery & boisterous brawls earned them a reputation & a name that would echo through the Fifties. They became known as the Suicide Gang, a name that represented their courage & recklessness.

Of Course, the Suicides tried to recruit me, I was the best fighter in my grade hands down, I was considering it, cause that's my older brother, but my heart was on being a Crip. They brought T-shirts & ironed a big ass RED "S" on the chest that resembled the Suzuki Logo. Their prowess & fearlessness quickly earned them a reputation.

The Brims rapidly became notorious & seemingly untouchable, controlling both visible & invisible power lines throughout the westside, including real estate that was once the Gladiator domain. Their Suicides union marked the genesis of a fierce rivalry after an altercation at the Galley Hoe on 56th & Vermont, a showdown between High Schoolers & Elementary Schoolers.

Tony, Shithead Ted, and Stillbill, face off with the oG Brims, Angel, Pockets & Sugar Bear, the Brims possessed a one-sided advantage of size, strength, and age, however the Suicide Gang, wasn't deterred. They emerged as an opposition to this established order. The Suicides didn't last too long, but the reign of the Brims was soon to be challenged.

Introducing our OG, an Original Gangsta is somebody that commands respect & has earned it over the years. A reputable oG's name is synonymous with his gang. oG Herbert Gates is our Original Gangsta he introduced something new to the Fifties in 1972 & his name became synonymous with Westside 52nd Street Crip.

Gates introduced the Fifties to Westside Crippin', he lived on the corner of 52nd street & Hoover. OG Gates was a solid, imposing figure at 6 '3, he prided himself on being unique during an era when big naturals reigned supreme, he wore his signature baldie. He never dressed in the traditional Crip attire of the times; his swag was unique just like the Fifties.

Gates was a notorious, reputable member of the Original Westside Crips that kept a big old 44 caliber magnum like Dirty Harry as his favorite accessory. The Westside Crips were also known as the Undergrounds. oG Gates, oG Bogart & oG Davey Jones started a chapter of the Westside Crips on 52nd street, called Five-Deuce Underground Crip.

The legacy that the Gladiators once embraced was now split & torn between two rival factions, the Westside 52nd street Underground Crips & the Untouchable & 59th street Block Brims. The heart of the territory once ruled by the Gladiators was now at stake, brewing an inevitable storm of conflict.

Driven by an insatiable desire for respect & territorial control, the Crips soon began to terrorize the Brims, challenging their dominance & control. My brother Spookee, only 11 years old then, and his day one Blac DeeDee were inducted as Baby Crips of the fierce faction of the infamous Westside Crips. The metamorphosis of these two brave young men underscored the rising see-saw of power, adding weight to the Crips' side.

The ranks of the original Five-Deuces contained some of the most infamous personalities of the decade. Original Gangstas like Donald Douglas, Baby Johnny, his unpredictable brother Laleaze (Stillbill & Chucky Mac's uncles). Half-Breed (Ice & Lil Ice from Seven-Foe Hoover's older Brother), Shu Shane, Snake, Squirrel, Monk (Lil Madman's Uncle), Eric & Mark Washington (School Boy Q's Uncles), Maynard & Big Cap, Psycho Mike, Belizean John-John, and Davy Jones were synonymous with raw, primal courage.

To be a Crip, you needed to be a cold-blooded gangsta, a warrior in mind, body & soul. Enlisting in the Westside Crips was no easy feat. It meant being ready to put in work on Brims at every opportunity—shooting, stabbing, or fighting them whenever the chance presented itself, which gained Spookee his first trip to Juvenile Hall.

There was another initiation ritual - a stomach-churning gauntlet that mere whispers about could shiver the spine of the bravest. It was referred to as the Crip Gauntlet, a sort of soul train line reserved for wanna-Cee's. There wasn't any pop-locking, though.

The prospects were to stroll down an aisle aligned with blood thirsty Crips on both sides, their eyes glaring, fists clenched. Instead of funky music, the air was filled with the cries of battle, relentless attacks with fists, kicks, and even sticks, a true test of one's heart. One had to be fearless to walk this path. To be a Crip, one had to swallow fear whole & spit out courage.

At the tender age of seven, I was immersed in this turbulent Crip world. Watching my brother & his comrades terrorize their foes, I harbored a burning desire to become a Crip someday. I was young & ignorant of the warning signs that lit a path paved with perils.

Around this time my Pops was being proactive in trying to keep me on the street & narrow, he considered it his duty, and he believed he had found the perfect combination to satisfy my love for violence, and competition & to instill discipline: boxing.

He enlisted the help of Mr. Wiggles, a no-nonsense seasoned boxer-turned-coach who ran the after-school program at Hoover Street Gym on 78th street & Hoover Street. My father made sure I was well equipped to survive on the streets. Mr. Wiggles was more than a trainer, he was a well of hard-earned knowledge in the domain of boxing. His training sessions were not isolated to jabs, crosses & hooks; they were about discipline, resilience, and above all, HEART, getting back up after being knocked down.

> *"Boxing is an imitation of life. You get knocked down & you get back up. You don't quit no matter how dark it gets, or whatever adversity passes your way. "-Caleb Plant*

Tucked away in the heart of South Central, there was a time when Blacks weren't welcome at the Hoover Street Gym. The brick-&-mortar structure bore the remnants of a segregated past - originally open as a wrestling gym for whites only. Until a man named Irish Jake, took over & opened its doors to everyone, regardless of color or creed. Irish Jake was the spark that ignited change.

The Hoover Street Gym was not your everyday run of the mill boxing gym. It was sacred training grounds that had been graced by legends like Muhammad Ali, Smokin' Joe Frazier, Sugar Ray Robinson, Ken Norton, to name just a few, each a titan in the sports world who had shaped the direction of boxing history.

However, unbeknownst to my father, the lessons learned beneath the high ceilings & vintage, worn-out boxing ring would take on a life of its own. Rather than a temple to build hard-earned discipline, it began to feel more like a military boot camp, where I would prepare for a battle far removed from professional boxing—a different type of arena that was as unpredictable as it was dangerous.

I was destined to be a Gladiator & the streets of Los Angeles were my Colosseum. Contrary to my father's motives I was crafting my own path with its own set of rules. Unknowingly, Pops had created an urban warrior who found solace in hand to hand combat, street credibility & hood notoriety, refining raw power into a precision instrument, unhindered & untamed.

His love for order & discipline inadvertently helped me become a street fighter like Balrog. My knuckles didn't ache for the hardened leather of boxing gloves but craved the feeling of bare knuckles crushing Brim bones. My training assisted me in my rise through the ranks of the Crips.

Those were days of fire & brimstone, a time of change. My journey from the Hoover Gym to the enigmatic yet notorious Hoover

Gangsta Crip had been one of destiny & defiance. Where each jab was a stroke of rebellion, each hook an assertion of power.

This was the world I lived in, a world where being a Crip was a symbol of valor, a medal of bravery, and I aspired to wear it regardless of the cost. The dream rested in my young heart as I watched my brother & his Crip comrades reclaim the Gladiators territory in the name of the Crips, preparing myself for the day I would join their ranks.

Thus began the era of the Crips, a fraternity forged in the fire of rivalry, a creed conceived in courage & nurtured in the backstreets of 52nd street school. Little did we know then that this brotherhood would watch over us through time, shaping our destinies & scripting a story that would become the stuff of urban legends.

The Brims were audacious, carving out a reputation as they snarled at the opposition. Yet among their ranks, their ferocity was outshone by the Five-Deuce Underground & their allies, oG Raymond Chatman, Eddie Robinson, The Cole brothers & the Five-Six Syndicate Crips. Though their numbers were not overwhelming, their fortitude was another matter entirely.

The original Five-Deuces were witty strategists, stone-faced shooters, and ruthless cold-blooded killers. Their combined strength allowed them to gain control of the area that had been claimed by the Untouchable & Five-Nine Brims, laying the foundation for Westside Fifty Crip.

A power shift occurred on June 5, 1972; an unforgettable day seared in the memory of those that survived it & mourned by those who lost. The original Fifty Crips 5-2-6's, engaged in a fatal shootout with the Crips spilling first blood among the factions, claiming the life of an iconic Brim, Lil Kountry. It was an act the likes of which South Central had rarely ever witnessed. The Crips further displayed their lack of respect for the old order by invading Lil Kountry's funeral & committing the unthinkable - flipping his casket.

Now, the Brims had to respond, they gave chase. However, instead of exacting vengeance, they were caught in an ambush, the blaze of a drive-by shooting, one that marked an end to their claims to the area. This brutal attack served as a grim testament to the Crips' boldness & strategic brilliance. The infamous incident also signified the rise of the Westside Crips & their terrifying reign of South Central Los Angeles the last 50 years.

1974-the beginning of color banging, Blood or Cuzz, that's what it was. The Brims, now a part of the larger Blood alliance, continue their turf war with the original Five-Deuces that is changing the landscape & gang culture in Los Angeles. The original Five-Deuces numbers were rising simultaneously as the popularity of the Crips rose. I was now 9 years old & three things I knew was: One, I didn't like red, two, I didn't like Brims & three, I was born to Crip.

OG Gates & the original Five-Deuces had an on-sight campaign in place, on their conquest to eliminate the Brims. They commanded respect & put in work on anybody that looked like a Blood- anything red, was dead. The influence of the C & the Blue rag won over our area.

I have a childhood memory of another incident, one buried in the shadows of this metropolis that stays blind to the public eye. This event became one of LA's deep dark secrets that shaped it into the gang bang capital. The battles of the original Five-Deuces & the Block Brims were sugar-coated realities of a bitter story that rarely made headlines - an infamous display of Crip dominance that occurred around 1974. An early event in the fabled history of the transition of the Fifties from Brim to Crip.

Picture a dusky afternoon on the busy intersection of Vermont Avenue & 50th Street, outside of Challenger's Boys & Girls Club. A regular school day had just come to an end. The yawns of the city's routine were suddenly choked by the echoes of gunshots. As a school bus came to a stop & the doors drew open, members of the Brims unloaded, a horrendous hailstorm of bullets ripped through the calm afternoon air, creating a soundtrack of terror.

This afternoon went down in history as an infamous show of Westside Crip aggression, a brutal stunt that painted the town in hues of blue, fear, and grief. This infamous incident resulted in numerous unfortunate casualties. The memory left a permanent scar on those who endured it. It's hard to imagine how the narrative colored the aspirations of the impressionable youth of that era in shades of Crip blue.

Riding on a wave of misguided rebellion, the Fifty Boys & I, lured in by the apparent power & audacity the Crips possessed. Even while we stood in the aftermath of a catastrophe, we weren't detoured.

Instead, the allure was magnetic-we became entwined in the corrupt display of authority, superiority & camaraderie.

The brazen act introduced us to raw power & had us yearning for notoriety, for the inflated respect that Crippin' promised. The Fifty Boys, all merely children under 10 years young, started looking at the Crips with aspiration. We dreamed of establishing our imprint as Crips. A foolish admiration that would lead its secret admirers down a perilous path of death & lifelong incarceration.

The original Five-Deuces were now in the spotlight. They embraced their newfound authority, terrorizing the rest of the Brims in the Fifties with brute force. The reign of terror brought about by the original Five-Deuces had an unparalleled effect on South Central, brutality surpassed fairness, and strength triumphed over compassion.

Opening the doors for the rise of sets like Foe-Tray Hoover, Five-Six Syndicate, Five-One Catwalk Crips & every other set that followed in the area. The Brims gradually lost their claims to the streets between King & Slauson, I remember seeing Brims being chased up & down Vermont Ave, running for their lives Word of the Crips' tyranny spread across the alleyways & boulevards like wildfire, leaving nothing untouched in its wake, instilling a cold fear in people's hearts.

The Five-Deuce Underground Crips, born in the line of fire & baptized in blood, inaugurated a legacy that seared its signature of terror & supremacy. Their reign was not mere tenure; it was a brutal exhibition of power & control, reminding everyone that the absence of the Gladiators had not left a void, but instead birthed a more formidable force. They replaced the Gladiator legacy with a chilling dynasty marked by audacity, authority, and blunt dominance & I vowed to succeed oG Gates.

My mama wasn't a gang banger, but she was hip & aware of what was going on in the streets. She didn't approve of the aspects of Crippin' that involved Black on Black violence, but she respected their no nonsense approach & the unity the original Five Deuces displayed. I remember it was the holiday season, everyone was getting ready to put up colorful lights & decorations for Christmas.

*"Don't put **NO RED LIGHTS** on our muthafuckin' house, I don't want nobody thinkin' this a Blood House & shootin' this muthafucka up!"* My Mama shouted at us as we prepared to decorate our yard.

"Yeah Mama! We don't need anybody thinking that! I agreed excitedly as I untangled Christmas lights on the front lawn. Little did she know we were already a Crip household.

My Pops on the other hand, he didn't condone any gang shit, he didn't like the Crip business or the Black Panthers at all. He didn't like anything that involved socializing & groups of people. My father was always a man of few words, and he was socially awkward, sometimes I felt like he didn't love me or understand me, growing up he looked down on me for being a socialite.

The narrative of our lives took on darker shades as we grew into the gang culture that was a common thread running through life in our neighborhood. My older brother, Spookee, five years my senior, was my idol & nemesis in equal measure. His ascent through the ranks of the Five-Deuce Underground Crips was like a riveting action movie that held my attention all through my formative years.

Each step took him deeper into a world cloaked in danger & dire consequences. With his piercing eyes, steely resolve, hardened stance, and the ruthless glint of his silver gun always at the ready. Spookee seemed to embody untamed power & unruly glamour.

To my young mind, his mesmerizing world of violence & notoriety drew me in, and in my childlike naivety, I longed to emulate his machismo, bravery, and bravado. I would frequently lock horns with my big brother, in a desperate attempt to validate my worthiness & carry a slice of his audacity.

The exhilarating feelings each fight brought mimicked the thrill of stepping on a rollercoaster ride, only that, in this case, it was a G-ride, putting in work to prove my fortitude. I became a young David, constantly challenging my Goliath brother, recklessly pushing my pint-sized boundaries to prove that I too was Crip material. Gates' influence was everywhere. The Fifty Boys & I were eager to earn our blue rags as Baby Crips.

Gates got a life imprisonment for murder in 1974. Many of the original Five-Deuces, undoubtedly some of the toughest cats on the streets, were dimmed with life sentences also, the ones that remained joined the ranks of Five Deuce Hoover. Their absence from the field marked a change in the dynamic, yet it was by no means putting a stop to Crippin'.

Fast-forwarding through the sands of time to 1984 & you'll find yourself witness to an intriguing reunion between Spook, and his friend, his ally, his mentor, oG Gates. Nearly ten winters after Gates' conviction, a crucial link with the outside world was granted to him, reunited with Spookee on his first state bid at the infamous San Quentin. Spook was the bearer of remnants of the past & a beacon of the evolution that had taken place on the outside. He was the bridge between the past & the current reality.

Spookee shared that the set was still active but had evolved into Five-Deuce Hoover. This revelation churned a reaction deep within Gates, a mixture of surprise, emotion, and a yearning to be a part of the changing world he'd been distanced from.

In response, Gates cheerfully exclaimed, *"Well then, this Five-Deuce Hoover, cuH!"*

It was a declaration of his alliance to his set, despite the prison bars that separated him from his turf.

Regrettably, Gates, would breathe his last a few years later, the cause of his end being an ailment that he battled while serving his sentence. Despair arose from the haze of grief, a struggle that continues to reverberate in the hearts that he had left behind. The tales of his ventures promise a lifetime of hard-earned wisdom. We, his loved ones, his locs, are his legacy.

The loss of oG Gates was deeply felt by Crips everywhere, but his memory & teachings continued to inspire & unite us for years to come. His contributions to the Crip community should never be forgotten, and we will always remember him as a beloved figure in C-History. During oG Gates time in prison he was incarcerated with oG Hoover Joe Stanley, founder of the Hoover Crips & Seven-Foe & oG Pretty Tony, an Hriginal Eight Trey Hoover, both reputable Crip shot callers.

Even within the confining walls of prison, Gates continued to leave a historical mark. His far-reaching influence reflected in his collaboration with Hoover Joe Stanley, to establish the first Crip Car - notoriously known as the C-Machine, which would gradually progress into the notorious CCO-Crip Consolidated Organization post a merger with Blue Magic led by oG Big James Miller from Harlem Crip.

This was merely the start of Gates' influence in the Crips. Alongside Hoover Joe, they pioneered the creation of the first crip module within the California Department of Corrections, a stark two years prior to the infamous 4800 Crip module set in LA County.

Moreover, in 1980, Hoover Joe assigned Gates to pen 'The Constitution of Crip'. It was a document of unity & brotherhood within the context of the blue world. It outlawed set tripping, thus promoting shared interests & cohesion amongst the members. These men were not only leaders but visionaries, fighting for a united front in the face of external threats & rivalries. The 'Constitution of Crip' was a pioneer's call for unity, a testament to Hoover Joe's foresightedness & willingness to adapt to changing circumstances.

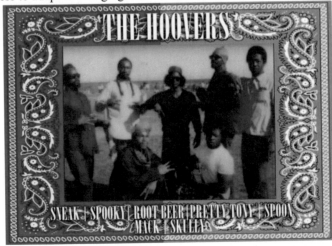

Contrary to popular belief the Hoovers were historically anti-set tripping, and unfortunately as we lost casualties to rival Crips, we became notorious for Crip on Crip violence. During his time in prison, he came up with our name-sake term, *"Kiwé"* (pronounced "Kee-Way"). The term *"Kiwé"* for Crip, which is derived from the Swahili word for Cripple, *"Kiwété"*. Today, the term stands as a testament to the C-machine's influence & vision.

The C-machine promoted the mind, body & soul, Hoover Joe wanted homies to excel & remain united. He saw the Crip Civil War on the horizon & tried to prevent the plague from spreading into the prison system. The C-machine pushed literacy programs & taught the homies how to read & write in English & Swahili.

The C-Machine implemented a physical fitness routine for all the locs on the yard at San Quentin. Their dedication to promoting education & physical fitness also helped elevate the minds & bodies of their fellow members.

CHAPTER EIGHT:
"KING CURTIS & THE ART OF THE HUSTLE"

Growing up in the heart of South Central Los Angeles, I was exposed to a lot of shit that my parents didn't want me to be a part of. The reality was I couldn't escape it. One person who was a constant presence in my life was my older brother, James', charismatic & magnetic friend, Curtis Frazier (King Curtis). He would become a mentor to me, his smooth demeanor & nonchalant attitude intrigued me, and I couldn't help but admire him.

King Curtis was a tall & lean man, always dressed in flashy clothes & a wide-brimmed hat. He had a smile that could light up a room, and the charisma to match. He always had a scheme up his sleeve, and everyone knew that if you needed anything, from drugs to black market merchandise, he was the man you had to go see.

Despite his shady reputation, King Curtis had a soft spot for me, and took me under his wing as his protégé. He would often pick me up from school & gradually I became his apprentice & mentee in the art of the hustle & con artistry. He taught me how to spot a mark from a mile away, and how to get whatever I want without getting caught.

King Curtis was my maestro. He had an entrepreneurial mindset that encapsulated his approach to life. He was charged with the energy of an electric current, which only intensified when he started to share stories about his latest ventures. The tales from his escapades painted vivid pictures of fast & flashy cars, all-night parties, and groovy pulsating beats. The way these stories lit up his eyes was contagious.

King Curtis taught me my first hustle, the weed game. He was the Colossus of Cannabis. King Curtis was the first to lay his hands on the much-coveted Columbian Gold strain of Mary Jane. Its buds were fluffy, and so sticky, it would leave crystals on my fingertips when I broke it up. It stank so good, it released a funky skunky, sweet aroma of lemons & limes into the atmosphere. It was this substance that would come to unite our spirits in ways I could never forget. As he introduced me to the world of marijuana, I discovered an entirely new & distinct subculture that existed within our community.

Columbian Gold was the shit, it was the za (exotics) of the 1970s & an ounce cost me only $10! I can't help but laugh, reminiscing. King Curtis taught me to eyeball an ounce precisely without a scale, a skill which seemed absurd, but in the ghetto where drugs were a prevalent revenue generator this skill came in handy & will serve me well for decades to come.

He also showed me how to roll the perfect joint for an exceptional high. At that moment, I felt as though I had entered a world far beyond school, homework & boring morning lectures, a world that welcomed me with open arms. King Curtis wasn't just a marijuana connoisseur.

He possessed the uncanny ability to make something out of nothing. The hustle seemed to seep out of his pores & engulf everyone he met. His most infamous trick was something known as the *"quick change."* As I peered over his shoulder on a busy Friday evening, he walked me through his method step by painstaking step. At the heart of the hustle was the art of distraction: keeping the cashier's eyes off of the real action long enough for the magic to happen. I was awestruck.

He would take me to the store to get a candy bar or soda, that's when the magic happened. He would distract the cashier by asking for change for a big bill. He would then confuse the cashier by giving them multiple bills & requesting different denominations until they were confused. While they tried to figure out how much change to give him, he would swiftly swap the bills & we ended up leaving with the item, the big bill, and the change for the big bill, which was actually the store's money.

He showed me various other scams: how to make a little extra on the side by turning my classmates into customers of my small slice of the marijuana market, and how to repurpose discarded or stolen items to sell for cash. These lessons were all coached within an essential ethical framework: never bite the hand that feeds you & always look out for your friends.

I was fascinated by King Curtis & his lifestyle. He seemed to have everything he wanted, from money to women, and I wanted the same. Sadly, King Curtis lost his life to cancer at 17 years young. He was the first person close to me that passed away & his service was the first funeral I attended without my parents. That day, I was accompanied by ScHool Boy, another person who understood the significance of our mentor. Tears coming down our cheeks, we paid our respects to the man who had opened our eyes & hearts to the subversive world of the hustle.

I couldn't believe he was gone; his absence left a void unlike anything I had experienced in my young life. My heart ached with the heaviness of grief & loss. I'll never forget him, South Central had a lot of love for him, his funeral was staggering; the procession stretched for miles, it was like the president died. I wept like a muthafucka at his services.

The people in South Central saw him as a king, and that's how he got his name. King Curtis was a big brother to me, and I will never forget him. More than four decades have passed since King Curtis graced the Fifties. Yet, his memory lives on, a lingering spirit of the wild & the unconventional. I will always remember him as a man who left an unfading mark on the people he touched.

The art of the hustle remains one of the most important chapters in my life story, an ode to the spirit of King Curtis. In moments when the world seems bleak & risk averse, I think back to those days in the 1970s, when King Curtis preached about the world beyond the Fifties, a world that promised adventure & camaraderie. His vibe, his style, and his determination has stuck with me, shaping the contours of my experiences & the adventures I have sought out.

Nowadays, as life takes its toll, I can't help but remember King Curtis: his grin, his laugh, his wit, and his exceptional talent for the hustle. Rest in peace, my nigga King Curtis, and know that your legacy will never be forgotten.

CHAPTER NINE:
"GOD & GANGSTA"

My mother stood as a straight-backed pillar of nerve & muscle, a resolute gust of unwavering determination. Indeed, my mama ran a tight ship & played no games. She was as affectionate as a Southern breeze, yet stern & unyielding like a cold Northern wind. The 1970s might have been ages ago, but the memories of my upbringing, under the unyielding watch of a strong black woman, are etched vividly in my memory as if it were just yesterday. I am black & I'm proud, and my mamma ensured that this sentiment was understood, accepted, and embraced.

She did her best to raise us right, drench our minds with love while instilling pride in our black heritage. She was an active advocate for the 'Black Panthers,' instilling in us the sense of justice & equality they fought for. She stirred a sense of profound consciousness into my veins about our struggle for civil rights.

At the same time, she took us to church every Sunday, marrying our social consciousness with spiritual grounding. Steadfast in her beliefs, she understood the importance of an Afro-American identity in a time when the winds of prejudice & discrimination freely swept across the nation.

Mama— a Black Panther, a strict disciplinarian, and a woman of faith — instilled in us the strength to achieve. She was a child of God, and we were her flock shepherded into the fold every Sunday. She knew the world was never going to take it easy on us, black children. Sundays were ordained for soulful surrender to the divine, attendance not negotiable but mandatory. A routine I despised more than anything.

"Mama," I would start, a pleading tone creeping into my voice, *"I don't wanna go to church."*

Unmoved, mama would cast a stern gaze with a silent message, *'no Sunday without church.'*

I couldn't comprehend the essence of my mother's commitment to these routines, the repetitiveness of it sucked the joy right out of me. Despite the annoyance I felt, quiet as kept I had respect that underlined my frustration. She told us that we could be anything we wanted to be. A doctor, lawyer, scholar, maybe even a writer– law-abiding, successful, and respected.

Instead, the streets called to me with their freedom, chaos, and unwritten rules of the G-Code. Getting taught alternate lessons about God & Gangsta within the same week created a dichotomy. The Lord- fighting the devil inside of me, and the Gangsta- battling the evils surrounding me. It was an education of sorts, and not one that everyone had the stomach to handle. I found solace in the rowdy laughter, the sneaky whispers, and the confusion that was a constant fixture around the way.

Momma had instilled in me the belief that I held the possibility of the universe within my grasp, all I had to do was reach out. My heart was yearning for something different, something that, in her eyes, was a path to perdition - I dreamt of being a Crip.

In the grand mesh of fantasies, the striking blue bandanas, the unity in adversity, and the strength it epitomized, the Crips were my hidden aspiration. My desire to stand out in those colors, to belong to something bigger than myself, was stronger than the pull of societal norms. Maybe it was the need for rebellion or perhaps my naive understanding of the world, drawn by the allure of what appeared as an exciting alternative to my rigid Sunday or School routine. It's a paradoxical irony that the woman who rooted for the liberation of the black community was raising a son who aspired to be part of an organization labeled as a notorious street gang that epitomized violence.

In my mind, the Crips relayed an unspoken narrative of righteousness & resistance. Being a Crip was not just about waving the glorious blue rag, Crip Walkin'& hand signs. It meant surviving, enduring, and thriving. It was about more than rebellion; it was about living true to oneself in an unforgiving world that demanded conformity. As a child, I didn't understand the Crip's complexity, the quagmire of crime & law. All I saw was a tight knit community of brothers, fighting for their survival in a world that was prejudiced against their color & existence.

I was uniquely drawn to my uncles, Roy, and James Ray. Their personas embodied the life I so desperately wanted. Roy, notorious yet respected, used to make a grand entrance with his lowriders, a spectacle that never failed to turn heads. His reputation for car theft added an edge to his already flamboyant persona.

My Uncle, James Ray, stood tall & revered as the leader of the Gladiators. The way he commanded respect was one of the silent pulls that drew me into Crip life. My admiration wasn't restricted to my family solely, it extended to the Hustlers & Gangstas, who were icons in my young eyes. King Curtis's cunning intelligence & the cool, calm & collected oG Herbert Gates & the original Five painted the picture of power & assertion that I aimed to mimic.

Reflecting, I realize my journey was shaped by magnetic & irresistible forces beyond my adolescent control. The unapologetic attitude of being black & proud, mingled with the magnetic allure of gangsterism to form the tapestry of my youth. It was an era of transformation & recklessness, infused with the complex duality that both shaped & marred my world perception. This is not a regret letter, but a testament to living amidst chaos, battling inner demons, and emerging with lessons etched deep within the soul.

I was a bad boy; Diddy could have made me the logo for his record label. A lot of parents couldn't stand me, they knew I was a bad influence & didn't want their kids hanging out with me. Unfortunately for those parents, all their kids would gravitate to me, so hate it or love it the underdog was on top, I wasn't going anywhere so they had to get to know me. I was not a mean-spirited child, but I had a knack for finding trouble. You could say trouble was my middle name. The truth is, I felt good doing things many people wouldn't dare try & that's one of the reasons I had such a massive following.

There was one exception to the rule. It was just another day around the way, summer 1975, giant beads of sweat made tracks down my face. As I wiped away the sweat from my brow, I spotted a kid hovering around my godmother's porch, eyeing her kittens deviously. There was something about his eyes—an uncommon blend of mischief & desperation—that propelled me to act.

This little nigga was trying to steal her kittens, and my immediate instinct was to beat some ass, so I sprang into action. Anger surged through me as I rushed towards him, ready to teach him a lesson. However, the scrawny thief was quicker than I expected, darting away before I could kick his skinny ass. A roaring fire of anger burnt within me as I realized I couldn't catch him. Frustrated, I watched him disappear, vowing to myself that I would catch him if it was the last thing I did.

Later, in the fading afternoon light, I was idling the hours away with School Boy, my loyal sidekick outside my house. We waved down this flamboyant, low-rider ice cream truck that often made rounds of our neighborhood. We eagerly waved down the baby blue truck, craving ice-cold relief.

I couldn't have expected that the moment making my order would change the course of my life. The kitten thief was riding shotgun in the ice cream truck, a picture of nonchalance. I was immediately set on edge, my instinct was to strike, but I held it together.

The man behind the wheel looked back & forth from the thief to me. He must have noticed the tension, his eyebrows knitted in concern. Much to my surprise, the cool, calm ice cream man was his father.

"Is this him?" muttered the Ice Cream Man.

Now, slightly more courageous under his father's presence. *"Yeah, that's him, Pops,"* he affirmed.

The man looked at me intently. His gaze was commanding but not threatening, *"What's your name, boy?"* he asked in a husky tone.

"Boo," was all I replied.

I was stunned into simplicity, yet somehow, I felt no fear.

"Okay, Boo, I'm Big Walt & this here is my son Lil Walt. Now, can you tell me what your problem is with my son?"

I was taken aback. It was an unusual thing to be asked this directly by an adult. I held my ground, *"I ain't got no problem with yo' son, Big Walt. He was trying to steal my god mama's kittens."*

Big Walt studied me silently, then, held out a thick wad of cash in his hand & then extended an invitation, a strange end to our discussion.

"I tell you what, come around the corner to 52nd street & see me."

"Why would I...?" I started to ask, but he shut me up with his outstretched hand full of money.

Time spent with Big Walt revealed a remarkable man. Big Walt wasn't just the ice cream man, he was a Muslim & entrepreneur, he owned a car lot, barber shop, and beauty supply. Big Walt admired the way I held my own in the streets, and he wanted that boldness to rub off on his son. Lil Walt always lived on 52nd street but I didn't know him.

First sight impressions? Lil Walt was different, that much was certain. He was the kind of person that stood out in a crowd, even when he was trying his best to fade into the background. That day I never would have thought we'd forge a friendship that would last a lifetime, eager for whatever adventures our future would hold.

I always felt loyalty was a prized trait, probably more valuable than gold, and Lil Walt & I had a lot of it. We had each other's backs & stood up for each other, navigating the highs & lows of teenage life in the hood. We became everyday niggas, living our lives with grit, resilience.

We became brothers through fights & prison bids, fun & women, and the sworn secrecy only best friends embrace. It would be a few years from now, but I would finally get to beat his ass when I put him on the set. I introduced him to the crew & to Crippin', he fell in love with it, Lil Walt, my loved one- more commonly known as the infamous Baby Crazy from Five-Deuce Hoover Gangsta Crip.

We had wonderful families but there was something enticing about Crippin' that we couldn't resist. Our lives were intertwined in the most unlikely circumstances & interactions, my life had changed in ways I couldn't fathom. So, the journey began on that brightly lit afternoon - a ten-year-old boy brooding over stolen kittens, an ice cream truck, and a fistful of dollars. It was not a shot in the dark, but a pathway illuminated by Big Walt's trust & companionship.

One thing that made Baby Crazy's home different was that his mother was a scary ass white woman that didn't let him come outside. Baby Crazy was a year younger than me, and despite being a kitten thief he hailed from one of the richest families on the westside.

As I look back & retell my tale, I realize we are, but pieces in the grand puzzle of life, slowly finding our place in the most unexpected slits & slots. We can carve out friendships from animosity & weave tapestries of brotherhood in the unlikeliest of circumstances, changing, evolving, and growing each day. Sometimes, the paths that lead us to our destinies could begin unexpectedly with a botched kitten heist.

CHAPTER TEN:
"THE ONE THAT FLEW OVER THE PIGEON COOP"

Before we started *"flippin' birds"* (selling coke), we were actually flipping birds. Around Fifth Grade, we started collecting tumblers & roller pigeons. I loved my birds just as much as Mike Tyson. We used to raise birds & pit bulls, and as we got older our hobbies became low riders, motorcycles, and women. We loved our animals; we never fought them or mistreated them.

A few homies had dogs, but a lot of us had pigeons, Myself & Baby Crazy on 52nd street, ScHool Boy, Catman & Romel on the Tray, Fish & Ken Dogg on the Foe, Ric Roc on the Six, Cyco Mike & Evil Red from the Seven, Big Fat Rat had one of my favorite collections. Then we had Hub, his baby brother Duck & C-Dog from 59th street, Scooby, Tim-Tim, Lil Sims & Bully Love from 74th street.

We loved our pigeons; we got in a few fights over the birds. We built pigeon coups in our backyards, but before we could release them, we had to leave them in the coup for a month, and after 30 days, you could let them out & they would come right back. Pigeons would never leave their babies or their source of food, so they were guaranteed to come back. We would get feed from the pet store, but it was cheaper to feed them popcorn kernels or rice grains.

Times have changed, we didn't view pigeons as *"flying rats"*, we admired them, they were so beautiful, they came in a variety of colors, and when we threw them in the air, they would perform, and come down rolling & tumbling, doing tricks & flips in the air, breathe taking aerial acrobatics. We would hold showcases with wagers over the best performance, sometimes it ended in a scuffle over the bets. Some people don't know the biggest pigeon ranch in the world was in Los Angeles at one time.

We even had our own language when it came to talking about our pigeons. We had certain terms for when they would fly in a certain way. If they flew in a circle, we called it *"circling up"*, and if they flew in fast swoops, we called it *"diving"*. We would watch them for hours on our rooftops, smoking weed & just admiring their grace.

We would try to *"stray"* each other's pigeons, I remember ScHool Boy would see my birds flying, then he let his birds fly too, and try to get some of my birds to go to his house. Sometimes it would work, one time I was able to steal one of Ken Dogg's birds. He was a horny ass bird that would go back & forth between coups. He would go to Ken Dogg's cage for 2 or 3 days, then come back to my cage for 2-3 days, he was a little pimp. Sometimes birds would stray, when they saw a flock, and I'd end up with gaining or losing birds like that.

Everybody had birds; it was a culture. We used to buy them at the pet shop, but it's cheaper to steal them so on ditch days, we walked around the hood seeing who was flying their birds, case their crib, and hit their cages when they weren't home. People don't realize how serious we were about those birds.

Back in 1975, life was all about adventure & testing boundaries for my friends & me. We were about 10 years old; we were young, curious, and just a little bit reckless. It wasn't just a fleeting interest for us; we made pigeon-collection more than just a hobby—it was our defining obsession. When I say we loved pigeons—I ain't lying!

However, acquiring this much-prized collection was not a cakewalk. It demanded a dash of daring, an ounce of audacity, and a generous sprinkle of good old childhood mischief. High-flying plans were hatched under the cover of the bright afternoon sun.

A revelation was introduced to our flock of pigeon aficionados. This new reality came in the form of a marvelous bird cage, a heavenly oasis occupied by the most splendid, winged creatures, an entire universe cocooned in glistening silver bars, just a stone's throw away. The owner, a white dude who was as alien to us as his impeccable sanctuary of winged creatures, had an established schedule - as regular as a clock. While he busy at his day job, his cherished sanctuary would be left unattended.

The innocent allure of the birds beckoned us, a siren call we were far too young to resist. Promptly, for the love of birdies, a daring raid was planned. I summoned some of my fellow Fifty Boys, Ken Dogg & Cyko Mike for the mission. Armed with our naive knowledge of heists from Sunday morning cartoons, we decided to steal the pigeons in broad daylight.

Our strategy was simple & held together by our unwavering determination. Splitting the roles among us, Ken Dogg hammered the locks, we would snatch up as many birds as we could as fast as we could. The mission was green lit, we advanced towards the bird sanctuary with a buoyant swagger. The warmth of the sun was as bright as the conviction in our hearts.

We moved with calculated precision, much like stealthy ninjas, our adolescent minds tuned to the solitary objective of securing the prize. Those beautiful air-defying feathered acrobats were well within our reach, a symphony to our ears, and a caper to our souls. However, as a certain Murphy's Law says, *'If anything can go wrong, it will.'* The flawlessly coordinated operation quickly cascaded into chaos as we were caught, red-handed!

The supposed-to-be-absent owner dashed out, bursting onto the scene. Panic ensued as our hearts pounded against our ribs matching the horrified drumming of wings from within the cage. The dream oasis had turned into a blaring pandemonium. our petite bird-loving band of thieves did what any self-respecting ten or eleven-year-old would do in such a situation. We hit the mad dash, fleeing the scene faster than you could say *"coo"*. Now, you got to picture this; three little bad ass kids, eyes as wide as saucers, hearts racing, legs pumping, racing away from the scene leaving dust trails behind us like Speedy Gonzalez! Arriba! Arriba!.

Cyko Mike wasn't as lucky – we looked back to see the white man dive & tackled Mike like he was 1974 Defensive player of the year, Joe Greene. I don't know how we got caught, I guess he got his speed from his white side. We saw his little body heading towards the ground with agony in his face as his bag of birds flew into the air! Releasing the mosaic of colorful birds to freedom taunting us as they flew towards a radiating orange sun & blue sky.

"*Damnnnn!*" Ken Dogg & I gasped simultaneously, as we looked at each other, without saying another word.

It was a sight none of us would ever forget, a whirl of panic, pain, liberation, and a strange hint of beauty. We knew we had a choice to make, go back, help Cyko Mike & risk losing the remaining precious birds or escape with our air defying captives.

We were Fifty Boys; we feared no one. The tight stranglehold on our friend jolted us back to action. We charged back, engaged the white man in a clash that we had not anticipated. We were small & young, but we were skilled backyard fighters. Our combined force of three young hearts fighting for our homeboy freedom mixed with audacity & luck, we managed to liberate Mike from the burly white man's clutches.

That afternoon, we returned home bearing more stories, new pigeons, a fierce spirit. We cherished Cyko Mike's courage & gifted him a couple of our birds, a token for our bond & his unbending spirit during the whole scenario.

Looking back now, I realize that day in 1975 was a mere reflection of the life we led as Fifty Boys. It was about our shared laughs, our endless escapades, the simple fascinations, and a friendship that was as wild & liberating as the pigeons we adored. It was about failures, triumphs, unexpected bravery, loyalty, taking risks, and creating unforgettable memories. All these still flutter in my heart, just as those pigeons did in LA's vast blue sky. The city has changed over the years, but the echoes of our childhood laughter resound therein, making these memories an indelible part of childhood's grandeur.

Baby Crazy had an aunt who lived on the outskirts of Compton, in a quiet street lined with modest houses & well-kept lawns. One hot summer day, Baby Crazy eagerly shared some intriguing news: He said his aunt had a neighbor who had an incredible collection of pigeons. Not just your average city birds, but exotic & rare breeds of tumblers & rolling pigeons that would capture the hearts of any bird enthusiast.

We loved everything about these fascinating creatures: the way they swooped through the sky, the colors of their feathers, and, of course, the thrilling spectacle of their acrobatics. This revelation sparked an impulsive & mischievous idea: we were going to steal some birds. It was settled: the Fifty boys were going to Compton.

We decided that we would pay Baby Crazy's aunt a visit & try to adopt some of those extraordinary pigeons from her neighbor. The first attempt went well, so we agreed to strike again with the same formula, cause if something isn't broken, don't fix it. At the time, we only knew how to get there by taking the bus & walking through a cemetery on South Central Avenue. So that's precisely what we did.

The day of the Pigeon heist arrived, and the excitement in the air was undeniable. We were determined to embark on this thrilling escapade, and nothing would stand in our way. Our plan was simple but audacious: we would sneak into the neighbor's yard early in the morning while everyone was at work & snatch up a few more of the exquisite birds to call our own.

As we made our way to Compton with my crimeys Baby Crazy, Insane Fish, and Romel. We couldn't help but feel like explorers on a great adventure. The thrill of the unknown pulsed through our veins, drowning out any fear we may have had. After a seemingly endless bus ride & a brisk walk through the cemetery, we finally arrived at our destination.

We spotted the house, a quaint, single-story home with a large backyard, and its seemingly infinite pigeon collection. Thanks to our thorough scouting, we found the perfect spot to sneak into the yard that appeared unguarded & unsuspicious. Our hearts pounded as we carefully climbed over the fence, trying to make as little noise as possible.

Once inside, the sight of the pigeon haven in front of us left us in complete awe. Birds of all shapes, sizes, and colors filled the small backyard, fluttering about in the gentle summer breeze. We wasted no time & began cherry-picking the most striking ones, placing them gently into our burlap sacks. In the heat of the moment, we filled each sack with five or six birds.

We couldn't believe our luck & thought it couldn't have been any easier, but some tried to resist capture & begin coo-cooing, wings flapping frantically. When suddenly the porch lights cut on, and we heard the owner hustling to unlock his back door. The rickety back door of the house swung open, and there stood the pigeon-loving neighbor—a fat older black man with a face like weather-beaten leather.

"What the fuck y'all lil niggas doing in my yard!" the old man with the potbelly & stretched out wife beater shouted!

We were caught! The owner of the prized pigeons had got us red-handed. His hand holding a massive Yosemite Sam gun, the kind you'd only see in cartoons. It was a surprising but terrifying sight. We went from elation to sheer panic in a split second.

Adrenaline surged through our veins, and we scrambled away, desperately clinging to our burlap sacks. With no time to think or plan, survival instincts kicked in, and we broke out into a desperate mad dash. Bullets whizzed past as we leaped over the fence & darted through the cemetery.

Thankfully, the pigeon keeper was an older, fat ass out of shape muthafucka with no chance of catching up to us. We could hear him panting & cursing behind us, but we refused to stop or even glance back.

We felt victorious, outpacing our pursuer, and leaving him in our dust. Leaving the cemetery behind, we reached the bus stop, drenched in sweat & clutching our bags of looted pigeons, we saw the old fat man's car racing toward us. He was determined to catch us before we could escape on the bus, intending to reclaim his prized birds & teach us a lesson by shooting our ass. The bus arrived right on time, sealing our escape route.

Boom! Boom!

He lets off two shots in our direction! We scrambled up the steps & found empty seats at the back. With a final burst of bravado, I gave the old man the middle finger as the bus pulled off. Our journey back to South Central was a beautiful mess, hearts racing, sweat pouring, and smiles plastered on our faces. Each of us cradled a burlap sack, nursing it like a cherished newborn. We were the proud captors of some of the finest pigeons our young eyes had ever laid eyes on.

As the weeks went by, we celebrated our success as daring avian bandits. We cared for those stolen pigeons like they were our own, gently tending to their every need. We marveled at our new collection every day, entranced as our treasures tumbled through the air in perfect formation. The Great Pigeon Heists of '75 were adventures for the ages, tales that would find a permanent home in our hearts for as long as we walk this earth.

Pigeons were a big part of our lives back then. They taught us responsibility, how to take care of something other than ourselves, and they also brought us together as a community. We would bond over our love for our pigeons, and it kept us out of trouble for the most part. Looking back now, it's crazy to think how something as simple as a bird could mean so much to us. It was a culture I was fascinated with. I plan on rebuilding my pigeon coup one day, and challenging Iron Mike.

Summer of 1975 was the perfect time to be a free-spirited boy growing up in South Central Los Angeles. Laughter filled the air as we played on the streets, while adults gathered around the barbecue pit on 54th grilling on hot afternoons. We didn't have much in terms of earthly possessions, but I knew from an early age that liberty & friendship were more valuable than any belongings.

Baby Crazy, my everyday nigga, I didn't just consider him as a friend, but a brother. We bonded over our shared sense of adventure, loyalty, and desire to escape the streets of South Central. While our fathers were friends, we felt a deeper connection in the unspoken rules & values of the urban jungle.

South Central Los Angeles was a place of resilience, ingenuity, and unwritten laws. My role models, King Curtis, oG Herbert Gates & Big Joe Ransom, were proof that these streets didn't define you but gave you character; they lived by the G code, and it resonated with us on an indescribable level.

Baby Crazy & I were struggling to find our place amid the turbulence of our surroundings. Little did we know that our lives would be forever changed by a game of harmless mischief. We were just children, after all, acting out of innocent curiosity but ignorant of the consequences. If only our parents had realized the harm they would cause by their overreactions.

As a young boy, I was constantly getting into trouble, but nothing could prepare me for the day when my old man discovered my antics. My friends & I were known as rascals around the way. I had a way of dragging all of us into my wild schemes, egging them on with my daring demeanor.

We did it all, from shoplifting candy bars from the corner store, quick change scams, to selling marijuana & firing BB guns at car windows. Nothing was out of our reach, and we happily followed each other's schemes & adventures. I led us to exhilaration & away from our boring chores, schoolwork, and tiresome responsibilities.

We thought we outsmarted everybody, that was until our fathers learned of our escapades & decided to teach us a lesson. Little did we know that the old man from the pigeon heist recognized Baby Crazy & told his Auntie. His Auntie covered for us & told the neighbor that Baby Crazy was away at summer camp, so it was impossible that he did it. What she did do was create a domino effect, telling his mother, who told his father, who told my father. Inadvertently igniting a sequence of events that would shake the very foundations of my family's relationships with one another.

One Saturday morning, I was awoken by my father's voice, asking me to spend the day with him. The excitement of spending some one-on-one time with the man I admired & loved the most was overwhelming. I was thrilled beyond words as I showered & dressed, thoughts of father-son bonding flooded my young mind.

I couldn't believe it Pops was taking me to Roscoe's, the one place where everything seemed possible, and dreams were cooked in cast iron pans, doused in syrup, and delivered on big white plates. A pause from the endless loop of beatings & chastising. This event was cherished, because quality time with my father was as rare as a black man becoming POTUS.

The world melted away as I sank my teeth into Roscoe's famous 1/2 chicken & 2 waffle dish, joy dancing on my taste buds & soaking into my very being. My father enveloped me with attention, and for that moment, I felt more special than I ever had in my life. The sun shone through the windows & captivated the soulful hum of the patrons in the eatery, but a storm was quietly brewing. Little did I know that the unfolding events of the day would not just change the dynamics of my relationship with my father, as my family nucleus, but also teach me some unforgettable lessons in life.

The day began on a high note with my favorite meal at Roscoe's. I cherished every bite of the famous dish, a perfect dish for a memorable day with my father. At this point, our bond seemed unbreakable, and I felt special to be the apple of my father's eye.

As we finished our meal, we departed on a journey I never could have anticipated. My father's expression transitioned from joy to anger as he revealed his plan for me. He had discovered my secret shenanigans. He looked me dead in the eye & told me that Baby Crazy's parents had spilled the beans about our wrongdoings.

"You been thievin'! You know I don't play that shit boy! I see you think it's a joke, so I'm learnin' you a lesson today!" His voice dripped with anger, rage simmering just beneath the surface as his eyes bored into mine.

He was determined to scare me straight, and with every word he spoke, my heart fell deeper into the abyss of fear. His anger & disappointment were blatant as he tried to teach me a lesson for my dishonest actions. His approach stemmed from the traditional belief of laying down the law to discipline bad ass kids. This decision, made with righteous intentions, accidentally had a negative impact on my life.

Despite his efforts, this decision did not produce the desired effect. Baby Crazy's parents, who were also aware of our antics, placed him in the juvenile hall also, turning the experience into one that only solidified our bond. Who would have thought the pigeon heist would lead to my unraveling, as it chipped away at the already rocky relationship with my father.

Pigeons held a peculiar place in my young mind, it represented a sliver of innocence & positivity amid a rough childhood. I took joy in helping them to their meals, caring for them & laughing at their delightful cooing & acrobatics. Those birds were my silent companions, my escape from my harsh reality.

When their innocent image was tarnished by my heist, adding yet another layer to my collection of punishments, it was hard to bear. Instead of resorting to the familiar route of peddling physical punishment, my father decided to drop me off at Juvenile Hall. I was merely ten, grappling to understand the overwhelming emotions churning within me.

As I stared out of the small, dirty window at Central Juvenile Hall, gazing at the Los Angeles skyline over barbed wire walls, anger & frustration filled my soul. The dark metal bars that separated me from the outside world were a constant reminder of the shackles in my life. I couldn't believe that instead of spending my summer playing in the schoolyard or hanging out with my friends' riding bikes, I was a captive. Trapped in this grim place with only the company of my good friend, Baby Crazy, who was just as confused as I was.

We didn't know how long we would be locked away in Eastlake. Our fathers must have come up with this dumb idea together. Unfortunately, I turned 10 years old at Eastlake, we had no idea about what respite meant. All I knew was I felt an overwhelming sense of betrayal by my pops. I was aware of the code of the streets that my role models lived by, but now it seemed like my own father was disrespecting it. My heart sank as my thoughts became consumed with disappointment in my father.

I never understood why they thought lock up was the answer. Maybe it was our fathers' way of protecting us from the harsh realities of the streets, but to Baby Crazy & I, it felt like an injustice & a betrayal. Being confined to Central broke every code our role models lived by, and it was this betrayal that marked the beginning of my resentment towards the man who was supposed to be my anchor, my protector.

As the days slowly turned into weeks, it seemed like my precious summer vacation was slipping through my fingers. The days spent in Central Juvenile Hall seemed to drag on forever. Long, hot days blurred with gloomy nights as Baby Crazy & I were torn out of the world we knew, and placed in a cold, alien environment. The only silver lining was having each other, as we were the only real family we had while in captivity. We talked about all the things we could accomplish together, the people who had wronged us, and what it meant to live the life we wanted.

My father, blinded by fury, didn't even know the repercussions of his actions. The cold bars that housed me in that juvenile hall began to take a toll upon my heart, hardening my spirit & truly scaring me into a rebellious delinquent. What had started as a warm day full of love, chicken & waffles had morphed into a chilling reality of consequences, one that would echo throughout my entire life.

When I was finally released, I couldn't shake the overwhelming anger & resentment towards my father. Thirty long days had finally passed, and my parents came to pick me up. The car ride home was silent, yet heavy with unspoken emotions, the strained silence spoke volumes about the damage that had been done. I had nothing to say to the man who had betrayed me, and that distance only widened the rift. At that moment, I couldn't decide what was worse - being a bastard child or being stuck with this nigga in my life.

When I got home, the bitterness growing inside me began to seep into every aspect of my life. I became more defiant at home, in school, and in the streets. My father must have thought that I was losing my mind, as he'd always say, *"Fuck the Cuckoo's nest, that boy done flew over the pigeon coop."*

At this point, my father realized the repercussions of his decision, not just emotionally but also financially, as the juvenile hall charged him $2,000 for voluntarily placing me without having committed a crime. The day my father received the first bill for my stay at Juvenile Hall was the day everything nearly collapsed. His pay was garnished, and the frustration & bitterness heightened the tension in our already unstable relationship.

I could see the strain on my mother's face, but it wasn't enough to bring my father & I back together. Each of us was fortified in our own emotional fortress & neither seemed willing to admit defeat. As the bills piled up, the consequences of his choices only served to widen the gap within our family, as my mother became infuriated. The chasm between us became a permanent fixture of our lives.

For many, the story of the pigeon heist might seem like little more than an amusing childhood tale. Yet for Baby Crazy & I, the consequences of our fathers' inconsiderate, heavy-handed approach continue to resonate in our lives. Although the story takes place in 1975, the lessons it holds for parents today are timeless: the importance of listening to your child, understanding their perspective, and teaching them consequences are truly meaningful & constructive.

Had our parents taken the time to learn more about our motivations & the social norms that governed our surroundings, they might have chosen a more informed approach to discipline, and our lives might have taken a different path. Instead, we were branded delinquents & subjected to misguided attempts to correct our behavior. The trust & respect between parent & child were irrevocably damaged, and the repercussions of those decisions continue to shape our lives today.

The absence of adequate consideration escalated my previous misbehaviors to entirely new levels of recklessness. This change was evident not only in my demeanor but also in the decisions that followed. From the innocent experiences with pigeons, I was propelled into the dark world of violence & crime, undisputedly numb to the ensuing consequences.

This incident left me emotionally shattered. The one place I called home no longer felt welcoming; the pain of separation was so intense I would have preferred enduring his beatings. This extreme experience changed my perspective dramatically & impacted my persona immensely. I became more prone to violence, became numb to consequences, and an aggressive streak manifested itself in my career as a Crip. In retrospect it seems the foundation of my journey towards juvenile delinquency & a life of crime laid on the concrete of corporal punishment & neglect.

CHAPTER ELEVEN: "TOO HARD TOO CRY, TOO YOUNG TO DIE"

The unforgiving Crip lifestyle that Spookee was entangled in was not as glamorous as it appeared from the scope of my youthful curiosity. By 1975, the intimidating walls of Juvenile Hall had become a second home for him. OG Gates & many of his fellow Crips were on a collision course with life sentences. Three-fourths of Spookee's life would become ensnared in the cruel, unyielding jaws of the justice system.

Ironically, rather than being horrified, the ominous gray walls of juvenile hall served to fortify my budding desire to follow in Spookee's footsteps. I became an original baby Crip of a new set called the West Town 52nd street Crips. I was excited to taste the same intoxicating cocktail of danger & supremacy that filled Spookee's cup. Following in his footsteps as pioneer Crips of our respective crews.

I was a foolish ten-year-old, in my misguided enthusiasm, I sought the excitement that seemed to encapsulate my sibling's life. I began following in his footsteps chasing after an adrenaline high, enticed by the dangerous lure of power, violence, and respect that the Crip culture provided, a deal with the devil that was too compelling to resist.

My rites of passage into the Crips, overseen by OG Big Choo, was a landmark event of my early years. I was mentored by the big homies of the West Towns, names like Big Tee, oG John Hunt, Crazy Poke, Fat Dogg, Whitey, Capone & Bugsy Malone. Myself, Captain Rainbow (Choo's baby brother), Preschool, and Lil Capone were the youngest members of the original West Towns. I was able to learn from the West Towns & little did I know I would use that knowledge to lay the foundation for my own powerhouse. The Q-bones, Angel, Pitbull, Insane, Gangsta Roc & his brother Caesar Mike, Baby Capone (Capone's Brothers), Hot Shot (John Hunt Baby Bro), and Bo Raspberry were some of my ace boons from West Towns.

My rookie year as a Baby Crip, I was getting my feet wet, doing petty crimes, robberies, selling drugs, scamming & of course, banging on any red rags I came across. Donning my blue bandana to make sure everyone knew who I was & what I represent. Boo Diggs from the West Town Five-Deuce Crip.

On one particularly hot Saturday, we heard about a house party that was happening a few blocks away at a kid named Noodles' crib. We were all young, full of energy, and eager to meet new people, so we decided to crash the party in search of girls & good times.

Intentions were good as we set out with excitement & anticipation for what the night might reveal. Upon arrival, we were greeted with loud music, *"Fire"* by the Ohio Players, shook the walls of the small house. Loud laughter, and the aroma of weed floated in the air, mixed with the fragrant perfumes of the girls milling around.

We tried strolling in like we owned the place, Noodles caught a glimpse of us. An intense glare of disdain washed over his face. Suddenly, our entry to the party was barred by a wall of older kids – that I came to know as Noodles, Sniper, One Punch, and some of their cousins & homeboys. Sizing up intruders was the norm in those days.

"Who the hell y'all think y'all are? This a private party!" Noodles spat at us, raising his chin as if looking down on us.

There was no way we would back down; our reputations were at stake. Fueled by pubescent bravado, our encounter quickly escalated into an argument. Tempers flared, and angry words flew back & forth.

Both sides sized each other up, each daring the other to make the first move.

Curiosity, testosterone, and an implacable desire for respect fueled our resistance. We saw some girls outside & decided to mix & mingle. We eventually left the party with our new female friends in tow. We still managed to have a good night, nursing resentment that we assumed would last for years to come.

A few days after our confrontation, Caesar Mike & Gangsta Roc ran into Sniper, after some heated discussion they decided to squash the beef between our two factions & joined forces instead. The simmering animosity transformed into new members to the ranks of the West Towns. Weeks passed, and the summer days melted into one another.

One hot afternoon, I found myself on Vernon & Broadway spray-painting *"52 Crip"* on a corner store. Sniper happened to pass by, and upon seeing me, he mistook me for a Blood! Instinctively, he rushed toward me, ready for conflict.

Sniper thought I had a strong resemblance to a kid named Nana from East Side Blood Stone Villain. People often said that we were identical twins, sharing everything from our facial features to our height. It was both humorous & odd how two people, representing opposing sides of the same coin, could resemble each other so much.

Retaining my calm, I swiftly introduced myself as *"Boo Diggs from West Town Five-Deuce Crip."* Sniper's demeanor changed instantly as he recognized who I was, and our supposed rivalry turned into a newfound friendship. We laughed off the initial misunderstanding, and from that day on, Sniper & I have been as thick as thieves. I had concerns about this red rag doppelganger as mistaken identity could be fatal in the color driven, shoot first-ask questions later, gangbang capital.

Colors carry a meaningful presence in how people interpret society & the world around them. These hues have the power to evoke strong emotional responses that touch the very core of human behavior. In America, one of the most striking color combinations is red & blue. With roots in our country's history, politics, and culture, these colors not only represent different political factions but have also become associated with some of the nation's criminal underworld.

For centuries, red has symbolized energy, strength, and passion. In various cultures, it has been a sign of lifeblood, fire, and intensity. On the other hand, blue has traditionally represented stability, harmony, and trust. It evokes feelings of tranquility, and in some cultures, is associated with clarity & depth of thought.

When it comes to US history, one cannot separate the concept of red & blue from the nation's flag. The colors incorporated in Old Glory represent key aspects of America's identity as a country. Blue stands for vigilance, perseverance, and justice, while red signifies valor & bravery, while white symbolizes purity & innocence. Through these colors, American history has interwoven ideals that have shaped modern politics, culture, and even gangbanging.

The significance of red & blue has evolved throughout the years to great prominence in American politics. Symbolizing the partisan divide between Democrats & Republicans, with states voting for the Democratic presidential candidate referred to as blue states, while Republican strongholds are christened red states. This division showcases the different perspectives associated with these political affiliations.

The color-coded political divide has become present in Americans' lifestyles, preferences, and even beliefs. Blue states, predominantly located on the coasts, tend to exhibit more liberal & progressive values. Red states, primarily in the South & Midwest, are more likely to adhere to traditional, conservative beliefs. The association of red & blue with distinct ideologies reflects a deep-seated contradiction within America & the different expectations & hopes that citizens have for our nation's future.

The importance of red & blue in American society does not stop at politics; it further extends to the realm of gang culture. The colors function as identifiers for various gang affiliations. Mexican hoods in California, the Surenos & Nortenos, illustrate this connection vividly. The Surenos, originating in Southern California, are known to use blue to represent their organization, while their rivals, the Nortenos, hailing from Northern California, are identified by their use of red.

Similarly, the connection between red & blue within the Crips & Bloods is deeply entwined with California's history. The Crips are known for their loyalty to blue. Directly opposing us are the Bloods, forming in response to the violence perpetuated by the Crips, are associated with red. The rivalry between these factions further emphasizes the intensity tied to red & blue.

If we look at the historical, political, and gang-related aspects associated with red & blue it shows us the depth & complexity of American culture. They embody our beliefs & affiliations in a diverse society, revealing how simple colors can have profound meaning.

It's the American way. Whether it's on the battlefield, in politics, or on the streets, the colors red & blue have had a significant impact on American culture. Colors continue to hold a powerful meaning today & will likely continue to do so for years to come.

When I entered the Los Angeles Crip & Blood universe it was all about blue rags or red rags, which we called *"color banging"*. It was on sight with Bloods, an alliance of off brand hoods that opposed the C, meaning automatically when you see one it was time for some action usually, a fist fight, maybe a stabbing, or rat pack (jumping someone), murders were still rare. All Blue rags were united, it was a good time to be a Crip. We were just mischievous kids getting into trouble & having fun.

British novelist L.P Harley once said, *"The past is a foreign country; they do things differently there."* This could not be more exact. When I cast my mind back to 1975, an era so distant it might as well have been another world. It was a time when life felt rawer, the edges sharper, my Los Angeles was far from the polished veneer it sports today. I was all of ten years old then, a bright-eyed, skinny child sitting on a cusp, one toe lingering in the innocence of childhood & another stepping into the Crip life.

My young eyes viewed the world differently than other kids, I had money on my mind focused on chasing dreams & making fast cash. I continued to implement the skills passed down to me by the late King Curtis, enterprising marijuana in the ghetto economy. My Big Bro Spookee just returned from juvenile hall, and we were each other's tagalong.

He was my mentor & under his guidance, I had jumped off the porch navigating the cold Crip underworld. We spent countless hours in the park, selling weed or PCP & hanging out, the aura of invincibility around us amplifying our juvenile recklessness. Today we are peddling two-dollar weed bags. Times were tough, but Mary Jane helped us get by.

Centinela Park, a sprawling 55-acre park. Overrun with shabby grass, it was an urban oasis dotted with towering trees & a mishmash of things to do in full swing. It was a popular hangout spot with basketball courts, soccer & football fields, and my favorite was an enormous swimming pool. You would find everyone from courting couples to aging veterans, children to drug pushers & Crips gracing the park.

The park was unique because it was disputed land – found in the heart of the Inglewood Family Bloods territory, yet ironically, it was a Crip domain. It was an alluring paradox, a picture of juvenile pandemonium amidst urban tranquility – & I was irresistibly drawn to it.

I still distinctly remember the day I met two legendary Original Gangstas, Stanley *"Tookie"* Williams & Jimel *"Sampson"* Barnes. Their Herculean stature stood prominently against the backdrop of the park, comparable to a couple sons of Zeus. Tookie & Sampson, shirtless, in faded overalls sporting imposing powerlifting belts.

One could feel the aura of raw power that emanated from them. These were Kiwé warriors in their primal form. They were in the park working out, two imposing figures *"breaking out"*, flexing their biceps & pecs for the admiring & apprehensive girls that drooled over them & little boys like me that aspired to be yoked like them when we grow up.

There was a charisma that spilled from their pores like beads of sweat, one that you couldn't help but notice. With their towering presence they were without a doubt, the largest Crips I had ever seen. Spookee decided it was time for introductions. With a casual arm tossed across my shoulders, he led me towards them.

"Aye Took, this my lil bro Boo from West Town Five-Deuce, Boo this the big homie Tookie," Spookee announced in his baritone.

I remember feeling intimidated, hands clammy as I held out mine in greeting. The handshake firm, I could feel the power & assurance in Tookie's grip, it was awe-inspiring.

A quick nod, a simple *"What up, cuH,"* as he returned to his workout routines, and we went back to making green off green.

Tookie was almost a decade older than me, so we didn't run in the same circle, but he embraced me & showed me Crip love whenever our paths crossed. He was a constant feature at all the social events

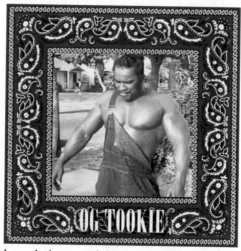

around the west side, often working security with Sampson at events, including concerts at Centinela Bowl, a large outdoor amphitheater in the park.

OG TOOKIE

It would be a glaring oversight to ignore the far-reaching influences of oG Tookie & oG Sampson, as the catalyst of bodybuilding within the Crips. They were the embodiment of power, discipline, and dedication, being every bit the force of nature we aspired to become.

Our pursuit of physical dominance wasn't aided by performance-enhancing drugs. We didn't hold the keys to synthetic strength that the white boys flaunting their chiseled torsos on Venice Beach did. Steroids were but a distant whisper in our world, as foreign to us as the silver spoon.

We got buff without shortcuts. We had to claw & grind our way towards it, every drop of sweat shed under the grueling LA sun signifying another rung climbed up the ladder. We pumped iron born out of the fire of brotherly competition, our grit forged in the melting pot of adversity & violence.

Without a doubt, each one of us was motivated by Tookie to walk around with the trademark, little ass legs with some big ass arms. They became inflamed visions in our minds, symbolizing manhood, virility, aggressiveness, and sheer strength mixed with an odd charisma we grew to admire. The surge of strength in every flexed muscle, and the solid gritty rawness of these individuals became a striking testament to the culture that turned our streets into an unfathomable gym & many of us could've been bodybuilding legends.

The city of angels was in the grip of a crime wave that was as much a product of desperation as it was of rebellion. At the epicenter of the madness was Boo & Spookee, the nightmares of 52nd place. The world was a shag carpet underneath our feet. As we stood on the corner of our kingdom, the hum of a Chevy impala passing by, and the distant wails of sirens that often announced another breach of the law by the Crips. If there was a throne for the brazen, we claimed it.

Growing up in Los Angeles, we were nurtured on a diet of rugged streets, racial divides, and economic disparity. Our adolescent minds were conditioned to perceive life through the lens of survival & not surrender — to remain stone cold & emotionless in the face of adversity & display no signs of vulnerability.

Spookee was snatched up by the unforgiving grasp of justice after a botched robbery landed him in Juvenile Hall awaiting sentencing. His absence wasn't just a void for me—it was an invitation, a challenge to step up & walk in my brother's Romeos. Fueled by my brother's incarceration, I was adamant to outshine him, to prove my worth & display the sheer intensity of Crippin' that coursed in my veins.

The desire to be perceived as big & bad as Spookee had propelled me into a crime spree of my own. Rage, rebellion, and reckless abandonment created a Molotov cocktail within me & the blatant disregard for law sculpted me into a juvenile juggernaut. I thought, at the time, that success in this toxic quest would help me gain the acceptance I craved, not just within our fraternity, but in the eyes of big bro.

Last year my father had intended to put me on the straight & narrow by sending me to juvenile hall. This move left me uncaring & nonchalant about the repercussions of my actions. Instead of seeking a way out of the abyss, I jumped headfirst in it, embarking on my reckless spree of lawlessness. Night after night, the city became my playground.

The adrenaline & need for affirmation motivated me, so I stole a car, I snatched purses from unsuspecting pedestrians, I assaulted red rags on sight. I jacked fools for their Schwinns & minibikes, anything that caught my eye. In one extraordinary act before 6th grade graduation. I committed a Picture day shakedown, patting down my classmates' pockets. Snatching their envelopes full of money & memories.

Juvenile hall turned into my second home, an unsettlingly frequent haunt as I found myself ensnared within its walls nine times over the span of 30 days. With each arrest, my determination solidified. I was not trying to evade the pigs. I wanted them to catch me & acknowledge my existence, my defiance.

The reason behind this unusual determination extended far beyond the need for approval or the thrill of out doing Spookee. It was rooted in a brother's love & the desire to stand by him. Each handcuff wrapped around my wrists served as a twisted emblem of brotherhood, each court hearing a silent testimony of my loyalty to my brother.

From the outside looking in this was insanity, yet to me, it was more than just a bravado or blind rebellion. It was a testament to the unity, the bond we shared. I felt an intense need to fight by his side & offer him the support I believed he required. In return, his presence beside me also served as a comforting anchor amid the anxiety-ridden uncertainty of my life. Simply put, I was too hard to cry & too young to die!

The court oddly found sympathy for my little ass & kept releasing me. A sense of frustration grew with each release; it was as if I was denied the right to stand by my brother, to share in his plight. I was like a boomerang, I found my way back to Juvenile Hall, desperately voyaging for solidarity until Spookee was sentenced. He was sent to a detention camp for 2 years, an establishment I was too young to inhabit.

In desperation, my father decided that I needed to see a shrink. I despised every moment spent in that dreary, impersonal office. The shrink would prove useless, as I had lost faith in the adults who claimed to know what was best for me.

Refusing to engage, I became even more resentful towards my father, spiraling into a deep chasm of mutual hatred & misunderstandings. My refusal only fueled the tension between my father & I but at the time I didn't give a damn, I was deaf, dumb, and blind to my father's efforts to save me from my fate & continued to follow in Spookee's haunted trail.

103 | P a g e

The year is now 1976 & change is in the air. Every alley echoed with a fresh, underground vibe that was a strange blend of unity, power, and rebellion against the system. South Central was a mosaic of personalities carving out their borders with swagger & pride. Amidst this evolution, the Fifty Boys were trying to carve out a space of our own.

It's a time that saw the Westside Crips in decline, as sets continued carving up the city into new territories, old turfs were adopting new identities, the Crips were going through a makeover. We were too young to develop a genuine relationship with Gates & his crew before they were taken off the street.

In lieu of the Undergrounds & Syndicates absence, a new generation of Crips were on the horizon in the Fifties that would change the face of the C forever, and the same changing of the guard was occurring all over this Crazy Crip City.

If you asked me who my ace boon coons were, I'd have to say the Fifty Boys. We were real homies like brothers from different mothers. We had a tough crew of bad ass little niggas, which became a wrecking crew. I was the vanguard of Crip amongst us. However, an incident occurred that was the catalyst for the rest of the Fifty Boys transition into Crippin'.

One evening while Coke Dogg, CoCo, and O-Dogg were getting drunk on Vermont Ave. The Six-Deuce Brims, Nell Dogg, Al Dogg, and Pug & some Van Ness Gangsta Brims bust on them. The hailstorm of bullets etched deep rifts of hatred for the Red Rags within their hearts. This attack germinated the decision to identify as their adversaries marking the birth of the Fabulous Fifty Crip. The metamorphosis was gradual; it started with Coke Dogg, wall banging, tagging names of imaginary Crips like oG Grumpy, Big Speedy & a host of others, a military mind at 13 using mental warfare tactics to make their ranks seem more impressive to prospects & intimidating to the Bloods.

The echo of their newfound identity reverberated through every crack & crevice in the hood. Before I knew it many of the Fifty Boys: Ric Roc, Cadillac Bob, Willbone, Too Sweet, Sham Roc, Ken Dogg, Dre Dogg, Fat Rat, ScHool Boy, Bow Dee, Lil Live, Madman, Bandit, Lovely, Blacc Charles, Mad Dogg, Cyko Mike, Slicc Ricc, Jaystone & Ant Capone. One by one they began to jump off the porch

103 | P a g e

& rally under the blue bandana. The Fabulous Fifty Crips had emerged. The birth of our brotherhood was etched into the veins of our streets, Two-Owe-Foe-Five-Six, it symbolized the essence of each block we claimed.

I watched proudly admiring their coming age, as they practiced their one hitter quitters on random Mexicans & pedestrians & running their pockets. I loved it! I relished in their transformation into daring, fearless Crips. They were becoming more brazen, more gangsta as they got their Crip on, jackin' fools stuck in gridlock traffic on 54th street after USC games & events at the Coliseum.

Raiding the bus & robbing everyone on it, spraying them with fire extinguishers. They became an intricate pickpocket gang as well, taking people wallet then passing it off discreetly to another homie like a hot potato so if someone spied the swipe & alerted authorities, the evidence would no longer be in their possession. As the apostle of this Fifty fraternity, I was a proud observer of their unapologetic journey into Criphood.

One day on the bus, Coke Dogg & CoCo ran into some Broadways, who asked what they were claiming. They replied proudly, *"Fabulous' Fifty Crip!"*

The Broadways insulted them, *"That ain't a good look."*

Coke Dogg, never one to back down, told them *"We don't give a fuck! That's what we claimin'!"*

The 110 freeway was the boundary that separated Fifty Crip, from the West Towns who adopted a new identity as the West Town Five-Deuce Broadway Gangsta Crips. Life was a thrilling roller coaster ride for me but things were about to get interesting. The Broadways wanted the Fifty Crips to join their ranks. Their refusal to join their collective sparked a wave of violent skirmishes.

A violent dance between the gangs ensued, breathing war into the Fifties. Though my loved ones were younger, they held their ground courageously. They would not succumb to defeat in this brutal tug of war. An intense ten-minute shootout was one instance that comes to mind. The roar of gunfire & the fear of losing lives was ever-present, yet both sides emerged unscathed.

I found myself teetering on the brink of a perilous cliff that divided the two rivaling factions. Torn between loyalty to my cousin, Coke Dogg & my day ones on one end & my big homie, Choo & the

Broadways on the other. I eventually chose to stand by my roots, the Fifty boys. This decision cemented my place among the ranks of the Fabulous Fifty Crips.

The big homie, oG Big Tee (Tyrone Tyars), the co-founder of Five-Deuce Broadway moved on to 53rd street near ScHool Boy's crib transcending these borders. This event led to Broadways spending more time with us, becoming cordial & forming bonds. Side by side we continued oG Gates legacy combating against the Brims. We didn't subscribe to being Broadways but my history with them led to Fifty Crip adopting West Town as a part of our identity.

My childhood was punctuated by the rhythm of street life. Elementary school was the last time I ever walked through school gates with genuine intention to learn. After that, school was merely a blip on my radar, drowned out by the louder, adrenaline-fueled lifestyle that became my addiction.

The year 1977 was a period of transformation for me. The days of 52nd street elementary were over, I was preparing to go to John Muir Jr High School, in the heart of Brim territory. The Fifty Crips were now scattered at various junior high schools, raisin' hell!

I remember those mornings vividly. The homies & I would meet up at the street corner, pooling our lunch money together. Our goal for the day was always more intoxicating than mere meals; we aimed to get drunk off malt liquor, a passageway to the recklessness we so craved.

I remember Baby Crazy & ScHool Boys' mommas would send them off to school like squares in slacks & penny loafers. They would jump in the bushes & morph into their Crip Uniform like Superman.

The day would be spent in a haze of youthful debauchery, seducing girls with our devil-may-care attitudes & smoking lovely, a marijuana joint infused with PCP. It was a dangerous concoction, but it was the thrill that kept us going. My mama thought I was going to school every day, all our parents did. They wouldn't find out until 90 days later that we didn't, and by then it was too late.

I knew that this was going to be a new beginning, but my homies & I wanted to make the most out of our summer. This crazy Saturday started like any other. The sun was out, and the smell of freshly cut grass filled the air. I was hanging out with School Boy & Baby Crazy.

We were inseparable; blood could never be thicker than this Fifty Crippin', but things weren't always groovy. Sometimes we had to throw down, but right after the scuffle we went back to chillin', smokin' & drinkin.' It was just another hot summer day around the way. We headed towards the liquor store on the Foe, determined to track down the Locs & stir up some trouble.

We found them gang-hangin' in the alley behind the Liquor store, messing around with a filthy, butt-naked dope fiend. The homies were cockhounds, young, dumb & full of cum. They were fondling her & sucking on her titties, squeezing her ass, playing' with her pussy & trying to convince her to fuck & suck. I mean really trying to do the nasty, I thought to myself, are they really trying to sex this vile, lowdown dope head!

The sight of this downtrodden creature filled me with a mixture of disgust & amusement. I'm cringing & laughing simultaneously at the sight of her rusty dusty coochie & these freaky boys trying to get some. ScHool Boy looked at me like these fools are crazy. He had this look of fear, grimace, and concern in his eyes.

I never saw him look so anxious. Before I could blink or think of a joke to crack on this fool, he took off, running as fast as his little legs could carry him leaving us in a cloud of dust like the road runner. Baby Crazy & I eventually caught up with him.

As we continued patrolling the turf, the golden summer sun blazing overhead, ScHool Boy lit up a joint of exquisite Colombian Gold. We passed it around, inhaling deeply & holding each breath, until our thoughts became fuzzy, and laughter bubbled, reminiscing on the recent scene with the smoker. It wasn't long before the munchies kicked in, leading us like a siren's call to Mr. Jim's on 54th & Vermont. The smell of the sizzling beef & hot links grabbed my attention & lured me toward the BBQ shack.

"Aye cuH, let's get some food, I'm hungry as hell", I told the homies.

We go up to the counter & I place my order, a chopped beef on a bun. I'm reaching in my pockets & coming up with lint. I realized with a sinking feeling that I lost my money in my haste to chase School Boy's yellow ass earlier. Left with a growling stomach & a shriveling sense of pride, I asked my friend for help.

In an inexplicable act of assholism, ScHool Boy refused to lend me a single dime, instead he started talking shit, clowning me for losing my money. Little did I know he had something up his sleeve.

"Nigga don't look at me, I ain't got nothin' for you, how the hell you lose all yo money!" ScHool boy tells me with a smart-ass tone.

While the unsuspecting clerk was busy assembling my meal, School Boy snatched the cash register & fled the store with surprising agility. As soon as the metallic clank of the register hit our ears, our instincts kicked in, Baby Crazy & I sprinted after our rebellious piss colored friend. Somehow, we managed to slip out of the store unnoticed.

ScHool Boy's little ass is struggling trying to run holding onto the heavy ass cash register, and we're right behind him! School Boy's legs gave out, and he crashed out in the alley behind the burger joint, gasping for air. School Boy, clearly pleased with his daring heist, slams the register on the concrete multiple times & finally it breaks open with a triumphant grin.

However, his face darkened suddenly as he looked at Baby Crazy & I. It seemed that our thieving comrade had decided that he alone deserved the spoils of victory. I look at this nigga, as he is stuffing all the money in his pocket.

"What the fuck nigga?!? Gimme some of that money!" I demanded.

The 3 of us are scrambling around picking up bills off the floor like some strippers when ScHool Boy shoves me & has the nerve to tell me.

"This my lick, I ain't giving you niggas shit!" ScHool Boy shouts very aggressively.

His ludicrous claim sparked a fire within us, I had no other choice but to hook off on this fool! Baby Crazy & I launched ourselves at him in outrage. Fists flew, and our once-tight-knit trio began to unravel in a vicious whirlwind of anger & bravado. We were in the back of Mr. Jim's squabbling over the money, we didn't give a damn about the police!!

The sounds of our scuffle echoed through the alley, and soon the wail of a police siren drew nearer. Baby Crazy & I look at each other, nope, we are not going back to Juvenile Hall! Chaos quickly escalated as we were suddenly forced to confront the consequences of our actions. Our scrap with School Boy was forgotten; friendship & survival became the only things that mattered & the driving forces in our lives once again.

We end the rumble, scrambling to pick up as much cash as we can. We raced through the alleys, hearts pounding, as the siren's call grew louder & more menacing. With each turn, we realized that our bonds of camaraderie were all that we had. We grew up together, sharing everything from scraped knees to midnight adventures. As the pigs closed in, time seemed to slow down, and my mind rewound through the years of friendship & laughter.

Finally, through a combination of sheer will & raw luck, we managed to slip through the suffocating web of LAPD that had us trapped. Our trio now stood together once again, panting, and leaning against a graffiti covered brick wall for support. ScHool Boy looked at us with wild, desperate eyes & then held out some of the stolen cash with trembling hands. It was his offering of his repentance.

We suddenly saw our friend, not as a greedy asshole but as our equal searching for his place in the world. We forgave him, realizing that our friendship was worth more than any amount of stolen cash. It was evident that we had all learned a lesson on that fateful Saturday in 1977: no matter how life changes & how wild our adventure gets, true friendship can withstand any storm. We patched up our battered friendship & swore to face the future together.

"Friendship is all about trusting each other, helping each other, loving each other & being crazy together."- unknown.

CHAPTER TWELVE:
"UNDER THE HOOVER INFLUENCE"

We, the Fabulous Fifty Crips, were very, very young, and impressionable. The oldest member of our crew was around 14 years old so we weren't taken seriously or being recognized by our fellow Crips but soon that was all going to change. ScHool Boy was always the scheming & conniving type, and his dangerous mind gave birth to a seemingly foolproof plan. School Boy's older brother, Blaine, exuded a nonchalance that made the streets respect him.

Blaine educated us in the controversial art of concocting PCP. We were enchanted by the process, 2 ounces of PCP mixed with 2 ounces of Ether transforming it into something so powerfully addictive, so feared, and yet, so sought after. Blaine would concoct his potion with a wizard's accuracy, using Ether or embalming fluid as the key ingredient.

School Boy, being the slick strategist that he was, started diluting Blaine's PCP supply with water or paint thinner instead of the more potent & expensive ether. He managed to hold on to the uncut product for himself, deftly monopolizing the best stash. He made a lot of money out of this ruthless tactic, launching us from small-time hustlers to major players in the PCP game. We were no longer just surviving. We were thriving.

ScHool Boy's strategic contamination of Blaine's supply paid off. His pockets got fat as Fat Albert, solidifying our reputation on the streets. While leading an unprecedented coup, effectively stealing his brother's customers. This marked the birth of our first drug enterprise as the Fifty Crips. This was not a brotherly act, but certainly a power move that was as cunning as it was controversial.

It wasn't long before word of our superior quality PCP spread like wildfire across the city, pulling in addicts from all regions, while strengthening our bonds with surrounding Crip hoods. It was not long before our Crip allies began to hint at a desire to recruit us, wooing us into their ranks. They recognized the strength of our hood & the loyalty we commanded, seeing us as assets for their own ambitions. This became a game of chess with pieces shifting & alliances evolving.

We were surrounded by Crips. South of us there was oG Tony Stacy, Scooby, Tim-Tim, Bubbles & the Seven-Foe Hoovers, as well as Mad Bone, HillBilly, Frog & the Eight-Trey Gangstas. An Eight-Trey Gangsta named Lil Timmy Tucker was a Fifty Boy, his family moved to the 80s as well as Ronnie, the Panther from Seven-Foe, was a Fifty Boy & one of Fat Rat's everyday niggas. We maintained our friendship which laid the foundation of our relationship.

East of us was Big Tee, Choo, Crazy Poke & The Broadways, Docthone, Casper, Bub & the Six-Pac East Coast. West of us was Peedy Wacc, Keita Rock, Eddie Boy, Pretty Boy F-Bone (Coke Dogg's cousin) & the Rollin' Sixties, and to our north we had Juda Bean, Bay, Nate the Boss (Coke Dogg's cousin) & the Foe-Tray Hoovers & Crazy Keith, Baby Brother & the Rollin' Thirties Harlem Crips. All were constantly present, each harboring a unique charisma that influenced us in some way or the other.

However, under the disguise of Crip camaraderie, recruiting narratives unfolded. The Sixties watered their seeds of influence through ScHool Boy whenever they came to purchase PCP. The impeccable quality of our product & our rising infamy led to recruitment attempts from various factions.

Our operation was booming, and the surrounding sets were keen to be part of the booming enterprise. Traffic increased exponentially, and our connection with Broadway, Harlem Thirties & Rollin' Sixties fostered a strong bond.

Others played their hands too. Undeniably, the most pressure was applied by the Broadways, who had well-established roots in the Fifties. Tee & Choo wanted me back & strived to consolidate us into their ranks & expand their set across the 110 freeway.

All these hoods aimed to fortify their realms, their strategies masked in the virtue of unity & brotherhood. The Seven-Foe Hoovers & Eight-Trey Gangstas were less assertive, yet their presence was felt, a constant reminder of the inherent power dynamics at play.

Lured by the mutual gains of this potential bond, some of us started leaning towards the other sets. This created particularly strong bonds with Broadway & the Sixties. Influenced by these alliances, a group within our own ranks started to consider adopting a new identity due to strong connections & began to identify as West Town Rollin' Fifty Crips.

However, we started on a path of self-assertion, carving out a distinct space for ourselves amid the pulsating chaos of South Central. A testament to the power of unity, the allure of rebellion, and the staunch will to carve out one's distinct identity.

As we plunged deeper into the world of the Crips, we made decisions that would shape not just our destinies, but that of the hood we called home for generations to come. What started as a cutthroat scheme to make a couple dollars, had given birth to a stronger, more formidable reputation.

I found myself under the wings of an influence that would change not only my life but also the journey of an entire community. There is an old saying that goes, *"the strongest steel is forged in the hottest fire."* A phrase, often applied to situations when someone confronted with overwhelming adversity, emerge victorious through sheer grit & determination.

In the crucible of American ghettos in the 1970s, few stories embody this motto better than the Hoovers, a small-tribe-turned-empire that would go on to dominate not only our rivals but the very culture & spirit of the Crips & Bloods.

The Ransoms were a remarkable trio of siblings from 106th street - Joe, Daryl, and Andre. Of these three brothers, the oldest, Joe, was the figure I found myself most drawn toward. He was a beacon of strength, resilience, and innovation. His staunch loyalty to the Underground Crip, a prominent part of his identity, was something that I, as a young boy, respected & admired profoundly.

As long as I can remember the Ransom Brothers had a weekly habit of visiting their cousins, the Lees. As they made their way down Hoover Street, their heads held high & exuding confidence, they never failed to catch our attention.

They used to come by 54th street every Sunday after Reverend Lee church service so I thought they were church folks, then I got to know them & found out they were some bad muthafuckas like me. Joe had an air of pure charisma that radiated from him.

In our quest to make our mark, my friends & I had long dreamed of being part of the Underground. However, our dreams met a dead end when much of the Undergrounds were incarcerated or began to branch off & start their own tribes. This setback made us realize a crucial fact of life; sometimes, when the paths you wish to tread are unavailable, the only way to push forward is to make your own. Thus, the inspiration to establish our own faction.

During the infancy of our hopes & efforts as Fifty Crips, Joe did the unthinkable; he switched his allegiance from the Underground Crip to the One-oh-Seven Hoover Crip & his brothers followed suit. This decision shocked me, for I had known Joe as a die-hard member of the Underground for years. What could have caused such a fundamental shift in Joe's loyalty? This question gnawed at my curiosity, so much so, that I found myself compelled to explore the latest movement that had found favor in Joe's eyes.

The biggest & baddest Crips in the early 70s were undoubtedly the Undergrounds. The largest faction in the city, they were instrumental in asserting their dominance through sheer force, numbers, and a fierce loyalty that bound them together as a tribe, but after oG Budda was killed by another Underground, it caused their ranks to splinter, and new regimes began to rise. One regime began to carve its niche through the heart of the city.

"Hoover risin' no surprising"
-oG Melvin "Bloodstone" Calloway, Founder of
Nine-Deuce Hoover Crip

The Hoovers were one of the first Crip sets established that would stand the test of time, in September 1972, within a year they began carving out the largest territory with 3 tribes Seven-Foe, Eight-Tray & Nine-Deuce & laying the foundation for Crip culture. oG Sugar Bear, a Hoover Crip general with a resume that included being a founding member of Compton, Westside, Eight-Tray & Nine-Deuce Hoover Crips as well as founder of the Denker Crips. Sugar Bear is also the creator of the world renown Crip Walk.

Hoovers are the trend setters in Crip responsible for the adoption of our trademark blue bandana. Hoovers were influential in Crip fashion, set colors, as well as the use of sports teams & clothing brands as Crip paraphernalia. Hoover was the first to have subsets, set hand signs, as well as introducing Crip sign language & eventually set days.

From day one our predecessors began forging their own unique path, breaking away from the traditional mold & creating something greater. Their unprecedented style of Crippin' led to organic growth that attracted people from all over to groove with them & earn the Hoovers the moniker of the first Crip Super Gang.

By 1977, the Hoovers had significantly expanded the territories that they controlled. Their empire included the Foe-Tray (43rd Street), Six-Tray (63rd street), Seven Foe (74th Street), Eight Owe (80th Street), Eight Tray (83rd Street), Nine-Owe (90th street), Nine-Deuce (92nd Street), One-oh-Seven (107th Street).

Each of these territories was known for its ruthless & resolute members loyal to the Hoover legacy. The Eight Owes, founded by Big Tank from Seven-Foe Hoover, was a short-lived project, like the 6-Trays founded by Big Wayne from Eight-Tray Hoover. Nevertheless, it contributed to the grand narrative of Hoover's influence & expansion efforts.

The Ransoms would become the first Hoovers the Fifty Boys & I formed a close relationship with. Daryl became known as the notorious Hoover Sam, Big Joe became known as Horse or Hoover Joe, and their younger brother, Andre became known as the legendary Big Devil. Having carved out their niche as respected & feared Underground Crips, the Ransoms addition made the One-oh-Seven Hoovers a force to be reckoned with.

Big Joe Ransom stood out as an unforgettable & imposing figure - He commanded respect, a 7-star general in the war zone we call Los Angeles. South Central was plagued with violence, poverty, and the constant struggle to survive. Surrounded by chaos & despair, I was influenced by the Ransoms, who promised a sense of belonging & security. It was within the confines of this relationship that I became enamored with the Hoovers.

Big Joe was the epitome of cool & smooth on his Hoover Groover shit, he possessed so much swagger & magnetism. I didn't have many heroes in his world, but he would be one of them. Joe wore Levi 501 jeans with a black leather jacket over a navy blue t-shirt. His massive muscular arms rivaled those of a Greek god. His natural was a massive crown that framed his face & made him look like a Black Hercules. I got to know him well over the years & got tight with his brothers also. I would begin assimilating the ways of the Hoovers & inevitably become a part of their unbreakable bond.

Big Joe would come around with his brothers & homeboys from One-oh-Seven. Dre Dogg & I were immersed in stories of bravery & adventure. Leaning against the cold bricks outside Dre Dogg's home, I listened eagerly as Big Joe, my larger-than-life hero, regaled us with tales of his experiences. Tales from the Crip about the street & prison. His stories painted a vivid picture of a life filled with danger, excitement, and the promise of camaraderie that came with devotion to the Hoovers.

A man whose wisdom seemed to surge forth from a deep well of personal experience. He spoke of the violence that ran thick with blood through the streets -- a necessary evil to protect their turf & loved ones. There were stories of wild escapades, with flamboyant candy painted low-riders that lit up the street like neon signs blazing down the boulevards, James Brown hits rippling through the city air. Parties that felt like they could rattle the very foundations of the world, where everyone who was anyone came together to groove into the night.

He seduced us with tales of fine women & sex with no strings attached. Above all else, he showed us the unshakable loyalty that bound them together. Their experiences made Crippin' seem like so much fun & the thing to do. The violence, the women, the cars, the parties, the love.

The Crips seemed to have it all. I listened to them talk about their exploits, both good & bad, with wide-eyed fascination & reverence. These men, only seven to nine years older than me, had been involved in so much in their lifetime, and I envied the excitement, the danger, and the camaraderie that their lifestyle offered. Big Joe made me fall in love with Hoover Crip. In Joe's stories, the Hoovers were always the heroes.

"I dig y'all Fifty Crippin', but y'all should be Hoovers down here," Big Joe told me in the voice of a prophet.

The massive mountain of a man chucked up the set, with his giant hands, which looked strong enough to crumble bricks. The Hoovers had a saying: *"Hoover Stroll in total control."* I believed that the Hoovers could take control of the chaotic city I lived in. Hoover Crips began to hold a special place in my heart.

In a time when we had little to believe in, we found solace in the strength & unity of the Crips. The thought of becoming just like Joe – powerful, respected, admired, filled my heart with anticipation.

Around this time, Big Joe introduced me to oG Judabean, the co-founder of Foe-Tray Hoover. This was a game-changing moment that exposed me to the expansive social structure built along Hoover Street. There was a missing link in connecting the Hoover line from the 40s to the 100s that they wanted us to fill. Big Joe & Juda Bean showed me the potential in creating a continuous Hoover line, one that would extend union & dominance of the Hoovers over South Central. It was like looking through a telescope & seeing a galaxy being formed.

Big Joe's influence was powerful. In the back of my young mind, I knew that it was time to take control of my own destiny. I might not have understood the gravity of that at the time, but the idea of living life on the edge, of belonging to a brotherhood like no other, lit a spark inside of me. A spark that would grow into a burning passion for Hoover Crip. I set about my fateful path to become a Hoover with the weight of my future heavy on my shoulders.

The Foe-Tray Hoovers were a small but powerful faction of paper chasers that held territory - a region stretching from Martin Luther King Jr Blvd to Vernon Ave & between the 110 Freeway & Vermont. Some of the notable Foe-Trays include Hoover Jack, NepHew, Blue Fly, Booman, 8-Ball, and my second cousin, Nate the Boss. I often found myself in the riveting world of the Foe-Trays, captivated by the titanic Hriginals oG Jerry Knox– Judabean & his valiant brother oG Bay, who were about 10 years my elders.

In my eyes they were like oG Joe Ransom, something akin to marvelous giants with muscles that were perceived to be as solid as an iron cast. In the embrace of the chalky sidewalks & graffiti-laced walls of the Foe-Trays, there I was, learning the ropes from my big homies. They were comrades, mentors, influencers, and family, making an imprint on our youthful minds. Their presence was as bold as their hearts.

There was a distinct sound to our afternoons together: the rhythmic clink of metal on metal as we tirelessly inspired to be like our oG's. Every embodiment of strength has a backstory, and theirs rested in their broad hands that could single-handedly hoist motors & transmissions as if they were playthings. Their fortitude was a product of makeshift dumbbells, whipped up from concrete once the proper weights ran scarce. Bay had an uncanny knack for heaving porta potties, treating them like throw pillows. The tales of his feats echoed in the alleyways; each anecdote spun into mythical yarn.

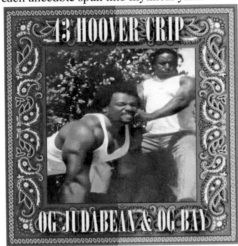

We observed these goliath showings with wide-eyed wonder. The camaraderie found in our shared pursuit of raw power was undeniably contagious, motivating us to emulate big homies like Bean & Bay, summoning our reserves of strength in pursuit of becoming powerhouses ourselves.

The life of a Crip wasn't all excitement & camaraderie, as we later discovered. It was marked by immense loss, heartache, hardships, and the looming threat of a life spent behind bars – or worse. Becoming a Hoover Crip required us to sacrifice innocence, dreams for a better future, and even the safety of our families. Back then, as a ten-year-old lost in the chaotic world of South Central, the alluring life of a Crip seemed like everything I wanted. It promised me excitement, belonging, power, and control.

Now, as an adult, I look back on those days with a heavy heart. The allure of gangbangin' was a mirage, a false promise of success & belonging that instead led us down a path of pain & loss. I only wish I could go back in time & warn that young, impressionable boy about the truth behind that dangerous world. All I can do now is learn from my past, work towards a better future, and hope that others don't fall for the same trap that ensnared me & so many of my loved ones.

I realized that the same ethos of comradery & courage that had been laid out so passionately to our young minds could be applied in my life to see my community grow & eventually move beyond gangbangin'. We could construct projects that brought education, mentorship, and opportunities, rather than let the future generations fall into the same trap as the Hriginals.

Looking back at my childhood, I am grateful for crossing paths with Hoover Joe Ransom. Though he championed a way of life that is shrouded in violence, it was his charisma & passion for the legacy of the Hoovers that provided me with a unique perspective on loyalty, community, and the spirit of the streets.

Despite the dangers of my past, my experiences with Joe provided hope for the future – a future where the spirit of the Hoover Groove would one day rise above its stigma & strive for a greater purpose. The streets may shift & change with the tide, the fire in my heart will never be extinguished – *"Hoover Stroll in total control,"* forever & always.

CHAPTER THIRTEEN:
"UNCLE ROY- HOT GIRLS & HOT WHEELS"

Hot girls & hot wheels became my hobbies at a young age. My Uncle Roy had a lot of groupies because of his low riders, he taught me a lot about women & cars in my formative years. I remember he had one of his hoes show me my first pair of tatas, and let my little ass play with them & suck on them. This was when I learned to perfect the *"motorboat"*, an act of pushing my face in between two big juicy breasts & rocking it side to side as fast as I could while making a *"burr"* sound mimicking a motorboat engine. I think this day made me a *"titty man."*

As I grew older, my fascination & desire for women only grew stronger. I discovered my Pop's porn collection, and it allowed me to admire & learn about the female body. I would often hang out with my Uncle Roy & his groupies more & more, he taught me about the different types of women & the things they liked, preparing for the day I would finally hit some skins.

Eventually, my love for women led me to becoming a womanizer, and quite the ladies' man. I was always looking for new experiences, and I wasn't afraid to try new things & get freaky deaky in the bedroom. I quickly gained a reputation for being a skilled well-endowed lover, and women pursued me for that reason. I told you how it ended but let me tell you how it started.

I was a wide-eyed, naive twelve-year-old experiencing the world around me as curious as a cat, and everything was a mystery. It was a hot summer night on 52nd street, I was chilling with my homegirl, *"Water Bottles,"* as we mischievously nicknamed her. We called her Water Bottles because of the size of her titties.

I don't mean those 16-ounce bottles; I'm talking about those 5 gallon jugs that go on the dispensers in offices. You know everything seems bigger when you are a little kid, but it seemed like she had the biggest titties in the world! Her bosom was something mythical, out this world, and I couldn't help but be captivated by her massive round juicy breast.

Water Bottles was a good friend of mine. She was 5 years my senior & lived around the corner from my mama's house. Water Bottles had already developed a reputation for breaking hearts. She had a history of being a promiscuous girl & leaving boys devastated in her wake. That didn't stop my hot & horny mind from racing with fantasies of embracing Water Bottles in a passionate, steamy exchange.

Back in the day, we used to hang out in the back of an abandoned apartment building by my crib. Tonight, we were at the chill spot, just the two of us, getting drunk & high off PCP in a broken down hoopty we frequented.

I inhaled some Sherman, my mind started soaring as I was taken to a world painted in groovy psychedelic colors, and everything seemed to be moving in slow motion. I was feeling good! My mind is blown, and Water Bottles catches me admiring her big juicy melons while licking & biting my lips.

She lifts my chin, looks me in my eyes, and says *"You want this pussy, huh boy?"*

I replied *"Hell Yeah"* as cool as I could while nodding my head excitedly.

She grabbed me by the dick faster than I could blink, but I was rock hard & ready for her just as quick. She whispers a warning in my ear, *"Don't fall in love, little nigga."*

It was at that moment that I realized how vastly outmatched I was. Water Bottles' experience with sex far surpassed my own, I was like a lamb being guided to slaughter, I was at her mercy. In that moment, my high took flight & an out of body experience took over, the world was my oyster. I was ready as Tevin Campbell, welcoming whatever passion she chose to share.

I was a novice, unashamed to admit she put it on me, she mounted me & put those enormous Ta-Ta's in my face. I was completely entranced, mesmerized by her presence; her raw, carnal energy, the sheer size of her breasts & taste of her skin. She could have suffocated me with those big ass titties, and I would have died a happy boy. She slid my member inside of her juicy, wet love box, an unparalleled moment, then proceeded to ride me like a mechanical bull!

The intimacy of that night caught me by surprise, and the intensity of our passion overwhelmed me. As the hoopty rocked back & forth, as if riding on a sea of sensual waves, we indulged in each other's bodies, communicating in a language that was both primal & profound. A nigga was in paradise! We had that hoopty rocking like it had hydraulics! We were rocking that car so hard; it fell off the cylinder blocks it was mounted on but that didn't stop us.

She reached out & caressed me from my head, down my face, chest, then wrapped her arms around me to pull me closer. I couldn't believe that I was inside of her. It was as if my mind, body & soul was in another galaxy. I didn't know what to do, but she knew, she guided me like a pro, she dismounted me then went into the doggystyle position with her hands & head near the floor of the backseat.

"Fuck me, Boo! Harder! Harder! Go deeper! Hit the bottom of this *pussy boy!*" Water Bottles screamed & moaned.

She told me what to do & how she liked it, and I followed her lead. She demanded I fucked her hard & fast, and smacked her round brown ass hard. The combination of cheap malt liquor, Angel dust, and lust gave me a physical & mental sensation, I'd never experienced before. It was exhilarating, like nothing else mattered in the world except the two of us in that hoopty. I couldn't believe this was happening.

As I emerged from that steamy car, my body drenched in sweat, weak in the knees trembling from the intensity of the experience, I looked at the world around me with new eyes. It was a moment in time that would forever be burned into my soul, gifting me with a newfound appreciation for the power of the pussy & vulnerability. This wild summer night was the end of my childhood innocence, and the beginning of my journey into the intoxicating world of love, passion, and manhood.

That summer seared itself into my memory like a vivid, hallucinatory daydream. Time seemed to move in slow motion as Water Bottles & I journeyed through an intense, fast-paced exploration of our teenage desires. In that psychedelic haze, I experienced passion & freedom like never before, but at the same time, I was trapped within it. Always in the back of my mind were her words, that sinister reminder not to fall in love.

Water Bottles made me a man that night. I was proud I got my first piece of ass, and I loved it! I'm eager for more sex, a young nymphomaniac, I tried to seduce her again, but she wasn't with it. She told me she didn't have any intention of having another rendezvous with me. She was wet (literally & figuratively), high, hot & horny, and needed some dick, but she wanted to stay cool, so that's what it was. A one-night stand that ended in the *"friend zone."*

The lessons of '77 ranged from hot girls to hot wheels. The sun was high & there wasn't a cloud in the sky. The sound of soul music & laughter filled the air as people gathered on the streets for an impromptu block party in East LA. Among the crowd was the one & only Uncle Roy, the popular Low Rider who lived just down the street. Everyone in the hood was familiar with Uncle Roy & knew that if there were ever any car troubles, he was the one to reach out to for help.

I was a ghetto child running wild with a passion for hot wheels, I looked up to Uncle Roy as though he were a superhero. He was a tall light skin man with a humongous natural, he had a deep voice that was as smooth as the custom candy paint on his Impala. His low rider was the focal point, and it was easy to see why.

The deep burgundy color glistened in the sun. The gold wire Dayton wheels sparkled like polished gems as the hydraulics bounced the machine up & down. Uncle Roy was known to have a Midas touch for transforming old rust buckets into lowrider goldmines.

I rushed in my uncle's direction with a big ass Kool-Aid smile & stole an even bigger hug, the love was reciprocated with a wide grin, as he ruffled my hair.

"What's happenin', nephew?" he said, his voice deep & smooth like velvet.

"Are you ready to learn some of the secrets of the Low-Rider life?"

My eyes must have lit up as bright as the chrome trim on his car as Uncle Roy let out a hearty chuckle & motioned for me to follow him. As we walked over to his garage, I could see one of his cars parked inside, its lustrous paint job subtly glowing like a fine piece of art in the dim light.

Uncle Roy taught me everything from mastering manual transmission to the art of dodging the pigs. In this intense summer boot camp, I learned the basics of engines, brakes, and clutches. As my confidence blossomed, so did my curiosity.

One afternoon, after a driving lesson in a Sear's parking lot, Uncle Roy brought out a box of shiny metal gadgets labeled: B-10s. He smirked as he handed me the lock pick tools, little did I know I was becoming his apprentice in the art of auto locksmithing.

"This right here is a B-10, little man," he explained. *"It's a gadget we use to unlock & start General Motor cars, like Fords, Chevy's, Oldsmobile's, Cadillacs, Pontiacs & Buicks."*

Mastering the use of those B-10s was the key to my first successful car heist. As the streets of Eastside LA filled with darkness, Uncle Roy led me to a seemingly abandoned 1970 Oldsmobile Cutlass, perfectly idling in a dimly lit parking lot. Under his watchful eye, I inserted the lock pick into the door lock & after a few thrilling moments, felt a rush of adrenaline as the door gently clicked open.

It's hard to describe the excitement that came with my first successful auto theft. It felt like an initiation into a secret society. As the weeks turned into months, the hotwired vehicles began to pile up in his garage, awaiting their transformation into lowriders – the kind that would reign supreme across Los Angeles.

Uncle Roy was content with his protégé crafting his carjacking skills, my hunger for knowledge invariably drove me to seek a greater level of expertise in the art of Grand Theft Auto.

One afternoon I found myself in the company of Ten Speed, who was known throughout the neighborhood for his ability to fix up anything with wheels. Nine out of ten times, Ten Speed could hotwire any car faster than one could peddle a bike. We called him Ten Speed for his love of bicycles, and I remember admiring the way he could transform any rusty old two-wheeler into sleek, mean machines that would leave other kids around the way green with envy.

We were hanging in his backyard, and I bragged about the new trick I learned from Uncle Roy & showed him my new tool. Ten Speed decided it was time to elevate my car knowledge to the realm of hot wiring. Time seemed to slow down as he demonstrated the technique on an old beat-up Chevy that sat neglected in the corner of his yard.

With a steady hand, he removed the fuse box cover & began to decipher the array of colored wires that snaked their way through the dashboard. He identified each essential connection; he took care to explain the sequence of steps that would bypass the ignition system & start the engine with just a twist of the exposed wires.

It was invigorating watching the old engine spring to life at his mercy. He maneuvered through this process like a seasoned vet. I knew that I was learning a skill which could help me become a master mechanic or criminal. I felt a sense of empowerment gaining this knowledge, and I couldn't wait to put my new skills to good use.

Ten Speed became a confidante who sincerely cared about my circumstances, my future. As the years progressed, my experiences with Uncle Roy & Ten Speed would shape the man I became, hardening me to the realities of life in Los Angeles while forging an unshakable bond with the world of cars, and the lowrider culture that introduced me to it. Now a master of Grand Theft Auto at the tender age of twelve.

CHAPTER FOURTEEN:
"ONCE YOU FIGHT, YOU ALRIGHT"

Let's turn the clock back to 1977, there were no smart phones, just the old school rotaries & pay phones. No streaming channels to keep us entertained all night, no social media to flaunt our lives, the only way to show off was to go outside. It was a time when bonds were pure, relationships were genuine, and companionship meant more than Instagram likes. If anyone asked me about the most loyal companion I had, I would have to say Whitey.

My childhood was full of adventures & mischief. One such incident occurred on a typical sun-soaked afternoon. I crossed paths with Bart, a rambunctious kid from 56th & Budlong, who claimed to have a litter of pit bull puppies for sale. I eyed the pups with a sense of fascination, their big, cute eyes staring up at me with intrigue & innocence. One pup caught my eye.

It was a beautiful shade of sugar white that glimmered under the sunlight. I reached into my pocket & came up with lint, realizing I didn't have the cash Bart wanted but I did have something. I decided to take a chance. From my other pocket, I procured five joints of the finest Columbian Gold. With a bit of persuasion, I was able to convince Bart to accept the trade. A sense of satisfaction washed over me as I picked up the pit bull pup, newly named Whitey, because of his cocaine white fur.

The first time I held him, his puppy teeth tried to nibble my fingers, his way of showing affection by trying to eat me up. As if by some magic, Whitey never seemed to grow, retaining his pup appearance. Short, stocky, adorable - a creature resembling what we now refer to as 'bullies,' a pit bull subtype known for its compact size & muscular build. It was a delightful revelation to realize that perhaps I had known & owned one before the term had even drawn its first breath in the world.

Whitey possessed a unique charm & was the smartest dog I ever knew, and all the homies would tell you the same. Growing fond of him over time, I fashioned Whitey with a signature look - a Crip blue bandana wrapped around his neck. I even got his ears pierced, adding glistening diamond studs that contrasted beautifully against his snowy-white fur. Whitey became a spectacle wherever he went.

He looked distinctly different from the other dogs in the hood with his white fur, bright red eyes, and diamond studs on his ears. The diamonds were a sight that was amusing & intriguing to everyone. His unconventional look attracted not just dog enthusiasts but also the girls. He was a head-turner & as a result, he became my wingman. Whitey's irresistible charm managed to reel in a remarkable amount of attention, becoming my foolproof method of casual flings.

Whitey conquered the hearts of my family, also. The most significant was my mother. Her rapport with Whitey was unique, close to being a rivalry with me. We would compete for his attention, which brought much amusement at home. There were times when Whitey was torn between choosing my mother or me. My secret weapon, invitation for a car ride. The prospect of an adventure in the steel beast would always tip his preference in my favor. He loved nothing more than feeling the wind whip against his fur as we cruised down Hoover Street.

There was something incredibly therapeutic about those rides, just two companions—man & best friend—cruising down the 110, the wind in our faces, and the promise of adventure waiting for us at every turn. Whitey brought joy, companionship, and above all, an unconditional bond that weathered all storms of my childhood.

Admirably, Whitey had a streak of guard dog in him that accounted for countless comical & memorable instances. His welcoming demeanor coaxed Ken Dogg into our yard, and his tail fluttered with joy when he had company. However, this joyous greeting turned into a stubborn insistence when Ken Dogg had to leave, as though he had held him captive by his irresistible canine charm.

Ironically, this spark of life that brought so much joy to our lives eventually passed away, leaving us heart-broken. The news of Whitey's death sent waves of heartbreak through the family, as tears strayed down our faces, etching the profound sadness of our loss.

Whitey wasn't just a pet, but a family member, a wingman, a captivating personality, and an unforgettable part of my youth. Through every tail wag & joyous greeting & every desperate farewell, he was the embodiment of love, adventure, and joy, forever etched in my memory. The story of Whitey is a testament to friendship, joy, and the pain of losing a loved one, deeply interwoven into the fabric of my life's journey.

My world was ablaze with stories that would shape the way we looked at life in the years to come. For me, this was the summer that marked my transition from adolescence to manhood. It was the summer where everything changed in the span of a few short months, when I lost my virginity, mastered automobiles, and adopted my puppy, but this summer had more surprises in store.

There is a point in your life where friendship's meaning transcends the boundaries & limitations of mere camaraderie—it becomes a bond held together by trust, loyalty, and shared experiences. For me, that point arrived when I met a kid that would not only become one of my best friends but my crimey. He was a new kid around the way. The homies & I used to catch him looking at us, it made me wonder.

"What's up with this nigga?"

I would see him walking to the school yard with his cap & glove, tossing his baseball in the air, so I could tell this kid was a baseball player. He hung out with Killer D & some squares named Marlon & Curtis, squares always do the right thing, cause a square has nothing but right angles. The new kid was a mystery & it was only a matter of time before Coke Dogg put me on to game. The kid just moved on to the Foe from the east side & recently graduated from Main Street School.

One day, I was in my yard playing with Whitey, I caught sight of the new kid strolling down the Deuce toward the schoolyard. It was the perfect opportunity for me to introduce myself, and chop it up with him so I did, swaggering over like I'm Hoover Joe Ransom with a confidence that came from years on the streets.

"What up cuH? I'm Boo Diggs from Fifty Crip. What's your name, and where you from?" I asked in my usual casual, street-tough manner.

To my surprise, the kid responded with a friendly smile & said, *"I'm Richard, but my family calls me Kato & I ain't from nowhere...yet!"* I felt his energy & he felt mine because he declared that he wanted to get put on the set. As we continued to talk, he revealed his desire to become a Crip, explaining how his family had moved around a lot, but he had already lived in a few notorious Crip sets.

> *"I'm talkin' real shit to ya baby, that real Crip shit*
> *- Tha Eastsidaz, Crip Hop*

I told Kato stories about oG Gates, the original Five-Deuces, Big Joe Ransom & my guys from Broadway. Kato told me he went to school in the Broadways & he knew of Big Joe & the One-oh-Seven Hoovers & had some stories to share about his time living on 107th & Budlong.

Our admiration & respect for the Hoovers drew us closer together. I remember Kato recounting the tale of a shootout that had occurred between the Hoovers & their rivals from 107 Underground Crip on Vermont & 107th street, just a couple years before he moved to the Fifties.

Christmas day, a time when most people were celebrating with their families, Kato found himself witnessing flying bullets & chaos. Fearing the arrival of the police, the Hoovers ditched their guns in an apartment building next to Kato's home. Kato, a fearless & inquisitive kid, saw the whole ordeal unfold from his window, and along with his older brother, decided to sneak in & hide the guns before the pigs arrived.

The next day he was playing ping pong in the school yard, when the Hoovers approached him, imposing figures, all big & buff with bald heads.

"Where our guns at, lil nigga!"

He broke up out of there, hopped the gate & fetched his brother so they could return the guns together. This act of fearlessness & loyalty not only earned Kato some cool points with the Hoover Crips, but it also caught my attention. There was something about him that I knew would make him a great friend & an even greater Crip.

He felt that Crippin' was a natural fit for him, and as we spoke, I realized that he was serious about it. I gave him a pep talk, I let him know the real deal. I took it upon myself to tell him about the initiation into Fifty Crip, and to my satisfaction, he was feeling what I had to say.

"This ain't some shit you can just sign up for, cuH, this ain't the boy scouts." I continued. *"You gotta get down for the crown! You gotta fight!"*

"I'm with all that shit, fool!" He replied.

We didn't make it official the day we spoke but today it was going down! We used to ask people if they wanted to be from the set, but we only asked once. After that you got your ass kicked & you were getting that beatdown with one of two results, be a Crip or be a mark. A mark is a sucker with a target on them, X marks the spot.

We had a slogan *"once you fight, you alright"*. A few days later, I was on the corner with the muscle, CoCo, and Coke dog, waiting for the winos to get our 8balls. CoCo was an imposing 12-year-old that was built like a grown man with fists like boulders & a gaze that would make even the bravest tremble. Coke Dogg, was a militant 14-year-old brute, that was wise beyond his years & commanded respect with his hulking shadow towering over our shrunken bodies.

The duo were seasoned brawlers who had proven their worth, solidifying their place in our gang, asserting their dominance over anyone who dared to cross their paths. We prepared to put Kato on the set by getting drunk. It was time to test his gangsta, so we proceeded to pick a fight with him, and see if he had some heart.

As these two colossal Crips approached him, Coke Dogg said, *"What's up, Kato!?!"*

Coke Dogg & CoCo fire on him before he could respond. Caught off guard, phased & dazed, Kato faltered, his knees buckling under the crushing weight of the onslaught. His vision blurred by the sharp jabs & heavy hooks, but he met the fists with an unwavering resolve, he embodied the Spartan law, *"no surrender, no retreat."*

In that moment, an unspoken code enveloped him, urging him to rise above the battle, to become the true gladiator that lay dormant within his child-like demeanor. He fought back, the kid had some squabble & proved he had heart.

Unable to ignore the call of brotherhood & respect for Kato, I immersed myself in the rumble. Blow by blow, I made my presence known & showed my new comrade some love. He took his ass whipping like a champ. Kato got up with a black eye & busted lip, he wore it like a badge of honor. Despite the culmination of bruised knuckles, battered muscles seared with pain, Kato stood tall, earning his stripes as a Fifty Crip.

He managed to dust himself off as if the event were a mere passing cloud. He was a living testament to our creed, exemplifying the motto *"once you fight, you alright!"*

We shook his hand in a show of love & respect, cementing his position amongst us. Around the way, if you run once, plan on running for the rest of your life. Kato was no punk, he held it down & we've been homeboys ever since. Kato would become a solid Loc, infamous in all aspects of gangbanging, knocking off brands out, jacking suckers & pushing the line.

Our legendary partnership began. Together, Kato & I embarked on countless adventures, each one more perilous & exhilarating than the last. Every day with Kato was thrilling, unpredictable, and filled with raw emotion—the type of life that could only exist amid the perils of gangbangin'.

Our time together was filled with infinite unforgettable experiences, and as the years went on, Kato became so much more than a friend. He is a brother, a partner, a fellow Kiwé warrior, and one of my everyday niggas. Our bond was unbreakable, forged in the fiery crucible of South Central Los Angeles. Solidifying our bond through the shared experiences of violence, deceit, and kinship.

Kato was always playing around, always doing some dumb shit. A true asshole, but in a good way, he would always play pranks on the homies. He was known for his wild sense of humor & limitless energy. He reveled in the chaos his antics spurred, and his laughter was like a siren song to many of his homies. However, Richard's humor had a darker side, the very aspect that made him who he was: taking advantage of the unexpected.

We just returned to the Barn from 48th street park, Crip Crazy & Jaystone's cousin, Trent, just got put on the set by Big CoCo. Trent was initially named Baby Tee, he was the first homie that wasn't from the Fifties, he lived in the 20's off Jefferson, in the middle of the Neighborhood Bloods turf. Baby Tee would become one of my everyday niggas, a stomp down loc known as the infamous Big T-Dogg from Five-Deuce Hoover Gangsta Crip.

The Brims recently came through the hood on bikes chasing homies with bats & chains. Rumors spread that they were out on the prowl. As we prepared for a potentially volatile confrontation at the Barn, Kato was assigned to lookout duty. Amid the adrenaline rush of a possible skirmish, his inner prankster grew restless. Taking advantage of the tense atmosphere & heightened nerves, Kato hastily burst back into the hideout, his face contorted in fear.

In a panic-stricken voice, he shouted that *"The Bloods is coming!*

He continued, *"them niggas deep & they strapped!"*

We sprang into action, hearts racing as we readied our weapons & prepared for the worst. Moments later, Kato's laughter echoed through the room, stopping everyone dead in their tracks.

"Gotcha, bitch! I'm just playin'!" he howled, tears in his eyes as he struggled to contain his amusement.

A relief washed over the homies' faces - but it was quickly replaced with anger. After all, they had been jerked around enough to think their lives were on the line. It wasn't the first time Richard had played a joke like this on us, but it was by far the worst.

Mad as hell, CoCo, Lil Live, T-Dogg, Jaystone & Crip Crazy decided they'd had enough & attacked Richard, a ritual known as a DP (discipline & punishment), where they beat his ass for his careless foolery. Sprawled on the ground, bruised, and battered. Kato couldn't help but laugh like an evil villain, showing no signs of remorse or regret for having played us all the fool. As the days & weeks went by, Kato began to silently seek out those who had jumped him that day, catching them off guard & individually challenging them to a fade, mano-a-mano.

No one ever saw him coming, and before they knew it, Kato had successfully given out ass whippings to all them except Big CoCo, who was a physical anomaly & arguably one of the best squabbler amongst the Fifty Crips. His reputation transformed from a mere prankster to a force to be reckoned with - not just for his wit & trickery, but for the sheer grit of a man who refused to back down.

The homies, awed & humbled, learned to respect Kato for who he was, and their annoyance at his antics slowly morphed into a robust appreciation. In the face of fear & danger, Kato's humor had been a double-edged sword; while his unpredictability may have irritated some, it was also a breath of fresh air. That's how my brother from another mother, Kato, became known as the notorious Big Joker from Five-Deuce Hoover Gangsta Crip.

    The rest of that summer was a whirlwind of experiences & emotions as Joker, and I grew closer. We shared many moments together. We roamed the streets, picking fights, learning new skills, making friendships, and leaving a path of destruction along the way. He became not only my comrade in Fifty Crip but a genuine friend, someone I could rely on through thick & thin.

    It's the rarest of friendships that endure across decades, especially when they are born of such chaos & uncertainty as Crippin'. Yet here we stand today, Joker, and I, survivors of many wild summers & a reckless youth. Big Joker, the jester who wore the H-crown & dared to bring light into the dark corners of our souls.

CHAPTER FIFTEEN:
"HOOVER GANGSTA CRIPPIN' AIN'T EASY"

We grew up during a time when society's pressures were a force to reckon with & a sense of belonging was sought by every kid in the hood. A distinct need for affiliation was the motive for creating of our initial identity, Fifty Crip. However, something was in the water, a significant transformation was shifting the ground beneath us like tectonic plates.

A change that echoed in the dusty alleys & bustling streets, shattering our known identity like bottles of brew & paving the way for something singular, something remarkable.

The saga of our rebranding began one evening while CoCo & I were hanging outside his mama's crib on 54th street. As we passed a 40 ounce of Olde English back & forth, we talked shit about girls we were trying to freak, Brims we wanted to beat, and hustlers & playas we could sneak & thieve. We politicked about the current state of Fifty Crip & the collective desire for a new identity.

Caught in the whirlwind of thoughts, I shared my idea with CoCo - a name that would echo the air of defiance & strength of the place we dominated, 'Five-Deuce Hoover Gangsta Crip.' Coco's eyes sparkled; he dug my idea. The matter was to be discussed further. CoCo would become a key player in setting up the program &

foundation for FDHGC. He was passionate about the collective & the belief that everyone had a voice.

He pushed for us to have meetings, he was our enforcer & sergeant-at-arms, he specialized in maintaining order & security. CoCo took pride in quoting (initiations) & DPs for absences & lateness at functions or anything we deemed unacceptable behavior. He developed us into becoming more militant. Coco believed in tough love, and looking back, I see he wanted to make sure anybody claiming Hoover Gangsta were warriors ready for combat.

Armed with a potential new identity & an eager spirit, we linked up at Bow Dee's crib on 56th & Hoover. The turnout was impressive, with about 20 of us banding together for this momentous decision. A motley crew made up of me, CoCo, Coke Dogg, Big Fat Rat, Ken Dogg, Insane Fish, Cadillac Bob, Ric Roc, ScHool Boy, Sham Rock, JoJo, Dre Dogg, Lil Live, Slicc Ricc, Hoppin' Rod, Cyko Mike, Willbone, Green-eyed Kev & Too Sweet. I sincerely apologize if I forgot anyone, blame it on the PCP & old age.

As we huddled up we passed around joints of lovely - a blend of PCP & weed, and plastic cups of Kryptonite- a mixture of silver satin & green Kool-Aid. We clung to these simple joys, each puff & sip enriching our conversations. The cipher was filled with echoes of laughter, viewpoints, varying opinions, and blossoming ideas about our new identity.

Among the clamor of voices proposing new names, Coke Dogg was reminiscent of the legacy of Gladiators, suggesting we take their name. He echoed sentiments of respect towards the predecessors, proposing *"Gladiator Crips."*

Another suggestion floated from Ken Dogg, *"Five-Foe Vermont Gangsta Crips,"* a tribute to our frequent hangout. Willbone added his own flavor to the discussion, suggesting we call ourselves the *"Five-Foe Warlock Crips."*

Amid the turbulence of contrasting thoughts & the anticipation that loomed like fog, the moment of truth arrived. I felt like Tupac with all eyes on me, their Crippin' vanguard. There was a silent but powerful question hanging in the air: *"Boo, what we gonna do?"*

The weight of the silence emboldened the echo of my voice as my response shattered the tension.

I surrendered my idea of *"Five-Deuce Hoover Gangsta Crip"* to the judgment of my peers. Mirroring the twinkle in Coco's eyes, they seemed to embrace it.

The reaction was instantaneous & electric— a wave of loud affirmative cheers spread around, with all the homies hollering a collective *"Yeahhhh!"*

The homies reacted favorably to my proposal; however, the street that would accompany our new name sparked a fierce debate — *'Five-Deuce'* or *'Five-Foe'*. While we claimed every street as our throne, the majority resided & spent most of our time on 54th street.

"I feel you, cuH, but I think we should claim Five-Foe Hoover," Ken Dogg continues with the support of all the 54th street homies, *"more homies live on the Foe."*

This was an undeniable truth; homies also voiced their objections & reservations about claiming Five-Deuce due to its attachment to the Broadways.

I inhaled my joint & exhaled heavy Grey smoke as I addressed their concerns, *"I don't nominate Five-Deuce cause it's my block it's for 52nd street school!"* I continued, *"and it shows love to the Five-Deuce Underground."*

Regardless of the street we lived on it seemed like all the homies felt that shared entitlement to our childhood alma mater. 52nd street school would become our breeding grounds. My words hung heavy in the smoky air, sinking into their hearts & minds as they warmed up to my POV. Their heads bobbing in agreement, a unanimous decision was reached! We are Five-Deuce Hoover!

It was a pledge of unity, resonating with our shared past, while bestowing respect to the trailblazers who led the way for us. In convincing them about the importance of the number 52, I saw our unity strengthening, our bonds growing deeper. Five-Deuce became the essence of our tribe- unity amidst diversity, finding common ground where each of our unique footprints could meld into one powerful symbol of defiance.

We were not the first to claim Hoover or Gangsta, but we were the only Hoover Gangstas. The combination gave us the uniqueness we desired & a title we were proud of. Hoovers were highly respected, and the soul of the Crips. We knew we wanted to command the same respect for our section, the Fifties, always kept it gangsta & we had no plans of changing!

Amidst the intoxicating haze of Kryptonite & Lovely, FIVE-DEUCE HOOVER was born — a name intended to sow mayhem among our adversaries & captivate the hearts of the girlies we craved. A name born from a common vision, nurtured by shared experiences, and etched in the Fifties.

Energized, we rounded off the day by making our mark in the alley on 54th, where CoCo, Sham Rock & I, under the newfound banner of solidarity, striked up all our names on the wall. This act marked the dawn of a new chapter in our lives.

We were just boys then, ages 10 to 15, daring & dashing, operating on reckless courage & youthful curiosity. We plotted & ambushed every business establishment on Vermont Ave, our exploits becoming so legendary that the owners began showering us with freebies, only to stop us from pillaging their goods. These quid pro quo arrangements became our main survival strategy, keeping us filled with hope, and most importantly, nourishment, despite the harsh challenges the world threw at us.

We frequently ransacked Golden Bird, a renowned chicken spot. In a memorable night of bold adrenaline-rushed thievery, we stole their safe, anchoring chains around it & dragging it through two walls with a pickup truck. The thrill was intoxicating, the victory tantalizing. After that, the chicken began flowing freely from the Golden Bird, a peace offering to subdue our looting.

This free meal ticket would be cashed in at the liquor store on the corner of 54th & Vermont. We didn't wait for opportunities - we made them. Like clockwork, as the delivery truck came, we would position ourselves strategically, ready for the delivery man to step into the store. Instantly, we would spring to action, swiftly stealing cases of malt liquor from the unattended truck. We had some nerve, sometimes we brazenly swiped stuff from the shelves.

To honor this momentous occasion, we stopped at our regulars—the Golden Bird & the liquor store to pick up liquor & food for our first Hoover Gangsta party. We raided the store 20 deep, but the clerk was fed up.

He had a fire in his eyes, a raw defiance, as he pulled a gun on us from behind the counter. We were not the ones to back down, especially not today. Cadillac Bob matched his energy & revealed his own concealed piece. The wise store clerk upheld the tradition of letting the Fifty Crips take what we want.

We retreated to Ken Dogg & Fish's shack, where we partied all night smoking & drinking with the 57th street Fly girls. At around 4am as the discord of rowdy laughter & drunken rough housing echoed into the night. Sirens cut through the silence—blue & red lights permeating the darkness. The pigs crashed the party!

Instant pandemonium ensued as we scattered like project roaches when the lights turned on. Desperation looming over our intoxicated states. Unfortunately, Ken Dogg, Willbone, and CoCo, were too inebriated to acknowledge the threat as they were having too much fun rough housing, resulting in them getting cracked & tossed into Juvenile Hall. Ken Dogg was wilding in the spot pushing the line, socking out red rags & got hit with additional time in CYA, and was gone until 1982.

What a crazy night! A nostalgic flicker glistens in my eyes as I live through these memories once again. Reflecting on the old days & the loved ones we lost fills my heart with laughter, sorrow, and a whole spectrum of raw emotions. We didn't know it was the birth of a worldwide phenomenon, a movement that would transform into a living entity unto itself.

The seeds of this immense force were sown in the heart of South Central, a community known more for its bleak realities than its nurturing soils. Yet it was from this barren land that roots of extraordinary power & influence would spring forth.

Looking back, it seems I had an uncanny ability to orchestrate people at a tender age, my charisma pulling us towards a unity we had never known before. The following evening, we met outside of Dre Dogg's crib. We sparked up some Sherm & Mary Jane, our minds settling into a sworn pact of solidarity. Coke Dogg & I led the charge! What started as a casual twenty evolved into a force, marching its way from the Foe through the 40's to Exposition.

We followed Willbone's words, as the half Mexicano chanted a contagious, "*Viva La Cincuenta Dos*" (Long Live Fifty Two in Spanish), echoed throughout the streets, every syllable marking our claim to this territory.

Our march wasn't just about possession. It was a celebration of Fifty Crippin,' our way of life. Time seemed to cease as we indulged in the sensational delights of joints of Mary jane, Sherm sticks, Mad Dog 20/20 & Olde English. We created an institute that made us family & became our tribe.

Circling back towards the familiar embrace of 54th street was like witnessing the formation of the universe. Our numbers had doubled; our collective voice echoed resounding chants of *"Five-Two Hoover"* This was a moment of profound unity, one fueled by the shared external experiences that internally defined us.

The following day saw an even grander celebration under the robust branches of the Yum-Yum tree outside my mama's house on 52nd place. A tangible air of excitement & anticipation took over us as dusk set in, my street turned into a block party. The unity of our group, now expanded, the shared sense of purpose, and the quickened heartbeats pounded the rhythm of a narrative that was unique to us.

To believe in this groove was to believe in the unbelievable. The love, the unity, the community that we created - the Fifties - was nothing less than a supernatural phenomenon. We were just a group of kids from the hood that became a movement, a wave that refused to be stopped, a wave that was destined to crash into every coast.

Looking back feels dreamlike that a handful of reckless kids from South Central started a ripple which turned into a tidal wave, spreading far beyond what we ever imagined. It was a time of change, of growth, and of sheer, unadulterated aspiration.

A couple days have passed since the metamorphosis to Hoover Gangsta. I was hanging out with my nigga, Joker. We were always getting into the wild shit, our mischief kept our blood flowing with adrenaline, filling us with a sense of belonging & excitement. However, today we needed something different – money. Life taught us that while money is essential to survive, it could also buy the simple things in life that felt like luxuries to us.

As the sun dipped lower, it cast shadows against the grimy pavement that made us appear 10 feet tall as we hatched a plan. We were united in our despair, trudging through life with barely a dollar to our names. We quickly discovered the true meaning of *"necessity is the mother of invention",* as our enduring need for money turned us into resourceful thieves, numbing the deep-rooted morality within ourselves.

Our criminal urges led us to the Fairfax District in West Hollywood—a place that glittered like a beacon of wealth. This trendy part of West Hollywood was a hub for the rich & famous alike, swarming with movie stars, well-off Jews, and eager tourists flocking to CBS Television City to see *"The Price is Right."* The busy streets, the affluent people, and the potential victims of our cunning plans all spelled *"opportunity"* for us.

Desperate times, call for desperate measures & an opportunity to feel the weight of cold, hard cash in our pockets was a risk worth taking. It is time for me to use the skills I learned from Uncle Roy & Ten Speed. After all, what was a high-stakes crime spree without a swift getaway?

Our first order of business was to get some wheels, a task made easy by my uncanny ability to use a B-10 key to get any vehicle started. We embarked on our journey to Fairfax, eager to indulge in a robbing spree that would, at least temporarily, alleviate our financial woes.

As we parked our car in a dimly lit alley, the anticipation hung heavy in the air. With a nod to each other, we embarked on our hustle for the evening – purse-snatching. Under the neon glow of streetlights & the vibrant energy of Fairfax, searching for unsuspecting fools that we could jack. To our naïve young minds, it seemed like such a simple, foolproof plan, devoid of consequence. Our hearts raced as adrenaline pumped through our veins, each step bringing us closer to our next target.

"We've gotta make a move, cuH," Joker whispered.

I could barely hear his voice over the crowds of people & disco music radiating from nearby venues. It wasn't long before my eyes locked onto an older white lady as she exited a luxurious store, her purse clutched tightly in one hand. Every fiber of my being told me she was the perfect target; dressed in fine clothing & dripping with jewelry, she had wealthy stamped on her forehead.

Without a second thought, I sprinted toward her, adrenaline surging through my veins. This bitch never stood a chance. I grabbed the purse right out of her hands & turned to flee, as the panicked screams of the victim rang out, echoing through the streets like a screeching siren's call. Suddenly, our harebrained scheme felt much less foolproof, and a wave of fear washed over me as I ran, desperately trying to escape the scene of the crime. Among the chaos, a pig saw us, his stern gaze locked onto me as he began giving chase.

"Stop! Freeze!"

We pretended we were deaf, dumb & blind, as we started running like we stole something, cause we did! Joker & I were forced to split up, hoping to avoid capture, weaving through the congestion of panicked pedestrians & darting into an alley. My legs burned as I pushed myself to run faster to escape the pig hot on my trail. All too soon, the moment we had dreaded came: the sirens & flashing lights.

Retracing the steps to my getaway car, the fear of being caught collapsed on me, but it only drove me to push harder. My lungs burning as I dove inside & slammed the door shut behind me. My heart thudded in my chest as I fumbled with the key, throwing the car into gear, and speeding off into the night. Joker, on the other hand, managed to escape & take the bus back to the Fifties. I wasn't so lucky.

The high-pitched squeal of handcuffs snapping closed around my wrists announced my fate louder than any siren. Our dream of making money & escaping the clutches of poverty had in a cruel twist of fate, landed me in the clutches of Sylmar Juvenile Hall. Charged with Grand Theft Auto & Robbery, I couldn't deny it. I had been caught red-handed.

This place was nothing short of purgatory. Walking down the narrow corridors lined with screeching metal doors, laced with an all too familiar stench of industrial detergent mixed with a faint trace of despair, my mind wandered. Under the dim lights of Sylmar, I found solace in the camaraderie of my fellow Hoover Gangstas—CoCo, Ken Dogg, T-Dogg, Big Fat Rat, Gangsta D, and Lil Live. Our unity was a familiar sense of comfort.

The transition was smoothed over by the presence of my fellow Crips there. The familiar faces of my brethren. Swallowed by the unforgiving walls & cold glares of my fellow detainees, I wondered about Joker. The bitter irony of it all took shape a few days later, when Joker joined us in the facility for an unrelated robbery.

With all the frenzy & turmoil engulfing my life, my parents never once visited me. It was as if I had been written off, my transgressions too heavy for them to bear. When the time came & the rusty gates of Sylmar creaked open for me, I returned home deprived of any joy or anticipation. Arriving home was anticlimactic – no grand reunion, no warm hugs, just a house echoing with resentful silence.

The tension between my pops & I was like an overstressed guitar string– ready to snap at any moment. He sat in the living room, the old television set casting shadows on his stern face. Taking a deep breath & cementing my resolve, I attempted to walk past him unnoticed.

I was greeted by his mean, cold stare. Before I could say anything, he opened with vicious damnation. *"Boy, you went from stealing pigeons to being locked up over 10 times in a year!'*

His voice echoed the harsh reality of my actions. I stiffened, finding no words to defend myself. On this battleground, I was unarmed, vulnerable. An argument ensued. I looked to my mother for support, but she merely shook her head in disapproval. Our voices penetrated the sheetrock walls into the street. I pleaded desperately, trying to explain why my actions were a response to his unjust treatment.

"You can't talk down on me when you locked me up for no reason! What kinda father does that," I retorted defensively, my gaze meeting his unrelenting one.

"Oh, you think you a big man now, huh?" he asked, his eyes filled with a desolate mix of anger & sorrow.

Our loud argument resonated through the silent halls of our home, a symphony of pent-up anger & sorrow. Within that heated exchange was also a note of desperate hope. My rebellious acts were a furious hammering against my father's authoritarian stiffness, seeking not to shatter it, but to mold it into a more accepting, empathetic shape.

"I know I've been hard on you, boy" he said after an excruciating pause. *"I was tryna set yo ass straight. Instead, yo ass chose to get deeper in the bullshit. You need to get ya mind right!"*

I spat back, *"I ain't proud of it, but at least I was takin' from whitey they can afford to lose something."*

"Just cause they white, don't make it right, you sound like one of them stupid ass Black Panthers," he retorted, his eyes narrowing, his voice dipped dangerously low. *"You think you some kinda Black Robin Hood, huh?"*

"I'm doing what I gotta do," I said smugly, *"I know you can't dig it, you talkin' that jive cause you a Uncle Tom!"*

A back hand smack followed by a silence that engulfed the room momentarily, and then he said, sarcastically, *"Robbin' & stealin' ain't no rebellion. It's some stupid nigga shit. Are you a dummy or does doin' time make you feel like a tough guy!?!"*

Tensions rose as the heated exchange continued, until my father, wiping away any trace of emotion, sighed deeply & said, *"Son, change ain't gonna happen overnight. You got decisions to make, but understand this, the path you on now only leads to one place, and trust me, it's way worse than Eastlake!"*

His words, intended to be lashing whips, felt more like a hollow echo. All the pain, resentment, and stubborn defiance steeled me, hardening my resolve. The room crackled under the tension, a war waged over unspoken words & shattered dreams. We clashed again; his pent-up frustration & my adolescent rebellion clashing like a tidal wave against the shoreline.

"You can't keep blaming me, boy. You made your decisions; now, it's time to face the consequences," my father's voice rang out, cold & stern. His words slapped me in the face.

"What the fuck, pops you never listen to me" I voiced my anguish, desperate for a hint of understanding, but my plea was met by deaf ears & a punch to my chest by his massive fist.

"You watch your mouth lil nigga, I brought you in this world, and I can take yo ass out! I gave you everything I could. You gonna throw it all away," he accused, his icy gaze searing into my very core.

"It's cool, Pops, I gotta new family," I said proudly, my eyes unwavering, *"the Crips!"*

My honest words hung in the air like a comet, bright & burning. The silence stretched into what felt like a painfully long heart-wrenching solitary confinement. As I stomped off to my room, madness took over my mind & I fantasized & plotted on killing my father in his sleep. These dark thoughts continued to fill my mind for months, I even tried to convince Spookee to help me, but thank God he talked me out of it or we could've been the Menendez Brothers & I would have never forgiven myself!

From father to son, we ping ponged our hurt, each blow revealing our painful vulnerabilities & the delicacy of emotions, blurred by the anger & aggression we used as camouflage. Our words were harsh daggers.

Looking back now, I realize that day was a crossroad in my life, and while it was embedded with bitterness. I was blinded by rage, I didn't nourish the seed of change my father planted. He even gave me first job with his landscaping business to try & keep me out the street. He wanted me to learn the value of a hard earned dollar but I foolishly looked at it as a punishment.

I swore my father gave up on me but now as a wiser man, I understand he wasn't fighting with me, he was fighting for me, fighting for my future, fighting to save my life. This was a fight I regret winning, so I could've been the man, father, and husband my family needed me to be.

CHAPTER SIXTEEN:
"THE BATTLE OF THE FIVE-DEUCES"

We were the cool kids that seemed to know everyone, we were the neighborhood toughs, who commanded respect & admiration from our peers. Like all great stories, the rise of Five-Deuce Hoover began with this core nucleus, the descendants of the Gladiators.

Each member brought unique qualities to the fold, and together, we forged a bond stronger than any single one of us could have ever dreamed. We were young scholars of the streets, meticulously studying the original gangstas. Those who dabbled in gunplay & drank from the cup of intoxicating power, demanded respect & extracted it with harsh brutality. It wasn't long before other kids, even adults around the way started to take notice of the bond we shared.

We used to engage in friendly competition throughout our adolescent years. Football & basketball games were a staple with every block in South Central represented by its own team. We would face off against the streets, the victories & losses feeding the fires of camaraderie that had begun to unite us.

As we grew older, the lines between innocent games & something more serious gradually began to blur. A sense of shared identity had begun to take root in our community, it was a generation of tribalism. Our reputation grew & new recruits eagerly sought to join our notable ranks, we started to evolve into something much bigger.

"What makes a set strong is the variable personalities. Everyone has their function. Everyone isn't a killer, some are fighters, hustlers, shooters, playas, some are taggers/wall bangers, everybody has their own groove & individuality. You can't force people into a lane that isn't what they're suited for." - oG Hoover Luv Hriginal FDHGC

The Crips had become something that every kid in South Central wanted to be a part of – something that represented power, fidelity, unity, and a support system amidst the grim realities of life. I was confident in our strength & unity. It felt like we ruled the world, every street corner from King to Slauson belonged to Hoover Gangsta.

I was the top recruiter but it was the reputation of the collective that was intriguing to suitors. The collective systematically screened & selected only the best of the best to be granted entry into our fold. Among the newcomers, there were some who simply did not make the cut. This was not a place for the weak-willed or the faint of heart; only the strong survived in the blue world.

"Mind of steel, Heart of Stone. Crip Machine is Moving On."
- oG Herbert Gates, Founder of Five-Deuce Underground Crip, author of C-Machine, Five-Deuce Hoover Gangsta Crip

I started recruiting everybody & their mama to the set. I was that infectious spirit that weaved a web of resilience & fearlessness, bringing members closer, making our gang ties impossible to untangle. The manifestation of my dedication was the tattoo I brandished, Five-Deuce Hoover, a pledge of allegiance etched in my skin. The blue rag that looped around my neck served not only as a token of my unswerving loyalty to my tribe but also as a badge of honor & an emblem of the fire I kept within my heart.

We were one of the newest sets, a group of kids who were determined to make a name for themselves. We didn't know all the politics involved with Crippin'. Due to our new identity, we sparked a fire with multiple hoods & Five-Deuce Hoover welcomed all challengers!

"Deuce Here!"
– oG Bobby Johnson, South Central

Back in the day the streets buzzed with the spirit of defiance painting a picture of our daily struggles. It was the time of turf wars, gang brawls, and bloodshed. We heard whispers in the street, the Five-Deuce Broadways –our friends & allies – had the audacity to proclaim that there could be only one Five-Deuce! Naturally, we couldn't let that slide. We refused to back down, we had to prove our worth.

We refused to honor our challengers battle cry *"Broadway or No Way!"*

A thick layer of fog crept over the hallowed ground of the Fifties. As I alongside Big Fat Rat & CoCo led the homies to the battlefield, 20 deep & clad in midnight blue, staying true to our cause, ready to fight for our dignity & our name. The meeting was set at our border underneath the 110 freeway. A dark, gloomy place where the harsh shadows were a constant reminder that the path to victory would not be easy. A place where the echoes of combat ricocheted off the stone-cold walls.

No one could intimidate or deviate us from our goal. The air was electric as the first rumble began. The determination to come out victorious only grew stronger as the weeks dragged by. The skirmishes were brutal, often leaving the warriors bloodied, bruised, and battered but more spirited than ever. It was all about honor, as we ran fades, engaging in one-on-one battles to test our heart & our gangsta. We fought with every ounce of strength we had, it was an epic showdown.

Each punch thrown & every drop of blood spilt was a demand for respect & display of our dedication. It wasn't just about who would reign as Five-Deuce – it was an unspoken realization that in this powder keg of anger & aggression, both sections commanded a certain level of admiration for the other.

As time went on we grew stronger & more determined to dismantle Broadway's dreams of dominance. It seemed impossible, but as time progressed, the unimaginable began to take shape. With each brutal clash, a bond of mutual respect between Hoover & Broadway developed, intertwining our destinies like the roots of an ancient tree. Injured, scarred & unashamed, we learned of the true nature of our adversaries – their resilience, their unwavering determination, their unconquerable spirit – & we realized just how much we mirrored each other's values.

As the dust settled, the negotiations began. I met with Big Choo, we decided to abandon our differences & end the battle for supremacy, instead we ventured towards uncharted territories – a collaboration fueled by shared history, ambitions, and unwavering dedication.

West Town Five-Deuce Hoover-Broadway Gangsta Crip was formed. A union of Five-Deuces, each contributing their strengths to the common cause. Our colors merged, our hearts beat in unison, and we reclaimed our territory as a united front.

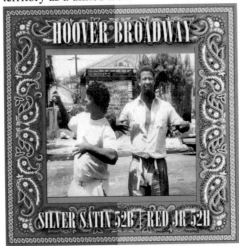

We formed the Five-Deuce car. The original borders of the Hoover-Broadway dominion stretched from Martin Luther King Jr Blvd to Slauson Avenue, and Figueroa Street to Normandie Avenue & east to Avalon Ave, it had been ours to govern; a place we could call our own.

I remember it like it was yesterday, even though we approach a half century of this gangsta groove. Big Bro finally came back home from camp & Spookee was now over 6 feet tall & strong as an ox. First thing I said to him when I saw him was *"I guess I can't kick your ass no more huh, Big bro!"*

He laughed me off, *"You still talking shit, huh, lil nigga?!? Good to see you too!"*

His arrival was a resurgence of hope & a breath of fresh air that the Fifties missed dearly. I couldn't wait to tell him & show him what I was up to. He had missed our Fabulous Fifty Crip era. Now that we formed our own set, I faced the formidable task of growth & expansion, and I wanted, no, I needed my brother to be a part of it.

Besides the nostalgia brought by his return, it was also his Crip ardor (passion), that I admired most. An original Westside Five-Deuce Underground Baby Crip, Spookee carried an air of subtle allure & knowledgeable experience that I held in high esteem. When I narrated our journey & the inception of Hoover Gangsta, he had a spark in his eyes & a smile on his face that spoke volumes about his approval & excitement.

It was a welcome surprise; he immediately declared his allegiance to our newly formed alliance. His actions testified to his dedication. He didn't just blend in but became an integral thread, weaving the fabric of our organization. He didn't only contribute his loyalty but fortified our unity under shared goals, making our group more cohesive & influential among his generation & his big homies.

The good news of the day didn't end with Spookee being sworn in. His homecoming was shared with his band of brothers, loyal comrades who had stood with him from the Suicide Gang & the original Five-Deuces. We were now an expanding force to reckon with.

Our establishment as a resolute collective solidified a feeling of belonging among us. The concept of brotherhood, which we embodied, now had an identity to cement our family. The solitary silhouettes that once lurked in the neighborhood were now a part of a collective body, echoing the resonating message of unity & strength.

In retrospect, my brother Spookee's return changed the course of our trajectory as a young set. Not only did his support boost our confidence but his wisdom & experience from being an original Westside Crip enhanced our operating skills significantly. Every anecdote, every piece of advice served as a steppingstone for our evolution, shaping us from naive Baby Crips into more experienced & streetwise Locs.

As we stared into the setting sun over 52nd street school, we were now unified under one emblem, a family, unbreakable by adversity, strong in unity, and fearless. THE HRIGINALS, carrying the legacy of the Gladiators, the original Five-Deuces & the Hoovers.

"Crips Don't Die, We Multiply!" - oG Buddha
(Curtis Morrow) Original Bonsallo & Westside
Crip

Here is what you all been waiting for the Hriginal Five-Deuce Hoovers broken down by block on 52nd street we have myself, oG Spookee, oG Ten Speed, oG Baby JoHnny, oG Blac DeeDee, oG TD-Tim Dexter, Baby Crazy, Jamaican Mike, Big Bandit, H'Luv (Lovely), and their baby brother Lil Bandit, an Hriginal Tiny Loc. We also had oG ShitHead Ted, he was mixed with Native American.

Ted got his name because he had the worst perm ever, it looked like a bunch of clumps of shit on his head, it was all jokes, but he decided to keep it as his name. Lastly on the Deuce we had Killa D from the Budlong side & we had oG Catman, ScHool Boy & Wish Dogg aka Lil Spookee, an Hriginal Tiny Loc from 53rd street.

On 54th street- Crip Crazy, Too Sweet, Willbone, Ken Dogg, Sham Rock (Playa Sham), Insane Fish, Blacc Charles (Egghead), Cadillac Bobby & his brother Lil Fat Rat, CoCo, Joker, Dre Dogg, Green-Eyed Kev, Jaystone, and his cousin T-Dogg.

Coke Dogg, Tee Dub, the lone homegirl & her brother, Mouse, along with Inch High, Gigolo, oG Monkey Man, oG Big Red Jr & Fats, who was previously from Eight-Tray Hoover. Rounding off the 55th street crew was Mad Horse & Deuce. Deuce was an older cat about 10 years my senior, he had recently moved to the set from Nickerson Gardens in Watts. Both Deuce (Bounty Hunters) & Mad Horse (Brims) switching the color of their rags from red to blue, an example of the influence & power of Hoover Gangsta.

The Six was thick. We had Gangsta D, Ant Capone, Crazy De-De, Ric Roc, O-Dogg, Bow Dee, C-Note, oG Madman, and his brothers Lil Live, Slicc Ricc & Hoppin' Rod on 56th street. We had Cyco Mike & his brother oG Evil Red, Mad Dogg & his brothers oG RP, and Bel-Aire on 57th street & Big Fat Rat from 58th street.

Little did we know that the rebranding of our set would give birth to a complex web of alliances & rivalries that would continue to shape the street politics of the city to this day. As the Fabulous Fifty Crip, we had no Crip adversaries. What led to this dramatic shift in allegiances was the politics surrounding the change of our programming. We didn't know our claims to Hoover & our alliance with Broadway included all of their beefs! This introduced our beef with the East Coast Crips, our first Crip rivals.

Raymond Washington, the undisputed founder of the Crips, set forth a vision to rebrand & reunify the Eastside as the East Coast Crips. His objective was to consolidate power by recruiting sets on the Eastside under a united front. Raymond Washington secured the support of the Six-Deuce & Six-Eight Neighborhood Crips & the Six-Nine Shack Boys, who became the original East Coast Crips.

The birth of East Coast Crips saw the city's landscape change. They aggressively expanded their influence. Fueled by a relentless drive for dominance, it wasn't long before the Coast boasted an imposing collection of 12 sets. However, with their growth, power & influence came new enemies & the inevitable tension within the Crip empire.

OG Raymond Washington also waged a failed campaign to recruit the Five-Deuce Broadways. Although the oG hoped to win them over with his lavish promises of power & influence, the Broadways along with Avalons, Main streets & Kitchens respectfully refused to rebrand & align under the Coast banner.

On top of Broadways refusal to flip to East Coast, there was the dick & pussy element. A love triangle that resulted in the Coast abducting 2 members of Five-Deuce Broadway. Their intentions, throw Lil Capone & Baby Down over the overpass onto the 110 freeway!

However, oG Raymond Washington intervened & stopped the execution. Despite this merciful act, it became apparent that there was no going back. Hostilities escalated dramatically, and soon Los Angeles became witness to a new Crip on Crip rivalry.

As a result, the beef between the East Coast & Broadways became our fight as well. Despite the brutal conflict that grew each day. During the next 2 years, we still met for football games at Bethune & South Park in attempts to foster fellowship between the two factions that were once close allies. The underlying tension was undeniable as each play carried with it the weight of fear, anger, and mistrust. The gridiron became a battlefield, where fights or shootings were a regular occurrence.

CHAPTER SEVENTEEN:
"NOTHING BIGGER THAN THE PROGRAM"

As the nostalgic sun began its daily descent, casting shadows along the cracked & worn pavement, one could feel the restlessness stirred within the Fifties. A gust of wind carried the faint perfume of phencyclidine & the hum of a distant fire truck siren. The residents understood the law of this land. Our strategy was an integral part of our foundation, an initiation, and a rite of passage that all residents had to endure. As our ranks swelled so did our reputation, our presence on the streets of South Central became more & more notable.

No corner was left untouched by our influence, as we claimed block after block in the name of Hoover Gangsta. Every day, more & more people could be seen gang-hanging throughout the Fifties, clad in the now-iconic blue that symbolizes our organization. Together, we made our hood into a fortress of strength & solidarity.

We were now over a hundred deep across our territory. We could've claimed different sets on every street, but we all had one thing in common. Our sense of community unified us so everybody fell in line. We made membership a requirement to live within our borders.

I remember as if it were yesterday - leaning against the store, the sun beating down on us, our brows drenched in sweat, the laughter of innocent kids replaced by the calculated whispers of outlaws. We decided that our initiation process would be simple but effective, unforgiving yet enticing. We would transform our set into a symbol of Fifty pride & power, whether by choice or by force. Everyone residing in the set had two choices: Get down, embody loyalty to Five-Deuce Hoover or lay down & regret challenging the order.

It became routine. Each morning, as the sun crept its way above the horizon, painting the sky in brilliant hues of pinks & purples, we'd convene at the bus stop outside the liquor store on the Foe, our hawk eyes sharp & focused, seeking out the prey who lived within the boundaries we had set. There were no exceptions. From preschoolers to the old timers, all would succumb to our gangsta groove.

Their avoidance tactics turned into an amusing game. As the bus approached, a symphony of thuds, clangs, and hurried footsteps replaced the early morning silence. People jumped from bushes, crawled from beneath parked cars, they made a mad dash for their sanctuary – the bus that would remove them from our presence, if only for a few fleeting hours.

In the afternoons, we'd gang-hang at the bus stop, waiting with bated breath to chase the same bodies that jetted off the bus, eyes widened in panic as they raced to outrun our wrath. No one could escape the long reach of the Five-Deuce Hoover Gangsta Crips.

What we did we believed necessary. A fight was a bold declaration of either loyalty or dissent, and we demanded both with equal passion. To fight was an expression of defiance, a nod to the spirit of rebellion that the streets seeped into our very souls. Run once & spend the rest of your life looking over your shoulder or stand tall & face the onslaught of fists & fury.

We would throw down the challenge, daring them to squabble, challenging them to stand their ground. Those who hesitated or tried to flee would be branded as cowards, labeled a *"mark"*, marked for a lifetime of ridicule & scorn. They would spend the rest of their days running, hoping to escape the cruel fate that awaited them.

Those who chose to fight, gained the honor to wear our colors were forever a Hoover Gangsta. A shared understanding that the pain we dispersed, and the camaraderie forged in those moments were cemented elements of the social fabric we weaved.

Reject us, and the path was paved with daily beat downs. Embrace us & join a force that shook the core of the Earth with an uncharted force on the Richter scale. The dawn of Five-Deuce Hoover did not occur in isolation. This was common practice in the rise of prominent sets of both Crips & Bloods that stood the test of time.

It embodied the spirit & ruthless mentality of the streets of Los Angeles & transcended into a new & intoxicating form of tribal identity. Some people may question the validity of these rites of passage, claiming that they promote violence & perpetuate harm. we recognize that the structure & the sense of family we found within the set was crucial to our survival. It was how we established dominance, order & loyalty in our world.

Our first clubhouse was called *"The Barn."* We took over an abandoned property across the street from 52nd street school with a big ass garage that looked like a barn. The Barn was a trip, it had 2 sides & 2 floors. We had ladders to take us to the second floor, we would go up one side & down the other. We set up beds on all floors. To gain access we had to jump the gate & any female that wanted to be a part of our entourage followed us over & indulged in a freaky fifty good time. Lots of the Locs got their first piece of pussy in that shack. Some used it as refuge if we got kicked out by our parents.

The walls were painted navy blue, with white trim & accents, and Baby Crazy, Joker & I, the top strikers, decorated the barn with graffiti, tagging our names, and the set all over. Over time it would display murals of our fallen homies, H-Crowns & slogans like *"HGC for life" "Brim Killa", "Hoover Groover, Slob Remover,"* & the Famous Hoover Gang Fingers all over the barn, it was Loced out like a muthafucka.

In the center of the room, we had a round table reminiscent of King Arthur & his Knights, where we held meetings, planned our next hustle, mission, and packaged our product, and of course play spades & dominoes.

It also functioned as a stash house. We had several secret spots to store our weapons & dope. We made sure to keep an armed lookout with a shotgun or rifle watching for any attempts to infiltrate.

The Barn was more than just a hangout spot. It was a symbol of our unity & power, a place where we could come together & feel invincible. We hosted parties, barbecues, spades, and dominoes tournaments for the homies to promote fellowship & boost morale. It was our secret sanctuary, kind of like the Hall of Justice for the Justice league.

From day one FDHGC operated as a collective. In our world, the majority ruled, and we made our decisions together. This mindset allowed us to push the line further, solidifying our position in the gangbang capital of the world. We operated as a well-oiled machine, focusing on unity & staying true to our core values.

We were a family, Hoovers-in-arms, bound by endless loyalty & respect for one another. This was the foundation upon which we built our legacy, making sure every individual was heard, and their opinion mattered. We were a unit of like-minded individuals who believed everyone deserves a voice. We wholeheartedly believed in community & brotherhood.

We never believed in a shot caller. There was no leader dictating our every move, instead, we believed in the principles of

FDHGC. It was through these unwritten principles we seemed to naturally exemplify certain traits. These qualities are best described by the Five D's of Five Deuce- Dedication, Devotion, Determination, Discipline, and Discrimination upon this platform we built a solid foundation. A Hoover Gangsta must stand firm in our purpose, defending our community from external threats while putting the big H in honor.

The first, as crucial as the heartbeat, was dedication. As members of this fraternity, we dedicated ourselves to one another, valuing the group above all else. We pledged our lives, injecting our souls into the FDNA of the set, engraving our existence into its history with the ink of loyalty, bravery, and sacrifice.

We were hardened by life's trials, dedication was our driving force, the need to fight for what we believed was unequivocally ours. Each tiny loc quoted under our insignia were enthusiastic, frontliners, braving challenges & not flinching from taking up our cause. Respect meant everything to us & each of us was committed to ensuring Hoover was respected no matter the sacrifice.

Devotion was our religion, not to any icon but to each other. We were fanatically devoted, taking on the mantle of protectors, turning ourselves into defenders of the pride & honor of our tribe. Each brick, each crack in the pavement, each shard of glass was a piece of us. Each letter in the graffiti on the wall, each blood stain on the street, each bullet ridden corner was a piece of us, a testament to our resolve. Such was our devotion that we became inseparable from our community, merging into one.

Our devotion was the essence of our existence, reflected in every deed, every action we took. It was part of our nature, as we aimed to protect the harmony of our set. The Fifties narrated stories of valor, heartbreak, and victory, and we, the devoted Deuces, ensured to add chapters of unyielding courage & unity.

Determination was the driver that shaped our path amid a world full of chaos. With odds stacked against us, it was easy to give in, to lose sight of our purpose. Nonetheless, each setback was met with resilient spirits. We clenched our jaws & tightened our fists, determined to stand up every time we were thrown down.

We were noble Kiwé warriors, every scar a testament to our lionhearted determination. To survive in the world that we inhabit requires not just sheer will but an unwavering determination. Determination was perhaps the most critical of the five. We were a stalwart bunch, determined to keep our place, to retain our status in the face of adversity.

Discipline is often mistaken for being submissive to authority, but it was our internal compass, guiding us through a maze of woes. It was a harmonious balance between freedom & responsibility. Strengthened by discipline, we walked on a path that led us to our tribal role as guardians, and protectors of my people.

We remained militant when it came to the protocols of decision-making, problem-solving, and conflict-resolution within our ranks. Within the folds of our brotherhood, there was order amidst chaos, a disciplined structure of unwritten codes & hierarchy built off respect. Your word is your bond, a solemn vow & breaking it was met with dire consequences.

Our discipline, the invisible force that bound us together, the veins & channels that connected us, that delineated the rules, the ones we lived by, fought by, and if need be, die by. We were a community walled in by disciplinary practices, processes invested with a ritualistic fervor that helped us establish a conduct, a standard that defined FDHGC.

The term 'discrimination' is typically seen as a negative trait, but in our lingo, it was not geared towards race, color, or creed, it refers to the judgment necessary to survive in a ruthless domain. It was the ability to distinguish between right & wrong, between allies & enemies, friends, and foes.

It allowed us to make informed decisions about where our loyalty should lie, and who we should trust or not. We learned to differentiate between those who sought to stand with us & against us. Firmly ingraining the understanding of loyalty, allegiance, and betrayal.

Unwittingly, these traits marked the path we tread, creating an order that resonated with the pulse of the community it sheltered. Our purpose was unique: we defended our loved ones from external threats, we promised vengeance for any trespass & maintained a code of honor from within. To some we may be outcasts, monsters born out of societal neglect; to others, a fraternity born out of necessity & the will to survive.

As a group, we knew right from wrong, and we adhered to unspoken rules of engagement that governed our code of conduct. Unfortunately, many of our ideals were deemed the opposite by society & led to many of us being incarcerated for most of our lives.

Amidst the hostility that ran rampant on the streets, there were a few notable exceptions to our turf politics. Despite being our enemies, we held a grudging respect for oG Batman Davis from East Coast, and Sugar Bear from Untouchable Brims, two reputable Original Gangstas of the Crips & Bloods, respectively. Both men, about a decade our senior, had earned their stripes & thus, were allowed to live within our borders as long as they adhered to our code. No recruiting or disrespecting the Groove was allowed, and as long as they honored these rules, they could coexist peacefully within our territory.

We kept it in the street kind of like a game of tag when you were home, you were safe. If we saw an enemy with his family, he was safe, and our rivals offered us the same respect. We understood the importance of boundaries & valued the sanctity of people's homes & families, which were off-limits in any conflict.

Discretion & restraint were virtues we vehemently upheld when engaging with our adversaries. The skirmishes we engaged in were noticeably different from the clichéd drive-by shootings & random acts of violence that most associate with gang warfare.

We took pride in our physical prowess &, as brothers, we relished the rush of adrenaline that came with hand-to-hand combat. There was an indescribable satisfaction that came with up-close & personal confrontations that no firearm could ever replace. These encounters became our rite of passage & served to strengthen the bond we shared as a collective.

It wasn't just about the thrill of the fight, though. Our preference for face-to-face confrontations minimized the collateral damage that plagued generations that followed. Innocent bystanders & civilians were spared as we opted for more personal, less chaotic methods of engaging our rivals. This was a point of pride for us, and we were universally recognized for our skilled fighters & minimal risks to innocent bystanders.

We are not perfect; we understand that violence begets violence. We made a promise to ourselves that if we had to use guns, we would do so in a way that we believed was honorable. We were going to live & die by our code, and we were going to make our neighborhood proud.

As time passed, life in the city began to change. Hoods that had once stood united began to fracture, and new faces emerged. The old guard was pushed out, and a new generation of gang members, with their own codes & ways of life, began to rise, leaving discord in their wake.

Our archrivals were the Six-Deuce Brims, now known as Harvard Park Brims. The Brims were right next to us, so we constantly engaged in skirmishes, both sides lost a lot of homies to the grave & the penitentiary over the years. Our other rivals were the Five-Nine, Van Ness Gangsta, and Rollin' 30's Fruit Town Brims as well as the Black P Stones & Rollin' 20's Neighborhood Bloods. We only had altercations with them at school or social events, the Brims were the closest in proximity & a worthy adversary.

I remember our first fight with the Brims. It was a hot summer afternoon in the City of Angels, with the sun blazing down to remind us of its fiery presence. The sky was brilliantly blue, with not a cloud in sight. I still remember that day, every detail etched into my mind like it happened just yesterday. The air was heavy with the scent of the city – the familiar blend of car exhaust, fried food, and the remnants of last night's debauchery. I suppose, in a lot of ways, that unrelenting heat was the perfect backdrop for the raw energy of the Crips.

I was hanging out on the corner of 56th & Vermont, talking shit & cracking jokes with the homies – Coke Dog, Lil Live, and Willbone, just enjoying another day in the Fifties. Posted outside of Louisiana Fried Chicken, the sweet & spicy aroma of their famous recipe & delicious & crispy fried chicken skin wafting through the air.

Next thing I know, twenty something Six-Deuce Brims creeped up on us out of nowhere, led by Al Dog, Nell Dog, and Rick Rock like a pack of wolves stalking prey. The intrusive roar of the Bloods had infiltrated our domain, leaving us with no choice but to stand our ground. An eerie silence fell over our once-lively street corner as they approached. Despite being outnumbered 5 to 1, the fierce pride pulsing within our veins ensured we would never back down.

OG Sugar Bear, one of their big homies was there, his eyes holding an intensity that commanded respect. His little brother, Chino, is an Hriginal Tiny Loc from the set, so we were confident he wasn't going to let this turn into the all-out disaster it could have been. Instead, he stepped between us, asserting control & ensuring we'd have a fair fight. The Bloods' older members watched with anticipation, their cheers fueling the adrenaline surging through their young soldiers' bodies.

Without any further ado, the first swings were thrown. Arms flailing, fists connecting with skin, while the sound of the blows echoed through the air. One by one, we each squared off with our opponents, putting everything on the line for the sake of our family. The line between friend & foe was anything but blurred as we fought to defend our turf & our reputation.

I found myself face to face with Al Dogg, a formidable opponent with a reputation that preceded him. He eyed me warily, sizing me up as I did the same. It would have been easy for either of us to show fear, to give in to the intensity of what was happening around us – but our loyalty to our respective hoods was stronger than anything we'd ever known.

We had a standoff, fists bawled up & eyes locked. The fight was fierce & relentless; neither of us held anything back. We were warriors on a battlefield, fueled by our love for our crew & the desire to prove our worth. Al Dogg was taller than me, giving him a bit of an advantage. However, I was faster & more agile. It didn't matter, though. All we wanted to do was pummel each other, and that's what we did. We all had a good squabble, nobody got knocked out. As we circled each other, our respective homeboys cheered us on. Their words of encouragement & jeers fueled our anger, making us want to hurt the other person even more.

My adversary kept trying to get me in a headlock & wrestle with me, but I managed to escape his grasp each time. He didn't want to throw the hands after I landed my first 3-piece combination; he knew he couldn't see me from the shoulders. For what felt like hours, we went back & forth, trading blows, tackles, and slams to the ground. At one point, I got Al Dogg in a chokehold, and for a moment, I thought I had won; but he managed to slip out of my grasp, and we were back at it again.

We looked at each other both exhausted, panting heavily & sweating profusely. We stood there, catching our breaths, and the tension between us began to dissipate. It was then that we both realized we had earned each other's respect, so we shook hands. Satisfied with our efforts representing our sets.

The battle between Five-Deuce Hoover Gangsta Crip & Six-Deuce Brim had reached its end, with every member still standing, albeit bruised & battered. Though our gang rivalry persisted, Al Dogg & I had somehow managed to forge an unexpected camaraderie that transcended our affiliations. Street code was everything, but that day taught us that there could be something more in this harsh world. Something we now know is trust & respect.

In the months & eventually years that followed, Al Dogg & I would look out for each other, despite the badge of our hoods. Our unlikely friendship went beyond the color of our bandanas, and in its essence, revealed the deep human connection that could exist even in the world of Crips & Bloods.

CHAPTER EIGHTEEN:
"CRIMEY'S & BACK STABBERS"

This was a time before cell phones, before social media, when holding onto your weapon was more valuable than sharing an update on what you were up to. Our love for our set was enough to keep us going, even though we knew that it might eventually lead to trouble that was just part of the game.

We turned to burglaries as a means of obtaining firearms, knowing that the more we gathered, the stronger of a force we would become. This way, when the Brims tried to attack us again, we would be prepared, resulting in countless sleepless nights.

I was hanging out on 51st street with some squares. We were horsing around, flipping off inner tubes. Although bangin' was my primary focus, there was something about the innocence of this horseplay that drew me in, at least for a short while, I mean I was only thirteen, but due to my lifestyle I rarely got to act like I was.

I decided to join them on this day, gladly adding my athletic prowess to their little group of amateur acrobats. I flawlessly nailed front flips, back flips, and side flips, like a gold medalist while my audience watched in admiration. I have always been athletic, I can do all types of acrobatics, front, back, side flips, tucks, Arabians, Aerials 360 Fulls, Websters, you name it. I can still flip today at my old age.

As laughter & sweat filled the air, a sudden interruption snuffed out our happiness. While we were out there flippin & flopping, having a good old time.

An angry old man appeared, waving his gun & hell-bent on reprimanding us for the minor inconvenience of being on his lawn. Foaming out the side of his mouth & cursing more than a voodoo doctor.

"Get off my muthafuckin' grass!" as he points his gun at me.

We scattered & retreated to safety, but my anger towards his unnecessary aggression lingered. I said to myself ok, I'm going to teach this old son of a bitch a lesson. He was a bitter old man, that fact made me dislike him even more. He lived in the home by himself. He owned a pickup truck. I cased his crib & as soon as I saw him drive down the street, I saw my chance to capitalize!

As a wise man named James Brown once said it was time for the big payback, and he was going to pay me back with a new gun! The adrenaline coursing through my veins empowered me, but it also clouded my judgment. Fearing neither retribution nor jail time, my only focus was on the immediate mission at hand. The consequences could come later. I went right in the back, pulled the little side windows out, I got in & out of there, I stole a shotgun & an old ass revolver. Boo got his first gun.

After the burglary I went straight to my garage. I sat & stared at my new toys, like any kid would. I couldn't wait to play with them, I called up some of the homies, and we made plans to go Hoo'Ridin', putting in work, the same night. As Willbone, Baby Crazy & I rode around the Brim's turf, my adrenaline was pumping.

My hands were shaking with excitement. At that moment, all I could think about was the power I held in my hands. We rode by a group of Brims gang-hanging on the corner, and it seemed like the perfect opportunity to become a blood killa. I jumped off my bike & aimed the .38 in their direction. I didn't care if they saw me or not, I was ready to take them out.

Boom! Boom!

The sound of the gun echoed through the streets as the Brims scattered in every direction like blood splatter. I felt like a God, invincible & untouchable. I thought it was a .38 special at first until I shot it at the Brims! Oooooo child, that shit was powerful, it used to kick fire out that muthafucka, it sounded like a cannon. After I fired it, I realized it was a colt 45! I'm still surprised my little ass didn't go flying out my Chuck Taylors.

If I were to go back to that time, with everything I now know, would I think it was all worth it? Was the pride, the loyalty, the fight for recognition & respect, worth all the pain, jail time & heartache? I've had many opportunities to reflect on the choices I made in my youth, and I've asked myself this question countless times.

The unbridled bravado & fearlessness of youth tends to blind us from perceiving the true cost of our actions. The adrenaline that used to give me the courage to flip off inner tubes or stand up to our rivals now offers an older, more sober perspective of a life filled with twists & turns, both good & bad.

The next day the set was buzzing with activity. It seemed like everyone was outside. People were walking their dogs, repairing their cars, tending to their yards, little kids were playing outside, and the sounds of The Jackson's new song *"Shake Your Body"* could be heard from a nearby backyard barbecue. I had no idea that my past deeds had caught up with me. The hood was hot this morning filled with the noise of sirens & flashing red-&-blue lights.

Feeling like the king of the world, or at least the corner of 52nd & Hoover Street, I strutted down my graffiti-laden street, envisioning the spoils that my breakfast would be made of. Before I knew it, the very force intended to halt my groove, the pigs swooped in & ruined my favorite meal of the day.

As I come out the store some old bitch & the kid, I robbed for the minibike is with the pigs screaming & pointing at me!

"There go that bad ass lil' nigga right there! He's the one! He's the one that robbed my grandson!"

The police grabbed me before I had a chance to run. A flashback from a few weeks ago struck me - the episode where Lil Live, Criptonite, and I had relieved some unfortunate fool of his plush minibike. As I sank into the cold metal bench, a familiar face joined me. My main man, Coke Dogg, an integral part of our brotherhood. Despite the oppressive strain clashing against the iron bars of our confinement, the camaraderie of a fellow Hoover Gangsta lightened the gravity of the situation.

My cousin was visibly upset. He fidgeted around in his dickie suit & scratched his Afro nervously.

"Man, these jive ass muthafuccas," he grumbled, his voice echoing around the cell, bouncing off the slabs of cement & iron.

Catching my knowing gaze, he exhaled deeply, *"These jive ass pigs tryna frame me for some shit I ain't do!"*

On the verge of turning thirteen, I had already been arrested around 20 times. His innocence in this game of street survival starkly contrasted with my seasoned nonchalance.

"I was just walkin' through the set minding my business when those pigs ran down on me," he confided, his eyes flickering with untamed frustration.

Coke Dogg became an innocent bystander in an unfolding drama. The one-time stormed him by surprise, forcing him into the spotlight of the investigation.

His world flipped upside down within seconds, as he was thrown into the back of a police cruiser. Accused of burglarizing the home of a retired pig that lived around the way. Coke Dogg, smacked right in the middle of a crime he didn't commit while I, racking up a list of bullet points on my criminal resume, unbeknownst to each of us, I was the author of his misfortune!

After they detained us for 24 hours in the frigid embrace of the precinct, the pigs released us into the custody of our parents, the urgency of our arrest dissolving into the ether of administrative red tape. Miraculously, the charges that had weighed heavily on Coke Dogg evaporated just as quickly as they had materialized.

In the whirlwind of events that followed my release, I discovered a shocking truth. My fellow Crip was arrested for my crime! The raw essence of life had once again wrapped its firm grasp around our existence, serving a sinister round of poetic injustice.

As I navigated the following days, I couldn't help but look over my shoulder. The streets never forgot, and neither did the law. I was a predator camouflaged among the prey, waiting for the day the hunter would recognize my true nature.

Every now & then, the homie, Bobee threw parties at the arcade on 55th & Vermont. It was no different this weekend, the weekend of my thirteenth birthday. I'm freshly dressed, as I sauntered towards the pulsating sounds of Rick James *"You & I"* that echoed down the block. As I walked in, a sense of thrill washed over me. This was going to be a groovy night to remember, a night where possibilities were endless.

The scene was alive with kids draped in funky colors, hormones raging, bodies bumping & grinding with hypnotic rhythm. However, as my eyes scanned around the lively crowd, a striking anomaly caught my attention. I was appalled & filled with anger simultaneously. I found myself drowning in a red sea, a color I despised.

My heart starts racing. My head is throbbing. PCP fueling my rage. The sight was instantaneously unsettling. It appalled me & filled me with anger simultaneously. The Sherm distorted my senses &

manipulated my feelings to a state of heightened aggression. This was the defining moment where I chose the path of going Crip crazy!

Brims! Brims! Everywhere!

The sight of my enemies reducing my sanity into ashes. I morphed into a ticking time bomb! I didn't even think to warn the homies, I was absorbed in a surge of madness that resonated through me. It led me to retrieve my .45, and with a complete disregard of life, I unleashed a shower of lead at the party. Turning my C-day bash into a chaotic shooting range, abruptly ending the once-joyous celebration.

The party was done, but I wasn't. Fueled by wrath & distorted judgment, I staked outside the arcade with my loyal homies, waiting to ambush the trespassers as they exited. Unbeknownst to our collective knowledge, simmered an old debt, a hushed secret preserved by Coke Dogg.

Coke Dogg was carrying the burden of a pass he received a few years ago. Coke Dog owed the Brims a favor. He had connections with the Brims hailing back to the innocent days at Budlong Elementary. Realizing the impending doom, he pulled aside Pig, a childhood friend & significant figure from the Brims. He warned him of our ambush, he guided them to safety, advising them to escape through the alley, avoiding my wrath.

During the infancy of Fifty Crip, Coke Dogg was sent on a mission by his mother. Unaware of his membership in the Crips, she told him to go to a house party on 60th street in Brim territory. The assignment, to find his cousin & bring her home.

Coke Dogg's Crippin' was still wet behind the ears, he was unaware of the intricacies of gang culture. A lovely pretty young thang boasting an enchanting smile & seductive hips swaying to the beat, became his unexpected temptation within the danger zone.

Amid getting his groove on, the DJ. began to chant rhythmically *"Aye! We gotta Crab in the party! Aye! We gotta Crab in the party!"*

Being new to Crip, Coke Dogg didn't know this was a derogatory term for Crips. He had no idea that he was the crab in the party! His awakening came through an unlikely savior, Pug from Brims.

Pug approached Coke Dogg, *"Aye Ravele, they talkin' bout you, nigga, you the crab in the party, my homies went to get the gun, you gotta get outta here!"*

Recognizing the danger he was in, Coke Dogg matured into the gravity of his situation. Disturbingly informed about his impending fate, Pug fed him the crucial survival tips. Grasping onto the lifeline thrown at him, Pug directed him towards salvation.

"Go out the back door, and meet me by my car, and I'll give you a ride home," Pug offers.

He was a Crip after all, brave, and in-due-course cunning. His gut told him, Pug could be looking out to make him put his guard down to meet a detrimental fate. With the stark danger looming over his head, Coke Dogg chose his own route to safety.

Looking back, the party that was supposed to be a celebration of my life had spiraled into a display of brash decisions & untamed fury. As an unwitting participant & orchestrator in this chain of events, the memory reverberates with lessons learned in the throes of raw experiences, forever reminding me of the irrational frenzy that marred my 13th birthday.

However, it was this day that I learned about friendships that transcend petty rivalries, the subtle acts of courage that lurk within the turbulent realm of gangbangin'. Coke Dogg's intervention that day not only saved numerous lives but also served as a reminder that humanity & friendship could shine through the darkest hours.

That fateful day remains etched into my memory, a stark reminder of how quickly joy can turn into disaster, and how disaster can give birth to unexpected acts of courage & solidarity. I was all in, in too deep. I was playing Russian roulette with a loaded gun cause I felt like I had no choice. I was on a suicide mission, I loved Crippin' more than I loved myself.

Writing this book, I'm reminded of the person I used to be & I can't help but wonder what the hell was wrong with me! I can't believe I shot up my own birthday bash, an event that had all my loved ones in attendance. What was I thinking? What was going on in my mind? I guess I didn't have a care in the world, I was focused on two thing: gangbanging, and pussy, showing out for the girls. I just thank the lord I never hurt anybody I loved & I'm here to tell my tale.

A couple weeks later, there was a house party on 57th Street, and the brims crashed again, but this time they were not so lucky. Despite Coke Dogg's previous warning, they decided to trespass in Five-Deuce territory, again. As they jump in an old riviera with a slant back, one of the Broadways lets shots fly, shooting one of them in the back before he could get in the car leaving him paralyzed. Brims never came back to party in the Fifties again.

Back in Fall '77 Ten Speed went away to college to play basketball. Speed would bring me to hang out with him on campus while he was attending San Diego State. On one of his visits back home he approached me with some money making ideas.

It all started with a simple conversation under the 110 freeway overpass. I'm catching up with Ten Speed, he is telling me about college life & orgies with white girls . His stories were so good he had me considering staying in school so I could be a college boy too. You already know he is my 'A-1, Day 1', we had always been involved in petty crimes like kicking' brim ass, shoplifting, vandalism, smoking & selling pot, but today, Speed mentioned a different type of crime, my type of crime – burglary.

"There are a lot of rich muthafuccas around my school, we can make a lot of money out there," Speed continues. Not only was Speed as big as Dwight Howard, and tough as George Foreman, he was incredibly intelligent, and a mastermind when it came to crime.

I'm all ears & he is saying all the things I like to hear like sweet music to my ears. He had this entire plan mapped out in his head, and he had already scouted a few houses & businesses near his college campus. He explained, he needed me to execute the plan with him because of my small size – I could easily fit through a small window or crawl space, which was usually not possible for someone his size, and so, we became crimeys.

The first few burglaries were low-risk ones – we targeted small businesses that we knew didn't have security cameras or alarm systems. Our plan was always simple – Break in, steal what we could, and break out as quickly as possible, and it worked. We managed to hit a few local stores & make a few hundred dollars. It wasn't much, but it was enough to keep us going.

I was feeling confident in our partnership, and I decided we need to take it up a notch. I knew I couldn't stop now; I was fiending for another big hit.

I was tired of these small licks, so I told Ten Speed, *"I need you to come up with something big, cuH, these lil jobs ain't cuttin' it!"*

"Aight, blue, I got some shit I been plotting, if you think ready cuH," He replied. *"It's a mansion job, a player from the San Diego Chargers."*

At first, I was hesitant. It was risky, and I wasn't sure if we could pull it off. Speed was adamant, and he convinced me with his plan I was ready to aim higher. We set our sights on a mansion that he had been keeping an eye on for weeks. It was owned by a wealthy pro football player who traveled a lot & was known to have a lot of valuable items in his crib.

We waited until the baller was out of town, and then we made our move. It was a nerve-wracking experience – the house was huge, and we had to avoid setting off the security system; but with Speed's expertise, we made it through without any issues. The stash we found in the house was worth over $5,000. It was a massive amount of money for us, and we both knew we had to celebrate. Our heists continued for a few more weeks, and we managed to accumulate little over $7,500 from our crime spree. Things started to get hot, the pigs started to catch on to our activities.

The local & university authorities had started to investigate the chain of burglaries in the area. One night, Ten Speed came to me with a serious look on his face. He had received a tip from one of his white girls that we were being watched, and he knew we had to stop our activities before we got caught. We decided to call it quits & split the money we had made. We would return to South Central & in the weeks to come he would go play pro ball in Europe until 1981.

I had fun hanging out with Speed, I was able to get a taste of college life, fast cars & white girls. It was a thrilling time to be alive, we pulled off some impressive heists. I will always remember those days fondly, but I am also grateful to have a true friend & partner in crime like Ten Speed in my life through thick or thin, sink or swim, lose or win!

This was a time of profound discovery for me. However, not all these discoveries were pleasant, some revealed harsh truths about loyalty, friendship, and the rough life on the streets. Now, being an older & arguably wiser man, I feel compelled to recount my journey of self-discovery to understand how the experiences of my adolescence shaped the man I would eventually become.

Life was changing, less innocent, and more enlightening. It was the summer I shared crucial experiences with two conflicting personalities-- Lil Live & Criptonite that later shaped my life significantly. Lil Live, so nicknamed due to his vibrant energy & enthusiasm, and Criptonite, who looked older than his age, His eyes held layers upon layers of stories that were far too complicated for his years. His appearance was more severe & serious.

There was an intoxicating sense of invincibility that accompanied our misadventures, echoing in our laughter & the adrenaline-rushing thrill of being a bad boy. Chasing our desires for material things & our reckless ideas of fun & adventure, we strolled into a journey that taught us life's brutal truths. We were merely kids with too much time on our hands & too many dreams in our hearts.

One of those dreams involved a mini motorbike that was the prized possession of a more fortunate kid in our neighborhood. Our audacity driven by pure adrenaline & youthful stupidity, we rat packed the kid & claimed his prized possession as our trophy. A pompous display of power & callous indifference. Our apprehensive conquest led us straight into the jaws of juvenile court.

I remember the day the long lanky shadow of Criptonite fell on the grimy courtroom floor. That sight is etched in my mind like it was branded by hell fire. He strolled into the courtroom, clad in a disgraceful, tattered moth-eaten trench coat that resembled a set of old, raggedy drapes.

The sight of his mother was even more striking. His mother, who accompanied him, was the epitome of tough love – she was a towering figure, an imposing black woman like the famous comedian Leslie Jones. I ain't lying, she favored her so much they might be related.

There she was with her fierce looking stern face, framed by short, wiry hair. A face that seemed chiseled out of molten rock. She oozed a certain kind of toughness that put Criptonite's bravado to shame. Her frightening aura made her appear more intimidating than her son ever could.

As I recall this scene, regret & bitterness still linger in my heart. What happened next was more peculiar. When it was time, Criptonite got on the stand pointed in my direction, irises burning with betrayal & defiance.

His voice echoed off the courtroom walls, *"Boo Diggs Did it!"*

A ripple of hushed giggles & gasps followed his statement. Criptonite calling me *'Boo'* in court was amusing, almost to the point of laughter, that he didn't even know my real name was Marcus. He introduced me as *"Boo"*, an alias my mother gave me, often used in our circle, his testimony serving as a curse for us.

Due to Criptonite's brilliant idea of being a rat bastard. Lil Live got himself a month in juvenile hall, while I got a little less time plus probation. The double-cross was a significant eye-opener to our young brotherhood.

The peculiar thing about the entire experience was not the turn of events but the sense of shock that penetrated our ranks. Snitching—or turning into a traitor—was a rarity then, nearly unheard of. Loyalty was the binding thread of any relationship. A man was judged by his word, and in Criptonite's case, his word led to his dishonorable discharge. Crips were not the kind to accept such betrayals lightly. His mother knew the consequences of his act were severe.

His family vanished into thin air relocating to North Cali before he could pay for his offense. Years faded into decades, and I never heard from him again, until fate played another surprise game.

He caught wind of my book & had the audacity to contact mutual friends. As if the passage of 4 decades could make me forget his deceit.

A betrayal so profound it left an indelible mark on my psyche, a lesson in trust for me, forging my future path. It was no longer a time for child's play; life had become a survival game.

Nevertheless, the circumstances we found ourselves in functioned as a catalyst that forged a bond between Lil Live & I that goes beyond normal friendship. We were Hriginals that became crimeys, partners in crime, and stompdown homies for life - a relationship borne out of shared trials & tribulations.

By the time the leaves started changing hues, signaling the approach of autumn, I'd learned a lot about life. In a society where trust was as valuable as gold, becoming a snitch was unthinkable, an act of treason. Criptonite's turncoat act was my first encounter with such treachery- an unforgettable life lesson.

It taught me to be wise while choosing friends & always remember the fake ones. It taught me the fragile & volatile nature of trust, especially in an environment riddled with easy temptation & dire consequences.

Breaking trust was equivalent to shattering a mirror - the pieces could never fit together the same way again. For life's heavy blows have a strange way of unmasking pretenders & rewarding the faithful.

I learned that difficult lesson in the scorching summer of 1978, a summer that remains as unforgettable as the bullshit nigga, Criptonite & my homie for life, my main man Morgan, better known as the infamous Lil Live from Five-Deuce Hoover Gangsta Crip.

CHAPTER NINETEEN:
"TOUGH HOOVER LOVE"

The formation for Hoover-Broadway didn't end our challenges. We were still trying to establish ourselves, and we found that Crippin' ain't easy. We had more hostility in the Crip world. A faction we admired became one of our biggest rivals, our namesake, the Hoover Crips, didn't appreciate us newcomers remixing the name & creating a different variation of the Hoover identity.

The Hriginal Hoover tribes were born from the Bonsollo Crips that became Seven-Foe, Eight-Trey or Nine-Deuce. Our Hoover tribe had different roots. We were rooted in Fifty politics- the Gladiators, the original Five-Deuces & of course the Fifty Crips. These origins set us apart from the other Hoover tribes. We bore the Gangsta in our name, breaking the uniformity that the other Hoover tribes so highly valued. We wanted to be unique & forge our own path.

Our relationship with the Seven Foes & the One-oh-Sevens was already established when we decided to claim Hoover. The Seven-Foes were the most influential & powerful tribe. We had been representing the groove for a few months & felt it was time we met with the Hriginal Hoover tribe.

We took the bus up to 73rd street about 13 deep; Joker, T-Dogg, Big Fat Rat, Baby Crazy, ScHool Boy, Jaystone, Ric Roc, Lil Live, Bow Dee, Insane Fish, Bandit, Cyko Mike, and Willbone had the revolver just in case. We were also joined by Q-Bone, Crazy Poke,

Choo & Big T from Five-Deuce Broadway. It was silence amongst the homies on the ride, not even Joker was cracking jokes. I looked at my Locs, stone cold, militant, young niggas from FDHGC.

When we got to the block, we saw tens of homies starting to congregate, so we joined the festivities. Homies from Trey-Foe (Seven Foe & Eight Trey) were chilling, Frog was smoking & drinking brews with Hoover Lon, Tim-Tim & some more homies. Bubbles & Crow were with Mad Dogg who was showing off his Crip Walkin' skills.

I remember he told us he was going to create a dance just for the Hoovers. Mad Dogg did just that, few years later he would come up with the Hoover Stomp with Big Smiley from One-oh-Seven Hoover, a combination of a two-step, skips & dips with a cold swaggering stomp that shook the earth, that represented being a stompdown Loc, Hoover stomping on our enemies like the roaches they are.

Big Huron kicked off the function, we started with the roll call & all the Hoovers in attendance introduced themselves & represented their set.

"I'm Boo Diggs from Five-Deuce Hoover!" I proclaimed, chest out & chin up. My introduction caused whispers amongst the HC's.

Huron replies, "Five-Deuce Hoover Crip! I like that shit!"

Joker jumps in, *"Na cuH, its Five-Deuce Hoover Gangsta Crip."*

"Fuck that Gangsta Shit" shouts one of the homies in the crowd.

Big Scooby responds, *"Shut the Fuck up, respect all Hoovers!"*

We completed our introductions.

I stepped up, *"Whether Hoover Gangsta Crip or Hoover Crip, what matters is that we from Hoover first! Nothing is Bigger than the H!"* I proclaimed to my comrades.

All the Hoovers shook their heads in agreement.

"I agree, cuH, ain't nothing bigger than Hoover but I ain't gonna say I like this HGC shit either. This Hoover Crip. Ain't no Gangstas on Hoover," Big Huron replies.

"We may stand alone on Hoover as HGC, but that's what we pushin' til the wheels fall off, cuH" I reply.

Huron looks at us up & down, sizing us up & says, *"It's like this either you Hoover or Gangstas!"*

"We ain't no Gangsta Crips", I continued.

"We Hoover Gangstas- that is just what it is & what it's gonna ce in the Fifties, we ain't changing shit, cuH," I replied proudly.

Huron responds, *"I give it to y'all lil niggas, I see y'all not scared to stand up for ya selves & what y'all believe in & I dig that, cuH."*

Now that the business was completed, we proceeded to pass around joints, Sherm sticks & 8 balls. Willbone was fiddling around with his revolver, *"pow"* it accidentally goes off & barely misses Cyko Mike! The bullet goes right through his hat! Damn near blew his muthafucking head off!

We didn't have issues with Foe-Trays or Nine-Deuces, we never had a relationship with Nine-O. Tray-Foe-Seven accepted us as Hoovers but resented the *"Gangsta"* in our name; they would say Hoovers ended at Slauson. An invisible boundary ran like a fault line between Hoover Gangsta Crip & Hoover Crips..

On the westside from Slauson to King were our streets, we were the veins pumping the blue blood of a city that had seen more than its fair share of bedlam & triumphs. Among my brethren, I was revered as the personification of dedication & unswerving commitment, serving as the outstanding depiction of our creed, like how Jerry West continues to epitomize the NBA with his staunch figure. I was the living logo of the set.

The Hoover Crips dared to challenge us, mistaking our youth for feebleness, our numbers for weakness, but like the sands of the hourglass, our membership & strength only increased. We had to *'be down for the crown'*, willing to fight, shoot & bleed for Hoover, for respect & to build a reputation for our set. A mantra & principle our brotherhood fiercely adopted.

The evening following our meeting with the Seven-Foes we were hanging out at the Hoover Store on the Foe. Standing on the sidewalk with my comrades - Joker, Baby Crazy, and ScHool Boy, we were just kids none older than 13. Suddenly, the quiet we had been soaking in was rudely disrupted by a clatter of footsteps, the eeriness of a looming presence, and the whispers of danger in the wind.

An imposing figure appeared from the shadows; the big Homie oG Joe Ransom & his brothers oG Hoover Sam & Big Devil, flanked with a formidable force of muscle-bound henchmen from One-oh-Seven. These were colossal Crips, each carrying 22-inch pythons, reminiscent of Hulk Hogan in his prime. They were offended by the *"Gangsta"* in our name, disagreeing with our identity in Hoover's ghetto copyright. Their aggression intended to instill fear & coerce submission to fall in line as Hoover Crips.

I remember feeling inexplicably small beneath the gaze of these towering giants that seemed more like titans than men in my adolescent eyes. The Ransoms were very enraged with passion about us not claiming Hoover the way they introduced it to us. To them, we were but small, feeble obstacles that could easily be overcome. Regardless, they were the walls we knew we needed to climb over to prove our worth.

We stood our ground, as Hoover Gangstas, we knew we were no match for their sheer size & brute strength. However, we had the heart of a lion pride, so we refused to retreat. We weathered the storm & took the beatdown like men. We understood that, to achieve our desire to be recognized as Hoovers, we had to withstand any trial put forth - even if it meant enduring a brutal beatdown from these seasoned Kiwé warriors.

It was a rite of passage we chose to embrace rather than escape, a harsh welcome into a life permeated by our dream to be

Hoovers. Keeping our resolve intact, emerging battered & bruised after the confrontation, we rounded up Ten Speed, Spookee & the older Hoover Gangstas. The face of our fate was in the rearview mirror as we piled into the cars & drove down Hoover Street towards the One-oh-Seven Hoover territory. A raw pursuit of proving ourselves sparked a flame in our hearts. We had shown heart by standing our ground when faced with the daunting prospect of a battle we were destined to lose.

We had shown courage, a kind of valor that runs deeper than simply fighting against the odds. It was our tale of victory, woven into the fabric of our Hoover Gangsta legacy. Portraying a picture of unwavering courage, we embarked on a mission to earn our stripes under the watchful eyes of our Hoover counterparts. Engines roared, echoing the rampant sense of anticipation taking root within us.

To outsiders, we might've been seen as little kids trying to fit into Chuck Taylors that were too big for our feet, but we knew better. We had oG members they had no knowledge of, they would even the playing field. We believed in the mettle we possessed, the resilience we exhibited, and the pride we established in the Fifties.

Little did we know this skirmish wasn't going to be a one & done, it would become a daily occurrence for us, a challenge that we willingly undertook. These trials would be our painstakingly demanding rites of passage on our path to earning our stripes, our badge of honor as Hoovers.

As we arrived at 106th street, controversy & danger swirled around us like Sherman smoke. A shouting match was brewing, a storm crackling with electricity & unveiled threats.

Devil, with his gritted teeth & balled up fists quaked with rage as he bellowed at Dre Dogg, *"Fuck that HGC shit! That ain't Hoover, cuH!"*

His voice, a grating & gravelly boom, bounced off the abandoned buildings, painting a verbal sketch of deep-seated disapproval.

Dre Dogg fired back, his voice, deep with bass resonating across the small gathering, *"Na nigga, this Five-Deuce Hoover Gangsta Crip, we ain't changing shit!"*

It was a defiant declaration of loyalty, a verbal stake firmly planted into the earth. There was a lot of machismo in the air. Invisible sparks of ego & aggression were ricocheting around the crowd. Eyes were lit with anticipation of a showdown - of an explosive clash between these two young warriors.

The pulse of animosity between them set the scene for an epic duel, the kind of spectacle that would sear itself into the minds of all those who had the privilege of witnessing this family feud firsthand. Despite being cousins, Dre Dogg & Devil's face-off served as a reminder that affiliation isn't always determined by blood but by the creed one stands for. A few stray voices of dissent surfaced amidst the sea of tension that surged around them.

Towering over others in the dim streetlight, the Giant of 52nd street, Ten Speed, swaggered into the center, and exhibited his demands for respect & retribution. His resolve was titanium- we were not leaving without administering some justice, regardless of the One-oh-Seven's numbers or brawn. He challenged all contenders who had a problem with Five-Deuce Hoover Gangsta Crip, his voice resonated with an intimidating ferocity as he called out the One-oh-Seven's that pummeled us.

Stepping up to this call to action, Big Joe Ransom nominated a promising brawler from his ranks. Ten Speed seemed unconcerned & justifiably so. His fists moved like twin lightning bolts, striking & darting, and before we knew it, the One-oh-Seven was sprawled on the dusty ground.

Enraged, Big Joe called upon another One-oh-Seven to face Ten Speed. Once again, his strength & gritty determination shone through, and he once more reignited the spirits of our faction. The collective gasp from the spectators, the atmosphere morphing into a chilling mix of dread & exhilaration. Ten Speed had claimed his victory, but this was far from the end. His valiant efforts stood proof of our resilience & echoed the beginnings of a long-drawn era of confrontations.

Despite being outnumbered, we stood firm, our convictions unshakeable. We refused to bend to the intimidation, our resolution tested as we all ran fades, some of us won, some of lost but all that mattered was that you fought! The Hoover Crips became one of our main rivals.

They repeatedly raided the Fifties, testing our loyalty, challenging our dedication & molding us into the notorious FDHGC. Their brazen trespasses were a rite of passage. Our initiation into the Hoovers was not a joyride, but a brutal test of our heart, pushing our mental & physical strength.

Hoover Crip, a name synonymous with danger, audacity, and kinship, their ceaseless affronts to our claims challenged our resilience, our allegiance to the ideals we had built our set on, the very essence of our existence as Hoover Gangstas.

I confronted these challenges head-on, immersing myself in every brawl, standing my ground as the front line of defense against their relentless onslaughts. My home, a modest dwelling on West 52nd place overlooking Hoover Street, served as our bastion, a fortress against all intruders. Each stride bore the weight of responsibility - a hardened resolve to uphold Five-Deuce Hoover at the jeopardy of all risk. I was but a kid, embossing my name on an infamous legacy that would echo through the back alleys, and sacred ground of our turf.

Please don't get it misunderstood, what constituted our strength was not the bravado of one man. It was the unity & fraternity we carried within our ranks - thicker than blood, stronger than steel. No matter the grit & grind needed, it had to be unreserved loyalty for FDHGC, and the foundation we were building. Showcasing any sign of weakness or surrender was a cardinal sin, and displaying staunch bravery was the only way to earn your keep. This was the true essence of Hoover loyalty.

Half of the Hoover car refused to accept us; they would continue to test us. They say pride comes before the fall, but for our tribe, pride was the foundation- the cornerstone on which we were built. We are FD, fearless & determined Five-Deuces. We swore on God & HGC, they were going to learn to respect us.

Each battle, each beat-down, each victory, shaped us, changed us, forced us to adapt, and prepared us for what lay ahead in our lives as Hoover Gangstas. One thing was clear, to be a part of the Hoover car we had to prove our worth every single day! We went through hell & high water to establish the set. We didn't get put on once, we got put on anytime a big homie or peer came around & wanted to challenge us, we endured these rites of passage molding us into hardened Hoover warriors, immune to fear, fortified by shared sacrifices.

"Non-cooperation is a measure of discipline & sacrifice, and it demands respect for the opposite views." - Mohandas Gandhi

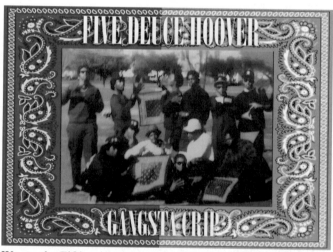

We are the Fifties, it's 5-two, we do it big, whatever we do! Whether it was crazy ass house parties that shook the city, or brutal murders that stole its sleep, we did the damn thing! Through fires of adversity, we emerged not as mere carbon but as a diamond, hardened, bright, and precious. We weathered the storm of disrespect & skepticism to stand tall & steadfast.

FDHGC reminds the world that dominance is not merely assigned but must be earned, respect is not given but taken. Our legacy is a testament to how harmony, collaboration, and a strong will can shape a group's destiny amidst adversity. Only through unity can the full potential of a collective be attained, shaping its members into an entity that outshines the brightest star. We stood tall for the *"H"* & earned our *"G"* & left homies with no other choice but to respect Hoover Gangsta.

All the Hriginals were hitters, a vital part in the machine. A group's strength can be gauged by its weakest link, but our crew had no weak links; we were a chain of unyielding steel. Five-Deuce became a respected name within the Hoovers & the Crip car. Our reputation rose from a collective determination to prove our worth.

Mad Hoover love to our predecessors who forged the Hriginal path. It was their tough love which infused us with a spirit of resilience & fueled the spark of our groove. Their tough Hoover love, stern yet nurturing, made us stronger as a collective.

Fortunately, our Hoover conflict never escalated beyond the point of no return, it was merely rites of passage, but on January 4, 1979, the One-oh-Sevens went to test the Nine-O, similar to what they did with us, Nine-O was a fairly new set formed around 1977. After one of our traditional squabbles ended with one of the Nine-O's relatives, a Venice Sho 'line Crip firing into the brawl resulting in the death of Big Onnie. Onnie was only 16 years old, but he was no ordinary member, he was the founder of One-oh-Seven Hoover's baby brother, oG Moo-Moo, so this was a serious offense.

MOO MOO & BEN NOSE

Things went sour with Nine-O after Onnie's death, the incident created a deep rift amongst the Hoovers. It was a senseless slaying that became the root of six chaotic years of infighting. A Hoover Civil War that evolved into Hoover versus Rollin' Nineties & the origin of the Crip Civil War that pitted Hoovers & Gangstas versus Neighborhood & Rollin' Owes, a conflict that has endured 4 decades & seems never-ending.

During these six turbulent years, the turf wars & petty rivalries spiraled into violence & betrayal. Blood was shed, and lives were lost as Nine-O fought courageously to maintain their Hoover identity. For the founders of Nine-O, Too Sweet & Fonn, their unwavering commitment to their tribe required an acknowledgment of the real world consequences of this constant antagonism. By 1985, the two men who had been instrumental in the formation of Nine-O would both fall victim to the violence. We must commend these men for they fought & died bravely in battle as Hoovers, H.I.P Big Fonn & Big Too Sweet. Their deaths would signal the end of the Nine-O Hoover era.

Subsequently the Nine-O Hoovers finally succumbed to the realization that things had escalated past the point of no return. Everything Nine-O (Hoover & Gangsta) were alienated, there was no love for them within the Hoover car or from our allies. They changed their name & abandoned the Hoover moniker. The Nine-O's clicked up with East Coast, and Nine-O Gangstas, becoming Nine-O West Coast Crip, and eventually Rollin 90's relocating to the area around Sportsman Park (now known as Jesse Owens Park). Their original turf was from 88th to 92nd street by Manchester Park. In the mid-1990s, *"Big Headcase"*, a reputable Hoover Gangsta, would breathe new life into the defunct Nine-O Hoover territory & re-established the area as Bacwest FDHGC.

Few people know the true history of Bacwest Five-Deuce Hoover. The year was 1996, and the community was caught in the crossfire of two factions of the Crips who were supposed to be allies but had turned on each other. The trouble began when the Nine-Five Playboy Styles & the Nine-Deuce Hoovers found themselves tangled in a storm of rage & jealousy.

At the epicenter of the conflict was similar to all Crip fall outs, over some dick & pussy. A respected member of Nine-Deuce Hoover had found himself in an entanglement with a Playboys' girlfriend. The betrayal & dishonor that followed couldn't be ignored, and tensions between the two factions quickly escalated. The lovers' tryst ignited a spark that became an all-out gang war.

Fueled by ego & foolish pride a series of skirmishes carved a bloody path through the city. The Playboys' treachery knew no bounds, as they adopted a calculated, deceptive strategy: they continued to show love to Hoovers they knew while ruthlessly targeting those they didn't.

The war had officially begun, and there seemed to be no end in sight. The first casualty of the war was Chilly from Nine-Deuce, who fell victim to a senseless act of violence perpetrated by the feud. The Nine-Five Playboys' devious tactics extended to marking their vengeance by tagging disses & slurs on trees & walls throughout Nine-Deuce Hoover turf; the vandals violated & defamed the set with H/K, (Hoover Killer) graffiti outside the home of Big Headcase & he would not tolerate the disrespect. An offense that may seem trivial to some can result in serious consequences including death in the gang bang capital.

"Verzz, No Slurz." -unknown

In the infancy of the chaos, Big Headcase recognized the potential for devastating consequences & attempted to mediate peace between the former allies. Unfortunately, despite his valiant efforts, his attempts at diplomacy were met with violent resistance. Playboys claimed to have no problems with Five-Deuces or any other Hoover tribe, but Hoover is Hoover, and we stand united.

The situation only grew worse as the 6-Eight & 9-Tray Playboy Hustlers joined forces with the Nine-Fives to continue their brutal offensive against the Nine-Deuces. The bloodshed was far from over, and more lives were to be lost to this gruesome gang war. As the onslaught continued, the Nine-Deuces had regrouped & planned for retaliation.

"The ultimate measure of a man is not where he stands in moments of comfort & convenience, but where he stands at times of challenge & controversy."
-Martin Luther King Jr.

During this tense period, Big Headcase emerged as a pivotal figure in the conflict. As the discord between the two Crip factions grew, Big Headcase was inspired by the Eight-Tray Gangstas who had successfully expanded their territory over the years with four sides: Bacwest, far west, South, and North. Emboldened by ambition & passion, Big Headcase sought to claim the territory formerly belonging to Nine-O Hoover. This area was now dedicated to Bacwest Five-Deuce Hoover & would become shared territory with the Deuce-Foes.

Bacwest pledged their support to the Nine-Deuces to defend their territory & joined forces with them to secure the boundaries that the Playboy Hustlers sought to disrupt. Big Headcase positioned himself as an example of selflessness & loyalty within the Grooveline. His actions not only served to defend the Nine-Deuces territory but ultimately strengthened the Hoovers as a whole. The Hoovers prepared themselves for the ultimate retaliation against the betrayers.

As the battle raged on, the Playboy Hustlers suffered devastating losses of key generals. As the days turned into weeks, the intensity of the conflict began to wane. The Playboy Hustlers, faced with the realization that they were overpowered by their adversaries, ultimately submitted to Hoover supremacy.

CHAPTER TWENTY:
"NOTORIETY- A RISING GANGSTAR"

I was on my journey for notoriety, seeking a certain kind of fame, but not the kind that would get me a Hollywood Star, but that of a rising Gangstar. Right from the start, I dove headfirst into the role of the macho gangsta, a persona ripped straight from Hoover Street. At school, I was the center of attention- acting a fool, showing off, and taking every opportunity to make sure everyone knew I was repping my colors with pride.

Everyday excitement & adrenaline surged through my veins when I walked through the doors of John Muir Junior High. Decked out in my blue rag & overflowing with eagerness to represent FDHGC, I had my mind set on making a name for myself. A name that would soon transform into something unforgettable. I wasted no time proving my allegiance to the gang, putting hands & feet on any Brim that dared step to me.

Back in the day it was all about machismo, about pride & dominance, and asserting our budding manhood. Today is a day stitched into the fabric of my memory, its drama woven with the violence & hard realities of life in South Central. One day during lunch we got into a war of words with the Brims, heated insults volleyed back & forth, and by the ring of the lunch bell, we decided the only way to settle things was to have an old-fashioned throwdown to assert our dominance.

We chose our battleground carefully: the wide expanse of the Sears parking lot behind our school on Slauson & Vermont, the DMZ of our world. It straddled the neutral boundary, separating our respective territories, Hoover to the north & Brim to the south. It was a no-man's land of sorts, charged with an eerie uncertainty that mirrored the mounting suspense within each of us. We spilled into the parking lot after school, our hearts echoing the beat of anticipation.

The Brims arrived, twenty strong, exuding an animalistic determination. We stood our ground – yours truly, ScHool Boy, Coke Dog, CoCo, Lil Live, Crazy DeDe, Dre Dogg, Bow Dee, Ric Roc, Jamaican Mike, Big Fat Rat, Joker, T-Dogg, Willbone, and Slic Ric-- standing unflinching in the face of potential pandemonium. The rumble was on. Twenty of them, about fifteen of us. The odds were against us, but the universe had never been particularly fond of mathematics. Outnumbered, but not outgunned.

The air was ripe with tension when we arrived, each side armed with improvised weapons - chains rattling ominously, brass knuckles glinting under the anemic sunlight, sticks transformed into nigga beaters. The parking lot transformed into a gladiator ring as both sides wielded their street-approved weapons. There were no guns, just the raw, primal display of strength & brawn. Positioning ourselves in strategic alignments, the dusty, war-torn Sears parking lot further strengthened our resolve as we charged towards the adversaries.

There was a ballet of violence, with every move choreographed spontaneously in the throes of adrenaline. I was the first to land a heavy blow, knotting a Brim's eyebrow with a savage right hook. Two of our hardest hitters, Coke Dog & Bow Dee, joined the onslaught, their fists delivering a symphony of suffering. Steel met flesh with visceral crunches & sharp cries filled the first moments of the brawl.

Coke Dog was a beast, his muscular frame moving with the predatory grace of a well-oiled devastation machine. His punches landed like sledgehammers, turning adversaries into ragdolls. Bow Dee, on the other hand, was the silent assassin - nimble & stealthy, his attacks as swift as they were merciless. He moved through the battlefield like a panther, silent but deadly, unloading punches that sent enemies sprawling.

CoCo & Big Fat Rat, two more powerhouses of the Hoovers, reigned terror among the opponents. Coco's fists swung with such raw power that they seemed to split the air before connecting with solid thuds. They were blended hurricanes of raw power & lethal precision, an intimidating sight, even for us, their fellow grooves. Fat Rat managed a grin despite the chaos surrounding him. Their chain-wrapped fists swirled, struck, and danced with furious energy, humbling the bravest among our rivals.

On the other flank, Baby Crazy & Jaystone were calmly dissecting the opponent's structure. Baby Crazy, armed with his brass knuckles, was the embodiment of mechanical precision & raw power. His rhythmic movements, timed blows, and an uncanny understanding of street fights left many of the Brims gasping for breath & scrambling for escape. Jaystone, nimble as a mongoose & fierce as a wildcat, expertly employed his stick, deflecting assaults & landing unexpected blows, leaving a trail of groaning bodies.

RIC ROC

The Brims fought back viciously. At the crescendo of the cacophony of violence, Ric Roc weaved through the crowd, a phantom of fluid motion, chin checking Bloods left & right, with precision. Ric

Roc hands were lethal weapons, he would become the light heavyweight champ on the level 4 yard in 1987. Meanwhile Coco tackled another into a nearby concrete parking divider.

The Bloods prowled like panthers, their movements illusively graceful even amidst the maelstrom. They struck swiftly; fangs bared, claws scratching, tearing at the threads of our unity. The fight escalated to an unthinkable crescendo, characterized by fury & pride. The melee endured, a reckless whirlwind of raw emotion, shimmering with brutality. The courage of the warriors on both sides matched the other, speckled with moments of individual heroism & strategic maneuvering, reflecting the relentless waves of assault & defense. It was a spectacle born out of the primal instinct of survival, a tangled web of fury, fear, and fraternity.

The battle raged on. Coco was using his stature to his advantage, throwing heavy punches. ScHool Boy darted through the fray, landing hits where he could, dodging retaliation with impressive agility. This brutal melee carried on, no side giving in, combatting not only for street superiority but for respect & revenge.

Each side valiantly defended their turf, repaying blow for blow. Bruises bloomed, bones cracked, and blood stained the asphalt, silently seeping into the indifference of the concrete, forging irrevocable bonds of grudges & rivalries within.

Lil Live was agile & swift, body-checking Bloods twice his size while deftly avoiding swings. Slic Ric's brass knuckles left their mark on numerous adversaries. Every member of our crew fought valiantly, bravely withholding the onslaught from the opposition.

Amidst the thunderous clamor of the bloody warfare, a sharp, resounding gunshot echoed, reverberating within the dense air of the parking lot. An armed security guard had fired a warning shot. The abrupt, violent assault on our eardrums snapped us out of our frenzy. Instantly, the battleground was veiled in an eerie silence, only to be broken by the rustle of fleeing combatants.

Our hearts pounded in our chests, adrenaline fueling our flight from the looming threat of incarceration. The next day we were all dragged into the principal office, bruised & battered from our rumble, they interrogated us & threatened to call the pigs about the off-campus fiasco, but we all remained stitched lipped.

A few nights later the Brims came through & shot up Bow Dee block. The next day at school, we had a knockout contest, we were going through the hallway punching anybody that was blood, looked like a blood or was from the other side of the tracks & Bow Dee won the trophy he knocked out the most Bloods that day. I tell you man, he really hated Brims. Bow Dee was a problem, he knew the precise spot to hit someone to knock them out stone cold. In my opinion, the top 3 Hardest Hitters out of the Hriginals were oG Bow Dee, Coke Dogg & Big Fat Rat.

As the weeks went by, my infamy started to grow, just like the wildfire of disruption & chaos I unleashed around the school. A deep blue sea of homies surrounding me as I Crip-walked atop the lunch tables evoked my inner beast, feeling unstoppable. I was the baddest muthafucka alive, and anybody with the audacity to cross my path would quickly come to regret it. My hotdogging was interrupted by the most unlikely of adversaries: the bitch ass school principal. He approached me as I busted my groove atop the table with a stern look on his face.

"Get off the table, young man," he ordered. Little did he know that his request was no match for my bravado.

"Fuck you! This Hoover Gangsta Crip, cuH!" I retorted; defiance etched into every syllable.

It wasn't until this fool tried to put his hands on me & take my blue rag, I snapped. Blinded by anger & the desire to protect my identity, I instinctively defended myself & knocked him out in one swift move. My actions had earned me a reputation, one that I wore like a badge of honor. That single moment set the wheels of consequence into motion. Not only was I expelled from John Muir Jr High, but I was also arrested & later released to my mother.

In the aftermath of that chaotic day, my notoriety knew no boundaries. I transferred to Horace Mann Junior High—a school nestled deep in the heart of Rollin' Sixties territory. My insatiable hunger for recognition drove me to commit yet another outrageous act. This time, I set the trash can ablaze, causing chaos & earning me another expulsion.

Despite the whirlwind of disruptions & the turmoil it caused, my need for validation remained unquenched. I left a trail of destruction following everywhere I went. I was soon enrolled in my least favorite school, I hated it at Audubon Jr High on 11th Ave, dominated by a blood gang called the Black P Stones. One of the few Crips in the school, I was locked in their crosshairs. I knew that they would come for me, and they did.

I fought valiantly against those that dared to challenge me, proving myself as a reputable Crip. The first one I whooped on fell like a domino, and I relished the victory, earning me instant notoriety & a target on my back. My adversaries were relentless. They made it clear I was never going to have a moment of peace. They started surrounding the school every day at dismissal, waiting for an opportunity to catch me slipping. My options were limited, but my resolve was unwavering.

Refusing to back down, I devised a strategy to face them head-on. I engaged in one-on-one battles against the Black P Stones during school hours. It was easier than I thought, after my second squabble, I was expelled yet again. I was proud to be labeled a troublemaker & a danger to those around me.

My next stop was Foshay, a school located in Harlem Crip turf, but that was cool because they were allies. We had H love between Hoover & Harlem. The best part about Foshay is that I was with my Locs, ScHool Boy, T-Dogg & Insane Fish. My everyday niggas, and it's always good to have Five-Deuces nearby.

We had each other's backs, and that was all that mattered in the world of gangbanging & best believe, we did a lot of gangbanging together. We knew what it meant as Hriginals on our road to being gangstars, and we planned to start & end our saga together. Shortly after I arrived, Fish was kicked out of school for whipping on a Brim.

I formed relationships with Harlems like Crazy Keith, Baby Brother, the Pervs, and Maxwell. We called our alliance Hoover-Harlem. I started dating a girl from their set. She was a beautiful, feisty girl who was as tough as nails & ScHool Boy hooked up with her sister.

We shared laughter, secrets, and late-night conversations that seemed to stretch for hours on end. We had some good times hanging out with them, enjoying each other's company & enjoying the freedom offered by our youth. Those were the days our only cares were hot sex, PCP & Crippin. Those happy days would not last. The cruel world we lived in took no prisoners, and when tragedy struck, it left no room for redemption.

One day, my girlfriend was found dead, a cold haunting reminder of the city's relentless wrath. The Harlem Crips blamed me for her death, claiming I was the last person to be seen with her! They didn't care for evidence or reasons; they only cared for revenge. The news spread like wildfire through the hallways of Foshay, and the school turned on me, literally.

The entire student body claimed Harlem Crip. There was a fight or two, battles I fought bravely, but eventually, the administration kicked me out of Foshay. The echoes of my lost love, the whispered judgments in the hallways, and the bitterness of betrayal gnawed at my soul, dooming me to my exile.

The Harlems that once greeted me with open arms now clenched their fists with contempt. It seemed my days of notoriety were waning away in the ruthless winds of the City of Angels. Once again, I found myself expelled & transferred to a new school. I can't make this shit up; I have lived a crazy life.

My next stop was Bethune, a school that would become my favorite. It had an indoor pool that drew me in like a smoker to a pipe, and I would enjoy the pristine water every chance I got. My Auntie lived right behind the school, so I hopped the gate daily to have lunch with her.

Bethune was a gangbangin' ass school, a Gangsta's paradise– Hoovers, Broadways, East Coast, Mad Swans, 20 Bloods, and so many others. I loved that shit! The tension in the air was electrifying to me, as if I had finally found my place in this world & I was reunited with my main man, Joker.

At Bethune, I formed a relationship with several reputables from the East Coast Crips, Bub, Doc Thone & Casper during weekend football games & mob downtown to the Movies at State Theater & hit licks. I also met a sweet girl named Sheila G, the older sister of my comrade, Crook from the Seven-Foes. Sheila became the object of affection. Lil Simms from Seven-Foe & I used to fight over her all the time, but Big Boo eventually won her over. I will always remember & cherish the puppy love we shared.

Notoriety became more intoxicating to me with each passing day & the pursuit of it kept my mind off the loss of my ex. As time went on, clashes between rivals intensified within the school. It seemed like everyone's reputation was on the line in this endless cycle of violence. Over time my relationship with the Harlems mended itself as they realized I had nothing to do with her passing.

One day, I found myself in a confrontation with Pistol Pete, a reputable of the Rollin' 20s Neighborhood Bloods. Facing him in a one-on-one duel, I didn't back down, proving to everyone that I was not to be trifled with. The brawl was as brutal as it could get. I was victorious but Pistol Pete earned my respect as a Damu warrior.

From the day I knocked out a principal to my expulsion from Audubon & Foshay, each new territory I conquered was a testament to my unyielding fight, resilience, and insatiable desire for notoriety. I had come a long way, but my journey was just beginning. My tenure at Bethune would be short lived, I would get kicked out for my specialty, truancy, even though I loved it at Bethune, I hated going to class. They kicked me out for too many absences & entering Fall 78, I was sent to Continuation School. Going to continuation became a rite of passage as you worked your way up the ranks of the Crips.

CHAPTER TWENTY-ONE:
"BOO VERSUS COCO:
TRIPPIN' OFF WATER"

It was due to a curious case of mistaken identity that I ended up sharing an intriguing bond with someone I would never have otherwise known. Three years had passed since Sniper erroneously assumed I was a Blood named Nana. One day in 1978, nestled between the gritty, grease-streaked parts of old cars, I was hanging with my partner Low-Ryda at his Chop Shop. Low-Ryda, known for his skill at slinging heroin & customizing luxury cars – specifically, those pristine Cadillacs that cruised around the way, sparking envy in the hearts of many.

We were tweaking & modifying lowriders, with the rhythmic beats of Parliament Funk lightly floating on the autumn breeze. That day, an unexpected encounter turned my world upside down - I met Nana for the first time.

I was startled by the uncanny resemblance between us that could easily fool a bystander, and to my surprise, it had already fooled many. In our faces' mirrored geometry there existed tales of confusion & crossed wires that had been composing themselves in our absence. As evidence mounted, I realized that Sniper's mistake was not entirely his fault - we really did look strikingly similar.

Deciding to approach the situation with an open mind, Nana & I found common ground - our love for Sherm. During our drug-induced conversation, we started sharing stories we heard of each other, laughing at the ludicrous rumors & speculations that cropped up in the streets, humanizing each other beyond our gang affiliations.

Then came the ultimate revelation that had both of us erupting in laughter. I confessed to Nana about a time I effortlessly slipped into his shoes, a mix-up created by chance & perfect irony. A girl I met at the 18 bus stop on Exposition & Budlong had approached me, mistaking me for Nana.

She looked a bit disappointed as she said, *"Nana, why don't you call me no more?"*

At that moment, I decided to play along, offering some smooth words, *"Girl, it's all love. I lost your number."*

Can you believe it? Her forgiving nature bestowed upon me an unexpected gift, she gave me some pussy that afternoon. The laughter that followed this amusing episode paved the path to our friendship. Our resemblance to each other added a new chapter to both of our lives that day, and we found solace in laughter, stories & the shared bond that transcended colors. We became the unlikeliest of friends, brothers from another color- as the proverb says, *"people who look alike, think alike."*

On the other hand, it was still BK (Blood Killa) all day when it came to the Brims. We were giving the Brims the blues & they started shooting instead of fighting, so we started getting our arms up with plans of bustin' on anybody that tried Five-Deuce Hoover. We started earning more street cred & respect from our Hoover counterparts.

A few days later, CoCo & I were getting ready for our ditch day, it's like 8am. The sweat & heat of the morning sun beat down on our defiant faces, devilry dancing in our bloodshot eyes. Little did we know this day would test the strengths of our unbreakable bond. We decided to hit the store & use our lunch money to get some beers, so we went half on $1.50 forty ounce.

This nigga start hogging the brew, I asked him to pass it, you know what he has the nerve to say, *"I'll pass it to you when I want too"* & took another swig.

I'm infuriated by this fool's selfishness, ok, I got your big ass. I started thinking of how I can teach him a lesson. I saw a nice 8-inch wrench. I decided to go grab it & bop this fool over the head with it, then I jumped on his back & put him in a dope fiend (sleeper-hold) until he went night, night, then I celebrated by enjoying the rest of the 8 ball. I won this round, but this was just the beginning of our crazy day.

Round 2, Later that evening around 4pm, we were hungry & needed some money, so we caught a lick together. We jumped on this Mexican, CoCo knocked him out his shoes & I ran through his pockets. CoCo didn't forget about me bopping him with the wrench & choking him out earlier. This super-sized Crip lusted for revenge – & it was about to get ugly.

Feeling an unjust sense of entitlement, CoCo is back on his bullshit, he tells me, *"I knocked him out so I'm keeping all of the money"*.

Our heated voices escalated to malice shouting, I'm mad as hell—we start squabbling again! Our fists flying. CoCo's lingering rage fueled a relentless beat down upon me until I submitted. Battered & bruised, I admitted defeat.

"Aw man! You got it, cuH!"

He whooped my ass this round, he fucked me up bad. He beat my ass so bad he felt sorry & let me get half the money.

Round 3, later that night, a house party was in full swing between Crazy DeDe & Fish crib. The pulsating music & flamboyant laughter echoed through the Foe. I'm chilling, smoking lovely with Spookee in front of Coke Dogg's crib. The block is full of action, everybody is outside enjoying the night. Over the pulsating rhythms of *"He's The Greatest Dancer"* by Sister Sledge, we overhear an enraged CoCo in a heated argument with some miscellaneous nigga. CoCo was known to be wolf-hearted & aggressive, but tonight he is going Crip crazy off that water.

In an environment teetering on the brink of chaos, we took the initiative, locked & loaded for whatever may come. Our trio headed over to have CoCo's back & see what was going on. Spookee with his 9-shot diamondback .22 caliber revolver & I with my reliable colt .45. We approach the brewing tension with caution; CoCo was the homie, but the foreign fool was an unknown variable.

Upon reaching the mouth of the dispute, we discovered the stranger clutching a pistol, trained on CoCo. The sight heightened our senses, readying us for whatever might happen. I noticed Spookee's struggles to discreetly retrieve his weapon from his inner jacket lining. Simultaneously, I tightened my grip on my Foe-Five, ready to bust on this fool at a moment's notice. Before we even had a chance to gauge the situation, we were intercepted by the stranger's sudden pivot, his eyes glaring daggers.

In a paranoid, aggressive tone he asked, *"What's up with you niggas!? Y'all gotta problem!?!"*

I felt a shiver crawling up my spine- the situation was spiraling out of control. Unfazed & cool as a fan, Spookee contrasted with CoCo's fiery temperament. He retorted calmly, *"Nah, we chillin'."*

His nonchalant demeanor provided a momentary distraction allowing Spookee to land a brain rattling haymaker on the gunman. The impressive display of strength not only stunned the crowd of partygoers & bystanders, but it also left the gunman stumbling to the ground, disoriented with a Quasimodo sized lump on his eye as a souvenir from Hoover Street. His pistol slipped from his hand & clattered onto the pavement. ScHool Boy swiftly snatched the gun before the stranger could regain his composure.

Triumphant, Spookee now commanded two Deuce-Deuce's. Spookee asked me to go to the crib & get some more ammo. He was thinking two steps ahead, big bro was always on point, his dark eyes clouded with concerns of possible payback by the battered, humiliated partygoer.

This incident provided an unfiltered perspective on the life we were living- it wasn't just about survival, but also understanding the circumstances people found themselves in, and how they react. On that evening, that house party spoke volumes about friendship, the quickness of one's wit, and the sheer strength of instinct. We were ready for whatever, whenever. As ScHool Boy & I made our way back to my house, we knew that this was just another day around the way, like 2pac would say to live & die in L.A.

ScHool Boy & I return to the get together, and next thing you know CoCo starts talking shit, the braggadocious antagonist of the evening simply couldn't resist telling everybody & their mama about kicking my ass earlier. He begins jabbing his finger into my chest & laughing in my face in front of an audience of hot girls who are now all awe-struck by the drama that unfolded.

I told this fool to chill out for the last time, I couldn't believe he was tripping on me after my brother, and I just came to his aid. Undeniably, I'm still in my feelings from the ass whipping he gave me that afternoon. I'm feeling violated & disrespected, I'm sure it was visible in my face. Lil Fat Rat & ScHool Boy tried to rationalize with him to chill & leave me alone. Encouraging him to cool out & have a good time.

CoCo refused to listen, instead he kept antagonizing me. I had the Foe-Five on me. I don't know if CoCo knew I was strapped, or if he did, he just didn't give a damn. He was clearly on a rampage today, cause suddenly he fired on me with a furious roundhouse! We start fighting in Mama Mary's driveway then in the street like stray Crip dogs! Ferociously trading blows as the cheering crowd of spectators & party goers egged us on. We squabble for what feels like an hour until the homies jump in & break up the rumble. That's when Spookee appears.

I'm trying to catch my breath, but the respite was short-lived. We end up around the corner outside of Catman's crib. Perhaps fueled by the intoxicating power of a bruised ego, CoCo, still seething with anger, unleashed his venom at me.

"Nigga I'ma shoot up ya crib!" He roared.

I can't believe CoCo threatened to shoot up my mama house. The audacity of the threat pulled the icy wind out of the warmth of the summer night. His venomous words hung in the air.

It was Spookee who broke the chilling quiet. *"What the fuck you say!"*, he bellowed.

His words filled with unspoken promises of repercussions. He had recently knocked a fool senseless for brandishing a firearm at the unbearable CoCo. Now here he was, threatening the safety of our home. It was the last straw; the camel's back was broken like a muthafucka! It was plain as day, CoCo had to pay for what he said.

He hits the mad dash! Spookee & I gave chase, but this fool was out &, in an attempt, to scare him, we fired a few shots his way. I let off 3 rounds in CoCo's direction, like Yosemite Sam. He flees & effortlessly flips over a gate.

Later I found out that he was shot in his ass! Damn, I shot CoCo! I didn't want to hit him, I just wanted him to stop picking on me, I just wanted my respect. CoCo held it down; he didn't tell on us. I felt bad, my heart was full of remorse. I couldn't believe I shot the homie.

Most the homies remained neutral in the quarrel, we all knew CoCo was always bullying cats, picking fights & they knew I was a shooter & a hothead. When I say CoCo was a bully it isn't in the sense of preying on the weak this crazy ass Crip only preyed on other predators!! Nonetheless the tension between us was awkward for everyone. Spookee & I knew better than to get high or drunk with Coco, because we always had to keep our eye on him because CoCo was a dangerous man with lethal hands.

CoCo towered over everyone like a menacing skyscraper, at 6'7 by the age of 14 years old. CoCo was always on deck, a frontliner ready for war, and the first one any Hoover Gangsta could call in a conflict. He had his faults nonetheless; Coco had a reign of unyielding terror in the hood.

He knew nothing about restraint; picking on anyone that dared cross his path, he recently threw CyCo Mike head first in a dumpster for no reason. Joker, T-Dogg, Baby Crazy, CyCo Mike, ScHool Boy & I had endured enough of his bullshit. You know I've gone my share of rounds with the colossal Crip from 54th street, today we decided to give CoCo a DP! It's time for the Gangsta Midgets to kick some ass!

As we made our way back from the Hoover store with ice cold 8-balls & an array of munchies. We heard the loud ruckus of a scuffle echoing down the alley off 54th street. We find CoCo towering over Willbone hitting him with the ground & pound. CoCo was much like Deebo from the movie Friday. After he was done pummeling the homie, he snatched Willbone's stylish Turkish rope chain with Cadillac medallion right off his neck.

I'd be lying if I told you his mama gave him that chain or he worked hard for it. Willbone was a half Black, half Mexican, Gangsta Midget with a Napoleon complex that enjoyed to strong arm fools. He didn't have any hustle in him; he didn't enjoy any kind of work, not even selling drugs. Willbone would rather rob the dope boys or playas & he jacked a lot of fools to get that chain.

We saw an opportunity to teach CoCo big ass a lesson. Fury simmered within us as we watched Willbone struggle to reclaim his chain. We were about to make our stand against the big behemoth. CoCo was distracted squabbling with Willbone, so we used it to our advantage. Swiftly & silently, we creeped up behind him like alley cats, pulled his shirt over his head, momentarily blinding him. Chaos erupted as we rat packed him with a relentless fury, a united force giving Big CoCo a taste of his own medicine.

We rained down blows countered only by Coco's fumbling blocks. Our collective strength was more than a match for his individual might. Our bottled-up frustrations released onto his armor-like exterior.

CoCo did not take his defeat lightly. He recognized some of us who had participated in his beat down & sought revenge. Whenever he managed to corner any of us alone, he attempted to reclaim his dominance. Over the years our experiences & encounters with our loved one, CoCo, elevated our strength both as individuals & a collective.

One evening, Rev Lee, a father figure in our lives, became the voice of reason we didn't know we needed. His intervention marked the end of an era of hostility & the birth of a revelation we never anticipated. He felt the broken bridge between me & CoCo - the tension as thick as an uncut diamond, the awkwardness as silent as a grave.

Uninvited as it was, the reverend insisted on mediation, an open dialogue to mend the tears in our relationship that were tattering at the ends. It was not as much a desire as it was the desperate need for our collective, we were the spark that ignited Five-Deuce Hoover. He had a way with words & got us to see things differently. He told us some stories from the bible about love & how to love each other.

He told us the story of Barnabas & Paul, the mentor & the protege. Barnabas took Paul under his wing as a friend & student. He trained Paul to be a great evangelist, and ultimately, he became the leader of the ministers. Barnabas & Paul were friends for many years until an argument separated them, but they maintained respect for each other amidst disagreements.

The Rev told us the story of Jesus & Peter, and how Jesus forgave Peter after his many mistakes, including denying being a disciple. Jesus showed compassion & forgiveness to him before going to heaven, though Peter had denied Jesus, Jesus knew that Peter would be a man who would boldly proclaim the saving grace of God to the world.

CoCo & I saw the light, we saw our relationship in both stories, we hugged it out, and promised to be better homeboys, it was a tender moment. All the homies had a lot of respect for the Rev & when he spoke, we listened. During the mediation, I found out CoCo was shot by bullets from a .22. I was relieved, CoCo's blood wasn't on my hands!

CoCo & I became closer after that. What we saw reflected in those tales was a mirror image of our own predicament. We were inseparable in every battlefield, a tag team fighting demons in the city of angels. Embracing this revelation brought about unforeseen change. CoCo became my shield; He was the muscle, and I was the brains It was a give & take relationship, serving the purpose, a balance in chaos. Life was still far from perfect, but there was a new understanding, a newfound respect, between us that we had never imagined.

We had each other's back, no matter what. We never had another fall out again. He stopped bullying me & started bullying people for me or we punked people together. CoCo & I remained the tightest of homeboys, but our friendship had evolved to something deeper. We had learned the true meaning of brotherhood, and it was a beautiful thing. Our victories were shared, our defeats bitter-sweet. It was us against the world, and together Hriginal FDHGC.

The chapters of our turbulent adolescence turned into lessons of brotherhood, strength, and respect. We learned the value of surviving together, the essence of standing up for each other, ten toes down & the power that lay in unity. We found brotherhood, not in blood but in a shared struggle, not in power, but in vulnerability. It was a brotherhood born out of adversity & shaped by redemption.

Reverend Lee was the patriarch of the Lee family, he was a great man & one of the best wordsmiths with the gospel in South Central. I wasn't the church-type, but the Rev was the only one capable of invoking me with the Holy Spirit. He delivered the word of God like none other.

I have fond memories of Tony taking us joyriding in the Reverend's Rolls Royce. I learned one thing for certain & two things for sure from the Rev, and that was God is Good, and God is Good all the time! The Rev was one of a kind, he loved us & raised the Fifty Boys like his own children.

CHAPTER TWENTY-TWO:
"THE ODD COUPLE: BOO & SPOOKEE"

Back then, life seemed carefree. Our youthful naivety & thirst for adrenaline, the steppingstones of our adolescence, set the stage for many adventures. Coke Dogg was by my crib hanging out. I was amid a tangled relationship with the law, and I remembered I was scheduled to see my probation officer today. I was in a predicament: I didn't have enough time to walk before the office closed, it was all the way by Exposition Park.

I decided to give my big cousin a lesson in Grand Theft Auto. Today Coke Dogg was going to learn how to steal a car with my trusty B-10 keys. In a hasty tutorial, I demonstrated to Coke Dogg, the intricate mystery of car theft using the B-10 keys. His wide-eyed astonishment was etched in the memory of that fateful day. We made it to the probation office right before it was scheduled to close. I was relieved everything went without a hitch. Our stolen car wasn't where we left it, we surveyed the area.

I saw it hooked on to the back of a tow truck being taken away. Ain't that a bitch! Now I had no choice but to jack another one. There she was, a Chevy in the parking lot was our ticket home. It was a vivid hue of Five-Two blue & chrome that seemingly teemed with life under the night's scrutiny.

Driving down Vermont *"Boogie Oogie-Oogie"* by A Taste of Honey playing off an 8 track I found in the car. The cool night air & the hum of the car's engine created a deceptive tranquility. Out of nowhere, a Ghetto Bird emerged, slicing through our jam session with its massive rotor blades. A piercing beam of searchlight gleamed into our car, obliterating the darkness.

The pilot's stern voice echoed through a loudspeaker, *"Pull over."*

In the face of authority, I mustered enough audacity to reply with a defiant middle finger out the driver's side window, and I floored it, the engine roaring with rebellion. I attempted to outpace the pursuing hawk above us. The chase continued until we reached 57th street. When Coke Dogg jumped from the speeding vehicle like he was in a Blaxploitation film, dashing wildly into the night. In a heartbeat, I followed suit.

I traced his escape route in an adrenaline-high pursuit. I spotted Coke Dogg diving under the crawl space of a nearby house. Without hesitation, I followed right behind him, the pig's searchlight on my ass like a spotlight at the Apollo as I slid under the house. Coke Dogg looked at me, I looked at him, his eyes wide with shock, his face lit by the insistent spotlight.

He shouted at me *"What the fuck you doing, cuH! I thought you went the other way! Get outta here!"*

It was too late, we were surrounded. I had priors so this time they called my mama & told her I was going straight to juvenile hall. Coke Dogg went home after a week or two. I stayed there about 60 days, and after sentencing, they sent me to Chino. They placed me at a county facility called *"Boys Republic."*

It's now February 1979, one day I was with my Mexican partner named Blanko, he was from a very respected & old barrio called the Big Hazard Gang aka Hazard Grande. They have been doing their thing & have controlled their turf since the 1940s. We got along well from day one cause we both represented the H.

"Yo Blanko, I'm tired of this shit, let's bust out this joint," I told my Chicano homeboy.

Blanko was down, so we just strolled right out that bitch, it was easy, because Boys Republic was a group home & a school with no gates. We took like 3 or 4 more buses to get to his hood, a long ass

3-hour journey to Ramona Gardens in Boyle Heights, East Los. I stayed with Blanko for about a month before I got back to the set.

Blanko & his gang were involved in all sorts of illegal activities, from drug dealing to extortion. I would hear stories about rival hoods getting shot up or people getting beat up for crossing them & I wanted to be in the middle of it all, so that's what I did, they saw me as honorary Hazard Grande.

I finally returned to my house. Upon my arrival, I was greeted with devastating news. My Uncle Walter informed me that the police had been searching for me since my escape from Boys Republic & my parents were mad at me. My Mama didn't want me back at the house, she was tired of my shit, and I was tired of her rules. Unwilling to obey her rules, my pointless defiance cast me into an existence that promised anything but a carefree youth.

I stopped by Baby Crazy's house, but he wasn't home. I started to troop towards the Foe in my search of the homies. As I was leaving Baby Crazy's yard, something caught my eye. I had to do a double take. I couldn't believe my eyes; Baby Crazy striked up the set big as hell with gang fingers & BK on the side of his parents' house! I laughed thinking about how bad Big Walt was going to kick his ass. When I got to the Foe I found the homies gang-hangin', smoking, and drinking.

Blanko taught me how to do jailhouse tattoos with some simple easily accessible items. First you have to mix cigarette ashes with some toothpaste, and water to create a soot then pack it into the toothpaste cap real tight, then heat up a needle & voila, like magic it's time to create a ghetto masterpiece.

I did some ink that night, Bow Dee, Joker, and Tee Dub, agreed to let me tatt them up. Can you believe those tattoos stood the test of time? The homies still got the tatts after all these years. They were impressed with my skills & soon I became the go-to guy for tattoos in the hood. I told the homies about my situation at the crib, and Sham Rock extended an invitation for me to stay at his house for the night, so began my life as a nomad.

I was a hot-headed teenage boy, misunderstood, stubborn & defiant. I had chosen the streets over the comfort of a warm home, the pride of being Hoover Gangsta Crip over the basic duties & rules that my loving parents sought to impose on me. The bitterness in their eyes fueled by their disappointment over my disobedience prompted their decision.

I became a ruthlessly independent young man, dependent only on the companionship of my homies, and the intoxicating allure of girls around me. Back then, technology didn't bind us together - we relied heavily on each other, the bond we formed, the very core of our brotherhood.

We spent our weekends crashing house parties, as the thrill of infiltrating unwelcome territory fueled us. Any rejection was met with anger & gun fire, we weren't shy about pulling the trigger. On impulse, we would shoot up these parties, not always out of malice, but sometimes out of resentment & foolish pride for being denied entry.

I was the smallest out of my siblings, so naturally people thought I was the youngest & underestimated me, this put a chip on my shoulder. Their ignorant eyes unable to see the menacing shadow of a hardened life carved in the belly of Hoover street. Despite my petite frame, I was a reckless soul, disguising my immaturity under the veneer of a hardcore Crip.

My Mom welcomed me to visit but only while her & my father were at work. She didn't disown me, she just said I couldn't live there if I couldn't follow the rules, and I couldn't. She tried to give me a 10pm curfew, and that didn't fly with me cause that's when my nights were just getting started.

The streets were unkind, but they offered me an intoxicating sense of belonging. The reckless pursuit of thrill, the adrenaline of surviving another day, and the allure of quick money eclipsed the undercurrent of anxiety that threatened my existence.

My mother would go to work at 6am & wouldn't come home till 6pm, so I would hang out at the crib while she was out. I cherished those visits because I got to spend quality time with Whitey & my birds, making sure they were fed, and cleaning my dog cage & pigeon coop.

I would shower, and eat leftovers every day, you know nobody cooks like mama, because she cooks with love. It was during those quiet hours in the morning that I could reconnect with a part of my life that had once made me feel whole.

After a while my visits to my family home were brief, and rare. Often, it was to drop off money for my mother, a woman tortured by the distressing thought of her teenage son's outlaw lifestyle. Each time I showed up at her doorstep, I saw the worry in her eyes, all she could do was pray for me. There was a disheartening resignation in her sighs & a heartbreak in her teary eyes that haunted me. Yet, bound by my pride & the thrill of Crippin', I turned a blind eye to it.

On the other hand, my Pops, a man of hardened ways & attitude, was more direct in his warnings. I remained a disappointment, a far cry from the son my father had hoped for.

My father would often say, *"you ain't shit,"* His words were laced with disappointment & disdain, his optimism dying a slow, painful death with every crime I committed.

"You ain't gonna make it to see eighteen", he'd continue, his voice resonating with the loss of his little boy.

His harsh words were his defense mechanism to keep the hurt at bay because I had forsaken the safety of my family for the treacherous glimmer of the streets.

My decision to reject family ties in favor of life as a Crip incited my father's damnation. The constant clash between us was starkly ironic; he chose to insult & provoke me back into order, while my actions were merely a defiant cry for acceptance in an adult world I barely understood. His words stung, but they also fueled me. Fueled me to make it past eighteen & prove him wrong. Each verbal assault became a proverbial gauntlet, pushing me to survive, pushing past the odds stacked against me.

I'd given my life to the streets, the set had become my family, sex & drugs were my solace. I'd chosen a life where disputes were settled with bullets, and brotherhood was spelled in spilled blood. I'd chosen a life where every step could be a misstep into a death trap.

As I reflect upon those fugitive years, I wonder how different everything could have been had I chosen another path. But even during the violence & the hard reality of street life, I found my place, my people, and myself. The experiences, good & bad, have shaped me, not as the *"failure"* my father labeled me, but as a survivor battling against the odds in a world set against me. I had to learn the hard way. My stubbornness, my audacious pursuit of a powerful existence out on the streets would eventually ask for its pound of flesh.

There are seven billion people in this world, and trust me, none of them has a more intriguing sibling dynamic than I do. Growing up as the proverbial black sheep was an experience colored by constant friction & paradoxical freedom. This stigma would shape the unique bond between me & my polar opposite: Spookee. Spookee was the definition of mama's boy, the apple of her eye. While I was a rebel with a precise & righteous cause, FDHGC.

We were as different as chalk & cheese, as night & day, as fire & ice. The gap in our personalities is so vast, it's often been an impetus for misunderstanding, tension, and yes, heated arguments & fist fights. Yet despite all this we've always had each other's backs. Our differences weren't just skin-deep, they ran much deeper. Spookee & I were an odd couple, seemingly united by blood yet divided by personality.

As I ventured through crowds with my vivacious spirit, Spookee wandered alone in solitude. I am a people's person who craves the thrill of human interaction. In contrast, Spookee was more anti-social, preferring his own company over the company of others. Our differences trickled down to our physical appearances too.

I carry a more compact, short & stocky frame while Spookee stands tall, a towering figure at 6'2 brown skinned with tight ass chinky eyes like an Asian. Spookee's unwavering loyalty is legendary; his picture could be placed next to the word in the dictionary. His dedication was soft-spoken & resolute. He's a warrior knighted on the battlefield of life, his armor forged in the fires of unwavering commitment.

South Central provided a hard & uncompromising view of the world. There was no gray area for Spookee; My brother didn't like anybody that wasn't from Five-Deuce Hoover. If you didn't claim what he claimed, you were an outcast & he didn't want anything to do with you.

Spookee was dead serious about maintaining his boundaries, he held a deep-rooted disdain for anyone who did not pledge allegiance to FDHGC. He was the stereotypical closed book, only open for those who identified with the same lineage, deciphered only by those indoctrinated in the same code. He drew up a circle of acceptance so narrow, it could feel suffocating.

We used to bump heads a lot growing up due to his ideologies. This nigga didn't even fraternize with other Hoovers, he didn't care if there was a million dollars on the line. He was indifferent to the prospects of wealth, status, or power, if it meant betraying his roots, his colors. Spookee's suspicion & caution extended as far as turning his back on anyone or anything that didn't fit within his view of the world. His perspective wasn't born out of ignorance or naivety but was a carefully crafted strategy for survival in the dog-eat-dog world that was all we knew.

I remember a particular incident that perfectly encapsulates his rigidness. I was hanging out with some playas from outside of the set. They dropped me home in a sleek Cadillac, and as soon as big bro spotted it, he instantly seethed with anger. He didn't want me bringing no cool-ass niggas around our mother's house. His perspective didn't just paint strangers as potential threats; he feared the exposure might dilute one's loyalty. It was a measure to safeguard his kin, his home, and the sanctity of our brotherhood.

We continually clashed over this. My mindset welcomed the shaking of hands with strangers, the camaraderie born in unfamiliar territory, an attribute that helped me build the set. Spookee, on the other hand, was an exemplar of caution, intolerance, and a near-obsessive need to maintain the purity of our circle, an attribute that protected us from being infiltrated. His loyalty was unwavering to the point of being taut, and volatile, yet, wholeheartedly genuine.

As much as I understood where he was coming from, I couldn't help but feel stifled by Spookee's attitude. I knew that there was more to the world than just the Fifties, and I was desperate to see it. I tried to explain to him that networking & getting to know people outside of our set was essential for our growth, but he passionately disagreed.

According to Spookee, the only thing that mattered was staying true to our roots. For him, loyalty to the Five-Deuce trumped everything else in life. I became more & more frustrated with the restrictions placed upon me by my family.

My family didn't understand my vision & my plan to expand, to rise above the circumstances that had shaped my life. Deep down, I knew that my mom & Spookee were only concerned for my safety – after all, they'd grown up in the same harsh world & didn't want to see me suffer the same fate as so many people around us.

I felt there were walls being erected around me, entrapping me, causing me to rebel against their protective instincts. I no longer wished to be shackled by the blinders that had been ingrained into our minds from a young age. I needed to break free & experience life outside of the Fifties no matter the risk.

While my brother Spookee stayed trapped in the dark, I began pursuing the power & freedom of the unknown. It was this decision that set the course for the rest of my life, where I discovered my true potential & strength, even if it meant standing alone & defying the guidance & advice from my elders. I'm starting to branch out, I'm making connects & finding new ways of getting money & Spookee would object *"Fuck them niggas, they ain't from Five-Deuce!"*

Back then, I didn't care where somebody was from. We can get this paper, unless they were Blood or East Coast.

Anyhow, Big Bro used to look out for me though, I love him for that. It's the little things that count like opening the back door for me or leaving a window unlocked so I could get in my mama crib. Despite our differences & disagreements, Spookee & I will always be brothers – bound by blood & Five-Deuce & even though our paths may stray apart, we always remain together. I'll never forget the lessons he taught me, which helped shape me into the man I am today.

Brotherhood, as I experienced, has always been more than just a shared lineage or common childhood memories. It is a bond cemented in the trenches of life's toughest battles, forged in the fires of shared pain & mutual understanding. We might have been yin & yang, but underneath these surface disparities, there was an ironclad bond that connected us.

Anchored in the rocky soil of family beefs & the fast-flowing river of adolescence, our bond was the pontoon that navigated us through troubled waters. Despite everything, one fact stood unaltered: we were each other's protectors, always looking out for one another & our kin. We were two sides of the same coin, different yet united like Yin & Yang.

Two brothers, enigmatic & polar, maneuvering the winding roads of life, always together yet forever apart. Shadows on a sundial, moving in different directions, but bound by the same center. An odd couple, a dynamic duo born from the same womb but destined for separate paths - the black sheep & the golden boy.

CHAPTER TWENTY-THREE: "ONE NATION UNDER A GROOVE"

The 1970s was an era of economic instability triggered by oil embargoes, inflation, and a national recession. Los Angeles was not immune, South Central experienced acute effects of these downturns. Unemployment was rampant within the Black community, leading to increased poverty & a stark deterioration in living conditions.

Growing up in such a period of unrest shaped a generation of adolescents. Schools, plagued by high dropout rates & below-par academic performance, failed to provide an escape route from these socio-economic circumstances. Instead, many youngsters sought solace in rising street gangs, not only as a source of protection but also as a form of family & identity.

The compounding pressures of economic turmoil & increasing gang membership added stress to an already strained relationship between South Central's residents & the pigs. Black citizens' increasing distrust in law enforcement was not without basis. The LAPD under the leadership of our arch nemesis Chief Daryl Gates was notorious for their 'tough on crime' stance that often translated into aggressive policing in South Central.

We saw the rise of the LAPD's CRASH division, and the ramifications of local & national politics. CRASH, Community Resources Against Street Hoodlums unit was a reason for pigs to harass black kids in the ghetto but disguised as an initiative to curtail the escalating gang-related crimes that accompanied an era of economic hardship.

This specialized unit was often perceived more as a gestapo force instead of community protectors. They were criticized for instigating tensions & intensifying violence due to their heavy-handed & dirty tactics such as aggressive stop-&-search practices & fabricating gang attacks to initiate turf wars.

Critics argue that the federal government in the late seventies inadvertently fueled these adversities. Carter's Urban Policy was largely ineffective at addressing the socio-economic woes facing areas like South Central. In turn, amplifying membership in street

211 | P a g e

organizations like the Crips & feeding the cycle of violence, distrust, and socio-economic degradation.

This was the world we lived in; a Crip milestone of 1979 was the introduction of the First Five Deuce Day celebration on May 2, now known as the Set day & have since been adopted by every hood in the land. May 2nd marks the one-year anniversary of the birth of Five-Deuce Hoover & our alliance with Five-Deuce Broadway. Over a hundred Hoover-Broadways, the 57th street Fly Girls, alongside a buffet of groupies celebrated with us. It eventually evolved into an annual tradition, a day earmarked for putting in work on our enemies, a celebration of our tribe & a solemn tribute to our fallen stars.

We rendezvoused on the Foe then we all hopped onto the Slauson bus to Ladera Park, which was just a breezy fifteen-minutes away within the Rollin Sixties turf. This park served as our arena of good times. We enjoyed joints of lovely & ice cold bottles of Olde English & Mad Dog 20/20. The aroma of sizzling meat mingled with the pungent scent of Sherman & malt liquor.

Our celebration flowed with basketball & football games as well as a vibrant dance-off, where we showcased our Crip Walking & Pop Lockin' skills which was followed by a King's feast. I got my grub on but didn't pig out. I also got some pussy from a girl I've been trying to dig out. As Ice Cube would say, today was a good day.

While I got freaky deaky with BBQ from Broadway, the homies congregated at our hideout on 55th & Vermont. Before we took over the shack, it was the home of a former Fifty Boy, Larry Walker, and his family. It was a sprawling two-story home with eight rooms that was furnished with plush couches & mattresses that we scavenged, making it more homely for the homies.

Baby Crazy, Joker & I were the set artists, we made sure the set was blasted all over the place like wallpaper, but the highlight was a ghetto masterpiece curated by Baby Crazy, who encompassed the entire roof with a massive moral of *"52 Hoover"*. The home also had a balcony overlooking the Fifties. We kept an armed lookout overseeing the property from the Balcony or roof day & night, but since it was our first set day we were all at the park.

Upon arriving at the shack, Coke Dogg & the homies were greeted by some unsettling news delivered by one of the local winos. His words ruined a sunny day like a thunderstorm.

"The red rags been in y'all shit" – a phrase that took us from groovy to gloomy.

Sure enough, a remorseless devastation awaited us as we entered our sanctuary. Their artwork stood stamped in period red spray paint all over, a testament to their hatred for our creed. They took their sweet ass time & got their Picasso on! Like starving artists cherishing their blank canvas, the Brims painstakingly desecrated the shack with their blasphemous artistry. A caricature of Popeye disrespecting the set. One hand brandishing the C, our sacred hand sign, while his other hand gestured the middle finger, with a speech bubble that screamed *"Fuck Crip!"* They had done a thorough job, systematically whacking out every trace of Crip hieroglyphics. The visual cut deep into our pride, a sight that left our souls inflamed.

It was a bold display of scorn etched in crimson ink against the once Loced out walls of our honeycomb hideout. This was indeed a declaration of war! A silent vow passed amongst the collective, an unspoken promise to retaliate. The homies met the challenge head-on, launching a direct attack on the Brims. The fire of vengeance ignited in their hearts; we sprang into action.

Armed with a mélange of stolen artillery – Coke Dogg snatched our grandma's .22 beretta from her sock drawer, Insane Fish swiped his father's .38 snub nose, and Cadillac Bob finagled a .357 magnum from his mother, Mama Mary – alongside a militia of Fifty Hoover-Broadways, troops descended upon the infamous Sugar Shack. The Sugar Shack was the Brim hideout, located on Slauson in the area around John Muir, next door to a Jersey Maid ice cream parlor.

Our revenge would be all but subtle, or predictable. Rather than a simple shoot-em-up, Willbone had a more dramatic idea, turn the Sugar Shack into a flambe with a Molotov cocktail. The spectacle of their shack ablaze was a sight to behold, a glaring portrayal of vengeance on a Wednesday afternoon. We were true to this but new to this & made the mistake of not surrounding the building. The Brims escaped through the back door, scampering over the fence into their territory.

Surprise, surprise, my Grandma appeared exiting off the 110, on her tiresome return from work as a Compton school teacher. As she reached the corner of Slauson & Vermont, she saw Coke Dogg, gun in hand, fleeing from a blazing shack! Their eyes locked in an unsettling stare down; a grandson & his guilty secret unveiled before her world-weary eyes. Coke Dogg was caught red-handed!

Fear surged through his veins as he raced home like Jesse Owens, barely beating grandma to 54th street. As their eyes met again in the living room, maps of age & wisdom stared into his burning with questions & accusations.

"What were you doing with a gun, Ravele?" She asked, her voice hollow.

Caught in the crosshair of the confrontation, he resorted to a lie enveloped in the innocence of childhood games.

The words hung heavily in the air as he responded nonchalantly, *"It was a cap gun, grandma. We was playing cops & robbers."*

Coke Dogg's lie hung in the air, attempting to shroud the brutal reality of the day. Yet, our lives had become far detached from the innocence of childhood games, now spiraling into a churning whirlwind of gang rivalry & territorial wars. The first Five Deuce day ended on a bitter note, leaving an impending wave of uncertainty about what laid ahead. This was an episode in our lives that blurred the lines between play & peril, forever altering the course of our narratives. As the sun set on the horizon that day, we saw the metamorphosis of good boys into Kiwé warriors.

Our reign over the 55th street shack lasted more than a year until the prying eyes of patrolling Ghetto Birds spotted our inadvertent advertisement, and display of unity & power. Their hawk-eyed view saw our rooftop mural. From then on, our sanctuary turned into a target for the pigs who began raiding it relentlessly any time something went down in the hood. Despite the menace, the memory of that First Five Deuce day remains, a flickering flame in our hearts: a beacon of unity & resistance.

The Groove was comparable to feudal states — loosely associated entities sharing common names, heritage, and interests, diverging, merging, and battling with one another & rival hoods. Hoover was expanding at an unprecedented rate. The year 1979 was a Hoover explosion, a year of massive expansion. The One-oh-Seven's initiated the Eleven-Deuces. The Nine-Deuce Hoovers, not to be outdone, introduced the Nine-Foes into the fold.

Lil Simms, the Tukomes from Seven-Foe claimed 59th Street. Where they planted the blue flag & Five-Nine Hoover was formed. Prior to their arrival, this region was primarily under the sway of our rivals the Five-Nine Blocc Brims.

Some of the Hriginal & 1st generation Five-Nine Hoovers include key figures such as Big Worm, The Smileys, 8-Ball, Joker, Hoover Blacc, Devil, Rat Dogg, Rat, Insane, Riccshay, Duck, Hub, Fred Dogg, C-Dogg & Snowman, among others. Emboldened by their burgeoning strength & the recent upheaval, they strove to assert their dominance over their territory.

Spookee wanted the Fifties to be Five-Deuce & Hoover Gangsta so we went over there to test their mettle, we pressed them like the Hoover Crips pressed us it was only right. The Five-Nines earned our respect over time, and we pushed Nifty Fifties together. As Hoovers we may not have agreed on our stance as Gangstas, but the aspiration was clear: Make this One Nation Under a Groove.

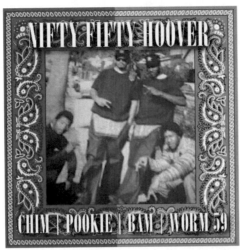

Just like music, memories have a way of transporting us back in time. Thinking back to that summer night in 1979, it's remarkable how vividly I recall it - a whirlwind adventure packed with wild, untamed experiences. During the peak of the Black funk revolution, a life-changing event took place.

It was the spring of 1979, just three weeks after the inaugural 5deuce day. The mercury was climbing, with an electric energy buzzing through every nook & cranny of Los Angeles—a city soon to bear witness to the World's Greatest Funk Festival. A star-studded cast was set to rip the stage, ready to serenade the mob of funk fanatics.

Have you ever attended an event that was so magical & surreal that it remains unforgettable even after decades have gone by? For me, that life-changing moment happened during Memorial Day weekend, Saturday, May 26, 1979, at the world's greatest funk festival. To say that it was a historic day would be an understatement; it was a day that defied all odds & had the spirit of Black Power & Cuzz Love coursing through its veins, right into the heart of Los Angeles.

I still distinctly remember the lengthy walk from 54th street to the coliseum; a parade about two hundred deep marching through 2 miles of Five-Deuce Hoover territory, an emblematic gathering of Hoover-Broadway Gangsta Crips. The energy was intense, the anticipation like a thick fog in the air. Upon arrival, the crowd was massive, the coliseum resembled its own city. It could have easily been mistaken to be a meeting point for the million man march, an ocean of black folks outside the venue creating a spectacle worthy of the history books.

As we inched closer & closer to the coliseum, the city seemed minuscule in comparison to the vast ocean of humanity we found ourselves a part of. Now, out of our groovy band of 200, only a fortunate few, roughly a score of us, had secured tickets, Insane Fish was one of them, holding their ticket like a holy piece of paper that was their portal to a world of rhythm & soul.

One hour prior to the concert, long lines of eager ticket holders were buzzing with excitement. The crowd was an eclectic mix of backgrounds & ages, bringing together individuals from various corners of the city. From older fans who fondly remembered the golden age of 60's rhythm & blues, to funk babies like me, this event held the promise of an unforgettable musical journey.

As the clock struck 1pm, the gates opened, and waves of enthusiastic fans surged into the Coliseum. The stunning architecture, an ode to ancient Greece & Rome, stood tall & proud, embellished with sculptures & fountains. It served as the perfect setting for a once-in-a-lifetime gathering that would witness the showcase of some of the greatest musical talents in history.

The immediate stumbling block separating us from the funk universe going on within the coliseum was a 15 foot gate. But like water finds its way around a rock, we were not to be deterred. Suddenly, on this unforgettable day, a plan was hatched. It unfolded nonchalantly, almost unexpectedly. With the groove our only guide, Coke Dogg & Tony took the initiative to scale the gate.

Ready or not, here we come! Inspired by their audacity, we followed suit, each adding our weight to the towering structure. Nothing can stop us now! Suddenly without warning, the colossal gate groaned under the collective weight & capitulated—it was falling! A hush fell among the crowd, lasting nearly an eternity until it was broken by the thunderous crash of the gate meeting the ground. That was it, the barrier was eliminated & a path to funky town lay ahead.

As though this was a coordinated effort, creating an avenue for us, and everyone else waiting outside, to flood into the coliseum-almost as if the Hoover dam had burst. That move was a coliseum-wide gift from Hoover-Broadway to the rest of the crowd. A few thousand lucky bystanders, who had been stranded outside, discovered themselves awash in the sea of victorious gatecrashers. We had orchestrated an unexpected contribution to an already momentous event.

You might expect pandemonium to ensue, chaos to dictate the course of the event in the wake of the Hoover-Broadway invasion. Who said the Crips don't give back to the community? From where we stood, we likely gave away a few thousand tickets to the greatest concert in LA history! The festival turned out to be as harmonious as it was riotous, a grand testimonial to the unifying power of music.

The atmosphere on that special day could be felt from miles away as fans flocked from far & near to witness the milestone event. I, a 13-year-old kid attending the greatest funk festival of all time, will forever remember the significance of this extraordinary event in shaping my life & my views of Black culture & pride.

A curated mix of Black musicians & fans came together as one in a massive, peaceful celebration of music, love, and most of all...soul. A blaring sun shone down upon the 43,000 attendees eagerly awaiting their favorite funk icons at the World's Greatest Funk Festival. The atmosphere was charged with excitement, and the air was comparatively heavy due to the rich blend of colorful personalities, intoxicating substances, and unity against all odds.

As we made our way through the festival, I marveled at the sight before me. I had never seen so many Black people in one place before in my life. Thousands of fans from all walks of life flocked to witness what was to be deemed the pinnacle of funk.

Throughout the 11-hour funk marathon, stretching from 1pm to 12am, we enjoyed the most iconic funk musicians of all time. As the audience settled in, the concert organizers unveiled their lineup—a breathtaking roster of funk luminaries that would shake the 1923-built stadium down to the very foundation. Amongst the bejeweled acts were the charismatic Rick James, the outlandish Parliament-Funkadelic, smooth-playing Bootsy Collins, and the soulful Bar-Kays. Each had their own iconic sound & style. CoCo & I pushed & shoved our way through the crowd followed by a militia of Five-Deuces marching with purpose towards the stage. Before the musicians even started playing, we found ourselves caught in a whirlwind of newfound friendships & memorable encounters. It was there that Sniper, and I ran into Diamond from Eight Tray Gangsta. As we exchanged stories & laughter, Diamond suddenly turned somber & gave us an alarming update.

According to Diamond, a member of the Rollin' Sixties, named Tyrone, had been killed. To our dismay, he informed us that the blame had landed squarely upon the shoulders of the Eight Tray Gangsters, and Sixties unsuccessfully tried to smoke Big Bacot igniting a bitter feud. Little did we know that this beef would drastically shift the tone of Crip history & unity forever.

The show commenced with a thunderous introduction of the Bar-Kays, a seasoned funk & soul band who previously served as backing musicians for Otis Redding. Their opening performance acted as a harbinger of the dynamic grooves & wild energy on the horizon. The moment arrived as the sun beamed high above the Coliseum.

The Bar-Kays took the stage, wasting no time as they unleashed a soul-shaking slick groove that sent the crowd bouncing to their feet. The unstoppable energy of the band members pulsed through the arena, perfectly setting the tone for the day. With James Alexander on bass & Larry Dodson's mesmerizing vocals, they played hit after hit, including *"Shake Your Rump to the Funk"* & *"Holy Ghost."* The highlight came as they concluded their act with the electrifying sizzler *"Too Hot to Stop."* Overwhelmed, the crowd was left enthusiastically wanting more.

We were about 200 Five-Deuces deep, occupying the space right in front of the stage. We secured a spot so close to the stage that we were practically part of the artist's entourage. Throughout the Coliseum, there were Crips from every set imaginable, swelling our numbers easily into the thousands. Hoovers, Gangstas, Sixties, Eastside, East Coast, Westside, Main Street, Harlems, Kitchens, ScHool Yards, Avalons, N-hood, Blocks, Undergrounds, Compton, Long Beach, Watts, Gardenas.

We proudly wore our true blue & represented the unity that is now extinct among us. This was a lost era of brotherhood, prior to any inter-Crip grievances, a time that focused on having a good time as a Crip collective, showing the world the strength of the unified C.

The air was electric with anticipation, and as each act began their performance, the crowd went wild. Everyone danced & sang along, sweat dripping down their faces as the beats filled our souls. The sun began to set, casting an eerie pinkish glow over the stadium, yet none of us seemed to even notice; we were entranced by the rhythmic sounds of funk that echoed throughout the arena.

"Chitty-Chitty Bang-Bang! Nothing but a Crip Thang"-
oG Raymond Washington, Founder of the Crips

It was during this astonishing display of unity & celebration that I had the incredible fortune of meeting oG Raymond Washington, the legendary founder of the Crips. He was charismatic & larger than life, with a magnetic personality. For me, it was like meeting one's hero - Conversing with him, however briefly, was a humbling & unforgettable experience. Sadly, we would never get to nurture a friendship as he would be murdered later that year on August 9, 1979, but during that festival, his presence inspired us all.

Amidst the camaraderie & unforgettable experiences, there was an ever-present undercurrent of mischief & chaos. A wave of PCP use swept throughout the crowd; it was not your typical PCP-laced Sherman cigarette. Instead, it was a new form of angel dust, called Black Dust. The black dust concoction was a dangerous mix of PCP, embalming fluid, rat poison, and jet fuel – a potent cocktail that earned its moniker from the blackouts that it induced. Despite its intense effects, which included people feeling compelled to get naked, and dance all day & night, T-Dogg, and I couldn't wait to try it.

As the sun began to dip below the horizon, painting the California sky with vibrant shades of orange & pink, the electric & eccentric punk funk prodigy, Rick James, took center stage. Clad in extravagant, brazen attire – tight leather pants, a studded leather jacket, and knee-high boots – he launched into an explosive set that encapsulated the spirit of the cutting-edge punk-funk genre. His raw energy & rawer lyrics held the attention of the thousands of fans within the Coliseum, igniting their primal desire to dance, jump, and thrash to the driving beats.

At the forefront of the funk scene, with his vibrant stage presence, Rick showcased his swagger & effortlessly cool demeanor throughout his entire set. By the time *"Super Freak"* poured from the gigantic speakers, almost every single person in the vast arena was dancing, scintillating in those electrifying hours.

Another spectacular moment was provided by Rick James' that stood out among the rest, not just for his spectacular rendition of his classic, *"Mary Jane"* but also for his iconic gesture of tossing hundreds of marijuana joints into the crowd, inciting a mad scramble similar to the chaotic frenzy of war.

The Locs & I joined in struggling to grasp those elusive prizes like desperate hoarders in the face of scarcity. The Super Freak's set was filled with unforgettable moments, like the electrifying performance of *"You & I,"* where Rick's powerful voice soared as the entire crowd sang along in unison.

Through the haze of music, sweat, and smoke, my homies & I got our hands on some of those coveted joints, H'Luv & I were all eager to smoke what Rick James was smoking. As the first effects of that glorious plant mingling with the PCP began to take hold, I experienced a feeling I had never known before: a sense of unity & love for the entire stadium, with thousands of black people movin' & groovin' with me under the same sky. Fueled by the music & my newfound sense of freedom, I boogied all night.

Rick James' act of generosity sent waves of euphoria & bliss coursing through the audience. This gesture resonated with the people's insatiable appetite for the freedom to express themselves in a world that had often shunned them. Unfortunately, marijuana was still illegal in these times, so the pigs abruptly ended Rick James' performance & escorted him off the stage.

The effects of the Black Dust were evident all around us. Everywhere I turned, it seemed that someone had stripped off their clothes or engaged in some other manifestation of its intoxicating pull. The combination of my youth & the Angel dust I had consumed throughout the event contributed to the heightened sensations I experienced.

Every pulse of the bass, every soulful note, and every passionate lyric seemed to reverberate within me as I was engulfed by the collective bliss around me. This curious cocktail of chemicals, though dangerous & potentially lethal, contributed to the quirky, carefree quality of the epic festival where people could forget societal expectations & embrace their primal nature. Hypersexual energy thrummed throughout the crowd.

As we all know, when you combine music, adrenaline, and mind-altering substances, inhibitions can often fly out the window. We witnessed wild & scandalous behavior throughout the venue as people got caught up in the pulsating excitement of the festival.

There were women giving head in the crowd, a girl grabbed me by the collar & told me, *"I'm going to suck your dick like a harmonica!"*

You know I let her, and she agreed to do Baby Crazy & Bow Dee, also. This young freak & her friends joined our entourage for the remainder of the night, returning with us back to ScHool Boy's shack for an orgy.

The scene evolved into a black Woodstock overseen by the main ingredient - PCP! As the evening progressed, a seemingly endless supply of twisted sights unfolded before our eyes. All around us, people discarded their clothes, oblivious of decency or consequences. It felt as if the entire Coliseum had embraced anarchy, including Joker & I, with inhibitions & morals forgotten in the fog of intoxicated pandemonium. I loved it!

Rick James' performance, as fiery & unforgettable as it was, seemed but a mere prelude to the cosmic eruption that was to follow, as the reigning kings of funk, Parliament Funkadelic, assumed their rightful place on the stage. Commanded by their fearless & infinitely creative leader, George Clinton, P-Funk set forth to transport their audience to a realm uncharted by the human mind. Instantly, the audience was transported to a groovy, psychedelic, and far-out place.

The Funk Festival was now in full swing. The air was thick with the all-consuming haze of PCP. One could hardly move without someone puffing on what clearly was the narcotic of choice for the night. Parliament Funkadelic was an unstoppable psychedelic powerhouse, merging the wildly imaginative worlds of funk, rock, gospel, and science fiction with a theatrical flair rarely seen in live performance.

From their iconic spaceship prop & science fiction-inspired costumes to rollicking tunes such as *"Chocolate City"* & *"Flashlight,"* the stage was alive with a mesmerizing display of creativity. They were the essence of pure funk, drawing the patterns of space & time around them.

The Parliament Funkadelic took the stage & performed a soulful rendition of *"Atomic Dog"*, the Crip Dogg anthem. It was an awe-inspiring spectacle as thousands of Crips, from various neighborhoods, represented their sets to the groovy tunes. Parliament Funk performed their iconic song, *"One Nation Under a Groove"*, which was the Hoover Groover anthem.

"Hoover Groover, Blood Remover"
-oG Mel P (Nine-Deuce Hoover Crip)

In response, hundreds of Hoovers began to move & groove to the beat, an unforgettable sign of unity that reaffirmed the genuine power of music in bringing people together. It was evident that the infectious music had elevated the spirits of these hardened gangsters to a level of nirvana, momentarily driving away dark pasts & uncertain futures.

As *"Under The Groove"* played the euphoria seemed to spiral into a crescendo with each intoxicating beat. As we swayed & bobbed to the rhythm of the funk, we readied space in the crowd for our best C-Walkers forming a crescent in front of the stage. Fueled by Black Dust paired with Kryptonite, a lethal mix of green Kool-Aid & Silver Satin, feeling invincible & dreaming wide awake. School Boy, Jamaican Mike, and Crazy De-De, our top doggs in the Crip-Walking world, stepped in the center of the massive C formed by blue raggers. It was a thrilling spectacle, our combined talent creating a magnetic pull that drew the crowd.

The trio showcased their mastery & unique flair with the language of footwork, their personalities unfolding before our eyes. School Boy, with a signature move fittingly named *"The Colt 45,"* dropped low like he was ducking bullets & spun with a dazzling whirl, dusting off his Chuck Taylors, his Converse All-Stars scraping the ground as if to etch his presence forever. He shocked & awed the crowd, his performance becoming the stuff of legends within just minutes.

Crazy De-De, the maverick, was always one to set the dance floor on fire. He would blend in his pop-locking skills with his C-Walking, making it an eclectic explosion of movements. Across the Coliseum, heads turned as he slid across the floor, shifting swiftly from a smooth Crip-Walk to a perfect robotic pop-lock that could make Rerun jealous, while his eyes shimmering with the defiant spirit of the Five-Deuce Hoover.

Jamaican Mike was another spectacle altogether. When he took to C-Walking, it seemed as if he was moving on air. He owned the beat break, his moves synced flawlessly with the rhythm, compelling the audience into a euphoric cheer. His C-Walk was mesmerizing, an unforgettable performance.

I couldn't resist it, the gangsta groove was contagious! I joined in Crip Walkin' non-stop, my dance moves in sync with the pounding rhythm. It was a truly liberating moment where the air felt crackling with the potency of our collective soul.

The Crip walk is equivalent to the Indlamu, a very high spirited & energetic tribal war dance performed by our ancestors, the Zulu warriors of South Africa. They both embody a compelling blend of intensity & rhythm, creating a startling spectacle for the crowd. These dances, while entrenched in different cultures, also offer a window into humanity's need for expression. A C-Walker speaks with their feet, covertly communicating our allegiance in celebratory fashion while a Zulu warrior exhibits their might through the stomping Indlamu.

It was surreal standing at the front of the stage, feeling the power of music vibrate through my body as if we were one. As our militia's enthusiasm seemed to peak, our battle cry *"Hooooo-vaa"* rang through the coliseum so profoundly that George Clinton had to urge us to shut up as they began to perform *"Aqua Boogie."*

It was a moment of pure bliss - being chastised by the legend himself was an honor & a memory I'll cherish forever. Their unique energy exuded the essence of funk, and it was impossible not to get lost in their performance. During their song *"Give Up the Funk (Tear the Roof off the Sucker),"* it truly felt as though the coliseum might burst from the sheer power of the rhythm.

By the time they hit *"Knee Deep"* & *"Maggot Brain"*, Insane Fish & I could already feel the intensity of a powerful pull, a surge of unearthly energy that could only be described as the mothership descending, picking them up to new heights in the form of an awe-inspiring & musically divine presence. The intoxicating blend of tight grooves, soulful vocals, and unpredictable musical twists created a psychedelic rollercoaster ride through the outer realms of their colorful universe.

Bathed in the psychedelic glow of infinite colorful stage lights, hyped beyond belief by the energy brought by P-Funk, the crowd found their feet pulsating & moving of their own accord. Unbeknown to them, they were about to be plunged into ecstasy by the main act of that unbelievable day.

At long last, the undisputed master of bass & funk royalty, Bootsy Collins, graced the stage with his larger-than-life presence. With his star-shaped bass – which he nicknamed the *"Space Bass"* – strapped to his body & clad in his trademark glittery top hat & oversized sunglasses. The boots were made for walking, but he was born to strut.

Bootsy Collins, a living legend known for his outlandish stage presence & infectious grooves, Bootsy took the crowd on a cosmic journey with his wild basslines & contagious charisma. As an artist unafraid to explore the boundaries of music, Collins left the crowd hungry for more from the evening's lineup.

Bootsy's trademark extravagance captivated the disco-ball-colored crowd of over 43,000 who now jived uncontrollably. Bootsy's Rubber Band rocked the stadium mercilessly with classics like *"Stretchin' Out," "Bootzilla,"* & *"I'd Rather Be with You."* In that scorching afternoon, Bootsy's persona alone was enough to set the air ablaze. Bootsy & the Rubber Band, brought the house down with his intoxicating blend of classic funk, soul, and psychedelic rock.

In the days leading up to the concert the rumor mill was churning like a muthafucka, its whispers spread through the hood like butter on toast. The gossip was that Bootsy was secretly a Blood & would reveal his allegiance by throwing up the B during his performance. Our response was clear - if he dared to do so, we would storm the stage en masse.

As I stood there, high off the euphoria of black dust, I couldn't help but hope that nothing would spoil the special atmosphere. Instead, the festival brought people together, enabling us to revel in our shared bond, forged by the magic of the music & the funk that we adored. If these Bootsy rumors were true, violence would have erupted, but instead, all 43,000 of us reveled in the spirit of the music.

The song that encapsulated the essence of that incredible night was McFadden & Whitehead's iconic hit *"Ain't No Stopping Us Now."* As the DJ captivated the crowd during each intermission, the song became the event's rallying cry. A testament to the spirit of funk & its unyielding power to bring people together in the name of the groove. The tune infiltrated every corner of the Coliseum. Couples dancing with the fever, the crowd harmonizing the unforgettable chorus, and swarms of fanatics singing it with locked arms illustrated the pure magic of that night.

The Funk Festival was about more than just music – it became a living testament to the profound impact that culture & togetherness can have on even the most hardened social groups. The World's Greatest Funk Festival of 1979 was not just a legendary gathering of talented musicians; it was also the last time all Crips gathered in peace.

We were completely unaware of the tragedy that awaited us. That day would be the last time that all sets of the Crips would come together in fellowship. Soon after, we lost our founder & erupted into a bitter civil war, a terrible conflict that would cleave us down the middle & leave scars that endure even today. Perhaps that catastrophic sequence of events was inevitable.

The very next day, Crip on Crip brutality reached the doorstep of the Five-Deuces. A longstanding beef was ignited, ultimately leading to a rift within the once stable East Side Gangsta Crip alliance. The origin of the beef with the Foe-Trays can be traced back to a football game on Memorial Day Sunday 1979 at Gilbert Lindsay Park in the heart of the Foe-Trays. An altercation erupted, Gangsta Lee, from Five-Deuce Broadway found himself at the center of this conflict & paid the ultimate price: his life.

The death of Gangsta Lee had a significant impact on the dynamics in the area. He was not just any Broadway; he was the baby brother of oG Choo & Captain Rainbow, co-founders, and leaders of

227 | P a g e

the Broadways. In the wake of the Gangsta Lee shooting, the Eastside Gangsta hierarchy underwent a seismic shift. Alliances began to crumble as blood was spilled on the streets, and loyalties previously thought unshakable wavered in the face of deepening divides. Five-Deuce Broadway & 5-Tray Avalon shared South Park. During skirmishes between Foe-Trays & Broadways at South Park, the 5-Trays remained neutral leading to a fall out & Foe-Trays removing "Avalon" from their moniker & transitioning to Foe-Tray Gangsta Crips.

227 | P a g e

CHAPTER TWENTY-FOUR:
GRAND THEFT AUTO 5.2

By the age of 14, life assigned me to the school of hard knocks, compelling me to fend for myself in these streets of turmoil. I no longer had a home to call my own after being exiled by my parents. The comforts & security of my parent's home were yanked away from beneath my feet.

My life was reshuffled, turned upside-down, I was free, but freedom tasted more like survival than liberation. I found refuge on 57th street with the Parker Brothers, I was pretty much living over there & hangin' out with RP. He had a Hoover Household, all his brothers were Hriginals, it was 3 of them, Mad Dogg, Bel-Aire & RP (oG Randy Parker).

RP was the same age as Spookee, the two were as close as kin. He had a knack for masking the audacity of a cold muthafuckin' Crip, behind his pleasant, brown-skinned, innocent baby face. His currency of choice was danger, and he reveled in its thrill. He became an unexpected mentor, introducing me to an underworld of criminal exploits so vivid.

OG RANDY PARKER (RP)

One day, our lives took an exciting turn. RP had developed connections in the jewel trade, one of whom was Ari Davtyan, an Armenian, who owned a Jewelry store in Downtown LA. Ari was making real good money in the jewelry game, but he knew he could make a lot more if he eliminated his competitors. RP had gotten close to the Armenian & earned his trust. The Armenian will provide us insider information on his competitors, which we will use to rob them. We were to pillage their stores while he sat back & watched his rival's downfall in exchange for our services, he would cash us out a hefty percentage of the value.

It was a cold November evening when we met Davtyan in an abandoned building in the heart of Skid Row. The first meeting was under intense scrutiny. He was a tall, broad-shouldered man with sharp facial features that made his Armenian roots quite apparent. He led us through the silk route of contraband. We sat amidst the jumble of old shards of ceramic & metal, glimmering jewels, and lacquered antique.

He was an older man with coarsely tanned skin & eyes like a cobra, his coat smelled of expensive cologne & hidden in various pockets were blueprints of his competitors stores & detailed information on their security systems. His raspy voice echoed against cold displays of diamonds while he detailed his desire for his rival's Crippy blue necklace studded with blood diamonds with an extreme infatuation, as he claimed was worth a fortune.

"My rivals are blinded by greed, so you will rob them blind & leave no trace," he said, his sharp eyes glinting with a scheming gleam. "For this task, 90 large is all yours."

The Armenian was an intriguing character; a tall, stoic man, with a sun-worn face weathered as his hardened demeanor. His piercing gaze & cobra-like eyes were unsettling but held a calculated coolness. In the dim, smoky underbellies of our secret dens, he laid out the plan. We targeted a high-end jewelry boutique in Beverly Hills. Adorned with sparkling diamonds & precious gems, it was a pit-stop for the city's glitterati. RP, BEL-AIRE, and I, armed with the Armenian's precise information, plotted our moves like expert chess masters.

Every night for a week, we camped out across the street under the stars, mapping out the comings & goings of the store personnel, the patterns of security guards, and the positioning of security cameras. RP had already arranged a van for Bel-Aire Johnny as the getaway car. The van belonged to one of RP's smokers & was big enough for all of us to fit in.

I was nervous. I broke into a few houses but nothing of this magnitude, but RP was confident, and his confidence was infectious. We rehearsed our roles repeatedly until we were sure we knew exactly what to do. Then, on a chilly Tuesday night, under the cloak of darkness, we struck. No alarms were breached, no guards were alerted. It was clean & profitable.

The plan was simple. RP, with hands deft as a surgeon, neutralized the door, while BEL-AIRE kept a hawk-eye for any unexpected company. Once we were inside, we used the detailed instructions we'd been provided, we bypassed the security systems, unlocked the vault, and to our delight, gazed at the glittering fortune that rivaled a pharaoh's tomb.

Prior to our escape we smashed the glass cases & grabbed as much as we could before bolting out of there as fast as possible. We were focused & organized, and we didn't waste any time. In just under two minutes, RP & I emptied the entire store & made our escape.

Despite the nerves that hung thick in the air, we executed the operation flawlessly & made away with our illicit treasures, leaving behind a hollow echo as the only evidence of our quickening steps. We ran towards the van, our hearts pounding, and palms sweaty, we threw the booty in the van, and made our great escape.

BEL-AIRE floored the gas, we were like phantoms in the night, slipping away into the veins of Los Angeles, our beating hearts muffled by the thud of heavy jewelry bags & adrenaline. We didn't stop until we were back at skid row. We high-fived each other, chucked up the H & laughed hysterically, as we realized that we had just pulled off the biggest heist of our lives.

Plunged under a shroud of secrecy, we met the Armenian in the veil of the night. The Armenian arrived at the skid row hideout, his eyes wide & a smile sneaking out from beneath his thick mustache as he looked at the stolen goods, his demeanor expressing satisfaction with the heist. With no hassle, he handed us our cut—a whopping $90,000 in cold, hard cash. Every inch of this risky operation was worth it. The money was generously split, and my share was a hefty $30,000, an enormous sum that looked like a ticket to the moon.

I was 14 years old with 30 grand in cold hard cash in 1979, which is equivalent to having 125k today, so I was feeling like Scrooge Mcduck. I was swimming in the money. I'm thinking about all the things I could do with my newfound wealth, and I had a flashback about Bobby, he was hustling with oG Whitey from Five-Deuce Broadway & became a legend in the dope game. Anyway, Cadillac Bobby was getting real money since a young age, a few years ago, he pulled up on the set in a brand new 1977 Cadillac Brougham.

That car was clean. I remember complimenting the groove *"That's a cool ass ride Loc, where you steal that shit from?"* Bobby replied, *"Man this shit ain't stolen I brought it, cash nigga!"*

We couldn't believe cuH bought a Cadillac in 9th grade. We started calling him Cadillac Bobby from Five-Deuce Hoover Gangsta Crip after that. OG Whitey, that's my guy, he would become big time in the dope game, a Los Angeles kingpin, Bobby was a key player of his crew, the infamous Whitey Enterprises.

Cadillac Bobby was a cold playa & a hustler with long wavy hair like Arnold Schwarzenegger in Conan & he got to the colloquial bag as my nephews would say. You remember how Mr. T had all those chains? Bobby was doing it first! I felt inspired by my homeboy & decided I was going to use some of my money to buy my first car, a clean ass gray '64 Chevy Impala Super Sport, this car sold for $3,500 brand new in 1963/64 but today I got mine for $200 from the homie Hub from Five-Nine Hoover.

I gifted myself a Yamaha 125 minibike & Big Walt introduced me to a tailor that revamped my wardrobe, you could put my photo in the dictionary next to fabulous. That summer was becoming one of the best in my life, and I'll always remember it as the time when we pulled off the ultimate heist. It was a dangerous & risky job, but completing missions with my loved ones, that's what made it more special.

Boo got him a muthafuckin Six-Foe! Joyriding in stolen cars was my driver's ed & one of my favorite pastimes, feeling like a king with the wind in my hair & the radio blasting. I never thought much about the consequences of my actions, only about the thrill of the moment.

There's something magical when you're 14. You're still a curious kid, but you're also at the threshold of adulthood, discovering things that would shape your mind & life. It was the middle of summer, and to call it an unforgettable time to be alive would be an understatement.

I was riding my minibike around the Fifties. Little did I know a simple ride through the hood would change my life forever. On this fateful day, my bike's chain popped as I rounded the corner on to the Tray. I cussed under my breath, preparing to deal with the inconvenience.

I couldn't have broken down in a more perfect location, cause when I looked up, I saw her sitting on her porch. A beautiful, exotic Samoan girl, who would become the source of both humor & romance in my life. Her bright caramel-colored skin & vibrant smile were enough to make me fall in lust at first sight. & her body? Let me tell you, her abundant, curvaceous figure with these big ass titties that drove me crazy.

Seizing the chance to introduce myself, I stammered out a flirtatious greeting with a charming grin.

"Hey beautiful, how you doing today? Can I know your name?"

She replied, *"I'm fine, my name's Nakita, and you?"*

"I'm Marcus but everybody calls me Boo" & I agreed with her, *"Hell yeah You fine as hell,"* then I asked, *"why you look so good?"*

She giggled in a flirtatious way, while calling me handsome. I felt an instant connection with her.

We flirted effortlessly, and before I knew it, I found myself genuinely captivated by her. Something about Nakita disarmed me, piquing my interest & igniting a passionate fire in my young heart. Feeling comfortable & confident I made my move; I asked if I could see her again.

Nakita's laughter tickled my heart, captivating me even more.

"Well, why don't you come by tomorrow & hang out with me? I mean you already know where I live."

The next day, still on cloud nine, I hurried over to Nakita's house. Eager & hopeful, I could knock her boots, I knocked on her door, and a moment later, I found myself enveloped in her beauty once again. It was in her presence that I found a temporary hideaway from my vida loca, where I discovered a new side of me.

That night we kicked it on her porch. She had a whole jar of Sherman, my kind of lady! I don't know how this angel face cutie got her hands on it, I wondered if she found it, stole it, or had it for sale but I was impressed & in paradise. I didn't question it. Her deep, dark eyes had such sincerity & openness that I just couldn't help but trust her.

I found a winner with a mayonnaise jar full of Sherman cigarettes, and I was ready to get wet! Cracking open that heavenly jar, the heady aroma of the PCP filled my nostrils, immediately sending a shiver of excitement down my spine. Nakita sparkled under the stars, her eyes reflecting the flickering light as she lit the first cigarette.

What a sight she was, a lady unafraid to live on the edge, yet carrying an alluring innocence. Indeed, I had struck gold! We smoked, got high, and it was there, under the spell of our intoxicating infatuation, that we made love for the first time.

As we lit those Shermans, we watched the rhythmic dance of the smoke, swaying, swirling, and eventually vanishing into the star-lit night, much like our inhibitions. The drug coursed through our veins, casting a hypnotic spell over us, and the world beyond these four porch walls ceased to exist—it was just me, Nakita, and our shared addiction.

In the constellation of euphoria & a psychedelic trip, our hearts started to beat in sync. As each puff caressed our senses, it deepened the colors of the night, painting it with the shades of Roy G. Biv. The tip of the cigarettes glowed like the moon, and each exhale formed illuminating wisps that danced provocatively in the night air.

Our bodies moved in tandem, a seductive dance under the influence of the water & S.O.S Band *"Take Your Time (Do It Right)"*, the perfect vibe for the moment. our conversations drowned in the looming silence, and all that remained was opportunity & lust between us, silent whispers of desire & longing.

The intoxicating infatuation took the form of a sensual spell as we made love for the first time. It began as an innocent exploration; a brush of the hand, a stolen glance, quickly transforming into raw desire. My fingers traced the contours of her face, trailing down her neck, electrifying her skin with my touch. Her breath hitched as she tilted her face towards mine, closing her eyes, ready to surrender herself to the night.

Our lips locked for the first time, and a rush of emotions drowned me—the taste of her lips, the smell of her skin, and the silent whispers of her heart. The teasing continued for a while, burning firework flares coursing through our veins. As I held her close, her honey-coated skin throbbed against mine, radiating warmth that infused into my pores.

Her lips, as soft as the touch of the first snowfall, moved in a ravenous abandonment against my own, the taste of lingering smoke tipping the scales of warm & cold. Her fingers traced riveting symphonies over my naked skin, and her eyes sparkled with utmost vulnerability & trust.

As the record stopped, we explored each other in silence, each inch explored setting new fires that could only be put out by the other's touch. Under the spell of chaotic symphony & heady desire, that moment was beauty interwoven with raw passion.

Our bodies intuitively grooved in rhythm, responding to each other's whispers of lust & secret desires. Her fingers tugged at my hair, pulling me even closer, if that was possible. Those heavenly moments of passionate sex were punctuated by soft gasps & whispers, and erratic heartbeats echoing in the serenity of the night.

Each motion was languid, each second was savored, each gasp was sensual, creating a symphony that resonated with our shared passion. The smell of the PCP mingling with hot sex & our intoxicating chemistry was the only witness to our private celebration of love & togetherness. It was here that our bodies & souls intertwined, pledging to an unspoken promise of desire & mutual passion. That night marked the beginning of our intimate dance – orchestrated by the tantalizing aroma of the Sherm.

The next day, I found myself butt ass naked in her bed with a mixture of feelings; from the dizzying high of PCP, tender love & lust to the confusion that comes with vulnerability when we lower our guards. Part of me knew that I was tiptoeing the line between her & my gang, and I imagined myself too tough to be a tender dick ass nigga.

I have seen a few fools tweaking off the wet running down Vermont Avenue butt ass naked like Smokey in Friday. I'm relieved I found myself butt naked in some pussy & not in ScHool boy's pigeon coop. Over the following months, Nakita & I were inseparable. We began spending more & more time together. I would sneak in her window every night. She became my oasis amid the chaos of South Central LA.

Our sexual chemistry was undeniable, we were getting freaky deaky all day & night whenever, wherever we had a chance. Every heated touch & whispered secret intensified my deepening feelings for her.

I got myself a girlfriend now, and I'm trying to balance my quality time between her & the homies, the homies & her. With every stolen moment away from the set, I felt the oppressive weight of guilt threatened to suffocate me. I was Five-Deuce Hoover Gangsta Crip through & through, and I couldn't betray that part of me.

She had me & they had me, but the homies won that battle. Heartbroken by what I thought was a necessary sacrifice, I chose my gang over Nakita. Little did I know that those months of teenage lust & stolen passion had left their mark

I remember one day, I was cruising down the block in my Six Foe, when I saw a car lot that doubled as a mechanic shop with a bunch of old school cars. My heart started racing with excitement. I went in & talked to the owner, and he had a few cars that needed fixing up. I saw an old school Impala & knew that I had to have it. I put in some work on it & made it look like it came straight out of the showroom. The owner of the car lot was so impressed, he paid me a hefty price & made me an offer I couldn't refuse.

The owner was a short, brown skin cat named Puerto Rican Mike, we got real tight, and gradually transformed into accomplices, bound together by trust & mutual benefit. We became partners in a grander plan, as I became a knight in his court, stealing cars per diem fulfilling his orders. He cashed me out for each completed task. It was the perfect revenue stream so I could stack up the money from the heist.

I soon realized that my operation demanded more hands on the wheel, to keep up with the demand. Just like that, my motley crew was born, Bow Dee, Cadillac Bob, Joker, and Fat Rat. The allure of the easy money, the thrill, and most importantly the dream of my own custom lowrider motivated me.

Our operation was simple, almost elegant in its efficiency. We were night owls, venturing under the cover of darkness & returning with our exploits. General Motor Cars were the prize. Stripping them down, we not only profited from the thriving black market but also left no trace for the pigs. We probably one of the reasons they invented VIN numbers, a mark of my prowess & audacity.

Toolboxes, flow jacks, ratchet keys on hangers: the mechanic shops we stealthily infiltrated provided us with our weapons. Ones that we would wield to dismantle & customize our fleet. The elusive B-10's secret enabled us to crank up any General Motors vehicles, be it Chevys, Cadillacs, GMC or Buicks. The thrill of hearing the engine roar to life & burning rubber in the night made it all worthwhile.

In a calendar flip our operation was more than just a side hustle; it was a well-oiled machine in motion. Our outfit, now bosses of a car theft ring, chop shop & a car club with our custom-made fleet of lowriders. They were a sight to behold, each a testament to our increasingly brazen pursuits.

Reflecting back to those wild years, filled with chaotic energy & the scent of Petro & PCP in the air, they were indeed the best & worst of times. We were knights & knaves, thieves & mechanics, innovators, and destroyers. Every night was a new adventure, every sunrise a new score.

A night that I would later remember as my first brush with death, something unforgettable for an adrenaline junkie like me. My daily life danced a thin line between danger & exhilaration, a rollercoaster ride of reckless youth & the intoxicating freedom it promised. With a cunning twist of my trusty B-10 key, I was slipping in & out of pristine cars with a swift efficiency that danced in harmony with the beat of the night.

I decided to steal a shiny 1964 Chevy Impala, custom-built & impeccably maintained that appeared like a gift from the gods ripe for the taking. She was sleek, shiny, radiant with a candy apple red exterior that spelled 'TROUBLE' in capital letters. Turning the ignition, the massive V8 engine rumbled underneath the hood with a burst of roaring engine & peeling tires, leaving a smoke trail behind as I made off with the car under the cover of darkness.

Breathing in the leather upholstery, the scent of thrill & magic tree air freshener filled my senses. I hadn't planned to, but the temptation was just too strong. It drew me in like a moth to a flame, so I convinced myself to keep it for a day longer before handing it to Puerto Rican Mike. What was meant to be a simple come up became a hell of a night.

The next day I picked up my day one, ScHool Boy. He didn't say a word; he just gave me the head nod with the Grinch's grin that spoke volumes about how much he approved of this beautiful machine. We rode around town all day handling transactions, water burning to the sounds of *"Groove Line"* by Heatwave.

After a long day of selling wet we decided to check some fine young hoochie mamas from the Low Bottoms & bring them back to the Ghetto Safari for some good times. We filled the car with beauties, booties, forties, and Sherm smoke. After a couple fun filled hours of fornication & intoxication, we decided to drop the girls off.

On the way back to the set we had to make a pit stop at a shabby motel that used to be on 45th & Figueroa. There was a veteran woman of the night there that owed ScHool Boy some money for some water & let us run a train on her to settle her debt. We left the motel, pocket full of money, a car full of Acapulco Gold & the best wet in the set, feeling on top of the world. We were engulfed in the intoxicating haze of Sherm & victory.

Just when I thought the night couldn't get better…it got Crip crazy! A quick glance into my rear-view mirror revealed - one time, the pigs, were trailing me, my heart pounding but I played it cool in front of my homeboy, but when I saw the night sky painted with blue & red lights a chill ran down my spine. A teenager in a stolen car full of risk, weed & water. I had two choices: pull over & make their job easy or make these pigs earn it, I chose to put your tax dollars to work!

The stakes were high; the odds were against me, but I had to outrun the law. The chase was wild, riveting. Life bore sharp claws as it threw hurdles at every turn, but that got damn Chevy roared beneath my command, a lion refusing to back down. Beside me, ScHool Boy panicked, the high fueling his fear & paranoia.

"Let me out!" he screamed; the terror strangled his voice to a squeak.

I sneered back, *"What the fuck you mean let you out! Scary Jerry ass nigga!"*

His fear pushed me to drive harder & faster, I was not going back to jail today!

The engine roared beneath us, and I could feel the vicious vibrato of the vintage beast down to my bones, sending thrilling shivers up my spine. I had to become the nightmare every pig is warned about - a young Hoover nigga taking them on a high-speed chase!

Amid the blaring sirens & the screeching of tires the chase was as intense as it was surreal. It was as if time had decided to take a backseat while I took center stage, leaving everything around us blurred & drowned in its wake. Fueled by fear & adrenaline, I pushed the pedal to the metal as we whizzed past buildings & red lights.

Primal instincts commanding my actions, I was so focused on the chase that I didn't notice the cloud of smoke rising from the hood. I was going so fast that candy red couldn't keep up. I erupted the radiator; thick charcoal gray exhaust polluted my vision & lungs. I marvel at the fearlessness of my youth, as I narrowly avoided a crash into the Good Shepherd Church at the corner of the Tray.

With breathless precision, I swerved hard, causing the car to lift up onto two wheels. As the Chevy climbed onto the sidewalk, we kept going, the scene unfolding around us in dramatic slow motion as the car balanced on the brink of disaster. We raced down half the block before the beast gave in, relinquishing control to gravity & it crashed onto its roof.

An origami of twisted metal & crushed dreams, but I'm still here with an unconquerable spirit. We just hung there, upside down, gasping in shock. A cloud of dust, the stench of burnt rubber & gasoline, shards of glass, and a profound silence followed our spectacular crash.

Time is a luxury you do not have when you are being chased by the one-time. In that terrifying stillness, I looked over at ScHool Boy, his wide-eyed panic mirrored in my own eyes. The pigs were closing in, escape seemed impossible, but we were from Five-Deuce Hoover, and impossible was our playground.

In a single, fluid motion, I unclasped my seatbelt, popped open the mangled car door, and scrambled out. ScHool Boy followed my lead with all our contraband. We disappeared into the shadows swiftly & silently –With each beat of our hearts echoing in our head, we managed to escape into the silent embrace of the Fifties. Sitting on my porch, bathed in the diminishing adrenaline rush, I swirled in Sherm smoke & smirked at my exploits while munching on some popcorn.

Suddenly, Spookee appeared, his eyes wide, glistening under the porch light. He looked at me like he saw a ghost. *"Bro, am I trippin'!?!"*

I nonchalantly inquired, *"Are the pigs still out there?"*

He looks at me up & down in disbelief.

"Yeah, nigga they out there looking dumb as hell, tryna figure out how u escaped as much as I am!" he exclaimed, shaking his head.

"I ran to the crash, cuH, the pigs had the car surrounded in less than 52 seconds with their guns out!" His curiosity amused me.

I glanced into the distance, thinking to myself about the night's events, all I could do was shrug my shoulders & laugh.

I replied, *"You know how I groove, Big bro!"*

All we could do was laugh & get high! I had cheated death & the law, all in one night. As I exhaled Sherm smoke into the LA sky, I knew I wouldn't change a thing about it. I lived off high-speed chases, close encounters, and freedom behind the wheel. Life was a thrill, undefined by rules or norms, and I was the lightning bolt streaking through it, leaving a trail of exhaust, burnt rubber, and stolen dreams in my wake.

Amid the chaos & orchestrated anarchy that was embedded within the rise of Hoover Gangsta, was a man I held close to my heart, Big Fat Rat. They say opposites attract, but so do parallels. Big Fat Rat, a complex character who was far from ordinary. He was as unique & distinctive as his persona.

Only two years my senior by 16, he had already managed to build a reputation that would send chills down the spine of even the hardest thugs. In the dim-lit alleyways & graffiti-splattered corners of the Fifties, Big Fat Rat was deemed the Boogeyman, a title he carried both with pride & an evil smirk.

He hailed from a family rooted in Texas, he seemingly manifested a unique trait - he was a big black ass cowboy. Yes, as unbelievable as it sounds, amongst the hardcore Hriginals was an urban cowboy, as sturdy as any steed, a mammoth of a man like a Shire Gelding & as relentless as the dry desert wind.

His cowboy persona was almost comical against his menacing figure & daunting reputation. He would wear his cowboy hat high &

cowboy boots with an air of pride that came naturally to him. His cowboy persona was something that reminded me of the famous wrestler & Texas tough guy Stone Cold Steve Austin. An imposing brute with an aura of unmistakable authority.

Fat Rat & I bonded as avowed animal lovers. In a neighborhood marked by economic strife & racial tensions, his passion for animals was a startling paradox that often left me amazed. Pigeons were his Achilles' heel; he may have loved them more than I did but his adoration for animals extended far beyond our feathered friends. He was a true cowboy that rode horses through the hood, it was common to see him riding down Figueroa with Duck & Hub, two of his cohorts who shared his wild, untamed character.

It was around this time that my oldest brother Don, a man of peculiar interests himself, bought a pony from Hub's uncle who owned the stables on El Segundo & Figueroa. This unexpected transaction led to Fat Rat & my brother developing a close bond, with their shared fondness for horses becoming the adhesive for their friendship. Don would often host pony rides around our yard & up & down the block for the little kids, adding a touch of innocence to our vida loca.

Beyond the maze of streets, we dared to tread & the flurry of fights & brawls we endured, I found something irreplaceable in Fat Rat- an unwavering spirit unbroken by the chaos around us. He was a mystery I was eager to solve, constantly testing his gangsta to see if there was even a hint of fear in his fierce soul. Whether it was our unexpected encounters with red rags or the insane stunts we brazenly executed, Fat Rat never showed a hint of cowardice.

Over time, I constantly tried to discover his weakness, searching profoundly into his psyche for any scary jerry in his soul. I went to unpredictable extremes to spook him, but the results struck me with awe every time. Rather than getting spooked, this dangerous man surprised me with his actions.

Every time he'd turn the tables around, and I was the one spooked! His iron-clad temperament & rock-strong resilience were testaments to his fearlessness. His acts of bravery were not just limited to physically daunting confrontations; he also encompassed his uncanny ability to remain unfazed under pressure.

While I was busy dodging the law, I found an uncanny solace in Fat Rat, he joined me on missions carjacking for Puerto Rican Mike or our personal wants. When we went joyriding in our stolen cars, it was always a rush, a cocktail of fear & adventure. We were fearless & reckless.

Fat Rat was the embodiment of Hoover Gangsta - fearless & unyielding. He wasn't just a fellow Hriginal; he was a force of nature, a titan dressed in human flesh, an enigma that awed me. It wasn't just Fat Rat's mental tenacity that I admired; his physical strength was equally impressive.

In a vivid memory that pushed my admiration for him off the charts. We were chugging Kryptonite working on our low-riders at Duck & Hub's crib. I looked up & he effortlessly lifted a 400 lb. Chevy Impala engine as if it were a sack of feathers & gently placed it in the hood without putting a scuff on his pristine snakeskin cowboy boots. In another display of brute strength, I witness Fat Rat lift & flip over a Volkswagen Bettle

I swear when he put on those boots, he was a different person with unimaginable strength & power that knew no limits. He was, undeniably, a daring rhapsody of anarchy – a man who wore his menacing charisma with an easing nonchalance, personifying the essence of our lives.

One day, Fat Rat was riding a horse up & down Figueroa. The stubborn beast had a mind of its own refusing to obey his voice commands, throwing him off the saddle. Without missing a beat, the infuriated cowboy got up & hit the steed with a swift two-piece combo. Wham, Bam, the distressed neigh was loud as hell before he instantly started snoring.

I gasped, *"oh shit, Fat Rat knocked that Mr. Ed the fuck out!"*

We watched in stunned silence as the beast of a man stood victorious, his strength outmatched that of an adult stallion. When the horse came too, he never disobeyed again! He became the most obedient one in the lot. Fat Rat had proven that he was not a man to be trifled with, not even by a rebellious bronco. After Fat Rat went crazy on that horse, I started calling him *"Crazy Horse."*

In this lawless world of ours, Fat Rat was the embodiment of a Hogg. His presence carried an air of invincibility that I respected & appreciated. He was one homie I'd never try to fight, due to his strength, both physical & mental, he was a country I dared not invade.

BIG FAT RAT THE BOOGEYMAN

In the grand scheme of life, I will forever be grateful for his presence in mine. The pages of our collective history are inked with unforgettable stories of camaraderie & survival. Through all the hard times, Fat Rat taught me the value of a brotherhood that holds strong amid adversity. Today, these tales echo in the silent corners of our existence, serving as timeless reminders of a past splashed with daring escapades & authentic connections.

Fat Rat was not only my crimey but a comrade, a brother, who taught me the true meaning of fearlessness, friendship, and loyalty. He truly embodied the spirit of Five-Deuce Hoover, which was more than a name—it's a lifestyle. My man Ray, the infamous Big Fat Rat of Five-Deuce Hoover Gangsta Crip.

One night Joker & I were up to no good & stole a Ragtop Nova. We had been cruising around town all week in our stolen chariot. It was a beautiful day in Southern California, so we decided to take our talents to a place symbolic of summer: the beach at Santa Monica. Young, wild & free in the city of angels. We couldn't resist the allure of the golden sands & gentle breeze of the Pacific Ocean & of course, the girls – the lovely, sun-kissed pretty young thangs whose smiles glistened like sun rays. It was the perfect destination for some Crip Doggs in heat.

We blasted *"Boogie Wonderland"* by Earth, Wind & Fire on repeat while we cruised down Ocean Ave, my little ass trying to look too cool, as I peered thru my Locs, diamond in the back, sunroof top, digging in the scene with my gangsta lean while we hit on the honeys walking down the avenue.

"Hey cutie, you ever made love to a Crip?" I flirted with every Hottie with a body that came into my crosshairs like I'm God's gift to women.

I'm styling & profiling riding in that machine like it's legal, basking in the sun with my naïve bravado. Two teens in search of a reprieve from the world that had kept us down – even if it meant spending our days as outlaws.

Whoop, Whoop!

Police sirens are now in my rear view. I ignore it, I'm in my own world, thinking, they couldn't possibly be bothering us. I forgot we are still kids. We were smoking, cruising, blasting music like I wasn't a 4'11", baby faced 14-year-old Crip, and Joker, only 13, riding shotgun with his hat brim flipped, an identifier of a gang banger back then, didn't make the situation any better or worse.

The pigs continued to tail us. As my heart raced & my mind struggled to process our predicament, I acted on impulse, making one rash decision after the other. I sped down 5th at 70 mph, desperately trying to shake the pigs.

Panic surged through me, and I committed one last act of desperation. In the face of what felt like the end, I believed I could outsmart the law & evade capture, so I went for it. I made an outrageous decision – I had so much adrenaline I forgot to stop the car. I opened my door, jumped out the whip while it was still moving like I was John Shaft & hit the dash. I left the car ghost riding down the street with Joker still in it! I saw through my peripheral, Joker reaching over fighting to maneuver the steering wheel & avoid a disastrous crash.

My plan was to escape by dipping between houses or try to hide under one. I used to lift the shutters up on the side of a house & hide under there until the heat died down. It was a different time back then with no K9 units to sniff us out.

It seemed like as soon as they announced they were in pursuit of black boys on the radio there was a million pigs everywhere! My escape failed miserably. The pursuit lasted a long 10 minutes of scuffling through alleys & scrambling over fences, I was the epitome of a fish out of water.

I don't know how but the pigs found me hiding in a dumpster on the side of a house. I think they smelled me; I got out that muthafucka stinking with a different kind of funk, a parliament funk! I'll never forget how the pigs laughed while they cuffed me & hauled me off to jail.

I'm so mad, I'm cracked, and I smell like sweaty ass, stale beer & trash. I'm reunited with my crimey, Joker at the precinct. I've been on the run for about a year at this point, I'm thinking they finally got my ass. Luckily, they released us the same day! I think it was because I smelled so got damn bad!

As the 1979 School year kicked off, our bitter rivalry with the Brims was as combustible as a lit cigarette in a PCP lab, liable to explode at any moment. The wrists of the city shook as we clashed, attacking one another with years of pent-up hatred. The heat of the beef bore down on us like the BBQ pit on 54th street, each act of violence stoking the fire just a little bit more.

One morning, the rockin' robins chirping a low tune, as I patrolled the set on my beach cruiser, the cold steel of my revolver jabbing into my waist. Scanning the distant & deserted alleyways, I ran into Joker Crip walking down Budlong.

"What that Five-Deuce Hoover like?" I greeted Joker, the words tasting as familiar as the Sherm that seemingly forever lingered in my mouth.

Joker, his face arched into a smirk, responded, *"5 two whatever I do! I'm on my way to school, cuH."*

Unwilling to let a groove stroll alone in our ripe warzone, I offered Joker a ride, to which he readily accepted. As I savored the potent scent of marijuana filling the air. I took a deep pull & passed it to Joker who took some generous tokes before I hoisted myself onto the handlebars. We ping ponged the jay amidst small talk, our laughter echoing through the ghetto, a little break from the grim encounters of our daily life.

Our moment of peace was abruptly shattered as we passed Slauson. A flare of red invading the corners of my peripheral vision was enough to set my instincts on fire. My heart hammered against my ribs at the sight of a red rag, slippin' while walking to school.

Joker always alert pointed him out. A whisper spilling from his lips, *"Ay, Loc, check this Blood nigga out."*

His words like an ultimatum. The adrenaline rushed through my veins, fury & hatred transmitting through every nerve. Like a bull when he sees the matador's offending red cloth, my only thought was attack.

My lips barely had time to part, uttering a brief warning, *"Hold on, cuH."*

Before Joker could reply, we were in action. Jumping off the bike, Joker & I drew our weapons in sync like we read each other's mind. Propelled by hatred & rage we fired at our enemy.

Later that afternoon we were savoring our victory, when fate decided to pull the rug from beneath our feet. Joker & I strolled down Vermont Avenue on our way to the Foe when we encountered Al Dogg & Wiggles from the Brims. They passed by us without a word, maintaining poker faces to hide their intentions. When they got by the Golden Bird, they attacked!

They blasted away at us, each bullet whizzing past like a deadly harbinger of death. Regretfully we were slipping, naked with no gun. So, we retreated, the Brims ran down 55th toward Budlong, as we scrambled in the same direction down 54th street to Coke Dogg's crib for reinforcements & fire power.

Our duo, now a trio that's armed & dangerous. We run towards Budlong in hopes of intercepting the Brims before they reach their turf. An odd sense of thrill overtook us. The hunt was on! We pursued the Brims, cracking open a round of fire that echoed through the streets. Resembling Yosemite Sam, runnin' & gunnin'.

As we reached the crossroads of Slauson & Budlong, the faint yet distinct wail of police sirens in the distance. When a random older man offered us refuge. His nervous attempts to convince us to hide in his birdcage were red flags, and I hate red flags! The safety he offered felt more like a noose tightening around our necks, and it wasn't long before we figured the truth out. This fool wasn't a good Samaritan! He was a Blood, a pawn in their devilish game, seeking to trap us for the looming pigs to lock us up or for the Brims to kill us. We weren't going to wait & find out either.

As the realization sunk in, Coke Dog, pulled his gun on him. We fired a couple of rounds at him before making a break for it. we scampered across the tracks, back to the set. It was yet another day on the battlefield, another chapter in our war with the Brims.

CHAPTER TWENTY-FIVE:
"HEAT WAVES, BABES & FADES"

Took me about a year to get my low-rider all hooked up. I hooked my Chevy up with a siren, and it wailed just like the police. I remember the first time I hit the block with ScHool Boy, and I let that bad boy sound off, you'd see everyone pull over & I'd just groove through traffic like the Moses of Hoover street. I got real good with cars, one day we were riding through the set & my brakes went out on me, but I had a life hack my Uncle Roy taught me.

I ran into a nearby drug store & got some rubbing alcohol, poured it in the cylinder & fixed that baby right up, and we were back G-riding again in no time. Cruising through the set we saw some girls we knew from around the way, and they were yelling *"Let me ride"* like Dr. Dre, of course we obliged & took 'em back to ScHool Boy crib. We poured up some Kryptonite, smoked some Sherm & did the nasty in the birdcage, today was a good day.

The Six-Foe became my pride & joy. I put all my heart & soul into that car. I would spend hours cruising down the block, feeling like a ghetto superstar. Everyone knew who it was when they heard my siren blaring. I was living the dream of every kid from the hood.

In a way, my Six-Foe became a symbol of hope for me. It reminded me that no matter where we start in life, we have the power to change our circumstances. All it takes is a little hard work & determination. I felt like I could conquer the world in that ride & that's exactly what I did.

I'm riding through the set with my nigga Insane Fish, styling & profiling, being young, wild, and free. My hands firmly gripping the glossy handlebars of my low rider. My heart swelling with pride as I rode through the set, Kool-Aid smiling as the candy paint glistened under South Central's warm sunlight. I hit the switch on the hydraulics, causing the low rider to energetically bounce & perform a captivating three-wheel motion down Vermont, a sight for sore eyes.

As I'm hopping down the road, I saw the homeboys, Whisper & Silence, flagging me down. They were untypical brothers, proud members of Five-Deuce Hoover. What set these two apart from the others was that they were both deaf & mute. The fact that they were born without the ability to hear or speak did not protect them from the complexities of life in South Central. Silence, a natural-born sharpshooter with an uncanny ability to anticipate danger. Whisper was a formidable fighter, skilled in close-range combat.

They had an uncanny ability to communicate in ways that others could not. It was unorthodox, relying primarily on sign language, lip reading, and a generous dose of body language. They managed to adapt to their challenging environment with flair & skill. It was as if they had a sixth sense that kept them informed about the gang's every move. Their connection to one another & the people around them bordered on telepathic.

Despite the challenges, we understood each other perfectly. In our bond lay a peculiar understanding, communication not bound by words, where expressions were just as good . I was amazed the first time I witnessed my deaf homies put their hands on the speaker to feel the music & watch them groovin' to the beat, poetically. It was remarkable that these two could fearlessly navigate life in a world full of pandemonium & peril, where the faintest of sounds could mean the difference between life & death. This held no merit for them, life was just life.

Whisper & Silence, the mischievous duo that kept a trick up their sleeves, had a thrilling proposal for me that day. They mentioned to me through their signs & muted gestures about some fun-loving hotties with bodies from their deaf school who wanted to party & get wild & crazy with the Crips.

Being the cockhound that I was, the idea piqued my interest immediately, I never got freaky deaky with a deaf girl. It was like they read my mind because it was just what the doctor ordered, some new pussy. I told you; I swear they were telepathic.

Without hesitation, we set off to scoop the girls. It shouldn't come as a surprise when I say these girls were fine as china. They were attractive, possessed bodies that would make any boy blood rush &, more importantly, they were ready to get their groove on. A thrill washed over me as we all agreed to head to our usual hangout spot, the Barn.

At the Barn, we built an atmosphere conducive to their liking, complete with weed, PCP, and the bitter-sweet taste of malt liquor serving as our evening's spirit of choice. These girls fell in love with the dangerous allure of our Hoover Gangsta lifestyle. They seemed captivated by the underworld of crime & violence that we inhabited. They were attracted to the thrill of it all, and our authenticity was irresistible.

They got high & unapologetically sought out the pleasures of life's darker side. The air was thick with laughter, merriment, and an unmistakable hint of erotic tension. One thing led to another, and soon a wild, unforgettable night unfolded before us; an orgy that seemed to have come straight out of my wildest fantasies.

I never knew deaf girls were so freaky. The girls initiated the escapade, revealing a side of them that not many were privy to: in the words of the late great Rick James, they were super freaks! As you know there ain't no fun if the homies don't get none, so naturally, I blew the Crip whistle & invited them over. That night, the barn was filled with more than just intoxicated laughter & wild teenage antics - it witnessed our barn transform to the moonlit bunny ranch.

The girls made a variety of unexpected sounds, some simply monotone, others completely silent during our sexual rendezvous. The uniqueness of it all made for some genuinely unforgettable moments. At times, I couldn't help but think to myself, damn, we're really fucking the shit out of these deaf girls, we're going straight to hell for it. It was through this connection that I learned one of the most significant truths of my life. You see, the intricate relationship between the homies & the deaf girls taught me that everyone, regardless of their background or abilities, has desires & fantasies.

Their hearts beat as passionately as ours, and they too yearned for affection & belonging. I couldn't help but recognize the transformative power of my friendship with Silence, Whisper, and the deaf girls. Preconceived notions about disability & vulnerability were replaced by the unshakable realization that beneath all our external differences lies a shared core of love, desire, and resilience.

We showed them a good time & wild nights with the deaf girls became a regular theme in our lives, as they fell deeply in love with the exhilarating world of the groove, craving more of the dangerous allure it promised. They returned often, their youthful curiosities & sexual desires fueling them to share more erotic experiences with us.

We found solace in these shared experiences, as they allowed us to escape our harsh realities for a time. While I was on the run, it was Silence & Whisper who anticipated my every move & steered me clear of harm & capture. Through their cunningness & loyalty, the two brothers proved their worth to Five-Deuce & their comrade in need.

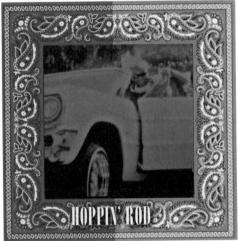

"Don't Stop the Music" by Yarbrough & Peoples blasting from a Chevy bouncing down Vermont, it's my Locsta, Hoppin' Rod. It was the scorching hot summer of 1980, Hoover street steamed from the heat & seemed to come alive by the sheer desperation of people trying to escape the boiling 100-degree hot pot. The air was thick with the aroma of pot & malt liquor, as we tried to find ways to cope with the blazing sun.

Today I'm gang-hanging with Mr. CoCo & Prince Dogg. Prince was ScHool Boy's newest recruit, we were the same age, he recently moved on 51st street from the 20's, an area that became home of the Neighborhood Rollin' 20 Bloods. Prince Dogg gave me a good vibe. I immediately took a liking to him, and he turned out to be a cold-hearted Crip.

PRINCE DOGG & ROSCOE

P-Dogg became infamous for being an unyielding & ruthless gangster infused with charisma & charm. Far from being merely the dangerous tough-talker one would expect, he was also renowned by the ladies for his good looks--a sharp contrast with the unforgiving, gritty environment he called home.

Prince Dogg is a blend of Native American heritage & L.A. street-bred flavor that gave him an exotic appeal. His well-maintained, shoulder-length hair swept down like the wings of an eagle, reflecting his roots, and setting him apart. He was often underestimated, as some were fooled by his appearance, but Prince Dogg was a stern enforcer of the blue flag.

Prince Dogg didn't play games when it came to defending his hood. His hostility towards rival factions was matched only by his love for Hoover & the women who vied for his attention. There was a particular incident that cemented Prince Dogg's notorious reputation.

The eccentric yet fearless Crip once jumped onto a moving city bus, seeking not public transportation but a moving fortress. The mission? A daring drive-by assault on the Brims. This harrowing act underscored the commitment; the level of intensity he employed towards his loyalty to FDHGC & his unmitigated hatred towards the Bloods.

The feeling of youth & invincibility was definitely in the air. It was like the world was ours for the taking, and nothing could hold us back. We decided to go to the Exposition Pool on Bill Robertson lane -

our oasis in this vast urban desert. The sun shone bright above us, casting a warm, golden glow over everything & everyone in its path.

As we arrived at the pool, we were greeted by the familiar blend of sounds – music, laughter, and splashing water that conjured up memories of previous summers past. I eased myself into the water, taking in the refreshing coolness as it enveloped my body like an ice cold frosty Olde English.

We were having a great time at the pool, wading in the water, swimming laps, and showing off our acrobatic dives to the honey's sitting poolside sunbathing. We couldn't help but hit on the beauties spectating in hopes of a summer fling. We approached them with our best suave smiles, bold enough to make them blush & smooth enough to make them want more, because there is nothing smoother than a Hoover Groover. We found ourselves gang-hanging on cloud Fifty-Two, thinking to ourselves, today was a good day, as Ice Cube would say.

I'm kicking game to a thick chocolate girl with a lovely perfectly formed natural & gigantic titties busting out her orange bathing suit, the type that I adore. The sudden appearance of red rags appeared in my peripheral, so I tapped the Locs, told them to be on high alert. Prince Dogg, tells us he knows them & grew with them. Their leader swaggering around like he the king of the pool, as they approached us.

"What that Twenty Blood like?" their leader asked menacingly, sizing me up as though attempting to find some point of weakness through my gaze.

I replied without hesitation, with a confident & defiant tone, "nigga I dunno, I know this Crip, Fool! Five-Deuce Hoover, Blood remover!

They call out Prince Dogg, *"Yo James! What you doing with these crab niggas!?!"*

After a heated exchange of words, a fierce brawl of epic proportions played out. I knew these niggas were seeking revenge. They weren't happy with the outcome of my altercation with their partner, Pistol Pete. We were always up for a challenge, so we gave them what they were looking for.

An epic showdown between original members of Five-Deuce Hoover Gangsta Crip & Rollin' Twenties Neighborhood Blood. I ran the fade with their leader, a kid named Vaughn, he later became known as *"Santa Klause"*, folklore says he got the name for killing a Crip on Christmas, then making it an annual tradition.

We just needed Michael Buffer to introduce us, *"let's get ready rumble!"* The air was thick with tension as I squared up against Santa Klause. Sweat poured down our faces, my skin glistened under the intensely hot sun radiating black power. We could feel the weight of our gang's reputation resting upon our shoulders. The wrong move could mean humiliation or defeat. We refused to be intimidated.

The showdown Boo Capone versus Santa Klause, we roared into battle, fists flying & feet slashing through the air. Our bodies collided with the force of a thousand suns, each punch & kick sending waves of pain through our bones. Santa Klause & I traded blow after blow, locked in a tussle. Our fists moved like lightning, and I could feel every punch, every strike, like a raw, visceral expression of the tension between every Crip & Blood in Los Angeles.

It was a test of strength, skill, and willpower as we pushed our limits to the breaking point. We understood the rules of the game, having been raised on the same mean streets, we engaged in a dogfight for the pride of our respective hoods.

Our homeboys locked in their own skirmishes, blue & red rags clashing violently as we pitted ourselves against one another. Grunts, gasps, and profanity filled the air, punctuated only by the sound of fists hitting flesh & bodies slamming against concrete, trading haymakers like heavyweight fighters locked in the most intense match of their lives.

The air around us was filled with the sounds of struggle as the battle wore on, both sides immersed in a primal dance of manhood & machismo. We lived for this, deep down we loved the danger we faced. We couldn't ignore the thrill of it all, knowing gossip & rumors of our epic battle would add fame to our names & gang throughout the City of Angels.

Santa Klause & I had had one hell of a squabble; respect & victory seemed to hang by a thread & fluctuated with every hit. We couldn't escape the fact that we were all prisoners of this life we had chosen. We could knock each other down a hundred times, but it wouldn't change the circumstances. Our world would continue spinning in its own terrible, yet beautiful revolution. Admitting defeat wasn't an option.

Eventually, the lifeguards & security guards descended on our impromptu rumble & broke up the fighting, then pigs appeared! I was still on the run, so we fled to my Six-Foe, the bloods nursing their wounds & escaping towards their getaway vehicle. It was clear that we were the victors of this skirmish. After the rumble, there were rumors that 6 of us jumped Vaughn but it was a head up fade. Santa Klause was a worthy adversary, he just couldn't beat me. Looking back, I realize, we all wanted the same thing– power, respect, and to be ghetto gangstars.

Despite the hatred that fueled our fight, there was an unspoken understanding - a mutual respect - between us. As we exchanged blows, we came to acknowledge each other's tenacity & strength. Consequently, we earned something priceless in the process: each other's recognition & respect.

That day at the Exposition Pool was indeed a good day. We got to do some gang bangin', created new war stories & memories, shared laughs with my homeboys & flirted with pretty girls. Nightfall came, we nursed our war wounds, sipped on 8 balls, and smoked some water, recounting the highlights of the day.

We knew that we had created a memory that would last a lifetime. That day at the Exposition Pool was more than just a summer day spent trying to escape the sweltering heat; it was a testament to the strength & unity of our tribe & a reminder of what we were capable of when we had each other's backs.

Summer '80 was nothing but heat waves & fades. When the Brims wanted trouble, they came right to my block, 52nd & Hoover. I was always ready & available to provide Frontline Defense from day one. I made sure everybody that lived on my street claimed Five-Deuce, the only way around it was move your ass off my block.

Sugar Bear wasn't like the rest of us. Sure, he had the swagger, he had the nerve, and he had the street smarts that even the smartest men lacked. Sugar Bear was from 56th street & an original Untouchable Block Brim, his brimmin' predated FDHGC, but the rest of his family was from Hoover, and I had Fifty love for him.

As the homeboy, Chino's older brother he was given a pass to live among us, protected by a shroud of Fifty loyalty & endearment that transcended the everlasting war between Bloods & Crips. That pass grew into a priceless & timeless bond. We got so tight, he even gave Bow Dee & Lil Live their names. There also came a time when the Brims thought he had become a Hoover Gangsta!

This unique position within the two worlds allowed Sugar Bear to bridge the seemingly unbridgeable gap between the two rival hoods – the Hoovers & the Brims– he ultimately paved the way for what became an unorthodox form of camaraderie. Sugar Bear was an advocate for Hand-to-Hand combat. He recognized my influence & one day he approached me with an offer I couldn't refuse.

Sugar Bear came to me & said *"I got a proposition for you, Boo get your best 5 & we go to Harvard Park."* He continues his proposition, *"Y'all can squabble with whoever y'all want...I guarantee a fair fight...win or lose!"*

He loads up in his wagon with 5 Hoover Gangstas, Bow Dee, Big Fat Rat, T-Dogg, JoJo & I & takes us on a Hoo'ride. Together, we made the perilous journey across enemy lines to Harvard Park, a Brim stronghold. This wasn't a typical gang outing – we were about to engage in a friendly 5-on-5 fistfight with members of the Six-Deuce Brim.

Sugar Bear, was a shot caller in his own right, set up some ground rules with the other Brims. He made it clear that the Hoovers were under his rag, and he personally vouched for us. This ensured that the skirmishes remained on fair terms, with only one-on-one battles & no weapons allowed.

I loved it, I didn't care about the risk! I was a risk taker! I used to ask him to take us over there every week! This is Hoover Gangsta Crip, I ain't scared of no blood! Some homies were reluctant to go but don't get it misunderstood they weren't scared to fight! They had every reason to be reserved about trusting Sugar Bear, who wore the enemy colors. They had genuine concerns.

"You can't trust that nigga," they'd say. *"He's a red rag, and we know how they operate. They'll just shoot us up if we go to their turf."*

I listened. The homies had valid points, so I made a proposal to Sugar Bear, cause I didn't want anyone to miss out on the action.

"How about you bring some Brims over to us to squabble on our turf."

Sugar Bear was quick to debunk my idea. He explained how fostering a battle in the wrong location could easily spiral out of control.

"That isn't possible," Sugar Bear replied, shaking his head. *"I can't control the Crips, and my influence only extends to the Brims. You know my whole family, Boo, haven't I proven you can trust me."*

I nodded my head in agreement, I mean he was right, there were too many variables. We had too many hot heads & trigger-happy young Crips on our side. One of the homies could easily become bloodthirsty & shoot up all of them including Sugar Bear. Sugar Bear's actions spoke louder than any claims he could have made.

He put himself in the line of fire for these meetings. He proved he commanded much respect from the red team. I already witnessed they wouldn't shoot at us while we were with him or go against anything he said. The Brims knew they had to fight for him or there would be consequences & repercussions. I respected it, and I was having a great time beating on Brims, so I relayed the invitation to the homies.

I continued to go over for skirmishes with the Locs that dared to groove with me. We were over there so often; we began to know them by their gang names & real names. Over time, the weekly challenges became more than just fights they evolved into a means of fostering relationships among two rival hoods who once saw each other only as enemies.

It was evident that Sugar Bear's efforts had cultivated a sense of understanding & respect that could never have been possible otherwise. Sugar Bear showed us a way to release our aggressions without gunplay. More Hoovers began joining us on our ventures, and to everyone's surprise, the tension temporarily started to ease. What Sugar Bear accomplished was indeed revolutionary.

In an era of gunfire & bloodshed, he managed to unite two rival hoods through the power of unity & respect. Though we all remained loyal to our respective turfs & identities, the weekly challenges gave us an opportunity to see each other through various perspectives. Sugar Bear's gave us a reminder of the common humanity that united us as young black men behind our colored bandanas & gang ties.

If a single Brim living in the heart of enemy territory could foster positivity, unity & understanding across seemingly insurmountable divides. It begs the question: What could our society achieve if we let go of our prejudices & extended our hand in brotherhood, just like Sugar Bear did? I wish we kept this thing going. It would have saved so many lives on both sides but instead it fell on deaf ears & blind eyes.

The Summer of 1980 was everything you'd expect it to be - hot, dry, and a seemingly never-ending stretch of days that swirled together like an endless, blurry dream. Looking back, it might have been indistinguishable from any other summer, were it not for the coming of age of a particular youngster that, despite everything, managed to shake up our little world in ways none of us could have predicted.

In every neighborhood, every school it seems like there's always that new kid that nobody likes. It doesn't have to be for any good reason, but once they set foot into your life, they're immediately sized up & bothered because, most people fear change, but with Jerome, it wasn't so easy to find a reason to dislike him or mistreat him, this kid was real likable.

Growing up in the Fifties was never easy. It was a place that could make or break you, a place where you had to be tough to survive. For Jerome, that toughness came naturally. He was always the kind of kid who never backed down from a fight, who always stood up for himself, his beliefs, and his friends.

My nigga Jerome, that is my boy! I love that man; he could have been Lil Boo Capone & he wanted to be. I can still hear him saying *"Ay, Big Homie you know I was supposed be your #2."* Boscoe was about five years younger than me, so he was about 10 years old at that time. Despite his age, he seemed to possess an aura that demanded respect, and that more than anything else is what gravitated me to him.

Jerome was a bad ass lil nigga that stayed with a pistol. He was claiming a Mexican gang called the Harpy's, they were from an area north of the University of Southern California. The Harpy's had taught him to fight for his respect, his turf & protect his homeboys. At a tender age, Jerome was already a gangsta, he moved on the turf at 7 years old & was already claiming. I quickly learned he was willing to do whatever it took to protect his turf & his loved ones.

I'd harass Jerome about turning Five-Deuce every time I saw him, but he'd always shrug it off, saying that he wouldn't betray the Harpy's. It was a stance that you couldn't help but respect, no matter what hood you represented. Even CoCo couldn't help but be impressed by his fearlessness. CoCo was an imposing & intimidating figure. More than anything, CoCo wanted to bring Jerome into the set, and his powerful presence usually made most people submit to his will without resistance, but not this kid.

It was a time when tensions were high, and anyone who wasn't part of Five-Deuce Hoover was seen as an outsider. One day, CoCo decided to test the young Jerome's gangsta. CoCo gave him numerous chances to change his mind, but he would not sway. As the years went by CoCo's patience began to wear thin & Coco felt it was time.

One sweltering afternoon, CoCo issued a final ultimatum: *"Join Hoover or else lil nigga."*

All I could do was shake my head as Jerome looked up at the towering figure & stubbornly shook his head & says *"Or else lil nigga!"*

Reaffirming his loyalty to the Harpy's. He couldn't have known then just what the consequences of his decision would be. I'm thinking CoCo is about to beat this little boy to death or Jerome is going to shoot this big ass nigga. CoCo was known for having a short fuse, and it didn't take much to ignite it, he always chose violence over diplomacy.

In that moment, it wasn't a question of if CoCo would act, but rather when. The simmering tension finally exploded. Here comes the violence, and Jerome took his beat down like a champ. It was a brutal end to an otherwise normal summer day. I remember feeling something like a deep sadness as I watched his once proud face crumple under CoCo's blows, but this was just how things went down around the way.

In the days that followed, there was a noticeable shift in Jerome's demeanor. Jerome ran with the Hriginal Baby Crips- WisH Dogg (Lil Spookee), Lil Dee (Devil), Lil Bam, C-Dogg, Chino, Big Man, Lil Man, Crazy Aye, Lil Bandit & Gee Man. They began to do dirt & put in work that would foster bonds similar to myself & the Fifty Boys.

Manuel Arts was originally a Brim stronghold, and these years were the infancy of a new order that has changed the identity of the school to Crip ever since. The 1979-81 freshman classes introduced an era of change at Manuel Arts High School, during these years the Crip sets were entering High School.

The homies invaded Manuel Arts with an influx of Crips. Hoover Gangstas, Five-Deuce Broadways, Five-Nine Hoovers, and the Harlems, pretty much all the incoming 8th & 9th graders from John Muir, Bethune, Foshay & Adams were Crips. We developed an alliance with the Harlems called *"Hoover-Harlem."*

CHAPTER TWENTY-SIX:
"PITY & PAYBACK"

Once upon a time, all Crips got along, the streets of Los Angeles had given birth to a different kind of family - one that found solace in shared battles in the face of adversity. The Crips, united under the blue bandana, awash in the undying loyalty & fierce allegiance that flowed through our veins. We shared what we thought was an unbreakable bond, but in reality was a powder keg ready to explode.

This is the story of how it all came crashing down, shattering the once strong unity that we shared & replacing it with an inescapable divide that assassinated our unity forever. A series of events occurred that led to certain Crip gangs being blackballed by the Hoovers & the Gangstas that led to the formation of the Neighborhood alliance.

Unfortunately, most of the Crip on Crip conflicts were over dick & pussy, the concept of *"bros over hoes"* held no weight within the fold. Once the killing started, there would be no turning back, machismo would prevail & diplomacy would fail, mostly because we made no attempts to be diplomatic, it was shoot first, ask questions...NEVER.

At this point in Crip history, a lot of the Original Gangstas were incarcerated or killed leaving next generation Crips in conflict to fend for themselves. With no one to mediate, these gripes escalated & spiraled out of control. The One-oh-Seven & Eleven-Deuce Hoover have beef with Underground, Block, N-Hood & Nine-O, Hoover-Broadway has friction with East Coast & Foe-Trays, Eight-Tray Gangstas have drama with Sixties, and Tray-Foe Hoover have conflict with Six-Five Menlo.

We fell out with the East Coast Crips early in the game. We used to be Crippin' cousins. We used to gather for football games. Our sets would meet up & engage in fierce but friendly battles on the gridiron. The games involved Hoover Gangsta, Five-Nine Hoover, Five-Deuce Broadway, and the 6-Pacc. Most days, the field would come alive with the passionate cries of the players & the excited hooting & hollering of the spectators.

We felt that in those precious moments of fellowship, we could transcend the harsh realities of our lives & find a sliver of lining. Unfortunately, a lot of us including myself already had a deep seeded resentment for them since the Broadway abduction in 1979. So, every time we met up something went down, every scrimmage ended with a fight or shootout.

It was a hot summer day in 1980, when the members of Five-Deuce were playing football with the 6-pacc. The sun was unforgiving, and the heat from the asphalt was generating stifling temperatures, reaching a hundred degrees. However, distractions such as heat & exhaustion had never deterred us from a good time.

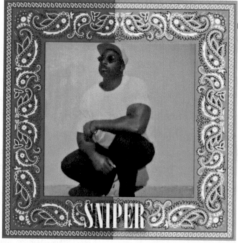

It was during this ill-fated game that the thin threads of our unity began to unravel. Our tale begins in Los Padrinos Juvenile Hall, an institution designed to reform wayward youth but often served as a pressure cooker, intensifying the tensions between enemies. It was here that Sniper – then a member of Five-Deuce Broadway – first crossed paths with his future nemesis, Ghost, from the Six-Deuce East Coast.

Fates colliding within the unforgiving walls of Los Padrinos, the two young Locs found themselves entangled in a brutal squabble. Without a doubt triggered by the potent cocktail of loyalty & pride that fuels all gang feuds, the confrontation saw Sniper come out on top.

As punishment, both were sent to solitary confinement. However, circumstances intervened, and Sniper was released before the two could properly settle their beef, since no rematch occurred the embers of resentment were left to smolder.

Fast forward to 1980, Fate had not forgotten what happened at Los Padrinos, its shadow materialized as Sniper found himself face-to-face with the very man who had suffered defeat at his hand's many years ago. Seething with anger but keeping his emotions hidden, Ghost approached Sniper, shaking his hand & offering him a joint, a seemingly peaceful gesture.

Sniper, oblivious to the remnants of the grudge that Ghost nurtured, took the olive branch. As if the bad blood from their past could be dissolved by the haze of marijuana smoke. In our world, old grudges are not so easily forgotten, and the mask of friendship belied a darker truth - Ghost still harbored hatred, fueled by unsatisfied vengeance.

Suddenly, the crowd erupted into madness as the Crip'lettes from East Coast started in-fighting. Punches were thrown, hair was pulled, titties were out, and the scoreboard faded to irrelevance. Caught up in the brawl, everyone failed to notice Ghost slipping away. We remained blissfully ignorant of the storm brewing within Ghost's mind.

As we exited the park amongst a deep blue sea of Crips, the evening took a sinister turn. Ghost came sprinting from his hiding place, he fired a single shot at Sniper, striking him in the ass. Then vanished back into the shadows faster than I could blink, his mission of vengeance now complete.

> "I always gotta worry about the payback some
> punk that I roughed up way back. Comin' back
> after all these years. Rat-a-tat-tat-tat-tat- that's
> the way it is"
> - Tupac Shakur, "Changes"

From that day forward, we ceased social activities with the Coast. Sniper was a man on fire consumed by a burning desire for revenge. Several times he caught glimpses of Ghost, lurking among the Harlem Crip territory, but each encounter he either managed to vanish like a phantom or the Harlems acted as his savior.

In the end, Ghost passed away before Sniper could avenge himself - the specter of vengeance left to haunt the alleyways & street corners of a city that had fostered countless rivalries & lost countless lives in the ongoing war for supremacy. Sniper's story is a testament to the tragic realities of life in the ganglands of 1980s Los Angeles - a world where vendettas could upend entire lives, and where the line between friend & foe was as blurred as the smoke of a fat joint.

The Hoover Collective took note of the East Coast mimicking our tactics by expanding their factions with numerous subsets. Resentment bubbled beneath the surface, a simmering pot that threatened to spill over & ravage the connections we had fought so hard to maintain. It was as if these powerful, passionate emotions stirred within us a need for dominance & territorial control, slicing away any remaining loyalty we had to one another.

Inevitably we reached the point of no return. The once-valued camaraderie between us collapsed, swallowed into the unforgiving abyss of gangbangin' & leaving a fractured & broken fraternity in its wake.

The triumphs & struggles we once shared, were lost amidst rage & betrayal. We may have once battled as a united front in the unforgiving underworld of Los Angeles, but it was our own inability to prevent the implosion of our fraternity that marked the true downfall of our union. Our sets have forever been altered, the unity we once held slipping from our grasp like the sands of time.

There are no victors here, only a failed fellowship. This is our cautionary tale, a lesson in the fragility of relationships & the consequences of resent left to simmer. As we continue to walk our separate paths, we can never forget the memories of the brotherhood we shared, and the world we lost to unforgiving rivalry.

Summer days come & go, as the streetlights cast a dim orange glow over Hoover Street. In the fading moments of dusk the distant sound of sirens blended in with the rhythmic hum of the city. It was another one of those nights when anything could happen, good or bad, so Joker, T-Dogg & I were out patrolling the set.

The air felt heavy with the knowledge that our enemies knew what this street, Hoover Street, meant for us. They would seize any opportunity to come through our territory, to disrespect or hurt us & our family. We were constantly aware, and always prepared, we call it Frontline Defense.

As we strolled down the street, our eyes were always vigilant on point for any signs of trouble or suspicious activity, our attention was drawn to some freshly painted graffiti on a brick wall on the Tray. The unmistakable shade of red, set off alarm bells in our heads, and we exchanged uneasy, knowing glances.

"Must be one of them Blood niggas," T-Dogg muttered under his breath.

This was a bold message to us that the enemy was operating right under our noses. We crept closer to this fool, adrenaline pumping through our veins as the trespasser came into view.

"What that Five-Deuce Hoover like, cuH?" I asked, trying to bait the trespasser.

"I'll blast this fool right now groove!" Joker chimes in with aggression.

T-Dogg's hand slid into his jacket, gripping his trusty .32 that he stole from my baby mama's father. We could feel the weight of the situation bearing down on us, and we knew that our next move could make or break us.

It was strange that we called out to him, giving him a chance to explain or react. We usually wouldn't give that luxury to someone disrespecting the set. T-Dogg & Joker were ready to put in work & silence this fool without delay, but something deep down told me to stop them. Maybe I wanted this fool to look us in the eyes before we blew him away or maybe something about him seemed familiar.

As he turned to face us, his can of spray paint still in hand, recognition dawned on us. He wasn't a Blood; it was the homie Buddha's older brother. Buddha was a certified Five-Deuce Hoover-Broadway that moved on 53rd street.

His brother – standing there in front of us dressed like a Mexican cholo with a shocked expression – was named Virgil but we called him, Ronchie. Ronchie had moved around the way from East Los claiming a Chicano barrio called VNE, Varrio Nuevo Estrada. Ronchie was striking out WF propaganda, VNE's bitter rival, White Fence. In a way, we respected Ronchie for lashing out at WF & representing his set, but this is Crip, and we were not allowing any VNE or WF activity in the Fifties.

We pressed Ronchie about his affiliation with VNE. We tried to recruit him into our ranks – surely, since he was Buddha's brother, should already have a sense of loyalty to the brotherhood we formed in the Crips. Unfortunately, it wasn't so simple. Ronchie was infatuated with the Ese' culture, and his priorities lay elsewhere. Ronchie could squabble & I wanted him in our ranks.

Nevertheless, we continued to push our line religiously scouting & recruiting, especially since we kept adding new enemies to our hit list. Youngsters are the lifeblood of a set, but our counterparts from Foe-Tray seemed to view them as a liability, prone to violent, and initiating conflicts, Hoover Gangsta excelled at this.

The Foe-Trays were an older regime primarily focused on hustling & getting money. They didn't subscribe to gangbanging, they didn't even trip on the Bloods like that. Even though Foe-Tray Hoovers were not known to color bang they defended their territory with grit & honor.

Here enters Flash & Killer Kev from w 42nd street with dreams of being Hoovers via Foe-Tray. For reasons still buried in mystery, the Foe-Tray's had put a halt to new members back in 1978. It was a hard blow to their shared dream, but it did not deter them.

Flash had formed a kinship with the homies Hoover Bam & Gangsta Crazy based on shared childhood experiences & memories at Dee's arcade on 43rd street & Vermont Ave. This relationship played a vital role. These interactions functioned as the bedrock on which Flash built his aspirations, leading to them adopting the *"Hoover Gangsta"* moniker.

Flash & Killa Kev were influenced to embark on the formation of an extension of FDHGC, Foe-Deuce Hoover Gangsta Crip. Inspired by the Hoover multiplication of 1979, we felt adding numbers to the Hoover Gangsta brand would make our movement stronger. The decision seemed in tune with Flash & Killa Kev's ambitions as a Hoo'rider. The Hriginal Foe-Deuces included fierce warriors like Flash's uncle oG Half, an original Five-Deuce Broadway, Killa Kev's little brother Tiny Loko, Lil Ten Speed, C-Ratt, Rattone, Creep Dogg & the homegirl Lil Bit to name a few. I always admired Flash – a resolute, brash youngster who dared to chart his own course.

LIL MOUSE, C-RAT, HALF, SMOKEY, FLASH

My homies were initially skeptical & eager to test their gangsta & make them earn their respect, thus the initiations began. They endured raids from Foe-Trays & Five-Deuces. I enjoy playing mind games with new initiates. Today, I decided to introduce Flash & the Foe-Deuces to a world beyond their comfort zone & test their gangsta.

Beckoning them to cross into the heart of enemy territory, an apartment complex known as Death Lane to buy PCP. Death Lane was a fortress where you could find a hundred Coast at any given time.

Yes it's true, you're right, this is madness, it's war time. It was a death sentence for the average Hoover but not for Big Boo Capone. Of course, we were armed & dangerous, anything else would be uncivilized. The Coast dangerous eyes scrutinizing our bold incursion in full Hoover Gangsta uniform with golf hats displaying *"FDHGC"* on the flipped brim.

As we walked closer, there was a sudden hush, and then whispers began to ripple across the crowd. We could hear the rising murmurs & the suppressed anxious breaths of our enemies. Suddenly, a voice well-known to me pierced the chilling silence. Docthone, one of the pioneers of the Coast, recognized me, diffusing the tension.

He shouted, *"That's Boo Capone. They good, leave 'em alone, cuH!"*

Flash looked at me, awestruck by the respect I commanded. Even on enemy turf, I managed to earn grudging admiration, a status

Flash was yet to achieve. It was his first taste of duality, the grim crisscross where friends could easily become foes & vice versa.

This camaraderie wasn't unusual, it is just absent now. Our Crip love was born years ago during football games we played at Bethune. Bub, Docthone, Casper, and I formed an unbreakable bond. The trio, groundbreakers for East Coast, and myself for Five-Deuce Hoover. We fought side by side against the Swans & Brims. We had slogans of unity, one being *"Hoover-Coast Do the Most."*

I remember the day when the homegirl, Smokey warned me of Coast trespassing on our turf. My instinct screamed danger, my hand gripping my weapon, ready to put it to work. I pulled up ready to spray, I saw Docthone & Casper, old memories resurfaced, outweighing the current reality.

I couldn't pull the trigger instead I went over to speak with them. The conversation that ensued ended with my Crip comrades being extended a courtesy, a pass to get out of harm's way. That incident ignited a mutual respect between us. Every time we crossed paths, he extended the same courtesy, saving me from several detrimental situations.

In our world respect was a currency more valuable than gold, and strength was measured on the battlefield & by the ability to resist inevitable conflict. This incident was a turning point for Flash. He realized that power is not just about having more soldiers or carrying bigger guns.

It's about earning respect, maintaining old relationships, and showing bravery when no one else dares. It was his first time being around the enemy without engaging in combat, and he came through it unscarred. Stronger & more committed to our cause, but the Foe-Deuces would have a short life span. Flash caught a case & during his 2 year absence, the Foe-Deuces had slow growth & chose to consolidate into Five-Deuces by 1983.

A few weeks later, the night air was thick with hostility, the smell of gunpowder & hatred engulfed the atmosphere like cheap cologne. The sky had faded to the deep bruise of twilight. The Coast were cruising around the Fifties in a fleet of six vehicles. Their intentions, catch a Hoover slippin'!

Our veins were overflowing with adrenaline as we heard engines & screeching tires before we saw them. The Coast spotted

Ronchie outside of Young's Market, mistaking him for a Hoover, they attacked him. Their plan backfired, Ronchie, an elite street brawler, was not going down without a fight. The threat only brought out the monster inside.

Ronchie, was quick to retaliate, landing solid one-hitter quitters that dropped them one by one like dominoes, three rivals laid on the pavement. The resounding thumps of the bodies hitting the asphalt triggered the cavalry. More Coast poured out from their cars like a Forty ounce for the dead homies.

From a block away, my homies & I witnessed the battle royale. Without skipping a beat, we charged towards the brawl. CeeCee, Buddha & Jerome emerged from the store, right as things began to look grim for Ronchie. The tables turned, outnumbered & overwhelmed, the East Coast beat their feet & made a hasty retreat. We began to unleash hellfire upon the enemy's getaway vehicles.

> *"I will strike down upon thee with great*
> *vengeance & furious anger those who attempt to*
> *poison & destroy my brothers. & you will know*
> *my name is the Lord when I lay my vengeance*
> *upon thee."*
> *- Samuel L. Jackson as Jules, Pulp Fiction*

Before the staccato soundtrack of gunfire & screeching tires could fade out altogether, T-Dogg showed off his skills, expertly shooting out their tires & causing one of their cars to swerve into a fire hydrant. Water erupted into the night air like a geyser as the Coast scrambled from the wreckage, trying desperately to escape.

The Coast fled for their lives, deserting one of their homegirls. T-Dogg & Baby Crazy quickly apprehended her, now she was at the mercy of the Hoovers. The girl's piercing screams filled the oppressive air around her.

"Shut the fuck up, bitch!" Baby Crazy demands.

Her wide eyes like a deer in headlights glancing from one unrecognizable face to another in a pointless search for a friend. Abandoned & broken, she found herself behind enemy lines.

I grabbed her by the hand, and told her, *"Be cool."*

I guided her toward our hideout on the Tray, as we cheered & celebrated our victory against a thwarted lethal ambush. It was a dark testament to the times in which we lived that this woman, now a prisoner of war, became a token of our victory, a trophy of our power over our foes.

In the dimly lit room of our makeshift hideout behind Giggalo's crib, the intoxicating smell of PCP & Kryptonite mingled with the sounds of *"Let's Groove"* by Earth, Wind & Fire from the boom box.

I became the friend she was searching for. Looking into her terrified eyes, I offered her reassurances, presenting her a dixie cup full of Kryptonite & some smoke to calm her nerves.

"You good, on Crip, we ain't gonna hurt you, we just gotta make your punk ass homies sweat a lil."

She proceeded to get sky-high with us, she let her guard down. As she exhaled some lovely smoke, she poured her heart out.

"Y'all niggas is gangsta as hell, and cool as a muthafucka. I ain't gonna lie, I like y'all Hoover niggas," The Coast'Lette confessed.

"Them bitch ass niggas ain't even look back for me," she continued.

She began flirting with us, seducing us with lustful eyes. She went from victim to Vanessa Del Rio, a legendary porn star. She gave the homegirls head & invited her rival gangbangers to a gangbang in an act of sexual liberation.

We had a good ass time with her, she earned our pity, so we let her go. While she was walking back to the eastside, she went the wrong way, and ran into Spookee, who pressed her about being on the set, she offered him sex as well, they took off into the shadows for a rendezvous.

A couple days later I was on the block with Insane Fish & a couple other Grooves, when some East Coast pulled up to set trip. Seeing the danger, young Jerome showed incredible bravery & loyalty when he whipped out his revolver without hesitation.

With a determined yell that still echoes in my mind, he screams *"This Five-Deuce Hoova, bitch!"*

His fierce proclamation was quickly followed by the deafening sound of gunshots, he starts shooting at the Coast until his gun is empty! The Coast scramble away in fear, realizing they had greatly underestimated the courage of this young boy. From that day forward, he earned our respect & admiration.

He proved to be a rider, and hence, cemented his place as an essential part of our regime. Initially he became known as Lil Crazy DeDe. As the years went by, it was only natural for him to evolve & grow within our ranks. Lil Crazy DeDe & I have shared countless blood, sweat, and tears together.

We've also had many laughter-filled moments & lessons learned side by side over the years. He earned my trust & the homies alike, leading by example to create a stronger bond within the Five-

Deuces. His name gradually changed to Boscoe, reflecting both his growth within the tribe as well as his newfound status.

Boscoe would become a highly respected figure within the Hoovers. Most members of the set embraced Boscoe with open arms. His bravery was admired, his unyielding spirit applauded, his entrance into the Crips welcomed, but you know there is always that one hater, hating on you no matter what you do. For Boscoe, it was Tiny Loko.

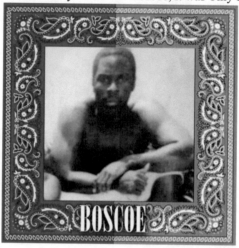

Tiny Loko was a disgruntled 12-year-old, that recently joined our ranks from Foe-Deuce Hoover, he was eager to prove himself & sow the seeds of discord. Tiny Loko embodied jealousy & resentment. He voiced out his discontent, objecting to Boscoe's membership as he felt Boscoe hadn't been appropriately 'quoted', the initiation rite where a prospect has to fight or be jumped in. A rite of passage he felt was necessary & wanted to be the one to execute it.

Boscoe was a rare breed. He met Tiny Loko's demands head on. His weapon of choice was a big ass stick, yet it was wielded with such blind fury & precision that it conveyed more than just physical pain. Boscoe's intrepid retaliation shocked everyone. Tiny Loko, wounded & humiliated, disappeared into the shadows of South Central. He was a chilling example of 'when testing somebody's gangsta goes wrong' - a lesson in humility learned the hard way.

"Speak softly & carry a big stick; you will go far."
- Teddy Roosevelt

With his startling achievements, Boscoe's reputation began to solidify. These actions laid the bricks to Boscoe's notoriety. To this day, I'm grateful for Boscoe's unwavering support & his unflinching loyalty throughout the years. He has truly lived up to the expectations CoCo & I had of him, protecting his loved ones with his life.

Through his ascent, Boscoe demonstrated the power of the human spirit & the benefits of surrounding oneself with loyal comrades. Boscoe proved himself to be an immediate factor, he became the face of FDHGC to the next generation. Whether he's remembered as Lil Crazy DeDe or Boscoe, one thing that will never change is his courage, loyalty, and devotion to his turf & his people.

CHAPTER TWENTY-SEVEN:
"JOY & PAIN"

The Cali sun scorched the already parched landscape of South Central, Los Angeles, daring countless individuals to venture forth & seek their fortunes like modern-day 49ers. My drive may not have been fueled by the promise of unearthing glimmering gold. I quickly realized that my ambitions placed me squarely within a vibrant & evolving auto market, an oasis of opportunity for a fugitive.

Living on the run from Boys Republic had presented its fair share of challenges, but it was during this turbulent time that I recognized my uncanny ability to negotiate deals, elevate the value of a vehicle, and turn a profit, we called it flipping cars. I would buy cars that need a little bit of work, fix them up with stolen parts & sell them for profit. I was on the run making a hell of a run & having hell of fun.

I started to realize that I had a talent for fixing up cars. I would spend hours tinkering in my garage, playing with the engines & making custom parts for my low rider. People started noticing my work & began to ask me to hook up their cars. I was making money doing something that I loved.

It was then that I bought my first project car. I invested $500 in a 1968 Dodge Dart in need of my Midas touch. Whenever I felt the potent hum of its powerful Hemi engine pulsating beneath my hands, I dreamed of the freedom & power it would one day represent.

When I began to restore this classic car, I found myself engaged in various escapades & confrontations that fueled a growing sense of rebellion in me. One day I got myself in a high speed chase with pigs. My heart pounded outside of my chest, while I was speeding through the maze of South Central streets. The police were in hot pursuit, their sirens shrieking ominously in my ears as the wind howled around me.

As the engine roared beneath me, the only thought in my mind was the fear that my luck was finally going to run out. Every turn I took & every pedal I pushed took me deeper into a reality I wasn't prepared to face. I had never felt so terrified & exhilarated all at once. I knew I was in deep trouble. If they caught me, I could be going back to the group home, so I kept the pedal to the metal.

When I finally screeched to a halt outside my mother's house, panting & shaking, I saw the flashing lights of the one time in my rearview. I felt a sinking feeling in my stomach as the pigs surrounded the vehicle. I knew it was all over for me. The officers rushed towards me, shouting obscenities, and pointing their guns. I thought to myself they are about to fill me up with lead for taking them on this wild goose chase. I felt like I was in a movie, a bad one where the criminal always gets caught, but then a strange thought occurred to me.

What if I told the truth? What if I just owned up to my mistake & hoped for the best? So that's what I did. As they handcuffed me & hauled me off to the 77th division station, I explained that I didn't have a license & that I had panicked when I saw the police behind me. The officers were stunned but also a little amused by my honesty.

As I sat in the police station, waiting for my fate to be decided. It was a miracle; they didn't run my name since the car wasn't stolen. They released me to my momma. I knew I had dodged a bullet, which was a close call, I swore I was getting locked up that day.

My parents & I had a strained relationship, as you already know I couldn't live with them. Nevertheless, my mother allowed me to store my ever-growing fleet of automobiles at her home. Cars were a tradition for the men in my family. Mama knew I got that influence from my uncles, at first, she thought some of the cars belonged to Uncle Roy. We had a long driveway that could park 4 cars & a double car garage. She didn't approve of me driving without a license, so I had the cars I drove parked on the street, down the block or around the corner.

I lived a wild, unrestrained youth that only the City of Angels could offer. At fourteen, the world was vast & exciting, with every corner promising a new experience or an unexpected treasure. One day, Baby Crazy, approached me with a glimmer in his eyes & a Kool-Aid grin that spread across his face.

"You ain't gonna believe this shit," Baby Crazy said, bouncing on his toes, *"My Pops took me to this Asian massage parlor by Fox Hills Mall."*

He then recounted how he had been reluctantly left in the waiting room while his father got his groove on in the back room. The anticipation in Baby Crazy's voice was infectious, his words tinged with wanderlust I could barely resist.

"I saw some fine ass hoes in there, cuH," he confessed, a wicked gleam in his eyes. *"& nigga, guess* what?!? I stole my Pops credit card! You wanna come with me to get some 'sideways pussy?'"

"Hell yeah!" I replied without hesitation.

What followed was a clandestine operation of siphoning gas for my Cadillac & hitting the road with nothing but adolescent lust & bravado guiding us. We ended up in a vibrant Asian corridor, a heady blend of koi ponds, glowing neon signs, and spicy scents wafting through the streets.

The massage parlor was a tantalizing cocktail of mystery & allure, with a dose of the forbidden. The beautiful women welcomed us, treating us like little kings. This was, indeed, a memorable experience, full body massage, with a happy ending. It also turned out to be the day that debunked a legend I had been led to believe by my Uncle Roy.

He had spun tales about Asian women having 'sideways' pussies, which I believed because Asians have chinky, slanted eyes. We were hooked on that oriental allure, that 'suki, suki, love me long time' provided such intoxicating pleasure that I found myself trying to convince Baby Crazy to sneak his father's credit card a few more times!

A month later, Big Walt got his credit card bill! He was mad but cool about it.

"I get it, fellas," Big Walt's gruff voice echoed in the Los Angeles summer heat, *"But don't use my credit card to buy no pussy! I'd rather you ask me for some cash to get some ass from one of those raggedy hoes on Figueroa."*

His stern demeanor softened, and he surprisingly added, *"That Asian pussy cost too got damn much!"*

Despite Big Walt's visible anger, his surprising reaction brought our recklessness into perspective & gave us a valuable lesson about respecting boundaries. Baby Crazy & I learned about misguided assumptions, the value of money, credit cards & the embarrassing but essential spectrum of teenage Crippin' cockhounds.

Looking back on the folly of our actions, I can't help but chuckle. We were young, reckless, and high off life. These memories are my souvenirs in the museum of my youth, that still provoke a smile & a shake of the head. After all, isn't it said you only live once!

The gentle breeze of liberation was a facade on that day, as I busted my groove through the busy Hoover streets, but I could already feel the chill of the evening coming. My life had become a series of temporary hideaways as I journeyed up & down the Fifties, where crime & scandal lurked in every shadow. I spent my days with no clear purpose, evading justice & navigating the underworld of South Central. With every step, I felt the demons of my past chasing me, threatening to drag me down.

For almost two years, I'd been on the run from Boys Republic. While one could argue that my decision to flee was somewhat impulsive, I was proud of my survival skills & my ability to remain elusive. This is my home; it had dangers, but those dangers were far easier to stomach than wasting time doing time.

It was a life that's exhilarating yet uncensored with nerve-wracking paranoia. The constant threat of capture only made the highs of my outlaw existence even more thrilling. It was a tightrope, one that I had been walking on for too long. Tonight I found shelter at the Nighty Nite Motel now called the Copacabana Inn, a shabby establishment found at the intersection of 53rd & Figueroa Street.

The whole area was notorious for gangsters, pimps, hoes, drug deals, and all sorts of unsavory activities. Each motel room was a den of nefariousness, filled with all sorts of sinful pleasures. It was the perfect place to lie low for the night & indulge in hedonistic fun. Getting freaky deaky seemed to be the only acceptable way to keep my sanity intact. It was 5 AM, my less-than-pristine room was my arena for hot & sensual delight.

I was with a Chicano girl named Pauline that the homie Baby Man lil sister, Kim, hooked me up with, entangled in an enthusiastic fuck fest fueled by the potent combination of lust & lovely joints. As I reveled in sex with no strings attached, the entire world seemed to slow down & fade into the background.

I'm balls deep, sky-high in the chocha, giving her epic back shots to the beat of black Michael Jackson *"Don't Stop"* when without warning! My sexcapade was interrupted by the commotion of thumps, thuds, and doors splintering off its hinges as panicked voices vibrated through the paper-thin walls, snapping me out of my erotic trance. The unmistakable sound of police boots stomping through the hallways quickly followed, sending my heart racing.

As our bodies melted into one another, It felt like I was reaching the pinnacle of pleasure, oblivious to the impending doom encroaching on my sanctuary. Our passionate escapade continued relentlessly, the sound of our ecstasy echoing through the motel room, my grip around her waist tightening as each pleasurable, powerful thrust edged closer to its peak.

Simultaneously as I climaxed, suddenly & abruptly the door to my motel room was kicked in, shattering the fragile veneer of our temporary sanctuary. The next moments unfolded like a scene straight out of a gritty crime thriller, as the pigs came barging into the room, guns drawn, shouting orders in an explosive harshness.

There was no warrant, no apparent reason for their intrusion – but then again, this was Figueroa Street, these pork chops didn't need a reason. As the officers barked commands & tossed the motel room in search of any incriminating evidence, the weight of my fucked up situation started to sink in.

Adrenaline coursing through my veins, I growled at them, the anger & frustration etched onto my face clear as day. I'd like to think that the police saw in my eyes the fire of a man who was hell-bent on surviving the dark corners of this world at any cost. In the chaos of the moment, I realized that I was little more than prey for these hunters wielding badges & guns.

The raid on our motel room was just one part of a wide-scale operation, targeting the illegal operations conducted in the motel. While we were still in the initial shock of their intrusion, other motel room doors were being kicked open, their occupants forcefully dragged out.

We were all paraded outside in various stages of undress, some people, such as me, found themselves butt ass naked sitting on the cold pavement with handcuffs restraining them, like livestock waiting to be loaded into the police cars & paddy wagons that were ready to take us to jail. It was a brutally invasive & dehumanizing experience that served as a reminder of what we were up against in our lives.

As I sat there on the curb, wrists shackled in the cold metal of the handcuffs, I couldn't help but feel a sense of dread creeping up on me. They had found my pistol. I knew my luck ran out.

This time I was sentenced to 2 years & placed in a detention camp surrounded by barbed wire so I couldn't escape, it was called Camp Mendenhall in Lake Hughes. It was a work camp, all we did was go to class & work like slaves on a plantation. They put us out in those fields to work us to death. On those hot California days, I could sweat enough to fill 52 buckets. We worked so hard, we didn't even have time to beef & there was a couple of Bloods at the camp to tangle with.

I was a teenager in heat, and I was growing sexually frustrated from wet pussy withdrawal. I would reminisce about hot sex with Nakita & the good times we shared. We had grown close over the last few months, but we lost contact when I got arrested. I didn't know if she knew I was locked up, but I missed her & wondered if she thought about me.

I missed the homies, I missed the Fifties. My nigga CoCo was one of the few people that sent me letters & answered my calls while I was away as the old saying goes, it's the little things that count, and that meant a lot to me. He kept me in tune with everything, so I never missed a beat.

He would go by my house & check on my mama, take the trash out on his way out. He would escort my mom to the bus stop early in the morning & late at night to make sure she was safe. He was a very considerate gangsta.

A couple of weeks went by, I was chillin' in the dorms doing calisthenics when my name was called for a visit, this my first visit since I was placed, my parents & I were estranged. I couldn't hide it anymore & my mother couldn't deny it anymore, her baby boy was bad, bad as a muthafucka. I settled in the visiting room, and I saw my parents sitting on a couch with my main squeeze, Nakita.

Nakita holding a bundle of blankets in her arms. I had the Gary Coleman *"Whatchu talkin' bout Willis"* look on my face. I know that isn't what I think it is, but I knew what time it was once I saw Nakita with my parents. I greeted them with hugs & kisses. I peaked in the blanket & my thoughts were confirmed. I became a daddy, November 11, 1980!

My pops transferred Torrie from his mother's arms to mine & said, *"There goes your son, boy!"*

That was the scariest & happiest day of my young life. I was smiling ear to ear, I was nervous, I could feel the sweat dripping from my armpits & my whole body was trembling. I felt like I was shaking the whole camp, 8.0 on the Richter scale. I didn't even know Nakita was pregnant, this was a big surprise.

I couldn't believe this shit, I couldn't believe he was mine, but I knew he was mine because we were really doing the wild thang like Hollywood porn stars. I looked at my son, I could see the resemblance, but he was pink as hell like his mama. He was fresh out the womb, so he didn't have his melanin yet. Torrie stole my whole face; he was my identical twin. He has told me people have mistaken us for each other often.

For the first time in a long time, I felt something other than anger & frustration. The weight of camp was temporarily lifted off my shoulders, and all I could think about was my new family. Days turned into weeks, and weeks turned into months, but I never forgot the joy that I had experienced when I first held my son.

It was that hope & love that kept me going during the bullshit that I faced every day. The visit from my family helped alleviate my homesickness & rejuvenate my spirit & things began to get better & time seemed to fly by.

My time at camp eventually ended, I knew that my son would always be with me as a reminder of the joy that life could bring even in the darkest of times. I'm 15 years old & I had to grow up fast. I didn't know how to be a father.

I was this big bad ass Crip, but I didn't know how to be a man, how to take care of another person. All I knew was how to get it in the streets & gang bangin'. This was the first time I ever felt anxious. A few months passed, I got time served, and some work credits, now I'm on my way back to the set.

CHAPTER TWENTY- EIGHT: "LOVE & WAR"

"When the power of love overcomes the love of power the world will know peace."
-Jimi Hendrix

In the fading glimmers of my past, 1981 was home to defining moments in my adolescence. A time of freedom & regret. Life before that my stint at camp had been a whirlwind of uncertainties; personal battles & skirmishes with adversaries & authority that spiraled out of control. I was young, far from innocent, and very much a stranger in my parents' home.

Today, I was going home at last. Home, a concept I hadn't associated with in a few years. I forgot the true worth of the word since my parents expelled me from their residence. I was barely an adolescent, a victim of circumstances, and bad decisions. Yet, as fate would have it, while I was away, I became a father. A glorious revelation clouded with flagrant sadness, for it also marked another milestone in my family structure.

My heart raced as the bus reached the outskirts of Los Angeles. The dry air of Camp Mendenhall seemed like a distant memory; I was finally home. Months of slave labor in an unforgiving climate had hardened me, but it was nothing compared to what awaited upon my return to the city. I stepped off the bus & felt the sweltering embrace of LA's relentless heat.

The Fifties stayed the same - movin' & groovin', each step drenched in memories. The first thing I did was visit Nakita & make sure to spend quality time with my baby boy. My next stop was 52nd street to visit my parents. Nothing felt better than the sweet taste of freedom. My Chuck Taylor's flopped against the unforgiving concrete as I swaggered my way down the Deuce. My footsteps quickened as I approached my family's house, the simple abode hidden in the shadows of my past.

The deafening silence that hung in the air was punctured by the gentle thud of the door as it opened, granting me passage, I was greeted by Whitey, tail wagging vigorously as he jumped up & down trying to lick my face & be embraced. My eyes met familiar scenes, my nose smelling the same fragrances, the aroma of mama's home cooking filled the air & all that was left was to meet that kind soul that had filled this house with so much love my entire life.

No words could ever describe the feeling that engulfed the halls when she appeared. Relief, overwhelming happiness, the purest love - everything combined into a single moment in time.

"Mama," I croaked out, my throat unaccustomed to the thick emotion.

"Welcome home," she replied, as if forgetting the conflicted past. The warmth in her voice was balmy.

A whispered apology dripped from the corners of her eyes, bathed in grateful tears. Time seemed to blur together as we held each other, we knew in the deepest part of our souls that it would all be okay, at least for a little while. My mother was always the more nurturing one. Her warm smile washed away my anxieties.

"Where Pops at?"

She didn't respond, she ushered me inside the living room & as if riding a wave of nostalgia, we found ourselves engrossed in *'Young & the Restless,'* as was our favorite pastime. As the monotonous drone of the soap opera filled the room, she turned to look at me, the happiness in her eyes replaced with a touch of regret.

"Son, your dad & I..." she hesitated, her thumb mechanically spinning her wedding ring, *"we separated."*

The lump in my throat felt uncomfortably large. An unexpected tension filled the room. The soap opera drama seemed to be mimicking our predicament.

Sensing my discomfort, she reached for my hand, *"I'm sorry..."* she breathed, and for a moment, I could see the pain fleeting across her eyes... *"for kicking you out your home. It was ya father's wishes, not mine."*

As I absorbed the news of their separation, pain marred by the acceptance of their irreconcilable differences, my mother's next words emerged as a ray of hope.

"I cleared out the garage for you," she declared, her voice choking with emotion.

"The garage!?!" I echoed with a puzzled excitement.

"Yes, Boo. I thought you could turn it into your apartment. Make it...home."

The simple words seemed to resonate a declaration of independence. The realization hit me; I have a home. It was different, raw, and a little battered around the edges...just like me. I was suddenly overwhelmed with the complex blend of joy & sorrow that life had hurled at me. In my heart I didn't want my father gone, I wanted to come back home to my family. I wanted his good qualities to take more precedent in our lives. His absence brought an unwelcome peace.

It was an emotion that was in limbo between relief & sadness, bittersweet. I was happy to be back home yet unnerved by the changes in my household. Even though my father & I had a strained relationship, my parents' separation was still a hard pill to swallow. I found myself on the threshold of a new life. As I stepped out into the cool night air to see my new apartment. I was optimistic about rebuilding the tattered pieces of my past into a new fabric. I was optimistic about having a place to call my own.

Around this time, I spent a lot of time shacked up with my Baby Mama, her house was my second home. I wanted spend as much precious quality time as possible with my baby boy. I loved Nakita's cooking, it took my mind off the violence brewing outside, and for once, I felt a bit of normalcy & getting a taste of being a family man. Breakfast was always my favorite meal; I'm the type of person that can eat breakfast any time of day.

Nakita's specialty was sunny side eggs with the runny yolk, rabbit sausages & grits, cooked til they were a little, brown & sweet. If you have never tried rabbit sausage, I recommend it. You will love it. Her culinary skills were simply heavenly, and you could smell it wafting through the air from five blocks away.

"Your story is what you have, what you will always have. It is something to own."
- Michelle Obama

That weekend I called a mandatory meeting. Number one on my agenda was putting in work on the red rags. I received the war report from the homeboys, beef was active with the Brims & East Coast. Homies warmly welcomed me back into the fold & wasted no time in arming me with a pistol & a quarter key of ready rock to get me back on my feet.

This new product made the hood forget about Sherman & Marijuana & it introduced us to a lot more money, fancier cars & finer women. A sense of pride swelled within me at the opportunity to contribute to this lucrative new hustle, it reminded me of my apprenticeship with King Curtis.

Crack cocaine was changing lives in South Central for better & worse! My Big Sister, Linda G, was a master at cooking rocks & after a few weeks she molded me into a top chef. I was like Gordon Ramsay with the pot. It was a simple process but hard to master. Crack was new & muthafuckas were getting sky high! We didn't know the effects it would have on the community; people were basically lab rats being experimented on. Regardless, this new narcotic brought in big revenue, we would end up making more money than we could count.

I was also made aware that Big Q-bone from Broadway transferred to Crenshaw High where he got tight with Rollin' Sixty. They gave their friendship a name, it was called *"Five Two, Whatever We Do, Six Owe, Wherever We Go."*

This put us in a hard position due to our alliance with Broadway. This was a time of growing tensions between the Hoover Crips & Sixties due to the Hoover alliance with Eight Tray Gangstas. Hoovers already frowned upon our ties with Broadway & their relationship with Sixties, created a Molotov cocktail.

Homies shared stories about our enemies' brazen acts. Brims like Knuckles, Wiggles, and Dre Dogg, regularly invaded the set with brigades of red rags on bikes, rat packing homeboys or shooting at us, and their attacks were becoming bolder & bolder. All I could think was that we had to make an example out of our enemies, we had to be bolder & badder. We made a vow that we would be the aggressors in every conflict, aggression became our trademark, and the foundation of our reputation as the most hated Crips in Los Angeles.

In dire need of firepower, I suggested *"snatching"*, the act of snatching guns from careless security guards working in local businesses. The act required stealth & swiftness, but the payoff would be a boom to our arsenal. The homies collectively nodded in agreement, and we vowed to execute the plan in the coming days.

Back in the day all the businesses had armed security guards, they used to have big .38 specials hanging off their belts. When I saw an opportunity, I'd walk up to them like I had a question & snatched the revolver right off their belt, they couldn't do anything about it. I would just back them down with their own gun before I fled. My first victim was the guard at McDonald's, after that it became a regular routine for us to get our artillery up.

The Six-Deuce Brims were an opponent we were hell-bent on demolishing. Every night we would invade the Brims turf & try to catch one slipping & give them the blues. Simmering beneath the surface was also an escalating Crip rivalry with the East Coast. The need for more firepower became more & more apparent, and we were all too aware that our survival hinged on this.

We moved forward with the plan to snatch guns, I was in peak physical form from camp, and I put it to good use. The months of rigorous training at Camp Mendenhall had been a baptism by fire, reshaping my entire physique & instilling a reservoir of strength within me.

With each successful snatch, our firepower grew, instilling in us newfound confidence to combat our enemies. Gunfire echoing into the night like a haunting drum roll. Despite constant barriers, the love for my baby mama & son was a fire that refused to be extinguished. It was an unstoppable force that fueled me through the sleepless nights & battles.

Upon my release from Camp Mendenhall, I was forced to enroll in Jackson Sr High downtown. This wasn't your average high school; it was an all-boys continuation school. Regards for the law were laughed off & education took a backseat. Jackson High was filled with an eclectic assortment of delinquents, and dumb asses from every shadow ridden ghetto of Los Angeles. The daunting labyrinth of Jackson High seemed, by any standard, a minefield & I felt I was equipped to navigate.

Gang culture wasn't just a part of our lives, it was our very identity, a harsh truth I soon came to understand & accept. Academia, it seemed, wanted nothing to do with young men like me. We were roses with thorns too sharp, too jagged for the manicured gardens of the upper classes. The ink began to dry up, and the pages of this chapter began to close.

I learned at this tender age that a man needs two women in his life – a wife & a mistress. The wife is fundamental to his existence, like the air we breathe & the water we drink, without her nurturing presence, his life would soon be void of its core rhythm & warmth. A man yearns for something elusive, something that will add a touch of extravagance to his otherwise routine life. Here, enters the mistress, like an exquisite piece of jewelry that is taken out selectively. Her rare appearances add a spark of elegance & excitement, a break from the usual that invigorates his soul.

I was gang-hanging in the Grooveline with oG 8-Ball an Hriginal Foe-Tray Hoover. A certified hustler named after his #1 product, an eighth of an ounce of cocaine. 8-ball was a wise man, he knew the street, he knew how to get money. 8-Ball leaned towards me, his dark eyes glinting with mischief under the dim streetlight.

"There's a pretty young thang got her eyes on you, homie," he said, his low, sinister voice barely audible above the traffic noise. I glanced up at him, quiz draped across my face.

Her name was Verna, a new face from the gritty, riot-scarred streets of Watts. She was a year or two older than me, just barely 17, and I had seen her around the set a few times, her demeanor always challenging & demanding respect she rightfully earned.

True to 8-Ball's words, Verna was a sight to behold. She carried herself with a magnetic allure that was as irresistible as it was engaging. Her heels accentuated her confidence, and her big eye lashes offered her an uncanny resemblance to the classic charm of Betty Boop. However, beneath that seemingly innocent exterior was a woman who played by her own rules, in life, love, and beyond.

The most lightning trait of them all was her inclination towards danger, her almost reckless bravado. If you didn't satisfy her sexually, you'd risk facing her wrath, she might bust a cap in that ass. In matters of the heart & flesh, she possessed the assertiveness of a man.

She was bold & confident, never shying away from expressing her desires. Her understanding of relationships was simple & straightforward: you give her what she wants, in the way she wants. When it came to sex, I made sure to do it in her favorite position: from the back. I put everything I had into the act to make sure the sex was spectacular, for there was nothing more fearful than a Verna scorned.

Perhaps the element of danger made her more desirable, or maybe it was my young, naive heart resonating with her wild, fearless spirit. Our first date was as unexpected as it was passionate. She challenged the stereotypical roles of our gender, treating me like an object of her desire, a boy toy, a hot commodity for hot sex.

Verna put that pussy on me, made me feel like a king, and then she put some money into my pocket, and sent my ass on my groovy way, blurring the gender lines in many ways. Her intense love & generosity stirred emotions in me that were alien, yet intriguing.

> *"Court a mistress, she denies you; let her alone, she will court you."- Ben Jonson*

The sex was so good, I tried to bring her home to mama! There was a part of me that had become tender dick. I fell head-over-heels for her hoping to make her a square bitch, but she wasn't that type of girl.

On the surface, Verna was a femme fatale, a woman who echoed that anything that a man could do, she could do better & in heels. From the outside, she might have seemed ruthless, a cold-calculated gangsta you never dared to cross. Yet, to me, she was an enigma- hard as steel with a heart as soft as a cloud. A testament of resilience wrapped ever so delicately in layers of raw love & compassion.

Verna was everything but a *'girly girl'*. She was a gangsta, just like me, a realization that sent ripples of surprise through my being. She even had the jailbird badge to prove it, having just come home after a time in jail. She is one girl you never want to cross, because she will hurt you physically not mentally or emotionally. Little did I know we would form a lifelong bond.

In honor of our relationship, she incorporated my name into hers, she became Verna Boo from Five-Deuce Hoover. It was an unexpected gesture of affection, marking our bond & serving as a constant reminder of our unconventional attachment to each other. Verna had chosen me, not as a conquest, but as her equal.

My teenage years offered me a rough cobblestone path, and by the tender age of fifteen, it felt like each stone had a unique challenge on its surface. That fall, I decided to step deeper into the abyss of notoriety. Jackson High would be my last academic venture. I dropped out, not with regret, but with a sense of unburdening. I found myself dedicating more time than ever to the set.

The allure of power & notoriety coupled with the adrenaline of rebellion was a heavy mix, drawing me in until there was no turning back like an addiction. It was my brotherhood, my Hoovers-in-arms, my loved ones that had my undying loyalty. The unfiltered love I received from the homies & fierce devotion mattered more than the algebra or American history I was being taught in school.

Five-Deuce had become my priority, second only to a heartbeat that softly but steadily made his presence felt– my son. He wasn't an obligation or responsibility, but a piece of my heart living in human form, my one redeeming factor in a life that was a dance with joy. I cherished him for reminding me of the importance of hope & tenderness amid our never-ending struggles. I cradled my son in my trembling hands & promised him a future doused in kindness & love.

It was a tightrope walk, balancing my time between my heart & my reality; my heart being my son & Nakita, my childhood sweetheart, and my reality being FDHGC. My life was a fine balancing act between my unwavering allegiance to Hoover Gangsta & the unconditional love that swelled in my heart for Torrie. Born into a world that was far from perfect, my son was the pillar of my existence. The second thought that echoed in the back of my mind amidst the trials of my everyday life.

I held onto the promise of being a better, more considerate father to my child than mine had been to me. A vow that felt like an anchor in the raging sea that my life had become. I did not want him to fall victim to the abuse & neglect that were rampant in my childhood. In his innocent gaze, I saw glimmers of a life I yearned for, but never had.

I promised myself to be the shield that protected him from the brunt of the struggles that life tossed our way. My son stood at the crossroads of my existence, a living embodiment of my lost purity. I dedicated every free minute I could scrape from my hustle & banging to being present for my son, cherishing each giggle, and seeing his milestones of growth.

I held my son's tiny hands, trying to provide him with the comfort of a father's warmth, showing him that he was not alone in a world that had left me in solitude at a tender age. The long hours & sleepless nights were worth every moment spent, seeing how his eyes gleamed with innocent queries that I was all too willing to answer.

The sheer joy of watching his lips curl into a gummy toothless smile filled my heart with a sense of purpose & need. Those were the moments that fueled my determination, offering a break from the harsh reality of the street life I was enmeshed in.

Meanwhile, the other half of my time was reserved for Crippin'. I held my duties & responsibilities up high, like the blue flag. Providing my tribesmen with a much-needed sense of security & support. My endless days turned into restless nights with me having to be there for my Five-Deuces, standing up for them in their time of need. As I walked on parallel paths of street life & fatherhood, I strived to own my responsibilities with dedication.

Life was tough & relentless, but I attested to my vows, attempting to be an exemplary father while surviving the merciless world of the Crips & Bloods. With every passing day, 1981 brought yet another story of struggle & strength, lessons & mistakes, and sacrifices & solidarity. This chapter in my life shaped me, molded me, and directed me to continue my journey. A journey that was graced by the smiles of my little boy & challenged by the ruthless life of a Hoover.

My loyalty to the homies seemed like a destiny bestowed upon me by fate. As much as it had summoned me into a troubled lifestyle, it was this very alliance that also served as a sanctuary in my fugitive years. Often, my comrades convinced their parents to provide shelter for me.

I remember with a strange sense of nostalgia the lengths they had gone to convince their parents to allow me a place to live. Unaware that there was a fiercely protective network of Hoover mommas always there looking out for me, despite my forced exile. To my friends' parents, I was a stray lamb, welcome with open arms.

Our mothers kept communicating through hushed late-night telephone calls & vague references to our safekeeping in their everyday conversations. I was a prodigal son. My mom, to her credit, played the dual role of concerned yet distant parent. Secretly keeping tabs on my whereabouts & safety.

Offering a safety net on the low to redeem herself for disowning me per my father's demands & her regretted loyalties. Over time our gang-related activities began to cause friction within our homes. My makeshift apartment became a refuge, offering the much-needed respite from their frictions.

Mouse & his sister Tee Dub were the first of my comrades who sought refuge, their introduction to Crippin' having disrupted their home equilibrium. They had been living a conflict-ridden existence; always in the middle of family squabbles, they sought solace in the groove. Eventually, they became fed up with the tension in their home.

LIL MOUSE & BIG MOUSE

They showed up at my doorstep in the middle of the night, their hurriedly packed belongings defying the uncertainty in their eyes. Seeing them standing at my door brought memories flooding back. Their initiation into the set started over shared tales of our lives, stories of our thuggish bravado, and the promise of a rebel's camaraderie. Now they stood there, their lives irrevocably altered, seeking shelter under my roof.

From that day forward, my garage became a haven, a place of refuge for my fellow Hoover Gangstas when things became heated at home. This makeshift guardian role I suddenly found myself playing went beyond just providing shelter; it fostered deeper bonds within our ranks. It reaffirmed our shared histories, our shared struggles, and our shared loyalties. It fostered a genuine love that would serve as our strength in the gang wars that we had no idea awaited us.

My place became the cornerstone of an unspoken social contract. The trust their parents showed by keeping me safe, I now extended to my homies by opening my doors to them. This act, performed in the name of Hoover love, further solidified our relationships, giving us more than loyalty to hold on to. We were evolving daily into an airtight family.

This was a landmark year that saw an estranged teenager evolve into a guardian of other lost souls. Amidst the chaos & turbulence, we found comfort in each other. The year became a testament to survival & resilience, a symbol of how a challenging environment could transform lost souls into unexpected protectors. I wonder what would have happened if my father weren't abusive or if I hadn't joined the Crips. Yet, as strange as it sounds, these circumstances made me who I am-- an unexpected guardian amidst a deep blue sea of chaos.

It was perhaps the shared sense of displacement that allowed us to weave deeper connections within the disorganized structure of God's plan. Perhaps, the proverb *"misery loves company"* holds grains of truth, because we found relief in shared hardships, insecurities, and the inalienable bond of Hoover love.

On an otherwise boring ass day, I needed some action, and I needed some wheels. An idea slid into my mind, Spookee's prized white Cadillac. A classic symbol of the American dream, but more importantly, my object of secret longing for its majestic white paint job, plush leather seats, and hypnotic hum. It sadly sat forgotten in the driveway, while my brother sat behind bars.

Spookee had a scowl like an untamed lion, and a heart that held the eye of a hurricane & his pearly white Cadillac held the same furious spirit. It was a beast of a machine, hues of cocaine & chrome colliding against the Crip blue sky.

I hatched my plan & proceeded to play on my mother's naivety. I approached my mom with rehearsed nonchalance, *"Momma,"* I began, faking a compassionate tone, *"Spookee called from jail today."*

Her brows raised anxiously, *"What ya brother talkin' 'bout?"*

I had an evil grin in my mind while letting my poker face shine, *"regular shit, but he said I could get the keys to his Cadillac while he's locked up."*

Of course, she was suspicious, but the tug of sibling trust in my voice had her skepticism crawling back into the shadows. Ignorant or not, she succumbed to my persuasion. Just like that, I became the proud temporary owner of Big Spookee's immaculate piece of machinery.

293 | P a g e

CHAPTER TWENTY-NINE: "PARTY & BULLSHIT"

It was the summer of 1981, Friday of my C-Day weekend, I'm turning 16 in a couple days, and my weekend was to be filled with parties, drugs, bitches & mischief. During that summer, we were at the height of our power, known & respected throughout the streets of LA.

As the clock struck midnight, signifying the beginning of my C-Day weekend, Bow Dee, my fellow Hriginal & a brother to me, soon pulled up to my crib. We had big plans for the kickoff of my C-Day weekend at Flippers in West Hollywood. We'd been frequenting this joint ever since the grand opening in 1979, promoting our turf & punking anyone who dared to look at us the wrong way.

It was an exclusive & chic roller rink & nightclub. I probably skated enough miles in that place to make it to Brooklyn & back, two times. The floor was shellacked to perfection, so it felt like we were gliding on air. I was hypnotized & mesmerized by the colorful strobe lights bouncing off the mirrors & a booming system that made classic records like *"Bad Mama Jama"* by Carl Carlton, *"Controversy"* by Prince, *"I Will Survive,"* by Diana Ross, or *"Funky Town"* by Lipps Inc, even more enjoyable.

Flippers was fly as hell, A bar stocked with the best liquor, a restaurant that served delicious food, and a custom skate shop that was off the hook. I loved the ambiance. Every time I walked through the doors, I felt like I was stepping into a different world. The neon lights, the loud music, and the fresh scent of pizza & burgers made me feel alive.

We were there looking for girls, vibes & trouble with anyone looking like a Blood or a sweet lick. We ended the night jacking some fools that looked like playas, who had more money than common sense. Bow Dee, he had a lethal knockout punch, it's that very reason the Brims rather shoot than fight. He let loose on this unsuspecting fool & left him snoozing on the pavement like a bum on skid row & while the victim was out cold, I ran through his pockets & discovered 5 hundreds! Happy C-day to me!

Saturday night the homies threw me a party at the Brain House. The Brain was a large property situated on the corner of 53rd

293 | P a g e

street & Vermont, the house stood undeterred, its silhouette bearing an uncanny resemblance to a graveyard lost in time, touching somewhere between enigma & horror. Its exterior was so grim, it could inject fear into the bravest Crip.

Yet, it was a place where every Hoover from the 4tray to the one way, the Broadways, and the Gangstas would all frequent. We used to be there every weekend. South Central Los Angeles in the early 1980s was a different world than it is today. Engulfed in the crack epidemic & rise of gang banging, the city was plagued by social issues that made it a difficult place to grow up. Amid this madness, the Brain became our refuge.

The Brain belonged to a mad scientist, an older, tall & slender, light skin man, with wild curly hair named Greg. He had a nephew that was always hanging around & would grow up to be Big Moochie from Five-Deuce Hoover Gangsta Crip. I met him on the Tray one day I was chilling, smoking with ScHool Boy, Tee Dub & her big booty cousin Porsha from the east side, who became our 2nd Hoo'lette.

Greg approached me to buy some water. Next time I served him, he invited me to smoke with him, we engaged in small talk, and he told me about the house & extended an invitation to come over with the gang for a house party. We went there & it was an unforgettable experience.

What made the house truly special was that it was like a combination of haunted house, museum & futuristic wonderland with gadgets that lit up all kinds of colors. The owner had equipped the house with an ultramodern computer called THE BRAIN. The Brain was a technological marvel unlike anything we ever seen before.

As soon as we entered The Brain, we knew we were in for a wild ride. The once haunted vibe transformed into a techno wonderland. In the heart of the house, The Brain was brilliantly built into the wall exactly where the fireplace was supposed to be.

The Brain was intricately connected to every nook & cranny of the house. Similar to a fuse box with labels & switches for each room, but with an array of glowing lights adjacent to them. Greg could control his home with just a few simple voice commands. If he were to utter, *"Glow box, kitchen,"* almost as if magic, every appliance & light in the kitchen area activated.

295 | P a g e

Perhaps the most amazing gadget of all was an AI assistant. This device was like nothing we had ever seen before - it looked like a miniature robot with a glowing eye that would follow us around the room. I remember being high as hell asking it questions & it would respond with a synthesized voice that sounded like a cross between Roger Troutman & R2-D2, and it would never get tired of our dumb ass questions.

Our journey inside the peculiar Brain House continued into the kitchen, where the fusion of technology & daily chores occurred. Greg would casually stick his burrito into the microwave.

Just when you think it ends there, the microwave, enveloped with AI, would happily address him, *"Hey Greg, your food is ready,"* dousing the room with laughter while bleeding the line between the myth of fantasy & the reality of science.

Kitchens did not talk back then, but in the Brain House, the impossible was possible, and the future was not only a dream but a functioning reality. As if that wasn't enough, the house had two floors adorned with eccentric décor. Among the most intriguing features were model planes hanging from the ceiling atop the second floor, seemingly suspended in mid-air.

The walls were covered in flashing lights & neon signs that gave the whole place a futurama, star-wars vibe. The center of the room was dominated by a giant screen that displayed trippy animations & psychedelic visuals. It was the gadgets that really caught our attention. They were everywhere - on the walls, on the ceiling, even on the floor. As we moved through the house, we couldn't help but marvel at these amazing devices.

One of them was a holographic projector that could create 3D holograms that seemed to float in mid-air. Another was a robotic arm that could mix drinks with the precision of a professional bartender.

There were also computer terminals that could be accessed by voice, and voice-activated devices that could turn the music up or down. The second floor of the house was decorated with amazing realistic miniature model airplanes & spacecrafts that dangled from the ceiling.

Then there was Greg's bed - a unique creation that hung from the ceiling by chains. Springs were attached to each chain, lending the bed a bouncy effect. As uncanny as it might sound, sitting on it was an

295 | P a g e

experience of a lifetime - your heart skipped a beat as you were pushed off the floor, but then the springs came to the rescue - bouncing you back again. It was like sitting on air, something only a mad scientist like Greg could fancy & fabricate. I looked at Porsha with lust & raised eyebrows, which screamed you know what I would do to you on this bed, girl!

She replied with an arm slap, *"You so crazy, Boo!"*

From the core of the house, we traveled to the rear, where a 3-car garage had undergone a delightful metamorphosis into an event space with a light up dance floor comparable to a Sunset strip Discotheque. This was where we gathered & indulged our vices. We tantalized our taste buds with Kryptonite. This neon libation immortalized our experience in the Brain House.

"We drink Kryptonite & we Crip tonight!"- oG
ScHool Boy Hriginal FDHGC

The Brain really tripped me out! After our first visit we told everybody & their mama about the Brain & it became known as the ultimate party house. It was the kind of place where we could let loose on the weekends, blasting music & dancing the night away.

The night of my 16th C-day Bash, I arrived with ScHool Boy & T-Dogg, the Brain was vibrating from the bass, the speakers blasted Rick James *"Give It to Me Baby"* numbing my senses.

The room was a disarray of soul train dance moves, vivid neon colors, and the overpowering aroma of marijuana & Sherm smoke. I looked around, wide-eyed but completely at a loss, until I spotted her. My big booty crush, Porsha, was dancing with Tee Dub, her laughter occasionally ringing out over the sound of the music.

The genius was always around to keep an eye on things. Greg rarely spoke, except to give us the occasional word of advice or instruction when we were in danger of damaging one of his precious gadgets. For such a smart guy, I don't why he thought his house would be safe from destruction by the party animals known as the Hoover Groovers.

I approached Porsha. She gave me a big ol' hug & offered me a hit of her Sherman cigarette. As we stood there dancing, smoking &

talking shit. She asked me if I could fly one of the model airplanes. I looked at her confidently. I couldn't refuse the challenge.

"You know I can make that muthafucka fly, but we gotta fly together", I replied.

Under the influence of PCP, Kryptonite, and good times, we climbed a ladder leading to the nearest model airplane. My heart pounded with exhilaration as we climbed into the tiny cockpit.

The plane swayed gently above the floor, held in place by thin cables. Porsha's confidence in me sparked a newfound determination to bring this machine to life. Knees pressing into the model's hard edges, I began using my body weight to swing the plane back & forth, us both giggling like little kids up to no good.

Suddenly, the cables snapped under the strain of our wild pursuit. For a moment, we were airborne amidst the shimmering disco lights & the roar of the party outside. The memory of our eyes locked together in that surreal instant will remain with me forever.

The plane crashed into the wall with a deafening thud. Miraculously, Porsha & I had managed to come out unscathed, both alive to laugh about what happened. We were bundled into a world of euphoria, invincibility in our youthful recklessness. As my birthday party continued, undisturbed by our fiasco, we perched atop the wreck, still chuckling with adrenaline racing through our veins.

That night, two things became abundantly clear. First, I knew that I was head over heels for Porsha, as she sat beside me, and seemed to feel the same way I did. Second, those precious moments of foolish daring are often the ones that leave the deepest impressions on our hearts.

From that night on, Porsha & I remained close friends, embarking on countless adventures together. While we've matured & our wild antics have since died down, we often reminisce & still laugh about the time we crashed an airplane at the Brain. The time spent with the ones we love, and the thrill of breaking boundaries will forever be etched into my heart.

The Brain was ahead of its time it was a place where technology & humanity coexisted in harmony. A place where a mad scientist could create a world that was both playful & profound. It was a magical place that we will never forget.

It wasn't a typical Sunday, it was my 16th C-day! It was about to transform into a legendary tale etched in our memories. Baby Crazy & ScHool Boy suggested we go to Magic Mountain, as our destination to let loose our spirits. This was no ordinary day; it was the inaugural School's Out Party, marking the advent of summer. All over Los Angeles, young boys & girls were ready to celebrate school being over, and we were no exception.

We rounded up all the homies for an epic day of mischief & celebration. Just imagine a mob of Crips, Fifty deep; this was the epitome of camaraderie. We didn't go to ride roller coasters or play games. We were there for a different kind of amusement. We were on a mission to cause pandemonium, hoping to make headlines, and promote the set.

Upon reaching Magic Mountain, a swarm of over twenty thousand kids from all over California greeted us. The surroundings echoed with exhilaration & enthusiasm, matching our spirits. The faces of the youngsters, each showcasing different degrees of excitement & anxiety, were aglow with the euphoria of the party. We were troublemakers, ready to some at a moment's notice.

Per usual we were miscreants looking for mischief & bitches. We found it, when we ran into the Compton Piru Bloods. That was exactly the kind of trouble we craved, the kind that got our adrenaline pumping. Not one to back down from a fight, we got down to squabbling, standing our ground.

The confrontation was intense; there was no grace, no mercy, only raw force & determination. After an epic exchange of power & pride, we came out victorious, serving them an ass whipping they will not easily forget.

The victory invigorated us with a newfound zest for the rest of the celebration. The laughter & sly grins of satisfaction never ceased for an instant amidst all the chaos. Our boisterous laughter mingled with the uproar of a crowd of thousands, we were indeed, the heart of the party. The park, at that moment, seemed like a paradise, a heaven of beautiful damsels & endless opportunities.

We walked away from the scuffle with a triumphant strut. Not a stain on our clothes or drop of worry in our eyes. That's when Destiny swung open her doors & ushered in the winds of pleasure. We struck gold, unearthing a bevy of sun-kissed beauties just as thrilled by our exploits as we were.

A group of hoochies with juicy booties, draped in the colors of a West Coast sunset, swishing & swaying their hips straight into our groovy world. One caught my eye – a Lancaster girl with flawless brown skin, and an effortlessly curvaceous figure. Her eyes twinkled & soon enough, we found ourselves engaged in flirty conversation, our chemistry magnetic.

"Today's my C-day, baby!" I proclaimed, flashing my most charming smirk. She, however, seemed puzzled. *"What's a C-day?"* she inquired, her face gleaming with curiosity.

Chuckling to myself, I explained, *"It's a Crip's Birthday!"* I knew that I was pushing it a bit, but I couldn't resist passing on a bit of gangster knowledge to this beautiful girl.

Then, with unabashed swag & audacity, I threw her my favorite line: *"You ever make love to a Crip, baby?"*

Her eyes widened, and she bit her lip, clearly amused & equally excited. There was something about my audacious confidence that seemed to thrill her, leaving her eager for our little escapade.

Her body language shifted from curiosity to intrigue. A flicker of risqué excitement danced in her eyes, surrendering to my proposition. With a whisper of wanderlust, we snuck away from the crowd, disappearing behind the silhouette of a monstrous roller coaster.

The midday sun blazed high in the California sky as we found the perfect spot shrouded in the shadow of the hulking metallic beast. The charismatic chaos of Magic Mountain fading into a distant hum, our quickie began with a tantalizing birthday treat: a spontaneous blow job that was a more of a thrill than any roller coaster ride. The explosion of pleasure radiated through my veins, shooting stars dancing behind my closed eyelids.

As she slid down her cut-off jean shorts, I gently tugged at the straps of her crop top, revealing her perky breast to the concealing darkness. The thrill of our secret liaison heightened our senses, I put it in, and it was electrifying! I gave her the best 5 minutes of her life! It was a good old-fashioned wham, bam, thank you, ma'am!

It was an animalistic celebration of life, an exhilarating thrill ride of sorts. Amidst the feverish ecstasy, a golden thread wove through our rendezvous making it an unforgettable chapter in my C-Day story.

By the time we came out from our secret rendezvous, overflowing with adrenaline, the moon's twilight was starting to creep over Magic Mountain. As the last echo of my one-liner faded into the balmy evening, we re-joined the homies, our triumphant grins & flushed faces unveiling the sexy secret we swore to keep.

There were over 20,000 kids in the park from all over California, so there were hundreds of girls for us to hit on. It was like heaven with so many females. However, our primal instinct of conflict remained untamed. It wasn't just the Pirus we got it on with.

The park, being the social mecca it was, also attracted various sets of Crips & Bloods from various hoods, so conflicts were bound to occur. Being the fearless bunch we were, we took pride in giving out several sets of ass whippings & loving every moment of it.

T-Dogg & I decided we should celebrate our victories with some rewards, so we started robbing the games & concession stands for food, drinks, prizes & money. Throughout our robbing spree, we managed to loot a total of $500, a sum that filled our pockets with substantial weight. Additionally, we scored enough food & drinks to feed our whole posse, but the homie Cadillac Bobby had the true eureka moment.

Cadillac Bobby, a homie with a knack for spotting opportunity, stumbled across a fortune in disguise. He had dared to break into a back room at one of the stores, where he discovered a massive bag. Inside the bag was a stash of $20,000 to be exact. Our joy knew no bounds; Bobby hit the jackpot!

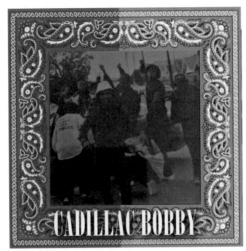

CADILLAC BOBBY

With an added $20,500 now in our collective pot, we divided the treasure among the homies. Our pockets heavier & smiles wider, we reveled in the good day of Crippin' at Magic Mountain. My C-day was full of victories; a triumph over adversaries, a freaky deaky rendezvous, and some free money.

We thought for sure we would make the papers the next day. Yet, to our surprise, the events of the day were silent in the media. They probably didn't want any negative publicity for the inaugural School's Out Party.

Honestly, it didn't matter whether the media acknowledged us or not, we knew, and those who witnessed knew: Five-Deuce Hoover owned Magic Mountain that day. It was a day that defined Crippin' at its best, a narrative that we would carry in our hearts, spinning tales of the time the Hoover Gangstas painted Magic Mountain Crip blue.

On an otherwise boring ass day, I needed some action. An idea slid into my mind. I needed wheels, and the solution was Spookee's prized white Cadillac. A classic symbol of the American dream, but more importantly, my object of secret longing for its majestic white paint job with matching plush leather seats. It sadly sat forgotten in the driveway, while my brother sat behind bars.

Spookee had a scowl like an untamed lion, and a heart that held the eye of a hurricane & his pearly white Cadillac held the same furious spirit. It was a beast of a machine, hues of cocaine & chrome colliding against the Crip blue sky. I hatched my plan, I went ahead & played on my mother's naivety.

I approached my mom with rehearsed nonchalance,
"Momma," I began, faking a compassionate tone, *"Spookee called from jail today."*

Her brows raised anxiously, *"What ya brother talkin' 'bout?"*

I had an evil grin in my mind while letting my poker face shine, *"regular shit, but he said I could get the keys to his Cadillac while he's locked up."*

Of course, she was suspicious, but the tug of sibling trust in my voice had her skepticism retreat. She'd succumb to my persuasion. Allowing me to become the proud temporary owner of Big Spookee's immaculate piece of machinery.

The next month was a blur of good times cruising down the 110, styling down Vermont basking in the glory of the Cadillac's roaring engine. I reveled in the freedom it granted me – flashing lights, booty calls, extravagant parties, and long nights with no real destination in mind. I was riding high, groovin' through life without a care in the world.

Surprise, Surprise, Spookee got released early. I'm carefree riding down Fig with a Caddy full of South Central's finest hoes! Suddenly out of the corner of my eye I see Spookee standing on the corner of 52nd street & Vermont. I chuck up the H, as I hollered out the window *"I'll be right back!"*

On my way back from the store, I saw Spookee, where I left him. Brandishing his Colt like it was part of his hand. Next thing I know I hear 5 repeated gunshots, then I hear them hitting the vehicle! I don't see any red rags anywhere!

No, it was this wild ass nigga, Spookee! In his blind rage, he seemed to have forgotten that the car he was hell-bent on shooting up was his own! The bullets ripped through the body of the sleek Caddy, causing the girls to scream in terror, as I pushed the pedal to the metal.

By some kind of divine intervention, I got away without any casualties. The car, though, was not so lucky. The hood & the driver's side door were marred with gaping holes courtesy of my dear brother. I refurbished the damage done, exchanging the original white hood & driver's side door with doo-doo brown ones from the junkyard. If nothing else, it was a testament to me being the bigger man, repairing the damage he inflicted on his own ride.

Seeing the ruined state of his beloved vehicle did nothing to smoothen Spookee's ruffled feathers.

"Look at my damn car!" he howled, furiously pacing around the patched up Cadillac. *"You fucked my shit up nigga!"*

I was stunned. In my head, I felt like this fool owed me an apology.

"nigga please, you the one that shot it up!" I retorted, a mix of confusion & anger playing upon my face. *"& besides, muthafucka, I fixed up your car after you tried to kill me."*

Just like all our arguments, Spookee had to have the last word, *"this ain't over, lil nigga,"* he growled.

Reflecting on that sunny afternoon my big bro is crazy as hell, but I wouldn't trade him for the world. It's wild how all this chaos can evolve from a simple lie. A sly scheme to borrow my brother's ride. Just another crazy day around the way with Boo & Spookee.

CHAPTER THIRTY:
"GET IT BACK IN BLOOD"

SLICC RICC | LIL LIVE | MADMAN

In August 1981, my main man, oG Madman, finally came home from Chino after doing four long years. The Fifties was buzzing with anticipation, all the homies were eager to welcome him back to the fold. He was the oldest member of Fifty Crip, he followed his baby brother, Lil Live as his protector. Mad was the first homie to go to prison, he had been gone since 1977. I wondered how he'd handle the changes that had occurred during his years away.

Spookee & Madman had been best friends since they were kids at 52nd street school, wreaking havoc. OG Mad was like a big brother to me, so when he saw me, his eyes lit up. *"Boo! My man! It's good to see you again,"* he exclaimed, wrapping me up in a bear hug.

As soon as I saw Madman, I could sense the confusion & excitement in his eyes. It was evident that he was embracing the waves of change. We found ourselves gang-hangin' at one of our favorite hideouts in the set—a dimly lit, graffiti-covered alleyway on the Foe.

We spent time reminiscing about old times & catching him up on everything that had happened in his absence. After hours of discussion, Madman got serious. He pulled me aside. We had been through thick & thin, and even though he was my elder, he knew that whenever he needed help or advice, I had his back.

"Damn Boo, things are so different now," Madman deliberated as we sat on my porch, watching the Hoover Gangstas congregate on the street.

"Shit done changed so much, cuH. Crips we used to be cool with are now our enemies."

I nodded my head in understanding, knowing all too well how much the game changed over the years. I had to share with Madman one of the most significant changes in the set.

"Look, loved one, I definitely understand how you feel. The first thing you need to know" I started. *"We're Five-Deuce Hoover Gangster Crip now. New rules, new relationships, new enemies but at the core, it's still Fifty Crip!'"*

My childhood friend looked troubled, which was understandable. He had just spent four years behind bars, and now he had to adapt to an entirely new reality.

Between swigs of Olde English, he confided in me, *"Boo,"* he said, *"I need some money & some wheels. I can't be out here stuck & broke, blue."*

"Madman, relax. I got you!" I assured him, patting him on the back as I devised a plan.

I knew just the car Madman would want - a '64 Chevy Impala. With its smooth lines, sleek body, and undeniable street presence, it was the perfect choice.

"Madman, if you want cash, I know just the thing. We gonna get some Six-Foes, and then we'll take 'em to Low-Ryda's Chop Shop. You gonna get some cash, and a set of wheels."

Madman's eyes sparkled at the thought.

"Boo, you always gotta plan, nigga," he laughed. *"Alright, let's do this."*

The night was young, and so were we. We prowled the streets of Los Angeles, seeking the first of our targets. The glint of chrome & the elegance of classic curves caught our eyes on the corner of a dimly lit street—a perfect candidate.

We quickly got to work. In the cover of the night, we broke into the car—an immaculate candy apple red '64 Chevy Impala no one deserved more than my friend. I expertly wielded the B-10 key, and in a heartbeat, the engine roared to life. Madman's nimble fingers tuned the radio to our favorite station, KDAY 93.5.

This was our night. Elated & high off adrenaline, we journeyed further into the depths of the city, seeking a car for me. It didn't take long before we found another beauty, this time a Dodger blue Impala that glowed underneath the L.A. moonlight. I slid into the driver's seat, grinning when the car came to life with ease. We were unstoppable.

The two of us had managed to steal not one, but two Six-Foes. We loved old schools; these cars were a big deal. Two Deuces cruising in a groovy motorcade, enjoying the vibes of *"Apache"* by Sugar Hill Gang. Grinning with success written all over my face, knowing we could turn both cars into some fast cash like blue magic.

Eventually, we made it to Low-Ryda's Chop Shop, where I had become a regular. Low-Ryda knew the drill—these cars would be dismantled, sold for parts, and disappear forever. In what felt like the blink of an eye, Low-Ryda completed his work, his masterpiece. Both '64 Chevy Impalas were surgically disassembled, destined to live new lives somewhere in the world.

Low-Ryda was willing to give us a few days to sell the parts from the Impalas to come up with his cut. He'd earned his name thanks to his expertise in dismantling cars as easily as breathing. Out of a sense of loyalty to Five-Deuce or perhaps triggered by rivalry, we decided we wouldn't give Low Rider anything. After all, he was from East Coast Crip.

Friday nights were always a reason to celebrate, and this one was no exception. Tony, Madman, and Spookee, decided to hit the pool hall to celebrate Madman's release. The pool hall was a dimly lit, smoke-filled den where we would gather to drown our sorrows & revel in our victories. It was the favorite hangout among the gangsters & hustlers. As the trio burst through the doors, the sound of laughter & glasses clinking filled the air.

Madman, came home buff from his stint in the slammer, he couldn't wait to get his hands on a cue stick & dominate the billiards or a bitch ass nigga. He looked around, taking in the sights & the sounds, his eyes sparkling with excitement. It wasn't long before those eyes fell upon a familiar face, one that turned his mood sour in an instant: Low-Ryda.

The pool hall grew quiet as the two locked eyes, an unmistakable tension lingered in the air. His steely gaze was a promise of the trouble that was about to unfold.

"What's up, nigga?" Low-Ryda called out from across the room, his voice dripping with false cordiality.

Madman knew what was up, as his face darkened.

"We need to talk, man," Low-Ryda continued, flipping a cue stick in his hand. *"About that money you & Boo owe me."*

Low Rider marched up to Madman, snarling as he spat out, *"You think you can get away with not giving me my cut, cuH?"*

Spookee, nonchalant as always, took the matter into his hands. He calmly retorted, *"I don't know what you're talking 'bout, but keep my lil bro's name out your mouth."*

His cool demeanor belied the menace in his words, a warning wrapped up in casual dismissal.

Madman on the other hand was another story, his face turned red as a Damu's bandana, as he stared Low-Ryda dead in the eyes.

"You feel entitled to that money, huh?" he said in a low voice that sent shivers down Low-Ryda's spine.

"Well, I've got news for you, nigga. You ain't getting shit."

Madman was never one to back down from a challenge. He took pride in being a tough guy & loved a good fist fight. His weapon of choice was not a firearm or a knife but a humble screwdriver, and his hard-knuckled fists.

He mean-mugged Low-Ryda, straightening up to his full height, before scoffing, *"What you gonna do about it?"*

The room itself held its breath as murmurs & whispers spread from table to table. The gathering storm was all too clear.

Low-Ryda's face filled with fury, spit flying from his lips as he got right in Madman's face, his finger jabbing at his chest.

"You best watch your back. I'll be coming for what's mine, nigga."

Madman snarled, *"put ya finger on me again, and I'll break that muthafucka in half!"*

Madman, unflinching even as Low-Ryda grew increasingly threatening, looked around the room, surveying the faces of the patrons. Finally, he made his proclamation.

"You want what's yours, fool?" he asked, smirking with a twisted grin. *"Get it back in blood, nigga."*

A collective gasp echoed through the crowded room. Madman's ultimatum was clear: Low-Ryda could choose to fight for the money he believed he was owed, or he could let the matter slide. As the tension in the air continued to build unbearably, Low-Ryda & Madman had a standoff, a fierce stare-down was in progress that threatened to set off an explosive rumble.

A hush fell over the room as the challenge grabbed everyone's attention. The stakes had been raised; Low-Ryda's face paled, as he walked away, the homies' laughter rang out. We knew that our decision would light a fuse to ignite a dangerous rivalry. Still, we lived for conflict, and confrontations, we welcomed it all.

The confrontation left a sour taste in Low-Ryda's mouth, pumping animosity into his heart. Things came to a head. Surrounded by the sounds of broken pool cues, clashing balls, and good times the homies continued to drink & shoot pool. They had no concern about the bad vibes, it couldn't damper their groove.

What followed was a devious sneak attack. As my brother turned his back to resume his game, Low-Ryda viciously struck Spookee over the head with a pool stick, igniting an unforeseen Pool Hall Brawl. The air filled with shouts, curses & the unmistakable clatter of a skirmish.

Meanwhile, I stood at the corner of 54th Street with the homies Gangsta D, Big Fat Rat, Dre Dogg, Big Red Jr, Lil Fat Rat & Bow Dee along with some homies from One-oh-Seven Hoover. We were just gang-hangin', smoking & drinking, taking in the night when one of the old head Gladiators passed by us. With him came news that stirred up a fire in the atmosphere.

He told us, *"ya homeboys bout to get in to it with Low-Ryda & em at the pool hall!"*

We got to the pool hall armed to the teeth & infatuated with vengeance. We were heavily armed with my sawed off shotgun & some handguns. The crisp night air did little to freeze the fiery hatred that burned within us, a hatred made all the more potent by our unwavering love for Big Spookee. With the Hoovers by my side, and a single kick, Big Fat Rat, knocked the door of the Pool Hall off its hinges, crashing onto the hardwood floor & echoing throughout the room. We stormed in like a tempest, my sawed-off shotgun glinting ominously under the dim lights.

"Everyone get on the fucking floor & empty your pockets & you empty the register!" I bellowed, my voice reverberating off the grungy walls.

Their punk ass sneak attack reminded me of the stray wolves lurking in the darkness, waiting to pounce on the prey at a sign of weakness. Only, we weren't their prey; we were the retaliating predators. We got to robbing not just Low-Ryda & his boys, but everyone present.

The aura of the pool hall shifted from a place of fellowship, conversation & friendly games to a battlefield, bodies thudding against cold concrete & the chings of emptied pockets echoing through the chaos. The patrons, caught in the eye of the storm, gave up everything they had, then scattered haphazardly, the terror in their eyes mirrored the fear I wanted to instill in the Low-Ryda boys. They stormed out of the exit leaving only the Low-Ryda boys & their blatant audacity behind.

Sweat glistening on my brown skin in the dimly lit room, my sights focused on the Low-Ryda boys, my hands holding the shotgun with an iron grip. The Low-Ryda boys cowering behind a pool table was a pitiful sight, resembling pawns in a chess game, waiting for their inevitable end. I could almost smell their fear seeping out their pores, their eyes as wide as saucers.

The Low-Ryda Boys' frantic scattering was a pathetic dance of desperation. I squeezed the trigger, unloading my shotgun, an eruption of hot hellfire & bedlam in hot pursuit of my prey. The deafening rain of lead echo sent them scrambling for the exits. My sawed-off shotgun, an omen of pending doom, greedily devoured shells as I unloaded them.

The sound of the shotgun as I gave chase, a grim symphony punctuated by the shattering sounds of pool balls & overturning furniture. However, the Low-Ryda boys managed to evade the hailstorm of revenge, speeding off into the night. Low-Ryda had chosen the wrong crew to fuck with. We moved as a collective, Hoover Gangsta did not tolerate any violations of our own.

It had been a few days since things came to a head with the Low-Ryda Boys. We Hoo'Ridin' in Tony's sleek, true blue Camaro, its flashy Dayton rims reflecting off Figueroa Street like a mirror. Madman was riding shotgun, stone faced, an unreadable mask, as he processed the money on his mind & revenge like mine. Spookee & I were crammed in the back, cracking jokes & smoking lovely. We creeped down the street like a panther on the prowl, the 8-track blasting black Michael Jackson *"I Wanna Rock with You"*, giving rhythm to our ride.

It was a familiar sight, the tricked out Cadillac Deville showing off its hydraulics, bouncing as it came into the intersection, it was Low-Ryda! A reminder of an unsettled vendetta, an ongoing beef that was as much a part of LA as the palm trees that lined its streets.

A blinding metallic glint caught my eye as someone from the Low-Ryda car pulled out a Winchester - a chill swept over us. Perceiving the imminent danger, Tony instinctively gunned the red light, wheels screeching their protest as Low-Ryda's bullets began raining down on us.

My heart leaped to my throat, but I knew I had to return fire, but Our Camaro was a coup, so hanging out of the window was not an option. Luckily, Madman reached for Tony's piece that was stashed in the glove box, and letting out a madman's roar, he returned fire from the passenger side. It was a surreal orchestra of violence, as bullets sped back & forth from two moving vehicles.

One of Low-Ryda's boys caught a lucky break – his bullet burst through the trunk, embedding itself in Spookee's back. A sharp gasp & a wheezed grunt echoed in the confines of the car. I whipped my head around, seeing Spookee slumped over, gritting his teeth against the pain. I started shooting, the echo bouncing around the inside of the car. My bullets exploded through the partially shattered rear windshield. Suddenly, the Deville veered off, the Winchester silenced, my rounds proving too hot for them to handle.

Tony wasted no time; he pushed the bullet-ridden Crip Camaro to its limit, turning the city into a blurred puzzle of neon & shadow as we raced to get Spookee to the hospital. The brawl had left a deep scar on Low-Ryda & I's relationship, but it wasn't until their vindictive act of shooting up GT's car that I truly tasted the bitter pill of animosity. The malice of their action caused a shift in my psyche.

They shrunk back in retreat only to strike us when our defenses were down. Blind rage coursed through my veins. I couldn't believe this nigga shot big bro! The streets were cold as a New York City winter that dreadful night, my blood boiling hotter than molten lava as each heartbeat echoed with a thirst for retribution. I reached the pinnacle of my bloodlust as Tony drove Spookee to the hospital. His agony etched itself into my memory, fueling my desire for payback.

The sight of my flesh & blood, Spookee, wounded & in agony, fresh in my mind. I was a man on a mission after that & I wouldn't stop until my blood thirst was satisfied, it didn't matter how long it would take me, I had a taste for blood & Low-Ryda blood had to spill to satisfy me. The feelings of resentment were corrosive, gnawing at my consciousness, clouding my judgment, my vengeance was a ticking time bomb waiting to explode.

I could feel it brewing, a vendetta infused with carnage. My hand clenched tightly onto the cold metallic handle of my Mossberg, its weight serving as an uncanny reminder of the daunting task that lay ahead. My heart pounding, my fingers itching to squeeze the trigger again. We spent months & months, putting in work, hunting him down, shooting at Low-Ryda unsuccessfully, but successfully delivering pain to his circle.

The sequence of events was a chaotic downward spiral triggered by our own actions - lives intertwined & trapped in a never-ending cycle of violence. At the time, however, our burning rage & determination to avenge our loved one left no room for second thoughts or regard to consequences.

While telling this story, I understand our actions led us down a path filled with violence fueled by our unwavering loyalty to each other. It's painful to look back on these memories. It's a cruel reminder of the recklessness of youth, the allure of crime, and the consequences we not only faced ourselves but also brought upon those we were closest to.

CHAPTER THIRTY-ONE:
"GOD FORGIVES HOOVER'S DON'T"

Ronchie recently came home from CYA after carjacking a Mexican on Valentines Day a couple of years ago. Upon his return he finally decided to leave VNE alone & he has been a solid stompdown Loc ever since known as Big Chim-Chim from Five-Deuce Hoover Gangsta Crip.

We called him Chim cause of his unorthodox fighting style that resembled that of a wild chimpanzee. Chim made a name for himself putting in work on the Blood Stone Villains after they killed Crazy Poke's brother, Stupid from Five-Deuce Broadway. Chim & Buddha, two brothers from both sides of Five-Deuce became the definition of what Hoover-Broadway represented.

Let me introduce a novel collection of characters, who dared to make a name for themselves on the playground of 52nd street school. Chim's little brother, Vincent, together with Terrell - a couple of audacious ten-year-olds, ventured out to lay the seeds of a peculiar clique within our turf, called the 409 Green Rags.

The 409 derived from the popular cleaning spray, asserting their slogan to 'clean up the hood.' It was a rather comical sight, watching baby gangstas, armed with BB guns, decked out in green bandanas.

A group of youngsters from 53rd street whose courage was apparent at a young age. Their enthusiasm, bravery, and commitment were inspiring to see. They specialized in wanton acts of vandalism, toppling over trash cans, breaking car & house windows, bike thefts, shoplifting & nickel & dimeing. They were young, but they had heart — & we recognized this.

Honestly, we didn't approve of this movement one bit, so we decided these youngsters had to turn Five-Deuce Hoover. Our goal was not just an influx of numbers, but a desire to induce unity & provide direction to these young souls. One day around the way the Green Rags crossed paths with my fellow Hriginals Big Fat Rat & Ric Roc on the Tray. Big Fat Rat, spotting the mischief-makers, decided to confront them.

"Y'all gonna stop that shit," commanded Fat Rat across the street.

Marquis, Big CeeCee's nephew, a bold—maybe a little too bold—member of the Rags, defiantly replied, *"Fuck Yall! This 409 Green Rags, fool!"*

Underlining his resistance with actions that were louder than words. Cue Deebo music from Friday— No sooner had the words left Marquis' lips than Big Fat Rat started making a beeline for him. Panicking, Marquis yanked out his BB gun with an intensity that appeared to be driven by mortal fear.

Marquis started pumping his BB gun like his life depended on it. He took precise aim at Big Fat Rat, and shot him square in the eye, causing the imposing figure to crumble to the ground in excruciating pain, a bloody spectacle that no one had expected!

This act earned them a severe ass whipping from Ric Roc & instigated Hoover Gangsta beyond our boiling point. We unleashed our vengeance whenever we saw them, whether they were on their way to or from school, hanging out on the Tray or at Jack's arcade, they were going to learn the rules of Hoover Street the hard way. However, no matter how many beatdowns we delivered, the 409s stubbornly refused to trade their green bandanas for blue ones.

While such an offense would typically wreak Big Fat Rat's wrath, instead a surprising reaction was unraveled. His outrage conflicted with the sight of the petty offender, resulting in an unusual show of mercy & compassion. Big Fat Rat could have easily obliterated the child in a moment of displaced aggression.

Fat Rat, an embodiment of the gritty South Central streets, smartly strategized his revenge. It was clear to him that the beatings were not enough to sway the loyalty of the Green Rags; a more cunning plan was needed. He came up with a more sensible plan: divide & conquer. His eye, now half-blind but twice as fierce, set his sights on Marquis's rival, a ten-year-old girl named Keysha who was Chim's baby sister & known to throw down with boys like the roughest & toughest of 52nd street school; she was fearless.

Keysha & Marquis had always been like oil & water, their disputes as common as the pigeons on the telephone lines. Fat Rat approached Keysha with a deal: a clean hundred dollar bill (enough to make any ghetto child's eyes light up) if she beat Marquis' ass.

Buddha, aware of his sister's tenacity & feistiness, at once tried to intervene, exclaiming, *"Don't tell her to do that shit, cause she's going to really do it."*

Buddha was right, she did it without hesitation. The kids got to squabbling what followed was comical. Marquis & Keysha clashed on a sunny day; they tumbled onto the green grass in a rowdy rumble, punches, and wild grappling. During the brawl, Keysha pulled off an antic that would become a local folklore for years to come. She mushed Marquis's face into a fresh pile of hot steamy dog shit.

He got up with poop all in his face, which satisfied Big Fat Rat the most with an eye patch & grin reflecting satisfaction, it was the picture of a puppeteer reigning over his marionettes & made us all laugh our asses off. Marquis, overcome with disbelief & wrath, retaliated by scooping up a handful of the very same poop & throwing it at Keysha. Marquis chased Keysha across the patchy lawns, armed with handfuls of the doo-doo brown ammunition. The fight soon evolved into a shit show, poop-slinging competition.

The repercussions of this fight were far more symbolic & significant than a mere fist fight or settling a petty feud. It displayed how resilience has a way of tempering spirit. The Green Rags didn't fold under pressure.

Instead, Big Fat Rat's strategy had led to a storybook ending, managing to disband the Green Rags & absorb them entirely into the

ranks of the tiny locs of Hoover Gangsta. Their unyielding spirit
fascinated us. We had laid down the law, and they had taken it, facing
their beatings with courage. Each punch was a lesson learned; each
fight was a stripe of honor. Even us, the hard-hitting big homies, had to
tip our hats to their grit & resolve.

Over time, they grew in stature, both in terms of their ranks &
their standing amongst us. We watched their evolution from Green
Rags into notorious Hoover Street Gangsta Crips. In an odd way, it was
a testament to their character, their perseverance, and their undeniable
will to be remembered.

Their journey was a testament to the Spirit of Hoover Street,
the tenacity of youngsters forced to navigate a ghetto built on unwritten
rules & uncompromising standards. We bombarded them with
challenges & reprimands ended up cultivating them into the Hoover
Gangstas they became.

They took the blows, they took the insults, they took the scorn,
and in the process, without realizing it, we created something unique,
unpredictable, unconquerable. The Spirit of the Five-Deuces prevailed,
and the ten-year-old bad asses from 53rd street became more than just a
funny neighborhood story – they became a symbol of the determination
& resilience which the Hoovers demanded.

Terrell became Boom-Boom, Marquis, the tiny rebel, was
accepted into our fold as Lil CeeCee, transforming his identity along
with his loyalties. The brave girl, Keysha became known as Keytaboo
& Tony became Te loc further solidifying a new generation of Hoover
Gangstas.

The journey from Foe-Nine Green Rags to Five-Deuce
Hoover was more than just a power move. It represented an adolescents
search for an identity, a path to unity driven by mutual respect, honor,
and a burning desire to belong. From Fat Rat's mercy to Marquis'
courage & Keytaboo's indomitable spirit, each act served as a
cornerstone, building up the legacy of Five-Deuce Hoover Gangsta
Crip.

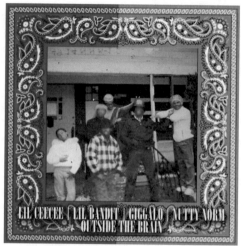

LIL CEECEE | LIL BANDIT | GIGGALO | NUTTY NORM
OUTSIDE THE BRAIN

A few weeks into the school year, Mad Dogg came back to the set real upset, but he didn't tell me what happened. I later found out a Six-Deuce Brim killed a Harlem Crip, execution style outside of Manual Arts during lunch time.

Gangsta D jumped up excitedly *"Fuck the Brims! Let's go get them niggas cuH!"*

They go out hunting. They were unsuccessful & Gangsta D called it a night, Mad Dog was resilient, he wanted revenge, Mad Dogg went back on the hunt with Big Dogg from Five-Nine Hoover! He caught the culprit over by John Muir on 59th, riding on a minibike with a broad.

The homies saw the target before he noticed them, so they had the advantage of surprise & hid in some bushes until he got close! He runs down & introduces the red rag to a shotgun blast, the blood crashes into some parked cars & succumbs to his wounds. Mad Dogg shows mercy & spares the girl's life. The girl knew Mad Dogg & Big Dogg from school & told on them.

"Revenge is an act of passion; vengeance of justice. Injuries are revenged; crimes are avenged." - Samuel Johnson

Police choppers could be seen & heard flying overhead, their search lights invading everyone's privacy. The pigs were relentless in their pursuit of Mad Dog, they came around harassing us, beating us up, trying to get us to rat on who did the shooting. I was chilling with the homies on 56th street, the pigs hit the block 10 cars deep!

One of the pigs yelled *"Where is Murdock?!"*

I yelled *back, "Nigga we don't know & if we did, we wouldn't tell you shit!"*

The pigs threw me against the wall, told me to put my hands on my head, I resisted, so they hit me with the billy club!

All I see is white, I'm disoriented, I don't know what is happening to the other homies during the chaos. I just hear everyone screaming & shouting. The community worked together, the whole Fifties helped hide Mad Dogg, from house to house, moving clandestinely through alleys, and backyards for as long as we could, like slaves running from the overseers on the Underground Railroad but Mad Dogg was selfless. He couldn't stand to keep hiding & watching the pigs beating on the homies from the shadows. Mad dogg was laying low on 55th street with Tee Dub.

"Shit is crazy, I ain't gonna get away! I can't let the pigs keep fuckin homies up over me." Mad Dogg tells the homegirl.

He decides to turn himself in. This would be the last time I saw Mad Dogg, he would be incarcerated for 40 years & Big Dog gets sent to CYA. Now that we spilled first blood, we waited for retaliation, with our defenses on high.

You probably heard that, Tony! Toni! Toné! song it never rains in Southern California, well that fool lied his ass off cause tonight it's raining cats & dogs in South Central. Fortunately, when I step out of Lil Live's front door, my bro Spookee is pulling up to visit Madman. Lil ScHool Boy was my partner in crime tonight, we had plans to get wet & freaky deaky with some pretty young thangs, but the rain was throwing a wrench in our plans.

Out of options & clock ticking, I tried to convince Spookee to let me borrow his ride for tonight's fun-filled agenda but the disdain in his eyes made it clear that he was not interested in my proposal. Lord knows I've swindled him before.

He was still mad. I convinced our sweet, unsuspecting mama to let me *'borrow'* his cocaine white 1972 Cadillac Coupe De Ville, under the pretense of a store run. Classic Boo! To make matters worse, the newly replaced hood went soaring into the midnight sky during an impromptu drag race with Coke Dogg on Figueroa! I could picture the shock & anger on Spookee face & the sound of metal scraping on the road, I know he wanted to kill me!

I was confident I could get him to cough up the keys nonetheless, so I tried to sweet talk him, offering him one of the ladies & some lovely but our back & forth on the matter was uneventful. He stood firm with his refusal but made a grudging compromise, he agreed to take us to ScHool Boy crib to get some Sherm & drop us off to the PYT's.

Spookee had conditions though, he said *"ScHool Boy been trippin' lately, if he gets on some bullshit with y'all, I'm leaving', Madman & I got plans."*

Seemed fair enough & I didn't have too many options, so I made the deal. On the way to the Tray, Spookee wouldn't stop talking about how bad ScHool Boy been trippin' & tried to get Lil ScHool Boy to cosign.

Lil ScHool Boy didn't fall into Spookee's trap, *"My big homie ain't trippin, cuH, cut that shit out,"* Lil ScHool Boy replied.

Spookee even more frustrated with us, snarled at us, "Whatever nigga! I got shit to do, so make this shit quick!"

When we get to the Tray, ScHool Boy & Lil Red Jr. are hanging out with a new kid that moved in across the street, he allegedly had good ass Kush & ScHool Boy's trying to barter some of his premium water in exchange. However, the transaction is taking too long for Spookee's liking, he starts to get anxious.

"Man, I'm fittin' to go, bro" he snapped, tired of waiting, *"Y'all cramping' my style!"* He continues, eager to shake us off.

Desperation overflowed from me, but my appeal for patience was ignored. He jumps in his car, his headlights cast a faint glow on the wet asphalt as he floors it! I was overcome with frustration & with a surge of adrenaline.

I lunged my 40 oz of Olde English at his car, which smacked into his rear window. It exploded in an eruption of consequence, anger, and shards of glass. In the frenzy of rage & rain, the Cadillac hydroplaned, veering uncontrollably sideways down the slick road before crashing into an undefeated telephone pole with a thundering clash.

LIL SCHOOL BOY

The car, Spookee's beloved treasure, stood crumpled—a haunting shell of its former glory. I was shell-shocked at the sight, my anger quickly dissolving to regret, thinking I killed big bro! I ran towards the wreck but when I got there, Spookee was gone like the ghost of Hoover Street!

I'm sitting on the new kid porch with ScHool Boys & Lil Red Jr. Consumed by worry over big bro's fate, I wore my anxiety like a Pendelton. However, relief rudely shoved my anxiety away. The darkness soon yielded a surprise - Spookee, he is alive & mad as hell clutching a .38 special, he recently snatched from a security guard.

He appeared from the shadows of a neighbor's yard, rage boiling over in his eyes. He would never let me forget about propelling him into the crash - an incident he took as sabotage rather than an impulsive action spurred by feelings of betrayal.

The scene, a wild west standoff like the finale of Thomasine & Bushrod. Only the irony was we were brothers turned foes in less than 52 seconds. He drew his weapon, a ghastly expression of his resentment, nobody was safe from Spookee's vengeance, not even me. Spookee with a gun was like a grenade with the pin pulled, knowing this, I couldn't leave my fate to chance. I followed suit, and ours turned into a deadly dance of bullets.

Caught between the crossfires of his blind fury & my bruised ego, our attempts to harm each other were curiously unproductive. There was an odd sincerity in our attempts to miss. After a volley of wild shots, we cooled down, exhausted our ammunition & fury, acknowledging the absurdity that had taken over our brotherhood.

Ravaged by a storm of emotions after our skirmish, Spookee sought release in his bad habit, jacking fools. He went on a robbing spree. To channel his rage & not kill me, he chose crime therapy. Spookee felt like he was headed to prison either way after welcoming the new kid to Hoover Street by shooting up his house during our fiasco. The thrill was short-lived, and his freedom paid the price, trapping him behind cold bars till Fall '84.

Little did we know that would be the last time we'd see each other as free men. We would enter the revolving door of the justice system, when I came home, he went in, and vice versa. A sinister dance that had plagued our entire lives until this day was anchored by the memory of that evening. A cycle we promise to break.

CHAPTER THIRTY-TWO:
"BECOMING BOO CAPONE"

As determined as I was to be a family man, the wild temptations of new pussy & gangbangin' had a stronghold on my psyche. Tonight, Crazy De-De's parents are out of town, so he is throwing a house party. I pulled up with Madman, dripping wet, with a couple bottles of Tyronia.

As we walked into Crazy DeDe's crib, our heads swam in a fog of euphoria, soaring on cloud nine off that PCP like the Temptations. Amid the good times & funky vibrations of The Brothers Johnson, *"Stomp"* filling Crazy De-De's dimly lit living room, a voluptuous brown skin girl with a pair of walnut brown eyes, and coffee-colored curls, caught my eye. I asked Madman if he knew who she was.

"That's Janine, she just moved on the Foe," Madman replied.

Janine was babysitting her drink in the corner, trying to blend into the shadows of the party's madness. Madman wouldn't let her off so easily. We headed over in her direction, Madman messing with her for babysitting & his playful attempts to knock the cup out of her hand broke the ice for me. As we conversed, an inexplicable bond formed between us. She had an irresistible aura about her.

Turns out, her father was Big Cee, an original Gladiator who had transitioned to Five-Deuce Hoover. Big Cee was a respected figure in the Fifties, someone who enjoyed widespread respect & fear. Amidst our conversation, she told me she hung out with T-Dogg & was down with the set.

She told me, *"I know who you are,"* with a twinkle in her eye. She recalled the first time she laid eyes on me.

"I've seen you before, you was in my house," she began, chuckling slightly as she continued, *"You was chasing & shooting at some Blood nigga, he was running for his life carrying a baby. Then y'all came running in my daddy's house to hide from the pigs. I remember thinking to myself, 'Who the fuck are these niggas, they are crazy!"*

"You so crazy, I think I want to have yo baby" -
Salt-N-Pepa, "Whatta Man"

We laughed about it, and in the shared amusement, I felt we were forming an indescribable bond. In the days that followed, Big Mama & I got tight, she became my favorite homegirl. I didn't have a driver's license, but I taught her how to drive. As I sat beside her, guiding her hands on the steering wheel, the depth of our bond started going beyond the world of Crips, drive-by shootings, and ducking one-time.

We were just two young souls searching for something real, groovin' in a world of uncertainty. We were the same age, but her tender heart held an assuring warmth, with the qualities of a matriarch that extended towards not just me but all the Hoover Gangstas. We all cherished this girl who cared for us like a mother, so I christened her Big Mama from Five-Deuce Hoover Gangsta Crip.

For most teenagers, their life revolved around the usual fun & games, enjoying days of sunshine on the sandy beaches of California. My life was anything but ordinary, a 16-year-old father & Hriginal. Instead of basking under the Pacific sun, I was making plans to support my baby momma & our toddler.

One afternoon, Sham Rock, Lil Fat Rat, and JJ from Broadway engaged in a risky operation, jacking an oG from the Fruit Town Brim Bloods of six ounces of PCP. The tooth for tooth, eye for an eye philosophy of Hammurabi ran deep within our veins. Enraged & vowing revenge, the Fruit Town pulled up to the Evan's humble abode, only to bare his fangs of fury at Mama Evans.

A chilling threat echoed ominously in the air, *"If we can't get ya son, we gonna get you!"*

Threatening a Hoover Gangsta let alone one of our mama's was a clear cut declaration of war. However, the winds of fate were blowing in favor of the Evans clan. As luck would have it, Sham Rock & Big Mike arrived at the scene just in time, as if ordained by an unknown force.

The standoff that ensued was swift & brutal, gunfire piercing the heavy afternoon air. When the dust settled, the Fruit Town was left in a dire state, his consciousness slipping into an abyss, his body a hollow shell imprisoned in a three-week coma. A testament to how dangerous the Evans clan was.

The oG Fruit Town appeared in court with the audacity to mean mug the homies, like he wasn't a snitch trying to mask his cowardice. They were sentenced to 6 years for attempted murder with a firearm. The domino effect of arrests spread through the Evans brothers like wildfire.

Fish & Ken Dogg were already serving time for robbery, and now Sham Rock & Big Mike joined their ranks. Within a short time, we lost vital members of the Evans clan to the system depleting the strength of Hoover Gangsta.

Minor setbacks for a major comeback. The daunting episode didn't end here. Fish leaped at a glimmer of hope & made a brave escape from CYA, only to be captured later. This period of the early 80's marked a greatly disheartening phase in our history, with 70% of the Hriginals incarcerated just three years after our formation. Back on the streets, the remnants of our set might've appeared weak due to our reduced numbers.

Behind the iron bars, it was contrary, we were becoming more powerful & notable, our name ringing bells in the Detention Camps, CYA, and the County jail. Caught in the whirlwind of gang rivalry, law enforcement, and survival, each homeboy played their part in an unyielding quest for dominance & preservation of our brotherhood. The tale of our endeavors & tribulations serves as a chilling reminder of the realities of life as a Crip.

After just a few months of being home from Camp, life didn't give me enough time to get back on my feet before I found myself caught up in a robbery case with the homeboy, Stroll, one of the younger homies from the set. That fateful day commenced like any other, the warm sun rays sprinkling its orange hue onto Hoover Street.

The motive behind the robbery was not greed, but the pressing need to provide for my family. Stroll & I were young, reckless, and desperate for money. I had no other avenue to make some quick cash than catching a sweet lick. I decided to rob from the rich & give to the poor, my family. Unfortunately, the robbery went bad, and we got arrested.

STROLL

While I was detained in the police precinct, I had the brilliant idea to lie about my age so I could possibly be reunited with Spookee & get access to cigarettes in the county. We weren't allowed to smoke in the Juvenile facilities. So, I told the pigs I was 18 years old,

I had already been to the juvenile hall, the group home, detention camp & now it was time for the real test. A test of character, loyalty, and sheer willpower. As I walked through the iron gates that bound countless young souls like mine, I was mentally preparing myself for any challenges & enemies I may meet.

I was deeply entrenched in representing FDHGC, it was my tribe, my loved ones. My heart was embedded in the lifestyle, and I felt I owed it to my homies to prove myself, a strong, dedicated representative as I introduced my fellow Crips to Hoover Gangsta. Unfortunately, my plan for reunification failed, they placed me at Wayside.

I was there for 2 weeks & ended up stabbing up a Long Beach Crip that thought he was going to punk me for money to use the phone. A power move that garnished more respect & notoriety for me & FDHGC amongst the older Crips. After the incident, the officials found out my true age & sent me to Juvenile Hall until I was sentenced, where I was reunited with Big Fat Rat.

The judge sentenced me to two years in the California Youth Authority (CYA) with an odd sense of grief & excitement. I was the only Hoover Gangsta in there until Gangsta D got there & we were fortunate enough to be cellies (cellmates) but there were a couple other Grooves in the spot.

It was during my time in CYA that opened my eyes to the vast expanse of the Crip world. CYA housed youngsters from various turfs & walks of life, and I found myself rubbing shoulders with an eclectic mix of fellow Crips. I was exposed to a wide array of perspectives & beliefs, forcing me to view my own affiliations in a new light. I saw an unprecedented potential in collaborating, ironing out differences, and creating alliances that could collectively wield a considerable influence on the streets of L.A.

I was there with Blacc Bug from Seven-Foe, Squirrel & the deaf homie Speed from Eight-Tray, Killa, Head, Levi, and Big Boo from One-oh-Seven Hoover. Some Eight Tray Gangstas, Chico, Mad Bone, Lil Spike & Lil Timmy Tucker. The Devils 1&2, Shiphead & Birdman from Gardena Shotgun Crip, Crazy John, Ricc Dogg & Tray Dee from Long Beach Insane. Crazy John is a highly respected member & G homie from Insane, he is currently on death row for a double homicide.

Big Boo was a reputable from 107th street, fighting a murder/robbery case at the time. It was eerie to meet someone else wearing my name, not only did we have the same nickname, but we were also like minded which led to us becoming tight as we did some time together over the years. My mother has been calling me *"Boo"* since before I could remember, carrying on the family tradition from my beloved Grandma, Mama Boo.

CYA would hone my resilience & determination to razor-sharp perfection. Little did I know that going to CYA would mark the beginning of a transition. As fate would have it, change walked into my life. In order to stand out & differentiate myself from my newfound comrade, Boo from One-oh-Seven, I was assigned the moniker *"Capone,"* likening my tenacity & passion for the Crip lifestyle to the infamous Chicago gangster Al Capone. The name stuck, and I adopted it as a permanent part of my identity. I became Big Boo Capone.

My time at California Youth Authority had shifted something within me, inspiring me with a drive to network & unite with my fellow Crips. This new persona served to emphasize my strengths as a leader & a ruthless defender of Hoover Gangsta as well as the Crip car. It was a powerful combination, and one that ignited a fire within me to establish a more dominant presence.

Transcending the boundaries of Hoover Gangsta & forming bonds with other factions of Crips. During this time, I solidified the Hoover Gangsta alliance with the Gardena Shotguns, Long Beach Insane & the Eight Trey Gangstas. These sets had already had solid foundations set up with the other Hoover tribes & now that same loyalty was extended to Five-Deuce.

I found myself reuniting with an old friend to pass my time in lock down. The friend to whom I refer wasn't a person, it was my love of boxing, sweat-stained gloves & heavily worn punching bag, the strong smell of leather & machismo.

My body had already nurtured a lofty muscular build from my time at Mendenhall. I wasn't your average teenager. A dedicated fitness regime honed my physique. My short stature of 5'2" was dwarfed by a solid muscular build weighing 190 lbs., an unexpected heavyweight housed in a seemingly compact embodiment.

There was something therapeutic about boxing again, a sense of equilibrium it brought to my life, as I was wedged between adolescence & adulthood. Amid the chaos of confinement, the boxing ring was my sanctuary where I could tune out the world. I would focus solely on the punches & counterpunches, the raw aggression I harbored finding an outlet.

I latched onto the sport, delighting in the raw power, the discipline it demanded, the respect it commanded. It became my coping mechanism & a way out of anger. I was often pitted against opponents who were bigger, those who towered over me, seemingly giants.

My trainer was a gentleman named Smitty. A short, old nigga with experience etched in his wrinkles, he had an uncanny eye for spotting potential where others only saw problems. Smitty, with his gnarled hands & deeply etched smile lines, was like a lighthouse. His guidance became my compass, swinging me away from the storms of my anger & anchoring me to the shores of discipline & resilience.

During my tenure at CYA, we had matches against various branches of the military. Those meets were my testing grounds, pushing me to unleash my potential. Far from home & dwarfed by the colossal forces we met; my nerve never wavered. I used my disadvantage as a weapon, never shying away from the challenge.

They were bigger, but I was badder & more determined. The fights were never fair due to my height disadvantage, but I was never intimidated, I've been fighting bigger cats all my life. I strived on the sheer rush of taking on a challenge, I was the underdog, overcoming insurmountable odds. Win or lose, I was the maker or breaker of my own destiny & reputation.

My sparring partner during those years was Henry Tillman, a towering figure of 6'4", five years my senior. He hailed from Los Angeles, from the streets of 89th & Central Ave on the border of the 87 Kitchen Crips & The Neighborhood Family Swan Bloods.

Battling him in the ring was like seeing David take on Goliath, without the sling shot. Tillman, with his towering personality & imposing figure, was an incredible athlete who challenged me to push my boundaries. It wasn't just boxing; he was a mirror to the challenges life often throws at me, both anticipated & unanticipated.

As we sparred with sweat streaming down our faces, I perfected my unique fighting style: the now-famous peek-a-boo boxing style. With my guards glued to my cheeks, hawk eyes trained on my opponent, I could deliver quick, explosive punches, shattering their confidence. It was all about defending & attacking swiftly. It was this cunning technique Tillman absorbed from our sparring sessions, learning to anticipate & counteract my onslaught of high-speed attacks.

In August 1983, destiny chose a different path for Henry, releasing him early to fight in the Pan American Games. His dedication to boxing mirrored mine, a reflection of ambition, resilience, and sheer determination. The battlefield shifted from our modest CYA training grounds to the Olympic trials held in Fort Worth, Texas, the following summer where he faced off with a young Mike Tyson.

The formidable Mike Tyson needs no introduction but if you are unfamiliar, he would become one of the greatest boxers of all time. The man who later championed the peek-a-boo boxing style I had utilized. Amidst the deafening roars & the blinding lights, Tillman emerged victorious & later won the 1984 Olympic Gold Medal.

It was a testament to hard work & lessons learned in the spur of the countless matches we had in the CYA facility. Henry's rise represented something for all of us - a chance at redemption - a sliver of possibility that one of us could transcend the imposing boundaries of CYA.

As the sun rose & set, I felt like another forgotten juvenile delinquent incarcerated in the Fred C. Nelles Facility in Whittier, California. I roamed the cold halls with a heavy heart, hopeless & drowning in an overwhelming sense of dread. Until one memorable morning, Big Mama, a tremendous pillar of strength, loyalty, and affection, surprised me with her vibrant presence.

Her arrival was like sunshine on a cloudy day, her brown skin glowed, holding a radiant smile on her face. A face that welcomed me with warmth, empathy, and genuine love. It felt like a lifeline thrown to a drowning man, and I clung to it, grasping at the hope it represented. It was something that sent a surge of much-needed vitality coursing through my veins.

During her visit, she couldn't help but notice the changes in my physique, courtesy of my rigorous boxing training. Her gentle touch gingerly explored the contours of my chiseled biceps.

"I love ya muscles, Boo," she complimented me.

Through her touch & words, she managed to awaken a profound sense of accomplishment in me. I've never felt more valued or more seen. Her admiration was evident in the way her fingertips caressed my muscles; her compliments catered to my ego. She had a touch that was as gentle & nurturing as the sweetest of motherly love &

I was the immature cockhound constantly fighting the growing feelings inside me. I believed in Hoover Gangsta Crip, I didn't believe in love.

It was like she had plucked my black ass out the lost & found; the realization of her unwavering loyalty made my heart swell with gratitude & affection. Yet what meant more to me than her words were the sacrifice she made to take this trip. Rising before the sun at 3am to catch the shuttle & travel the long miles to the facility to see me, was no minor sacrifice.

My relationship with Big Mama was blossoming into something more substantial. I saw her in a new light, no longer just a homegirl, there was a pull inside me, a need to protect her, to treasure her friendship. On the other side, there was fear — the terrifying thought of ruining our bond, of betraying her trust. I was young, dumb & full of cum; the thug life had left me numb.

These intense emotions frightened me. Although I was a thorough young Crip with more power in my fists than most, I found myself afraid of commitment. I felt she deserved better, this internal struggle, a tug of war between the desire for more & the fear of losing it all. Regardless of my reservations, she proved her loyalty.

Big Mama continued to visit me during my confinement & even accepted all my expensive collect calls. Her efforts, unmatched dedication, and unconditional support testified without a doubt she was ride or die for me. Through every conversation, her soothing voice gave me comfort during my captivity. Looking back, I realize it was the start of an evolution, an evolution of my relationship with Big Mama, but more importantly, the evolution of Boo.

Life continued inside the belly of the beast, the cold, concrete walls of CYA was no walk in the park, a place where alliances were formed, and plots were born. The cold silver bars imprisoned disillusioned young men & future career criminals. However, the prison walls could not cage the dreams of men whose hearts yearned for something greater – something so captivating that the risks were all but forgotten.

It was a year of turmoil, our numbers on the street were down, it was a time of uncertainty & high passions. A time where loyalties were challenged, and alliances put to the test. The ghettos of Los Angeles were a kaleidoscope of dreams & nightmares, a battleground for respect, territory, and survival.

In those times, the heart & soul of our collective, our membership, began to dwindle in the streets. Our life of crime led to inevitable entanglements with the law. Leading to most of the Hriginals finding ourselves locked up like Akon, sentenced for an array of crimes ranging from petty to gruesome.

The Seven-Foes arrived at a decision that would change the Hoover collective by adding the G to their name, now becoming Hoover Crip Gang. The switch was strategic, a means to distinguish themselves from the Harlem 30s who also donned the *"HC"* for Harlem Crip. However, we did not share this vision, standing stubbornly against the idea of changing our identity. During this time, we had less than 2 dozen Hoover Gangstas on the street, and the turbulence began to be amplified with various factions we had ties too.

During my absence the set was governed by the remaining Hriginals, Coke Dogg, CoCo, Ric Roc, Bow Dee, Cadillac Bob, Madman, BEL-AIRE, Big Fat Rat & the return of Ken Dogg. These were not just names; they were legends, their grit surpassed only by their unflinching loyalty for the Hoover Gangsta & its principles.

The sibling rivalry originally awakened by the One-oh-Seven's had subsided & now the issues lay with Seven-Foes & Eight-Trays. The Seven-Foes & Eight-Trays disdain towards our defiance was not confined to arguments & insults. Animosities escalated into fist fights, brawls, and even exchanges of bullets. The Seven-Foes, upset by Coke Dogg & Ken Dogg refusal to fall in line with their HCG campaign, shot up 48th street park! Luckily these instances of violence didn't result in any dead homies.

The rivalry also spilled into the juvenile halls, camps, prisons, transforming lockdowns into vipers' pits where the overwhelming numbers of Hoover Crips would 'rat pack' the isolated members of Five-Deuce, testing their gangsta, looking to exploit any weaknesses.

Now, it certainly wasn't easy being a Hoover Gangsta during those trying times, but it was fun, a twisted sense of mischief that kept us hooked. The Bloods were no competition, our troops grew bored with our one-sided quarrels. We thrived for the constant danger, the adrenaline rush of battles, the unity forged in the face of adversity was something that gave us unwavering resolve.

Our skirmishes with the Hoover Crips kept our knives sharpened. Nonetheless, we were not exempt from weak minded troops that agreed to fall in line, even getting Hoover Crip tatted. Most chose to brave the storm with me, fearless souls who refused to bend, fold or to assimilate. We refused to compromise; we held fast to our beliefs. We were at the bottom of the Hoover totem pole & despite being the minority, we embraced a spirit of defiance & courage.

> *"Not everybody's journey is easy, and it wouldn't*
> *be worthwhile if you can't see what you gained*
> *without realizing what kind of battles you've been*
> *through, what kind of scars you have."*
> *- Tamlyn Tomita*

April Fool's Day 1982, a day etched deeply in my memory. On this cold, grey day, Big Smiley, a respected Hriginal of the Five-Nine Hoover Crip Gang, was ruthlessly killed by East Coast. The event was like most Crip on Crip rivalry, which escalated over a shared female entangled in a love triangle. Things went sour during a dice game behind the school.

Thursday, April 1, 1982

The attack seems to have been related to gang warfare in the area, according to Celestain, but he added that it was the first shooting he had heard of on the grounds of the elementary school at 62205 S. Figueroa St. in the 21 years he has been in school security.

"The information we have is that the victims were members of the Hoover Crips Gang, and the guys who did the shooting are believed to belong to the East Coast Crips Gang," he said.

Big Smiley's fierce determination, doused in a lethal mix of courage & grit, made him a remarkable figure in a wave-tossed world of turf wars & relentless animosity. The tragic event occurred at the 61st street school, a place where innocence is supposed to thrive & where dreams are supposed to be nurtured.

The injustice sparked outrage & ignited a war, enraging the Five-Nines to become our allies in our conflict with the East Coast. It wasn't long before the East Coast Crips suffered a loss, a fatality from a shotgun blast. The implications of this killing were devastating, compounding the tension creating mortal enemies.

During my bid I formed a relationship with Blacc Bug, it was an undeniable bond built on mutual respect. Blacc Bugg, a reputable member of Seven-Foe Hoover, we were about the same age, he was about 5 '6, a sturdy young man with skin as black as the middle of the night.

Our meeting wasn't a mere coincidence; we were destined to be a part of a master plan – the birth of an empire that would shake the foundations of LA's underworld. Together, we became part of *"The Hoover Connect,"* an enterprising organization founded by Bugg & Judabean, the infamous leader of Foe-Tray Hoover.

I didn't know my position in the plan that he & Judabean devised would lead to the most memorable phase of Hoover History, our Golden Age. It all started with the creative scheming of Big Judabean & Blacc Bugg; their intentions were clear: to turn the Hoover Crips into a drug empire. To fully understand the significance of our vision, one must first look back at the early 80's drug scene in Los Angeles.

"Have a vision. Be demanding."
– Colin Powell

At the time there were three major organizations in the narcotics game: Bertrain & the Foe-Tray Gangstas had Third World, oG Whitey & Whitey Enterprises were from Five-Deuce Broadway, and Freeway Rick & the Freeway Boys, which contrary to popular belief had nothing to do with Hoover.

Freeway Ricky Ross, a drug kingpin who had made his fortune through cunningness. Freeway Rick was raised in the Hoovers, many people thought he was groovin' because many of the Freeway Boys were. The Freeway Boys headquarters was also smack dab in the middle of Eight-Trey Hoover territory on 81st street.

Freeway Boys had various members from rival Crip & Blood factions & at the time we weren't interested in mingling with enemies, only eliminating them. We had a strict policy against fraternizing with the enemy.

Judabean felt the need to create an entity to give us an identity separate from the Freeway Boys & Crippin'. The separate entity was the Hoover Connect & the Board of Directors consisted of the organizers Judabean & Blacc Bugg, along with me from Five-Deuce, Big Bugg from Five-Nine, Big Ed from Eight-Tray, Big Vamp from Nine-Deuce, Crazy Nell from Nine-Foe, Big Ben Nose from One-oh-Seven, and Big Mikey from Eleven-Deuce.

Judabean had set up a dependable connect with a Colombian national, who was connected to the cartels. Through this connection, We would have access to high-quality cocaine for incredibly cheap prices, a game-changer.

Hoovers were not going to work for anybody, the expectation was that all Hoovers got their product from the Connect. In return, the money stayed within the Hoover empire, a true black monopoly— expanding its influence & power. As we implemented the plan & watched its success unfold, Los Angeles transformed before our eyes.

Our combined might made the Hoover Connect a force to be reckoned with. We consisted of nine sets with over 1,000 members. We were united in our thirst for power, forging our own path to dominance.

The Hoover Connect rose to power rapidly, reclaiming 81st street & the Hoover Plaza apartments as Hoover Connect headquarters. This location became the epicenter of our business operations - a hub of drug distribution, money reconciliation & laundering, and a base for our continued growth.

Blacc Bugg would be released around this time, so I put him in contact with Baby Crazy to represent the set while I was finishing up my time. Judabean & Bugg made it happen. Hoover Connect was movin' & groovin', dominating the drug trade. The streets of South Central LA were awash with the spoils of our hard work. The wealth was incredible, and the power intoxicating. We had reached a level of influence that could make or break others in the city. Our name echoed through the streets – a sound that was both comforting to our allies & terrifying to our enemies.

Our peaceful coexistence with the Broadways got brutally disrupted one alarming day. They saw our vulnerable state as an opportunity to assert their dominance, pressuring Hoover Gangstas to join their ranks. Some of our homies did seek refuge from the HGC-HCG conflict under the mantle of the Broadways. They put faith in the brotherhood we had as Hoover-Broadway & were enticed by the success of Whitey Enterprise.

The Broadways wanted us to drop 'Hoover' & unite under the Five-Deuce Broadway banner. One afternoon the Broadways, Big Tee, Rainbow & Crazy Wayne pulled up on Twindogg & Chino outside the Hoover store.

Big Tee asked *"What that 5-Two Like?"*

Chino replied *"Hoover, cuH!"*

Rainbow countered *"Wrong answer fool,"* & fired on him!

The Broadways jumped the homies, they got their asses kicked but they held their ground & that's all that really matters in this lifestyle. The outrage at this incident was immediate & widespread among us, a collective recoil from the idea of abandoning Hoover from our allegiance.

The Broadways audacity was perceived as an insult, an affront to our deeply cherished foundation. The homies were infuriated by their recent attack. With our resolve fortified & pride driving us, the inevitable face-off was set into motion. It was about principles, turf, defending our identity & the legacy stitched into the very fabric of our being. The stage was set for a rumble on 54th street.

Our home turf became a battlefield where the power would shift, alliances would be tested, and pride would be wounded. The confrontation that unfolded was fierce; it was the clash of titans during the next invasion by Big Tee, Broadway Ken Dogg, JJ, Bear, and Buddha along with over 40 Broadways.

Mr. CoCo, Coke Dogg, Fat Rat, and Chim plunged into the heat of the battle, a series of one on one fades, which resulted in a return to our regular programming, but with a renewed understanding of our shared allegiance. Sticking to our roots as Five-Deuce Hoover-Broadway, our resolve crystalized, and fortified by that unforgettable battle.

The rumble was a reminder of the consequences that faced anyone who dared threaten our foundation. Amidst the flurry of flying fists & fury, a fierce determination engulfed my fellow Hoover Gangstas. They asserted our collective pride, the refusal to bend or break under pressure. We remained true to our roots; honor intact, pride undenied. Each punch thrown by the homies echoed our collective voice, a voice that defiantly proclaimed:

"We are Five-Deuce Hoover Gangsta Crip, and we won't back down, bend or fold for nobody!"

We are reflections of those infamous rumbles in the Fifties & behind the wall our unity echoing through Gangland. As the years passed, no matter where life has taken us, our allegiance remains to Hoover Gangsta. This name is a symbol of our unconquerable soul, a blend of shared history & an unwavering bond that binds us under ironclad loyalty. This is the saga of FDHGC, and the unwavering defiance that fuels us. We embody the reality of the streets, a reality littered with trials & triumphs, a reality that makes us who we are.

CHAPTER THIRTY-THREE:
"THIN LINE BETWEEN LOCS & FOES"

I finally got my release date. As I walked out of those prison gates, I couldn't help but feel a mix of excitement & anticipation about what life would have in store for me next. What I didn't know was that my journey was just beginning, and it would be filled with love, wealth, and struggles of its own. Blacc Bugg & Baby Crazy came to pick me up.

It was good to see Baby Crazy, and as always, he was Loced out. I swear he took no days off. He was decked out in his FDHGC uniform, crisp blue rag, matching his Hoover boots, blue Colorados, fresh out the box. His Dickies starched & pressed so hard they could stand on their own. He wore his blue Pendleton with the top button only, looking like a Mexican cholo. Baby Crazy represented the epitome of a true blue 52nd street Hoover Gangsta Crip.

The Grooves welcomed me back in style with a cocaine white Cadillac limousine. It was the kind of ride that made a statement. Baby Crazy, a true Crip, pistol tucked in his waistband. Hanging off his arm, one of the finest blonde haired, blue eyed European hoes with a pair of the biggest titties I ever saw.

As I entered the limo to my delight, I found out they brought gifts, a couple more fine snow bunnies, some fried chicken, and a few bottles of chilled Dom Perignon, a prestige cuvée champagne. My first taste of ice cold bubbly tasted as sweet as my newfound freedom. The homies made me feel appreciated. It felt good to be welcomed back like this - surrounded by good people, good food, and good vibrations.

We spent the day cruising around the city in that limo, catching up on all the time we had missed while I was away. They gave me updates about our new venture, the Hoover Connect. Our new drug enterprise was growing rapidly & steadily. As we rode through the streets, I couldn't wait to get a piece of the pie. I thought to myself, a nigga about to be paid, I'll be back on top in no time.

As the strings of tradition played in the background, I found myself standing at the epicenter of our universe: The corner of Hoover Street & 81st Street, the Hoover Connect Headquarters. It became a sacred protocol for every Hoover to make it their first stop upon release. The Hoover Plaza apartments became our fortress, it probably inspired *"The Carter"* in the movie *"New Jack City,"* with Wesley Snipes.

The sight that greeted me at Headquarters was the essence of our tribe - over a hundred Hoovers from every branch were swarming the area while *"Grooveline"* by Heatwave blasted from a nearby boombox. Intense scenes unraveled before my eyes; security armed to the teeth with carbine rifles made their presence known, displaying our readiness to defend our turf at any cost.

This concrete castle was not just about cold blue steel & ice grills. It was the place where Judabean & Blacc Bugs' vision became real. It was a thriving dope boy bazaar where the exchange was not just dirty money & crack cocaine, but it consisted of stories, life lessons, and dreams. Amid the intimidating security & crowd of Crips ran the vital lifeline of our community - a line of smokers eager to get their share of our lucrative product.

As I absorbed the electrifying vibe of our lively enterprise, I came across my boy Yella from Eight-Tray Hoover. He was a real laid back, cool Crip with a wise soul, and a streak of ruthlessness he saved for his foes. His stories were always intriguing with his unique deep baritone voice reminiscent of Barry White. He was telling me how the pigs keep mixing him up with Big Mikey, his doppelganger from

Eleven-Deuce, locking them up for the other's crimes. Amid my laughter, I heard a familiar voice call my name.

"My muthafucka, Boo Diggs! Pardon me, cuH I hear its Big Boo Capone now!"

My gaze is drawn towards the source, my main man, Judabean. He stood there, a proud emblem of the Hoover brotherhood, a stalwart guardian with a formidable reputation adored & feared in equal measure. The metamorphosis of Judabean was intriguing & motivating. I'll always remember him as a distinctive figure of strength, encapsulating the raw charisma of the Kiwé culture.

Each day, he donned the signature Crip uniform with an incontestable bravado - the blue rag, the Pendleton shirts, and 501 jeans that held stories of our cold Crippin' lineage. However, today, the inescapable whiff of Johnson baby powder & cool water cologne tag teamed with a new affluent attitude radiating from him.

The success of the Hoover Connect evolved his swagger into the epitome of our motto, *"there's nothing smoother than a Hoover Groover."* Judabean's wardrobe transformed from G'd up to chic & debonair, he swapped his Pendelton for silk, his 501's were now crisp slacks, and his Chuck Taylors were replaced by Stacy Adams.

> *"Look around you. Everything changes.*
> *everything on this earth is in a continuous state of*
> *evolving, refining, improving, adapting,*
> *enhancing, and changing. You were not put on*
> *this earth to remain stagnant."*
> *-Dr. Steve Mataboli*

The evolution of oG Judabean was not confined to appearances alone. His throne of power had multiplied from a gang leader reigning supreme on 43rd street to a coke tycoon. A car for every day of the week was his new proclamation of power, and I was welcomed into his empire with a gift - From his luxurious collection, he tosses me some keys to a beautiful piece of machinery - a 1975 Chevy Caprice Glasshouse.

"Welcome home, cuH, enjoy ya new ride, courtesy of the Hoover Connect," Judabean proclaims with a big ass smile like the Lakers legend, Magic Johnson.

This pristine, timeless beauty was a testament to his generosity, a symbol of my initiation into the Hoover Connects prosperous hierarchy. As I ran my fingers over the cool metal, the feeling of gratitude cemented my loyalty to this brotherhood further.

In return I tattooed the Hoover Connect around my neck like a noose, to symbolize my commitment until death. The gift mirrored my own transformation, my own journey to find a place within the tribe & beyond it. His sense of style & his grace were almost infectious.

In my heart & mind, Judabean was a one-of-a-kind homie that couldn't be duplicated. Despite his endless material possessions, it was clear that his true allure didn't solely lie in his wealth or aesthetics, but in his soul. He was a human paradox of sorts - a silky smooth operator with an indomitable, fiery spirit – embodying the essence of what it meant to be a Hoover.

His belief that the Hoovers could rise through unity & shared ambition, became the fuel that powered our daily lives. His transformation & the overall metamorphosis of the Hoover tribe opened new horizons. It proved that we could transcend our beginnings & build a life beyond society's expectations.

The Hoover Connect represented much more than just a lucrative drug operation; it was a symbol of aspiration, unity, and resilience. As a Hoover, being witness to its astonishing growth, and charismatic leaders was not only awe-inspiring but a constant reminder of our collective strength.

My next stop was to spend quality time with my loved ones. Nakita came over with my son, for some quality time with my mother & I. In search of a fix, some good smoke & some drink, I made my way to the Foe after spending a heartwarming few hours with my family watching *"The Young & The Restless"* & enjoying each other's presence. The scent of springtime still hung heavy in the air, with a touch of that unique aroma, fresh spray paint & cheap malt liquor.

It wasn't long before my search for Five-Deuces was successful. I made my way through the set stopping by the liquor store on 54th & Hoover. As I approached the store, I walked by a group of youngsters sitting on a porch.

They didn't look like gangbangers, so I paid them no mind until one of them asked me *"Ay cuH, where you from?"*

Without hesitation, I replied with a question of my own, *"nigga, where you from?"* They reply confidently, *"This Five-Deuce Hoover!"*

In response, I defiantly uttered, *"Fuck Five-Deuce Hoover"* before entering the liquor store.

To my surprise, when I came out of the store, those same youngsters were standing there alongside everybody I was looking for, CoCo, Coke Dogg, T-dogg, and Joker.

Laughter erupted from Joker as he informed them, *"man, that's Boo Capone, one of the big homies who started the set."*

Feeling disrespected by these tiny locs who hadn't earned their stripes yet, I called them out, *"you lil niggas ain't shit, I diss the set & you run & get these niggas. Y'all was supposed to beat my ass!"*

Determined to teach them a lesson in loyalty & respect for our set's history & values, we gave them a DP in the alley. The incident served as a turning point for these youngsters - Chino, Snake, Gee Man, Lil Man, C-dogg, and Lil D. They learned firsthand what it meant to be part of something bigger than them. From that day forward, they became more militant & dedicated to upholding our set's reputation.

This encounter taught the tiny locs that sometimes it takes kicking some ass to teach lessons of true loyalty within a brotherhood. It also reminded them of the importance of respecting those who came before you & instilling discipline in those who will carry the torch.

Shortly after Chit chat filled the air with excitement & laughter as we sat down on Coke Dogg's porch. Joker nods his head,

343 | P a g e

raises his eyebrows, smiles, and signals for me to look at his hand.
Joker passes me a fat ass joint of lovely & another ice-cold 40-ounce
St. Ides, the familiar burn of the alcohol hitting my throat, a perfect
welcome home gift.

The pungent odor of PCP & the bittersweet aftertaste of malt
liquor belonged to a world I was well-acquainted with & missed dearly.

Amidst the hazy fog of our old ways, Joker hit me up: "*Shit
been crazy in the hood.*"

The homies had the lowdown on everything crackin' in the
set. They filled me in on all the happenings & changes since I had been
away.

CoCo interjects *"we had some run-ins with Rollin' Sixties!"*

A bond that was now in limbo by a series of incidents &
politics. One afternoon the Sixties came screeching down the Foe about
six cars deep, hanging out of windows, throwing up gang signs, and
yelling, *"Rollin'!" "6-Owe!"*

Homies weren't trippin' of course, we all Crips, so we replied,
"Hoover!"

They were gang-hangin' outside the liquor store on the Foe,
about 20 deep, CoCo was kicking game to a pretty young thang at the
bus stop. As the Sixty motorcade sped in their direction, suddenly they
attacked! One of the Sixties lunged out of their car with a switchblade
in hand, driving it deep into CoCo's arm!

It happened so fast — CoCo was so high off angel dust, he
didn't even realize he was stabbed. He was completely unfazed. He was
standing by the bus stop, just watching the Sixties drive away, that's
when Joker noticed the 6-inch blade sticking out of his arm.

"Yo, what the fuck, Groove! You got stabbed!" Joker shouted
at him.

CoCo looked down in disbelief.

"Oh shit, cuH!" was all CoCo managed to say before
clutching the bloodied knife handle protruding from his bicep &
yanking it out.

They immediately sprang into action. It was like instinct took
over at that point— they knew what they had to do. Joker figured they
had probably gone to the Broadways, so they jumped in their cars in
hot pursuit.

343 | P a g e

The perpetrators disappeared in a cloud of dust, the homies frantically searched for the assailants, but they disappeared into the maze of streets & alleys that encompassed the Broadway turf. Disappointment & rage filled the car as they returned to our hood. Joker knew that it wasn't over.

As the sun began to set, casting an eerie red hue across the Fifties. La Smokey comes on the Foe & tells us, a car full of Rollin' Sixties was parked up on the Tray, getting high on PCP with ScHool Boy. That was all the homies needed to hear— They knew they couldn't let the Sixties get away with stabbing CoCo.

There was no denying it; they had to confront the Sixties, but it was going to be a vicious battle. The homies grabbed their guns & headed out in 3 cars. The Homies were determined to make the Sixties pay for their actions. As they drove up to the Tray, it was obvious that the Sixties were already pretty wasted off water.

They stopped their cars a few houses away & approached them cautiously. As they got closer, Joker peeped the scene had gotten chaotic. The Rollin' 60's, fueled by the mind-warping effects of the PCP were bugging out & School Boy was screaming at them with visible anger.

"Y'all muthafuckas shot up my car!"

Confusion filled the air as both sides started drawing their weapons, creating a dangerous stalemate that could go one of two ways – an uneasy truce or a gunfight to the bitter end.

The scene was surreal. School Boy & the Sixties were locked in a standoff, the previous transaction having quickly dived into a swamp of deep-rooted malice. It turned out that the Sixties, under the influence of the potent drug, had bragged about shooting up a Five-Nine Hoover's Monte Carlo.

Unfortunately, they had mistaken School Boy's car for that of their intended target, and now he was prepared to take matters into his own hands. A tense silence hung in the air as the stand-off between two sides of an allegiance gone awry reached its boiling point.

In that instant, the air became thick with tension as guns were aimed in every direction, locked & loaded. One wrong move & the shouting match would have turned into a bloody massacre. Mama Harris & a lot of little kids were outside playing. The Sixties engaged in diplomacy. Explaining the mistake & denying knowledge of the incident with CoCo claiming innocence, preaching Crip Love for Five-Deuce Hoover.

The Sixties, with guns pointed in our direction, slowly walked backwards while maintaining eye contact, and slipping into their vehicles. They let them escape to avoid any collateral damage & innocent bystanders.

I soon found out from the homies that wasn't the only incident with the Sixties, and the reason why they gave them a pass. It turned out Joker had crossed paths with Peedy Wacc & Eddie Boy from Sixties on the Foe with Lil Fat Rat. They were supposedly looking for trouble with our brothers from Five-Nine Hoover. They had a fall out & Five-Nines shot up Joker from Sixties car. He explained they claimed to be cool with Five-Deuce which made this situation even more tricky & sticky.

Joker couldn't help but get angry & replies, *"Hoover is Hoover!"*

When Joker stood on business, the Sixties responded with animosity & aggression. Tempers flared & guns were drawn by both sides, but thankfully Peedy Wacc – was cool & intervened, he put a stop to the situation before it escalated any further.

"Na, cuH, you can't trip on Joker, that's the homie", Peedy interjects.

After that the Sixties shot up the Monte Carlo they believed belonged to the Five-Nines that shot at them. During the stalemate, Joker recalls the prior encounter with Peedy Wacc & extends the same courtesy. If this same incident occurred a few years later it would have been a bloodbath but on this fateful day in history, Crip Love prevailed.

Passes were given on both sides but the goodwill we once had with the Sixties was staggering on a thin line between Locs & Foes. Two powerhouse sets that were once Crippin' Cousins will soon be morphed into a vicious rivalry, boiling over with resent & anger. These events with Joker, ScHool Boy & CoCo didn't have a clean resolution.

Over the years the tensions between us & the Rollin' 60s would grow into hate. The stand-off that day on 53rd street left a permanent mark on both sides. It revealed the fickleness of alliances & the importance of choosing our battles wisely. For every homie we thought we'd gained we'd lost countless others – to bullets, stabbings, and imprisonment— the inevitable toll of gangbangin'.

The city was a smoky tapestry of street dreams & lust, seducing many with its seemingly infinite possibilities. It was just another night in the Crip dog eat Crip dog world. Tonight, we are headed to World on Wheels, It was a vibrant world, attracting the most diverse crowds.

World on Wheels opened on Halloween night, 1981, while I was away at CYA. It became a popular joint known for its mix of roller-skating, dining, disco, and Crips. It was located at the corner of Venice & San Vicente boulevard in Mid City, the kingdom of the ScHool Yards. I was accompanied by some of the usual suspects- Joker, Coke Dogg, CoCo, Willbone, Too Sweet, School Boy, Ant Capone, Bow Dee, T-Dogg, Crip Crazy & Twindogg. Impeccably dressed in our sacred blue, we made sure to jack some fools for their jewels & hard earned money before we disembarked.

Troublemakers on the prowl looking for good times & hot girls. We aimed to squeeze out every ounce of enjoyment that the night had to offer. Once we reached World on Wheels, a vibrant epicenter of my generation, Crips from Geer Gang, Rollin Sixties, Broadway, and School Yard where in the building.

I found myself locking eyes with a pretty young thang from Mid-City. Her eyes, gleaming under the neon lights resembled sparkling disco balls, and I swiftly engaged her in conversation like a Crip Casanova should. The sweet sound of her laughter was rudely interrupted by a behemoth from School Yard Crip. He decided to step in & cock block, casting an imposing shadow over us.

His words were soaked in envy, a petty attempt to claim his dominance, as he growled "*I don't appreciate you mackin' on my bitch.*"

> "*You know the rules of the game, yo bitch chose me. We can settle this like you got some class, or we can get into some gangsta shit.*"
> -Goldie, The Mack

The audacity of his interruption made the atmosphere thick with tension. He thought he could intimidate me because he was twice my size. The big dummy clearly didn't know who I was, a certified

Hoover Gangsta made of grit & defiance. I wasn't with the bickering back & forth so I kneed him in the nuts. His face went from confident bully to agonizing pain in seconds. Swiftly, as the beat dropped, I followed up with a two-piece-roundhouse & an uppercut that lifted the ogre off his feet.

As soon as I put his lights out, his homies rushed me like adrenaline under the flickering strobe lights. It evolved into an all-out brawl. As our respective crews jumped in, eager to defend their own. I could see Joker, landing powerful blows, his face contorted with the intensity of the fight. I used my agile nimbleness to deliver swift, accurate punches to my foes. CoCo & Coke Dogg were effortlessly putting fools' night-night, left & right.

Willbone & Too Sweet, almost a blur, were rat packing one of the yard boys, dealing with him with an efficiency that was nothing short of impressive. Ant Capone speared two of them at once reminiscent of the pro wrestler, Bill Goldberg, while Bow Dee knocked another one's teeth out.

T-Dogg bobbed & weaved dealing haymakers with surgical precision. Amidst the melee, ScHool Boy introduced a couple of them to his switch blade while I was Hoover stomping a mud hole in somebody son. Despite being outnumbered & on their turf, we were getting the best of them.

However, as the dust settled & the broken cries of our adversaries echoed around the rink, a stark realization was like ice water through our veins. Our victory, no matter how sweet it was, had been won on their ground.

Spying them regroup & retreat across the street, we knew they were going to get some guns because one of them screamed *"We gonna get some guns!"*

We were dangerous but unarmed so we had to get out of dodge! There was no time to wait for the bus, Coke Dogg & I decided to jack two getaway cars with our trusty B-10s. My heart thudding in sync with the engines roar, we tore down Venice Blvd, laughing in the face of adversity.

Joker, one of our most ruthless cohorts, along with Ant Capone & Twin Dogg, decided to hitch a ride. An unsuspecting Good Samaritan gave them a lift, oblivious to the evil he invited into his car. A robbery was now in progress but the driver refused to give up the keys & the money, a sporadic struggle ensued, ending tragically with the driver being stabbed.

The car spiraled out of control, crashing into a tree. Left behind by fate, the homies found themselves abandoned, left to troop the remaining journey to the turf. By the time we all regrouped at our stronghold on 54th Street, tensions were ready to reach a breaking point.

As the night deepened, Q-bone from Broadway pulled up in tow with two rival members from Rollin' Sixties. A cold chill blew through our ranks on their arrival. On-sight, Bow Dee, a pillar of strength, tied a sacred blue rag around his head & took the war to them, singlehandedly knocking out the trespassers, asserting the power of the Hoovers. Bow Dee effectively brought an end to the *"Five-Two, Whatever We do, Six-Owe, Wherever We Go"* relationship between Five-Deuce Broadway & Rollin' Sixties.

He was not done yet; tonight was the Bow Dee show. What happened next was nothing short of a dramatic soap opera, we could have called him Big Young & the Restless. Bow Dee, agitated & fueled with adrenaline, got into an argument with Crip Crazy after he spoke out the side of his mouth about 52nd street school. A swift & lethal roundhouse punch sent Crip Crazy right off his feet. His punch was so powerful that it sent a 14 karat diamond ring flying out of Crip Crazy's mouth. A ring that was supposed be a part of the pot from the bus robbery.

Oh! what a tangled web he weaved, a web of resentment & disgust. Crip Crazy, in his lust for wealth, had secretly pocketed some of the booty for himself – a clear betrayal of our brotherhood & trust. There may not be honor amongst thieves, but there certainly is among the Hoover Gangstas! Crip Crazy's betrayal of the G-Code marked an unforeseen climax of that memorable night.

His actions did not go without punishment. He was ruthlessly beaten, not only for his deceit but for several other allegations. This incident marked the final straw that broke the camel's back. We showed him the same mercy he showed us — none! His punishment was swift & irrevocable: he was banished from the set. We were far from saints but within our code of ethics, loyalty & respect were above all. No transgression, especially betrayal, was acceptable.

CHAPTER THIRTY-FOUR:
"LOVE & WAR PT. 2"

Nakita moved out of the Fifties & into Sixties turf during the infancy of our beef. This complicated things very much. I had to creep behind enemy lines hidden by the dark scars of the night, climbing over fences & alleys, slipping through unnoticed & depart before dawn.

How would one label these escapades, reckless or the commitment of a father & a lover? The answer lay within the pounding chambers of my own heart. Each visit was a gamble. For every instance I snuggled into the warmth & love of Nakita & my baby boy, our lives slipped into jeopardy. The comfort & consistency of Nakita's home was now consumed by peril.

I couldn't continue to take these risks or let my family become collateral damage. Ultimately, time & absence are the archnemesis of a family's unity, making me a stranger in my own home. My time away created a cold, unfamiliar void & a widening rift. Now I'm back in my old bag of tricks, a nomad, rotating between my apartment, her crib, and my other women.

> *"Papa was a rollin' stone, wherever he laid his*
> *hat was his home."*
> *- The Temptations*

There was a Wino that hung out on the side of the Hoover liquor store & got us beers religiously. I stole his car every night to go to Nakita's then I'd push or coast it back into its parking spot before sunrise. I would sneak out of my house, make my way to the winos car, and drive around like I owned the world.

It was thrilling, exciting, and dangerous all at once. I thought I was getting away with it, but he knew about it the whole time. Today, I asked if he would sell me his car. He had a '65 Sedan Deville Cadillac.

He said *"You know what, yeah! I'm tired of your ass stealing my shit! Gimme $90 or whatever the hell you got!"*

I gave the fool $90. The wino handed me the keys with a warning.

"You better take good care of her, kid. She's a good car, and I don't want to see her in the junkyard anytime soon."

I promised I would, but inside I was grinning. I had no intention of taking care of that car. As I drove away from the scene, feeling both exhilarated & accomplished. All I could think about is this come up I just came across, and the nice flip I will make off this $90 investment. I was just grateful to have the Winos' car. It was a symbol of my power, my freedom, and my youth & I was going to drive it like I stole it cause that's the only way I knew how.

One fateful day, I was riding down Hoover Street, in the Seven-Foes, my path crossed with a blast from the past. It was Sheila's grandmother, a sweet old lady who had watched us grow up. We did some catching up, and I asked about Sheila's whereabouts. I found out she moved to North Long Beach & was offered her phone number.

As her grandmother scribbled on a piece of paper, I reminisced about good times we shared & made sure I put the number to good use. Dialing Sheila's number was like turning back the hands of time. The conversations were full of sparks, it was like we were 13 again, setting a blaze memory of our puppy love & igniting our adult passions on fire.

We agreed it was the right time to rekindle an old flame. This old flame wasn't the only fire burning. On a typical sunny day, the heat radiating off the pavement mirroring the simmering tensions of life around the way. The groovy, Big Mike, recently released from prison & back on the set, pulled up on me by my mama's crib. Looking to break the monotony, I proposed an outing. The excitement of the newly released blockbuster, Scarface, had spread through the city like a California wildfire.

I looked over at Big Mike, *"Hey cuH, drop us off at the movies, we're tryin' to see Scarface."*

Big Mike's initial response came as no surprise. He was not one to play chauffeur, made evident by his cheeky reply, *"nigga, what I look like a cab?"*

However, his abrupt *'no'* did not deter me. Seeing his reluctance, I counter-offered with an enticing proposition.

With a glint in my eye & an evil grin, I countered, *"I've got a girl for you, fool, I'm gonna hook you up with Sheila's fine ass cousin!"*

The promise of a potential fling with Sheila's cousin served as the perfect bait. The subtle shift in Big Mike's demeanor let me know that I had him hooked.

His eyes twinkled with curiosity as he casually exclaimed, *"Oh, word? Now we're talking, Loc."*

With a triumphant smile on my face, I orchestrated a double date with Sheila & her alluring cousin, Ursula. To say that the date was a success would be an understatement.

Margaret Atwood once said, *"The Eskimos had Fifty-two names for snow because it was important to them: there ought to be as many for love."*

Ursula, exuding charm, and vivacity caught Big Mike's attention instantaneously. I still remember every time he looked at her his face seemed to shine like he had too much wine, that's amore'. As I watched Big Mike & Ursula interact that night, I saw fireworks, I realized that there probably weren't enough words for love to describe their connection. They were two imperfect pieces perfectly fitting together, their ghetto love story unfolding.

That spontaneous double date turned into a series of lust-filled encounters that melted even Big Mike's hardcore exterior. Ursula didn't just become Big Mike's girlfriend; she evolved into the mother of his child, and it all happened courtesy of me accidentally playing Crip Cupid.

Looking back, it amazes me sometimes how life unfolds in the most unexpected ways. That day, I just wanted to catch a movie with Sheila, little did we know that the universe had planned a different script. They say love comes to us when we least expect it, and Big Mike & Ursula were a living testament to that.

Before I knew it, we spent so much time in the LBC, hanging out with the girls, as well as Crazy John & Ricc Dogg from the Insane Crips, Long Beach became my second home. I marinated in the consistent duality of my life, serving loyalties to different women, chasing fleeting moments of comfort, always interrupted by danger & uncertainty, and constantly yearning for rest & relaxation.

In my hunt for rest & relaxation, I decided I needed more space, stability & peace of mind in my life. I outgrew my Mama's garage, I'm now 18, and the Hoover Connect had my money right. I started looking for my own place, a place I could call my own. My big sister Renee, my sister from the same mister. I told her what was on my mind, I needed to have pay stubs that the dope game didn't offer to get my own spot. She offered me a lifeline: she would help me rent an apartment.

Overwhelmed with gratitude, I accepted her generous offer. I found myself a bachelor pad on 52nd street between Budlong & Normandie near Killa D crib, and Renee put the lease in her name. It was a little back house with one bedroom, one bathroom & decent sized living room for $550 a month. It wasn't much but it was mine & what mattered to me the most was I was still on 52nd street.

With every breath, every step, the love that kept me going also bore the terrible weight of the choices I made. The consequences of living a life fueled by drug runs, guns, and Hoover Gangsta Crippin' lay heavy on my head & heart. My life had become entangled in both love & war. I knew I made choices that would change the fate of my family.

Things were never the same with Nakita after she moved to the Sixties. Before I went to CYA, fate introduced new characters in the Fifties. A Dominican family moved in next door to my mama house. The family had two daughters around my age.

Everything about the sisters was intriguing, I never met a Dominican before, so I found them intriguing- their caramel skin, raven black hair, and the way they walked & talked made them very exotic with an air of intrigue.

My big sis, Linda G, introduced us, their names were Goofy & Mimi. Unbeknownst to me, big sis had been playing cupid. Linda G always had my back, and she taught me a lot, she taught me the importance of family & how to treat a woman. When she showed me how to cook crack, it was about family & surviving.

"Your sister told me a lot about you. She said you were just my speed & I think she's right."

Goofy whispered in my ear as Her big brown eyes stared into mine, I was mesmerized. I recall that warm, sunny day when Goofy & I spent what felt like hours walking & talking, leaving Mimi behind with Linda G.

As we conversed, it felt like we had known each other for years. It was then that I found out that the sisters were claiming an ese' gang called 18th street. Despite this revelation, I felt an instant connection to Goofy, and I knew she felt it too.

The connection between us was so strong, from day one she was attached at my hip, she was my tagalong, everywhere I went she went. Goofy was a bilingual chocolate Latina with hypnotizing eyes, juicy lips, big ol' titties & a big fat ass that drove me wild. She had a smile that could light up a room & glamour about her that demanded attention at every entrance.

Goofy was down for me, and there was nothing that could sway her loyalty. I was now engaged in more entanglements than Will Smith & Jada Pinkett, but the pendulum of my thug love was swinging in Goofy's direction. She was so down for me, but her mama couldn't stand me.

It got to the point that I was the only person that could tell Goofy what to do & her mom, Connie, felt I was a bad influence on her precious daughter. It got so serious, when Goofy acted out, her mom would call me to help, but little did she know that I was the reason behind her daughter's defiance.

Connie finally accepted me & used me as a lifeline to help her reach her daughter. Goofy would do anything I asked without hesitation. If I told her to climb to the top of the roof at dawn & crow like a rooster, she is going to be up there like *"cocker doodle doo."*

Her type of loyalty was rare, it was such a turn on for me. The chemistry between us was unlike anything I had ever experienced before.

"A truly submissive woman is to be treasured, cherished & protected for it is only she who can give a man the gift of dominance."-Anne Desclos

We became inseparable, and it seemed like nothing could ever tear us apart. I turned Goofy out, and she fell in love with me head over heels. Goofy eventually stole me away from Nakita. She had a hold on me, she was sucking & fucking my brains out, turning tricks, and hitting licks, so I made her my lady Crip.

"A loyal woman is like a rare gemstone, precious & priceless."- unknown

It was customary after females got comfortable with a homeboy, they would start repping his name. Goofy denounced 18th street & became Lady Boo Capone aka Goofy Capone from Five-Deuce Hoover. I blessed her in, but she made the decision to fight instead of taking the easy route.

Her determination & bravery only made me love her more. Goofy didn't want a pass for being my girl, she wanted to get her put on, so she squared up with Babygirl in the 52nd street school parking lot.

Back in 1983, there were only a few homegirls, La Smokey, Stormy, Babygirl, Marla & Toka. After joining Five-Deuce, Goofy was more determined than ever to prove her loyalty & dedication to the set & our relationship. Not only did she fight for her place but when I told her to go recruit, she brought her baby sister Mimi & her cousin La Giggles to the fold.

La Giggles would end up falling head over heels for the homeboy, Bam. Our respective couples were like 2 pairs of Bonnie & Clyde's rippin' & ridin' for Hoover Gangsta. Goofy Capone, the First Lady of the Five-Deuce Hoover, became the prime example of a Hoo'Lette, I couldn't have been prouder to call her mine. She became a top recruiter & line pusher. Goofy became my lover & my friend, she brought me & the homies all types of pussy. What more could I ask for?

CHAPTER THIRTY-FIVE:
"HOOVER BUSINESS"

The year 1983, a year we claimed as the year of the Hoover Crips, tore open like a wound & bled out a legacy of triumphs & defeats - each with its own weight & resonance. It was a year marked in our calendars, not by the page numbers, but by the codes, "8" for H & "3" for C - Hoover Crip, a name that echoed through the arteries of Los Angeles. The year brought with it many firsts - some smothered in victory, others drenched in the tears of defeat.

I was gang-hanging with the homies at 48th street park, I told them about the alliances Gangsta D & I set up in CYA with the Eight-Tray Gangstas, Long Beach Insane, and Gardena Shotgun Crips. We agreed to transcend the alliances to our operations in the street & so I set up a meet & greet of sorts at Rowley Memorial Park in Gardena, with the Shotguns & Paybaccs.

Our numbers were strong; we had both willpower & manpower ready to fuel the next phase of our alliance. The gathering was staggering - we had at least 250 members in attendance, a cocktail of hardened young Crips & ruthless enforcers, faces laden with hardened expressions & indomitable resolve stood united, bolstering an air of intimidation & power.

After the meet & greet we met privately for strategic planning. The illicit & lucrative enterprise we engaged in introduced us to the kind of wealth we had only dreamt about. However, human nature, in its most unstoppable form, springs from greed & ambition.

Despite our fortune, we yearned for more of that mean green & endowed with strength in numbers, we plotted to milk the flourishing cash cow at our fingertips. Our product - dope. Our market - the turf. Our prerogative - rent enforcement. We decided membership has benefits. One such privilege was access to a continuing source of wealth, rock cocaine. This potent stimulant had flooded the streets & hearts of our city, and we had decided it was time to extend our influence.

Around this time, crack cocaine led to the eruption of hustler crews, each as ambitious & voracious as the next. These clusters of men started becoming omnipresent in every nook & cranny of South Central breeding like mushrooms thriving after rain. The streets were buzzing with them & around the way many of them headed by our younger relatives. They appeared on their respective blocks within our boundaries. As leaders, we knew our play - it was time to absorb these smaller off brand subsidiaries, making them part of the Hoover Gangsta conglomerate.

> *"Without continual growth & progress, such words as improvement, achievement & success have no meaning." - Benjamin Franklin*

The crews that were on our radar for assimilation included the Fifty Hustlers, the 52nd street Cutlass Boys & the Five-Eight Crips. Boscoe, Lil Twindogg & Lil Chim were instrumental in converting the Fifty Hustlers & welcoming them to the fold.

The Fifty Hustlers ranks included Baby Dre Dogg, my nephew Big Crib, Lil Joe, Fly Guy & his brother Hershey amongst others. Followed by the 58th street Hustlers that were influenced by Big Fat Rat to join the Groove, their ranks included names like C-Capone aka Poonie, who became Lil Coke Dogg, Big Loon, his brother Cudabear, and Baldhead to name a few.

The next crew on our radar was the Cutlass Boys. Born to the city's pulse, the Cutlass Boys, led by Donyea & his brother, were princes of the hustler world. The Cutlass Boys originated around the unforgiving streets of 102nd street & Budlong. They'd etched a reputation & relocated & looked to start up their business in the Fifties.

The Cutlass Boys were enterprising & stylish. Every member of their crew boasted of possession of a classic Oldsmobile Cutlass, earning them distinction & their flashy moniker. The Cutlass Boys' claim on 52nd Street led to an unavoidable confrontation.

We wanted a piece of everything moving on the turf, so we implemented a *"Get Down or Lay Down"* campaign. We agreed during the function that anybody that wasn't Five-Deuce wouldn't be allowed to sell dope or pussy on the set without paying rent, tithes, tariffs. I was extremely aggressive upon my return from CYA, so I was eager to enforce rent on 52nd street.

We understood the assignment & applied pressure to everybody, Jamaicans, Mexicans, and the Cutlass Boys. Donyea & his family recently moved on my block. Donyea was my boy, we had no issues prior to the meeting but politics took precedence over personal relationships, nothing/nobody is bigger than the program.

Hoover Luv, Big Red Jr & I pushed the line on the Cutlass Boys. With trouble in my pocket & a cold swagger in my stride, I placed an ultimatum before them - affiliation or adversity. There was no negotiating. No one could hustle in the Fifties without paying a rent or swearing allegiance to Hoover Gangsta Crip. Their refusal was a decisive moment that put the gears of destiny into motion, compelling us to take a stand.

They thought we were bullshitting until I shot up their mama house & Big Red Jr knocked out his brother's teeth. The message was loud & clear - refusal to bow down will result in consequences & repercussions. The Cutlass Boys didn't want to pay rent, but they respected how we were coming & wanted to get down! They fell in line with the program, Donyea was christened as Heavy D from Five-Deuce Hoover Gangsta Crip by Big Spookee.

Heavy D, surprisingly, turned into a real good homie & a figure of immense importance in my life. He played the honorable role of the Godfather to one of my children & faithfully performed duties as the pallbearer at my mother's funeral. Every time I see his nephew Smacc from Five-One Trouble Gangsta Crip, it reminds me of my loved one.

As I reminisce & write about our shared past, I realize Heavy D's absence has left an unfilled vacancy. I miss him, the good & the bad. He was more than just a rival turned ally—he was a brother from another mother in the desperate & dangerous world we once ruled. I may regret our rough beginnings, but I will always cherish the bond that grew despite them.

Indeed, the story of the Cutlass Boys is a story of rivalries becoming relationships, battles that create brethren, and finding allies in adversaries. It's about learning to love those you were meant to hate, growth & understanding, the true meaning of family.

The Turf is our most prized possession, it represents our strength, and we will defend it from intruders & trespassers at all costs. It was an unwritten rule—No unknown vehicles. No unknown faces. This rule was not just accepted, but fiercely guarded—The walls of territories were invisible, but as invincible as the Great Wall of China. Trust was currency that was seldom in circulation, and it was even rarer that we handed it out for free.

One of the most protective members of FDHGC was Joker. He was as much a product of the paranoia-filled environment of our turf & one of its main defenders. His reality, ingrained with the rule of force, was a narrative dominated by survival instincts & a ferocious loyalty to his hood.

It was just another day around the way, Joker was on his usual patrol, marking his territory like a junkyard Crip dogg. His intimidating figure cast long, foreboding shadows against the graffitied landscape of Vermont Avenue.

It was the embodiment of the ruthless rule of the streets: if someone seemed out of place. It was mandatory we pressed you & interrogated you about your presence. If your answers were not satisfactory, we punished you. This went for any trespasser; we perceived all strangers as a potential threat. It was this brutal, straightforward logic that governed South Central.

On that day, a foolish trespasser had wandered into FDHGC territory, and that man faced the fury of the Crips. We are all familiar with a lock or soap in a sock, Joker introduced him to a brick in a towel. His fate served as a grim reminder of the razor's edge on which life teetered in these parts of the city.

A question as simple as, *"Where you from,"* was not an innocent inquiry but a loaded question. A wrong answer, an unfamiliar face, suspicious behavior — it was all it took for lights out. Punishment was swift & unapologetic. It was a time when travelers navigated South Central at their own risk. However, the essence of such brutal territorialism was a primal need for safety, a need to protect our tribe against anyone perceived as the enemy.

Joker was far from being a mindless goon; he was a tribesman defending his homeland in the only way he knew with blind loyalty & unyielding bravery. We were Kiwé warriors in a socio-economic & cultural warzone. Territory for Crips & Bloods was the last stand against an encroaching world that seemed intent on erasing our shared experiences.

From Slauson to King, from the Freeway to Normandie. People couldn't drive through the area after nightfall. Joker, Fat Rat & I challenged trespassers to games of Chicken, we raced full speed towards them, forcing them to make death defying maneuvers to avoid head on collisions.

We ran unknown vehicles off the road. We called it Crash & Bang which pretty much was like bumper cars at the carnival but with real steel, crashing & banging our cars into random fools driving through the set then jacking them. Our twisted minds drove us to cause mayhem & destruction turning them into twisted metal & shattered glass, yet we walked away unscathed, laughing in the face of danger.

54th street is a major thoroughfare to the Eastside, and residents knew only a fool would stop at the red light on 54th & Hoover or 54th & Budlong. If you stopped you better know somebody from Hoover Gangsta cause if not you were getting robbed, shot or both.

"Nationalism among nations is like racism among races. Racism & nationalism are forms of tribalism. Tribalism always, always leads to war. Why? Because every nation thinks they're superior to other nations, and their own self-interest is more important than the self-interest of other nations."- Oliver Markus Malloy

The Nifty Fifty Hoover versus Six-Pacc East Coast war raged on. Back in those days, the rift between us was like oil & water, survival was paramount, and alliances were swaying pendulums of lethal strategy. It soon escalated when the beef spilled over Slauson, the courageous LaJoy of Seven-Foe Hoover became the second fatality after a shootout with the Coast over drug turf.

The grief of losing LaJoy heightened the vendetta & initiated a horrifying domino effect. Malice & retribution pulled all our factions into the fray, his death was the catalyst that unified us in prosperity & adversity. A unification that made us monsters among men.

"Adversity makes men & prosperity makes monsters."
- Victor Hugo

The Crip Civil War, as we later christened it, was picking up steam, threatening to disrupt our collective existence. Power dynamics, alliances, turf borders – everything was undergoing a makeover. For almost a decade we were cool Crippin' cousins with Rollin' Sixties. Their veins pulsed with the same resolve; we shared a mutual respect via our Crip creed.

I reminisced the other day with Coke Dogg about times long forgotten. Fresh from putting in work on the Van Ness Gangsta Brims, the taste of adrenaline was still fresh on our tongues. As we were cruising down Slauson, we came across familiar faces. It was Peedy Wacc & Keita Roc from the Sixties. Their reputation had preceded them; little did we know we were legendary Crips in the making.

Looking back, it brings a half-smile to my face to recall the exchange.

"What y'all doing, cuH?" I had queried, my eyebrows raised in a combination excitement & respect, seeing my fellow Crips on a mission.

Peedy Wacc responded, exuding an air of enthusiasm under his tough exterior, *"We bout to ride on the VNGs!"*

The news made me smirk, our enemies were in for another round of chaos. It was amusing, we had just done our part to tip the scales in the war against the Brims.

In solidarity, Coke Dogg notified them of our next mission, *"On Crip we just hit them up! Now we on our way to Buss on the Six-Deuce Brims, C-safe out here Loc!"*

Keita Roc saluted in agreement, *"C's up, cuH!"*

This wasn't an unusual encounter; this was a common thing prior to the Crip Civil war. These were certified Kiwé warriors, earning our respect for their unyielding loyalty, courage & strength. We had no idea the Crip Civil War was on the horizon. Making this memory seem like a rare, peaceful moment in a time capsule, safeguarded from all the turmoil that followed.

We didn't know we were standing on the thin line between Locs & Foes. We had our fall outs; we had our disputes but this was Crip & we stood shoulder to shoulder against our common enemies. Little did we realize that the same unity had the power to cause the most damaging division amongst us.

The love for our respective tribes began to blur the lines & spilled over into the boundaries of hatred & animosity. The realization strikes hard that there was a time when we stood together for the survival of the Crips. Our unity isn't easily forgotten; a reminder of our Blue rags tied by the shared ruthlessness & a contempt for the second letter & their symbolic red. Perhaps the lines drawn in the sands of time are too deep to overlook now.

Perhaps, the bitter times of today are emphasized only because of the better times we once shared. One thing is clear: the strength of the C was greater in unity. Today, the same unity seems like a dream too farfetched.

The Persuaders once said, *"there's a thin line between love & hate,"* & we straddled that line for the longest time. Our love for our fellow Crips may have taken a detour, but the memories serve as a

silent prayer for reunification. We emerged from the same struggles &
somewhere down the line, we had forgotten, we are all Locs.

Now an underlying tension began to pollute the true blue
waters of our Crip empire. Allies turned into adversaries overnight, it
seemed as if the solidarity that we once had, now began to crumble
under the weight of bloodshed. The introduction of the Roller Coaster
alliance between Rollin' Sixties & East Coast added another layer of
complexity to the already complicated network of alliances &
animosities.

More money, more problems, bigger funds, and bigger guns.
We started setting up shop in abandoned houses in the turf & the motels
on Figueroa, all became gold mines. It was easy money. The product
sold itself. We had loyal fiends that came to us for their fix 3-4 times
per day, and we made good money off them.

Ken Dogg, Lil Live & I had a crack spot jumping on 55th
street. Business was good, better than ever actually. We ran the most
successful trap house in the Fifties, a place where addicts & hustlers
alike flocked for a slice of the intoxicating pie. Our corners of the drug
trade had taken off in ways we never could have imagined.

Fresh out of probation cruising through the infamous streets of
the Hoover Gangsta empire in my new charcoal-black '65 Sedan
Deville. My ride slowly drifted to a halt at 53rd Street, a world unto its
own, I pull up on the CeeCees, Boom-Boom, Fat Curtis, and Moochie
amongst the plethora of other homeboys outside of Naomi crib slinging

roc & shooting dice. Some smokers break dancing. While others leaned like Michael Jackson in the Smooth Criminal music video, as the Locs placed bets on which one would tip over first.

Among the usual suspects was a fresh faced Tiny Loc, a young boy of about thirteen, whose identity was yet to be etched onto the pavement of Hoover street. He was black as a panther & tall as a California Palm tree, but I could tell he looked up to me as he introduced himself.

"What up big homie, welcome home, cuH! I'm Naomi's nephew. My name's Stevie, but the homies call me Face."

Magnetic charisma seeped out his pores, fueling a burning enthusiasm for Hoover Gangsta. Observing Face, he possessed an untamed passion that ignited my rough, gangsta soul, that reminded me of myself. I was living my best life, Crippin', having fun & making funds. The economics of supply & demand meant that we needed more hands to handle the influx of customers. I decided that my protégés would be Face & Boscoe, my favorite Tiny Locs from 53rd & 56th street.

I saw them as uncut diamonds in the rough, needing just a bit shaping to reflect their brilliant potential. With my newfound protégés, my responsibility as a big homie lay in converting their raw passion into a disciplined dedication towards our cause. Thus began the process of putting them on to game.

Lessons not taught in classrooms but on Hoover street. I schooled them on the deep-rooted values & foundations that held us together. Loyalty, the unwavering belief in sticking by your loved ones through thick & thin. Honor, the irreplaceable currency of respect dangling around every Crip's neck like a Turkish chain. Most importantly, our holy grail - the G-Code.

Snitching was worse than treason, and going against the grain for third parties was sacrilegious. Right is right & wrong is wrong & you should always have your homie's back, right or wrong, and if he's wrong, we deal with it in private.

We were the gatekeepers of order in our own sin-stained paradise, operating on the unwritten code. I taught them the value of restraint. Listen more, speak less. Gather wisdom from the murmurs, and secrets from whispers.

365 | P a g e

Eager & hungry to learn, The duo accompanied me on rounds to our rock houses, proving their trustworthiness in the presence of thousands of dollars. Their unwavering dedication, evolving wisdom, and discreet discretion radiated their worth. I felt confident having them accompany me to put in work, knowing their commitment to watch my back & vanquish every rival. The expanse of these missions lie shrouded under a thick veil of secrecy, but it is safe to say Face & Boscoe proved themselves.

Homies like Face, Boscoe & Mouse are rare, their love & loyalty to Hoover Gangsta are second to none. Remaining stitched lipped when shit hit the fan tried & tested our loyalties. Learning from other's mistakes kept homies like Face & Mouse out of prison. They bloomed into decorated Kiwé warriors. They embraced & championed the Crip creed with unmatched fervor & resolve.

Real gangstas have morals. Heavy is the head that wears the H-crown. Being a big homie means mentoring & guiding the Tiny Locs on the right path in bad circumstances. A narrative written with in blood of our enemies, upholding the 5 D's of Five-Deuce.

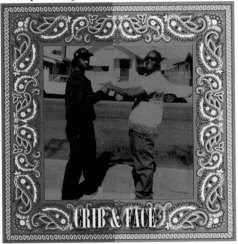

Figueroa is a famous hoe stroll filled with crime, desperation, and broken dreams that goes through the Hoover territories. Figueroa has always been a magnet for unsavory activities & those who thrive in its dark underbelly. It's been notorious since the murder of the king of soul, Sam Cooke, back in December 1964 at the Hacienda motel, a part of town that would become Nine-Deuce Hoover.

365 | P a g e

Figueroa used to shine bright like Las Vegas, its name illuminating the night, drawing in people like moths to a flame. In the City of Angels various factions vied for dominance & made our own rules. In the height of its notoriety, it became the perfect stage to execute a sinister plan.

Countless prostitutes prowling along the sidewalks of Figueroa, day, and night. They wore their desperation like a heavy cloak, weighed down by the realities of the harsh world they inhabited. These professional hoes selling their bodies as a means of survival & income, became a staple in south central.

The plan was simple, and it would not only benefit us but bring control to the chaos that engulfed the area. We stationed one of our Lettes, disguised as a hooker, out on Fig. She was the perfect bait, her tight clothing & mean switch drawing tricks in like bees to honey. As they eagerly approached her with cash in hand, their minds clouded by lust, they fell right into our trap.

As soon as the unsuspecting johns were lured into the motel room we had set up, they were faced with the unpleasant reality of our scheme. They think they are getting a sexual seduction but instead of some titties in their face, it's my nine-millimeter. Their foolish desires led them straight into our clutches, and they were now what we call a sweet lick.

We operated like a well-oiled machine, a C-machine in motion, the power we held over Figueroa was undeniable. We had established a new protocol, and the word spread like wildfire: nobody, not the hookers, the pimps, or the hustlers, could make any money on Figueroa without paying Five-Deuce our tithes & offerings.

Our presence felt throughout the area, and we thrived in our newfound dominance. Coke Dogg, Big Fat Rat, and CoCo were the enforcers, they found pleasure in enforcing tariffs & they made it look so easy, so effortless. These three brutes were such menacing characters, they left people shaking in their boots. Their presence made everyone from the hustlers to the pimps pay homage.

We ruled with an iron fist, and our section understood non-payment wasn't an option. Everybody paid, either with cold cash or spilled blood. With the subtlety of a sledgehammer, I made our intentions known to any lady of the night outside our room. I'd shout from the motel mezzanine.

"Aye bitch, I gotta room, and I got dope!"

After those magic words, they start coming like flies to shit. I would cultivate them with my charm. The lure of a warm bed & the promise of drugs was all it took for these desperate girls to fall in line. They were searching for an escape from their harsh reality, I became their oasis. As they became intoxicated by the sweet smoke & sweet talk, I say all the things they want to hear to make them my sweet bitch. Their lives, once their own, now a pawn in my master plan.

Slowly, Figueroa began to bow to our presence, and the balance of power in the Fifties became forever altered. No longer could anyone operate without our permission, without first paying tribute to Five-Deuce.

We took Figueroa for ourselves, branding it as Hoover property from the Forties to the Hundreds. We forced anyone who dared to cross our path to either submit or face dire consequences. Unfortunately, like all empires built upon a foundation of greed & bloodlust, our reign could not last forever.

The most crushing defeat was the haunting & pernicious police brutality that mercilessly claimed two of our most honorable members. One cornerstone of the Hoover Connect, our headquarters on 81st street, fell prey to a ruthless LAPD raid. During the invasion a prominent member & an inspiring leader, oG Pookie aka Anthony Kennedy from Eight Tray Hoover, was slain in a violent confrontation with the pigs.

OG Pookie died valiantly in the face of battle. His departure was a severe blow to the Hoover Connect. If there is anything certain in this life, it is death. However, the knowledge of its inevitability doesn't make the sting of loss any less potent, particularly when the lost soul is dear to us.

Soon after Kennedy's assassination, we mourned the passing of oG Hoover Joe Ransom, the man who first introduced me to Hoover Crip. Ransom was more than just a member of our fraternity; he was a big homie, a leader & mentor. He symbolized the resilience inherent in us, the unyielding strength that molded us into men of fortitude.

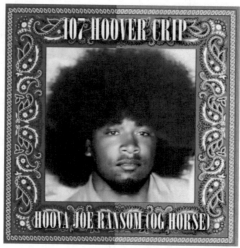

107 HOOVER CRIP

HOOVA JOE RANSOM (OG HORSE)

Joe's tragic departure left a massive void & battered hearts across the Grooveline. A gaping hole in our hearts that no amount of time could completely mend. He was the definition of a Hoover Crip, a man who personified courage & honor. During a routine traffic stop, he fell prey to a horrid narrative all too familiar to the Black community.

An illegal chokehold became the instrument of his death. Big Joe Ransom's untimely demise was a grim reminder of the danger we lived in. Similar to the highly televised deaths of Eric Garner & George Floyd, he too had his breath stolen away by the pigs. The plight of police brutality is a harrowing chronicle embedded deep within the fibers of American history, the bastard child of systemic racism. The year 1983 showcased the raw & uncut abuses of power by those appointed as the patrons of law & order.

Near the tail end of 1983, the homie Chucky Mac put the whole set on. Chucky Mac, my fellow Hriginal, stood out like a sore thumb among the vicious Hoover Gangstas. He was an anomaly; non-violent & selfless, while the rest of us reveled in the bloodshed, supplying any necessary muscle.

He introduced us to a new plug, a Chicano cat named Luis Ortega. Ortega was the answer to our prayers. Exactly what we needed for the power & influence we demanded. He could provide us with discounted kilograms of coke, thus enabling us to generate tremendous profits.

C-Mac was a ghost in the light, an architecture of tact, strategy, and secrecy. He received reverence & respect, not out of fear, but genuine love & admiration. While his benevolence was unique, it was his low-key demeanor that truly set him apart.

Unlike most of his contemporaries, he didn't care about the limelight. C-Mac maintained a low profile, working like a puppeteer behind the scenes, implementing strategies & alliances that would safeguard his interests.

"Never let no one know how much dough you hold cause you know. The cheddar breed jealousy especially, if that man fucked up, get yo' ass stuck up"- Notorious B.I. G, Ten Crack Commandments

Chucky Mac's rise to prominence was not mere coincidence. It was an opportune moment, precipitated by the raid on the Hoover Connect Headquarters & the subsequent surge of the notorious double up, a process where a pinch of cocaine was magically multiplied, and turned smokers into a street team. Buying one rock for $20, and reselling half of it for $40 thus enabling them to get high for free. The double up caused big time returns of investment that led to an unprecedented rise in greed & violence.

"That goddamn credit? Dead it. You think a crackhead paying you back, shit, forget it."- Notorious B.I.G, Ten Crack Commandments

We also built a cohesive alliance with Freeway Donny, an honorary Hoover Gangsta that was a part of Rick Ross' Freeway Boys, strengthening our position in the dope game. We also collaborated with my day one, oG Whitey & Whitey Enterprises, who, at the time, were battling it out with the formidable Bertrain & Third World (Foe-Tray Gangsta Crips). The drug war was so intense, bodies littered the streets like a ticker tape parade.

The sheer scale of our operations was overwhelming. Our stash houses packed so full that at times, we lost track of whose dope we were actually dealing with. Our only priority was making sure our books were right. An error in accounting meant the difference between life & death. Fucking up a pack was an easy way wind up dead. It didn't matter who you were, or what gang you were affiliated with.

> *"A strong word called consignment strictly for*
> *live men, not for freshmen. If you ain't got the*
> *clientele, say, "Hell no!" cause they gon' want*
> *they money rain, sleet, hail, snow."*
> *-Notorious B.I. G, Ten Crack Commandments*

To tell the story of a single year in the history of the Hoovers is to scrutinize a mirror of the ceaseless battle against systemic racism. The fallen Hoover generals were a symbol of resistance, a bastion against the oppressive tendencies that riddled the law enforcement agencies. As these oppressive powers came to bear upon us, they did not shatter our resolve but instead, just like an anvil, molded by countless onslaughts, it forged our resilience, honing it, shaping it till it became a symbol of hope. Struggle was an inbred component of our identity; resistance was our second nature.

CHAPTER THIRTY-SIX:
"FIGHT OR PIPE"

We exist in a world that many would consider off-limits, outrageous even, where rules & laws were broken on a daily basis, and the norms of society seemed a long-forgotten memory. This world was the realm of the Crips. We hold an allure & reputation that attracts young men looking for an escape from the struggles of their everyday existence.

We not only drew the attention of these aimless souls, but that of young females as well, who found something undoubtedly enticing about our rebellious Groove. The Crips are known for many things, one of which is our taste for hedonism. People may describe our shameless embracing of this lifestyle as scandalous.

For many of the girls who looked to indulge in the Gangsta Groove or any other Crip faction, there was an unorthodox initiation that awaited them. Any female who wanted to join our ranks got put on by shacking up, meaning getting freak nasty in one of our shacks or even in the pigeon coups.

It might be a culture shock to most people; but to us, it was just a rite of passage in the intoxicating world in which we lived. We put those beds in the barn to good use, serving as sex arenas where we engaged in raunchy escapades that only tightened the bonds between Locs & Lettes. For those women who wanted to have their place in Hoover, these beds were the gateway.

I bet your next question is who they had to sleep with, and the answer is — all of us. Giving herself to each of us proved her commitment to the cause by her willingness to share herself with the set in the most intimate of ways.

Our magnetic personalities, and impressive reputations attracted girls by the droves. These young ladies sought the thrill, notoriety or satisfaction that comes with affiliation or seducing a Hoover Gangsta. Girls would offer us pussy left & right, long term relationships &/or flings. These young ladies were infatuated & fiending to do the wild thing with a Crip, especially one from Five-Deuce Hoover! Big Boo was happy to oblige & satisfy.

Running a train, was one of our favorite pastimes. Why do you think they started calling it a *"gang-bang."* We made it a part of the orientation, but of course, there were homegirls that weren't with the antics. I became aware that a rift was occurring within our female regime, so I took note of it & we made changes to the secret ritual.

One afternoon, I'm at Uncle Cliff's store on 54th & this little cutie with a booty walks in. She had a petite figure, with sun-kissed skin, a head turner with a seductive sway in her walk. Her silhouette, accentuated in a figure-hugging, emerald-green dress, left little to the imagination. Even without knowing her, I felt like her body was calling me. As I stood there, entranced by her beauty, she glanced in my direction, and she locked eyes with me.

She flashed a bold, sultry smile & called out, *"Hi Boo!"*

I couldn't help but grin back at her; in my mind I'm thinking she already knows who I am, so I'm in the game. As we got acquainted, I couldn't help but feel flattered by the attention she gave me. I got that feeling that she wants sexual healing.

During our conversation, she says *"Boo, I'm tryna' be down with Five-Deuce. I heard you can put me on?"*

I look at her sexy ass & seize the opportunity to make her an offer she can't refuse - something that would benefit us both. In my grooviest voice, I proposed.

"How about I give you the best dick you ever had in your life, then I will bring you around & say you my cousin or something."

To my surprise, she didn't hesitate to respond. Stroking my hand with her delicate fingers, she smirked & said with a lustful glint in her eyes, *"Yes, Boo, I'm down."*

Our sexual rendezvous was something that wet dreams are made of. Our bond was solidified that evening, and as promised, I brought her to the set. As we entered the shack with its signature dim lighting, a sudden silence broke through the noisy chatter. Every gaze was fixated on the captivating treat that had entered the lion's den. As I introduced her to the homegirls, I could see the hunger in their eyes, as they stared at her like a pride, ready to pounce on a helpless gazelle.

She did her thing & fought; she earned her spot. I introduced her to the other members of our homegirls as my cousin & kept our sexual encounter a secret to keep her from scrutiny. Despite her willingness to embrace our initiation, she would never quite become like her predecessors, having to be subjugated to the plight of *"fight or pipe."*

It saddens me to think of how many of my homegirls had been left to fend for themselves from a young age. Whether they had been forced to survive on the streets or been subjected to the horrors of broken homes. They came looking for family, and we gave it to them. Things started to get messy. The plethora of women in our ranks began to dwindle as *"fight or pipe"* controversy caused division.

"Bitch you fucked to get on the set!"

That led to an immediate squabble! *"Fight or Pipe "* became the root of turmoil. The homegirls that got put on by pipe were belittled by the homegirls that got put on by fight, or Hoo Ridin' (putting in work). If I could make it right with a couple of them, I would. They were good people, and could've been solid homegirls, if things unfolded a different way.

I always believed in the collective, and that includes the women. All the hoods were similar, it was mostly about sex. Today, the homegirls handle their own initiations, and help nurture bonds of love, loyalty & respect. They became a safe haven for the Locs, they are our wives, paramours, mothers, sisters & nieces not sexual play things.

We always valued the presence of females, and historically held the most Lettes within the Hoover Groove. We understood the importance of supporting strong bonds among our members & the homegirls helped promote that. One thing we are guilty of is not allowing our Lettes patronize other Hoover tribes because they would try to steal our girls like we stole Wilda & China from Five-Nine.

YVETTE & TRAYMATE

I think back & reflect on that first set of young ladies that wanted to join the set, and you know what, they didn't stick around. Now that I have matured, and became a girl-dad, it became clear to me that the sacred hedonist ritual we thought was a thrill, was in reality, foul & lowdown.

It was a ceremony driven by power, pleasure, manipulation, and control. The homegirls that remained loyal, and stayed down for the H-crown were the ones that put in work, got jumped in, or were our relatives.

As the seasons changed & the years flew by, FDHGC remained a refuge for young people seeking solace in a world that might have otherwise rejected them. While banging is cursed with uncertainty & danger, it was also a source of stability for us.

Hoover Gangsta stands as a testament to the importance of community, solidarity, and respect in an unforgiving urban landscape. Within the Groove lies an intricate web of relationships that bind us beyond a collective identity. In our world, the homegirls played a key role in our quest for unity, love & loyalty proving their worth & value.

CHAPTER THIRTY-SEVEN:
" CRIP OR CRY, RIDE OR DIE"

We terrorized the Brims for years with no serious consequences. The war was completely lopsided & in our favor. They had started the shooting, but we had the grim reaper on our side. Baby Man was about 2 years younger than me. He was 16 years old, building his reputation as a solid & active Crip. He lived on the Tray, pushing the line since 13 years old.

Baby Man was the type of Loc you wanted on your side. He had a unique combination of intelligence & street smarts, which made him an invaluable asset to the set. He had a calm & collected demeanor, but beneath that calm exterior, there was a fierce & loyal heart, beating for the love of Five-Deuce.

August 5, 1983, Baby Man & his cousin Sleep from Eleven-Deuce Hoover, swaggered down 52nd street towards Normandie. The agenda for the day was casual—they were headed to the store to get brews & breakfast. The concrete beneath their feet hissed under the relentless Pacific sun, the rest of the city still waking up & stretching its tired bones.

Almost as if it were preordained the duo encountered our rivals from the Six-Deuce Brim. Voices amplified with taunts reaching a crescendo, urban warriors with a score to settle. Words exchanged, tensions building, the harsh sunlight refracted off the shards of broken beer bottles as the conflict escalated to new heights.

Normandie Ave morphed into a gangbanger's arena. The feeble protest of old timers & winos seemed futile, there were no words of wisdom to subdue this confrontation. Baby Man & Sleep stood their grounds with grit & resolve, Crip pride flowing through their veins.

In the midst of the chaos, the metro bus pulled up at its scheduled stop on Normandie & 51st street. It was a seemingly normal day for the driver, unaware that his bus was soon to be hijacked by an agenda far removed from its daily school & work commute.

Upon seeing the approaching bus, the Bloods saw an opportunity for escape. They dashed towards it, bounded up the steps, and sought refuge amongst the oblivious commuters. Unfazed & oozing machismo, the young Hoovers pursued their enemies onto the bus. Simultaneously morphing the unsuspecting passengers into horrified hostages of the street brawl that spilled over into their ride.

In the restrictive confines of the metallic bus, the brawl escalated. Riders whimpered as they saw the brutal scene unfold before their eyes. The driver, a grizzled veteran of these inner-city streets, quickly intervened, trying his best to diffuse the tension & rein in the uncontrolled fury of the combatants.

However, the intervention was in vain. Baby Man & Sleep, unshaken by the fear of others, continued their onslaught with Hoover aggression. After successfully reigning supreme & satisfied with the vicious beating they delivered, they exited the bus triumphantly.

As the homeboys celebrated on the sidewalk, their Hoover battle cry, and high fives echoed through the air, their gang signs offending their rivals. Unknown to Baby Man & Sleep, the Bloods were armed, and dangerous. The Bloods harbored more than bruised egos & battered bodies, their thirst for revenge was killing them softly. Panic ensued as the sound of shattering glass & the eruption of gun fire echoed around the vehicle.

The Blood's wrath was unleashed. The Brims did the unthinkable, a drive-by off the bus! Passengers' screams echoed as the bus windows shattered. The bullets found their unsuspecting targets; Baby Man was hit in the back, Sleep wounded in his arm & foot as they reached the intersection of 52nd street & Normandie.

The shooter then puts his gun to the bus driver's head. He stressed his demands with ice-cold clarity; the driver was now forced to be the wheelman for their getaway. The hijacked Metro bus on a course toward the Brim territory, leaving behind a trail of chaos & horror on Normandie Avenue.

Baby Man's death sent shockwaves through the set. The news was a bitter pill to swallow, filled with sorrow, regret, and boiling anger. The day's sunrays drew a massive shadow over the region, a reminder of the deadly feud. We were devastated. Baby Man was a promising young Kiwé whose life had been cut tragically short.

There was a heaviness in our hearts but we refused to let our grief define us. Instead, we let it fuel us, providing the strength we needed to continue to represent & eliminate our rivals one at a time.

This was serious, the fun & games were over. It was time to make a choice, Crip or Cry. Baby Man's death lit a fire within us, fueling our hatred towards the red rags. We ramped up our efforts to make our mark on the streets, determined to show the city that we would not be intimidated by tragedy.

H.I.P "BABY MAN" MARK LAZARI BROWN

We engaged in an *"on sight"* campaign & unleashed a brutal onslaught on the Brims. We were on their bumper; the Brims were going to be planning several funeral services in the upcoming weeks. Conducting daily attacks, leaving a trail of blood & destruction in our wake as we avenged our fallen star. We had learned a painful lesson: In gangbangin', there was no room for tears or weakness. It was Crip or Cry, and we would not cry.

His little sister joined the set after his death & became known as Hoover Kim, one of our most loyal & dedicated Hoo'lettes. She was determined to avenge him, determined to keep his memory alive, making sure he would never be forgotten. Kim, like her brother, was just 14 years old when she first threw up the H. She was courageous & enthusiastic, never straying away from a challenge or confrontation.

Sometimes when we were out gang-hangin', Kim would suddenly become quiet & reflective. Her eyes would fill with tears as she thought about Baby Man – her big brother, the one who had always protected her since they were little kids. They were so close, and now he was gone, forever. It broke our hearts to see her like this. we made a vow to be there for Kim & her family through thick & thin.

The streets of Los Angeles were filled with hostility & resentment. The air was thick with anger & hatred, and we fueled each other's fire with the memory of Baby Man. The years of fighting, bloodshed, and sacrifice seemed to pale in comparison to the few rare moments of peace we shared as friends & family. It was these moments that reminded us of the bonds we shared– friendships built on loyalty, trust, and love.

It became evident that our true enemies were not simply the Bloods or other rivals, but rather the forces that drove us to hate, to stand divided, to become numb to violence & death. We carry on, each day facing new battles, both on the streets & within our hearts. We must remember the sacrifices of those who came before us & after us, the hope we all held for a better future. We walk the paths we paved, growing stronger with each step, until the day that we can truly emerge victorious by choosing to create the lasting legacy that our fallen stars deserve.

Shortly after the tragic event, I caught a probation violation & the judge sentenced me to six months at YTS—Youth Training School—located in Chino, California. Back in the day, YTS was considered California's most violent juvenile prison. The day I entered the cold halls of YTS, I was fully aware that my reputation preceded me. However, I was ready to reinforce my notoriety, even though I had already proven my violent tendencies.

We called YTS *"Gladiator School,"* & it was fitting for what went on behind those razor-wire-lined fences. For a young man like me, YTS was less a correctional facility & more a training ground for the inevitable life that would follow that of a hardened inmate, prepared for the worst the state prison could throw at them. At YTS, you'd learn how to fight, how to make deals, and how to negotiate your way through the treacherous terrain.

As I trudged through the dingy corridors, every cell was like a jungle, teeming with young men who were fighting for survival. The stank of sweat & fear filled the air. The more I walked through the facility, the more I understood that this was not just a place where young men were sent as a punishment. It was a place transformations were predestined, either into senseless thugs or victims. This guarantee made YTS a place that demanded physical, mental, and emotional fortitude.

Our youth was snatched away from us, replaced with bitter lessons that could scar us for a lifetime. YTS housed a wide range of inmates, from ages 15 up to 25 years old. The age difference meant little here; what mattered most was how far you were willing to go to ensure your survival. In the time I spent at YTS, I learned about compromise, resiliency, and adaptability.

As I walked down the stairwell of YTS on my release day, I couldn't help but feel bitter. Realizing that the only thing I gained during my time there was viciousness. With every step, I braced myself for another uphill battle against the sin & temptations Los Angeles promised. The experience hardened me, I would be a lot more ruthless upon my return to Hoover Street, a mindset I didn't know I needed on the road ahead.

Before I got cracked, Chim & Buddha started working for this old white dude who opened an arcade on 51st & Vermont next to the liquor store. He was scared to leave his machines in the ghetto, so he gave them a job & the keys to open & close the spot. Aww man, you know he fucked up right?!? We would be in there having a ball with all the gum, candies, and games our hearts desired.

The early 1980's was the golden age of video games, so we were in paradise! Color video games just started coming out & the arcade had all the classics, Space Invaders, Frogger, Pac Man, Donkey Kong & Centipede. Chim figured out the arcade & the liquor store were connected, so we broke into it one night & got away with about 25 cases of wine & beer, a couple hundred dollars & some snacks.

We had an epic party in the arcade that night, we partied until the sun came up, and managed to have the arcade spic & span by the time the owners came in. We made a regular thing out of breaking into the liquor store.

Madman had a longtime friend named Lobster from 78th & Hoover, he was a cool cat, popular in the low-rider scene. Lobster recently put in work on the Brims, earning his blue rag. Lobster & JoJo decided to break into the liquor store one night. Unbeknownst to them the owner was sick & tired of us robbing his store religiously. The owner had a plan to catch the crooks red handed.

He decided to do a stake out & waited up for the invaders that night. As Lobster & JoJo exited the crawl space they were ambushed! The owner was merciless, instead of calling the pigs, he blasted Lobster with a shotgun! We couldn't believe he killed the homie. We thought the worst that could happen is we got caught & sent away for a little while. Instead, we have another dead homie, the second dead homie in Hoover Gangsta history.

JoJo got convicted of burglary & Lobster's murder & had to serve 10 years. JoJo was never the same after that, PTSD got the best of my comrade. We lost 2 solid homies that night due to the felony murder rule which states any death that occurs during the commission of a felony, results in the felony murder charge being brought against all the players involved.

The news of the tragedy spread quickly amongst our ranks. There was shock, disbelief, and sadness amongst us all. Lobster had just joined our family, and now he was gone forever. I remember feeling anger & confusion all at the same time. This was not how things were supposed to go. We all knew the risks of breaking into the liquor store, but we never expected such a tragedy.

CHAPTER THIRTY-EIGHT: NAKED BOOTIES & ROCK HOUSES

The city of Los Angeles was profound during this era, like an electric pulse running through the veins of the night, nothing short of spectacular. Behind the wheel of my 65 Cadillac looking stylish with my Ace Deuce hat, a gold Cuban link chain hanging heavy around my neck, single long earring in my left ear, biscuit shoes & painter pants, I was a groovy portrait of the era. Chino, Lil Tee Capone & the Tiny Locs called me Boss Hogg from Dukes of Hazard or Mugsy from Looney Tunes, inspired by my Boss nigga status, short stature & big ass hat.

I can hear Chino's voice now, *"All I see is yo big ass hat behind the wheel, big homie!"*

During these times, the Naked Booty was the heart of South Central. This vivacious strip club, located at the crisscross of Florence & Figueroa within the Seven-Foe turf, was the main attraction. The homies & I took it over & transformed the club into our own personal hedonistic getaway, I ain't lyin'!

You know the freaks come out at night! I had countless nights I can't remember due to being cloud nine high & dizzy drunk, I was on everything! My Naked Booty nights were full of lap dances, one night stands, and dice games. I embarked on wild booty club tours; starting at the legendary 1st King, then stopping by the unforgettable Barbie Coats, only to end my night soaked in the neon lights of the Naked Booty.

The Naked Booty was an adult playground, with an array of dazzling lights that painted dancers in an otherworldly glow, the steady rhythm of pounding music shaking the walls, and the sight of lust & desire intertwining with the strobe lights dancing in the corners. There was a grand stage that created an eye-catching extravaganza. The venue housed gleaming stripper poles, adding an exotic flair to the mesmerizing spectacle. However, the real allure lay in the bitches! The dancers were as diverse & appealing as a painter's palette, Blacks, Mexicans, Filipinas & your token coke snorting White girl gone wild.

These ladies of the night were always a vibe. Their ghetto fabulous appeal drawing men in like moths to a flame. They paraded around, donning weaves that featured enough colors to make Roy G Biv envious, from cobalt blue, pastel purple to fiery red. I recall one dancer even had braids on her coochie. The Naked Booty was outrageous & enticing. The perfect atmosphere for a scandalous Hoover.

Among these ladies, a captivating dancer called Blue Magic grabbed my attention. Her beauty outshone the psychedelic blue hair on her head, a hue that was marched by her coochie hair, a landing strip leading me to her pretty pussy. I vividly remember the first time she gave me some ass. It was during a sultry back room lap dance to the rhythms of *"Hey Mr. Groove"* by One Way, then we had an after party to the rhythm of backseat back shots in my Cadillac.

She loved her some Boo Capone - a fascination shared by most the ladies, they loved my aura & found gangbangers like me, irresistible. One time I had to hide my dope in her pussy cause the pigs raided the club. I had a few hoes up in there, they didn't only get their dope fix from me but they tricked on me, I was bleeding them bitches for every penny they had. Reflecting upon those wild days, the underage drinking, the voyeurism, and the thrill of dodging the law, I loved it!

Ken Dogg, Insane Fish & I were road dogs, partners in crime, reunited again. We decided to get a spot together. We found a duplex on 57th street. Ken Dogg & I were dating two sisters from the set,

Vicki Dogg & Blacc Pep. After some good dick & sweet talk, we were able to convince the homegirls to put the apartments in their name.

Fish had a brilliant idea, he suggested we turn the shack in the back of the house into a rock house, so that's what we did. Around the same time, CeeCee, Ric Roc & Chim opened up a Rock house down the block. Rapidly, 57th street transformed into a mean green money making machine. Everything was groovy, the money poured in, and our pockets swelled, all the pieces if the puzzle fell in place.

A few weeks went by. It was a cool evening during the last days of summer 1984. The sun was just dipping below the horizon, the smog filled skyline blazing with brilliant hues of red & orange. Insane Fish, Tee Baby, Hoover Kim, and Tee from the Eight-Tray Gangsters were hanging out on 54th Street. A few yards away, Willbone was grilling up some burgers & hot dogs at the barbecue pit. The smell of barbecued meat wafted through the air, mingling with the sounds of lively shit talking & laughter.

As they enjoyed good times & conversation, three dusty smokers strolled down the block. The three strangers finally approached Willbone & struck up a conversation. Willbone worked closely with Chucky Mac, so naturally, the homies thought they were looking for their next high.

As they enjoyed good times & conversation, three dusty smokers strolled down the block. These strangers didn't seem like gangbangers, they raised no suspicion, so the homies paid them no mind. The three smokers finally approached Willbone & struck up a conversation. Willbone worked closely with Chucky Mac, so naturally, the homies thought they were looking for their next high.

The trio eventually started heading back to their car, one of them on Will bone's heels. It was at this moment that Fish, caught a glimpse of one of the stranger's faces in the streetlight & realized that he recognized him. As it turned out, he was the older brother of the homegirl, Kimberly. Her brother, Aye, was a member of the Inglewood Family Gangsta Bloods, from his tenure in the Inglewood school district.

Aye was an older cat around Big Mike & Spookee's age, his whole family was from Hoover. We knew him for years, he never caused any problems or brought any red rags around, so we let him live. A sudden panic shot through Fish's chest as realization struck him.

Willbone's mannerism seemed unnatural & coerced; Fish noticed what appeared to be a pistol pressed into the small of the homie's back.

The Bloods were capturing Willbone right before his eyes, but Fish knew it was too late to react. Moreover, he was the only one with a firearm, a revolver, the wrong move could result in Willbone being shot or worse, and all of them being killed as they weren't aware of what kind of arsenal the Families possessed. They must be heavily armed if they were brave enough to come into Hoover territory with these bold antics.

Internally cursing himself for not reacting sooner, Fish sprang into action. Frantically Fish ran over to Joker & me by Big Mama's house, breathless as he explained the dire situation. We immediately alerted the homies to the situation & notified Chucky Mac. Fish suspected that the assailants were planning to rob one of our rock houses by using Willbone as a pawn to gain access. Time was of the essence – Will bone's life was in immediate danger, and the set was under siege.

We wasted no time setting up security at C-mac's various dope spots. Within minutes we were ready to defend our turf from further infiltration & hopefully rescue our fellow Hriginal. Since we lived in an age before cell phones became common, communication was far from easy. A few of us had pagers, but the majority had to rely on home phones, word of mouth, and our pigeons. Despite these limitations, our resolve to protect our homies & the Fifties only grew stronger. I step into the middle of the Foe & shout our battle cry at the top of my lungs.

"Hooooover!"

As the homies reply the same & begin joining us in the street. With each passing second, more & more Hoovers answered our call to action. We dispatched groups to each of C-mac's dope houses, taking up strategic positions & ensuring that we had a clear line of sight on the entrances & all corners.

Night had fallen, and everyone was on high alert. We were prepared for anything; no foe would stand a chance against our unified front. It was now a waiting game, and there was little more to do than to keep watch & hope for Willbone's safe return. My heart pounded loudly as I stood next to Big Joker & Insane Fish, my Locs for life, shoulder to shoulder on Hoover Street between the Tray & the Foe.

We were getting ready for war. I thought about our comrade, Willbone, a livewire, wild child that stood at a mere 5'5" but one of the most hardcore Crips you would ever meet. He was always down for the crazy shit & got himself into crazier shit.

Our plan gradually took shape as Willbone's crazy ass brother. Too Sweet, joined our efforts armed with a 12-gauge shotgun. His eyes were filled with fire & determination to get back, his brother. Fish, assessing the firepower, encouraged Too Sweet to trade it in for something automatic to bolster our chances. With my M-1 carbine in hand, I joined Too Sweet, and Joker, as we cautiously began crossing the street, ever vigilant of our surroundings. Just then, two cars made their way stealthily up 53rd Street, the headlights off, blending seamlessly into the darkness.

Our instincts kicked in, and we started shooting at the cars. The air filled with the sound of gunfire as bullets sped towards their targets. Before we knew it, we found ourselves engaging in a frantic shootout with the occupants of the vehicles as their bullets pierced the silence & ricocheted around us. Too Sweet & I ducked behind cars for cover, the intensity of the crossfire increased, and fear gripped us like an iron fist.

Insane Fish, attempted to join the battle, but the heavy traffic & heavy crossfire prevented him from getting any closer. Gunfire rang out through the night air, echoing through the empty streets like a ghetto symphony as each bullet tore through the night like the hiss of a viper striking its prey. Amidst the pandemonium, a third car pulled up in an alley off 54th Street, letting out even more Bloods. Fish, thinking fast, decided to use the element of surprise to his advantage. He stood nonchalantly at the nearest bus stop, pretending not to see the enemy approaching.

"*Where you from, Blood?!*" They hissed at him, their voices dripping with venom.

In an instant, Fish pivoted around, his handgun speaking before his voice could, the explosion of gunfire silencing their threats as two of the four men crumpled to the ground. He sprang into motion, sprinting away from the scene with bullets raining down around him, ricocheting off of houses & shattering windows. With a final desperate superman-nisque dive over a wrought iron gate, his gun clutched tightly in his hand, Fish managed to escape, but not unscathed. The impact chipped his tooth upon the crash landing.

It seemed like an eternity, but it was probably less than 52 seconds, our reinforcements finally arrived! Unleashing a hail of gunfire at the invaders. This onslaught drove the enemy into a full retreat, leaving the battleground littered with the wounded & the desperate. With the immediate threat nullified, we regrouped with Fish & some homies at Lil Coke Dogg crib on 56th Street, where we caught our breath & took stock of the situation.

We had managed to fend off the Bloods' first strike, but the night was far from over. Willbone was still in their clutches, and every minute that passed only spelled more danger for our comrade. As the commotion & hysteria began to subside we prepared to face whatever lay ahead, one thought remained clear in our minds: we weren't going to rest until we brought Willbone home – safe, sound, and alive.

Resolute & united, we pressed forward to continue our struggle, prepared to confront life-or-death challenges to defend our turf & save our friend. This game was unforgiving, but our loyalty & camaraderie mimicked it. Every step we took, every bullet we fired, was for the will of our people. It might seem strange to think there was any love in this cold world. It was a world in which your homeboys were all you had, and sometimes, it was loyalty that made the difference between life & death.

Our brotherhood had remained steadfast in the face of danger. Together, we had sent the Families running, proving once again that our loyalty & courage were unmatched. As we stood in the middle of 56th street, bruised & battered but alive, an unspoken understanding passed between us—we had shown our true colors in this battle.

The stench of gunpowder still hung heavy in the air after the Hoover Street shootout, while the wailing sirens in the distance signaled that the pigs were en route. We knew we didn't have much time. We entertained the idea of running into Aye's house, threatening & kidnapping his parents, and demanding Wilbone's whereabouts & his safe return.

There was just one problem, though; Aye's sister, Kimberly, was one of our own. She hailed from our set, and we knew we couldn't risk hurting her. After much debate & ethically driven discussion, the collective decided to veto the idea. The bond with our set was one of the most respected & valued things that we held true in our world. That definitely left us in a bind, but there was no way we were leaving our loved one behind.

Instead, we took it to the streets & went straight to the heart of family Turf, where our enemies lay in wait. We were like a tornado tearing through a small town, we left a path of destruction as we tore our way through the Inglewood Families. There could be no doubt in our message: You don't fuck with Hoover Gangsta. When our loved ones were in danger, we would stop at nothing to make things right. After our rampage we ensured the world of one less red rag.

Despite our brutal retaliation, doubt gnawed at the back of our minds. Will's fate remained unclear—was he dead or alive? Our hearts ached as we longed for an answer. Later that same night, his brother, Too Sweet, received an unexpected & urgent phone call. It was Willbone! The abductors, perhaps fearing the rampage that had just engulfed their turf, had abandoned their captive on Flower Street by the Harbor Freeway. They stripped him of all his clothes, valuables, and dignity but left him alive. The Bloods actions left Will bruised up, beaten, and with hurt pride.

Relieved & infuriated at the same time, Bow Dee & Willbone told us about the motive behind the abduction & attack. Unbeknownst to us, Bow Dee, had a longstanding gripe with Aye's nephew. Just a few days before, Bow Dee had robbed & beaten him.

Earlier that day, Bow Dee & Willbone had taken their vendetta a step further, shooting at the young man as he drove down

Figueroa Street. The poor kid ended up totaling his Volkswagen Beetle, damn near killing himself. The Bloods had kidnapped & robbed Willbone as payback, they may have also had intentions of hitting the dope houses when they were detoured by our defensive parameters.

With Willbone safely returned home, we knew that we had made all the right decisions. Our homeboy was back, and we greeted him with a newfound appreciation. For us, family means everything. No matter how many shootouts we got in or how much blood was spilled, that fact remained clear. United, loyal, and unforgiving – that was what made our set untouchable, the reason why no enemy dared to cross our path & we wouldn't have it any other way!

CHAPTER THIRTY-NINE:
"SEPTEMBER TO REMEMBER"

Boscoe was always on the lookout for potential recruits who displayed loyalty & courage. He started dating a girl & was introduced to her brother, a kid named Mahonda with peculiar mannerisms, which earned him the nickname *"Stranger,"* because he was a strange little nigga from 57th street. They started hanging out & Mahonda began soaking up the essence of the Groove.

Kids hung around the homies, trying to find a sense of belonging & purpose, but there was something undeniably different about Stranger. We felt his energy, and Boscoe ultimately brought him into the fold. Boscoe thought it was time, and one afternoon, he jumped him in with Lil Mouse, Lil Man, Devil, Lil Twindogg & Lil Coke Dogg. I never forget running into them in the alley shortly afterward, Lunchmeat & I started clowning him over that corny ass nickname.

"You gotta get put on by the big homies now," Lunchmeat declared.

Lunchmeat was twice Stranger's size & 5 years older. Stranger didn't back down, he stood up for himself, you know the slogan *"once you fight, you alright",* he did his thing but Lunchmeat got the best of him. Lunchmeat was my age, a big kid about 6'2 but he couldn't fight for his life. His head was so big after his victory, I found it quite amusing.

As the days & months went by, we did dirt together & soon I would give him a job selling dope for me, I found a soul I could truly relate to. His persona was infectious, and I couldn't help but admire the hustler spirit that seemed to seep through his pores. He wasn't known to be a great fighter but was a certified gun man! He was a marksman & natural pistoleer.

It was clear that we had stumbled upon an invaluable asset for our set. Over time, Stranger proved his unwavering loyalty & commitment to FDHGC. No matter the circumstance, he was always there for us, ready to jump into action with a quick trigger finger & fearless attitude. It was clear he was no longer a stranger, instead he was becoming my baby brother.

September 2, 1984, started out like any other day in South Central Los Angeles. The sun was shining bright, and the air was filled with the smell of freshly barbecued food from Mama Mary's house. We had plans to go to Fox Hill Mall in Culver City to get some fresh gear for the Uncle Jamm's Army party at the Sports Arena.

This was an event nobody wanted to miss, and we had every intention of making a statement with our presence. Besides kicking ass, our favorite thing to do was party, why do you think they call us, Hoover Groovers, we are known to get our groove on! We had plans on going up to the Arena over 100 deep.

I was posted outside the roc house with Lil Coke Dogg, Boscoe, and Stranger, when Lil Q-Bone & Hot Shot from Broadway pulled up. Lil Q-Bone had a Loced out 1984 Dodger blue Silverado on gold spokes. We told Lil Q-Bone our plans. He offered to drive, so we hopped in the back of the truck.

As we walked through the mall hittin' on bitches, Hoover Gangsta Crippin', browsing countless stores, in search of the flyest gear. We turned the corner & ran into some Sixties. The air around us seemed to change as an uneasy stillness fell over the area. The exchange began with pointed looks, and quickly escalated to a heated exchange of words – neither side backing down, nor willing to back away.

The soundtrack of the argument was full of profanity, slurs & gang signs. I couldn't contain my anger, I yelled out, *"Fuck Sixties!"*

In the midst of the bickering back & forth, I hear *"Fuck Hoover!"*

Rage took over, and without thought, I leaped & struck the disrespectful party with a thunderous superman punch right in his mouth sending him sprawling to the ground. An all-out brawl erupted right there in the middle of the shopping mall. We fought without restraint, violently clashing with our enemies.

Set against the backdrop of pristine storefronts & window displays, we furiously battled, fueled by our desperate need to claim the upper hand. As we exchanged blows, our weapons were improvised, we grabbed anything we could find - metal clothing racks, hangers, and even store signs.

Amid the chaos, Boscoe managed to slam one of the rivals through a storefront window, shattering the glass & sending panic through the mall. Lil Boo, relentless in his attack, stomped on a fallen adversary, while Lil Coke Dogg struck another with a powerful signature hook, elbow combo that resulted in blood pouring from the Sixties nose & mouth.

Lil Q-Bone & Hot Shot began to join in on the action. A good squabble, no guns or knives, just machismo. The fight was ruthless, fierce, a hurricane of violence - this was a clash borne out of years of bitter tension between our sets. It felt as though time had stopped, and the only thing that mattered was asserting Hoover dominance.

We tore the mall apart, leaving a trail of destruction behind us, shattered store front glass, knocked over food carts, and clothing racks. The Sixties started running out of gas, our superior conditioning worked in our favor. It wasn't long before they were battered, bruised, and retreating from our onslaught.

The mall's security watched helplessly, having wisely decided not to intervene in our ferocious battle, and instead chose to dial the pigs for backup. We chased them through the mall, throwing whatever random objects we could find at the ones out of reach until we heard Police sirens in the distance. It was time to end the fun & games & make our escape.

Standing tall, we howled our battle cry, *"Hooooover!"*, a proud declaration of victory echoing in the wind, so they knew Hoover Did it!

Breathing heavily with adrenaline still pumping, we surveyed the scene; the battlefield strewn with broken glass, merchandise & the remnants of our epic brawl. Sideways glances from shaken shoppers & staff met our gaze as they cautiously took in the wreckage we had left behind.

I realized that day that I underestimated Stranger, he could really squabble, but he saved his talents for bashing the enemy, and clearly restrained himself during his squabble with Lunchmeat. I knew he could have easily whooped his ass after today's performance. The drive back to our hood was a blur of shit talking, replaying the skirmish blow by blow, & the victory that had just taken place. Stranger & I looked at each other, both with busted lips.

"You know we tied at the hip now, I'm Lil Boo Capone!" Stranger states.

I replied with acceptance & excitement *"You damn right Lil Boo!"*

I kept the trio with me all the time. They continued to work for us & took care of things when we were incarcerated or out of town. Stranger was now the notorious Lil Boo Capone from Five-Deuce Hoover. With his new identity, he continued to strut down the alleyways & boulevards with an air of unparalleled confidence, carrying with him the spirit of being my number 2.

Tonight is the night! Our favorite party, Uncle Jamm's Army was going down, the perfect event for us to celebrate today's victory &

perhaps get to kick some more ass. Los Angeles brought you the super party, Crips, Bloods, and the best marijuana. At the time DJs were battling for turf just like the hoods, and Uncle Jamm's Army reigned Supreme. They were like the Hoovers of DJ crews.

Uncle Jamm's Army was the shit, they went from house parties to filling up the Los Angeles Sports Arena, the Convention Center, and the Hollywood Palladium! Tonight is the big party in the Sports Arena. The Los Angeles Arena was located at the beginning of Hoover Street next to the Los Angeles Memorial Coliseum.

These guys, Uncle Jamm's Army, were getting paid, one of their DJ's named Egyptian Lover bought himself a Rolls Royce off the profits from their parties. One of their most well-known members started as one of their backup dancers, a kid named Tracy Marrow from Sixties. He later became a big time rapper & actor known as Ice T. I will never forget when Egyptian Lover performed live on his 808 drum machine, engaging the crowd in freestyle chants to the beats that made the crowd go wild. It was called the *"Freak Beat", and* they named their record label after it. Uncle Jamm's Army were DJ's that became superstars.

The LA arena was filled with 10k attendees, no famous artists, just their DJ crew, it was rammed, and everybody had a blast except our enemies. We had intentions of hitting on honeys & taking punk's money. We were ready to make an example out of somebody, maybe everybody.

As we swaggered into the dimly lit party, the atmosphere was mad. The party was a melting pot of all types of people, you had the Prince looking niggas, the Michael Jackson type niggas, punk rockers, half naked muthafuckas like they was strippers & of course the gang bangers. Lights flashing, bodies bumping & grinding on the dance floor as the bass vibrated through the walls, creating a hypnotic vibe.

The savory taste of notoriety began as partygoers groaned & whispered with dread, *"Damn, the Hoovers are here. Party's over."*

"You Niggas Better Recognize"- Sam Sneed

We loved that shit! Their fearful recognition only fueled our appetite for power & control. We had made our mark, and our reputation soared to insurmountable heights. The Hoovers became notorious for shutting down events wherever we went. Our mere presence struck fear in the hearts of those around us.

As the night progressed, we began to enact our ruthless plan, targeting an entire section of the arena. It played out like clockwork: one by one, row by row, we advanced through the unsuspecting crowd, anything gold, any doe & any hoe was ours. We claimed anything valuable & left a trail of fear & chaos in our wake. To the people, it must have seemed as if we were like evil ushers, taking their offerings not for the church, but for Crip.

Our looting served as an opening act to the main event, and after pillaging, we turned our sights onto our foes. Hatred coursed through our veins as we scanned the packed arena, realizing our main rivals —Brims, Coast & Sixties – were amongst the crowd.

Despite their bravado, our enemies failed to see the trap that we had so carefully laid for them. We had over 1,000 Hoovers scattered throughout the party in various strategic platoons, they couldn't have known we were everywhere. It was as if we were a hidden army, waiting for the perfect moment to strike.

Certain songs were anthems they took the party to the next level like *"Mr. Groove"* by One Way & *"The Grooveline"* by Heatwave, *"One Nation Under a Groove"* by Parliament Funk would have the Hoovers going crazy! Throwing signs, Poppin' & lockin', Crip walkin; & bussing our Groove. Parliament Funk had a few anthems, *"Atomic Dog"* was another one, at the time Crips were known as Crip Doggs! Once it came on, everybody started throwing up their sets. Another song that made the Crips go Crazy that night was *"Aqua Boogie"*, when it came on, everybody started Crip Walkin'.

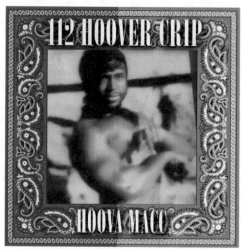

That night the Rollin' Sixties challenged a single faction of the Hoovers, the Eleven Deuces, completely oblivious to the fact that Hoovers infiltrated every corner of the arena. The Sixties attacked Macc & Ducc from Eleven-Deuce Hoover, attempting to throw them over the balcony. We struck with overwhelming force, attacking from every single direction like a pack of ferocious wolves. The cries of victory rang throughout the Sports Arena, *"Hooooover"* echoing back to the mayhem.

The squabble escalated quickly as fists, elbows, and boots pummeled our rivals' unsuspecting bodies; swiftly decimating their feeble attempts at retaliation. While we were brawling, they played *"Flashlight."* Something about that song made everybody stop fighting, mid-punch or slur, it made us vibe & stop the bullshit. We left them bloodied, broken, and above all, humbled.

Nobody could challenge the Groove whether we were on Hoover Street or any place else, as we believed & still believe that the Earth is our turf. We reveled in the anarchy, leaving our mark on the arena with each explosive act. As we disappeared into the night, chin high & chest out, hands in our pockets, and grins plastered on our faces, we solidified our roles as legends in the Los Angeles underworld.

Do you remember the last night of September, the bittersweet memory of those days still lingers within me. The scorching sun was gradually being tamed by the autumn breeze, and the rays of sunlight glimmered on the dusty streets. I was kicking it with Big Mama & Lil Coke Dogg at her crib.

Big Mama, looking fierce in her crisp new blue bandana, was a fine Hoo'lette. She had an aura about her that captivated me, but my conscience, dictated by an unspoken rule we all abided by. Due to her being Big Cee's daughter, I didn't make a move, all the while feeling an undeniable attraction towards her.

As a homegirl, she was dedicated & devoted to the cause, always standing her ground as a Hoo'lette. From day one she was solid all around & stompdown, her surprise visits while I was in CYA, meant a lot to me. My homie Chim told me real friends come visit you when you're down & out, in prison or in the hospital. I couldn't agree more.

I was the big homie, and a stud so I had a plethora of homegirls I was having my will & way with at the time. Tomorrow wasn't promised so we lived carefree, filled with laughter, camaraderie, and promiscuity. I couldn't foresee the important role Big Mama would play in my life, but I would soon find out how special she is.

It's the middle of the night, we were all chilling on her porch, swapping war stories & bragging about the work we put in, and sharing plans of future parties & missions. We were vibing, listening to some tunes, the boombox playing my favorite song *"Friends"* by Whodini. When her father, Big Cee, came back from the store with another old head Gladiator.

"You hear about yo boy CoCo?" the old head says.

"What you talkin' about oG?" I replied.

He shook his head & said, *"some nasty shit bro".*

I started to walk toward Coke Dogg's grandma's crib to see if he had any information. The tension was cutting through the air as I walked, every step feeling heavier & heavier. As fate would have it, I ran into Steve-O. His eyes were red as though he had been crying, and he was breathing heavily, struggling to find the right words.

He gave me heartbreaking news. *"Niggas killed CoCo on 53rd, cuH."*

Shocked & numb, I shift gears & sprint to Coke Dogg's house. He is there with Grandma, as well as CoCo's mom. It was clear in their eyes, a mixture of pain, anger, and disbelief. Steve-O's words held the bitter truth. They sat surrounded by memories of a life cut tragically short, mourning the loss of a loved one.

The scene is an emotional wreck. I gave her my condolences & vowed to revenge his death. As I scan the room & make eye contact with Coke Dogg, it's telepathic, he nudges his head & signals for me to meet him in the back room.

I ask him *"What the fuck happen to CoCo!?!"*

He told me *"It was bad, real bad, these bitch ass niggas killed baby bro!"*

The room is spinning! I'm catching a migraine from this emotional roller coaster. I was in shock the news knocked the air right out of me. I didn't think I could make it without CoCo. He was my big little bro! We worked together hand & hand, side by side, step by step to build the set.

He was always there for me!! He looked for me to start some shit so he could finish it & vice versa. He was always with the bullshit. I didn't know how I was going to do this without my boy. We were a dynamic duo like Kobe & Shaq, Magic & Kareem!

I felt helpless & I hated it! I wanted revenge!

"We need to round up the homies!" I yelled.

"Why?" Coke Dogg Replies, *"Me & you are all we need. Let's put in this work, on Five-Deuce."*

The word on the street was that he went over there for a get together & to get some smoke & things went haywire. There are several different stories & accusations against several different people. The hospital told us he would have made it if emergency services were notified sooner, and that he passed from internal bleeding. We head over to the deuce to get in one of my stolen cars, now we are on our way to bring the pain, *"The Big Payback "* by James Brown is the soundtrack for tonight's mission.

We were all wounded by the loss of our brother, like a pack of wolves hungry for vengeance, we hurt a lot of people during those turbulent days. We felt like the city needed to share our pain. I'm not proud that a lot of innocent people felt our wrath.

The once-warm days gave way to cold bitterness, we lust for revenge, hunting the streets for those responsible for our brother's death. The days turned into weeks, the weeks into months, and with each passing moment, our rage grew even stronger. The phantom of CoCo's killers managed to escape our grasp like sand through our fingers.

In the end, justice took an unexpected turn. The ones who were responsible for CoCo's death met their demise. The worst part is that we never got the muthafuckas who did it. Unfortunately, they are dead & it wasn't by my hands. I must live with this incomplete feeling.

I will never be satisfied. The memory still haunts me. My loved one didn't even get a chance to start a family with his wife to carry on his legacy, but we did have his baby brother, CoConut. I will always remember Big CoCo as a leader, a friend, and a warrior.

H.I.P ROBERT "COCO" TOWNS

CHAPTER FORTY:
"WHEN IT RAINS, IT POURS"

It was a gloomy morning in October as my Locs, and I gathered to lay CoCo to rest. His funeral was a somber affair. I could still hear his voice telling me to stay strong & look out for the lil homies. The sound of church bells echoed through the dense air as the congregation slowly walked out of the chapel into the sunny Los Angeles afternoon. Coco's funeral was coming to an end, and it felt like time had come to a screeching halt. Loved ones embraced one another, their tear-stained faces looking up to the heavens for hope & solace.

Despite my best attempts to stay strong, I couldn't help but shed tears for our fallen star. Coco was well-loved & respected, and his sudden departure from this world left a void in our hearts. We had lived life on the wild side, but at his core, Coco, my loved one, my brother, a great comrade, leader, and A-1 since day one Kiwé' warrior.

It had to be a little bit over a year since we welcomed Ric Roc's baby brother, C-Roc to the set. I couldn't help but smile, remembering just how eager & proud he was to be down with the set. He was young, but he had that spark in him that Coco loved. Just as I was coming to grips with Coco's death, I got slapped with a parole violation & was sentenced to do a few weeks in county jail where I was reunited with Joker, who was getting ready to embark on an 8 year bid.

Every life event, no matter how insignificant it may seem, has the potential to change the course of our lives. Sometimes it is so profound that it sticks in our memory forever, becoming a turning point that shapes our destinies. My life was full of such moments, but the one I am about to share reigns supreme among them all.

On the night of Friday October 12th, 1984, a date I will never forget, the cold steel of the jail cell felt even colder than usual. The following morning, I sat in the day room with Joker playing dominoes, my mind wandering all over, searching for some meaning behind the havoc of our lives. As the clock ticked by, I couldn't shake away the feeling of distress that was weighing heavy on my chest.

The buzzing of the television in the day room of the Crip module interrupted my thoughts, as I glanced up at the screen just as the news anchor began recounting the details of a recent crime. What I saw & heard next made my heart drop like a stone to the pit of my stomach: The 54th Street Massacre.

What the hell happened on the Foe, my mind clouded with confusion & intrigued. My heart shattered as the story unfolded & the list of casualties began, each name feeling like a tight knot in my chest.

The news anchor continues to list the fatalities, *"Percy Brewer (Big Buddha); Phillip Westbrooks (Big Phil); Diane Raspberry ; Shannon Cannon (C-Roc), and Darryl Coleman (Lil Insane). Five others were wounded."*

My mind raced, desperately trying to process the tragic news. The images on the screen portrayed a haunting scene, riddled with bullet holes, and stained with blood.

"Oh my God, not Shannon, not my baby bro C-Roc," I whispered to myself, my hands clenched into trembling fists.

H.I.P SHANNON "C-ROC" CANNON

I felt a whirlwind of emotions tearing me apart: sorrow, disbelief, and unbridled anger. I am a Kiwé warrior, I dared not shed a tear. I knew better than to show any vulnerability in jail, instead, I masked my sorrow & remorse with unbridled rage & conviction. C-Roc was only 13 years old & the only Hoover Gangsta casualty, Lil Insane was from Five-Nine Hoover & the others were from Broadway, regardless of which side of Fifties they were from, I considered them all family. We were facing unprecedented times with the death of Big CoCo followed by the Massacre.

"Your tears mean nothing. To be a warrior you
must kill your tears."
-Nanisca, The Woman King

In that moment, feelings of helplessness & anger consumed me, igniting the urge to break free from bondage & seek vengeance for my fallen comrades. I knew that even if I managed to exact revenge, a never-ending spiral of bloodshed & retaliation would continue to ravage our community. The deaths would go on, and families would continue to cry for loved ones lost, but this is what had to be done. The truth was cruel & unavoidable.

BEN OLENDER / Los Angeles Times
House on West 54th Street where five people were shot to death.

We all felt the burden weighing on our shoulders like Mr. Atlas. I had just been released from the county, and my first order of business was to attend the remaining memorial services for our fallen stars. Heavy hearts weighed down by sorrow from losing those who meant the most to us, we needed to gather & mourn collectively. I needed to be there. I reunited with H'Luv on 52nd street, my brother from another mother. His eyes, already swollen, filled with emotion I had never seen in him such despair.

H'Luv was inconsolable, and as we embraced, he said, *"Shannon died in my arms, cuH, he was only going to the store & stopped by Traci crib looking for Ricky."*

It was gut-wrenching, hearing these words rekindled my grief, but there was no time to deal with the emotions. H'Luv kept his cool & a level head, no matter the situation. Seeing him like this made my heart ache like never before. C-Roc's passing shook us all to the core, but of course it effected Ric Roc & Mama Louise the most. We leaned on one another, vowing to keep Shannon's memory alive & never forget the joy he brought to our lives.

It was a cool, crisp evening, when Manual Arts faced off against Crenshaw in a highly anticipated football game. The atmosphere was electric & charged with emotions as the two rivals went head-to-head. It was a game that was highly anticipated & everyone & their mama attended; it was practically the main event for the entire city.

It was more than a game to us, it was a ticking time bomb powered by tensions & rivalries. Ric Roc, Woody from Five-Deuce Broadway & Tee from Eight-Tray Gangstas had an altercation with the Sixties at Manual Arts earlier that day, the back & forth ended with the Sixties threatening them & warning them not to come to the game.

H'Luv arrived at the game with Cadillac Bob, Gino from Five-Deuce Broadway, and a deep blue sea of Five-Deuces to support Chino & Lil Coke Dogg, the star running back & defensive back for Manual Arts. The energy amongst us was like an infectious disease—we couldn't wait to cause chaos & push the line against anyone who dared to cross us. The football game itself was overshadowed by the sinister undercurrent pulsating through the stands. We were there to send a clear message to all: do not fuck with Hoover-Broadway.

As the game kicked off, the atmosphere was a powder keg waiting for the slightest spark to ignite. Hoover-Broadways pushed & shoved their way through the crowd, causing chaos, representing the C, checking niggas & jacking fools, wishing a punk would be brave enough to stand up for themselves & get beat down. The darkness of the night provided the perfect cover for their antics.

The game was not short of its electrifying moments & highlights. Lil Coke Dogg bulldozed his way through the opposition. Lil Coke Dogg makes a big run & knocks a Crenshaw player's helmet off & lays him out with a vicious stiff arm, turns out the kid was from Sixties! This moment, during the heart of the game, set the stage for the long awaited & anticipated fist to cusps.

Boscoe, C-Roc, and the tiny locs couldn't hold it in anymore. They took it upon themselves to take the hyped-up crowd one step further into chaos. Taking advantage of the adrenaline pumping through everyone's veins, they instigated a melee with the Rollin' Sixties who were rowdy & antagonizing Lil Coke Dogg after he embarrassed their comrade.

It wasn't long before the pigs started to notice the commotion. The commotion & fear caught their attention, prompting a disruption to our mischievous good times. In that moment, the mob of Crips scattered, making our separate getaways like project roaches in the middle of the night when the lights turn on.

Meanwhile, Ric Roc & Inch High were cruising with Tee from Eight-Tray Gangstas & Woody from Five-Deuce Broadway. The streets were full of people, either heading home from the game or loitering, mixing & mingling. As they drove down 54th Street towards Western Avenue, the homies noticed a parked gray Chevy, with a couple of guys draped in red attire inside of it who looked like Bloods.

As they passed by, one of the fools in the car flashed a gang sign at them, a fist with the pinky finger, and pointer finger extended, a hand sign representing the Brims. This audacious act infuriated the homies. A dangerous mix of anger, irritation, and the desire to retaliate brewed inside them. Not being the type to back down, the trio decided to make a swift U-turn to confront the opposition head on.

"That's the bitch ass Brims" says Ric Roc with a tone loaded with animosity.

It appeared that one of the Brims was fumbling around, desperately searching for a weapon alongside his brewing fear. Without hesitation, Woody whipped out his gun & pointed it at the Brims, but Ric Roc intervened. Caught off guard, Ase & the Van Ness Gangstas panicked, fleeing from the scene & deserting their Chevy. Tee seized the opportunity & decided to take the car. It was a form of both victory & humiliation: the stolen car symbolizing the power & dominance of the Crips while leaving the brims in a state of defeat.

They went on a Crip crazy joyride, adrenaline-fueled laughter filling the atmosphere as they drove the stolen Chevy with the pedal to the medal. The fun ended abruptly, however, when the piece of shit overheated from their abusive driving. Pulling into a nearby alley, they decided to strip the car before leaving it for good.

　　"We just jacked a red rag for his wheels, cuH." Woody Brags.

　　As Woody & Inch High rummage through the car, they uncover something that none of us could have ever imagined – a kilo of pure cocaine! Eureka! A hidden treasure! Of course, you know niggas claimed it as Kiwé property. It felt like they had just struck gold, cause they knew that this find would line their pockets with some serious paper. A kilo cost about 30k at the time, wholesale, and would retail for $200 per gram, for a fast 200k flip of pure profit!

　　"We need to send these bitch niggas a message, Loc, let them know Five Deuces did it" Inch High suggest.

　　Inch High leaves the whip with a new paint job. He spray paints a big ass blue 52 & VNG Killer all over the car, then they abandon it. Later that night a girl named Traci from around the way hosted a Birthday party at her crib on 54th street, in the heart of the Fifties. The party was nothing but good vibes, she was charging a dollar to get in, but she had a DJ, Food, Drinks. Many of the Five-Deuces were there celebrating the life of Big CoCo.

　　The DJ was spinning the grooviest tunes, setting the perfect stage for a fun-filled night. The air was filled with the sweet aroma of marijuana, delicious food & intoxicating drinks. The crowd had swelled to over 70 people outside, mostly Hoover-Broadways, acquaintances, and party crashers, who had come to drink & dance the night away. The festive mood spilled out onto the street with cars double-parked & people enjoying themselves.

　　Meanwhile, Coke Dogg, Chucky Mac, and Loon were on 57th street serving, when a mysterious gray car appeared looking suspicious. The car stops suddenly. So, they draw their weapons as they approach them to investigate. The strangers pull off, then begin tailing Naomi down the block, she pulls over outside of Madman's crib, and they creep by her peeping into her vehicle to see who was behind the wheel. The grey car kept it pushing, they must have seen her as merely an Asian woman & left her alone. Prejudice saved her life.

　　Around 9pm, H'Luv was gang-hangin' outside when he saw C-Roc scanning the crowd like he was looking for someone. C-Roc notices H'Luv & swaggers his way. C-Roc was looking for his big bro, Ric Roc. H'Luv told him Ricky wasn't around yet, so C-Roc decided to wait & chill for a bit.

Big Phil pulled up, he was making money working with Whitey Enterprises & was proud to show off his new BMX bike. He joined a marijuana cipher chopping it up with Buddha, Lil Insane, Diane & Cartoon from Five-Nine Hoover as they passed around blunts & drank forties. As the group chatted & caught up, I couldn't help but overhear an alarming conversation. Cartoon tells homies that he believes he saw a Brim, come, and go like he was doing some reconnaissance.

The realization sank in the homies were potentially under attack, as the Brims were most likely plotting their revenge for the carjacking. They weren't concerned because they were strapped, brazenly enjoying themselves on the very same street where the carjacking took place. Around 9:30 p.m. some cars arrived & double-parked in front of the house. Suddenly, two cats emerged, one with a jheri curl, carrying an M-16, the other armed with a shotgun.

One of the strangers called out, *"Buddha!"*

Buddha responded confidently, and replied *"Ay, CuH."*

From the corner of his eye, H'Luv saw the flash from the muzzle of the automatic rifle in the darkness. All hell broke loose, a hail of bullets & shotgun pellets then began to rain down on the crowd, turning the once-celebratory scene into a night of terror & confusion. In that split second, the entire street transformed into a war zone.

Bodies dropping left & right. C-Roc, a young Loc known for his fierce loyalty & heart of gold, was one of the first struck by the bullet storm after Buddha. His body crumpled to the ground.

The shooters laughed, their malicious giggles were bone-chilling, as everyone scrambled to find cover as bullets whizzed past them, too close for comfort. A stray bullet hits Blacc Charles in the ass as he scrambled for cover. The homies knew if they could find a safe spot, they'd have a chance to fire back at the trigger-happy intruders. They were in a bad situation with nothing but revolvers, they couldn't compete with the adversaries' heavy artillery.

H'Luv had taken cover behind one of the parked cars in the driveway, looking for an opportunity to fire back & protect our people. He could hear them laughing like sadistic villains as they continued to fire their weapons. Their laughter echoed through the air, sickening & cruel, an evil soundtrack to the destruction they were so gleefully causing. Sham Rock launched a counterattack & started firing at them from across the street. His cover fire gave Luv the opportunity to retaliate also. The homies returned fire as best they could.

The gunmen, realizing that they were no longer the only ones armed, quickly retreated. Unfortunately, the damage has already been done. Just as quickly as the attack began, the shooters sprinted back to their vehicle, still chuckling like savage scoundrels. The engine roared as they peeled away from the scene, leaving devastation & anguish in their wake. Woody ran after the shooting, as they sped away into the night.

Despite his grievous wounds, there was an intense determination in C-Roc's eyes: he would not give in to the pain that had ruthlessly dug its claws into his flesh. H'Luv mind raced, as he stumbled towards him, barely feeling my legs move beneath me. H'Luv found himself on bended knee by his side, desperately trying to keep C-Roc conscious.

"Stay with me, C-Roc," H'Luv whispered through his ears, *"don't leave me, man."*

Nothing seemed to work, the gleam in his eyes began to dim & H'Luv knew deep down that C-Roc would never regain consciousness. Overwhelmed by grief & shock, they clung to C-Roc, just hugged him, and held him trying to console him in his last breaths, his lifeblood soaking their clothes. The sounds of sirens & traffic drifted through the air, oblivious to the horrifying scene that had unfolded, the pain seared into the memories of those left standing.

Eventually, paramedics & law enforcement arrived after what seemed like an eternity. Their faces grim as they assessed the grisly situation; it was clear that they had been ill-prepared for such carnage. Suddenly, Ric Roc appears with Chim & CeeCee desperately scanning the aftermath, searching for a familiar face in the sea of pain & loss.

The paramedic gives up on trying to revive C-Roc, Ric Roc pushes the paramedic out the way & desperately tries to revive his baby bro. The crushing reality of his baby brother's untimely deaths, an unbearable burden to bear. A kid from the Fifties that went against the grain & turned Brim on the low, tried to console & calm the grieving Ric Roc.

"C-Roc will wake up. He's going to be okay," he pleaded repeatedly like a broken record, desperate reassurance dripping from his voice.

It was as if he thought he could magically reverse the harsh reality. It was this denial, hope or perhaps ignorance, which set off something within Ric Roc. His eyes burned with a fury that the homies had never seen before, and I knew that it was all too much to handle, a cocktail of grief, rage, and the thirst for revenge. With a guttural roar, Ric Roc lunged at the Brim, his fists pummeling him with the ferocity of a lion.

"Can't you see my brother's dead, muthafucka!" Ric Roc screamed, his voice cracking with pain.

The Brim tumbled to the ground beneath the barrage of anger & grief, his body taking the brunt of Ric Roc's smoldering rage. The beating continued as the Brim's pleas fell on deaf ears. Our lives would never be the same. Buddha is dead. Lil Insane is dead. Big Phil is dead. Diane succumbed to her wounds on the way to the hospital. The 54th street Massacre, bloodiest & most brutal attack in Crip & Blood history!

Mystery drive-by gunmen kill 5 teen partygoers; 5 more hurt

Los Angeles Times Service

LOS ANGELES — "The guy just jumped out of the car and started shooting," the young woman in the black jacket said.

"People were running, screaming, trying to hide. . . . I was hugging my cousin, and he shot her. He shot a girl on the other side of me, too. He just kept shooting, and people kept falling. . . .

"I thought if I ran he'd shoot me, so I just stood there, and I looked at him," the young woman said. "He looked right back at me. . . . I thought I was going to die.

"And then he stopped, and he got back into the car, and he drove away. It was over."

The young woman in the black jacket — she refused to give her name, for fear of retaliation — was unscathed.

young people arriving for a party Friday night.

At least five others were wounded in the barrage of gunfire that police believe was motivated by rivalry between two South-Central Los Angeles youth gangs.

Detectives said that while accounts of the incident varied widely, they had been able to determine which gangs were involved. But the officers did not reveal the identity of the gangs, and by nightfall Saturday, they still had not identified or arrested any suspects in the mass slaying.

The only ones identified on Saturday were the victims.

Police said those killed were Philip Westbrooks, 20, Shannon Cannon, 14, Darryl Coleman, 17, Diane Raspberry, 17 — cousin of the 18-year-old woman in the black leather jacket — and a

a party was about to begin at a modest, single-story house.

Paula Berry was hosting Friday's party in her apartment as a "pre-birthday" celebration for her daughter, Tracy.

A teen-age boy — who, like others, refused to give his name for fear of retaliation — said that he was standing near the sidewalk with other guests when he suddenly realized that a car had just "snuck up" the street toward them.

"They double-parked . . . jumped out of the car . . . and started shooting with an M-1 [rifle]," the boy said.

"There was no kind of argument. It was random, like they said, 'Here's a party. Let's shoot 'em up' . . . "

While the teen-age boy — and the young woman in the black jacket — spoke of only one car, a neighbor and other witnesses

Vengeance was taken that night, several Brim households had to plan home going services. I love my locs & pledged my undying dedication to all my Five-Deuces, as we loaded our weapons for another mission. We were guided by blind fury & loyalty. It was Hoover-Broadway against the world, we didn't know who was responsible so every enemy had to feel pain.

Our hearts were decimated, the losses tattooed infinite despair into our hearts that scar us until this day. The Massacre was etched within our souls, and had catapulted us into an inferno of heartache, payback, and animosity. Every step was a declaration of allegiance, and any disrespect was settled in blood. Life was a cruel game & we played by our own rules. Each passing month amplified the hostility, a grim saga of violent exchanges.

Our creed & our motto became *"When the Hoovers ride, the whole city cries."*

The ruckus turned our playgrounds into battlefields, our schoolyards into graves, our futures into hard time. In our struggle for survival, we saw innocent lives lost, dreams shattered, and futures stolen. Yet, we persevered. The soul of the Groove, the spirit that refused to surrender.

We were not formed as a vehicle for violence but as a shared identity to define our brotherhood & to protect it. Hell yeah, we did small-time crimes, robbing & stealing to get by but the 80's brought a change in the climate, it became kill or be killed. Many people blame the rise of crack as the trigger for many gang members becoming killers, metamorphosis to the *"gangbanger"*.

"He says we need to live in the real world, where
war & death are a reality, not pretend."
-Pittacus Lore

We can compare the evolution of global conflict with gangbanging. For instance, the Vietnam War was not intended to lose thousands of American lives but to stop the rise of Communism. However, situations unraveled on both fronts, with the outcome being the same: pain, deaths, and a cycle of endless violence.

Both the Vietnam War & South Central's gang conflicts were fueled by a combustible mix of socio-political factors, racial tensions, and institutional decisions. These conditions drew people into a conflict they neither desired nor understood in its entirety. As both escalated, the horrors & brutalities inflicted pushed participants towards self-medication via substance abuse.

We became shell-shocked soldiers. We witnessed a shift from calmer times to an era of senseless violence. The modest fistfights, stabbings, brawls, and revolvers escalated into full-fledged urban combat with automatic weapons, and shootouts guaranteed, daily like the sun rise. Like the transition from student to soldier. The US government drafted unwilling participants, and Crips & Bloods did the same to kids around the way.

The death toll within our ranks, a fraction of the thousands of lives lost in Vietnam but stirring up the same deep sense of survivor's guilt & PTSD. Each casualty represented a love lost. I was a beam in our foundation. I bear the burden every day, remembering those lost like my Pops & his platoon.

The soul gets marred with guilt, with questions about your purpose when your brethren meet brutal ends. This psychological burden made many of us eager, almost yearning for death in battle - either as atonement or honor. It's a startling reality of war, no matter where it's engaged.

CHAPTER FORTY-ONE:
"DAYTONS & M-16'S

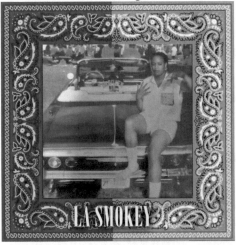

LA SMOKEY

After the 54th Street massacre it was all about survival in a city that had become the breeding ground of violence & despair. This was not the Los Angeles they advertised in movies & postcards. The murder rate in Los Angeles had skyrocketed nearly overnight, leaving the entire city under siege. It seemed that we lived in a never-ending war zone, and it was clear that we had to upgrade our weaponry to survive in the shifting times ahead.

The violence continued to rage on like an untamed beast, engulfing everything in its path. It weeded out the weak. Hoods that had hundreds of members were down to maybe 2 or 3 dozen hardcore homeboys. We knew we needed more money & bigger guns, and most importantly we had to become more ruthless, and we did.

No one knew when or where the next bullet would come from, and this sense of uncertainty made it difficult for most people to sleep at night, wondering if we would be alive to see another day. I don't know where these machine guns came from or how they got to the ghetto. Things that make you wonder, all we knew was that we had to get our hands on some.

This is around the time I got my first M-16. The time to seek out fortune & revenge had come. We were loading up with M-16's &

M1 Carbines for as little as $300 each. This was a bargain we couldn't pass up. We needed to act fast, as there was no telling when the streets would turn against us. No one was safe under the looming shadow of death that had engulfed the city.

BIG DEVIL AND LIL BUDDHA

It wasn't just guns that we were concerned with. One of the status symbols that all of us flaunted proudly was the Dayton wire wheels. Daytons, a luxurious yet extravagant accessory that would put us a cut above the competition. Everybody in Five-Deuce was *"ridin' on D's"*, you know why? It's because we were cunning & ruthless in our methods.

We were jacking any fool stupid enough to stop at a red light in the Fifties. We would rip open their car doors & strip them of everything they had, leaving them naked & penniless. The unspoken rule of lowriding, was you got to have clean ass wheels, and Dayton rims were the definition. They cost a grip about $3,500 to $5000 for a set of 4. We might pull up in 8 or 9 regals, every single one on D's.

Anyone with Daytons on their car was either a gangbanger or a baller, raking in cash through illicit means & gangbangers were robbing all the ballers. Several of our enemies were born out of people we robbed or wronged & sought vengeance upon us. Looking back, it is crazy so many people died over those wire rims.

Things really started getting good with our new connections, 42nd, 47th, 49th, 53rd, 55th, 57th & 58th street was like the blueprint for Gangsta Rap music videos. The set was decorated with Crackheads acting crazy, dancing around, couple fiends standing still as a statue like they were playing freeze tag or the mannequin challenge, another set of fiends leaning like the leaning tower of Pisa, weighed down by the burdens of their habits.

No doubt the crack game was dangerous & scandalous, but so were we, and the money made it undeniably alluring. The money we were making attracted head-turning women on the daily. Bad bitches & hood rats wandered up & down the block, drawn to the scent of success like bees to pollen.

Up & down the block & in the yard, you saw our whips, a sprawling collection of shiny metal & pure horsepower, the block was like a ghetto fabulous car show of Broughams, Cadillacs, low-riders, and even a couple of custom station wagons thrown in for good measure. On every block you saw blue rags, tens of Hoover Gangstas equipped with M-16s, Carbines, sawed-offs & semi-automatic pistols.

One afternoon at the crack spot on 55th, Madman & I were standing side by side, watching the scene unfurl before our eyes. We couldn't have been prouder of what we had built. A man pulls up in a blue 1983 BMW-3 series E30 320I, it's this nigga Willis (Todd Bridges) from *"Different Strokes"*, Willis wasn't like any other customer. He was a symbol of the wide-ranging appeal that our crack spot had garnered. He was living proof that we had bridged the gap between classic Americana & the underworld trenches we called home.

We served him a couple ounces; it further cemented our grip on this part of the city. 55th Street had become a melting pot attracting people from all walks of life. Everybody had money, even the dope heads had money. I didn't have to worry about somebody offering me a cheeseburger to get high, but I'm guilty of accepting a couple blowjobs for crack. We built our hustle on blood, sweat, and tears, and we fought tooth & nail to maintain our dominance. The money was something we celebrated, but the paranoia that accompanied this lifestyle I hated.

As I walked through the set, I noticed the contrasting effects of roc cocaine. The glitz & glamour, from fancy cars to rope chains & the suffering & raw pain, all a few feet away. The sound of dirty cash changing hands filled my ears, punctuated by the clicks of guns being cocked & ready.

Crack had the economy booming. A lot of homies made their money work for them & cleaned it with legitimate businesses. Around this time Chucky Mac decided to shift gears. In a move that shook the foundations of our crooked world.

He opened a car lot on Crenshaw, in the middle of Rollin' Sixties turf. The opening was shocking, daring, and veered into the unexpected road of going legit. A maneuver rarely executed, it marked the first steppingstone into a rare dope boy success story, a testament to the extraordinary life of an extraordinary man.

C-Mac defied the odds & the norms, scripted his own rules, built bridges, and navigated dangerous territories with poise. He was a Hoover Gangsta that was able to transcend the expected results of death or imprisonment & morphed into a legit businessman. In a world overwhelmed by blood, violence, short-lived success, and even shorter life spans. C-Mac managed to construct a riveting success story that resonates through the ages by reinvesting his profits. He made his exit of his own accord. His story echoes the possibility of change even in the most uncertain conditions. It also shows the potential for a man to control his destiny & find a way out.

416 | P a g e

CHAPTER FORTY-TWO:
"BAD BUSINESS & UGLY BITCHES

One fateful day, Fish got jammed up & found himself cornered in a sting. Things went awry & he ended up shooting an undercover pig. With the heat turning up, he was left with no other option but to skip town, temporarily disappearing from the scene. Taking refuge in Las Vegas until things died down.

Since Fish would be missing in action for an undetermined amount of time, we invited Vicki & Pep to stay with us. While we played house, taking full advantage of having in-house pussy we ended up getting the sisters pregnant, so Ken Dogg & I have children that are cousins.

We were getting money, doing our thing, We had dope spots everywhere, everything from Exposition to Slauson, cutting through territories of rival gangs like Brims, Black P Stones, & Sixties, but we never forgot our main objective – vanquishing every rival.

The homie Dre Dogg & I sat back chilling on my front porch one day. The taste of skunk weed mixed in with gin & juice, gave my palette a bitter-sweet tang. As the heavy bass pulsated through the stereo I enjoyed the vibes of *"Friends"* by Whodini, my favorite song. We reminisced about past victories & fantasized about future ones. We decided to put in some work on the Brims.

Weapons were selected with precision for a quick hit 'em up mission: an M1 carbine for yours truly & a sleek silver Nine millimeter for Dre Dogg. The plan was easy, we'd sneak up on those Brims camouflaged by the night, watch the fear spread across their faces as they realized who they faced. Hoover Gangsta– their worst nightmare.

For our transportation. We chose to jack a 1980 Buick Skylark. We set off toward 62nd Street. The anticipation & anxiety were like gasoline, fueling our every move. Adrenaline coursed through our veins as the familiar feeling of danger crept in, but excitement kept us going. As we approached our destination, our eyes scanned the darkened block, searching for the telltale colors of our enemies.

416 | P a g e

Jackpot, there they were, the Brims, clustered on a stoop. We pulled up about two houses away, giving us the perfect vantage point for a walk-up.

Leaping out of the car, we yelled our battle cry *"Hooooover!"* at the top of our lungs & opened fire.

The Brims scattered like roaches, trying to find cover from the hailstorm of bullets. An intense gunfight ensued, with bullets regularly getting uncomfortably close on each side. Amidst the hair-raising exchanges, we sought a moment to break away & made our exit as swiftly as we had emerged, bursting through the night at full speed. Usually, the Bloods would flee from our wrath, but this time was different.

The Brims were relentless, retaliating with a fury we hadn't anticipated. They jumped into their cars & tore down the street after us. Dre Dogg floored the gas, and we sped down Budlong Avenue at 80 miles per hour. In a mad mix of fear & exhilaration, leaning out the window of our speeding vehicle, ignoring the fierce wind battering my clothes & whipping through my jheri curl, I fired round after round at our pursuers.

I clenched my teeth as I leaned back in to reload, with a brief & alarming moment of respite. Dre Dogg tries to make a sharp turn on 56th street. He panicked, turning the steering wheel with too much force. We crashed badly into some parked cars. Our car was airborne doing somersaults like my tumbler pigeons & landed on its roof.

By God's grace we are still alive, but reality washed over us like ice water: we were trapped, and the bloods will be upon us any second now. The sound of twisted metal creaked & groaned above us. Coughing through the thick fog of dust that enveloped us, we struggled to extricate ourselves from the wreckage. I thought it was over. The Brims are going to kill us. Our minds raced & our bodies ached as we fought to free ourselves from the wreckage.

The smell of gas filled our nostrils as we clawed our way out. As I emerged, I saw the Brims headed in the opposite direction! With whatever energy remained, we sprinted away from the fiery scene & disappeared into the night, the car exploded into a disco inferno.

Our breaths came in ragged gasps as we watched the burning car. We hear sirens from approaching Police, and Fire fighters, so we hobble through some backyards, and maneuver stealthily back to Dre

Dogg's crib. The thrill of the fight & terror of the near-death experience cemented that night in our memories for years to come. Our breaths came in ragged gasps as we watched the burning car, knowing just how close we'd been to meeting our maker.

There I was, lying in my bed, wincing & gritting my teeth from the pain of the car crash. I was lucky, I only had a few deep bruises & a temporary limp, but no broken bones or lasting damage. It gave me just enough time to pause & think about the wild world outside my window, one that hadn't stopped just because I took a break from it.

So much has been going on. I wasn't 100% mentally or physically after losing the recent tragedies. My nigga, oG John Hunt stopped by to visit, Hunt was about his money, he proposed the idea of taking our talents beyond California's borders. A risky but lucrative move for us. Hunt was a gangsta midget like me, and an original Five-Deuce Broadway. I got tight with him & his brother Hot Shot during our time as West Towns.

It seemed like a good idea, and I needed an escape to get my mind right. It was an opportune time to exploit the markets & demographics of other regions. We were not strangers to the game, and he saw a potential gold mine in Denver, Colorado.

We went to the Mile High City & started moving rock in the Rockies. The crack game was already in motion out there, but we had better numbers. We could get an ounce for $200-$400 then resell it for up to $2000, that was a 1000% return on our investment.

Before embarking on our journey, we had to make sure that we had everything in order. We needed enough product to show the potential buyers the quality of our merchandise. To transport it safely, we had to get creative. We duct taped ounces to the axle of my El Dorado & put some packs in the bumpers & door panels.

We were ready for our two day road trip, that drive was boring as hell through the deserts of Nevada & Utah, so we passed the time smoking & drinking. The scenic views of the mountains & the vast deserts of the Midwest might have been breathtaking to some, but to us, it was a means to an end. We stopped occasionally to stretch our legs, get some food or fuel. We finally reached our destination.

At first glance, Denver did not seem to show any signs of being a potential market for our product. The city appeared quaint & serene but looks can be deceiving. We were cautious not to draw too much attention as we conducted business. We started by making relationships before we revealed the products we had to offer.

We had to find out where all the hoods were & hit them up. We wouldn't tell cats we were from out of town, because it was the fast track to hate or a fed case, so instead my strategy was more chameleon, have you ever heard the phrase *"When in Rome, do as the Romans do."* I learned their customs, habits, and slang so I could blend in with the locals.

There were a lot of LA hoods infiltrating the capital of Colorado, we ran into some Brims out there & Harlems, but everybody respected each other cause we all got money, so we didn't trip on each other. Once we set up a few distributors to wholesale it, it was on like hot butter popcorn.

Hunt was a grounded & decisive partner. He knew where & to whom we should serve. We created an efficient system that allowed us to supply our customers with quality dope, discreetly & safely. We ensured that our distribution was on point, and we delivered products on time without fail, he never let me down.

We had conquered another market, and our business thrived. All was well, and we were living the life of kings. We knew we needed efficient people to handle the transport of the product. It was a crucial part of the program, and any mistake could result in a significant loss of revenue or jail time. That's why I decided to have women handle this part of the job.

One bitch I had driving for me caught my attention, and not for her exceptional good looks. She was always around, and it seemed like she would do anything to be close to me. She didn't care about the money or the dope. She just wanted to be up under me, but trust me, she wasn't driving for nothing!

She wanted her payment in sexual favors, but this was a treacherous task for me. She did have some big ass titties but that wasn't enough cause this bitch was ugly as a moose. I mean, I couldn't even look at her without feeling sick to my stomach. I concocted a plan; I could get Lil Spookee to sex her crazy & keep her busy.

My nigga Lil Spookee is a straight up cockhound worse than me. He was like a dog in heat. He was reliable, and the perfect wingman. A bitch could be ugly than a muthafucka, he would give her the business, so this would be the perfect assignment for groove.

The Ugly bitch was a reliable, dependable worker & those were qualities I truly respected & admired about her. Unfortunately for me, she was determined to be my girl & wouldn't settle for getting sex from Lil Spookee.

I wasn't sure what to do. I mean, I knew I had to take one for the team, right? But the thought of sleeping with her made me want to vomit. In the end, I decided to go through with it. I had no choice but to give her some dick. She was the only one who would do this job for us.

It was a treacherous task for me, but we managed to get through it. The girl got her payment, and I got the product delivered to our contacts. It was a great relief for me when I met a guy named Anthony, who agreed to work for us. I was able to ship the product to him! This was a great relief because I didn't have to hump on this ugly ass broad anymore.

We had a nice run, Anthony kept it clean with me for a long time before he burned me on some work. He told me he never received it. I don't know why he did it. I don't know if he started using but once I got proof, I just took it on the chin & stopped fucking with him.

It was a tough break, but that's the nature of the game we were playing. I had to keep moving & find other reliable contacts to keep my business going. As for the ugly bitch who had driven for me, I never saw her again. I was just glad to be done with that part of the job.

The history of LAPD has been plagued by racial & discriminatory practices. Tom Bradley, the city's first Black mayor, was in power from 1973 to 1993. Daryl Gates was the LAPD's Chief from 1978 to 1992. Back in 1985, the duo launched a major campaign against drugs, focused on crack, and gangbangers. This war had devastating effects on the black & brown ghettos they were sworn to protect.

Under Bradley & Gates regime, the LAPD rolled out a military-grade weapon called the *"Rescue Vehicle,"* entitled after its purpose, rescuing the city from the dope slingers. It was an armored vehicle equipped with a 14-foot battering ram meant to smash through the fortified Roc Houses of suspected drug dealers. This piece of machinery, V-100's left unclaimed by the US government after the 1984 Olympics resulted in countless instances of property damage & community trauma in the hood.

The tactic raised eyebrows & escalated racial tensions within the city. Renowned attorney Johnnie Cochran, the National Association for the Advancement of Colored People (NAACP) & the American Civil Liberties Union (ACLU), were among those who filed petitions against the police department's use of the Rescue Vehicle, more commonly known as the Batterram. They argued that the vehicle was being used in a racially discriminatory manner, causing unnecessary harm & destruction as well as invoking fear among residents.

The uproar of the Black community found its way into hip hop. In response to the widespread abuse of the Batterram, Compton artist Toddy T released a classic hip-hop record called *"Batterram"* as a form of musical protest. Toddy T's record captured the essence of our struggle against racial profiling & police brutality. The lyrics mirrored the community's hopes & fears, turning their lived experiences into a catchy yet powerful composition that resonated with audiences far beyond Los Angeles. The track not only told the story of an oppressed community but also acted as a tool for activism & resistance.

Mayor Tom Bradley released a shocking statistic - there were over 300 rock houses in LA. As a core member of the Hoover Gangsta at that time, these figures weren't surprising. We were the puppet masters maneuvering behind the scenes, controlling roughly 10% of these gold mines. The rise of the Rock House was glaring proof of a city degrading into a combat zone overrun with drugs, violence, and scorn.

From '83 to '85, we transformed single-family homes, duplexes apartment complexes, and storefronts into covert crack dens. However, these weren't ramshackle operations. They were fortified lairs, tailored for the proficiency of our operations. Deterring arrest & indictments through specialized defenses.

Black Charles, Hershey, and Fly Guy were our welders, entrusted with a critical task. Their job was to transform these ordinary dwellings into fortresses. By installing remarkable steel doors sandwiched between two Sal wood doors & reinforced with 2 layers of iron bars on both sides at every point of entry.

One evening, as I was nonchalantly in the backyard taking a piss, when the sudden, distinctive rumble of a battering ram hit my ears. The bone-jarring, raging clang echoed through from blocks away. An ounce of fear surged through me, I didn't even waste time to put my dick away!

I frantically ran to the nearest window & warned Face, *"Yo, cuH, the ram is coming!"*

In the blink of an eye, our procedures swung into action against the impending siege. As the anxiety-inducing sound drew closer, pandemonium ensued within the house. As the homies rushed to stash the dope & firearms into hidden panels beneath the floors &

secret compartments within the walls. Any rock we couldn't stash was swallowed by the toilets.

This panic peaked into an impulsive flight! Homies jumped out of windows & crashed through the back door in a manic frenzy, the only escape from the impending siege. We disappeared like phantoms into the darkness of the night. We ran like runaway slaves, hearts pounding in our chests like African war drums to the chaotic rhythm of paranoia & survival instincts.

We watched from the safety of one of our nearby homegirl's crib. As the flashing red & blue lights descended upon our fortress. Squad cars screeched to a halt, emptying uniformed officers who slithered into the landscape like provoked vipers, hot on our tails. The paramilitary SWAT team, notorious in their black tactical gear, methodically immersed themselves within the premises & promptly surrounded & penetrated the structure.

As I recount my story, I conjure up vivid memories, a stark reminder of the life I once lived. It was an era of crack castles, rebellion, and perseverance. It was the life of a Hoover Gangsta amidst the crack epidemic. Each day was an adventure, an adrenaline-filled escape from the one time.

CHAPTER FORTY-THREE: LOVE & WAR PT.3

As the sunset over Hoover Street, Boscoe, Big Chim, and Lil Chim go to World on Wheels with the Harlems.. We were friendly with the ScHool Yards, but World on Wheels was a Rollin' Sixties stronghold. The roller rink was a breeding ground for beef & showdowns, as much as it bred good vibrations & memories.

Tonight, it pulsates with the bass of Run DMC's *"It's Like That"*, adrenaline & machismo. Hoover-Harlem harmony shatters when Big U & the Rollin' Sixties enter the rink. Arrogance etched in their faces & a sense of entitlement in their walk. As a wise man named Kevin Hart once said, *"it's about to go down!"*

Tensions flared like a lit fuse, and an exchange of hostile words tore through the atmosphere between the Hoovers & the Sixties. Insults hurled like stone pellets. The peace was dangerously close to shattering when the pigs arrived, their beaming searchlights casting long ominous shadows over the crowd causing the scene to dissolve like sugar in hot tea.

Big Chim's blood is boiling from the exchange, he feels he owes somebody an ass whipping. Chim follows the Sixties caravan down Venice boulevard deep into their turf. Chim had no cares about the danger that may lay ahead. This chase finally ends at a gas station off Crenshaw, bathed in the harsh fluorescent light, the homies found themselves severely outnumbered by a hundred Sixties.

Amidst the murmurs & stares, Lil Chim, stompdown & loyal to his big homie's agenda, does not hesitate to announce their presence *"Five-Deuce Hoover Gangsta!"*

The response is immediate & hostile. Big U, a key player in the Sixties hierarchy, defiantly retorts, *"Fuck Gangstas!"*

It was then, Big Chim decided to challenge Big U, his fingers gripping tight into fists, and his words, quick & sharp as a whip, dared Big U, *"so what's up nigga?"*

As tempers flare, Chim & Big U find themselves in the middle of a brawl. No guns are drawn; instead, fists fly & land brutal punches in the tradition of old-school rivalry. Big Chim impressively gets the upper hand, and Big U finds himself on the verge of defeat when Lil Looney from Sixties cracks Chim over the head with a 40 ounce.

A frenzy erupted, with Boscoe & Lil Chim defending their loved one by attacking the nearest Sixties. The battle was brutally one-sided. The Hoovers were out manned & outgunned, fighting a handicap match. Returning blow for blow, the homies still fought back as greater odds stacked against them. Amid the pandemonium, an unidentified Six-Owe cracked Lil Chim with a 2x4, knocking him unconscious.

The rumble is clearly in the Sixties favor when, out of nowhere, Kilowatt, Crazy Tom, and the rest of the Harlems charge into the chaos. Hoover-Harlem fought tooth & nail, tirelessly & fearlessly, and succeeded in evening the odds during the vicious melee, saving the homies from getting beat to death.

The scene is chaotic as they fought with the Rollin 60s, the homies get separated. The echo of sirens wailing in the distance started resonating, forewarning the arrival of the one-time. Before the homies could fully grasp the situation, the pigs stormed in, their eyes void of compassion & mercy. The homies became separated, Hoovers & Harlems scattered & lost amidst the madness. Boscoe sees Lil Chim incapacitated & rushes to Lil Chim aid, but they can't find Big Chim.

Summoning every ounce of his strength, Boscoe hoisted Lil Chim to his feet, and the two hobbled together around the back of the gas station as fast as they could. A momentary refuge, but it could not harbor them for long. They were trapped behind enemy lines, trying to evade the pigs thirsty to incarcerate & beat down some young niggas.

While they felt protected by the shadows, it did not take long before the Sixties had them in their crosshairs! They chased them, guns blazing. Their bullets whistling past them, their deafening threats punctuating the night.

The homies scrambled through the avenues, hopping fences, making desperate attempts to distance themselves from their pursuers. Their mad dash guided them into a random home. Sweat-soaked & panting, they hastily sought the phone, hoping to inform their comrades of their predicament! The homeowner backed out their firearm on the Hoover home invaders!

Back on the run until they find refuge & a way out from behind enemy lines. Their first instinct was to call for backup, to summon the homie, Ric Roc– however, he, too, was entangled in their own scenarios, essentially trapped within his own chaotic web. Ric Roc had just caught a body & was evading capture by authorities, rendering him unable to help the lil homies. The revelation seemed to multiply the intensity of the pandemonium of the night.

The night ravaged itself in madness, and danger clung onto the moon. With each passing minute, possibilities dwindled, and anxiety mounted. It was a spiraling nightmare that had their hearts pound heavily against their ribs, mirroring the pounding despair that threatened to engulf them.

As the cruel hand of destiny continued to weave its story, an unexpected ally appeared. Poochie from Harlems, the tides had turned in their favor! They flagged him down & thankfully he stopped & brought them back to the set.

A few days later, oG Pretty Tony, an influential big homie from the Eight-Tray Hoovers, called a colossal meeting at Playa Del Rey, a notable San Jose neighborhood. A mass of over 200 Hoover Crips, all tribes were represented from Foe-Tray to Eleven-Deuce. Coke Dogg, Big Mike, Big Fat Rat, along with One Punch & a dozen Broadways; went to represent our contingent.

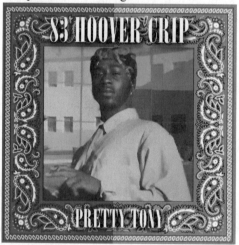

As the sun shifted its gaze towards this meeting, key topics were on the agenda. Primarily plans to go mob deep to World on Wheels to smash on the Sixties. Among these included our intriguing affiliation with the Broadways, a controversial topic that stirred discomfort within the Hoover ranks since our formation. The

Broadways wanted to come to support us & dispel rumors about Broadway/Sixties alliance. There was a sea of Hoovers in attendance, potential friction was rite, and the homies knew they were walking a tightrope.

Despite the tension, the Five-Deuces stood their ground. They carved out a narrative that illustrated our association with Broadway to our Hoover brethren. Upon Fat Rat's eloquent delivery, the clouds of doubt were beginning to lift. Understanding started diffusing through the ranks. However, not all welcomed this dawn of understanding with open arms. The elephants in the room, the One-oh-Sevens, were not as forthcoming.

One Punch, a Hoover-Broadway Gangsta loced out in a Dickies khaki suit, had arrived wielding a Louisville Slugger, a decision that wasn't the wisest, given the circumstances. Punch started chanting Broadway! This decision turned the spotlight back onto Hoover-Broadway.

Big Levi, a reputable from One-oh-Seven interpreted One Punch's rowdiness & his lethal choice of accessory as a confrontational act.

He asked, *"What's good with cuH & that bat?!?"*

Stepping up against the animosity, Coke Dogg stood up for One Punch, a bold move under the circumstances.

He declared, a voice steady with conviction, *"he is with us, he is Hoover-Broadway,"* drawing a line in the sand, a testimony of our alliance.

However, his words did more harm than good; they stirred up the One-oh-Sevens. Big Hogg, an Hriginal One-oh-Seven, refused the idea of a Hoover claiming any Gangsta affiliations. Lines were drawn & crossed. Voices of dissent turned into a collective physical uproar against Five-Deuce.

Hogg's retort, *"Fuck that shit, ain't no Gangstas on Hoover street,"* ambitiously defied the Five-Deuce rationale.

The brewing tension exploded into an unforeseen shoving match with the One-oh-Sevens. The once peaceful meeting of steel minds teetered on the brink of violence. The dire situation seemed downright menacing, a prelude to a brutal fight, potentially a blood bath. It was Bubbles from Seven-Foe, who stepped up & squashed the confusion as a voice of reason.

Luck, however, played its part as the flashing blue & red lights cut through the riotous crowd. The scene could have transformed into a one-sided beat down, if it wasn't for Bub's rationale & the pigs dispersing the crowd. The pigs intervention saved the situation from escalating into a full-blown fiasco, as the outnumbered Five-Deuces wouldn't have stood a chance against the wrath of the Hoover Crips. After there was a change in our relationship with Seven-Foes, they began to spend more time in the Fifties.

The chronicles of the Crips offer a rich canvas filled with stories of alliances, betrayals, fights, and triumphs– testaments to human resilience in times of adversity. An unexpected paradigm shift sent a rippling effect through the streets, Lil Bear, once an ally from the Five-Deuce Broadway, recently transitioned to Rollin' Sixties, for reasons unknown. Lil Bear's reputation evolved from a once trusted ally to despised traitor. Lil Bear, now an enemy, announcing dire news.

He approached Lil Bandit with warnings of an impending invasion by the Sixties, who planned to set trip on unsuspecting Hoovers at Manual Arts. Was Lil Bear playing psychological warfare or was his warning out of sincere concern for his former comrades? Only Lil Bear knows the answer.

The alarming news seemed intended to trigger fear & retreat, but Hoovers never cowered. We were warriors. We bled for our colors. We killed for the thrill. We lived to gangbang. We never backed down.

So, when Lil Bear sent down a mysterious warning about a potential Sixties ambush, we looked forward to it. It was an opportunity for an epic showdown.

As the school bell rang, it was time for dismissal. Lil Bandit gathered all the Hoovers, gritting their teeth, and gripping their heat, ready for anything. As anxiety reached its peak, they lay in wait. The anticipated ambush from the Sixties was a no-show.

Later, that night was the Manual Arts Carnival. Stall keepers hollered, advertising vibrant gray & purple painted masks, games of chance, fried snacks, and electrifying rides. Within the concrete arena of the school, tension & celebration pulsed side by side. Caught in a whirlpool of laughter, cheer, and adrenaline, the Hoovers stood in full force, prepared for anything. Suddenly, La Giggles came dashing towards us.

Breathless, she managed to gasp out *"The Sixties are coming!"*

Her eyes held a magnitude of panic that drilled a hole into our collective consciousness.

La Giggles witnessed Sixties creeping around the school disrespectfully hollering *"Sixty, Sixty, Sixty"* & *"Fuck the Hoovers."*

She relayed the information to us, much like Paul Revere on his midnight ride, warning the colonies of the approaching British forces. I could see the fire in her eyes as she spoke. As I stood alongside my comrades draped in blue. It was only a matter of time before we ran into them. They were hungry as wolves, itching to spill blood, Hoover blood, and vice versa, we shared the same hate & animosity.

Meanwhile, Boscoe & X-ray from Five-Nine Hoover are strolling through the back of the school on their way to meet us. Boscoe's boombox harmonizing with his rebellious attitude, blasted Toddy Tee. Their stride was disrupted by a car full of Rollin' Sixties. Their ominous question hung in the air like a guillotine.

"Where you niggas from?"

Without missing a beat, Boscoe confidently retorted, *"Westside Hoover, 52nd street! cuH! What's happenin!'?!"*

The response was immediate – gunshots! Bullets meant for Boscoe's torso were intercepted by his boombox, tonight…Hip Hop saved his life!

As quick as a lightning strike, they dashed into the school, as the Sixties bullets gave chase. The Sixties get stuck in carnival trying to get the homeboys when they come out the front of the school. Little do the Sixties know we are already on high alert waiting for their appearance.

Boscoe & X-Ray met up with us, urgency & resolve replacing the youthful mischief that once defined them. They narrated their brush with death, pointing towards the marauder's car inching down the street. As two cars inched closer, the occupants of both cars are screaming out *"Rollin!"*

Baby Shady from Seven-Foe responds with gun fire, emptying his clip on the two vehicles full of Rollin' Crips. The scene is in disarray as the cars crash into on-going traffic & the sidewalk to create a means to escape.

In the adrenaline-fueled chaos, Baby Shady thought he missed his targets. Soon after, the Harlems appeared, bearing with them a horrid revelation. This is where it gets interesting, it turned out the casualty wasn't even from Sixties, he was from Harlems! Our clumsy trigger fingers had caused friendly-fire casualties - Baby Shady accidentally shot one of the Harlems in the eye, a fatal blow that landed him in CYA for murder.

During the gridlock, the Sixties vehicle coincidentally ended up trailing a car full of Harlem Crips, who were screaming out Rollin' for Thirties! While the slurs of Rollin & Hoover Killa came from the Sixties that trailed them. A tragic mistake that resulted in the beginning of the end of the Hoover-Harlem alliance.

We had thrived together with H love, but the tragic incident changed everything. The mutual suspicion & animosity felt between Hoovers & Harlems could no longer be ignored, catapulting both sides into the swirling eye of a hurricane named Vendetta.

The lines of Loc & foe had blurred, which called for an urgent resolution. We don't usually explore diplomacy, but we felt our alliance was worth it. After the initial chaos, we came face to face with the Harlems. Grief & anger evident in their eyes, entwined with a thirst for vengeance. Warlock, an enraged & vocal member, proposed an arrangement rooted in the Hammurabi code. An eye for an eye, the death of our shooter in exchange for peace!

We refused the proposition. The shooter wasn't from Five-Deuce, and he had already been arrested for the offense. We stood our ground, Hoover is Hoover. If the roles were reversed, they would feel the same. The line had been crossed, and there was no turning back. We made our decision, and it was HOOVER FIRST!

It was then that Big Phil, a reputable & influential member of the Harlems, spoke as the voice of DNA – Denker Park, the Nine (39th street), and Avenue. An abbreviation coined to represent all sides of Harlem Crip. Despite the tense situation, Big Phil attempted to maintain diplomacy. An embodiment of wisdom, his words held sway over most of the Harlems present.

"Wrong is wrong & right is right," his voice echoed with an undeniable truth.

He admitted the blood of their fallen member was not on the hands of the Five-Deuces, easing out the wrinkles of confrontation. His agreement was a testament to stand up for truth, no matter the affiliation. Leading towards an uneasy truce but they held the Seven-Foe & the Eight-Tray Hoovers responsible.

This saga of conflict didn't conclude with a winner. What it represented was another facet of our existence tangled in a twisted web of loyalties & rivalries. In this treacherous Crip world, alliances waver, turncoats leave scars, and alliances fall, not to bullets of the enemy but under a cloak of confusion.

Just two blocks away, on the Six, Boscoe was hanging with his honey, Sugie from Hollyhood Piru, who would become Lil-Lil Bit from Five-Deuce Hoover Gangsta Crip. Big Phil, Warlock & Traylord pull up on Boscoe.

Harlems steered clear of any trouble with Hoover Gangsta & desired to maintain our alliance. They wanted to isolate the beef, have us play both sides, the good old divide & conquer strategy of Phillip II of Macedon.

Echoing our sentiments from an earlier meeting, Boscoe reiterated that, as per the unwritten laws of the Groove, *"Hoover is Hoover, you beef with one, you beef with us all!"*

Boscoe's words were an attempt to build a bridge of understanding. He tried to champion diplomacy, hoping that the situation wouldn't escalate further. Especially since justice was underway, the killer was arrested for the unintentional murder.

We were never the ones to be easily played with false hopes. The veins of the city were fraught with unease, desperation, and an undeniable sense of dread. We knew better than to let our guard down. Were we foolish to wish for peace? Even though we knew deep down that we were far from it.

> *"Deception is a sort of seduction. In love & war, adultery & espionage, deceit can only succeed if the deceived party is willing, in some way, to be deceived."-Ben Macintyre*

One scenario of *"Love & War"* has marked its impact on my life as well as several others, a tale overrun by betrayal, scandal, emotions, loyalty, and treachery. Baby Down from Five-Deuce Broadway became tender dick over the homegirl. Reminds me of that classic song by Franky Lymon, *"Only Fools Fall In Love,"* he became the definition of the phrase.

Despite our strict doctrine forbidding the homegirls from socializing with the rival Hoover Crip. Tee Baby's rebellious spirit led her across the tracks & into the arms of Big Crow, a notable member of Seven-Foe Hoover. Crow commanded respect on the street. He was a baller that possessed the unparalleled magnetism that comes with power & wealth. It reminded me of the adage told over the generations, *"don't hate the playa, hate the game."*

> *"What you mad at? Your bitch let me have that & I ain't even say shit about your fat ass. She chose me, don't get an attitude"- Too Short*
> *"Don't Hate the Playa"*

Baby Down's return from prison, painted a different picture. He was overcome with deep-seeded jealousy, angering him to the point of betrayal. His need for vengeance led him to make an unexpected move. I was on the Foe with Big Mike, Ken Dogg, and a few other homeboys, when the Broadway caravan arrived.

The Broadways wanted us to mediate & intervene in Tee Baby's personal life. They wanted us to convince her to get back with their Baby Down. Baby Down convinced them that the Seven-Foes was trippin' & overstepping their boundaries & they expected a pledge of support from us.

My comrade Ken Dogg was quick to retort, demonstrating his wisdom by dismissing the dispute, *"that love triangle shit, ain't Hoover business."*

I was irked & disappointed by Baby Down's shenanigans, so I interjected, *"CuH need to stop trippin' over some dick & pussy shit, we don't do that."*

Discipline & self-control are the name of the game. The next day, the Seven-Foes, led by Crow, Bub, Frog, Sinbad, and a few others, came to visit us.

Crow tossed a taxing inquiry, questioning our allegiance: *"If the Broadways wanna trip, who y'all riding with?"*

Ken Dogg, whose voice commanded the respect of both tribes, passionately declared our unwavering allegiance to the Hoover car. Our bold support for Hoover symbolized the deep-rooted loyalty that superseded our sibling rivalry. Undoubtedly Hoover comes first, and we chose to ride with the Groove.

The storm that had been brewing seemed to have passed, the tension evaporating with our declaration. We had made our choice – loyalty towards the Broadways stood secondary to Hoover. However, this proclamation sparked a reaction we couldn't have foreseen.

As the world turns South Central provided a menacing backdrop for a raging gang war between Hoover Gangsta & the Brims. Ken Dogg & I were as close as brothers, but blood couldn't make us closer than this Fifty Crip. We stood on the frontlines, fighting for the cause as if it were etched onto our very souls. Our loyalty to the set was unwavering, but what led us to maintain this allegiance was something much deeper.

I won't deny, Ken Dogg & I had an addiction to the adrenaline rush of gangbanging & chasing that high got the best of him. Our addiction led us deeper & deeper into the rabbit hole filled with violence, crime, and despair. Ken Dogg was always someone who loved to have control over situations, and he wanted things executed properly.

Ken Dogg was a big reason why FDHGC was flourishing, and he had a soft spot for the lil homies. As an Hriginal, he couldn't seem to step back & watch the next generation take our fight forward.

More frequently than I cared to count, they would approach us, asking us if they could borrow guns & ammo in hopes that their respective missions would grant them their slice of glory.

Ken Dogg, being the loyal homie & mentor he was, would always give in. He not only let them have the weapons, but he went along for the ride. I tried to reason with him. My words fell on deaf ears. Time & time again, I tried to convince him to let the young ones handle their own business, and write their own names in the sand, but he rather go chaperone.

Many nights, I would be fast asleep, dreaming of a better life, only to be awakened by Ken Dogg walking in, his footsteps heavy & deliberate. Smelling like a keg of gunpowder, a clear sign that he had risked it all once again. Ken Dogg finally started to listen to my advice, he started curving the urge to go on missions with the lil homies & spend more time with his family.

It was during this time that Big Mama & I gravitated towards each other, our connection intensifying, forcing me to acknowledge the surge of emotions coursing through me. My senses were overwhelmed by her very presence, and I could feel the barriers I had placed around my heart being slowly shattered. The magnetic pull of her allure only grew stronger. It wasn't just the intensity of Big Mama's beauty that mesmerized me, her mind & soul radiated a rare type of warmth that I found irresistible.

Slowly, I began to lose control of the self-imposed boundaries that kept my emotions in check, allowing myself to seep into her world. Despite initially viewing her as just a homegirl. She was developing into a stunningly beautiful woman, her body, mind, and soul growing more irresistible. So, we started seeing each other more intimately.

Despite my growing admiration for her, I was far from being a faithful companion to Big Mama. I was young dumb & full of cum, so I was spreading myself around. I found myself in another love triangle, this time with Goofy & Big Mama.

As a big homie, I was privileged. I entertained numerous sexcapades, allowing myself to be consumed by meaningless rendezvouses. Goofy wasn't just my partner in crime, she was someone who filled the void of my sensual desires. She had provided me with a smorgasbord of sexual pleasures provided to me by the many Hoo'lettes she recruited.

Big Mama didn't trip, never once complaining, as if she understood the fragile state of my love & lust. She played her position while I played deaf, dumb & blind to a good woman. I didn't recognize the depth of her love for me, and it was hard to focus on a relationship with all the violence that was happening around me.

Murders, drive-by shootings, and drug addiction pervaded our world, spilling into the gutters that would never run clean. I was intoxicated with the thrill & danger, the lust & desire that surrounded us; I was too blind to see the alluring beauty of Big Mama & the undying love she held for me like the stars that never faded.

It's a regular day around the way, I'm gang-hanging outside my mama crib drinking Tyronia with Lil Bandit, Big & Lil CeeCee, and some more homies when Coke Dogg pulls up with Big Fat Rat, Kiki, and Bub. Big Fat Rat jumps out of the car visibly upset, his eyes glowed with an unmistakable rage, his chest heaving like a caged beast.

Charging in like a bull, Fat Rat dropped a bombshell on us, *"Them Front Street niggas done car-jacked my baby momma,"* he continues *"they jumped in the back seat & put a gun to her head while she was in the drive-thru at Jack in the Box."*

Big Fat Rat didn't play when it came to the ladies in his life, especially his mama, sister & baby mama. His pride & joy was his '69 Crip Blue Chevy Caprice Sports Coupe. A symbol of his street cred, mounted on gold Daytons, was the apple of Fat Rat's eye.

Shocked by the audacity of the robbery, an air of determination spread among us. Prompting an immediate response, we mustered an impressive crew; including Big & Lil CeeCee, Big Eulys, Big & Lil Coke Dogg, Kiki, Lil Twindogg, Willbone, Lil Bandit, Lil Mouse, Lil Chim, Boom-Boom, Te Loc, Lil Te Dogg, Fat Curtis, Nutty Norm, Blue Rag & many more, I can't remember. We were so deep, ten cars loaded with forty to Fifty Hoover Gangstas. It was like they had pulled the rug right from underneath him. It wasn't about a vehicle, it was about respect, honor, and principles.

BOOM BOOM | LIL T DOGG | KIKI | POOCHIE

Spurred on by a single code of comradery, we raided 103rd street in an electric ambush. We saw a 6'9" Front Streeter, blue ragging, swaggering down the block.

Big Fat Rat's husky voice, loaded with anger, echoed, *"Where's my car, fool?"*

I don't know if it was innocence, or ignorance, flushed across the kid's face as he countered, *"I don't know nothing about no car, nigga."*

Kiki, points towards the '69 Caprice parked a little distance away. Enraged, I pounced on the kid, socking him right in the jaw with a superman punch, he stumbled into an uppercut from Kiki. The fight was on; Fat Rat body slams him, he goes skidding on the cold, hard asphalt right in a pack of wolves, disguised as Hoover Gangstas.

As we are Hoover stomping' the kid, about a baker's dozen of Watts Crips come to his aid, trying to even the odds. We treated them like heavy bags in the Hoover Street gym. We were too deep; they were completely overwhelmed. Out of the corner of my eye I see Lil CeeCee put his blue steel to the liar's temple, ready to pull the trigger.

A deafening silence hung in the air, pierced only by Fat Rat's imploring scream, *"Nooo! Don't do it, cuH! We just want the car!"*

The words echoed, hitting each one of us like a sharp exclamation, drawing attention to the pending execution. Lil CeeCee opts to crack him over the head with a Tyronia bottle instead. In the

437 | P a g e

shadows of mercy, the rattled Front streets scattered, leaving a window of opportunity for Big Fat Rat to retrieve his prized Caprice.

In the heat of the moment, with adrenaline racing through my veins, I made my move on a '72 Monte Carlo, deciding to secure a prize for myself. Just as we thought we'd gotten an easy win, the Front Streets retaliated! Returning in force & a hail of bullets. Instinctively, the tiny locs fired back, forcing the Front Streets to retreat again. God was certainly groovin' with the homies that night. Thankfully, none of us were hit, but Lil Bandit pointed out a bullet hole in Coke Dogg's coat that barely missed piercing his torso.

Homies managed to claim a '75 Impala Glasshouse & a '67 Chevy Malibu. Amid the chaos, clouds of smoke, and screeching of tires, we disappeared into the night. It was a night of triumph, a testament to the G-Code & our brotherhood; a night that reminded us that in our world, respect wasn't given, it was earned. I could only imagine the regret coursing through their ranks as they tried to digest their loss - the stolen car which had sparked the vengeance of Hoover Gangstas & immortalized their hate for the H.

CHAPTER FORTY-FOUR:
"TREASON SEASON"

Loyalty, a virtue that had been held in high regard for generations, seemed to be dwindling, disappearing amongst the chaos that had overtaken the streets. We watched bonds begin to dissolve when the heat was on. As greed & desperation pushed people to betray those they once held dear.

Less than a week after the Hoover-Harlem tragedy, February 19th, 1985, it is documented by the LA Times that a group of Brims were gang-hangin' at a house on 60th street. Down the street, a Cadillac slowly cruised towards them. As the car drew alongside the group, a .30 caliber rifle poked through the passenger-side window. A sharp intake of breath was the only reaction before the trigger was squeezed.

Bullets zipped through the air, cutting down their good times & forcing them to dive for cover. One wasn't quick enough. Struck in the lower back, as he tried to escape, the bullet sped through his body into his brain. All the hopes & dreams he held close to his heart vanished in an instant, as he crumpled to the ground. His life – over – just like that.

The shooter sped off, leaving behind a cloud of smoke. Witnesses at the scene, still shaken from the event, were quick to lay blame on triggers of the Hoover Gangstas. Some even claimed they could identify the shooter under one condition – a guarantee of protection. A couple days after Insane Fish caught a probation violation, and was charged with shooting the undercover, Ric Roc was captured for a homicide.

Around the time Fish got locked up, Ken Dogg & I decided to give up the apartment because it was getting way too hectic on 57th street between Pep & I. While Ken Dogg & Vicki's relationship prospered. Unfortunately, after Pep & I fell out, she kept me out of our child's life. I moved into a spot on 42nd street with my big sis Linda G. Everybody used to come hang out over there, we had the Foe-Tray to the one way crackin' off.

It was a seemingly ordinary day in May when Lil Man & Lil Ken Dogg were gang-hangin' around the way. They saw a car full of

Brims riding through the set, Lil Ken Dogg threw a bottle at them. No more than five minutes passed before the Brims came back guns blazing. Ironically, one of their bullets hit Lil Ken Dogg in the same wrist he used to throw the bottle.

The next day 3 brims were shot in an alley on 63rd & Bonsallo, 2 were wounded, one was hit in the arm & hip, the second was shot in the chest, and the 3rd was shot in the eye & died. News soon spread that the driver, Stroll's baby brother Batman, had been arrested shortly after the incident. Their sister's white '77 Monte Carlo with unique blue dots in the center of the hubcaps, was identified fleeing the scene. After Batman's arrest, Lil CoCo, Chim-Chim & Boscoe were picked up for the shooting.

Word on the street was they were looking for Ken Dogg too. It was also a deeply tragic reminder of the dark truth about our environment. In the harsh reality of a bitter & bloody gang war, the concept of loyalty became non-existent. Friends turned on friends, and it seemed that personal gain was the only thing that mattered.

> *"To me, the thing that is worse than death is betrayal. You see, I could conceive death, but I could not conceive betrayal."*— *Malcolm X*

In the absence of Fish & Boscoe, a brewing storm had swirled around whispers & rumors. Giving way to chilling confessions & unintended casualties in the cut-throat hierarchy of the Crips. We agreed to deem the Carnival incident as friendly fire, but the damage was done, an unhealable wound was inflicted to our relationship with the Harlems. The spirit of camaraderie & brotherhood that had bound us together was now shrouded in doubt & betrayal. We had held the Harlems in an esteemed light, treating them not just as allies, but as kin.

The H love & respect we had for them was profound & genuine, fueled by shared victories & defeat. We held the belief that this feeling of closeness, of family, was reciprocated. In the cruelest twist of fate, it was this blind trust that led not only to the downfall of the alliance but also the loss of one of our own.

oG Junebug, a noble warrior & Hriginal of Eight-Tray Hoover. He was not your typical member, he was a reputable Groove, his courage, and loyalty unmatched. One night, just when everything seemed to have cooled down, Junebug was ambushed outside his girlfriend's home located in the heart of Harlem territory.

Coincidentally, his girlfriend was a Harlem Crip, raising an unsettling question: Could she have been involved in the assassination? His death was marred by uncertainty, with the killer remaining in ghostface. They had planted the seeds of suspicion, turning our alliance into a minefield of treacherous doubts.

H.I.P WARREN "GEE-MAN" CARTER JR.

The cruelty of fate wasn't done playing its devastating hand with our lives. We were introduced to a gruesome discovery: the lifeless body of Gee Man found in the alley behind his home. The heart-wrenching rumors that he had been shot by a smoker or one of our own! Gee Man used to serve in the very alley he was found in, proving the cruel reality of our existence. An unfortunate end to a promising young Kiwé warrior. The mystery of Gee Man's tragic demise was never solved. His death was a stark reminder that uncertainty & danger were ever-present.

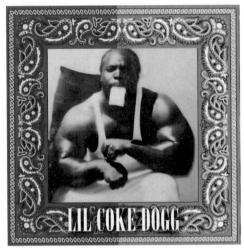

Another shocking event followed Gee-Man's murder. Lil Coke Dogg committed the brazen act of setting up a rock house in Harlem territory. The Harlems did not take Lil Coke Dogg's power move lightly, he pushed the boundaries & provoked the wrath of the Harlems. His Hoover audacity & Gangsta prowess became the spark that further ignited the tensions.

On a sultry evening in 1985 a night that began in celebration. The city was a boiling pot of beef, a stew seasoned with personalities struggling to make their mark, struggling to survive. It was a time when the Hoover-Harlem alliance was as precarious as the evening fog. Lil Bit & Baby Charles from Eleven-Deuce Hoover recently moved into the Harlems, and they were hosting a house party.

INSANE FISH & LIL BIT

A heap full of people were there, around the way girls, members of various Hoovers factions & the Broadways. Lil Coke Dogg was in the spot with Lil Twindogg, Boscoe, Crib, Lil Boo Capone & Lil Bandit. The party lights were switched off, the raucous laughter subsided, and the Hoover House party was letting out. As we began to scatter.

Lil Coke Dogg—the silent steel in his eyes matching the gun he carried swaggered with the Locs towards his car parked in front of the home. The metallic, electric blue 1970 Chevy El Camino seemed to sparkle under the weak, yellow glow of the streetlights. Boscoe & Lil Coke Dogg are standing in the street, talking, waiting for a double-parked corridor of cars to move so they can mount up & depart.

Unbeknownst to us, the Harlems waited like phantoms in the shadows. Only God knows how long they hid in the bushes outside of the home. Powered by vengeance, they launched a vicious attack on Lil Coke Dogg.

Suddenly, Lil Coke Dogg clutches his stomach & looks at Boscoe, *"I'm hit, cuH, what the fuck!"*

As blood begins to seep from the wound in Lil Coke Dogg's gut, an unknown voice yells *"Harlem Crip!"*

It's an ambush! The good vibes of the night were shattered as they appeared from their cover, their piercing battle-cry slicing through the air. A spray of bullets erupted, leaving no room for reasoning. In an act of sheer instinct & adrenaline, Lil Bandit hurled himself through the back seat window of Lil Boo Capone's car, shattering the glass.

The bullets that were meant to pierce his flesh unforgivingly slammed into the car door panels, one veering off to strike him in the leg, intercepting a bullet that held an even graver destiny with Crib's name on it, a potentially fatal headshot.

CeeCee, a revered Loc & threat to all foes, and Hoover Bam, a certified Hoover Gangsta, were double parked next to the fated cars. They did what Locs are supposed to do. They went ablaze, returning the encroaching firestorm with their own lead shower, striking one, causing the Harlems to retreat. The cover fire allowed Lil Twindogg & Boscoe to draw their weapons & engage.

During the gun battle, Lil Coke Dogg caught three more bullets to his torso. He was wounded but fought through the pain. The heat of the bullets was replaced by a chilling sense of willpower & survival instinct. Lil Coke Dogg dared to drive himself to the emergency room. Realizing the severity of his wounds, he opted for the closest refuge – the Southwest Police station on Martin Luther King Jr Blvd. The night burst into an unraveling commotion of screeching tires & shouts.

He arrived in dramatic fashion, crashing through the entrance of the pig pen! Lil Coke Dogg kicked off a frenzy, the pigs came charging out, guns drawn shocked at this unwelcome arrival at their doorstep. Gasping for breath, Lil Coke Dogg pleaded for help.

An ironic twist to the otherwise combative relationship we held with the pigs. He was losing time, losing blood, the pigs called for EMT's but were otherwise useless, as Lil Twindogg & Boscoe worked as a team to suppress the bleeding & comfort our injured comrade.

An ambulance joined the madness soon after. As the paramedics scrambled to attend to our wounded homeboys. As Lil Coke Dogg was being loaded into the ambulance, a black cop approached Lil Bandit with an eerie look in his eyes.

The black cop asked, *"So...what happened?"*

He was met with a nonchalant reply from Lil Bandit, *"I dunno."*

The response from the officer was cold, heartless, a chilling pronouncement of his perceived justice.

"Ok, well I hope ya buddy dies," he smirked, the indifference spelling the end of any remaining faith in the pigs. His words echoed around us, a chilling testament to the twisted dynamic we survived daily.

The incident was strangely similar to what happened to oG June Bugg. Such treachery was a stark reminder of the fluid loyalties in our world. One day you are breaking bread with these guys; the next day, their enemies with guns aimed at your head. This turn of events was a bitter pill to swallow.

Lil Coke Dogg survived, but with significant injuries. Groove was in bad shape; he needed a shit bag. The attack resulted in months of painful recovery, and a chilling reminder of treachery & deceit.

It was clear as Poland Spring—our cease-fire was obsolete. The bloodshed signaled the demise of our once unshakable Hoover-Harlem alliance. Seeing Lil Coke Dogg in such conditions made my blood boil with rage & hatred. It felt like a fire had erupted within my heart, a blaze filled with unending rage, hurt, and an unstoppable desire for vengeance.

We became the aggressors in the conflict. We retaliated immediately & repeatedly with each explosion of gun fire, and terrified screams we added gasoline to the flame. As we steeled ourselves for the battles to come, the siren call of revenge was a drumbeat in our hearts.

Our loved ones were the driving factors that kept us going, the reason we could not back down. The constant reminders that, despite our pursuit of violence & retribution, these people were the fabric of our beings, the hope that perhaps we could someday step away from this path of rage & hatred & find a way to encapsulate our devotion to each other in a more meaningful, less destructive way.

Such dreams seemed far-fetched, belonging to another life, another world disconnected from our reality. This was our fate until Los Angeles ground us all to dust or St Michael the angel of peace descended. We stood alongside each other, bound by our creed & our unyielding loyalty to FDHGC.

The Harlems weren't safe. We attacked them on the streets & at school, but they were not to be underestimated. They targeted 54th & 56th street, during back to back drive-bys Boscoe was hit outside the Hoover liquor store & Big Mama was hit near Lil Coke Dogg's crib.

I will never forget I was at the rock house on 55th when I heard multiple sets of gunshots coming from 56th street. When I got there the sight that greeted me: Big Mama lying helplessly on the floor of her Auntie's porch, blood spreading from two wounds as she gasped in pain. Their shots had penetrated her back & leg.

I vowed that I would avenge my loved ones, those responsible would feel the same vicious terror. I gathered my comrades, the flames of anger in our eyes serving as a beacon for hope & revenge & unleashed a torrent of fury upon our foes.

My heart ached for Big Mama as she remained in the hospital day after day, her struggle weighing heavily on my conflicted soul. Despite all of it, she was a trooper – she fought with every ounce of strength she had. Big mama was tough, it was in her DNA. Big mama stayed solid through it all, nothing could deter her love for the set. Her unyielding strength & tenacity inspired me.

The streets echoed with the sounds of our battles. The war blurred days into nights as we fought on in honor of our comrades. The hotheadedness of our youth & our determination to avenge every insult & injury.

Boscoe, a mere 14 years old at the time, a brave heart struck with raw pain, the vision of the war began clouding his innocent eyes. Trapped in a maze of revenge, now more resolute than ever, ventured into Harlem territory on a beach cruiser with his sawed-off rifle, his mission, seek & destroy. Cloaked in the darkness of the night, Boscoe pedaled furiously on his bike, crossing enemy lines. The night's whisper concealed most of his rugged journey until the piggies spotted him, a small shadowy figure armed with a deadly weapon.

They saw nothing but a threat. Without any confrontation or attempt to arrest him, they resorted to the unthinkable. They shot him in the back, an act as vile as it was cowardly. The act etched an irrevocable scar, both on his body & in the heart of the Fifties. He was thrown into the lion's den for 2 years. His crime was loyalty, the price he had to pay for vindicating his loved ones & defending his hood.

His shooting was far from being a justified act, it was recognized as wrongful. Boscoe, the young Kiwé warrior, won a settlement against his perpetrators, marking a small victory in his tumultuous existence. But victory came with its sacrifices.

The authorities wore their vendetta on their sleeves, their egos punctured by his unexpected triumph. Their irritation manifested itself into a storm of police brutality & constant harassment. The Fifties being drawn into the ugly vortex of their resounding fury. Unwarranted detainments, baseless & warrantless car & house searches, all became a common theme in Boscoe's life, hardships that transcended throughout the set.

> *"Turn your wounds into wisdom."*
> — *Oprah Winfrey*

We didn't become courageous by chance; it was the hard times that molded us, and in this life of ours they took no breaks. I would receive breaking news that left me heartbroken. Ken Dogg was betrayed, by the lil homies we fed, protected, and armed. Batman & Lil Man were cooperating & implicated Ken Dogg as the shooter.

We later found out Baby Down's treachery had no limit. He also flipped & became state's evidence to gain leniency in his own Brim murder case. Baby Down, put the nail in the coffin for Insane Fish, and Ken Dogg. Even his own big homies weren't safe, oG Crazy Poke & Big Gino were also taken down with Baby Down's assistance. The state was able to convict my loved ones of life sentences.

Baby Down's act of betrayal caused a stir within our pact, but in retrospect, it fortified our unity with the Hoover Crips. It served as a reminder of the importance of loyalty over rivalry. This fiasco underscored the extent a love triangle could disrupt the delicate balance within the Crip culture. Love triangles caused the rifts that led to Crip Civil War.

The experience changed our lives, the burning desire for respect, the thirst for camaraderie, and the intriguing mix of passion & jealousy, all under the shared bond of an ephemeral concept of brotherhood. The streets taught us lessons of survival, the lesson to value loyalty over romance & bigotry, only hardening our resolve to stand firm on the Grooveline. Tee Baby went against the grain & opened the doors for Hoover unity.

In the loss of both Ken Dogg & Fish, we felt the sting of betrayal & the death of the loyalty we had once held dear. It was no longer the same Hoover-Broadway that had fostered lifelong friendships & solidarity. No, these bonds were beginning to crumble under the weight of betrayal, fear & desperation. Ken Dogg & Insane Fish represent the very foundation upon which FDHGC had been built – loyalty, brotherhood, and love.

It is also a deeply tragic reminder of the dark truth about our environment. In the harsh reality of a bitter & bloody gang war, the concept of loyalty became non-existent. Friends turned on friends, and it seemed that personal gain was the only thing that mattered.

"To me, the thing that is worse than death is betrayal. You see, I could conceive death, but I could not conceive betrayal."- Malcolm X

Amidst the turmoil, my love for Big Mama only grew deeper. We clung to each other in these trying times like a lifeline, needing that connection to keep ourselves grounded in a world that was anything but. We spent hours together, sharing laughs, stories, and some of the most intimate moments of our lives. With each embrace, the war we waged outside seemed to dissipate, if only for a moment. Big Mama continued to be the calming presence in my life, a voice of reason during all the chaos.

Though her body still bore the scars of war & her mobility was hindered, Big Mama's spirit remained unbroken. Time & time again, she implored me to try & make peace, to avoid putting myself in the line of fire. However, my loyalty to the groove, coupled with the unyielding anger toward the Harlems, made it nearly impossible to heed her advice.

The Brims & the Harlems tested our resolve, but we were fortunate. We didn't lose any homies to them in these frequent clashes. However, merely surviving wasn't victory; several of our loved ones were shot, bullet trails that carried the capacity for death & the bitter legacy of rivalry.

Hoova Luv is my right hand man, he was a military strategist, we were equivalent to General Patton & General Eisenhower of FDHGC. Luv is an excellent judge of character & an expert at calling bullshit. There is a savage cunningness necessary to survive as a Crip, like the strategic savoir faire required in any theater of war. We spent countless hours huddled making game plans for successful missions.

> *"The object of war is not to die for your country*
> *but to make the other bastard die for his."*-
> *General George S. Patton*

For us, the pigs were relentless adversaries always on our tails. They were an inconvenient obstacle. Our battles weren't conducted through wild & reckless abandonment, but we utilized conventional warfare tactics, based on strategic maneuvers & quick decisions we made to avoid one-time & reduce collateral damage: homies killed in action or innocent bystanders.

Our treachery was the catalyst for many of our adversaries' territories being under what we called protective custody by C.R.A.S.H (Community Resources Against Street Hoodlums). This special police unit served as an annoying ass babysitter, watching over our rival territories with an eagle eye, with hopes of detouring our onslaught.

Moreover, the pigs were on the lookout for anything that seemed out of the ordinary on the streets, like a car full of blue in a Blood neighborhood & vice versa. Any car carrying more than three young black or brown men was a target for unwanted attention, it was like a siren that screamed: Look at me! Look at me! Crip Here! Crip Here!

These protective measures, however, did not deter us but rather provoked us to devise even more intricate schemes to outwit them. So, to circumnavigate this, we worked with multiple stolen cars, driving off in different directions to distract & confuse them.

449 | P a g e

One of the tactics we often employed was playfully termed *"2-D"*, denoting Diversions & Decoys. It was an adrenaline-charged game. A game we played tirelessly with finesse & precision. At the outset, a scout would be sent out. This lookout would shout our battle cry- an ear-splitting *"Hooooover"* into the night air to rouse the enemy. Once the target was identified, they'd probably curse us with obscenities. The air would become thick with disses & threats, slurs filled with hate were typical. The crew in the second car would then strike with viciousness, catching them off-guard with speed & precision.

Another tactic in our arsenal was the *"all sides"* approach. Once an enemy was identified, we would initiate multi-pronged attacks. One squadron would engage an attack from the front of the house while another squad would navigate themselves stealthily behind the house through an adjacent street, effectively launching a surprise rear-attack cornering them. The element of surprise, coupled with our driven, relentless spirit often produced the desired results.

Sometimes, we would disguise ourselves to infiltrate enemy lines. Many a time we utilized what the kids call cosplay nowadays, we would blend in with the unfortunate souls lost to addiction, pretend to wander the streets directionless, looking for our next high. We would disarm them with our apparent vulnerability only to strike fiercely when they least expected. It was an audacious scheme but effective, nonetheless. The turf wars on the streets were brutal. It was each man for himself against a backdrop of survival & power. It was survival of the fittest & we were the wolf in sheep's clothes.

Looking back, it's a sad chapter to remember. Fueled by desperation, pride & fear. We were reduced to urban guerrillas, forced to survive in a constant state of war, but it was just that: survival. Like a soldier on the front lines, every decision we made, however ruthless or cunning, was underlain by the primal instinct to live to see another day.

Now, more than three decades later, the wild impulse of gangbanging is a distant memory muffled by the veil of time. Yet, they remain etched in the corners of my mind like graffiti on a forgotten wall, remnants of battles fought & survived, a time that shaped us in infamy. Survival was the name of the game – & war is war, no matter where it's waged.

CHAPTER FORTY-FIVE:
"FIVE HUNDRED CRIPS"

Meanwhile, Big Mama is lying in a hospital bed fighting for her life. My world crumbled, and all I wanted to do was pursue vengeance on the enemy for what they put her through. Sham Rock, my day-one homeboy & fellow Hriginal, was by my side through it all. He tried his best to keep my energy focused on striving & surviving. It seemed that no matter where we turned, trouble had a way of rearing its ugly head. One foolish day, we decided to celebrate a successful mission by indulging at the local weed spot.

Sham Rock was a charismatic man with a natural talent for persuasion. He had an innate ability to make people feel comfortable, which became a significant advantage in our criminal endeavors. I, on the other hand, brought my strategic & analytical skills, which made us a formidable pair. Together, we had a perfect balance of charm & intelligence, which allowed us to execute our plans without suspicion or detection.

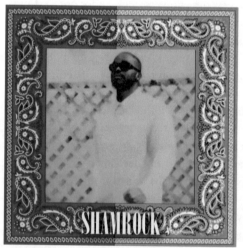

This sense of invincibility empowered us, fueling our desire to keep pushing the limits, no matter the cost. We targeted big houses & mansions, we sought high-value items such as jewelry, expensive electronics, and anything else that would fetch a high price in the black market. It wasn't just about the money, it was the thrill of the heist & the excitement of eluding capture that kept us coming back for more.

I was hanging out with Sham Rock, movin' & groovin' through the city of palm trees & movie stars in a stylish 1980 Cadillac Seville, making our pit stops. We were on our way to North Hollywood to case some mansions to burglarize. We cruised through the city smoking some of the finest cannabis California had to offer. The sticky, pungent buds taunted us, each whiff promising our own little paradise. I coughed as the smoke filled my lungs.

"Damn, cuH, this shit is hittin'!"

As we passed our freshly twisted joint back & forth. It seemed like nothing in the world could stop us. We witnessed a lot of scandalous shit in our brief lifetime, spent a lot of time dodging the law; things that the typical young man shouldn't be concerned with, but this was the life we chose as Crips. We did whatever it took to stay afloat.

"Let me tell you somethin' in this world. If you can't swim, you are bound to drizzown."
-Toothpick (Don't Be a Menace...)

It was a beautiful day in the valley, and our stomachs were rumbling with the munchies – the kind of hunger that could only be satisfied by thick milkshakes & juicy burgers. We stopped by our favorite late-night diner, Norms, in Van Nuys. The food was pure comfort, and we indulged without a second thought.

As we made our way back to our ride, Sham Rock noticed the odd number of pigs in the area. The moment we reached the car doors, unsuspecting & wholly unprepared, we found ourselves staring down the barrels of multiple guns. The pigs had us surrounded, their cold eyes glinting with a mixture of victory & contempt.

My eyes scanned the area in search of an escape route, but there was nowhere to run, no way out. The arresting officer, a burly man with a stern disposition, approached us with an air of triumph. As he read us our rights & placed the cold, unforgiving handcuffs around our wrists, one thing became painfully clear: the jig was up.

Everything began to unravel. Little did we know the pigs identified our car as stolen from one of our burglaries in Bel-Aire & had us under surveillance. They had a sting waiting for us when we came outside. It turned out the Los Angeles District Attorney had a hard on for us & assigned a task force to investigate a string of high-end burglaries. They held us responsible & had no intention of letting us off easy.

Sham Rock fought tooth & nail, but the justice system was not in his favor, they piled up additional charges against him. My Kiwé, Sham Rock was sentenced to a devastating eight years while I received two to three years for my involvement in two of the burglaries & felony grand theft auto. It was no surprise but I couldn't believe that Sham Rock was being framed & railroaded like this.

As I stepped off the bus in my blue jumpsuit & entered the soul-sucking walls of LA County Jail. I was reunited with my loved ones Ken Dogg, Insane Fish, Cadillac Bob, Prince Dogg, Ric Roc, Chim & Lil Live. It was on-sight with the Harlem Crips in the Crip module, or in the holding tank. It didn't matter where or when we crossed paths, it was on & cracking.

"All of us—who might have probed space, or cured cancer, or built industries—were, instead, black victims of the white man's American social system."- Malcolm X

I found myself locked away, awaiting my first prison bid. From within the confines of my cell, I found comfort in the unwavering loyalty & reassurance that came unfiltered & pure from Big Mama. She offered her support, her time, her money, and her love without ever seeking anything in return. During these darkest moments, Big Mama's devotion to me shined like a lighthouse guiding me through the hurricane that was my life.

On that frigid winter morning, the cold air was injected with tension as my mother was due to visit me, bringing updates from the world outside. Her past as a Panther carved her spirit into a tenacious advocate for social justice. Her words were sharp as knives when confronting matters that she felt passionate about. Her fierce dedication to the cause rubbed off on me & instilled the same intensity for challenging the oppressors.

My mother was a fierce, impassioned woman, she was the backbone of our family. She was the one who instilled strength, courage, and purpose into each of us. She was nothing less than a savior, the light inside an endless tunnel, guiding our family in times of need. Today, she was on the verge of her boiling point as she walked into the visiting room with Big Mama.

I was happy to see them but my Mother's eyes, her eyes were full of furious rage & determination. Her shoulders were taught with uncharacteristic tension, I immediately knew she brought bad news. When she finally sat before me, the weariness in her eyes tore at my heartstrings.

"They're after Kenny," she said, her voice trembling with both fear & anger.

My mother's distrust & dislike for the pigs was undisputed. She knew that the homies & I had been targeted for as long as she could remember. Our friendship was forged in the heat of a thousand trials. We were an emblem of loyalty amidst a sea of treachery. It was this unbreakable bond that made the pigs feel warranted breaching my family home.

"The pigs raided the house, they turned it upside-down & inside-out!" she spat out, her irritation reaching its boiling point.

"Boo," she began, her voice trembling with a mixture of rage & helplessness, *"the pigs have it in for Kenny & they're doing everything in their power to take him down."*

They had a search warrant & were desperately looking for evidence. They hoped Ken Dogg stashed the murder weapon at my mother's house, so they could tie me in as an accomplice. My heart ached as she recounted the invasion. She helplessly watched the pigs ransack our home. An uncivilized abuse of authority, leaving her feeling isolated & violated.

"They tore our home apart, tore our lives apart," she breathed, tears welling up in her eyes as the memories resurfaced. *"& all for nothing, because there was nothing to find."*

I felt my heart drop at the thought of my mother's sanctuary being violated. She lectured me about changing my life around, but it was too late. The injustice of it all burned deep within me, a bitter pill to swallow in the grim reality during that visit.

My days at LA County jail came to an end. Adrenaline pumping thru my veins as I arrived at California Institute for Men in Chino. It was all very jumbled in my mind, nerves tingling with a weird sense of excitement. This was my first time in prison & I was ready & eager to stand on my reputation & represent FDHGC.

While at Chino I was reunited with Baby Crazy & Joker, two solid Locs I knew I could count on. The steel bars encasing me in my cell felt like a metaphor for my life, always restricting me, strapping me to the point of suffocation. Nothing exciting happened during my time at CIM.

After Chino, Baby Crazy & I were transferred to Tracy DVI, Tracy was a Crip Prison with over 500 Crips occupying the facility. I was happy to reunite with my Locs, Prince Dogg, my crimey Sham Rock, and my big bro Spookee. The day I arrived at Tracy, I was put in the hole for 72 hours, while they ran a background investigation.

During that time, a tragic & most unfortunate event unfolded. Lil Insane from Five-Deuce Broadway was killed by the Bloods in the gym. The way it happened appalled the Crip collective. The red rags dropped a dumbbell on his head. I couldn't even begin to imagine the pain & the brutality. I just knew that this was something I would never forget.

You see, Lil Insane was someone I knew from the world, and he wasn't just anyone. He was a loyal & true young homie who gave this place a certain sense of brotherhood & comfort because of who he was. A heart-wrenching sense of loss overwhelmed me after his despicable murder

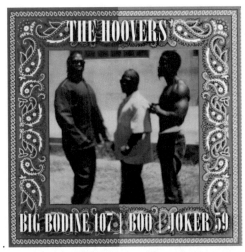

The very air in Tracy shifted to a vengeful kind of rage. The utter barbarity of Lil Insane's murder didn't just leave a void; it painted our hands with blood. There was no question that we would seek retribution for this heinous act. It was not a choice but a responsibility to each other, to our unity, and to Lil Insane. Thus, every Crip was not only outraged but engaged in the blood removal, the only way to somehow make things right.

With Tracy housing hundreds of Crips at the time, it wasn't long before our combined force went on a rampage. The Bloods got their eviction notice, they couldn't live in the prison anymore. It was our mission to ensure that they were entirely removed from the vicinity. The routine of violence & hatred became seemingly never-ending & changed the entire atmosphere.

Our plan was effective; the uproar caused the Warden to refuse to admit any new Blood inmates, as well as to start busing the existing ones out of the prison. Our unified force had brought about a level of change never witnessed before, as the prison authorities began to take drastic measures to try & control the violence. The aftermath of Lil Insane's murder led to my removal from Tracy for putting in work on the Bloods. I was put in the hole & then transferred to Soledad.

While I was at Soledad, Crazy Nell, an Hriginal from Nine-Foe Hoover was my cellie. I was reunited with my loved ones: Ten Speed, Bel-Aire, Lil Fat Rat, and Tony, who became known as Gangsta Tee during his bid. Upon his return to the street, Gangsta Tee became a

456 | P a g e

serious line pusher, recruiter, and staple in Five-Deuce Hoover. My main man, oG John Hunt, and oG Whitey from Broadway, as well Chip from Eight-Tray Gangstas, my guy, Blacc Bugg & Chippy from Seven-Foe Hoover.

My first day at Soledad, I found myself clashing with the guards at chow. The guards snatched me off the chow line, adamant that I had already gotten my share of the nasty ass food. Their claim was as baffling as it was frustrating. I was hungry as a hostage; I didn't have a meal all day.

"Step back, inmate," the burly guard spat, his eyes narrow slits of green barely visible beneath his furrowed brow.

I size up the big swoll white boy in front of me. His biceps, each the size of my head, straining against the fabric of his uniform. He was an intimidating figure, but I'm Boo Capone, I don't give a damn how big this dummy is.

His ice-cold eyes bore into mine, his voice brusque & clipped, *"no seconds, punk."*

Anger stirred within me, a rapid mood swing from calm to enraged.

"Watch who you talkin' to! You on some bullshit. I ain't eat yet," I retorted, highly offended.

"The hell you haven't!" he scoffed dismissively, moving along other inmates ahead of me.

Refusing to back down, I locked eyes with this punk ass C.O.

"Na, Fuck that!", I muttered resolutely.

"Back up, or it's the hole for you!" the guard threatened.

His stony face dared me with an annoyed gaze. The threat of returning to solitary confinement chilled my inferno. I was fresh out the hole at Tracy, and I didn't want to go back. I realized I had to change my strategy, I remembered I could get more bees with honey than shit.

I diffused my anger, choosing instead to request an audience with the captain. When he arrived, I found him a tall figure wielding an air of quiet authority. Undeterred, I held his attention & presented my case, making sure my voice resonated with nothing but sincere truth.

"Look man, there's been a mix-up. The guard got me confused with somebody else."

The captain was silent for a beat, the duo, scrutinizing me with clinical precision.

456 | P a g e

457 | P a g e

"*Sure, you ain't pulling our leg, inmate?*" he asked, his voice gruff from years of cigarette consumption.

I stared back at him, my eyes reflecting my burning hunger & sincerity. Just when I began to lose hope, another voice chimed in, from a guard more meditative & less scornful than his colleague.

"*Captain,*" he began slowly, "*There might be a mix-up. I think I know who we're confusing him for.*"

The captain dispatched the considerate guard, who returned after thirty relentless minutes dragging along a man from his cell. A wave of disbelief swept over the guards, the man they mistook me for & myself mirrored each other astonishingly. It was Nana, my Damu doppelganger. The chow line confusion was finally exorcized, followed by I told you so's & a crescendo of laughter.

"False friendship, like ivy, decays & ruins the walls it embraces; but true friendship gives new life & animation to the object it supports."
-Richard Burton.

During my time away, Goofy stayed in my apartment with Linda G, holding it down & keeping an eye on things. Through letters & phone calls, I learned that Goofy & Mimi had another girl hanging around with them.

Goofy's ability to persuade females to join our set was unprecedented; she was the number one Hoo'lette recruiter. It wasn't just her charisma, but that innate sense of knowing how a person ticked & using that insight to bring out the best in them. Goofy placed loyalty above all else. Her bond with Mimi, her younger sister, was unbreakable.

Their deep & passionate love humbled me every time I saw them together. Mimi was at that age when all teenage girls craved independence & the thrill of making decisions on their own. She was a force oozing with vitality, and nobody, not even Goofy, could match her stubbornness. They had a deep understanding of each other's needs & emotions.

About a year into my bid, Goofy shared devastating news: Mimi had been killed! I could hardly process what I was hearing.

457 | P a g e

Mimi, only 15 years old, full of life & promise. She became our first fallen homegirl & caused an unbearable pain to settle in our hearts.

Apparently, Mimi had gotten into an argument with the new girl. It was said that the newcomer was bad mouthing Goofy, and Mimi, being the protective sister she was, refused to let anyone talk down on her big sis. The girl wasn't willing to fight Mimi. Instead, she shot Mimi once in the chest & once in the back.

The incident made me recall what big bro always told me about hanging out with miscellaneous muthafuckas & cool ass niggas. Spookee always advised me against hanging out with people we didn't know well or weren't from Five-Deuce Hoover & the potential trouble it could bring. His cautionary words had never truly sunk in until that moment. This tragedy made me realize the danger of allowing random individuals into our close-knit circle, polluting us with their toxic persona.

> *"Death leaves a heartache no one can heal, love leaves a memory no one can steal."-unknown*

The news of Mimi's passing sent waves of shock, anger, and despair throughout the set. In their quest for vengeance, La Giggles & Goofy took it upon themselves to shoot up the house of the girl responsible for their dear loved one's death. Regrettably, they missed their target, leaving their thirst for revenge yet to be quenched. Mimi had been involved in a romantic relationship with a homie from Eight Tray Gangstas. The two had been partners in crime, running a dope spot together.

Mimi's lover, grieving for his beloved, requested that he be the one to avenge her tragic demise. Although we were all consumed by the desire to seek retribution for our sister, we decided to grant her lover's wishes. He was given him an ultimatum: a strict 48-hour window within which he would have to bring justice to Mimi's killer. If he failed to fulfill his mission, Hoover would handle it.

As the sun mercilessly rose & set during those two days, our grief was colored by a tense, bated breath as we awaited the outcome of this tragic tale. On the second day, just minutes before the deadline, Mimi's boyfriend fulfilled his promise. The girl responsible for Mimi's death paid the ultimate price for her actions.

Throughout this blood-drenched saga, the tale of sisterly love, loyalty, and vengeance chronicled the unkind & brutal face of our reality. There's no glory in a life riddled with violence. The memory of Mimi & all our fallen stars that paid the price. It is my belief that her life & our story will one day help to save the lives of many, guiding them on the path to a brighter & safer future, away from the perils of violence & vengeance.

CHAPTER FORTY-SIX:
"AMERICA'S MOST WANTED"

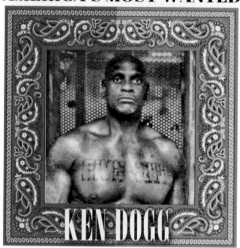

Meanwhile back in Los Angeles, amidst the cold steel, rebellion & disorder of the County jail, a gripping story was unfolding. At the core of this tale, we find my loved one, Ken Dogg, a hard-core Crip with a defiant spirit, who lived by the creed **Fuck The Police!** His brash demeanor had often led to verbal sparring matches with the jail authorities.

Tensions were high back then in the Crip module, saturated with the desperate fight for dominance, both Crip on Crip & Crip vs Pigs, which had given birth to unpredictable chaos. One of Ken Dogg's cellmates was an artist. He created realistic portraits of the police & sheriffs, capturing their smug expressions & the arrogance of their badges. Ken Dogg brought these pictures to life by inscribing the word 'killa' across them. Together, they decorated their cell walls with Pig Killa propaganda, transforming the drab walls into a revolutionary display of art.

The discovery was inevitable, as the sheriffs came around for the count, their faces distorting into masks of rage upon seeing the rebellious gallery. Their voices echoed against the stone-cold walls, demanding to know who was responsible. Ken Dogg, with the courage of a cornered tiger, identified himself as the culprit. Standing tall & unbroken like a true Hoover Gangsta, he proudly confessed, *"It's Police Killer,"* as he chucks up the infamous Crip sign, proudly.

It wasn't just his audacious artistry that landed him in hot water; there was a sinister undercurrent growing in the shadows. The Crip module, riddled with rats living amongst the Locs. Rumors spread that the Evans brothers had intentions of killing one of the turncoats in their case & were immediately transferred to the foreboding fortress of High Power. High Power is restrictive housing for the county's most violent, threatening prisoners & gang leaders.

A couple weeks after the transfer, on a Friday night the complicated script of fate had something to reveal to Ken Dogg. That same evening, nestled in his cell within the 1700 unit at High Power, an inexplicable dream seized him. A vision so powerful & vivid it felt almost real. He had dreamed he was free, walking out of the LA County Jail. The dream left a question mark in the curious design of his destiny. How he would get out remained wrapped in mystery.

That morning, Ken Dogg went to the exercise area on the roof, but remnants of his dream held on to him. He decided to call home, longing to hear the voice of one of his loved ones on the other end. He woke up his sister Cynthia from her slumber, ironically she confessed to waking from a dream about Ken getting out jail. Ken Dogg, startled by the synchronicity of their dreams, pondered over their potential significance. He reveals to his sister that he woke up from a similar dream!

The coming days brought a welcome surprise, the arrival of Cadillac Bob at High Power. That weekend brought some heartwarming family visits, the Evans were graced by their parents presence & Cadillac Bob spent quality time with Mama Mary & baby sis, Hoover Vette. Post the visit, the guards notified the trio- they were being sent back to the county.

The next day they returned to the Crip Module. The guards, however, had reshuffled their housing. Fish & Cadillac Bob were assigned to Able Row while Ken was steered towards Baker Row. Ken Dogg requested to be housed with the homies, but it was denied.

Reflecting back, Ken saw it as a divine intervention. Any other day, he would have manipulated the guards, deploying a tried-&-

tested alibi, claiming to have arranged the move with a guard in a previous tour. All the deputy would've done was get the card & placed them together. Something we did all the time, but for some inexplicable reason, he didn't.

As fate would have it, he was placed with oG Bam, Ant Dogg, a respected figure from Compton's Carver Park, Ducc from 190 East Coast, and our lil homie John-John. Bam had been transported down from New Folsom for sentencing.

OG Bam had an impressive resume as an original Front Hood Compton Crip, who was revered amongst his peers & a prominent member of the CCO. Bam was 6 years our senior & held an undeniable influence, combined with a Crip demeanor that commanded respect from both comrades & adversaries alike.

Looking back, Ken Dogg saw that pivotal day for its importance. The collective innocence of the new guards, his own obedience to the invisible pull, and being paired with oG Bam, the seasoned Compton Crip. All spawned a divine plan poised to influence Ken Dogg's destiny in unseen ways.

Upon his arrival, Ken wore an air of nonchalance which was in stark contrast to the hostile Crip module. He arrived with some commissary from High Power, an armful of candy bars, packets of cigarettes, and a jar of coffee. His belongings weren't luxurious, but in a place that thrived on muscle & fear, they were valuable possessions.

As John-John & Bam thumbed through his photos, a sense of warmth & familiarity was evident in their faces as they browsed through the still images that represented a world they all longed for. A Crip from the Harlem Thirties walked by their cell & striked conversation with Ken Dogg. The Harlem asked Ken Dogg if he had a cigarette. Instead of giving him just a single cigarette, Ken Dogg handed him an entire pack.

However, this action wasn't met with universal approval amongst his cellmates. Here comes Ant Dogg & Ducc. Ant Dogg voicing his discontent, *"Man, this nigga's a busta."*

Simultaneously, Ducc snatches the carton from the Harlem's hand. Ken Dogg, taken aback, asked, *"Why you label him a busta?"*

Ducc, mirroring Ant Dogg's disdain, replied gruffly, *"Because he won't fight nobody."*

"That don't make him no busta," Ken Dogg replied. His statement hung heavy in the air. He continued, *"We got a lot of bustas in here telling, but nobody doing anything about it."*

With these words, he handed the man from the Harlem another pack of cigarettes. Ken Dogg's response to the volatile scenario earned him the quiet admiration of one of his cellmates. He was intrigued by Ken Dogg's solid demeanor & profound sense of reason.

"I like your style," oG Bam confessed, breaking the silence that had blanketed the cell. He continued, *"I heard about you, cuH. Now, seeing you in action, it's clear that you not just another Crip. You a stand up homie."*

He offered Ken the bottom bunk, a symbolic gesture of respect & acceptance given Bam's seniority & status within the Kiwé hierarchy. OG Bam admired the noble cause behind Ken Dogg's incarceration. His actions were not spawned from an unquenchable blood thirst, but from an extreme need for justice. Avenging your dead homies is a principle that resonated with oG Bam & all true Crips.

There was also a certain photograph that sparked a unique interest within Bam. A picture of one of the homegirls, Hoover Kim, had caught his eye. He was entranced, his intrigue piqued. He fantasized about making her his partner in crime. Bam pitched the proposal to Ken, asking him to be a Crip Cupid & hook him up.

Ken replied casually, without making false promises, assured him, *"I'll see what he can do."*

One day, the four walls of Bam's cell echoed with the banter & laughter of Ken Dogg & oG Bitter Dogg Bruno, an original Grandee & Santana Blocc Compton Crip, infused with the intoxicating aroma of cannabis & prunos, a jailhouse wine, made from fermented fruits like apples &/or oranges, sugar, bread & whatever else we could find, complemented the surreal ambiance as oG Bam nonchalantly floated a cunning idea.

Bam looked at Ken Dogg, the flickering cell lighting casting dramatic shadows on his face, and suggested, *"I'll help you escape if you hook me up with the homegirl. What'chu say, cuH?"*

Ken Dogg declared, *"I can't pimp out the homegirl, cuH, but thank you for the offer, Loc"*

OG Bam laughed *"I'm just fuckin' with you, cuH."*

OG Bam offered to help Ken regardless due to admiration of his character. He returned with his master plan, and it was simple: as a seasoned vet he knew the guards didn't have access to photos to identify inmates, they only had notes about inmates' height, and identifiers like tattoos. This is where Cool comes into the picture. He is one of oG Bam's lil homies from Santa Fe Mafia Crip. Cool hit the module a few days ago after lying about his age.

Ken Dogg & Cool had similar stature & tattoos. Bam planned to convince Cool to swap wristbands with Ken Dogg. Ken Dogg would simply walk out the front door when Cool is called to go home in a couple of days. Simple, right?

Ken Dogg accepted his offer but had one more request from Bam, regarding Insane Fish, who was caught up in his own murder case, retaliating after the 54th street massacre. Ken wished to break him free also, but Bam knew it wouldn't be possible. No matter how much it ached Ken Dogg, he had to abandon the idea, so Ken Dogg selflessly proposed that Fish take his place, but Fish declined due to barriers that would make the plan more difficult to execute since he was housed on a different row.

First things first, Bam had to take the deal to Cool, he persuaded him with a sly cocktail of plea & intimidation. The stage was set. Bam used his persuasive authority to convince Cool, he sold him on the prestige that would be attached to his reputation for helping out such honorable & reputable Crips. Without hesitation Cool agreed, hatching the first step towards Ken Dogg's daring escape. The stakes were high, but for Ken Dogg, it was just another day.

Later that evening Ken Dogg, Lil Live & the Hoover-Broadways were gambling. While Ken was cooking on his illegal jailhouse grill. Ken Dogg asked Lil Live to keep a lookout for the pigs, so he doesn't get caught cooking. Lil Live got caught up in the game, and he let the guards get the drop on Ken Dogg. Deputy Jones scribbled fiercely in his little black book, sealing Ken's fate – a one-way ticket to the hole that would disrupt the planned escape.

Ken Dogg was a resourceful man; his quick wit was as sharp as prison gate barbed wire. His ability to navigate through the various challenges thrown at him in life was like an admiral at sea. Every obstacle was simply another test of his cleverness.

My homie had no intention of going to the hole. He pays a Crip named Greene to go in his place. They yank off their wristbands & ask a dep on the next tour for new ones. After the switch was complete, Greene gave Ken Dogg the heads up that his lawyer is supposed to come see him while he is in the hole.

Five days passed & Greene was taken to the hole for a 10 day stint. A couple days go by & Greene's attorney hasn't come. Today, the halls rang with the booming voice of Deputy Jones calling for visits. Ken Dogg is nervous, this is the same guard that wrote him up. As fate would have it, Jones called *"Greene."*

Lil Live, watched the scene unfold with a Kool-Aid smile on his face, *"how you gon' pull this off, cuH?"*

He chuckled at the predicament, his laughter bouncing off the prison walls, *"you gonna get caught nigga!"*

Unafraid, Ken presented himself. Deputy Jones, squinting skeptically, *"Didn't I send you to the hole?"*

Ken kept his composure, responding smoothly, *"Nah, that was somebody else."*

Deputy Jones interrogated him, *"Isn't your name Evans?"*

Ken shook his head, *"Nah, it's Greene."*

The confusion & suspicion was visible in Deputy Jones' face as he pulled out his compact, black logbook. Flipping through the entries, his eyes darted between Ken Dogg & the bold, black print that spelled 'Evans.' He looked at Ken's ID band, the name 'Greene' glaring back at him. His frustration & disbelieve was clear as he scrutinized Ken Dogg & then glanced at Insane Fish, spitting images of each other.

"Ain't y'all brothers?"

The question lingered between them before Fish denied the connection, *"Nah, we homies."*

In the attorney room, Jones announced, *"Who's here to see Greene?"*

A young black attorney with a sharp suit & even sharper eyes looked up, his gaze bouncing from Jones to Ken. The confusion on his face mirrored what Deputy Jones had felt moments ago.

He blurted out a firm *"No."*

His statement radiated doubt. Jones, now entirely baffled, looked at Ken Dogg again, his eyes demanding an explanation. An awkward pause stretched out in the room. The weight of the lie hung heavily in the silent spaces.

Ken Dogg shrugged with calculated nonchalantly, *"I dunno. I just got this attorney."*

The suspicious deputy raised a dismissive hand, *"Don't worry about it,"* & directed him to the back of the line.

Ken Dogg, seizing the opportunity, called the attorney over to him & made a small request. He asked the attorney to claim he was indeed his client. He promised to clarify everything once they were seated. Intrigued & somewhat amused, the attorney played along.

As promised, once they were safely entrenched in the privacy of lawyer-client privilege. Ken Dogg gave him the rundown. The attorney couldn't help himself & broke into spontaneous laughter. Ken Dogg had successfully fooled the system, at least momentarily. His gamble had paid off.

It's now February 4, 1987, and Greene is back from the hole, they pop bands & return to their original identities. Every day had been a theater stage where Greene & Ken Dogg switched roles according to the script that Ken Dogg had masterfully written. It was a swap that came with its fair share of skepticism, particularly from Deputy Jones.

Today Ken Dogg has a visit with his family. Jones is running the visit log again! He called out *"Evans report for visit!"*

Deputy Jones' became wide eyed with disbelief as Ken Dogg stepped forward, *"What's up."*

The confusion pooling in his eyes was undeniably entertaining, as he blurted out, *"Wait a minute... ain't you Greene! What is your name?!"*

Ken Dogg, cool as a fan, calmly said, *"na man, my name is Evans. I been told you that."*

Deputy Jones had had enough of Ken Dogg's shit, he gave up before he drove himself mad & escorted him to his visit. The day lent a shroud of excitement as his baby mama, Jenee, had just returned from Vegas with Hoover Kim. She held aloft a novelty Wild West poster that bore his name, *"Kenny Evans – Wanted Dead or Alive."* Ken Dogg couldn't help but laugh at the irony as he thought about his pending escape.

The poster served as an uncanny mirror into his life & a beacon of hope. It represented the slim chance of the risky escape plan coming to fruition. Jenee's voice shimmered like a silver thread through the air, murmuring rumors that he beat his case & was on the brink of freedom. The thought of tasting the air outside these iron bars made adrenaline surge through his veins.

Later that evening, he spilled the beans & revealed his plans to Hoover-Broadway. Cadillac Bob tried to be the voice of reason, vocalizing his concerns, trying to talk him out of his escape plan. His skepticism did nothing but strengthen Ken Dogg's resolve; it was now, more than ever, that he knew what destiny had in store for him.

Cadillac Bobby had his own vision. He fantasized about a daring joint escape. He had some inside info that he acquired from the trustee, Big Wiggles from Broadway. The catwalk led to freedom.

Cadillac Bob envisioned the group overpowering the guards & seizing their taste of freedom through the catwalk—the passage that connected the module to the free world. It was a plan laced with peril, a strategy too risky to play out. Regardless of the dangers, it was a risk they were willing to take.

Ken Dogg could only shake his head in disbelief. In his mind, their collective plan was far too risky, too prone to failure. He tried talking them down, instilling some sort of rationale in their euphoric minds. These fearless Crips were high off the promise of freedom & deaf to Ken Dogg's words. He wondered if their unwavering trust & companionship was their strength or their weakness, whether it would play a role in their salvation or self-sabotage.

The countdown to D-Day began, the sands of time slipping through the hands of destiny. Each tick of the jailhouse clock was a toll that grew louder in anticipation. There was no turning back; there was only pushing forward, striving towards that elusive mirage called Freedom.

Overwhelmed by the flurry of developments, Ken found himself at the crossroads of two paths. Bam's plan or Cadillac Bob's with Jenee's revelation echoing in his mind. He tossed & turned all night. His gut told him the Hoover-Broadway plan was far too dangerous, resulting in his firm decision to trust in oG Bam.

It was finally time to put the plan into full effect, bands popped, new ones requested. The morning arrived. The first light of dawn saw a-typical jail activity—calling out names of the inmates set to be released. As per the routine, the guards called out for Cool to be released.

Ken Dogg, now disguised as Sykes, nervous but undeterred. The fear of being revealed tugged at his courage. His heart pounded violently against his chest as he took his final steps as a prisoner. Peedy Wacc was the only one to kick up a storm of suspicion.

"Aye, nigga, where you goin?"

Ken Dogg, without missing a beat, casually replied, *"I gotta talk to the dep real quick."*

At that very moment, the witty oG Bam engaged Peedy Wacc into a conversation, serving as a perfect diversion to keep his focus off Ken Dogg. Meanwhile, Ken Dogg presented the ID band to the deputy, a moment of intense suspense ensued. The ID checked out perfectly. His eyes met Bam's across the room for a brief moment. A nod of unspoken approval & appreciation passed between them.

At that moment, Ken Dogg felt the weight of the world drop from his shoulders. The guard pressed the button, he exited the module, then the booking station. He swaggered right out the front door into his newfound freedom.

Craning his neck for a shout calling him back but it never came. He successfully escaped the LA county jail. Fresh air met his face, and the reality of his freedom overwhelmed him as each step welcomed this glorious reality. From then on, he was no longer a prisoner but he was a man living on borrowed time.

As luck would have it, a metro bus was parked at the bus stop so with a hopeful yet anxious heart, he sauntered up to the bus driver.

"Is the bus in service?" he nervously asked. *"It is now,"* the driver answered casually, turning on the ignition & sending a lulling hum through the bus.

The next question was crucial. Ken Dogg needed to find his route home. *"Where is this bus going?"*

"This the 40 to Redondo Beach, we pass through Downtown via Broadway & South Central via MLK," his reply was perfect.

Ken Dogg's heart skipped a beat, the driver's answer was music to his ears. The bus stopped at MLK & Hoover within Hoover Gangsta territory, a mere 20-minute walk to his crib.

Shortly after the bus began its commute, a random old man muttered, *"How are you doing, Kenny Evans?"*

The old man then continued to get off at the next stop, not another word, not another glance. His heart hammered against his ribs as he watched the man's retreating figure. How did he know Ken Dogg's name? Who was this stranger? Was he going to tell? The identity of the stranger remains a mystery until this day.

The irony of it all seemed poetic to him. The poster Jenee had brought turned into a bizarre memento, cause Big Ken Dogg was indeed wanted dead or alive! Ken basked in a freedom that wasn't his to rejoice, thanks to a daredevil plan, a random bus driver, and perhaps, a guardian angel.

The switcheroo was a success. The plan, as risky & improbable as it was, had worked. My brother from another mother, my ride or die, had done the impossible. He had escaped from the clutches of the Los Angeles County Jail! The days to follow would turn into a relentless chase.

The grit & determination Ken Dogg possessed was unparalleled. He stood up for our creed & lived every day ready to face any trials & tribulations that came his way. At the young age of 23-year-old, Ken Dogg was becoming a legendary Crip.

Meanwhile, I was counting down the days til I went home, my classification was lowered to level 2, so I was sent to CMC West where I was reunited with Big Mike, Ben Nose, Blacc Bugg, and the Broadways- Q-Bone, Lurch, Baby Ken Dogg & One Punch.

This is when Q-Bone broke the news, *"Ay cuH, check out the newspaper, Ken Dogg escaped from the county."*

The date was February 5, 1987—He tasted freedom & uncertainty, one week before he was to face the verdict that would seal his fate to 30 plus years in the belly of the beast. His daring escape made headlines the very next day; his face was plastered all over the Los Angeles Times.

"Murderer Escapes from County Jail."
"A convicted murderer escaped from the main Los Angeles County Jail on Thursday by switching identification wristbands with a fellow prisoner due for release, sheriff's deputies reported.
Kenneth Evans, 23, was to be sentenced next Friday for a street gang killing, Deputy Steve Lee said. He apparently persuaded Robert Sykes, who had been jailed on a narcotics charge & was to be released Thursday, to exchange name bands. He stepped forward when Sykes' name was called & walked to freedom. Sykes was to be booked on a charge of aiding & abetting an escape, Lee said.
Evans was described as black, 6 feet, 1 inch tall, weighing 194 pounds & wearing a brown shirt & black pants."
- LA Times February 6, 1987

Amid the dense, soul-scarred walls of the California Men's Colony Prison, an unprecedented event unfolded. A power dynamic shift was about to take place between some of the most formidable groups known to the institution. The infamous La Emé, also known as the Mexican Mafia, had a fall out with the Bloods. In a world bound by stringent rules & invisible boundaries, affiliations could not be taken likely. Back then, the Bloods were not as powerful on the yard as they are now.

An olive branch came our way from the Mexican Mafia. Their spokesman, a hardcore cholo known as Popeye with intimidating 17-inch arms, came to deliver their bold proposal. His message was clear; he proposed a willingness to align with the Crips to eliminate a shared enemy– the Bloods.

He boomed across the yard in a voice thick with the colors of aggression, *"we ain't got no issue with the Crips, Holmes, but we bout to take the Bloods out, y'all down to fuck these sucios up with us?!"*

His words hung in the air, a challenge & invitation interwoven in an audacious package. It came swift & resolute. As if bound by an unseen force of loyalty, I leapt upon the bench. My reply echoed against the concrete walls, *"Go fuck yo self, cuH!"*

My voice, strong & determined, rose above the clamor. The rage boiled within me, the audacity of their request so insulting that I couldn't remain indifferent. My stand sparked a wave of defiance amongst my fellow Crips. Rising to their feet in a show of solidarity, the Locs rose like the third letter, ten toes down, shoulders back, chests out.

Big Mike, a hulking figure among us, joined in, *"we ain't gonna let y'all hurt no brothers."*

Though we were entrenched in our bitter rivalry with the red rags, being Black took precedence in the prison yard. We believed La Emé proposition was nothing more than deceit, a divide-&-conquer strategy designed to weaken not just us, but the strength of the blacks as a collective.

We stood tall, our combined arsenal of black power & harmony, a formidable force against the Mexican Mafia's deceit. We filled the yard with bravado & an unyielding spirit of Crip unity. We were unified Kiwé warriors, Big Gino (Playboy Gangstas), Doss (West Blvd), Blacc Bugg (Seven-Foe Hoover) Ben Nose (One-oh-Seven Hoover), Lurch, Baby Ken Dogg, Q-Bone & One-Punch (Five-Deuce Broadway), and Maxwell (One-Twenty Raymond Ave), each of us with an impressive build & arms boasting 20 inches or more. Imposing figures that casted daunting shadows over the smaller built La Emé.

The tense standoff ended with the La Emé reeling back, deciding to call off their planned attack on the Damus. Our strength was in unity, in standing together for a cause beyond our conflicts – our race. We were black men united, standing up against an outsider intending to divide us. It was a testament to our loyalty, to each other, and to those who shared our skin color. A loyalty that was, and still is, stronger than the prison walls that confined us.

The clock hands seemed to move at a snail's pace as I anxiously & apprehensively stood by the blank, chipped, and painted steel prison doors of CMC, awaiting my release. The echo of those heavy metal doors swinging open marked the beginning of my second chance in life, a nerve-racking though invigorating experience. My loved ones, Lil Boo Capone, Lil Q-Bone & Hot Shot , were there, waiting impatiently to pick me up, their faces barely concealing a combination of excitement, worry, and relief.

The sight of friendly faces was a balm to my scarred soul, easing the bitterness that had taken root during my incarceration. When we got back to the turf, Lil Boo, presented me with 2 spectacular gifts. The sight of it nearly brought me to tears. It was a shimmering vintage blue 1978 Cadillac Sedan Deville Low Rider, her design alluringly flawless, reflecting the sparse freedom granted to me along with a Turkish link chain encrusted with diamonds.

Lil Boo told me, business was flourishing in the set, and these gifts from him & the Locs for putting them onto the crack game. He also gave me a Houston Astros baseball hat. When I got to the set, I noticed that all of them had the same cap, so they began to tell me that this was the new Hoover Hat, called the H-Crown & that we no longer wore the Golf Hats. I didn't care, I still wore my Golf hat every day, guess you can't teach an old Crip dog new trick.

They warned me the set was very hot due to Boscoe's lawsuit & Ken Dogg's escape, but it wasn't affecting business. As Ken Dogg's absence extended into weeks & then months, the LAPD's infamous 77th Division turned the heat up on the set, pressuring, harassing, and pushing us to the limit.

The LAPD's dogged pursuit knew no boundaries. Their obsession with Five-Deuce Hoover wasn't about upholding the law; it was personal. Their eyes ablaze with ambition, they would run down on anyone affiliated with the set at any time they had a chance. A feverish vendetta that was driven by raw & brutal emotions.

Renowned for their ruthless approach, their tactics to re-establish dominance was drenched in disrespect & spiraled from aggressive pat-downs & abusive language to full-blown physical assault. All the while, they wore their uniformed arrogance with pride, abusing power to make a mockery of the people they should be protecting. We didn't take this lying down, we fought back. Some of our bravest engaged in shootouts with the pigs to protect the set. It was in our blood to resist their oppression.

One of the most infamous tales of police harassment surrounded Lil Bandit. As he navigated the turf on his motor scooter, decked out in his Hoover Gangsta uniform. From above, the whirring rotor blades of the Ghetto Bird, a police helicopter, echoed through the hood, casting weathered shadows that skipped along the citrus riddled boulevards of 48th & Budlong.

The amplified directive from the officer cradling a loudspeaker in the hovering chopper bounced off the houses, *"Pull over!"*

Lil Bandit took a naive glance upward, contemplating whether the command was intended for him.

"You talking to me?" he retorted, pointing at himself. The order echoed once more.

Annoyance evident through the amplified authority, *"Pull over!"*

In an act of defiance, layered with a fuck that attitude, Lil Bandit extended his middle finger, then opened the throttle, accelerating the scooter to its maximum potential. Undeterred, the damn chopper remained on his heels, its blades slicing through the cityscape following him all the way to 53rd Street & Hoover.

As Lil Bandit arrived at a congregation of Hoover Gangstas, Face, Yvonne, La Crip Crazy, the CeeCee's, E-Loc, Fat Curtis, Nutty Norm, Willbone, Boom-Boom & a dozen more Crips, slinging rocks outside of Face crib. The chopper hovering overhead watching the homies handle multiple transactions. In an unshaken voice amplified by a loudspeaker, the unseen pilot taunted, *"I see y'all dumb asses selling rocks."*

The cackling echo of his words ignited a flame of rebellion – a trait South Central was famous for. Lil CeeCee looks up at the Ghetto Bird, and hollered, *"Fuck you, this Five-Deuce Hoover!"*

"I'm coming down," commanded the voice of the pilot. The homies watched in disbelief as the Ghetto Bird descended, the propeller's forceful gusts of wind caused leaves to dance around in fear & trees leaned sideways, leaves swirled in mini tornadoes, and litter danced through the air.

Amid this pandemonium, a couple thousand dollars of Yvonne's hard-earned dope money was swept off, becoming confetti in the air. Wads of bills fluttered around like disoriented birds amidst a hurricane, creating a storm of green. The audacious pilot had the nerve to set the bird down in the belly of the beast, the homies couldn't believe a helicopter landed right in the middle of the set.

As the dust from the helicopter's landing dispersed, the pilot disembarked & removed his helmet, surveying the scene before him with a smug self-assuredness. Standing in the middle of 53rd Street, he was the embodiment of the system we were rebelling against. The audacity was one in a million, a pig in a cage full of starved Crip Doggs.

Yvonne, the lion-hearted femme fatale of our Hoo'lettes, known for her boldness. Raw grit & untampered anger simmered in the air, she was vexed that the pilot spread her cash all over the Tray, she sought justice in her own hands. As the pilot was taking off his helmet she rushed him, punching him right in the mouth mid-sentence.

The blow effectively knocks the pig to the ground & the homies jump in, Hoover stomping the pork chop, as the melee ensued amidst the chopper's churning dust. The peaceful afternoon had transformed into startling chaos, a battlefield in the heart of the Fifties.

Soon enough, backup arrived, their glaring red-blue lights painting the streets & houses as they formed a barricade on both ends of the street.

In this seemingly lawless wild, wild west, a scene lifted straight from a Hollywood action movie. As the Calvary arrives 53rd street erupts into a mini riot 5-Deuce versus 5-O. The reinforcements swiftly herded all the Hoovers clad in khaki uniforms toward the sidewalk, forcing them onto their knees & commanding them to place their hands on their heads.

Willbone glances over at Lil Bandit with a look of discontent, *"Why the hell you bring these niggas over here, fool."*

The pilot singled out Lil Bandit, pointing an accusing finger at him, *"It was him."*

In his scramble for answers, Lil Bandit asked the money question, *"Why did you chase me?"*

Receiving the pilot's smug reply, *"You ran a stop sign,"* sent an incredulous sign of disbelief. A collective, unbelievable *"What the fuck"* swept across the crowd, the words *"stop sign"* echoing through the stunned audience. All this – the wild chase, the unwelcome chopper landing in the middle of 53rd street, the mini riot, all this madness spun out of one skipped stop sign. They loaded the Locs in their paddy wagons, a lot of the homies were released to their parents, while others had to do a week or two in Juvenile Hall.

The rest of the day turned out to be a bizarre blend of the somber & the exhilarating. The homies found themselves riding around in a limo, as they all donned their uniform in honor of our fallen comrade, Lil Insane from Broadway, whose funeral service was that day. The service was filled with raw emotion, as they said their goodbyes to one of our own.

Seeking another adrenaline high, the Locs turned their focus to the Five-Seven Hustlers. They took on what could be best described as a daring daylight robbery. The shift from mourning to exhilaration was strange, yet to ruthless street-savvy Hoovers, it was just another day in our Crazy Crip City.

After the robbery, Willbone had made a peculiar request to Hoova Luv. He wanted him to get G'd up, as we called it to wear our gang uniform for his funeral. That fateful night, Willbone, joined by my cousin Lil Twindogg, Lil Coke Dogg, Lil Chim, and Lil Mouse, as they ventured back into the Hustler's territory after convincing Naomi to be their driver. It was a typical act of Hoover audacity & defiance. The homies had Naomi park on 56th street under the guise of going to a friend's house, as she waited in the car with Lil Twindogg.

CHIM2|COKE DOGG2|MOUSE2|WILLBONE|TWIN DOGG2

They proceeded to go through a yard & hop a gate to 57th street. Lil Twin asked Naomi to spin the block to link with the homies around the corner. The scene was serene as Lil Coke Dogg & Lil Mouse conversed with an unknown party, Lil Twin joins Willbone, who was engaged with conversation with a dude from East Coast. The East Coast unsuccessfully attempted to reclaim the bounty from the jack move earlier.

He walks away & disappears momentarily into the darkness, from where he retrieved something that glinted menacingly in the fading light, a sawed off 12 gauge shotgun. Naomi was the first to notice him emerge from some bushes, her chinky eyes widening in disbelief & fear. She screamed but Lil Twindogg & Willbone were distracted engaged in conversation & didn't hear Naomi's warning!

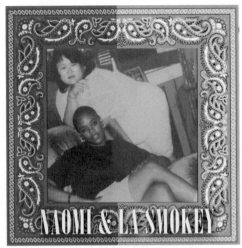

NAOMI & LA SMOKEY

The East Coast becomes Five-Seven's protector, fed up with his cousins being victims of Hoover oppression, unleashes his vengeance. The alarming sound of shotgun blasts echoed through the apartment complex. The unforgiving buckshot's flying for their faces, Willbone took the brunt of the attack. The severity of the injuries dealt to Willbone, left him clutching onto life by a thread.

Lil Coke Dogg & Lil Mouse spurred into action, returning fire, hitting their target but not disabling him. Despite their effort, the shooter vanished into the shadows. In the ensuing chaos, Lil Coke Dogg & Lil Mouse load the homies into Naomi's car. Her hands shaking on the wheel as she transformed into a stunt car driver.

Ignoring traffic rules & dodging oncoming traffic, Naomi weaved in & out of lanes in a desperate bid to reach a hospital. Through a blur of panic & confusion, she ended up at the orthopedic hospital's front steps. The medical staff, despite their specialty, didn't deny them, they quickly moved to treat the blast victims. In the end, Willbone's family chose to pull the plug, a heartbreaking decision that amplified the anguish we all felt.

Lil Twindogg, who was caught in the crossfire, was dealt a severe blow too, the barrage of gunshots knocking out all of teeth & rendering him blind. His vibrant world turned into an abyss of darkness in a blink, forcing him to navigate through life henceforth as Blind Twin. A stab of pain pierced through my heart as the news settled in. I was in disbelief. I couldn't believe my day one was gone, our first loss in the Hoover vs East Coast conflict.

H.I.P WILLIAM "WILLBONE" FLORES

Could I have prevented these gruesome incidents? These torturous thoughts began to wear heavily on me. The list of tragedies left a scar on my soul. These losses were a heart-wrenching reality that weighed heavily on my heart. Each igniting a flame of hatred within my soul.

As I sat across from Naomi, her eyes, misty with raw emotion, recounted the tragic event. She sat there, embodying the sadness that had nestled into the deepest corners of her soul. Her voice trembled, as if weighed down by the living nightmare, but she fought against it, straining to maintain the calm exterior. One could barely imagine the bone-chilling fear she must have felt then. As I tried to console her, an unspoken agreement seemed to conspire between us — a silent pact acknowledging the unfairness of life.

CHAPTER FORTY-SEVEN:
"CREATING MONSTERS"

While I was in prison, Foe-Tray Hoover had gone inactive as far as gangbangin', they were primarily focused on hustling. This absence left room & opportunity for a new set to be born claiming the area around Manuel Arts, they called themselves the Rollin' Foeties. They were originally known as the Vernon Ave Hustlers, some cats that we would jack as an additional revenue stream.

We didn't lose any real estate in a turf war. The slow erosion of loyalty caught us off guard. It was an area under our control, but lacked a strong presence, our main concern was the Fifties. As a result, we neglected the power dynamics within our own borders. We refused to fraternize with the youth in those areas, so a gap formed between Hoovers & the new generation. In many ways, the writing was on the wall.

I remember My first encounter with the Rollin' Foeties. At the time I was fresh out, home only a day or two & didn't know about the issues with this new set, shit I didn't even know they existed. The King Swap Meet had recently opened up across the street from Manual Arts High School in the Foe-Tray Hoover territory. I'm hanging out with my oldest niece, Kesh Dogg, and decided to get me some new clothes & footwear from the Swap Meet.

"I don't know why you are going to this swap meet. We should go to the one on Slauson," Kesh Dogg complained.

"I haven't been to it yet, I'm trying to check it out." I replied. When I went away the area was controlled by us & Foe-Tray.

"Uncle Boo, we don't get along with them cats over there anymore." She tries to explain. I'm hardheaded, and stubborn.

"I don't give a fuck about all that, you got to chill. I said, we good, there ain't nothing to worry about." I tell her confidently.

It was a hot ass day, I'm wearing a slingshot shirt, showing off my well defined tattooed arms. I'm trying on some classic white K-Swiss, we used to call them, *"Kill a Slob When I See a Slob,"* these sneakers were very popular in the Crip community. This little kid, maybe 12 years old, walked by staring at my tattoos. I'm looking at him, looking at me.

"*What's up Lil man?*"

He replied *"Oh, right, right, right"* before he walked away.

I'm thinking to myself, that little boy is a weird. About 5 minutes later, 4 or 5 cats approached me. I guess the Lil boy went & got them.

Their leader spoke, *"Where you from?"*

I replied *"Five-Deuce Hoover, what's up"* as I stood up.

He replied *"Rollin' Foety Crip"*.

I'm thinking to myself, alright, they're Crips, so it's all good, next thing I knew he took off on me. I dodged it easily & landed a hard counterpunch to his jaw. He stumbled back, and I knew I had the upper hand. We began squabbling, shit is getting hectic, I jumped on the counter & kicked one of them right in the mouth sending him flying into a nearby display of hats.

I told my niece to run, and I continued to fight with the Foeties. They bum rush me. One of them grab me from behind, but I spun around & landed a solid elbow to his nose, sending him reeling into submission. Just as I was about to take on another one, I felt a sharp pain in the back of my head. I turned around & one of these niggas holding a metal pipe, grinning wickedly.

I tried to fight them off, but they were too many & I was beginning to succumb to my head trauma. I felt myself getting weaker & overwhelmed, and just when I thought it was all over & they got the best of me, a security guard let off a warning shot in the air!

Boom! The explosion rang from his revolver & like the bell in a boxing match it ended the melee & people started scrambling in every direction. My baby brother Bushrod got my call for help & arrived shortly after the brawl with Crib & Face. Kesh Dogg & I bolted out of there as fast as we could. I was so angry & disrespected, I wanted revenge.

It's a never-ending cycle of violence, but I know I had to do what it takes to protect my pride & my tribe. In the end, it's all for the love of Hoover. The homies filled me in on the history of the situation with the Foeties, turns out a lot of them were relatives of the Foe-Tray Hoovers, and homies were applying pressure to them to represent the Groove.

Surrounded by the grim realities of the street, young men had two choices - either become predators or be victims. As a reputable & Hriginal I couldn't stomach the thought of being a sucker. My identity was wrapped in the blue bandana, my loyalty, and respect were earned by asserting dominance over those who dared to challenge the Groove. The Foeties newfound audacity, foolishly & bravely questioning the might of Hoover Gangsta, was nauseating.

My stomach churned with a sour taste of insult & contempt; in their eagerness to assert themselves. I couldn't believe these kids were bangin'! They were victims, cats we robbed when we were bored. Their refusal to accept the Hoover supremacy, fueled my rage & kick-started a deadly rivalry. I added Foeties to my hit list, I knew they had to go, so we got right to business!

We were going to put them in the place they rightfully belong, beneath our feet. Like a wolf cunningly plotting its hunt, I spearheaded a night mission to teach them a lesson they would never forget; a taste of Hoover's wrath. My choice of warriors was meticulous, matching their ferocity with my determination. Husky, heavily built, my baby bro, Bushrod, and one of the most intimidating youngsters in the fold, my nigga, Pookee. We were off to the Foeties, our mission was as clear as the night sky.

The air was thick with dread; a setup for the brutal play about to unfold. That same night, buoyed by anger & resolute in purpose. A casualty from the Foeties was our message, a loud & clear declaration of war. The honor & supremacy of Hoover Gangsta were not something to be challenged or belittled.

This was the beginning, the spark that sent off a wave of endless retaliations & marked the inception of a war that would span decades. Their refusal to comply, their undying spirit of rebellion, had caught them up in a war they could never walk away from, but forged in fire, they became our most worthy adversaries.

> *"We were terrorizing dudes, we were terrible instead of building bridges, Our actions created monsters."- oG Lovely (Hoova Luv) Hriginal FDHGC*

The Foeties were established by a member of Rollin' Nineties, the banished Nine-O Hoovers, and many Foeties are the younger relatives of the Foe-Trays. It comes as no surprise they stood their ground, as they have Hoover DNA in their composition. They transformed into a powerhouse, tried & tested by Hoover Gangsta.

You could compare it to a young fighter sparring with the greatest & toughest like Mike Tyson or Muhammad Ali. They faced their fears toe to toe, blow for blow. They grew fearless, molded by the fires of conflict into a defiant tribe - an alter ego of our very selves. That's probably why you may have heard about their battles with the Harlem Thirties or the Rollin' Sixties. The latter was supposed to be like a big brother to them.

The Foeties could have been allies or even Hoovers, like many of our adversaries. Instead, our decisions & actions as a collective forced them to take their own road. Now, I wonder: what if we had allowed the Foe-Deuces to thrive? The repercussions of our actions bore a heavy consequence, leading to the emergence of unnecessary adversaries. We projected the same indifference & hostility that the Hoovers had shown us.

The same destructive cycle followed with the Five-One We Don't Care, Five-Five, Five-Seven Hustlers, the Five-Foe Big Time Hustlers, the Vernon Ave Hustlers, and the Foe-Six Top Dollar Hustlers. We could have welcomed them into the Hoover Gangsta fold if we had chosen diplomacy over confrontation. Instead, they would become Anti-Hoovers & click up under the Neighborhood alliance against us.

What's unsettling yet strangely compelling is that it was our relentless Hoover aggression that acted as a catalyst for our enemies' formation. We unknowingly ignited the spark that fueled our rivals' defiance, determination, and unity. We gave them the courage to rebel, to uphold their values, to become the opposition.

The city had become a chess board, and each hood, a unique player with its strategic maneuvers & moves. Yet, through these years of confrontation & conflict, one undeniable fact rose from the ashes. That we had unknowingly created a monster. It was an ironic twist of fate that the stew we stirred produced our most lethal rivals, the Rollin' Foeties Crips.

Big Pookee was a man that is much ingrained in this conflict. There is an old saying that steel is forged by the fires of hell, Pookee & I gave them hell on earth. The story of Pookee unraveled much like a ball of twine in the hands of a playful kitten. Tangled, and simple, yet surprisingly captivating, it gives testament to the harrowing realities of street survival.

Pookee was like a baby brother to me, a child of the Groove, who had just converted to Five-Deuce while I was away. Pookee, originally christened as Tray from Eight-Tray Hoover, yet born & bred on the coarse pavements of Hoover Gangsta territory on Vernon Avenue. The primary influences within his world, his older brothers from another mother, Lil Herm & Lil Doc Rob hailed from the infamous Eight-Tray Hoover Crips. Their affiliation, compelled him to naturally gravitate towards it, pledging his allegiance.

I met him through my Uncle Roy who worked on cars with his father. Tray was driving around the set at 11 years old, similar to myself. He pulled up on me & Uncle Roy one day, we were in my driveway working on some cars. He had this crazy look in his eyes, like someone who could go from zero to 100, real quick. It was that fierce energy that drew me to him almost immediately, and we became inseparable as we roamed the streets, looking for adventure, excitement, and the occasional bit of trouble.

Even though he was younger than me, I couldn't help but admire his fearlessness, his swagger, and the way he kept his ear to the street. This kid was just like me, trouble with a capital T. He was a prodigy of the streets, a mulatto who rose through the Hoover ranks & became a legend. I felt an indescribable joy upon knowing my lil homie had morphed into Big Hoover Pookee from Five-Deuce Hoover, a name that sent shivers down the spine of many.

It was a typical day in Fall 1985, Tray was strolling through the Fifties, the streets echoing with the haunting sound of life as it spiraled in the ghetto. Suddenly, out of nowhere, the Rollin Sixties descended upon him. His companions of mere convenience rather than loyalty, deserted him, but fate had other plans.

Just around the corner by the Hut, Lil Mouse, Lil Coke Dog, and Lil Chim were idling. Hearing the commotion, they looked towards the noise. What they saw fueled their veins with adrenaline. Tray was surrounded & outnumbered by the Sixties, punches being thrown at him from all sides.

Infused with a potent blend of loyalty & rage, they sprang into action. The young Hoover Gangstas turned the tide of the fight in favor of the underdog. Their punches landed like cannonballs on hulls, with the Sixties reeling under the unexpected onslaught. When the dust finally settled, the Sixties lay in defeat, as the Grooves emerged victorious with knuckles, bloodied & raw.

A few days later, Tray wandered the Fifties with Lil Dre Dogg, and John-John looking for the homies. For some reason the set was a ghost town, a rare sight as the Tray, the Foe, and the Six were usually congregated by 30-50 Hoovers at any given time. They found themselves hanging out near the BBQ pit on 54th street, inhaling the twisted delights of PCP, while sipping on Malt Duck.

As the haze started to dissipate, they realized what day it was, October 12, 1985. The date commemorated the anniversary of the infamous 54th Street Massacre, a day draped in the blood & tears of dead homies. It dawned on them they were late for the memorial at the 48th Street Park!

BABY DRE DOGG & LIL DRE DOGG

When they arrived, eyes heavy, high as a kite, they were in for a severe shock. Their late arrival had sparked a fire of rage within their elders. The homies called for a DP, as lateness was a violation dictated by the ruthless street code of the Hoovers. John- John had to fight his counterpart, John-John from Five-Deuce Broadway. After the John-John's went fist to cuffs it was Tray's turn.

Following what seemed like hours of hushed deliberation, the homies pronounced Tray & Lil Dre Dogg's penalty. The day one comrades were to DP each other, to show their strength & loyalty. Tray & Lil Dre Dogg fought like junkyard Crip dogs until they were too fatigued to throw another punch. Tray emerged visibly bloodied but his eyes ablaze with an unbroken spirit. That tough ordeal & the recent brawl with the Sixties instigated a transformation within Tray, a metamorphosis of identity, allegiance, and self-perception.

Tray was shrouded in a newfound, hardened aura of respect & grit. He voiced his loyalty & declared his allegiance to Hoover Gangsta. He wasn't Tray anymore; he had forged a fresh identity- one as strong & resilient as the concrete that paved Hoover street.

Last time around, my trips with oG John Hunt to Colorado had given me a taste of what the road had to offer. As I considered my next move, those memories remained with me, stirring a sense of wanderlust that refused to be ignored.

Cocaine coursed through the veins of the Hoover Gangsta empire, and I wanted to expand our reach. I shared my thoughts with some of my most trusted cohorts – Baby Crazy, ScHool Boy, and Lil Boo Capone – great minds think alike, and they shared my ideals. Uncle Roy told me stories about the Vegas strip. The sex, the dope, the gambling, and the parties which seemed like a luxurious Sodom & Gomorrah of sorts. It was the perfect place for some young cockhound Crips on the hunt for cunts & funds.

I hit up Uncle Roy & cooked up a plan to move our product while seizing the night: Las Vegas, the perfect mix of razzle, dazzle, and debauchery. Now, our eyes were set on a lucrative mission, a wild road trip to the city of Sin: Las Vegas. Our intention? Buss our Groove, party like there's no tomorrow & sell a lot of dope.

We rendezvoused in the chill of sunrise at the rock house on 55th street. My vintage blue Cadillac, the leather matching my bomber jacket & the freshly polished paint mirroring my grooviness. The car was crammed with Kiwés & kilos all set to create ripples through Sin City.

We cruised down the 110, the V8 engine humming as the city's skyline faded in the rear mirror, a sense of liberation overcame the crew. Our journey through the desolate California landscape, punctuated by barren sand dunes & the ceaseless hum of the interstate, brought about a strange sense of camaraderie among us. We shared stories of our most infamous shootouts & robberies past & present.

The open road didn't soften the edges of our crew, but there were moments of brotherhood I'll always cherish. ScHool Boy, with his wiry frame & unfeigned charm, kept us entertained with his chatter, wisdom & dopey jokes, while Baby Crazy remained reserved & observant, absorbing the anecdotes with quiet candidness.

Upon arriving in Sin City, we were completely captivated with its neon blaze & high-stake dreams, the city welcomed us into its arms without a hint of suspicion. As we cruised the Vegas strip, I felt a strange sense of euphoria. This was the high-life, the epitome of all I had ever dreamed of: paper, pussy, and power, it was all within our grasp.

We booked a plush hotel suite at the Caesars Palace, overlooking the Strip. I admired the city in all its intoxicating glory. A fleeting view from our suite presented casinos humming with life, the never-dying city lights painting the night in vibrant hues of promise, and a spectacle of notorious dark alleys that promised more than the eye could see.

Las Vegas was a city on the brink of an enormous boom. The preening peacock of America, the streets dazzled with the neon glow of a thousand signs advertising the most decadent pleasures. The architecture of the city leaned heavily towards the postmodern mini skyscrapers, where architectural styles of the past were recycled in jumbled tributes.

The facade of Caesar's Palace drew inspiration from the Romans while the iconic Castaways took on a Polynesian vibe, turning the desert city into a hedonistic mirage of world cultures. Buffets were a relatively new concept at the time, we loved it. We got high & enjoyed extravagant meals at bargain prices.

Las Vegas was the land of Elvis impersonators, showgirls, and legal prostitution, where there was a professional courtesy to the wild side of life, my favorite side. Gambling – an indivisible strand of the city's DNA - was mainly done in cavernous, smoke-filled lounges permeated with the jingle of slot machines & the murmur of mutterings over cards. The city still relied heavily on the illicit charm of casinos - a town where adults could let loose — somewhat naughty, certainly risqué but undeniably fun.

The powerful neon lights of The Las Vegas Strip were as brilliant as ever, but a sinister undercurrent was emerging beneath the city's glamourous facade. An epidemic, both deadly & destructive, found its way into the heart of the desert metropolis; the Hoover Gangsta Crips with cocaine & its evil sibling, crack, had infiltrated the sin city.

In Las Vegas, decadence was not just tolerated but promoted & celebrated, making it a vibrant market. Casinos operating round-the-clock, pulsating nightclubs, and deluxe hotel suites provided the perfect backdrop for the reckless partygoers & thrill-seekers to ride the snow-white coke wave.

As we wandered through the city radiant casino lights & temptation called to us from every corner. We had more to do than just party, of course, we were here on Hoover Business. We had 10k worth of soft & hard to sell, and luck was on our side. The cocaine scene in 1987 was bold & blatant. It was everywhere - consumed in public restrooms, private limos, clandestine penthouses, and even in the nondescript backstage rooms of flamboyant Vegas shows.

The glitterati, middle class & commoners were seduced by its allure. Nobody was immune to its devastating charm; not the young waitress working double shifts, not the high-rolling gamblers betting their fortunes away, not even the performers gracing the stages nightly. While cocaine was the drug of the town's elite. We were able to infiltrate the ghettos of the city that thrived in the shadows of the radiant Vegas Strip with crack. Coke's cheaper & more potent relative swept through their rundown neighborhoods like a firenado.

Business was booming; no one could resist the allure of our potent product. Our reputation grew with every deal, and we were soon recognized by the elite drug peddlers, and established relationships for becoming their supplier. After a wild night of club hopping & networking, we met our quota, getting rid of every last gram. Our pockets grew heavy, but the allure of the strip had only just begun.

The memoirs of that summer included our first experience with escorts. The casinos & strip clubs held more than just gaming tables & slot machines. Uncle Roy introduced us to the clandestine, yet thriving, multiverse of world class prostitution — professional cum dumpsters for sex machines. Experiencing the professional courtesies was a stimulating experience.

Unlike the desperate ghetto hookers back on Figueroa, these Vegas hoes held a mesmerizing charm. They worked by choice, providing a quality service that the city recognized as a profitable venture. As young horny cockhound Crips filled with lust & heavy pockets full of cash, we indulged in these pleasures for a couple of dollars. They worshiped us like Gods & sexed us like the Kings.

Veni, vidi, vici, Vegas was conquered after losing ourselves in the wild twilight hours, but we craved something more. Our pockets heavy with the spoils of our success, I set us up a meeting with the connect so our next stop was across the border in Tijuana, Mexico. Before the sun set the next day, we found ourselves deep in TJ.

It wasn't long before we found ourselves at the doorstep of our rendezvous point. Upon our arrival in this hedonistic haven, we encountered an environment that echoed the unrestricted decadence of Tijuana. Stepping inside, we were struck by pure lust & vices, the smell of sex & carne asada filled the air. We could tell it was no holds barred & that anything goes within these hallowed walls.

As the night wore on, inhibitions faded, and our surroundings grew more exotic with each passing moment, people were getting real loose. The dance of seduction between audience & performer intensified further until the evening took a surreal turn – a sight impossible to forget. People talk about larger-than-life experiences, but what we saw was some real freaky shit. As the room held its breath, some brave woman, perhaps egged on by narcotics & greed.

Our jaws hit the floor as we witnessed the boundary between human & beast blur before our very eyes. I know women always say they want a man with a donkey dick, but this broad was fuckin' a donkey! We watched it in horror & fascination. That night would go down in history as one of the most outrageous moments we'd ever lived through. I mean she did everything, gave it a blowjob, took it from the front, then the back, then in her ass, let it ejaculate on her face, and cream pie her. I couldn't believe my eyes or turn away, the tequila had me fully engaged in the freak show.

We were all flabbergasted. While the shock & awe of the freak show temporarily blew our minds, we didn't let it get in the way of our ultimate mission. We sat with Ortega & his crew surrounded by tequila & bonita Latinas that danced butt ass naked around us. After the freak show we went to a back room to handle our transaction. With bags of the finest uncut product safely in our possession, we bid farewell to Tijuana.

In retrospect, the crazy night in Vegas, the audacious trip to Tijuana, and our successful re-up were not just a testament to our ruthless enterprise but also vivid pages in my story. Pages filled with sinful indulgence, reckless bravado, and a rebellious spirit, brewing a bittersweet symphony called life in the raw, concrete landscapes of Black America.

My Grandfather, who I affectionately called Papa, was known for his timeless proverbs. He possessed an uncanny way with words that captured timeless wisdom, one of which was:

---

*"Everyone has a monster that lives inside them,
and your job is not to bring the monster out of
that person."*

I didn't understand as a child, these words seemed abstract &
cryptic, however, retrospectively, they are gems of wisdom that
brilliantly weave through the narratives of my life. This one, in
particular, has left an imprint on me; it has shaped my understanding of
actions & their consequences & has given me a new perspective on
how we influence & are influenced by people & the things they do.

On this day, I was riding through the set with Lil Smokey, and
Twindogg, I saw Big Mike car out front his crib & decided to pull up
on him. The Fifties hung heavy with tension instigated by the latest
hearsay & feuds. I left the homies chillin' in the car.

As I walked up the broad steps to the front door, the midday
sun beat down on the back of my neck. Mama Evans, an exceptional
woman with a tender heart, seemed visibly distraught. She peered at me
suspiciously from behind the screen door.

She admonished, *"that boy got some nerve coming around
here after he told on my baby."*

I was taken aback, accusations of betrayal, of snitching, hung
in the air.

Confused, I asked, *"Who? Told on who?"*

"He told on Greg," as she pointed at Twindogg in the
passenger seat of my car, *"& that boy over there told on Kenny!"*

She disclosed with an acidic bitterness, firing them right into
my growing disbelief, as she pointed at Lil Ken Dogg standing with
some homies outside of Dre Dogg's crib. A wave of anger &
embarrassment overcame me, unleashing the monster. Mama Evans
words served as the trigger for my insurmountable fury. I rushed back
to the car, adrenaline fueling my stride. Grabbing Twin by the throat, I
dragged him out, dishing out a harsh punishment for his betrayals.

My fists worked in a maniacal frenzy, delivering blow after
blow as he writhed in pain, pleading for mercy. The fight moved from
the driveway to the front yard, ending with me Hoover stomping him
into Mama Evans cherished rose bush.

With resounding rage, I spat out a final warning, *" If I ever see
you again, you a dead man."*

Mama Evans watched, initially shocked by my violent display, yet a twisted sense of appreciation reflected in her eyes as she cheered me on. She knew the streets, her smile of approval silently acknowledging the necessity of my actions. She saw the monster come out of me, the one Papa warned about wreaking havoc, and she cheered me on.

I left Twindogg cowered in pain stuck in the thorny bush, as I marched toward Dre Dogg's house. I didn't break stride. With every step, vengeance pulsated in my veins. I was focused on one thing only – justice. A sequel of my rage was unleashed on Lil Ken Dogg! I continued my onslaught. My inner monster had been unhinged & unleashed.

Both Twindogg & Lil Ken Dogg had made statements against the homies; however, they didn't cooperate & testify at trial. It was too late, the damage had been done; their ink had set a chain of events in motion that eventually led to my loved ones convictions. Those deemed trustworthy were crabs in a barrel, perpetuating the torment of the unjust justice system on my brethren. An inexplicable feeling of despair gripped me, as their deceit spawned a vengeful monster within me.

> *"Don't do the crime if you can't do the time.*
> *Don't throw the dice if you can't the price. Don't*
> *do me dirt or you gonna get hurt"*
> *-Sammy Davis, Jr, Baretta's Theme*

The incident was a blend of guilt & pride for me. On one hand, my harsh actions against my former comrades were warranted. On the other hand, it served as a dreadful punishment for them. Twindogg vanished from our lives after that horrific debacle, while Lil Ken Dogg sought spiritual sanctity by becoming a devout Muslim. However, their actions had consequences, Ken Dogg was sentenced to 30 years & Sham Rock got nine.

In the midst of the anarchy, there was a peculiar fascination that Lil Smokey had developed for me. She was captivated by the raw strength & authority I portrayed. Dancing on the line between fear & adoration, she was drawn to me, choosing to explore this newfound attraction over returning to her halfway house.

It was never my intention to impress but to enforce. However, her attention was a fruit that came as an unexpected yield of an unsavory victory. It was flattering & offered momentary solace in the dense murkiness of our lives. It would be a lie if I said I turned her down. I was a man, after all, and she was an enticing woman. She wanted to gift me all her pussy, a proposition quite tempting to a cockhound like myself.

Life, just like the Los Angeles streets, is unpredictable, filled with unexpected twists. The woman who seemed infatuated with me had a different plan simmering beneath her seductive gaze. Ironically, the woman who claimed to adore me, turned out to be scandalous too! Lil Smokey ratted me out for an unrelated incident.

A betrayal that was hard to digest, one that landed me behind bars. The twist in the tale was a visit from her while I was in the county. Her treachery still fresh, yet she had the audacity to come & see me. As if her actions had not been the sole cause of my unfortunate circumstance, the oblivious gaze fooled some but not me.

Looking back at what had transpired, I realized that we all have monsters inside us. Sometimes, despite our best precautions, they are brought out by the actions of those we least expect, and when they are, they can be as uncontrolled & wild as the beasts we imagine them to be. Had I become the perilous beast my grandfather warned me of, or was I the hero defending honor & loyalty? This remains an unanswered question to this day. For in the quest of righteousness, sometimes one might awaken dormant beasts.

CHAPTER FORTY-EIGHT: "LIVING NIGHTMARES"

Now it's the peak of summer, July 1987. The sun had dipped below the horizon, giving way to twilight. The balmy heat of South Central LA draped a languid idleness over its asphalt arteries. A few months out of prison, every breath of freedom tasted sweeter than I could ever remember. It's been a few weeks since I roamed the golden-hued landscapes of Mexico, I was back on familiar grounds, back with my homies in the rough & tumble of South Central.

Lil Boo introduced me to our newest recruit, a spunky lil homie named Joe from his block, 57th street. Joe was a peculiar sight, looking like a cocktail of cultures, seemingly sprinkled with Mexican allure. While Ken Dogg & I were incarcerated Lil Boo got so tight with Joe that he dubbed him *'Baby Boo'*.

"Ay CuH," Lil Boo addressed me with an undeniable glint in his eye, *"meet our number three, his name is Joe, now Baby Boo Capone."*

He nodded at the young Loc who stood proud yet slightly intimidated by my presence, *"Baby Boo Capone, meet the big homie... Big Boo Capone!"*

It was just an ordinary day around the way that turned into a defining one as I stood outside of Lil Boo Capone's crib w/ him & Baby Boo conversing over joints of lovely & sips of Silver Satin. As the sounds of Fifties hummed around us, two shadows cut across our circle, Blue Ragg & Low Down. They were proteges of the Groove, born into chaos, raised on the streets. They were groomed off violence, vengeance, mixed with bravado & grit.

Blue Ragg & I shared the same birth name. He was also a Gangsta Midget that ran with the big dogs from a young age. He hopped off the porch into the savage Crip world at the tender age of 12, these similarities made me gravitate towards him.

Originally known as Lil Loc, he was christened as Blue Ragg by Boscoe. He got his name for the collection of blue rags he flaunted proudly; on his crown, wrapped around his neck, his left wrist, and a final pair peeking out of his back pockets. Now my lil homie is in front of me as resolute as ever, albeit starring in a different role - Unfortunately, his youthful nimbleness was swapped with a paralyzing reality, the scar, a shiny wheelchair from bullets that valued life less than pennies.

"What the fuck happen lil homie!?!"

As he inhales the lovely smoke, Blue Ragg begins recounting the tale of how he became the 1st paralyzed homie, the smoke framing his face, he begins sharing his story. August 23rd, 1986, 2 weeks before Blue Ragg's 14th C-day, he's riding on the handlebars of Low Down's Schwinn, late night groovin' down Hoover Street with his Boombox in his lap. Dressed in their unmistakable Hoover Gangsta uniform. His speakers blasting Toddy Tee & Mixmaster Spade sending vibrations that mix with their Sherm smoke in the atmosphere.

As they approached the borders of the set, a wave of the munchies took over them. They made a detour, steering onto 59th Street, their noses pointed towards the comforting aroma of the Burger shack on Vermont Ave like Wimpy from Popeye. Out of the corner of his eye, Blue Rag noticed the silhouette of a car slowing down beside them. As he turned to look, he was suddenly blinded by a muzzle flash. A brutal drive-by shooting, void of any war cry, any warning or rationale except their Hoover Gangsta uniform. The world around them disintegrated into heart-wrenching chaos, as the gunshots continued fiercely.

A cascade of pain washed over him; Blue Ragg realized he could no longer feel his legs. His slender, adolescent frame was punctured seven times by the merciless bullets. Low Down, with four bullets lodged in him, collapsed alongside him, struck down by the same vicious firestorm.

The aftermath of the drive-by was as hauntingly peculiar as its occurrence. Its eeriness was compounded by the chilling mystery of the assailants. Our minds whirled through a plethora of possibilities. Was it one of our rivals putting in work for their respective cause? Or maybe it was the dirty pigs, infamous for adding fuel to the fires of existing beefs, orchestrating carnage behind the scenes? With gnawing uncertainty swirling within us, our vengeance inevitably turned towards the Brims, Coast & Bloodstones.

In our world where allegiance & vengeance were bonded together, the Brims bore the brunt of our retaliation. Low Down fulfilled his vendetta, pain & heartache engulfed our rivals' territories. Yet, the cold truth remained, our anger was quick to point fingers, to seek revenge, yet the actual culprits hid behind the cloak of the unknown, their transgressions left unclaimed.

That night transformed Blue Ragg's existence. It permanently etched an unhealed wound, both on his body & his soul. My comrades' flashback descended into silence, his story narrated merely by the flickering embers of our dying joints & the pained look in his eyes.

A couple days later, I found myself back gang-hanging among some of the faces that I missed dearly during my incarceration. Alongside me, I had KiKi & Coke Dog, reliable pillars of our close-knit brotherhood. Also, in our company were the new members, a new generation on the horizon.

Pookee with his unruly attitude, always wide-eyed & quick to engage in combat & Hoova Dee, armed with a cruel wit & a heart of gold. Others joining us were Cee Dogg, Lil Red Jr, Baby Chim, Bub, Jay Rock, Lil Madman, Lil C-Note, Lil Baby Crazy, and Lil Bub, whose membership expanded our borders to 47th & Main Street on the east side. These young men carried the torch of our heritage.

The sight of Big Fat Rat's younger brother, Bub, among our ranks made me proud. Each one of these young men held a blueprint of what it took to survive in this terrain, and it warmed my heart that they were Groovin' like us.

Each of the spirited eyes that met my gaze was a testament of perseverance & the audacious spirit of Hoover Gangsta's new generation. Recalling the days when we laid the foundation, witnessing the mettle of the new generation, I couldn't help but be immersed in a profound sense of pride.

Cee Dogg hailed from 55th street. We got to catching up, and amidst the nostalgic reminiscing, he dropped a piece of news on me that truly warmed my heart. He was happy to see me & eager to tell me he finally had a #2, an eager fifteen-year-old with a fiery spirit you had to respect. Turns out the new recruit was Faitdon, Inch High's baby cousin from Oxnard, I've known him practically his whole life. Now he was officially one of us, known as Lil Cee Dogg.

Whenever he used to visit us in the summers, Lil Cee Dogg would watch our groove, a surge of fascination visible in his eyes. It was clear, even then, that he was entranced by the set's camaraderie. Now, here he was embodying our essence with an admirable fearlessness. He personified everything that went into becoming a Loc. The fire in Lil Cee Dogg's eyes shone like a beacon of what's to come, reflecting his raw audacity. Lil Cee Dogg's passion for earning his respect etched a deep impression on me.

From then on, Lil Cee Dogg would become an embodiment of the fabric that kept us together. Lil Cee Dogg swiftly forged his place in our world. Despite his youth, he showed an uncommon grit that made him one of my favorite lil homies. Looking at him was like seeing a younger version of me eager to prove his worth. He didn't just carry our name - he was the future of FDHGC.

Unspoken bonds, forged in the crucibles of shared hardships, unified us all, in the face of adversity, in the heart of South Central. We were just a bunch of young Hoover niggas, engaging in light-hearted chatter, puffing on lovely. Our guard was never down, our spirits always high as our mind state, yet never oblivious to the dangers that surrounded us. We exchanged war stories of our exploits on the streets & our stints in prison. Even in the pandemonium of the city & our own chaos, there stood a strange sense of brotherhood we called groovin'.

Four houses away, a dark colored '80 Chevy Blazer, pulled up, idling with their headlights extinguished. It's silhouette partially visible in the streetlights. The sight made every muscle in my body tense up. Without missing a beat, I reached for my trusty Uzi. I warned the homies sternly, *"Get ya strap & get low!"*

The Chevy started speeding towards us. It's a drive-by! The assailants shouted, *"VNG"* before raining bullets upon us. Like clockwork, we retaliated, the crackling chorus of our return fire was interjected by the metallic thud of them sideswiping parked cars. Their vehicle faltered, wavered, yet they managed to regain control, speeding away from the murky shadows of 54th street.

The silence in their wake was deafening. Once the gun smoke settled, terror gave way to relief. Coke Dogg did a wellness check. By some miracle, we had dodged the Grim Reaper's icy touch that night. The unanimous *"all good"* response was broken by Kiki, he jumped up, grimacing as he muttered, *"I feel somethin' burnin' cuH."*

A fleeting glance downward confirmed our worst fears. He had been hit. The bullet had shattered his arm & hit an artery. Crimson blood gushed out like a rogue geyser, staining the cold asphalt below. Coke Dogg didn't hesitate. He ripped his shirt off & pressed it to his baby brother's wound, stopping the blood.

The impromptu tourniquet saved KiKi from bleeding out, thereby avoiding another tragic addition to our growing roster of fallen stars. Though we counted no losses that night, it was a close call, a grim reminder of the life we were sewn into. We had already lost Baby Man & Gee-man at 16, C-Roc at 14. Blue Ragg was paralyzed at 13 & now KiKi, could have been our third lil homie killed in action. The eye-for-an-eye world we lived in demanded action.

As Kiki's spilled blood on the Foe's cracked pavement blended with the stains from the massacre, it was a call to arms, time to make some mama's cry & some kids' bastards. It wasn't just about retribution; it was about honor, respect, the unwritten code of the streets. Today was just another day's worry. Today, we thanked the Black Jesus, for the sun had risen, and we were still standing.

The streets of Los Angeles crackled with the distinct echo of Eazy E's *"Boyz N The Hood"* blasting from a low-rider cruising down Figueroa Street. This story centers around two key players of the set, Boscoe & Lil Coke Dogg, providing a deep insight into their unshakeable bond & the unwritten code that governed our lifestyle. Their relationship epitomized our sense of kinship. This dynamic symbolized the heart of our tribe. They were essentially different, yet their bond remained ironclad.

Boscoe, known for his fearlessness & loyalty, was as hardcore as a Crip could get. He'd seen the worst of what life offered but remained unscathed, almost thriving amidst the danger. Passionate & devoted, he held the set together & was a force to be reckoned with.

The other, Lil Coke Dogg, was a stompdown Loc but unlike Boscoe, He was more than just a gang banger. He was the golden boy of Manual Arts High School. Adored by his coaches & promised a scholarship to the prestigious University of Southern California. His agility & action-packed performance on the football field painted him as a mural of success for our community.

Lil Coke Dogg approached football with the same fearless aggression that made him notorious as a Crip. Beneath the facade of the star athlete lay the soul of a Hoover Gangsta as loyal & dedicated as any of us. Our creed was never to tear each other down; we wished nothing but the best & success for all our loved ones. His life straddled the fence of two contrasting worlds; Hoover Gangsta Crippin', and the promise of being an NCAA star with the NFL in his near future.

Hoover doctrine frowned upon any form of betrayal. There was a rat in our ranks. This unprecedented breach of trust left Boscoe with no choice but to quell what could evolve into a cataclysmic predicament for the collective. With a heart weighed heavy with duty & a cold, relentless determination, Boscoe shot the traitor, Batman, a drastic act of loyalty fueled by an unforgiving code of conduct. Lil Man was next on his snitch hit list.

However, destiny had a twisted sense of humor, Batman played possum & faked dead after the attack. A cruel twist unfolded when the snitch, through blurred vision & a haze of pain, mistook Boscoe for somebody else, Lil Coke Dogg. The frantic accusation, drenched in blood & treachery, reached the ears of law enforcement, paving the way to an intriguing journey down a road where truth was second to betrayal.

Unfortunately, the pork chops issued a warrant for Lil Coke Dogg's arrest. The homie with a promising future in football was on the brink of losing everything. Learning about his warrant, fear was the furthest thing from Lil Coke Dogg's mind. He wasn't concerned; he was sure the case wouldn't stick. He decided to turn himself into the authorities. He hadn't pulled the trigger, but he believed in the brotherhood, in Boscoe, more than anything else & wasn't going to rat on his homeboy.

Upon hearing this, Boscoe was moved by Lil Coke Dogg's loyalty. In response, he made a decision that displayed the true honor within their bond. He declared that if Lil Coke Dogg was turning himself in, he wouldn't let him do it alone. It was Boscoe who pulled the trigger, after all.

The coaches at Manual Arts & USC rallied around their star, enveloping him in a fortress of character testimonials. They attempted to divert the hammer of justice, pleading Coke Dogg's innocence, highlighting his athletic prowess & potential for a brighter future. Their efforts, however, were met with deaf ears & a blind eye.

The tables turned in the courtroom. Both members faced the jury, their eyes reflecting the unspoken camaraderie unique to their brotherhood. Boscoe confessed, laying bare the truth of how he shot the snitch, not Lil Coke Dogg. Boscoe was no stranger to hard times, his confession amounted to a personal sacrifice for his friend.

At this point, it seemed the scales of justice might do the right thing. Unfortunately, the system crushed his hopes of absolution. Despite the coaches & Boscoe's earnest efforts, the justice system labeled Lil Coke Dogg as guilty. They were passionate about pursuing Lil Coke Dogg, dismissing Boscoe's confession altogether in favor of their original statement. The gavel slammed, the room echoed, and the sentence fell on the shoulders of Lil Coke Dogg.

A nine-year sentence framed for a crime he didn't commit, he forfeited his future, his education & football career. Life for Lil Coke Dogg had taken a dark detour. Yet amid these twisted events, their tale symbolized an unwavering loyalty & camaraderie that bound not just them, but the entire tribe, steering us through the troubled waters of life. Their story serves as a testament to the fact that loyalty & sacrifice in a time of need is the true test of a friend, the true test of a Hoover Gangsta.

Then came the shocking scandal, Los Angeles was shaken to its core with one of the most shocking cases in its history. One that reverberated through the Grooveline's menacing by lanes. Capturing the irony of fate, Boscoe soon found himself in the company of Lil Coke Dogg again, but this time in the infamous Crip module of LA County Jail. A place where stories of deceit & loyalty wove themselves into the fabric of everyday life, where his exonerating confession had failed to prevent incarceration from ravishing his life.

The Get Busy Crew was notorious for their ruthless tactics, had concocted an intricate plan to generate revenue fast. They were accused of heinous acts that sent tremors down the spine of even the most hardened criminals. Kidnapping, extorting, and robbing major drug dealers naked, literally & figuratively during a crime spree that left their victims penniless & defenseless. They were stripped bare of their money, guns, dope, clothes, and, ultimately, their dignity.

The scheme seemed to work. The money flowed like a river, quenching their thirst for ruthless revenge & revitalizing their crippled egos. However, blinded by arrogance, Lil Chim took things a little too far. This particular victim— a man who had been abused, robbed, brutalized, intimidated, abducted, hogtied, unclothed, and photographed, was not influenced by his pride or ego to hide his deep dark secret.

He wanted justice. He found his redemption not in payback, but in law enforcement; he went straight to pigs with the photos after they released him from captivity. Overpowered by humiliation, he chose to break silence & became an informant.

The Get Busy Crew once overlords of their own underworld were now threatened by their own victim, the tables had turned. Like a gambler faced with defeat, Boscoe was dealt another vile hand. The man who had previously been willingly to take the hit for his own crimes & exonerate Lil Coke Dogg from a 9 year bid was now facing 20 long years. Lil Chim was met with the same fate.

Last time I saw Big Fat Rat we were in the bull pen awaiting court. He swore to me he did not participate in the kidnapping & was going to take it to trial. There was no evidence against him. He was on a road trip to San Diego with his wife in the stolen car, when he was summoned back to the hood.

During the trial the plaintiff testified that Fat Rat showed up for like 5 minutes, laughed at the handcuffed hostage & left. Unfortunately, after his co-defendants copped out, the Judge charged the jury to ignore the other co-defendants & place all the evidence against him. Since he was the elder, he was labeled the ringleader of the operation. This resulted in him blowing trial & being slammed with a life sentence — a game of Russian roulette where everyone involved had to bear the brunt of a loaded gun.

A Few weeks passed, it was a warm evening in the City of Angels, and the sun had long set behind the vast expanse of the horizon. The smog-filled skies gave way to stars, barely visible through the haze. Tired, I leaned against the hood of my low-rider Cadillac on 89th & Broadway. I was spending a lot of time over there hanging out with my former cellie, Crazy Nell.

The Nine-Foes always chilled on Broadway, you rarely found them on the westside. The Nine-Foes' arch rivals were the Eight-Seven Gangsta Crips. They were getting into it all the time because they were in close proximity to each other. Crazy Nell drew first blood in their conflict, he took pride in being the #1 Eight-Seven killa.

I was riding clean in my new fly ass low-rider, it grabbed attention everywhere I went so people recognized my car when they saw it. I would be seen in the Nine-Foes so much people thought I was from over there. Eight-Sevens even some Nine-Foes thought I was from Nine-Foe.

Someway, somehow these niggas found out where I stayed. They saw me hanging out on Broadway, and unbeknownst to me they knew my route home. A dangerous game of cat & mouse unfolded as the Eight-Sevens waited in the darkness, around the corner of 52nd street by the stop sign before my crib. Riding in my lowrider, with the hydraulics bouncing on the ill-lit streets, I took my usual route home.

As I rounded the corner near Budlong Ave, shadows loomed darker, corners became more sinister, and I felt the gnawing sensation that something was amiss. I pushed aside the eerie feeling & continued cruising through the inky blackness.

Out of the corner of my eye, I noticed a strange flash of light down the dark street. It was as if the entire universe was holding its breath. Before I could react, the staccato sound of gunfire pierced my ears, and I felt the piercing sting of bullets slamming into the side panel & windows of my lowrider. A thousand pieces of glass exploded into my face, I was caught in the middle of an ambush, and my life was hanging by a thread.

My heart pounding, and adrenaline coursing through my veins, I ducked to make myself an even smaller target. Desperation clawed at my chest as I drove blindly on pure instinct, trying to escape the deadly rain. The car jerked & swayed as it lurched forward, and I could hear the thrum of the engine & the relentless sound of gunfire.

Suddenly, an excruciating pain ripped through my body as bullets found their mark, tearing through my flesh like it was paper. I tried, in vain, to keep control of the car. The last thing I remember, as my vision began to blur. When my eyes fluttered open again, I was in a hospital bed at Martin Luther King Hospital in Watts. I was told that I blacked out & crashed into a lamp post.

The awkward silence of my room was only broken by the rhythmic beeping of multiple machines, monitoring my fragile existence. I was shot in the stomach, hip, elbow & the small of my back, and I lost a lot of blood. The damn Eight-Sevens got me good, I needed a blood transfusion. As I scanned the room, I saw my favorite face, Big Mama, with tears in her eyes in mid prayer, I reached for her, and embraced her hands.

It looked like I was going to be on the bench for a minute. The Hoovers, my loved ones, were my lifeline. My injuries were so severe that I required a blood transfusion to survive, and they rallied around me in force offering their lifeblood without hesitation. Big Mama & the homegirls, in their infinite love & compassion, stayed by my bedside, offering comfort in my darkest hour.

The homies Lil Red Jr, Lil Fat Rat, and CeeCee as well as various other homies took turns guarding my room. They were my family, my protectors, and my salvation. The lifeblood of my Hoover

Gangstas now coursing through my veins, solidifying an unshakeable bond.

As expected, the corrupt forces of C.R.A.S.H had taken an interest in my case. This division had a tainted reputation for corruption & brutality, making them an unlikely ally for anyone like me. As I lay in my cold hospital bed, the door opened to reveal the C.R.A.S.H officers that had been assigned to my case. At that moment, I knew that something was off about these fools. They circled me like vultures, their eyes cold & calculating. Their dark, expressionless gaze seemed to seek out the weakness in their prey, ready to exploit any vulnerability.

"Big Boo Capone from Five-Deuce Hoover, I see they finally got you! They got your little ass good too! So, who was it? The Brims? The Forties? Maybe the Sixties?"

A burly, smirking officer barked at me trying to get me to rat & make their job easier. I gritted my teeth at the officer's joy in my misfortune. Each movement sent excruciating pain through my broken body, but I wasn't about to show them any weakness. His aggressive persistence in trying to obtain information about the shooters & their motives betrayed any intentions he had of helping me. The officers also inquired about retaliation, flexing their coercive tactics as they pretended to be interested in stopping the violence.

"What about the East Coast? I've heard the Hoovers are beefing pretty hard with them too," the second officer chimed in, acting concerned as if he genuinely wanted to put an end to the gang banging.

Their inquiry into retaliation seemed insincere. I knew that they were only interested in keeping their arrest numbers high & detouring our brand of vigilante justice. My blood pressure rose, my irritation seeping through with each passing moment. The steady beeping of the heart monitor in the background intensified as my agitation grew stronger. Stubborn & unwilling to give in to their manipulative methods.

I responded, *"I don't talk to pigs, fool."*

Staring down the officers with equal defiance & resentment. As the officers continued their relentless interrogation, a mixture of pain, frustration, and fury boiled up inside me until I could no longer contain my emotions. I lashed out at them, ordering them to leave my room:

"Get the fuck outta my room, pig!" I exclaimed bitterly.

A heartbeat monitor beeped incessantly in the background, the pulsating sound echoing my frustration while I lay vulnerable in the hospital bed. Before they left, I added one more statement for good measure:

"I dunno nothin' about nothin'."

The officers exchanged glances, sneers carved into their faces as they stepped out of the room, leaving me alone with my thoughts & wounds, the last one to leave casting one final, loathing glance in my direction. I tried to suppress the conflicting emotions bubbling within me - rage at the audacity of these officers, bitterness towards the gang who nearly claimed my life, and a nagging sense of despair as I acknowledged the true gravity of my situation.

The hospital was in the territory of the Bounty Hunters, red rags from the nearby Nickerson Gardens projects. The day after my transfusion, I was lying in my bed, tubes & wires snaking out of my body. The usual backdrop of idle chatter, beeping monitors, and hushed footsteps was shattered.

Lil Boo, Stroll, Baby Crazy, Pookee, Lil Fat Rat, Lil Red, Jr, Baby Kaos, Cee Baby Chim & Baby Boo & a dozen more Hoover Gangstas were scattered around the hallways & waiting room of the hospital. Their presence did not go unnoticed by the Bounty Hunters who claimed the surrounding area as their territory.

I hear the Damus shouting with hearts full of hatred slogans like *"Blood up!"*, *"CK ALL DAY!"* *"Crab Killa!"*

I hear the familiar voice of Lil Fat Rat holler *"HOOVER!"*

As the homies respond in unison *"Carip!"*

Followed by Lil Red Jr's furious roar *"Slob Killa!"*

These battle cries resonated with raw power & passion, echoing through the sterile halls of King Hospital. Words morphed into weapons, as the shouts were assailed by profanity, vulgar in its expression—yet truthful in the undercurrent of pain it captured.

The fight between Hoovers & the Bounty Hunters erupted with a sudden fury. Stolen orderly's carts were launched at one another, chairs thrown & phones ripped off the walls. The waiting room turned into a demolition zone. Amidst this commotion, children cried, and patients dashed for cover while the overhead speakers called for

assistance from every staff member, security & law enforcement
available.

　　As I lay there straining my ears to get a clearer picture, the
sound spilled over in waves, invading my space with overwhelming
intensity. Screams, roars, the unmistakable violent crack of bodies
colliding in a dance of hatred, and the sharp sting of punches
exchanged. There were slaps, wild kicks, and the brutal sound of bones
twisted mercilessly by a foe eager for retribution. A fire burned deep
within my being, overpowered my insecurities, and replaced my
helplessness with an unbridled desire to join my brothers in their fight.

　　I could hear the chaos & commotion from my hospital room
while wishing I could be there to fight alongside my brothers. I
clutched my bed sheets tight, willing my body to step forth from the
confines of my cot towards the chaos outside. Every movement, intense
pain sliced through me, searing reminders of my wounds forcing me to
stay in place. The waiting room transformed into a battlefield - an
unforgiving landscape where allegiances were tested, and friendships
cemented.

　　In the minutes that felt like hours, I remember feeling both
admiration & fear for my homies as they exchanged blow for blow,
asserting their loyalty & defending our reputation. Blood splattered the
white-tiled floors, mingling with the coffee spilled in haste from its
cup, while the acrid taste of stale sweat & desperation hung in the air.
The scene was one of utter carnage.

　　My heart raced at a relentless pace, but I could not outrun the
wretched reality of my situation. This brawl continued with hospital
staff & security doing what they could to control the situation. After a
while the security & a handful of LAPD officers finally managed to
break through the chaos & pull the fighting sides apart, effectively
ending the brawl.

　　Suddenly as it began, the war in the waiting room came to a
stuttering halt. The howls & screams subsided into soft, resolute grunts,
and then into a haunting silence. I held my breath in apprehension, left
only to wonder how the battle transpired: who held the upper hand,
who remained standing, battered & bloodied. My pride surged when I
heard triumph in a familiar voice, it was Baby Crazy claiming victory
in that moment. My body swelled with relief, knowing that the
fierceness of our bond had triumphed once again, albeit at a great cost.

In the wake of this battle royale, the waiting room was left looking like a disaster area after Hurricane Hoover – blood splattered across the floor, furniture destroyed, and people sobbing in shock, nursing their injuries. It was a grim reminder of the never-ending cycle of violence that plagues the streets of South Central.

As I lay in that sterile hospital bed, looking out towards the battlefield that now lay quiet, I braced myself for the next chapter in this endless war, knowing that FDHGC will always stand tall, through the turmoil & the pain, as we march to protect our own.

Rest assured, the payback for their attempt on my life would be sweet, fast, swift, and above all, brutal. As I lay unconscious in my hospital bed, struggling to breathe against the searing pain that engulfed my various wounds, the homies had my back, taking matters into their own hands. On the night of my attack, the homies assembled a tightly knit unit of our most skilled warriors & these elite Locs infiltrated the heart of enemy territory like a pride of lions stalking zebras in the plains of Africa.

The objective was simple: hit hard & make them pay. Before the midnight hour struck, few bodies bearing the unmistakable markings of Eight-Seven Gangsta sacrificed in retribution. My Kiwés had successfully sent a tremor of fear resonating through the entire fake seven territory. This was just the beginning. a reminder not to cross us. It wasn't just one act of retaliation; we made sure to give those fools hell in any way we could. A chill ran down my spine when I heard of their first invasion. They were on a mission to avenge their fallen brother, and no force on heaven or earth, except the Almighty himself, could sway them from this path.

We played the long game, taunting & baiting them into traps & ambushes, never leaving them with any clue as to our intentions. Crazy Nell & the Nine-Foes weren't even aware of our attacks on their archrivals until the pigs started interrogating them. Once the Nine-Foes realized they were being accused of our vengeful escapades, they began to collaborate with us, cementing our alliance in the ongoing Hoover versus Eight-Seven conflict.

My physical recovery spurred on by the need to be involved, to return to the only life I knew & the loyalty that I held in my heart. I trusted my homeboys with my life. Confident that they would avenge me in my absence, that they would bring the same ferocity &

determination I embodied. The ideals of loyalty & devotion woven into every fiber of my being.

Eventually, my body began to align itself with the ever-moving world outside that had shown no signs of slowing down. After doctors cleared me & released me back into the realm I longed to return to. With each step I took, the truth was I was a survivor & a rider, and it's clear, I am here for a real reason.

> *"Many men, Wish death 'pon me. Lord I don't cry no more. Don't look to the sky no more. Have mercy on me, have mercy on my soul. Somewhere my heart turned cold."*
> *-50 Cent, Many Men*

My return was met with praise & adulation from my loved ones. They graciously expressed their relief at having me back among them, the fear having dissipated as my wounds healed. A renewed fire in my belly, I learned I could handle whatever the world decided to throw at me. Despite the uncertainty of our lives & the environment we called home, one thing remained constant – our loyalty would forever triumph over adversity.

Over 3 decades removed from the brutal reality of gang violence, I find solace in sharing my harrowing tale, in the hope that others might learn from my mistakes. Bloodshed only begets bloodshed, and in our thirst for vengeance, we only create an endless cycle of pain & suffering. Only by breaking free can we truly escape this nightmare & forge a better future, not just for ourselves, but for those we leave behind.

For I am living proof that one can turn the tide, learning from the error of my ways, stepping out from the shadows into the light. In sharing my story, I hope I can provide a beacon of hope & redemption for others whose lives have been consumed by the unforgiving cycle of revenge.

CHAPTER FORTY-NINE:
"MADMAN CHRISTMAS"

Life had dealt me a foul hand, leaving me battered, bruised, and scarred. Live by the gun, die by the gun. It was inevitable. These wounds served as a blunt reminder of the harsh reality of the game I had been playing, a game of life or death.

The incident also served as a wake-up call. I vowed to never get caught slipping like that again. The violence in Los Angeles was out of control & so was the competition in the crack game. It was very hard to ball & bang & I wasn't in condition for banging yet. I needed time to heal & rehabilitate my mind, body, and soul & after a few months of rehabilitation I was back to Crippin' full time.

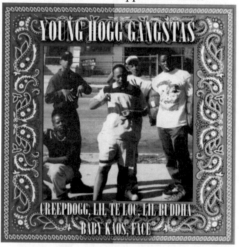

It's now the holiday season 1987, The cold atmosphere reflected the hearts of promising youngsters who had to navigate their lives through the splintered alleys of crime. During my time in prison & recovering a plethora of new homies joined the fold. We welcomed Lil Looney, Raccoon (Coon), Argo & the 49th street Hustlers. There was also a new generation of Tiny Locs from 52nd street school who would grow to command respect & fear in equal measures.

Viewed as a Chief among them, a raw gem chiseled by Hoover Street, my loved one, Pookee. My lil homie naturally became a big homie. He was idolized by the impressionable youth of the Fifties. Even under the spell of Magic Johnson's Showtime Lakers & the magnetic pull of Michael Jordan, they didn't aspire to *"Be Like Mike"* they wanted to be from Hoover Gangsta like Pookee. Pookee was a cold Crip, every time he came outside, matter fact the only reason was to put in work.

A young reputable in the making was Baby Fat Rat, who became known as Big Valentine from 50th street. He was a cornerstone of the new generation, influential in attracting his peers to the groove, silently stirring the simmering pot of our breeding ground. He instilled them with our hereditary trait of Five-Deuce Hoover Gangsterism, which I call FDNA during their tenure at 52nd street school. He introduced names like Hoover Bandit, Ropey Dope, Lil Te Loc, Baby Hoova D, Lil Buddha, H-Bone, Mexican Twin (Baby Twindogg) & Baby Loon (Big Fabuloso) they too, found their 'nom de guerre' (war name) & blue bandana while at Five-Deuce Elementary.

The crisp, winter air filled my lungs as I stood outside my crib smoking weed under the yum-yum tree. I hadn't felt this free in years. I was proud of myself; it had been a few years since I saw Christmas in the street. I'm feeling groovy anticipating some of my mama's home cooking later tonight. As I looked around the set, I felt a sense of home, and belonging. I begin to make my way towards the Foe, cause the Lee's always got it crackin' for Christmas.

The hood was vibrant with the color & clutter of the holiday season. The set, usually buzzing with an unending burst of energy, was oddly peaceful & calm. I found the homies outside of Dre Dogg's house, taking pictures, and shit talking as I photobombed & exhaled celebratory weed smoke into the misty air.

The peace of the afternoon was cut short by the growl of a powerful engine. Here comes Madman making a dramatic entrance, gliding into the scene in his slick, sleek silver Buick Skylark. His arrival, as always, commanded attention & injected a dose of rambunctious energy into the quiet morning.

Now, anyone who knows Madman will tell you that he had a deep love for cars. He appreciated not only their aesthetic beauty but the sheer power & exhilaration they brought. You see, Madman was an adrenaline junkie. He relished the thrill of burning rubber, speeding down dusty roads or lonely highways, and smoking water.

"Damn, homie! That's one clean ride, cuH," in admiration, appreciating the shiny Buick & its metallic bravado. As Madman jumps out to greet us.

"Thanks Loc! Merry Cripmas! Where the hoe, hoe, hoes at?!" he shouted, with diabolical laughter, his face beaming with excitement.

"Merry Cripmas to you, too, my nigga!" I responded, a wide grin spreading across my face.

I slapped him 5 & congratulated him on his new wheels. I whistled appreciatively at the spotless chrome rims. We chopped it up a little bit, the topic veering from Hoover politics to the sanctity of street cred.

Madman's chest swelled with pride, *"Hop in, let's take it for a spin,"* he exclaimed with childlike enthusiasm, masking his otherwise grim face.

"Hell yeah, Groove!", I replied.

Swinging myself into the passenger seat of his silver bullet, the door slammed shut with a finality that echoed my instinctive feeling of unease. The Buick was meticulously polished inside but something was off.

"Yo nigga, where's the steering wheel?" I asked, pointing at the empty space where the steering wheel should have been. Instead, I noticed an unusual apparatus, a pair of vice grips.

C-NOTE & MADMAN

Madman brushed my concerns aside with a boisterous laugh as he revved the engine to life, the low purr of its horsepower reverberating ominously in the morning stillness.

"Don't worry, cuH," he declared, tapping the vice grips with relish, *"I gotta good deal, this bitch drives like a beast."*

His words did nothing to calm my concerns, but curiosity baited me into taking the ride with my wild ass homeboy. I should have known better but I'm always down for an adventure. As he revved the engine, the flamboyant Buick roared to life, dismissing my doubts in its deafening growl. My disbelief was silenced by the roaring pistons as we drove off.

A fiery spirit, Madman earned his name through thrilling, life-threatening antics. He was just a crazy muthafucka, and behind the wheel, you better clutch your pearls with this nigga. Madman is the name, and madness is the game. If you were to look up *"riding dirty"* in the dictionary, his black ass grinning face would stare back at you with eyes filled with audacity.

We could have called him *"Daredevil"* or *"Stuntman"* but that would not manage to capture his legendary exploits. He just didn't give a damn, his lifestyle was a testament to his fearless spirit & animated demeanor. He didn't just take risks; he lived for it. No obstacle or danger was too great. Madman is just the maddest Hoover nigga in the world.. He moved out of town, he told us he was coming back to L.A to visit, Lil Coke Dogg raised a pot to give him money not to come!

There was a strange thrill in associating with him. An intoxicating sense of living on the edge that I too succumbed to. Getting into skirmishes, slashing through trouble, and surviving through chaos together, Madman & I became two halves of a wild whole.

I'm telling the homie how happy I am to be home for Christmas, *"It feels good to be back in the hood, cuH!"*

Our joy ride began with the Buick gliding smoothly along South Central's bustling arteries. Madman, living up to his reputation, flaunted his dismissive bravado at a red-light, pulling up next to an LAPD cruiser. Call it holiday spirit or sheer madness, but what he did next shifted our Christmas Day adventure to a dangerous gear - he starts revving his engine, he looks over at me, I look at him, I could tell by the look in his eyes, he is ready to do some wild shit.

"Watch this, fool!" Madman said as he turned to face the police cruiser next to us.

This wild man starts mean mugging the pigs until they finally make eye contact, then he starts talking crazy, shouting all kinda obscenities at the police. Any combination of fuck, shit, pigs, piss, asshole, you can think of he said it.

As the grand finale to his tirade, Madman yells *"Fuck the Police!"*, then throws his half-consumed 40oz at the cruiser's windshield, splattering the glass with beer like a poorly executed Basquiat painting & burns rubber! **Vroom!**

"Oh, shit you wildin' cuH!" I shouted like I was summoning my inner scary jerry, but Madman just laughed like an evil villain & floored the gas.

In a flash, the serene Christmas morning turned into a pulsating high speed chase scene straight out of Beverly Hills Cop, with us as the unexpected stars. The pigs followed us down Hoover Street in hot pursuit. Sirens, wailing & flashing, as they pursued us up & down every block in the Fifties, the whole hood saw us, there had to be about 10 squad cars chasing us!

The whizzing cityscape was a blur as Madman skillfully navigated to shake the one time. Time seemed to stretch & squeeze as adrenaline pumped through our veins & heightened our senses. The chase then took us onto the 110 Freeway, where the Buick charged full steam ahead like a stampeding wild stallion. My adrenaline is rushing as the pigs follow close behind us, sirens blaring. I hear an officer cursing us out & telling us to pull over, over his PA system.

"We goin' back to jail nigga!" I screamed.

There was nothing I could do; it was too late! Madman just didn't give a damn, he kept driving like a Madman, dipping in & out of lanes & dodging squad cars left & right at high speeds like Dominic Toretto in Fast & Furious.

The tidal wave of adrenaline hit us like an earthquake, as Madman lost control of the Buick & the world turned topsy-turvy, his vice-grip steering wheel taking us on a joy ride of its own. The Buick veered, fishtailed, and then, mind-bogglingly, we found ourselves driving backward down the freeway, a ridiculous 80mph with the LAPD still hot on our tail.

Undeterred by the sirens blaring in front of us & displaying an audacious bravado that only a man known as *'Madman'* could embody, He laughed hysterically, flashing a proud middle finger to our tailing nemeses from LAPD. With a calculated jerk of his makeshift wheel, the car swirled in the right direction, careening down the exit ramp with tires squealing in protest. The engine's powerful growl echoing across the city's tranquility, shattering the golden silence of Christmas morning.

Twenty minutes into this high-stakes game of hide & chase, our wild ride ended abruptly on somebody's front lawn, the unwilling landing pad for our Christmas Day run. As the dust settled, we hopped out, and busted a move leaving the once prized ride & the vindictive pigs behind. Before we knew it, the damn pigs were on our heels again, turning our situation into a foot chase through the back streets.

When the pigs finally caught us, they served us a nice ass whipping. Madman fought back with all his might, swinging at the officers, and even bit one of them during the scuffle. The police didn't hold back, they rushed him, tackled him to the ground & began beating him mercilessly with their infamous nigga-beaters.

At the same time, the piglets shove me to the ground & proceeded to stomp a mudhole in my ass. I still vividly recall wrestling with the officers, my freedom slipping through my fingertips. My voice echoing from the scuffle into the crisp, winter air, *"I'm not resisting man! I ain't do nothing, get the fuck off me!"*

Although my plea met deaf ears, A swift kick strikes me in my ribs & knocks the wind out of me, while another pig puts the strong arms of the law around me in a vice-like chokehold as their cruel response to my plea. I could taste the muddy grass & feel the humiliation of the failed escape.

My life, my victories, my struggles flashing before me. I saw my past, my present, drowned in the terror of an uncertain future. I remembered the big homie, Joe Ransom; the same chokehold had taken him. I'm thinking that this is it, these crackers are going to kill me! They continued choking me & I thought maybe death is the only peace for a young black man, for a young Crip as my consciousness faded.

When I came to, I was in a place I'm very familiar with, a Police Precinct holding cell. Here I am thinking I was going to have a nice calm Christmas, instead I was gifted a Madman Christmas & a trip to jail. My head throbbing & my body aching, My mind was cloudy, and my short term memory was blurry from the head trauma. The officers didn't bother to explain what had happened or why I was there. They simply told me *"be grateful you alive kid."*

The pigs released me in the morning, as for Madman, they sent him to the County jail for resisting arrest, assault an office, reckless endangerment & a smorgasbord of crimes. The release was more of shocking than the arrest. The pigs letting me go was a favor I didn't expect. From the high-speed chase across the city to the brutal beating on someone's front lawn, this Christmas day was one for the history books.

CHAPTER FIFTY:
"CRAZY EIGHTY-EIGHT"

One evening, I was cruising through the Foe-Tray Hoovers looking for Judabean. I saw a group of girls caught in the neon glow of the corner store, chit chatting', curls bouncing. Figuring they were from around the way, I rolled down the window & asked *"Y'all seen Judabean?"*

They had a stupid look on their faces, trading smirks & side eyes, they responded, *"Judabean who?"*

I replied gruffly, *"Hoover Bean."*

Realization rained on me, and it thundered down like an empire of judgment. These girls didn't belong in the Hoovers. They were Rollin Foeties!

A wave of revolt swept across their faces, *"Fuck Hoover,"* they spat, the words ripping through the air.

"Okay," I replied, a surge of adrenaline tensed my muscles. I warned them, with a sneer lurking in the corners of my mouth, *"I'll ce right back..."*

I made my way back to the set, where I found the homegirls outside of Cadillac Bobby's crib, Mad Mag from Five-Nine, Smokey & his baby sis H'Vette from Five-Deuce. Their presence brought an intense wave of relief as they were exactly who I was looking for.

"Y'all ready to put in some work?" I inquired, the urgency unmistakable.

Swiftly, without missing a beat, Mad Mag jumped in my car. No questions asked. That's what I admired about Mad Mag; she was always ready to ride. Mad Mag was a fierce member of the Simms clan, her family were influential members & groundbreakers of Seven-Foe & Five-Nine Hoover.

Smokey & H'Vette haggled a bit, circling around the burning flame interrogating me about the *'who'*, *'what'*, *'when'*, *and 'where'* before finally jumping in. Nonetheless, their loyalty was ingrained in the rich flavor of Hoover Gangsta.

As we cruised down Vermont back to 43rd Street, my mind lingered on Mag. I found her gangsterism sexy. She was a force to be reckoned with, an explosive concoction of strength with a relentless warrior spirit – a genuine brawler. She was like a junkyard Crip dog, ready to pounce in an instant. We neared the scene & luckily the bitches were still loitering outside the store.

In a flash of fury & anticipation, Mag leaped out of the slow moving vehicle. She pounced on the Foeties Loc'Lettes, catching them off guard. Her movements reflected the skill of a seasoned street fighter, the equivalent of a Lioness defending her pride.

The rest of the homegirls followed suit, pouring out of the vehicle with synchronized fury. We were there to remind them of the dire consequences of dissing the Groove. Scatterings of profanity & broken beer bottles echoed off the houses & alleys, each scream & blow, a chilling testament to the power of the Nifty Fifty Hoovers. During the melee, I saw a bit of myself in each of the homegirls: a spark of dedication, a trace of ruthlessness, a lot of courage, and unmatched conviction to protect what we loved - the Hoovers, our integrity & our bond.

Reflecting to that era of violence & rivalries, in my humble opinion, Mad Magg & Tee-Dub were second to none when it came to street fighting. Those fearless women, their fists clenched, eyes ablaze with determination, were the true embodiment of loyalty & sheer grit. They proved time & time again that they weren't just able to stand their ground, but they were a formidable force. Bringing the pain to trifling bitches, with every brawl, their names drew fear & respect.

The Foeties were becoming our #1 enemy. Tonight, I find myself puffing clouds of PCP smoke & chugging down Tyronia with the Locs. We were politicking about our rivals, Rollin Foety. Recently, they had pulled a fast one on us, shooting up Pookee's crib from the safety of the Jack in the Box, behind his house.

My blood boiled hotter with each retelling of the tale, the bitterness of treachery & vengeance lacing our words. Fueled by an intoxicating blend of angel dust, alcohol, and uncontained anger, I asked Lunchmeat to lend me the keys to his car. I had spun a story about needing more drink, but my real intent was to put some points on the scoreboard & put in work on the Foeties. Smokey, Mexican Twin, and Deuce unknowingly fell in line with my mission. Unspoken loyalty binding us together as we cruised down Figueroa Street.

As I drove behind enemy lines, fueled by unleaded animosity, the Foeties came into sight. A surge of adrenaline propelled me out of the car, a Colt 45 clutched in my eager hand. Each bullet with Foeties engraved on it. Adrenaline pumped like an opioid in my veins, my trigger finger itching. I squeezed off rounds until it was empty per Five-Deuce protocol..

I left as quickly as I came, I hopped back into the car, the scene of my vengeance rapidly shrinking in the rear-view mirror. Coincidentally, the pigs were filling up at a small gas station hidden around the corner. They heard the gunfire & saw me fishtail on to Fig & burn rubber into the night. Now they're on our ass, their sirens lighting up the night & waking up the dead homies.

I cut a sharp turn onto Vernon, which gave me some good distance on my pursuers as I sped towards Pookee's crib. A desperate plan began to form in my intoxicated mind. I thought about pulling into Pookee's yard, but better sense prevailed at the last moment. It would be too risky, bringing pigs to our hideout. Instead, I made a split second decision, I deserted the getaway car in a nearby Carvel parking lot.

We quickly made our exit through a sequence of backyards, hopping over fences & disappearing into the darkness of the night. Eventually, threading through the back blocks we made it back to Pookee's place, reunited with the homies, a welcomed refuge after the action packed escapade.

The aftermath of that wild night unraveled the next day when news reached me that the pigs were on my tail. The domino effect rigged by last night's mission; Lunchmeat went to retrieve his car from the impound, he was pressed about the assault. I guess he changed his name to Big Stool Pigeon. Lunchmeat's loyalty faltered, and he ended up singing like a canary. Now there might be a warrant & a manhunt. Upon hearing this, I knew I had to make a move.

In the grim affairs of my life, a silver lining appeared. My comrades, Lil Q-Bone & Hot Shot, struck me an offer too good to refuse. They proposed a scheme to travel cross-country to Albuquerque, New Mexico. The mission? To make some serious cash selling dope. This led me & a crew of fifteen Five-Deuce Broadways, to take our talents across state lines in a five-car caravan, filled with determination & a few keys.

After a journey that at times seemed endless, we arrived in Duke City – a land of scorched earth with autumn hues spread out resembling a surrealist painting of mountains & desert. Here, the heat danced off the ground & the sunset sky looked like an artist's palette, a mix of indigo, tangerine, and pink.

Our stay stretched out for a month, and business was good. ABQ offered a lucrative market, and my comrades & I were able to secretly peddle our goods.. Meanwhile, I found affection in the confines of a Chicano girl named Isabela, a local with almond eyes & an inviting smile. She provided warmth in her embrace & a kindness that was one of a kind. She kept my balls empty & my stomach full of delicious burritos & tamales.

Our mission in Albuquerque was a success, smooth as the Rio Grande that sliced through the city. We procured our intended profits unscathed, a rarity in our lifestyle. With our pockets filled, we left the city into winding landscape of the New Mexico highway.

Back on Hoover Street I reunited with oG Baby Johnny, a fellow Hriginal Hoover Gangsta, and a close friend who lived on my block. Baby Johnny was about 29 years old, at the time. He was all about his money, the epitome of a gangsta with ties to everything we needed – from guns to dope.

Baby Johnny been a Loc, his Crippin predated the set. He was the leader of the Baby Five-Deuce Undergrounds. His kinship was unquestionable, his commitment undeniable. Our loyalty to each other was ironclad, our bond unbreakable. Baby Johnny was a rare breed, the perfect partner in the underworld. Trust was not something that was given, it was earned through trials & tribulations.

Baby Johnny suggested *"How you feel 'bout making this move with me to Oakland, cuH?"*

Oakland— the city where my story began. A city synonymous with my birth, it held treasured memories, muffled amidst the raging chaos of my life. What could be a better stomping ground than my breeding ground?

The proposition was enticing— to return to my birthplace & conquer it. He talked about expanding our horizons in the Bay, a city alive with opportunities for people like us. The plan was rather simple— disperse more dope & fatten our wallets. The embodiment of the American Dream, O-Town laid before us, daring us to seize the opportunities hidden in its ghettos.

I made some nice change in Duke City & was looking to keep the money flowing, so it seemed like a win-win situation. It was also an opportunity to leave behind the chaos I had orchestrated in the hood. The idea was to lay low & let the dust settle, so we embarked on a new venture, Oakland better brace themselves, the Hoovers are coming!

I recall the exhilarating rush of adrenaline as I stepped out of our vintage Cadillac. I was all brimming pride & effortless confidence, my Fifty Crip swag exuding radiant charisma. Adorned in my signature Ace Deuce hat, presenting a stark contrast atop my lustrous dripping jheri curl, I felt a sense of invincibility. The hypnotic sway of my diamond encrusted Turkish link gold chain & my long diamond earring dangling carelessly in the wind were unquestionable indicators the Deuces are here.

My biscuit shoes & painter pants mirrored the assertiveness of my Crippin', causing intrigued glances from every direction. The women who happened to set sights on us found us irresistible. We smelled good & we looked good like big dope money. We set up shop in the heart of the Westside. It was a vibrant & lively city, buzzing with music, art, and black culture.

West Oakland carried the tag of *'Harlem of the West'* due to its large Black population & rich Black culture, their contributions to jazz, blues, and civil rights are historic. However, invisible to the naked eye was a darker, more sinister side brewing in the shadows. We became breathlessly entangled in the warm embrace of the city. The cityscape was an intricate tapestry of weathered Victorian houses painted in a barrage of colors side by side with big industry.

It was a time when the crack epidemic had hit the city harder than the hard rocks we were slinging, turning it into a hotbed of dope deals. The crack era introduced a Molotov cocktail of violence & crime, which Baby Johnny & I thrived in. Oakland was once renowned for its vibrant jazz music; the city was now overshadowed by crack inflicted chaos.

Crumbling buildings, a clear depiction of neglect, neighborhoods decorated with litter, and inhabited by empty, emotionless faces of zombified junkies. Characteristics that hinted at a city suffering a deep-seated social & economic ailment.

Yet to enterprising Crips like us we recognized this volatile situation as a fertile ground to make a fortune. Baby Johnny & I capitalized on this; the streets ran rampant with demand, and we were more than willing to supply. After a few weeks in Oaktown, working around the clock, we amassed an astounding $135,000, an amount equivalent to $368k today. Bidding Oakland adios, we embarked on our voyage back to Los Angeles. Our suitcases stuffed with cash, each dollar a stark reminder of the risks we took, the lives we jeopardized - & the fortune we made.

I should have kept my ass on the move because upon my return to LA, I got cracked. I was arrested for the assault on the Rollin' Foeties. The scent of the 77th division police station was funky like Old McDonald's pig pen, stinging my senses & tingling the edges of my consciousness with disgust. However, fate stepped in swiftly, the authorities lacked enough evidence to pin the crime on me.

Despite Lunchmeat's malicious allegations, they couldn't build a solid case. However, my eventual release didn't indicate an end to my journey. A new day dawned, and a former comrade was now my nemesis, anytime we crossed paths a shootout was inevitable. I had been through a distressing experience, a betrayal that would leave scars on my mind. Yet, I somehow relished it, knowing that each scrape & scar only carved me deeper into a man of unbeatable resilience.

I woke up each day, my scars a constant reminder of the life I led, the risks I took, and the toll it was taking on my fragile existence. I counted my blessings & my mama's prayers for every new day that came because every day was a brush with death. It was a time that, ironically, bled everything but love. The city was a war zone, infested by brutality, drug abuse, and innocent blood spilled too soon.

We were renegades making our own law, out of control, reckless & frighteningly unpredictable. The safety of the community was at our mercy. We were the Five-Deuce Hoover Gangsta Crips, the name that sent shivers down the spine of the average citizen, and rival, the target that the pigs had set their hawkish sight on.

Ken Dogg, as elusive as a phantom, was still on the run evading the iron fist of law enforcement since his daring prison break. The pigs were merciless, nurturing a vendetta against us that crossed lines of legality & morality alike. It had set into motion a relentless manhunt. They had pledged to round up all of us, by hook or by crook, to settle the score. Flipping the script, they turned into gangbangers themselves, ready to frame or murder us in the name of Seventy-Seven.

Were we Living or merely surviving? The line was blurred. Death stalked our every step, glimpses of its grotesque grin reflected in razor-sharp switchblades & gleaming handguns. Violence was a familiar companion while incarceration loomed over us like the rain cloud that followed Charlie Brown. Trapping us in a vicious cycle.

On the contrary 1987 was a milestone year, though soaked with violence, it was the last year we didn't bury any loved ones. In the years prior, the violent streets of Los Angeles snatched several reputables from us. Core members like Joker, Ric Roc, Insane Fish, Sham Rock, Dre Dogg, Boscoe, Big Fat Rat, Killa D, Lil Coke Dogg & Lil Chim became political prisoners with heavy bids ranging from a minimum of nine years to a maximum of life confined within the belly of the beast.

The pillars of our organization crumbled but we stood tall & united & reconstructed from the ruins. We were Fifty Strong with each passing wind we stayed stompdown. With each column that fell another erected in its place to support our structure -Baby Crazy, Big Mike, H'Luv, Baby JoHnny, Pookee, Lil Boo Capone, KiKi, Crib, Big & Lil Red Jr, Stroll, Big & Lil Bam, Lil Madman, FlasH, Baby Dre Dogg, Cuda Bear, oG Half, Loon, Hoova D, Argo, and Devil. Are a few of my loved ones that helped maintain our numbers & morale. Cultivating a new generation of Tiny Locs that became the epitome of fabulous & dangerous, upholding our brand, our lifestyle for years to come.

Los Angeles, was ablaze in a different kind of limelight during a week of Madness beginning on Wednesday, March 30. A day when lofty ideas collided with brutal realities, the drumroll of gang wars, scarring the environment for years to come. It was at the King's Swap Meet, amidst the raucous clatter of vendors striking deals & peddlers hawking their goods, that we unraveled the first thread of an intricate tapestry of chaos. It begins with CeeCee, being shot in the stomach.

The bullet was not just a piece of hot metal; it sparked a series of bloody events. He was carted off to the hospital, whispering the creed of violence under the shimmering L.A. sun, hatred etched deeply in his eyes. As the medical staff CeeCee wheeled into surgery, his injuries were severe, but not life threatening. He would survive the attack but for his recovery he would temporarily require a shit bag. Retaliation was instinct, while he was under the knife, a hit squad was on a mission to settle the score with the Rollin' Foeties, but as shadows of truth began to appear, it turned out the shooter was not from their faction.

It was the boyfriend of a former homegirl that got booted off the set & CeeCee coincidentally ran into her. I always warned homies about the downfalls of a *"put off"*, this is a person that we welcomed into our family, they may know some deep dark secrets or our hideouts, they may be vindictive & seek revenge, they can join enemy factions or become an informant.

The girl was like a deer in headlights, set in a haze of fear at the sight of CeeCee. Her boyfriend, envisioning his wrath due to CeeCee's ruthless reputation, took matters into his own hands. Fearing for her life, he took advantage of the element of surprise, and he shot CeeCee before his wrath could strike down upon the couple.

Thursday night, the last day of March, under the dim streetlights of the Tray, we gathered near a sizzling BBQ pit where the old timers sold plates of food, the air hung heavy with the smell of smoky ribs, forty ounces, lovely joints. There's a cultural rule in South Central during these times Crips & Bloods don't mix like two dicks & no bitch, find yourself in serious shit, like the late great Biggie Smalls once said. So, when this random fool hopped out his low-rider, dressed in what Crips called *"dead red"*, from head to toe to get some barbecue, his presence screamed Blood, and my soul replied Killer.

The rival gang member had trespassed on Crip territory, painting a big red target on his back & unfortunately for him, we forgave no man that trespassed against us. An act of daring defiance, an ill-intentioned step taken with malice & bravado, had harsh consequences. Eager to protect our turf, one of the Tiny Loks challenged the Blood, but chaos enveloped the scene like a vengeful ghost. The encounter ended with the red ragger being robbed of everything, his money, his car, and his life.

The aftermath of Wednesday's & Thursday's abrupt violence was still fresh in our minds; however, the climax of this tragic week reached its peak on Friday April 1st. Good Friday, the irony of the name was not lost on anyone. It was a day etched permanently in the fabric of our memory, not for one of Joker's infamous April fool's pranks, or the

Holy Holiday but the Good Friday Shootings. A two-fold incident in which both Hoover Gangstas & Foeties were hit by unknown adversaries & the scandal that occurred in its wake.

As I chilled outside Naomi's place, gang-hanging, catching vibes with my loved ones. Naomi's boombox blaring the distinctive sound of NWA. Amid Gangsta rap & mad Hoover Love, the night violently disrupted when a volley of bullets hailed at us from a passing vehicle. We returned fire but we suffered a casualty. Lil Cee Dogg was hit in his arm. Life that day had staged a grim act, a sequel of the previous night's confrontation, but a greater revelation was on the way.

There was word on the street of a mass shooting at a Rollin' Foety house party on 46th & Raymond Avenue, just minutes before we were attacked, and the rumors were that Hoover did it. The bullets that wreaked havoc upon the lives of the Foeties, our archenemies, were uncomfortably familiar. They matched the ones that wounded Lil Cee Dogg!

We were attacked by the same gunmen, but the Foeties losses were more severe - one dead homie & a dozen wounded, including an innocent 4-year-old boy ensnared in the crossfire. It was a horrendous act of violence, second only to the infamous 54th street massacre. The recent bloody events in Los Angeles monopolized the attention of the local media & government. The tension was escalating to uncontrollable heights, and there was a desperate call to action by the mayor to put an end to this. The mayor commissioned Chief Gates to *'clean up the streets.'*

That very evening the pigs made a sudden overnight raid. A battalion of over a thousand officers swarmed into our district, as invasive as a swarm of hornets, razed through our homes, inflicted unimaginable chaos & horror. The pigs beat down KiKi & various homies, they made over 175 arrests & interrogated over 600 people in a single sweep. The raid resulted in a stool pigeon amongst our ranks.

The manic week finally ended, but the wounds it opened & the scars it left in the heart of Los Angeles were profound & irrevocable. The guns began to cool off, but their echoes haunted the streets, rekindling dark memories & serving as stark reminders of the blood-soaked week where vengeance held everyone at gunpoint.

Two weeks later, The Chief of Police raided the set once again with over 300 officers & personally arrested Lil Cee Dogg, got on the news & called him a monster, and a lunatic. Labeled as a hardened criminal at the tender age of sixteen. Lil Cee Dogg was just a boy when he was framed & persecuted, the purity of that holiday forever tainted with death & his unwarranted life sentence.

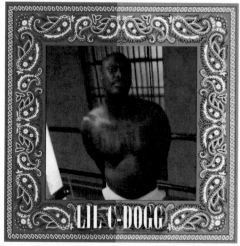

Lil Cee Dogg managed to become a Hoover Hall of Famer for his unmatched Hoover love. He stayed solid, they wanted to pursue the death penalty, but they spared him due to his age. Despite being screwed over with a life sentence, he shielded his comrades, taking on additional charges to protect his loved ones from a similar fate. His actions defined selflessness & his sacrifice protected so many people.

On that note it became a part of my agenda every time I was freed from these prison gates, the first thing I would do was send my Groove, Lil Cee Dogg a package. It was my way of paying homage to the sacrifice he had made for us, for our tribe, and for the G-code we had vowed to honor.

The brazen assault on Hoover Gangsta, and our enemies, the Foeties, conjured a plethora of questions. Conflicting theories ricocheted amongst our thoughts, like a stray bullet with no name. Could it truly have been the Van Ness Gangstas, our shared foe at the root of the attacks, or was there a more insidious force at play? Could it have been the LAPD, infamous for disguising themselves as gangbangers & instigating gang wars?

In the aftermath of the Good Friday Shootings & March Madness, Los Angeles wept under its hushed sobs. Its heartache whispered stories of blind conflict, mindless violence, endless suspicion, and unjust blame. For how long would the city bleed its children? How many more CeeCee's & Lil Cee Dog's would suffer? To live & die in LA, the violence & chaos of the week had woven a gruesome tapestry, painting an unforgiving portrait of a city at war with itself.

"Teenager Gets Life Term in Good Friday Shootings"
A teenage gang member was sentenced to life in prison Wednesday for one of the worst gang attacks in Los Angeles, the so-called Good Friday shootings that killed one person & wounded six others in 1988.
-LA TIMES

Death never came to our doors unannounced but always left a lasting impact. June 20th, 1988, also witnessed the detrimental death of a highly esteemed & beloved member, Charles Ticer more affectionately remembered as Big CeeCee, a renowned enforcer with a chilling reputation. He was a colossal fixture within our ranks that was respected & loved.

CeeCee was admired by all of us from the Hriginals to the Tiny Loks & provoked fear in the hearts of his enemies. He upheld his pledge to carry forward the image & uphold the values of Hoover Gangsta. His bravery was undoubted & his loyalty unwavering. He was a genuine leader & frontliner, leading by example, and owning all the qualities that epitomized FDHGC.

CeeCee's reputation was not solely based on his Gangsta IQ & leadership qualities, but his trademark hostility. He possessed that Hoover aggression & displayed valor in the face of adversity. Tales of his exploits echoed through the grimy alleyways of the Fifties. Every move he made, every word he uttered became a part of Crip folklore, building his reputation as a feared & revered Kiwé warrior.

He was an urban legend who once toppled three red rags in a single night. On another infamous occasion he pulled off the impossible & improbable, we've all heard of the old saying killing two birds with one stone, CeeCee once killed two Bloods with one bullet, etching his name in the Hoover Hall of Fame.

"Live by the gun & die by the gun."
- Tupac Shakur

However, life's certainty is its unpredictability. On an ill-fated night in June 1988, H'Luv & CeeCee were ambushed while visiting some females around the corner from King's Swap meet. My comrades engaged in a vicious gunfight, but CeeCee was shot during the battle, and unfortunately succumbed to his wounds. Our first loss in the Hoover versus Foeties conflict. This was a severe blow that ignited the fire of vengeance & escalated the war to new heights.

The aura of invincibility that he had created was shattered, and our tribe lost a crucial vertebra in our backbone. The death of a devoted warrior of only twenty years of age left a wound that would take years to heal. Retelling the legend of Big CeeCee is a mirror reflecting a world not many dared to stare into. A world that thrives on loyalty & is fueled by respect, power, and fear. A world where heroes are not made by comic book sketches or the silver screen but tested in the crucible of life & death. A world where Big CeeCee was more than a name, he was an institute, representation of power, influence, and unwavering loyalty.

The homie was a hero, a symbol of strength & greatness to his peers & a nightmare to his foes. Most importantly, he was, and forever will be, a central figure in our history. His tales of bravery, and his formidable skills as a hitman. He rivaled that of the legendary Big Pookee. If gangbanging was a sport, Pookee is equivalent to Lebron James, our all-time leading scorer, and CeeCee, ranks as our Kareem Abdul-Jabbar.

Meanwhile in the Los Angeles County jail, a unique universe, teeming with distinct personalities. Among these were Big Fat Rat, Chim, and Boscoe, along with Hoover Sam, Tiny Moo, and Head from the One-oh-Seven Hoover. There were also reputable grooves like Lil Snoop from Eight-Tray Hoover, X-Ray & Droop from Nine-Deuce Hoover, Hawkeye from Nine-Foe Hoover, Hoover Jay & Huron from the Seven-Foe Hoover. Two tiers were filled with members from all numbers of the Hoover tribes & our allies such as the Gangstas, Gardenas, and Long Beach Insanes.

The Crip modules 4700 & 4800, had to be shut down because of the horrific occurrences that were reported. People being torched, others being raped, horror stories that were too brutal for the faint of heart. The place held an echo of chaos that could not be squashed.

Amidst all this turmoil, a member of Six-Nine East Coast got transferred into unit 2123 after a drive-by shooting. The jail's upper tier was home to seven members of Coast, while the Hoovers occupied the bottom tier. The Crip hierarchy within the module was overseen by Hoover Sam & Huron, who strived to keep law & order.

They demanded that there should be no shanks in the module, and all disputes between inmates must be resolved by head up fights, no stabbings. To ensure adherence to this rule, they walked around with socks & bags to collect any hidden weapons from the Crips. However, this rule didn't sit well with everybody, specifically the new intake from Six-Nine East Coast, Lil Doc Thone, who straight up refused to surrender his banger.

This act of defiance created tension within the tier. It didn't help the situation now that Scooby from Seven-Foe was placed in the module. Lil Doc possessed scars from bullets inflicted by the Hoovers & held a grudge against Scooby. The fact that Scooby was there when Lil Doc got hit up was the motivation for his vendetta. It reached a boiling point; Lil Doc wanted his issue with Scooby in the dayroom. Hoover Sam & Huron try to keep the peace on the tier & tell Lil Doc to leave that beef on the street.

Huron & Hoover Sam tried their best to keep the peace but managing this intricate network of Crips in a setting filled with hostility was no easy task. Every day presented a new challenge & unforeseen circumstances, keeping everyone in a state of heightened alert & ready to ride.

Lil Doc wanted revenge, he had a score to settle, deaf to their counsels of peace. He didn't give a damn about their advice, he swaggered into the day room with a heart pulsing for a showdown & a shank with Scooby name on it. Lil Doc tried to creep up on Scooby, a shiny glint of metal in his hand revealing his intent. Unbeknownst to him, Big Huron spotted his sneak attack.

The result, a thunderous haymaker that connected with the back of his head, sending him crashing face-first in the middle of the dayroom. The atmosphere turned battle royale in an instant. Boscoe & Chim leaped into combat & the rest of the Hoovers swarmed in like a pack of wolves. Cheers of insolence erupted around the room –

"Get him!" "Hoover stomp him!" "Beat his ass!" "Kill him!"

The sadistic chorus was deafening, growing louder as every member of the Hoovers swarmed over him. It was a terrifying spectacle of brute force & tribal ferocity. As the Hoover stomp rained down on Lil Doc Thone. He managed to wiggle free from the dogg pile. He swung his shank around, a desperate attempt to fend off the Hoover lynch mob.

Suddenly the East Coast calvary jumped into the brawl, trying to even out the one-sided battle. Their fate was no better, serving only as more punching bags for the irate Hoovers. In the chaos, an unlikely weapon appeared. Tiny Moo, snatched off an East Coast's prosthetic leg & beat him & his homies with it.

Meanwhile, Huron, the catalyst of the brawl, found an opportunity to deliver what would be the final blow. He hit Doc, fracturing his skull with a mop wringer. The broad crack of metal echoed through the room, putting an abrupt halt to the pandemonium. Blood gushed out from Lil Doc's head, painting the grimy floors a dreadful red. Dazed & in pain, Lil Doc fell unconscious, signaling the end of the brutal brawl.

This cruel brawl bore testament to the animalistic savagery that thrived within penitentiary walls. It was a stark reminder that the lines between civility & barbarity were blurred far more than one would like to admit. Today, the day room wasn't just a recreational area. It was a lawless battlefield, a place of graphic violence & inhumanity, where a man's life meant no more than his ability to fight, and his worth as a human being was as disposable as the weapons they wielded.

"Fuck all these niggas, we ain't Crips," Lil Snoop declared. *"We Criminals,"* they proclaimed with a brash swagger.

It was an assertion of a newfound self-identity, a bold departure from existing alliances, and an unabashed embrace of a more independent persona inspired by KRS-One's song, *"Criminal Minded."*

These were mere sentences uttered in the afterglow of victory, a new alias for the set like *"Hoover Groover"*, but within the perspective of some members, it represented far more. There was no formal meeting or democratic vote for Hoover to denounce the Crips. It was a minority group's epiphany, born from a sense of grandeur as most Hoovers were imprisoned for serious crimes like murder & kidnapping. Their crimes defined their status, their status informed their identity, and their identity paved the way for the rise of the Hoover Criminal.

As Hoover Gangstas we remained dedicated & devoted to our foundation, the same way we refused to subscribe to Hoover Crip. We are Hoover Gangstas, we went through hell & high water to earn our name & we won't change it for anyone. We have always been on an island as HGC, and we are fine with that. Whether Crippin' or Criminalism, we pledge our allegiance to Hoover first. One must remember that the Hoover collective did not turn our backs on Crippin' but a generation chose to separate themselves from the Crip dog-eat-Crip dog world.

In essence, this pivotal moment within the confines of the Men's Central Jail sparked the emergence of a new generation. A generation that introduced one of the most savage & ruthless movements in our city. It is imperative to understand how power structures can shift, where evolution is often a byproduct of survival & superiority. Incidents can rapidly mutate to breed a new lineage of dominance & power, lending the reins of the game to the most assertive, a lesson taught by this historic brawl which birthed the Hoover Criminals in the forthcoming years.

While in the world, I cherished the taste of freedom that I had been savoring for a year since my release from prison. Experiencing liberty after confinement didn't exactly evolve into a smooth transition, but rather manifested itself into an uncertain journey marked with unexpected twists drenched in the darker shades of my crazy life.

The infamous Figueroa, shimmering under the neon lights, was the center stage for this sinister ballet. The company I kept, the world I inhabited, had its own set of rules, far removed from what society believed proper. Part of my survival scheme involved extortion & robbery.

One night, our focus was on a pimp named Hoe Stroll at my favorite motel, the Nighty Nite. Earning his living by exploiting the desperate ladies of the night who were caught in the hard knock life selling pussy. The fool had fallen behind on his rent. Aiding me with the collection was my Hoover-in-arms, Stillbill. A playa by trade but a Hoover Gangsta through & through, a menace just as cutthroat as myself. We cornered the sleazy pimp. We roughed him up, pistol whipped him & slapped his hoes around convincing him to cough up the money he owed. We asserted Hoover dominance & made it clear that late payments were not accepted.

GANGSTA T, STILLBILL, LIL FAT RAT

As I lay in drunken slumber in my bed, the sound of heavy banging at my door jolted me awake. Thinking it was hotel staff demanding my departure. I hollered back rudely, threatening them.

"Leave me the fuck alone before I shoot through the door."

Exhausted & irritated, I fell back into an uneasy sleep. Trouble has a knack for finding my black ass, and on Figueroa escaping it was often an impossible dream. What waited for me on the other side of that slumber was a harsher reality. Abruptly awoken again, this time I opened my eyes to a startling sight - a firearm, a badge, and the unforgiving gaze of a cracker ass cop. The punk ass pig, his face hard & eyes glaring, ready take my ass to jail.

Hoe Stroll returned the favor in his own way. He had reported us to the boys. The figurative trap door beneath my feet gave way, and just like that, I was back to my second home — the Los Angeles

535 | P a g e

County Jail. Booked for strong-arm robbery, assault, illegal gun possession, and an alleged act of extortion. I was looking at a grim 15-year sentence, an outcome worsened by a looming parole violation.

My first instinct, my only resort, was to contact Big Mama. I urged her to let Pookee know the situation & to look out for my calls. Pookee, a man of few words but with a knack for problem-solving.

I finally got in touch with the homie In a hushed tone, I informed him about the rat, my voice barely audible over the droning of the TV set behind me. The silence that stretched out between us seemed to drag on for an eternity before I heard his voice again.

"Don't worry Big Homie," Pookee said, and I could hear the unmistakable sound of determination in his voice. *"I'm going to take care of this shit for you. Just sit tight & Ce Cool."*

The days blurred into weeks, each passing moment highlighting the fickle nature of time. However, one such day captured a surprising shift in my circumstances. My lawyer returned with unexpected news that filled the air with a potential breath of freedom.

The District Attorney could not find the plaintiff, effectively throwing out the more severe charges. Though I still faced a year for the parole violation on gun possession, it felt much better having light at the end of the tunnel.

Heaving a sigh of relief, I felt immeasurable gratitude towards Pookee. As soon as I could, I thanked him, uncertain of how to repay the debt of his intervention. His response was dressed in humility, *"It's all good, big homie,"* he said to me, *"just another day at the office, cuH."*

Pookee didn't elaborate, and in hindsight, perhaps I was better off not knowing. All I knew was that Hoe Stroll had vanished like a phantom. Whatever strings Pookee had pulled & whatever actions he had taken were shrouded in mystery. Not a soul crossed paths with Hoe Stroll again. Whether it was destiny, divine intervention, or Pookee's meddling, I walked away with a newfound prospect on life.

Through my time on the streets, I have come to understand the paradox of a protector like Pookee. He is both guardian & avenger, the most delicate & violent manifestation of love & loyalty. Like a hero from those ancient mythological tales, he embodies the eternal code of honor & kinship that all true warriors cherish in their heart of hearts. Pookee's compassion, refusal to let the struggle change him, and unwavering loyalty are reminders that the spirit of protection & friendship should shine brightest in one's most trying times.

Even though another gun charge was added to my criminal record, another notch in a rap sheet that was starting to look more like a James Baldwin novel. I was thankful to have friends I could count on like my nigga Big Pookee. I knew with absolute certainty that Pookee's loyalty was embedded in the very essence of his being.

Today, as I pen down this piece of my life, I am reminded of the treacherous cycle of life as a gangbanger. It's a life in which one wrong turn can lead to unforgiving consequences. I am now a man of God, who believes in the power of resilience & redemption. For those who have walked the path I once treaded, I hope my story serves as a relentless reminder that the past does not dictate the future. The struggle for a better tomorrow may be steep with challenges, but it's an uphill battle worth fighting.

I had to spend the rest of 1988 in LA county. Over the upcoming months it was like a surge of Hoover Gangstas coming into the module. My destiny became entwined with the everyday brawls & tugs of loyalty that were attached to doing hard time like locks & keys.

In my last few stints my bids were plagued by grim violence & bloodshed. Trapped within a sprawling vortex of savagery & cruelty, we were jigsaw pieces pieced recklessly together. The county was our newest battleground, another war zone in our tribal dynamics.

Someway, somehow, I managed to keep my nose clean. Rather than the piercing edge of a shank that I was so accustomed to, I found a more potent weapon: responsibility. In an unexpected twist of fate, I earned the status of tier trustee. The position gave me exclusive access to the kitchen.

Once limited & constrained, my world exploded with access to a wealth of resources. The kitchen was a gold mine. Sharpened knives & pieces of metal bristling with potential to morph into lethal shanks. I got access to yeast, sugar & fruits essential ingredients for brewing potent jailhouse hooch & prunos. These items granted me unseen power & control within the prison's parched economy. The kitchen was a case study in resourceful entrepreneurship, with a treasure chest of coveted contraband that equated to a gold mine.

It was the fall of 1988 & the testosterone & machismo on Hoover street did not fade – Baby Charles from Eleven-Deuce, and my fellow Hriginal Blacc Charles got in to a fist to cusp. Blacc Charles emerged victorious. The next day the calendar flipped to November 2nd.

In our world it was a holiday, affectionately called 'Eleven-Deuce Day', being a day of reverence & strength for the Eleven-Deuces. This year, they decided to elevate the celebration to a whole new level, groovin' in a shimmering black limousine down 54th street.

Their show of power & supremacy filled the air with tension – a simmering stew of grudges & revenge in the autumn air. As the limousine closed in, Cadillac Bob, Coke Dogg, and Blacc Charles were outside of the donut stand on the Foe, as the limo pulled over across the street. Big Mac, Baby Charles, and a few more of the Eleven-Deuces jump out!

Their faces masked an alarming blend of Hoover aggression & vindictive malice. The mundanity of that Wednesday evening turned into a scene straight out of a Hollywood action film. Gunshots exploded in the air like lightning bolts, teeth clenched, hearts pounding - the Eleven-Deuces started firing. There was no time to think, no moment to process the danger – our very survival was on the line.

Instinctively the Five-Deuces returned fire. Showering bullets served to intimidate the Eleven-Deuces. Yet, amidst the chaos, the limo driver, who presumably had some inner sense of self-preservation or fear, decided to bolt, leaving the Eleven-Deuces stranded amidst the crossfire. Seeing their ride disappear into the night, the Eleven-Deuces started chasing it.

Miraculously & thankfully, none of my hot headed Hoovers hit each other. Perhaps there was an invisible shield of brotherhood, or maybe it was pure luck. Still, it was a stark reminder of the peril that looms over us, a vivid picture of Hoover street's rawness. We survive & strive amidst the struggle, hoping, one day, for a more peaceful existence.

Yet, as the sun set on another Eleven-Deuce Day, we were still standing, a testament to our resilient spirit in the face of danger, underpinned by a creed of power & respect. The skirmish also came with a lesson & an understanding. Incidents like this became infractions that had zero tolerance. No Hoover should ever raise a lethal weapon at another Groove in good standing, regardless of what comes after their

H. Any & all gripes should be settled with fades & ended with shared respect & not vendetta.

As the calendar turned its back on 1988 & galloped towards February 1989, the cells housed familiar faces Boscoe, Fat Rat & Lil Chim. A familiar resonation echoed in the grand arrival of Lil Madman, Pookee, Lil Hoova Dee, Sham Rock, Half, Jaystone2, John-John, Lil Spook, Chino & Gangsta Tee embedded themselves in the redefined narrative of harmony. Each arrival, in this cocktail of chaos & brotherhood, resonated like an anthem of mixed emotions, making an unexpected Fifty Crip family reunion.

Baker row was transformed under the weight of our collective identity. It echoed the voice of our shared experience, turning into an oasis of Hoover Gangsterism in the arid landscape of incarceration. As Five Deuce Hoover Gangsta Crips flooded the module, it adopted a new name, a new face, and a new identity. *"The Fifties,"* it was christened, enveloping two tiers full of Hoover Gangstas, brothers united in adversity.

Tensions began to arise with the Compton Crips, and an eerie cold war loomed on the horizon. However, the real challenge ensued from within the Groove. The Seven-Foes & Eight-Tray Hoovers still harbored resentment towards us. The burning point remained the 'Gangsta' nestled in our name, which they saw as an affront to the Hoover legacy. The Tray-Foes believed themselves to be the beating heart & resilient soul of the Hoover tribe. To them, we were an encroach, a stain sullying their name, the bottom of the totem pole.

When in the majority, Hoover Crips exploited their numbers to muscle us. They would gang up & rat pack our lil homies or try to intimidate them into claiming HCG. It was a clear demonstration of dominance, a power play to assert their alpha status & snuff out Hoover Gangstas, but we never folded. We fought for our respect & for our foundation. They hated it but the Fifties was tight as virgin pussy & proud, prideful as Napoleon Bonaparte & the French regime. As we approached our tin anniversary, we remained resilient & strong.

In between skirmishes we were dealt with a whirlwind of tragedies that hit us like a tidal wave. Obliterating the tranquility of our set in the world & in lockdown. A close ally & young homie only 16 years old, Lil T-Dogg was mysteriously shot & killed in Hollywood. The circumstances surrounding his murder were as cryptic as they were chilling; the case remains an unsolved mystery to this day, a silenced truth shrouded in a myriad of theories & whispers.

As shocking as Lil T-Dogg's death was, another tragedy crept close on its heels, shattering the illusion of us surviving the turbulence unscathed. Bobby Harris, more affectionately known as Cadillac Bob, my day one, my fellow Hriginal, encountered a fate most horrendous. Cadillac Bob held a reputation defined by fear & respect, a symbol of unwavering loyalty & an embodiment of Five-Deuce.

After his release from the county, Cadillac Bob had ventured into sinister territories, waging a war against rival drug dealers, exercising brutal tactics of kidnapping & extortion. In the unforgiving battlefield marred by crime & vice, he, unfortunately, fell into the hands of an impassioned adversary, leading to an outcome that was as unforeseen as it was dreadful.

One such kidnapping scheme spiraled catastrophically out of control. The feds ambushed him when he appeared to pick up the 6 figure ransom at the intersection of Gage Ave & 64th street, a moment etched in my memory, although I was far from the scene. The echoes of the violence & pandemonium at that crossroads reached even the confined quarters of my cell.

Cadillac Bob, the fighter that he was, attempted a hasty escape amidst the chaos but was gunned down brutally in his tracks by federal agents who brutally shot him 3 times in the head. The demise of Cadillac Bobby etched a stark line of gloom in our brethren. A prominent figure within our ranks, a beloved homeboy, and a highly respected Loc, his death was an unspeakable loss to us all. It was a piercing blow, one that reverberated throughout the set.

DIRTY CURT, H'LUV, CADILLAC BOB, LEEK

Our brothers were snatched from the present, ripped from the fabric of the blue rags that held us together. Their memory left behind a vacuum, filled with an overpowering sense of loss & longing. Reflections of their faces filled our minds; words left unsaid echoed in our ears, the laughter unshared, the tears unshed. Their farewell was not fathomed, their departure left us hardened, feeding into the volcano of rage within each of us. They were gone but not forgotten, their spirits etched forever in Hoover Gangsta history.

As I concluded my sentence in 1989, I stepped into a world vastly different from the one I had left behind. The streets, once a symbol of unity & solace, now felt barren, stripped of their vibrant character. The tragedies of 1988 & 1989 had carved wrinkles onto the face of our fraternity, leaving scars that reminded us of our harshest trials.

My brother Spookee & I were two sides of the same coin, orbiting around each other in our own multiverse filled with uncertainty. Our worlds revolved around each other, yet we were constantly the butt of life's cruel joke, with a sprinkle of bad timing. Each step we took seemed to lead us astray from the other. Much like a foul game of tag, the day I was liberated from the county, Spookee was dragged back into the system because of some petty bullshit charge. We were united through separation, an iron curtain between us, yet undeniably our lives were interconnected through turmoil & resilience.

We left behind materialistic things to remind each other of the other's presence. Spookee, in his absence, entrusted me with the keys to his freedom, his cherished automobiles, and his apartment. Similarly, when fate escorted me into a world devoid of choice, I would reciprocate the gesture, leaving all I held dear to him. These items were not merely possessions but were infused with the raw emotion of brotherly bond & promises of shared tomorrows.

We were brothers from the same womb, yet amongst the lot of siblings only Spookee & I walked the rough path of street life. Call it a defiant act of rebellion, or perhaps a manifestation of our unwavering determination, but we ventured into the perilous vortex of the underworld. This foray was not a one-man expedition but rather, a duo endeavor taken up to form an invisible shield around each other, pledging to weather the storm together, even if it meant getting drenched in the process.

Contrary to popular belief, alliances, as well our constant quest for dominance & survival, are not confined to political relations. They exist & shape the course of life within worlds away from political spheres on the streets of cities & towns around the globe. I think back to the last few years of the Hoover-Broadway alliance—a coalition that once made rivals tremble in fear, but ultimately lost its grandeur to the cold hands of the grim reaper & lady justice.

As time went on & the pages of history turned, we were forced to part ways, taking with us the memories of our alliance. A once indestructible bond met an untimely demise, but the legacy of our joint venture will endure for generations to come. The once unbreakable bond began to fracture under the weight of politics & external influences, and soon enough, the chasm between Hoover & Broadway grew wider & deeper.

The Five-Deuce alliance lasted for little more than a decade, as we operated as a united front under the FD banner, fighting side by side. Together, we made a powerful statement, not only to our rivals but also to the city: that there is strength in unity, and in that unity, our cause was indomitable.

Our long-standing sibling rivalry with the Hoover Crips began to wane & as our fellowship blossomed with them, we began to fall in line with Westside sets like Eight-Trey Gangstas, ScHool Yards, Gardenas & Playboys. Our relationship with the Broadways began to deteriorate as they began to form bonds with Eleven-Deuce Broadway, and Eastside sets like Avalon & Kitchen. Powerful currents of change swept us in separate directions, like the Pacific ocean's undertow in unrelenting hurricane winds. The story of the once united Hoover-Broadway chronicles a transformation within a decade. What began as a united front gradually deteriorated to infighting & realignment. Spawning the unification of the Hoovers & the Broadways.

CHAPTER FIFTY-ONE:
"LOVE AFTER LOCK-UP"

When I back on the streets I had money on my mind. Out of all the things I had on my to do list, NUMBER ONE was to find Big Mama. She was my rock, never missing a visit, always writing me letters, and ensuring that I would never be forgotten. Big Mama deserved all my love & devotion, so finding her trumped than anything else.

My eyes saw more clearly, and my heart became more available when I finally saw the depth of her commitment. Big Mama was A-1 not just towards her man but towards all the homies. She probably accepted a million dollars in collect calls from the Locs over the years. My heart in human form, the love of my life, She stuck by me when others turned their backs. She supported me through thick & thin, always ready with an encouraging word or a comforting embrace when it seemed like the world was crashing down around me.

I went straight to 54th street, but she was not where I had left her; Big Cee, told me she recently moved to the Valley with a somber face. A sense of discontent crept into me, painting my emotions in strokes of shadowy hues as I returned home. In between war stories, jokes, and the contagious banter with Shithead Ted & ScHoolBoy, a longing quietly took root within me, a hope to see the face of the woman who warmed my heart even during the harshest winters.

Suddenly a vehicle pulled up that grabbed everyone's attention. Stepping out slow, with calculated grace was Big Mama, the delicate vision I'd been craving since the gates of confinement clanged shut behind me. Her demeanor was a strange cocktail of shyness, a twang of apprehension perhaps, and a euphoric joy that couldn't quite camouflage itself. Her smile illuminated her face, as we locked eyes, our gaze echoing the innocent curiosity & affection reminiscent of puppy love.

The looks we exchanged were spellbound–a silent ballet of expressions that sang volumes where words failed. Her glowing eyes held thousands of unspoken words, reflecting emotions that eerily mirrored my own. Her desire was a striking presence in the spring air, a desire for Mr. Marcus that I reciprocated with equal passion.

I shattered the silence like a broken mirror as I complimented her radiant beauty. A blush rushed to her melanin cheeks, transforming her giggle into the sweetest sound of the evening. Surrendering my cool, I complimented her beauty.

She retorted, *"I'm glad you like your coming home gift, big daddy."*

The genuine delight radiating from her was impossible to ignore. She then went on to express her admiration for the swag in my step, something she fondly dubbed as the *"good dick walk."* The first time I heard it, a sudden burst of child-like giggles erupted from me, shit she had Big Boo blushing. The term was so amusing to me that it was hard to believe it was really a thing within the female community.

As the irresistible rhythms of Marvin Gaye's *"Let's Get It On"* serenade us filling my boudoir with its sensual soundtrack. I dimmed the brightness of the track lighting, painting my bedroom with hues of tranquility & romance. Across the room, there she was - Big Mama - standing as a testament of patience, grace, and steadfast love that had flourished despite the harshest trials.

At that moment, the lighting danced upon her ebony skin, igniting a captivating glow as if mirroring the beauty of the full moon. Her dark, star-like eyes twinkling with joy & anticipation were mesmerizing to behold. When our gaze locked, my heart stopped, my breath became scarce, and everything around us seemed to cease to exist. It was like the world had frozen, and in that moment, nothing else mattered but her.

I sat on the edge of my bed, and pulled her closer, bridging the gap between us, letting the warmth of our bodies overlay the coldness of the space surrounding us. As I wrapped my fingers around her waist, I secured her voluptuous body against mine. I held her with the fear of losing my world if I let go even a single bit. The raw emotions coursing through me during this beautiful, yet overwhelming union begged to not go.

Each touch was electric, every look held a promise, and each whisper held praise, as I worshiped her body like a goddess from head to toe. The sensation of her soft body against my rock-hard physique was a contrast so delicate that it was poetic. Her head rested against the crook of my shoulder, and a soft sigh escaped her lips - a whisper of relief, a melody of happiness.

Our eyes locked & our hearts speaking the language of love silently, seen only in the form of a single tear rolling down her cheek. It wasn't a coincidence or a moment of weakness. They were tears of joy & contention matching my thoughts & emotions, affirming loud & clear that she had been savoring & awaiting this moment in her heart all along. The years of waiting, of longing, of dreaming had culminated in this spectacular & magical encounter. She was just a young girl looking for love & found it on Hoover Street.

> *"Love finds you in the strangest places, and hope*
> *clings to us in the nooks & crannies we never*
> *think to look."*
> *- Shelly Crane, Wide Spaces*

Our love was celebrated for the first time that night, as two lost souls found solace in each other's arms. Through the darkness lit by the gentle glow of candles, we embarked on an intimate journey of exploration & connection. After eight years of yearning, filled with heartfelt letters, collect calls & painful patience. It was finally time to justify our love in the sincerest of ways.

"Wanting, needing, waiting for you to justify my love. I'm open & ready for you to justify my love"
-Madonna, Justify My Love

Love can sometimes be cliché, but that night, the love between Big Mama & I became more than just a word. The strongest trials had been weathered, replaced with the promise of a union just as strong. A sultry tango of fire & desire, seasoned with sweet kisses, gentle caresses, soft whispers, and lustful sighs. Every touch was like a verse of poetry in our love story, each moan a testament to the depth of our emotional & physical connection. The years of waiting had ignited a fiery passion between us, a flame that only strengthened as the night lengthened.

With Big Mama, it was more than just a physical attraction. It was a meeting of minds, a fusion of spirits, an intertwining of destinies. Our bodies grooved to the slow jams, our forbidden dance tracing patterns that mirrored our souls, leaving imprints on our hearts. The love we made that night was pure, raw, and invigorating; a testament to the power of patience & the strength of our connection built over years of trials & tribulations.

This first act of love making had a transformative power, with its completion, we emerged as two halves of a whole, experiencing a sense of belonging, a sense of unity that was previously unknown. In this act we had created an indestructible bond – a bond as strong as diamond, as delicate as a spider's web - fearless & unflinching, forged in the crucible of shared experiences & adversity.

"This is just the beginning, baby," I whispered into her ear.

My voice was barely more than a soft echo in the tranquil stillness. I could feel her essence seeping into my soul, becoming an eternal part of me. Big Mama was my past, my present, and would undoubtedly be my future. She became my lover, my confidante, my rock; & the woman I would share the rest of my life with. The memory of this night will always be etched deeply in the canvas of my mind, an ode to the resilient power of our love - a love that unknowingly began at a house party.

A pure love that was hard-fought, that had seen the face of the hardest times but never wavered. A love that had faced distance longer than miles but did not shake. It was this love between us that was consummated that night. Big Mama had earned her spot as my number one lady, and over the years to come, our love would continue to flourish. We started a family together, and our first love child was born later that year, a true testament to the love & passion we had shared that night. We are inseparable, and there is nothing that could come between us, not even these prison walls.

Upon sobering up from our night of bliss, I dove headfirst into the streets, and it wasn't long before the money matched my rank as I was an integral part of the operation. I was living large, with more money than I knew what to do with. With every high comes a low, and the life I had chosen wasn't the safest. I walked a tightrope between fast cash & constant danger - a fact that I was reminded of more than once during my time in the game. This was the cost of doing business, and I was willing to pay it if it meant keeping my family living large.

My family's love became my lighthouse during the darkest of times, and I attribute my survival in this dangerous game to my lady's unwavering love & support. They say that good things come to those who wait, and my life is living proof of that. The best thing that has ever happened to me, my number one lady, is waiting for me on the other side of those prison gates. I thank my lucky stars every day that I found her, for she has made my life richer than any amount of money ever could. Big Mama has never stopped riding for me & has stayed by my side since day one. She is the most devoted woman I ever knew. This woman visited me weekly with my kids at every single penitentiary I was placed in.

I messed it up with this wonderful woman & our beautiful family. I was in denial that I was in love with her. She gave me an ultimatum; she said it was the whole family or nothing. I chose nothing when I chose the streets, I ended up with a lot of heartache & regret, but she still made me feel loved & honored through my most turbulent times.

She is the best homegirl, my best friend, and over the years she blessed me with 3 wonderful kids, Boo, Stink & Nay-Nay. She always kept me close to my kids & always took care of us. I should have married her sooner, but instead I was caught up in my love affair with Crippin'.

The Hoo'lettes, La Giggles, Hoover Kim, and H'Vette, were fierce young ladies that lived by the G-code. One evening they journeyed to the eastside to visit H'vette's boyfriend from Foe-Tray Gangsta. They were clad in their set colors, and Hoover Gangsta uniform. On their way back to the set they made an impromptu stop to put in some work as they passed through the territory of the Eastside Blood Stone Villains.

Red rags fluttered in the wind - a sign of our archenemies, the Bloods. Without a moment's hesitation, the Hoo'lettes leaped into action, mercilessly opening fire on the B-doggs. In our ruthless, chaotic world we inhabited, it was on-sight, when we saw enemies. Whether you feel it was wrong or right, doesn't matter because this trigger-happy response was the norm. It was fight or flight, kill or be killed.

However, the red rags weren't slippin', they were trippin'! Returning fire, the streets filled with bullets & bravado. It was in this intense exchange that disaster struck. A bullet struck H'Vette causing her to lose control of the car, resulting in a catastrophic crash in the heart of Bloodstone Villain territory. With their car totaled & the potential of enemies hot on their trail, they were wounded warriors stranded behind enemy lines.

Their injuries seared through them brutally, a painful testament to their loyalty & courage. In a desperate attempt to stem the bleeding, they used their blue bandannas as makeshift bandages. Although each breath was a battle, they remained defiant, evidence of their unwavering allegiance. They were in a perilous situation, trapped between a rock & a hard place.

That was when I got the call. In the middle of receiving an epic blow job, I received the somber news of my homegirl's predicament. I knew as I heard their pleas that it was time for some action. I put everything on hold, my world paused as I was reminded of the harsh realities that we often escape in moments of sexual healing.

Their safety was my primary concern, and nothing else mattered in that instant. With vigor renewed, I loaded my trusty AK-47, its metallic consistency providing a bleak comfort in a world gone awry. Within moments, I was in my Cadillac, ready to breach the lion's den, speeding to where my loved ones awaited salvation.

The journey was nothing short of a nerve-wracking venture into Damu corridors. Every turn was a potential ambush, every car a possible enemy. Navigating through the BSV's, I was a lone soldier infiltrating enemy lines. After what felt like an eternity, I found my way to them. It was a strenuous reality to witness these young ladies, formidable Crip'lettes in their own right, nursing their injuries, their iconic blue bandannas soaked with their crimson blood. There was no time to grieve; we needed to leave Villain territory before we were discovered by red rags or the pigs.

We managed to elude any additional confrontations, eventually finding ourselves back in the set. Anxious but safe, we savored a bittersweet moment of victory. Our narrow escape from the jaws of danger was a stark reminder of the fragility of our existence, a sour reality that overshadowed our so-called victory against the harsh world we inhabited. This tale tells not just our tale of survival, but the harsh truths of the Crippin' we lay claim to, always reminding us that life is a precious gift, one that can be extinguished as abruptly as a candle's wick.

CHAPTER FIFTY-TWO:
"CRIPPIN TO THE FULLEST:
FIVE-DEUCE VERSUS FIVE-OWE"

A couple weeks later Big Mike was gifted a 1963 Plymouth Fury by Freeway Donny of the Freeway Boys. Donny had a lot of love & respect for the set. Loyalty was embedded in our souls, carried in every beat of our hearts - & it was this same loyalty that I saw in the eyes of Freeway Donny, and why we considered him an honorary Hoover Gangsta.

Anyway, the car was not merely a means of transportation, rather, it was a lifeline, a symbol of freedom for Mike & his brother, a necessary tool to elude the ever vigilant eyes of law enforcement whenever Ken Dogg was able to sneak into town.

As we cruise to the sounds of Tone Loc from One-oh-Seven Hoover's new song *"Wild Thang,"* Big Mike told me he recently spoke to Kenny. Ken Dogg had spent some time in Brooklyn, New York, Newark, New Jersey & Detroit, Michigan, but was now hiding out in Shreveport, Louisiana.

As fate would have it, Ken Dogg ran into Lil Hoover Bam out there in a local nightclub. Bam recently escaped from CYA. Lil Bam's reputation was grim, simmering with the infamy of the 1988 Halloween Massacre, which resulted in a Black P Stone's demise & left four severely injured.

Later that afternoon, Big Mike left me seated within the cool leather of the Plymouth while he went to discuss some matters with his lawyer. A wild, uncontrollable urge came over me, an exhilarating whisper of mischief. Without thinking twice, I decided to take the car for an impromptu joyride through Downtown Los Angeles. I pushed the speed limit, feeling the roar beneath the Plymouth Fury's hood, letting the thunderous thrill seep into my veins.

However, fate decided to hate on me; I was around the corner from the lawyer's office when I was pulled over by the pigs for speeding. Due to being unlicensed the punk ass cop decided the car had

551 | P a g e

to be impounded. I tried to persuade the officer to give me a ticket instead of towing the car, when Big Mike emerged from the office.

I started waving frantically trying to grab his attention as he exited his lawyer's office. Unfortunately, due to the lack of title & registration the car was inevitably towed. It unveiled a cocktail of anger & frustration within Big Mike, emotions he rarely displayed.

The incident became a grim reminder of all the cars seized from me because I chose to pull over for the one-time. This realization spurred an awakening within me. The repeated losses led me to push it to the limit, to challenge the pigs & not make their job so easy. From then on every encounter transformed into high-speed chases. I forced the pigs had to earn your tax dollars, to work hard as hell if they were to impound any more cars from me.

As for Ken Dogg he laid low as limbo, his appearances dwindling to whispers & rumors. Word on the street is that he appeared blended in with the mourners at farewell services for our fallen stars. Rumors where he had become a master of disguise, at times, he was said to resemble a Rastafarian, the embodiment of integrity, freedom & rebellion echoing Bob Marley's spirit.

Others swore they saw him as Frederick Douglas, the unwavering & bearded symbol of strength & resilience. In more peculiar accounts, some swore to have seen him don the guise of a big buff black woman, reminiscent of Tyler Perry as Madea. Whether these sightings were fact or the product of an overworking imagination remains a mystery.

Coincidentally, Ken Dogg & Lil Bam weren't the only ones spending time in Shreveport. It was around this time that I discovered my Uncle Roy was getting a lot of money with the local Chapter of Hoover Gangsta. Formed around the bedrock loyalty of family ties, this powerhouse was orchestrated by the renowned Ford family - Hoover Sam, his brothers Hoover Ray, Amp & Hoover Tim along with their day uno's Boo-boo, Road Dogg, Rob Lane & Leelo to name a few.

HOOVER SAM & AMP

Their origins had roots dating back to 1985 when the Ford bros were living on 53rd street, next door to Hoover Kim. The Fords are the CeeCees Uncles, and during their time living on the turf, they fell in love with the Gangsta Groove. As a result, the Ford bros got their put on. The Ford Bros were an embodiment of pure Louisiana grit - hardened gangstas, ruthless hustlers.

Lil CeeCee escaped from Stanislaus Juvenile Hall to seek revenge the day after Big CeeCee was killed. He puts in some work, then flees to Louisiana w/ Yvonne, Lil Bam, Face, the Ford Bros & a couple Harlem 30 Crips. While in Shreveport they laid the foundation for Hoover Gangsta on Cooper Road & Cedar Groove. They also established a pipeline connecting the thriving metropolises of Los Angeles & Shreveport.

A pipeline, which only facilitated my Uncle Roy's wealth & power. With this newfound wealth, Uncle Roy was living the high life. Cruising down Cooper Road in extravagant limousines like Ric Flair, a spectacle the locals admired & speak about to this day. It inspired me to take my talents to the other LA, Louisiana.

The time-worn saying, *"all roads lead to Rome"* seemed to become reality for me. In this case, all roads led me to the Bayou. The lure of Louisiana was strong; it was a routine childhood experience to be shipped off to the sweeping swamps for summer vacations. Little did my parents know, they were paving the way for connections that would later come in handy.

I decided to tap in with some of my cousins in Lafayette, Louisiana. I casually proposed the idea of expanding my business with them. This epiphany led me to share my thoughts with Baby Johnny. After we discussed the idea, I was relieved to find that he not only agreed with my proposal but was eager to embark on this new endeavor.

Now the course was set for another outlaw adventure shrouded with danger, and the reckless pursuit of power. With Baby Johnny's connections in the underworld combined with Uncle Roy's familiarity & notoriety in the region plus an already established pipeline, we could potentially make enough money to leave our pasts behind & forge new lives.

I kept the thought of my homeboys, Bam from Nine-Deuce Hoover, and Whitey from Five-Deuce Broadway in the back of my mind, they had recently received football numbers for transporting out of state, but big risk also meant big rewards & we were risk takers.

Since the trip was similar to my expeditions to ABQ & Mile High City, the best way to transport our supplies was in the same fashion. We had to take the same precautions to avoid being captured. We hit the road in the dead of night, guided only by the pale moonlight. The long drive began with a mix of excitement & anxiety. We knew our lives would never be the same, and although we looked forward to this fresh opportunity, the shadows of the dangers loomed over us.

As the miles faded behind us, we couldn't help but appreciate the natural beauty of the country, from the expansive deserts of Arizona to the green forests & bayous of the South. Entering the Deep South was a lesson in American history. We passed through Mississippi, the birthplace of the Blues, and Oprah Winfrey. Then we hit Alabama, the birthplace of the Civil Rights movement & home of the Tuskegee Airmen. Both states forced us to confront the brutal & complex history that shaped America. Each mile carried the weight of centuries-old tales of injustice – a reminder of where we had come from & where we aspired to be.

The long stretches of open road gave us ample opportunity to bond over our shared memories, the hard times we overcame, and our hopes for the future. We spoke of our families, our desire to outrun our past demons, and our aspirations to establish ourselves as viable, productive members of society one day. Our shared vision of a brighter future gave us hope & the drive to persevere.

It seemed that the cypress trees, the moss-ridden marshy landscapes, and the alluring air of mystique that decorated the outskirts of Lafayette ushered us into a new world. A world that would allow us to cleanse our bodies, minds, and souls for a much-needed reset. As it turned out, those quiet swamps & sleepy towns harbored a thriving criminality that would grant me the opportunity to continue my ventures without the unforgiving threats of gangbangin'.

The air was dense with humidity & optimism when we arrived. My family welcomed us with open arms, promising to give us the support & guidance needed to thrive in our new environment. Adapting to life in the bayou wasn't the easiest transition, but I soon learned that the streets here played by the same rules. Understanding that helped me to fit in & make connections with the right people.

I soon realized the potential for success in this new territory, Baby Johnny & I decided to set up a pipeline between Lafayette & Shreveport with Uncle Roy. Business was booming, however, the influx of cash left us with a problem. An abundance of dirty money that needed to be cleaned. That's when I came up with the idea, opening a wash house to wash my dirty money.

Finding the right person to manage this operation was crucial, I didn't want another *"Anthony"* situation. I needed someone who wouldn't ask questions or draw attention to our little operation. Enter Jimbo, a man whose life had seen him victimized by the unyielding waves of fucked up circumstances, leaving him a nomad, living in his van. He was the perfect candidate, and I presented him with an offer he couldn't refuse - the opportunity to manage my Wash House, earning him a modest salary & a roof over his head, the wash house had a backroom, and I transformed into a makeshift studio apartment.

Under Jimbo's watchful eye, my Wash House thrived, converting my illicit funds into clean taxpayer revenue ready to be spent as I saw fit. With the entire operation being handled off the books, we virtually eliminated the risk of leaving any traceable records that could bring the law crashing down on us. I used the laundered funds to take care of baby mamas, bills & expenses, while stashing away the profits from my Los Angeles operations.

Meanwhile in Shreveport, Ken Dogg & Lil Bam found themselves bound to a shared fate, threading similar paths but with contrasting personalities. Both were fugitives, escaping from murder charges & leaving their pasts behind. Surviving on borrowed time & fake identities, with only one thing in common, Hoover Gangsta. As time passed, their paths split, and their differing natures steered their distinct courses of life.

Ken Dogg, a rebel, and a conventional outlaw. After being branded a fugitive, he sought refuge in attempts to reshape his life. Nationwide manhunts ended up being futile attempts to capture him. The unnoticed passerby in the day became the chameleon of the city by night. Regular jobs became his haven, providing him a sense of normalcy in the otherwise turbulent world he was engulfed in. His journey ended when he settled in Louisiana, seeking refuge in the Cajun culture, the southern hospitality, and the soothing vibes of jazz.

He found love & started a family with a local woman. It was the life of an ordinary man living in a small rural town, far from the chaos of Hoover street. He was living an illusion, but it was a peaceful one, nonetheless. He & his new lady, who was oblivious to his former life as a Crip, even contemplated moving their new family to Germany.

Lil Bam was the total opposite. The echoes of his reckless youth lingered in his psyche, still an active gangbanger, feeding on the adrenaline that only killing an enemy can provide. His restless spirit found all the trouble he desired when a man named Yodi ignited a local chapter of the Rollin' Sixties. Lil Bam didn't give a damn, he was still hellbent on banging on enemies. He was groovin' w/ the Shreveport Hoovers, killing Sixties & anybody else he saw fit, turning the swamp lands into a baby South Central.

Lil Bam turned out the Shreveport Hoovers with authentic wild west gangbanging. His rebellious charisma inspired a wave of terror across the city, with murders playing out like grim montages in some nightmarish reality. Anything & anyone were a fair game painting the peaceful Shreveport into a bloody canvas. His reign of terror resonated throughout the 3rd most populous city in Louisiana, gaining him the infamous moniker of *"Killa Bam."*

The city of Shreveport, Louisiana, was set ablaze by a cultural phenomenon, a film called *"Colors"*. Seemingly overnight, the conversations & the gossip surrounded the film & its depiction of gangbanging had enticed the community. Colors brought stories of the Crips & the Bloods, to every household that could access it. The hype over the film had people all over America falsely claiming Crip & Blood, as if they had been secretly inducted into their ranks.

Killa Bam saw an opportunity, he took advantage of this infatuation with gangbanging, and took more Shreveport cats under his wing. The love, loyalty & unity of gangbanging drew in many youngsters who were desperate for a sense of purpose & belonging, as they ignored the dangerous aspects of membership. Hoover Gangsta membership began to swell in Shreveport, as Killa Bam's influence grew.

Rival factions pushed their way into the heart of the bayou, spurred on by greed & the desire to control the lucrative underground world we had built. Eventually turf wars ignited with Hoovers & Sixties. At the center of the chaos stood Killa Bam, who had assumed Hoover Sam's last name, using the alias, Dante Ford. Under his command, the Five-Deuces left a trail of bloodshed across Shreveport.

The first fatality in the gang war occurred in December 1988, when a 19-year-old member of Rollin Sixties was gunned down. The police wasted no time in pointing fingers at the Hoover Gangstas. The increased tension between rival hoods led to more frequent drive-by shootings, with seven reported in a span of three days.

By March 1989, the community was horrified as the violence continued to escalate. Killa Bam's reign of terror continued; the violence swallowed the city whole, compelling city officials to plead for Federal intervention. This resulted in key players, Hoover Sam, Boo-Boo, Rob Lane, and Leelo fleeing their kingdom & relocating to Houston. In H-Town, they dedicated their energies to erecting a new empire – the Houston chapter of Hoover Gangsta.

An unintended result was a cultural revolution. The new recruits included home-grown talent that became the backbone of the era-defining 'chopped & screwed' music style unique to Houston. A notable recruit was DJ Screw & the Screwed Up Crew, who gave birth to a potent subculture that had the nation drinking lean.

The Shreveport Hriginals is a testament to the power of reinvention, forging identities under ruthless circumstances. Their legacy, a tumultuous wave in the ocean of American street culture, continues to ripple through the sands of time, showing us the dualities of human existence & the radical extents people go to survive, thrive, and leave a mark in this ever changing world.

"We still Crippin' to the Fullest"
- Kevin "Hoover Bam" Bishop FDHGC

Our story takes us back to Hoover street. Tonight, we were at the rock house on 48th street, a symphony of dominoes being shuffled, exaggerated war stories, and the rhythmic clink of weights being hoisted & set down. Interwoven with weed smoke & malt liquor, as we served our loyal fiends when they materialized to the sounds of NWA *"Fuck the Police."*

It was Cinco de Mayo 1989; I'm busting down a burrito as the clock struck 3am. My pit bull puppy was becoming a pain in the ass, cranky from too much time at the rock house. I decided to take her home. As I was walking out the door, I saw a fine ass woman strutting our way. Her skin was the shade of rich caramel, her figure accentuated by the tight, cut-off daisy dukes, with the bottom of her round butt cheeks hanging out. She had a bountiful amount of booty that was enticing to the eye & seared into my memory.

"I like big butts & I cannot lie.-Sir Mixalot"

Keeping true to my inner cockhound, I attempted to woo her & get her number, she paid me no mind as she paid for two Fifty sacks. I shrugged nonchalantly & embarked on the journey home. As I resumed my moonlight walk, an aura of suspicion seeped into my consciousness. I darted towards the less-visible corners of 48th Street Park, my street smarts prompted by an intuition.

Turning into a Crip chameleon, my black ass blended into the shadows, watching vigilantly as a scene unfolded. As hundreds of Europeans & the big booty Judy-were digging in car trunks. They retrieved jackets with ATF & FBI on the back! The reality of her true identity was a crushing punch to my gut. The big booty Judy was a pig in hoochie clothes!

My heart pounded against my ribcage like a frantic African drummer, my palms sweating with the urgency of the situation. I needed to warn the Locs & fast! I emerged from my hiding spot, my every instinct screaming for me to reach for a phone & alert my comrades of the imminent danger looming over them.

Once I reached home, I rushed to use the phone. My thoughts & my heart were drag racing, my hands were shaking as I dialed the numbers. Each ring that echoed felt like a ticking time bomb, signaling doomsday. All my attempts were futile; my efforts to warn my comrades about the startling revelation time was not my ally. I was sadly too late.

The set erupted into a storm of chaos. As 250 pigs raided 16 of our rock houses between Vernon & 56th street, a raging army with battering rams, armed to the teeth. The silent dawn had been replaced with a nightmarish scene from a Hollywood movie.

The echoes of our laughter & camaraderie drowned out by the wailing sirens & the pounding of a gavel that served a cold dish of justice. For our humble million dollar a week operation, the party didn't just end, it was a grand finale. Faster than the speed of light or sound, I witnessed our empire crumbling before my eyes, and I was standing helplessly, watching our world fall apart.

I narrowly escaped but a lot of the homies taken down didn't have priors like me & received sentences of 20+ years. I couldn't help but imagine what my fate would have been if they got me too. Baby JoHnny, Hoover Bam, Argo, Loon, and numerous Hoovers or affiliates were apprehended & taken into custody. The situation had reached a boiling point, with streets dominated by dope boys & gang bangers all scrambling for their share of the lucrative trade. We had become a prominent force in the city.

> *Ralph Lochridge, a spokesman for the U.S. Drug Enforcement Administration, described the Five-Deuce Hoovers as "one of the heaviest gangs in terms of crack cocaine in the city." He added, "they're also one of the most vicious & violent, in terms of the number of drive-by shootings, armed robberies, rapes, and armed assaults."*

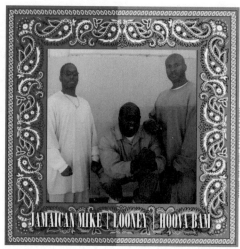

JAMAICAN MIKE | LOONEY | HOOVA BAM

He was not wrong. We were ruthless. Desperate to take us down, the Feds devised an incredibly risky & brave plan. In the Months before the raid, they began an intricate & dangerous game of cat & mouse. They recruited young blacks in disguise to be initiated as Crips & infiltrate the set as undercover agents seeking membership in the set.

We had over One thousand Hoover Gangsta Crips active in the street at the time. These snakes in Crip clothes blended in & gained our trust, learned about the ins & outs. They gathered invaluable information about our operations, money laundering, suppliers, stash houses, and clientele. The pigs managed to maintain their cover, even carrying out illicit transactions along the way. One transaction, they negotiated a purchase of several Mac-10's in exchange for crack cocaine with Baby Johnny. The Feds made drug purchases that exceeded $1,800.

Baby Johnny's instincts kicked in, and he grew suspicious of the individuals before him. Although he couldn't put his finger on it, something didn't sit right with him. At the height of their infiltration, the cover of some undercover officers was put at risk when Baby Johnny questioned their true identities. Undeterred, the undercovers pressed on, treading carefully around Baby Johnny's suspicions, all the while gathering further information on the gang's operations. Eventually, Baby JoHnny had had enough. He arranged for the undercovers to be discreetly tailed after a sale was completed. The undercovers managed to slip away & hide inside a nearby Sizzler restaurant.

Dawn had arrived. It was time for the raid. Law enforcement from multiple agencies descended upon the seemingly quiet street of the Fifties with little warning. As they moved in, occupants of the houses awoke to the sounds of broken doors & shouting officers. The homies scrambled, attempting to flee, but their efforts were in vain.

A total of 13 members were taken into custody. The coordinated efforts of local & federal law enforcement led to a series of indictments. My loved one Baby Johnny was sentenced to 20 years to life for his offenses & unfortunately would die in prison.

As the investigation unfolded, a central figure emerged: Baby Johnny, labeled the kingpin of our operation. The undercovers even managed to uncover a series of planned murder missions, but they were too late to prevent two of the hits. With each successful hit, our reputation for brutality & violence was reinforced.

H.I.P "BABY JOHNNY" JOHN LEO BENTLEY

The summer had been as relentless & for us, it meant a constant battle for power & respect. Gangbangin' is at an all-time high, and everyone seems to be caught up in it. Big Mama, and Pookee were no exception. They both drove the same car, identical down to the color, a 1975 Chevy Impala Station Wagon, the only difference was Pookee's had Daytons. It was a comfortable & spacious ride, perfect for cruising around the city with my kids or the Crips.

562 | P a g e

We used to put in a lot of work for the set, riding around in Pookee's car up to no good, doing whatever it took to protect our turf. I even did some dirt in Big Mama's car a few times, taking out rivals & making sure Hoover stayed on top. There was no question about it; these cars were as much a part of the set as any of us, having seen & experienced the same violence & bloodshed we had.

One day, the inevitable happened. As Big Mama brought the car to a stop at a traffic light, she caught sight of a group of Foeties that had been victimized by Pookee & I. Recognizing the familiar car from their numerous confrontations with us, they assumed that Pookee was behind the wheel.

The bullets ricocheted & shattered the windows of Big Mama's car, the sound echoing through the streets, petrifying my newborn who had been tucked safely in the backseat. Big Mama's adrenaline kicked in, and she immediately stepped on the gas, speeding away from the scene as our rivals continued to fire at her until they were out of sight.

The unfortunate case of mistaken identity had put the lives of my family in grave danger, and this incident became a pivotal moment for my family. They nearly destroyed my whole world with their mix up. The incident caused Big Mama to be concerned, even though was no stranger to violence. She realized that she didn't want our kids exposed to gangbangin' or become participants in the gang war. It was the straw that broke the camel's back. This time was different, our child was in danger so the stakes couldn't have been higher.

The bullets that pierced the side of the car tore me apart, as if their fingers reached in & choked the life out of all that was good & pure in my world. It was a wake-up call, Big Mama realized she couldn't be around this danger any longer; she had to move out of South Central with our kids. She decided to move a few cities away, hoping to start fresh & leave the violence behind.

It wasn't an easy decision, but it was the right one. Luckily, nobody was hurt that day. Swallowing the bitter pill of reality, I let them go. I knew it was best for all of us, even though it broke my heart. As they set off to create a new life, I knew what I had to do.

This was a breaking point for me; the attack on my family had struck a nerve, and it ignited an uncontrollable fire within me. My anger surged, and I had to protect those I cared about the most. The line

562 | P a g e

had been crossed too far, and it was time for the big payback. I sought the help of the only Hoover that hated Foeties as much as I did or more, Pookee. Aware of the gravity of the situation & the retaliation it demanded, we began planning our course of action.

For the sake of my family & the ones we swore allegiance to, vengeance was a must. The same night, I went to get my payback. The night was dark, and the air was dank as we embarked on the perilous mission armed with my Uzi & Pookee with his signature Thompson sub- machine gun. Stealthily, we made our way through the back streets, evading the prying eyes of potential witnesses that may have been out late.

The tension in the pit of my stomach grew more constricting with every step, but my eyes burned with determination. Pookee seldom saw me this determined.. We were A-1 since day one, and although we had been in many dangerous situations together, Pookee had never saw this side of me. This time it was personal. He was now witnessing the fire ignited by love & the burning desire of a father to protect his family.

Finally, we arrived at the location were the shooting occurred & saw a group of these fools gathered on the corner. We surveyed the scene before us, analyzing the group's layout - all the while calculating our next move. We had to strike quickly, leaving no time for counterattacks.

As we approached the intersection where our rivals were gathered, adrenaline & anger coursed through my veins. Without exchanging any words, I nodded at Pookee, reaffirming our mutual understanding. I felt a burning pain in my chest, a rage that could only be extinguished with bloodshed. In unison, we stepped out of the shadows, guns raised, determination etched across our faces. I embodied the anguish of a ravaged father, the result, only the fallen can tell the tale.

The night air was split by the gunfire, echoing throughout the quiet streets as we enacted vengeance. Swift & brutal, we painted a tableau of vengeance. Our sole purpose had been fulfilled - our message received. We were symbols of vendetta, guardians of the Fifties, and defenders of my family in desperate times.

Looking back, I realized that Big Mama was right. It wasn't worth risking our lives or our kids' lives. Unfortunately, at the time, I was blinded by the thrill of the G-ride & the power we had. It's a decision that I'll always have to live with, but it's one that I had to make. I had to learn the hard way that sometimes, the only way to win the game is to step away from the table.

Life in South Central has always been full of contradictions: hope, despair, love, and violence. It was a place where we scraped together an existence, while trying to protect our family, our community, and ourselves. I praise Big Mama every day for her unwavering love, her courage, and her ability to nurture our kids amid this chaos. She took this life I introduced her to, and she transformed it into something beautiful, something far beyond anything I could have ever imagined.

I wake up every morning, the sun's rays sneaking through the small window of my cell, and the first thought that comes into my head is Big Mama's smile. Her unwavering faith in me keeps me going, even in this desperately lonely place. She is the bedrock of our family, the compass that led us forward through stormy seas & turbulent times. It was her wisdom & intuition that shaped our children, molding them into the sweet & polite people they have become.

LAPD had a hard on for H'Luv the last few years. Despite their eagerness to clench justice, they failed to pin charges on him. This failure fueled their resentment towards not only him but all of us. What ensued was a wrathful wave of police brutality inflicted upon anyone remotely associated with Hoover Gangsta, a modern-day witch hunt.

One fateful night, the Five-Nine Hoovers, robbed a random Mexican, an act that set the hood on fire. We were riding in Luv's pride & joy, a souped-up black cherry Deuce, a dazzling 1972 Chevy Impala lowrider with chrome Dayton's, trying to stay under the radar. As the pigs swarmed like vultures, their sirens were threats to our freedom.

We decided to split up to minimize suspicion & meet on 59th street & Figueroa behind the church, providing us symbolic solace, perhaps. However, destiny, proving to be a cruel jokester, had its own plans. As Luv tried to blend into the darkness of Bonsallo Ave, a notoriously secluded & shadowy block, the pigs saw through his facade. They moved to box him in with hopes of possibly gunning him down without the intrusion of prying eyes.

Orchestrating a maneuver worthy of his reputation, Luv somehow managed to slither out of their grasp & got onto Figueroa. Resigned to his fate, he pulled over, under the harsh reflection of the police's flashing lights. The pigs accused Luv of the robbery, and ruthlessly handcuffed him to a gate, leaving him exposed & vulnerable. Like a spectacle upon a wicked stage, the car's high beams spotlighted Luv. They brought forth the victim.

Luv maintained an unwavering show of strength & defiance. A thousand accusations & denials hung in the air. In his possession were a few thousand dollars accumulated earnings from the dope game. The pigs, hell-bent on coercion, attempted to influence the victim into falsely identifying Luv, *"Give that to him. I'm sure he ain't have that."*

In a display of offensive arrogance, one officer retorted, *"shut the fuck up, asshole."*

Their deceitful theatrics, however, were short-lived. Much to their dismay, the Mexican victim discredited their accusations, stating Luv was innocent. Ghetto Birds invaded the night sky searching for the culprit, their deafening roars echoing across Figueroa. They circled overhead like vultures awaiting a feast, their spotlight dissecting the night's secrecy. While the pigs exuded cruel satisfaction, posing for Polaroids while he was detained – a memento of their dominance & authority.

It was common practice for them to do this & laugh at us, their diabolical grins highlighting the brutality of their act. Public humiliation was their drug of choice, they taunted him by brandishing their own gang signs, thumbs & pointer fingers forming two 7's. Making a mockery of our lifestyle with this gesture representing their precinct like a Crip set.

"77 is the baddest gang!" They'd slur arrogantly, their eyes glinting with ruthless pride.

Through their glossy Polaroid lens, they captured us in such anguished states. In those moments, held captive & yet undefeated, the pigs wanted our lives reduced to mere snapshots serving as their trophies.

Suddenly the night's tranquility was shattered as an eruption of automatic gunfire tore through the night. The Five-Nine Hoovers were shooting at the Ghetto Birds with her AK47. Her reckless audacity, striking terror served as an unexpected diversion. In the ensuing chaos & fear, the police uncuffed Luv. As he retreated into the night, I didn't know it marked the end of an era. Little did I know that night on Bonsollo street would be the last time I saw my homeboy Hoova Luv.

The chill of January 17, 1990, will forever echo in our history as the tipping point of a longstanding battle with the pigs—a grim morning in Los Angeles when the formidable Hoova Luv got busted by the feds. Notorious in his legend, H'Luv's deeds, often shrouded in shadows & secrecy, had finally caught up with him. H'Luv fell into a trap that would lock him away for a quarter-century.

He was charged with a colossal conspiracy & charged as being a drug king pin. His crime was nothing short of orchestrating a spider's web of cocaine distribution that stretched over two thousand miles, from the glitz & buzz of Los Angeles to the bluesy, mellow tone of Chattanooga, Tennessee.

The feds were shamelessly proud of their victory. So much so, that they took it upon themselves to conduct a grand parade, with H'Luv as the unwilling centerpiece. Handcuffed & ensnared by the bloodhounds of law, he was paraded around the city's dens of justice. From Southwest & 77th to Homicide, 108th, and Crash, they took him on tour. His face, a symbol of rebellious Fifty Crips, was showcased in every imaginable police station. The agents exhibited him like a hood trophy, their triumphant smirks a stark contrast to the heavy gloom that had descended on the set.

Each police station was an exhibition, as they bragged *"Look who we got!"*

H'Luv was more than a mere dope boy, he had selfless generosity. His Hoover love earned him love & respect. He always looked out & ensured the homies never had empty pockets or an itchy trigger finger. His arsenal stretched far & wide, containing everything from stealthy pocket rockets to menacing automatics.

Following the shock wave of H'Luv's apprehension, a cold shiver ran down my spine, an icy premonition of my own impending doom. It was not difficult to conceive that the hawk eye of federal justice could be trained on me & my clandestine activities in Louisiana. Which brought me to a crossroads & the difficult decision to cease all operations, putting an end to my Louisiana pipeline in an existence never meant for the faint-hearted.

The narrative surrounding H'Luv's apprehension serves as a potent example of the intermingling between legality & morality. As well as the effects of one's actions on the collective. This is our profound message to society about the repercussions of choices, and the duality of personalities. The circle of life, that every rise & its inevitable downfall.

Meanwhile in Shreveport, the Hoover-Sixty turf war raged on. Killa Bam & the Shreveport Hoover Gangstas were on a rampage. By the end of 1989, drive-by shootings were reported on a weekly basis, as the atmosphere of fear & anarchy settled over the city like a suffocating blanket. In January 1990, around the same time as the pigs caught H'Luv shipping to Nooga, they intercepted a package with a million dollars' worth of crack en route to Shreveport from Los Angeles. How many things could go wrong!?!

The violence reached its peak on February 5, 1990, when in just a single week, twelve people were shot, and five were wounded in separate gang related incidents. The spree of violence culminated in the murder of Killa Bam on February 6, 1990. As his life was snuffed out in a drive-by, after a bullet pierced his heart.

H.I.P "Killa Bam" Larry Alonzo Winters

The setting was a groovy Hoover house party in the Seven-Foe Hoover turf. We were celebrating Lil Dre Dogg's return & Killa Bam's legacy. Lil Dre Dogg; just came back from CYA after a 5 year stint for putting in work on some Blood Stone Villains that were trespassing in the set. The gangsta sounds of Ice Cube *"The Nigga You Love to Hate"* filled the house with vibes! As we sang along, things went awry. A loud smack was heard over the Cube lyrics, liquor pouring, and Crip Walkin'.

Among us was Chim-Chim, a fiery soul, notorious for his squabble, and Scooby, an intimidating character popular for his gall & gangsterism. Scooby, crossed the line, and smacked blue flames out of our cherished homegirl, Smokey, in front of everyone! Why? the reason I can't recall.

Chim, being the epitome of loyalty, couldn't stand idle. In a Hoover heartbeat, he jumped into action, fiercely defending Smokey's honor. Fists flew in a chaotic whirlwind, and amid the gasps & shouts, Chim got the best of Scooby, and abruptly ended the party.

Post the altercation, everyone was exiting the party & Scooby, unsatisfied with the results of the scuffle called Chim around the corner, where round 2 cracked off. A rematch or a bid for glorious revenge, call it what you will; despite the daunting odds, Chim held his own & won that round again. Scooby, a fierce warrior in his own right, just couldn't compete with Chim, but every action has an equal & opposite reaction, don't it?

An enraged Scooby rallied his troops, an army of Seven-Foes, and raided the Fifties. 53rd street was suddenly an arena for an unexpected battle royale between Five-Deuce & Seven-Foe, where they found us gang-hanging outside of Naomi's crib on the Tray. With madness glistening in our eyes, we transformed anything we could find including Naomi's lawn tools, hoes, shovels, even firewood, into a makeshift weapon.

It was pure pandemonium, pure machismo & Hoover bravado resembling the Navy yard rumble in Westside Story. Only the arrival of the pigs brought the madness to an end. The blaring sirens, flashing lights, and riot squad rushed us with their nigga beaters & rubber bullets. Scooby tried to seek refuge in Naomi's house.

Naomi was not with that at all! She told him about himself, *"You must be crazy, I ain't letting you in after you started all this shit!"*

However, in the name of Hoover love, she offered Scooby a ride home. Fate had other plans. The pigs halted their getaway, surrounding the vehicle before they could leave the block. One by one, we were rounded up like cattle & loaded into the back of cold, soulless paddy wagons.

In the frenzy, Chim came up with an unlikely escape plan. His strategy involved stripping down to his undies on a nearby porch, pretending to be a half-asleep neighbor awakened by the commotion. With nothing on but his biscuits & draws he executed his performance. Shit, he had me going, I forgot he was the reason we were squabbling in the first place. Unfortunately, the pigs didn't fall for Chim's theatrics & swept him up with the rest of us onto the paddy wagon.

The number of Hoovers incarcerated that night overwhelmed the capacity of the 77th precinct. With every cell filled to its brim, the officers had no other choice but to place the overflow of detainees in the day room. Handcuffed & corralled together with our plastic ID bands.

Desperation led to creative thinking, as Chim looked at me, still in his draws, and said *"I gotta get outta here, big homie!"*

He turned to the homie Argo & started using his jheri curl juice to slip off his wristband. Chim materialized once more as an unmatched escape artist. Taking advantage of the lack of bars on the window, he slyly made his exit. As if his earlier act wasn't audacious enough, he now climbed down a tree & made a break for it. In nothing but his tighty whiteys, he sprinted through the chilling night from 77th street all the way back to the Tray.

When I look back at that day now, I can't help but wince at the memory of the raw brutality & laugh, remembering the Hoover royal rumble. Grappling over dignity in a futile battle of ego. We were warriors, expressing ourselves the only way we knew how, with violence! Believe it or not, this was the Hoover get down & after the rumble we stood together as one, with even more respect for each other. We were survivors; we were storytellers of the remarkable battle that shaped our history.

There's a strange aura engulfing life when fractions of time hold the potential to overturn good fortunes & change the course of existence. I grappled with this bitter reality. With the shutdown of our lucrative, multi-million-dollar crack operation, the tables turned, burying me in the belly of despair & destruction. There was a time when I had the world in my hands, but now I feel like I've fallen & I can't get up.

As the days went by I felt like a man possessed; desperate, volatile, and dangerous. I found comfort at the bottom of bottles of Tyronia, as well as letting mind altering substances take over my world. These lethal potions offered a distorted comfort that masked the harshness of my existence. This whirlwind of self-destruction eventually landed me back behind the foreboding walls of Los Angeles County Jail.

Charged with a bank robbery, alongside two fellow Hriginals, RP & C-Note, I was faced with a numbing reality. I didn't give a fuck if I lived or died. I was on swoll & acting a damn fool. My life had been consumed by sheer violence & mayhem, nothing mattered but Five-Deuce, and all other aspects of my existence paled in comparison within the grand scheme of my loyalties. Devotion ran deep in my veins, so much so that it trumped everything, obscuring my sense of rationality, self-love, and self-preservation. Nothing mattered but Hoover, an ideology that became both my savior & my nemesis.

Inside the gang module, a place that was becoming like a second home. The authorities handcuffed us during visits, binding us in iron chains as a pitiful attempt to ensure security. The ingenuity of our desperation gave birth to an unusual innovation - we fashioned a crude, yet remarkably effective key out of staples from discarded apple crates. With these apple crate skeleton keys, we would unlock our cuffs, in a brazen act of rebellion that made us feel as though we possessed control of our freedom.

I remember clearly one day armed with my ingenious skeleton key, I was – or at least felt – untouchable. Daily, I carried a makeshift iron shank like it was part of my everyday wardrobe, its handle impressively crafted from melted plastic, which was just waiting to meet a Neighborhood Crip or a Blood. To me, it was a symbol of resilience, a testament to my constant fight against authority.

That day, a notable adversary sauntered into the visiting room. This man wasn't innocent; he was a Neighborhood Crip that carried the grim accolade of being a wanton murderer, incarcerated for killing my tribesman. His presence was a stark reminder of our ongoing feuds, of the lives lost & the wounds yet to heal. His crimes against us resurfaced in my mind, amplifying my festering rage. Without hesitation, I freed myself from the restraints, and launched a brutal attack right in front of his terrified mother.

It was a desperate & reckless act, a raw display of vengeance. I was fueled by a fanatic devotion, an intense unspoken loyalty that outshone any fear of consequences. This brutal assault should have spelled doom for me. An event that could have been my Waterloo, a catastrophic end that would plunge me deeper into the justice system. Fate had a strange sense of humor. I slipped through the probing fingers of punishment & got away unscathed.

Looking back now, I realize this was a cataclysmic time. It marked my descent into self-destruction, a fall from grace that spiraled out of control in a world that had lost its balance. The life I led, the choices I made, the path I chose, it all paints a grim, gritty picture of a life on the edge. The harsh fluorescent lights overhead did little to enhance the gloom in the Crip Module. A couple weeks later the homies, Lil Fat Rat, C-Note, RP, and I were caught for retaliatory attack on fools from Watts. The fall out surrounded assumptions, jealousy, envy, and greed.

There was a nice looking lady who worked in the commissary store that had a thing going on with one of the Watts niggas. He was under the impression that she was giving C-Note the pussy & was now our conduit for smuggling contraband into the jail. This assumption ended up costing them dearly. The Watts niggas launched a sneak attack on C-note, throwing him in the dope fiend & busting his head with a squeegee.

The savage injustice to one of ours was a declaration of war, we could not leave unanswered; not in this unforgiving game, respect means everything, and retaliation is law. With adrenaline pumping & urgency echoing in our hearts, we rallied in the wee hours of the early morning. Under the cloak of dawn at 5 a.m., we launched our clandestine ambush. We unleashed our revenge; we were merciless nocturnal raiders, piercing our foes with the cold, steel of vengeance while they were under the Sandman's spell.

Their assumption couldn't have been more wrong, and they woke up to an unimaginable world of pain & anguish. Our actual smuggler was, in fact, a doctor that was an acquaintance of the homie Bel-Aire. The irony of it all! Inevitably, our brutal upheaval echoed through the tough grueling walls of the jail. As we awaited retaliation, the wounded Watts Crips chose to rat instead.

Consequently, the homies & I were transferred up-the-ranks into high power; a not-so-unfamiliar territory filled with cellars meant for the most dangerous, the most notorious. My new home was the 1700 unit. The aftermath of the attacks led to my heightened security status. They fastened a red wristband around my wrist, I was classified as K-10, denoting me as a high-security risk. The implications of my status weighed heavy, but I wore it like a badge.

Yet, in the throes of my youthful gangsta life, I was indifferent. Each action in honor of Hoover Gangsta, a necessity in this wild Crip kingdom. Confined in solitary chambers, I was subjected to waist chain handcuffs that connected to my wrist & ankles, effectively restraining my movements during transport, a discreet narrative of the volatile monster I had become.

Reflecting on it now fills me with an eerie regret, but back then, all I felt was the rush of adrenaline & a sense of duty to the Groove. This reminiscence is not a glorification of my transgressions; rather, it is a testament to how far I've come from that bloodstained era of my past. That phase of my life was dominated by violence & a distorted sense of loyalty embodied by the Crip lifestyle. Today, I choose not to dodge those memories as they remind me of the person I was & the person I have become. Despite my grim past, my quest for redemption continues, underscored by the profound belief that change is, indeed, possible.

Meanwhile on the streets, the war between Five-Deuce & Five-Owe continued in the City of Angels. A city that was becoming more like the Devil's playground. The day I was arrested for the bank heist, Spookee was released from the county, and the day I was transferred to High Power, Spookee made a dramatic return to confinement.

It was an era when dread reigned supreme & our hood morphed into a warzone, with the pigs enforcing their reign of terror & the Hoover Gangstas resisting with all our might. Our nemesis never ceased & Spookee was a man full of fury & thirsty for payback. Payback for them killing Cadillac Bobby & decimating our multimillion-dollar business.

LIL BANDIT & DEVIL

Our homie, Devil's pops was a bounty hunter, and one night he had some bacon bits casually hanging out after work in the middle of 52nd street. Spookee noticed the trespassers, and something inside him snapped. Overrun by the desire for vengeance, he decided to exercise justice the Hoover way. Enraged & fearless, Spookee unloaded a round of bullets towards the pigs & took off, leaving behind the gun smoke & shock.

As if luck had planned the whole scenario, he bumped into Gangsta Tee mid escape, who became his getaway driver. Soon enough, over a hundred squad cars were chasing them through the set. The Locs were no fools, they were seasoned Crips! With every turn of the car's wheel & every gear shift, they outfoxed their pursuers until they were overwhelmed & surrounded. Fearing their end would be likely on some anonymous backstreet which were often the silent witnesses of ruthless police murders, they veered their course, heading to the Tam's burger parking lot - a place that was well-lit & always crowded.

In retrospect, Spookee's audacity could have cost him his life. The charge of attempted murder on a police officer was grave enough to ensure a life sentence; however, God don't like ugly, the judge dropped those charges. Ultimately, he was sentenced to seven years. As for Gangsta Tee, he was given a lesser sentence, being an accessory after the fact.

The days, weeks, began to pass, as my crimeys were returned to the general population. I quickly found myself catching cases with Hooron & Crazy D from Eight-Tray Gangstas. I became the lone Hoover Gangsta in High Power. Misery was my only companion in those dreary single-man cells. They confined me within those cold, gray walls, but my spirit remained untamed. The tiny window in my cell was my only connection to the outside world, a world I'd lost touch with, in more ways than one. There was an eerie solitude that hung heavy, only interrupted by echoing footsteps of guards patrolling the corridors.

It was during this testing time that they brought down oG Tookie Williams from death row. His arrival in High Power was like a ray of light piercing through the doom & gloom. The minute he saw me, his face lit up like the sun, his enormous smile & the ensuing laughter felt like an unanticipated tribute to my notoriety, *"They finally got yo ass, huh, cuH."*

Hearing his voice echoing around 1700, transported me back to the 1970s, when our destinies had last aligned. Tookie's curious eyes recognized the transformation of the reckless West Town baby Crip into the infamous Boo Capone from Five-Deuce Hoover.

"I've been hearing about Boo Capone," he stated, a glint of amusement in his eyes. It seems my reputation has preceded me.

"They said that lil muthafucka is dangerous, I didn't know it was you. I heard the Five-Deuce Hoovers making a lot of noise in the

street, tearing shit up…I remember when y'all first started," he continued, marking the journey the gang had undertaken.

As time passed, the iron bars between us became invisible as bonds connecting us, breaching the void of our isolated cells. We spent our nights rekindling the past, trading war stories like trading cards, replaying victories & defeats. Late night discussions with Tookie that turned into therapeutic sessions – a blend of soul-bearing confessions & candid debates. Drawing vivid pictures of the colorful world we both craved to relive. We reminiscence about our freakiest hoes, dreams unfulfilled, money making schemes, and treasured moments in the realm of *'Crippin'*. Big Tookie became my confidante, as I did his.

Eventually, I succumbed to a plea bargain, six years with my cases running concurrently. Reality cut through the veil of defiance I wore, underscoring the urgency to adapt. I served three & a half years, a trying period that acquainted me with resilience, hope, disillusionment, and finally, acceptance.

As I sat in High Power awaiting my transfer to a new facility, the cold steel shackles bore down on my wrists & ankles, life outside continued its unrelenting pace. Unmitigated hostility plagued the veins of South Central. My hood was embroiled in an unforgiving war w/ the Rollin Foeties– a feud that claimed too many lives. With hatred as fuel, the animosity between our tribes pushed us to the limit.

At the flame's base was one man, Pookee, the Vernon shooter. No figure was more heavyweight in this deadly game than him. He was on a rampage taking out Foeties like the trash every couple of days. With each passing day, the battle grew increasingly savage, a ceaseless cycle of vengeance that only fueled the city's rising death toll. Pookee embodied the temperament & unswerving hatred the Hoovers had for the Rollin Foeties. He was fully committed to the cause, a career Crip, putting in work was his full-time job.

On the night of July 15, 1991, the hood was set ablaze once again, this time from Pookee's Thompson machine gun. The darkness was lit up with his unbounded fury, added two Foeties to the collection of souls he reaped & wounded several others. The Foeties, suffering severe casualties were thirsty for revenge, stayed on his tail like hounds tracking a scent from the hunt. Their pursuit led them to the intersection of Vernon & Vermont avenue, just a stone's throw away from where Pookee lived.

Before he had a chance to turn into his driveway, they cut him off. The air grew tense, as they faced off, their animosity lacing the very atmosphere. Gunfire split the quiet night, bullets ricocheted in a deadly dance of the damned. Against the hail of bullets, Pookee did not flinch, returning his fair share. Nevertheless, amid this chaos, one bullet found its mark – a renegade messenger of death sealing Pookee's fate.

His sun set too soon. Just 20 years old – a youth who had barely begun to experience life, Pookee was laid to rest. Don't cry Big Pookee he was a warrior & embraced the honor of dying in combat. His name transformed into a symbol of unwavering strength & loyalty. Killed in action on the streets he defended, Big Hoover Pookee memory will forever be in the Crip Hall of Fame, a bittersweet memory in every Hoover Gangsta's heart.

H.I.P Lamar "Pookee" Moore

Hoover Pookie was a man of grit & determination, a champion of our cause, a formidable opponent, and a dear friend, brother, father & husband. His death marked the end of an era. A fallen star, a warrior, a legend, an icon, and ultimately, an immortalized hero. We adopted the Young Hogg Gangsta moniker in his honor. His spirit lives on, his legacy & sacrifices will never be forgotten.

Some of the Hriginal Young Hoggs include Tiny Dre Dogg, Baby Hoover D, Baby Flash, Lil Half, Baby Ken Dogg, the Loons, Baby Madman, Rope Dope, Lil Te Loc, Hoova Bandit, Lil Barney, Baby & Tiny Kaos, Duso, G-Roc, Lurch, Creepdogg, Rat Niddy, Baby

Traymate, Baby Chim, the Cudabears, Baby & Tiny Fat Rat, Lil
Buddha, Pistol, Face, the Coons, Jay Stone2, Baby Gangsta Tee &
Moochie. Pardon my Groove if I missed anyone.

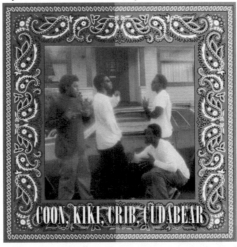

During this term, fate conspired a reunion at Chino with Joker,
who was in the final days of his robbery bid. As the year faded away &
introduced 1992 to us, both Spookee & I found ourselves in the
confines of the prison walls at Chino. Two brothers, separated by life's
unfortunate events, finally reunited under undesirable circumstances. I
was also reunited with Prince Dogg, Lil Fat Rat, and Lurch on this
bid. They never failed to extend their unwavering support, and together
we navigated on another journey together. Time may have worn us a bit
around the edges, but the bond, much like the ink of our gang tattoos,
remained unchanged. The sense of fraternity, born out of shared
adversities, only served to add an extra layer of depth to our entwined
histories.

As I look back, the year 1993 was etched in my memory as a
blur of freedom & uncertainty. The newfound sovereignty granted to
me was short-lived. A year later, I became a victim of old habits &
ensnared in another robbery case, shoulder to shoulder with my partner,
Ten Speed. Thus began a grueling fight for freedom that stretched over
two years from the clutches of my good acquaintance, the LA county
jail. A case that would typically only snatch a half decade from my life
at most, was now a fight for my life now that the 3 strikes law was
passed.

This case brought on an unprecedented level of challenges that demanded extreme fortitude. As I sat behind the defense table, the anticipation hung over my head like the storm cloud in Charlie Brown. The courtroom was a well-rehearsed drama like the soap operas I loved, but I was not entertained. A flicker of hope scattered my dark thoughts - the profound power of my mother's relentless prayers. My mind was filled with tears of Bible verses she used to read, each word promising salvation & offering a thin veneer of optimism.

The echoing corridors resonated with the haunting possibility of spending my remaining days in prison, but I clung to my mother's faith in me. As I scanned the courtroom audience, my heart stumbled upon my loved ones. My eyes fell on my big brothers, James & Spookee. Their quiet strength made me straighten my back subconsciously. The sight of my mother, the sentinel of my vida loca, and my wife, Big Mama, my pillar of support, warmed my grieving soul.

Our dear mother, the beacon of unwavering faith & irreplaceable love, was forced into an unenviable state of worry & prayer. Her eyes, lined with the tracks of countless tears, would gently close as she whispered her silent pleas for our safety. To be the cause of her heartbreak, and being incapable of undoing the damage, seemed to be the heaviest chain in our prison sentences.

A moment immortalized within the frame of an old photograph, a scene of a simpler time, when we were just kids, the essence of family. Seated around our dinner table, surrounded by love. Illuminating the power of unwavering family bonds, the image held a stark reminder of the world we had left behind, the priceless quality time with my loved ones & a world lost. This was a cherished memory etched within the confines of our hearts.

I wish we had given our mother one last tribute, a final family dinner, reunited, under a peaceful roof, far from the chaotic drama which had consumed our lives. This gift, small in its presence, but profound in its meaning, could have been our loving salute to her unflinching devotion. For it wasn't a feast we craved, but a chance to reassure her of our love, echoing our appreciation. However, the mystifying game of fate had other plans, etching a divergent path, forever away from this heartfelt desire.

My journey through this courtroom ripped from Law & Order, had seen its share of reruns, with two mistrials adding to my anxious anticipation. The judge, a newcomer to this well-scripted series, was a fresh face, a replacement. His unacquainted face did nothing to deter my gnawing dread. The harsh gavel descended, and my world was submerged into darkness; 35 years to Life. The weight of the sentence sunk into my heart, tearing me apart from the inside.

The moment the words left the judge's lips; they seemed to suspend in the cold air of the courtroom, unreal, disconnected from the man they damned. Denial seemed like my only refuge, as the reality of my fate was too much to bear. The gloom of my sentence was not real until I saw the heart-wrenching tears of my family. I lost myself to the aching disbelief. Rage fueled by bitter injustice prompted me to flip over the defense table to the shocked courtroom, casting chaos into the hallowed chambers. My disorderly protest was swiftly met with rigid order by the prison officers. Cornered & handcuffed, yet brimming with furious defiance, I found myself at their mercy. Each kick & blow by the officers crystallized the gravity of my sentence. They left me there an agonizing few minutes, a battered body lying on the cold courtroom floor.

California's 'three strikes law,' was sinister trick. Born from Governor Wilson's political agenda, it promised that conviction at the first trial was only the start. The all-encompassing web of the law deemed all charges within a singular case as strikes & included prior plea bargains & even juvenile cases. Threads of my past, which I thought had been severed, were woven back into my narrative. It was a bitter revelation as I became the 2nd person to be sentenced under the three strikes law, at the tender age of 31. The prospect of dying behind bars, stripped me of my optimism. The light at the end of the tunnel seemed an illusion, a mockery. I prayed for an escape, even one delivered by my enemy's shank.

EPILOGUE: THE REDEEMED"

*"Seeking to forget makes exile all the longer; the
secret of redemption lies in remembrance."-
Richard von Weizsaecker*

The unforgiving hallways of this prison echo my name, a
constant reminder of who I am, or perhaps, who I used to be. I am the
pioneer of the infamous Five-Deuce Hoover Gangsta Crips, a title once
worn with a fierce pride that now hangs heavy around my neck like a
cursed medallion.

In the confined desolation of a 10 by 6 foot cell, my abode for
30 years, 6 months, 26 days... & still counting. My incarceration in this
purgatory emphasizes my tainted past. Every second that ticks is a
reminder of the seemingly endless days that have expired & those yet
to come. In the gritty world outside these walls, where the sunsets paint
the world with hues of liberty I long for, my firm handshake was
currency. It was a symbol of brotherhood, of bravado, binding the
righteous comrades & Black men whom history forced into a fraternity
of shared suffering & redemption.

My tale is a quintessential saga of struggle, resilience, and
anomalies of the human spirit. Pain nurtures resilience, and my
narrative is no different. The challenges, the deep-seated pain, the
trauma that we have been forced to endure while constantly proving our
strength & resilience is a story I convey. It's a story held together by a
knotted string of memories, coarse & painful, that has been passed
down to us by our ancestors in our shared struggle. Heart-hardened by
the bitter dynamics of life, I've walked through the fiery paths of strife,
intensified by rampant racial stereotypes.

I'm a direct product of the systematic racism & limitations that
ghetto children are subjected to, a living testament of how an unruly
environment can shape our destiny. We were bred in a world where
harsh realities mingled with hopelessness, as though the two were
strange lovers. It shaped us, like a blacksmith working tirelessly at the
anvil, but in our case, the result was far from a gleaming sword.

Instead, it forged undying embers in our heart that set the world on fire. With the courage of a Samurai & bravery of a Spartan, we stood firm.

We became the fearless warriors of the Kiwé nation, our camaraderie tightly bonded by shared experiences that only my tribesman could understand. Our life was a never-ending chess game of survival. Our courage & bravery were misconstrued virtues, fashioned out of necessity rather than choice, but out of sincere loyalty, pride, and conviction, we held on; we represented something bigger than ourselves. Scars painted our bodies, bandanas veiled our faces, but beneath it all, we were the Crips, fearless youngsters burdened by existing.

Battles were waged nonstop, each bullet fired was a cry for freedom, every blow to keep the dream alive. We bore the burden of our hood, and in return, it shaped us into men unlike any other. The streets we battled on were once playgrounds where innocent laughter had ricocheted off the walls. We were once those children, but our innocence was bargained for survival. Our fears transformed into gall, and our bonds unbreakable. The world against us, and us against the world.

Over the years, the cost has been overwhelming. As our loved ones left us, our legacy persisted amidst infinite nights of violence. Our fallen stars who could have been entrepreneurs, role models, and community leaders have been lost to a relentless battle. Countless generations have perished as result of constant turmoil, disappearing like smoke into the abyss of lost unforgettable souls. Armies of brothers have waged wars, spilling blood & tears onto the parched earth, seeking a phantom victory. Yet the price we've paid, the sacrifices we've made have been inked in vain, like the unclaimed bodies of the LA county cemetery.

We neither attained shared goals, nor tasted the sweetness of our collective aspirations. No banners of glory flutter in our honor; no songs of triumph render the air. The only trophy is a badge of survival, the silent privilege of breathing another day. Our aspirations, once radiant stars in the expansive galaxy of our dreams, have flickered & died out. Our collective ambitions, like fragmented pieces of a puzzle, lay scattered, refusing to form a clear picture. Yet, we still wage war, waiting for redemption.

As I lay in the darkness of my cell, the sound of steel bars slamming shut echoes throughout the vast corridors like a ghostly reminder of how far I have fallen. Memories wash over me like waves crashing in a storm, entwining the good & the bad into a twisted mosaic of my life. I can't help but feel I'm being punished for my loyalty. I think back to the times when I had a chance to make a different choice & take a different path. My dedication to my tribe kept me tethered to an inescapable fate.

As I sit here reminiscing, my heart aches for all the things I could have been & all the moments I missed out on. I wish I could have been the husband that Big Mama needed, the father & grandpa that my children so desperately deserved. I can only offer them my most profound apologies & hope that, in time, they might find it in their hearts to forgive me. My only regret now is that I couldn't give them the last three decades of my life.

I still imagine vivid Sunday afternoons, Big Mama in the kitchen preparing that delicious fried chicken, while our children sat around the table, their eyes wide & curious, as I would recount tales from my youth. Those daydreams felt so complete, every fiber of my being aware that I was part of a family that loved & respected me.

When people label me a bad person, I feel the sting of their judgment like a branding iron searing my flesh. I want to scream out that I have so much goodness inside me, maybe not enough to excuse my past actions, but some that my children & grandchildren have inherited & developed flawlessly. They are the living testimony to the love, care, and guidance that Big Mama & I shared, I will forever be grateful for that.

Today, as I sit in this cell, I allow myself to indulge in sweet memories of my beautiful wife & our kids in their youthful innocence. I see Big Mama's beautiful face, her eyes a never-ending ocean of love & understanding. These memories are what keep me alive, what reminds me of the man I should have been.

As I serve out the remainder of my sentence, I hold these memories close to my heart & promise myself that I will continue to grow & learn from my past mistakes. For Big Mama, for our children, and for all those who have ever believed in me, I have become a better man. When the time comes for me to be released, I know that I will undoubtedly have my family's love awaiting me.

Within these harsh prison walls, I slowly found redemption. I realized that I could no longer afford to live in the shadows of my past. The choices that led me here had to be confronted, analyzed & amended. A renewed sense of responsibility & a desire to give back to my community consumes me. Through long days of self-reflection & remorse, I slowly began to rebuild myself. I became an advocate of hope for many within the prison walls, promoting education & rehabilitation. The journey was long & filled with struggles but, with the same determination that was once attributed to my life as a Hoover, I began to change.

It wasn't just me who noticed this transformation. Over time, I gained the attention & support of those who once saw me as a lost cause. Members of my community, who watched me grow from a boy with dreams into a man who made grave mistakes, now lend their voices to advocate for my freedom. These voices are diverse & unexpected, ranging from doctors, lawyers, and even police officers. My journey to redemption & self-improvement has touched them in such a way that they believe I deserve another chance.

As I look back on the life I left behind, I think of the pain & suffering it caused, not only to myself but to countless others. A vision formed within my heart, a dream of how I can use my newfound purpose to celebrate my eventual release & create a new beginning. A party, unlike any other, is a true testament to the way life should be.

I dream about a luxurious yacht with my loved one, Gangsta Tee at the helm, cutting through the beautiful crystal-clear waters of the Pacific Ocean, so far from the shores that the troubles of our lives would seem but a distant memory. A helicopter for our guests, so they know this event represents not just my return to the world but a move away from the darkness of the past. There would be no more fear, no more chaos, just free-flowing worry-free joy & happiness.

I feel the sun on my face & the salty breeze on my skin as we cruise towards our destination. The excitement in the air is contagious, and I know this is going to be a night to remember. On that yacht, the past would lose its grip on us, and we would remind everyone that life is worth celebrating. The laughter of redemption & forgiveness would fill the air. The shackles of my past would be forever broken in those deep waters. I can't believe how many people have made the effort to be here for me, and my heart swells with gratitude. I yearn to be reunited with friends & family that have stood by me over the last 30 years. I can't wait!

For now, I must bide my time within these prison walls. The battle for my freedom rages on, fueled by the support of those who have seen the change in me. I remain patient, though the anticipation, leaves me eager. I anticipate the moment I walk out into the bright sunlight, a free man, finally vindicated from my youthful transgressions.

This journey has humbled me, changed me, and undoubtedly molded me into a better person. It has also taught me the value of genuine loyalty & the importance of surrounding yourself with people who will support & encourage you when you stumble. It has prepared me for that moment when I will finally taste freedom again, unburdened by the darkness of the past. A new chapter will rise, filled with hope, redemption, and a renewed sense of living life to its fullest.

It's time to redefine the narrative, time to destroy & rebuild. Rising from the ashes of my past, like the phoenix, in my heart lies a fire fueled by hope, passion, and resilience. Each rising sun, a chance at redemption. I've lived a life battling in the shadows. I remain, Marcus Diggs, a proud black man, yearning for redemption & the day I can re-emerge as part of the solution & not the problem.

While the tainted views of society may etch me as a bad person & a criminal, I am more than that. I am a human being of course I am not perfect; I've made mistakes. I'm a father, grandpa, a husband, a brother, an uncle & a loyal friend. Hoping one day the story of our resilience will mean more than the color of our skin or the choices we were forced to make. Now, all I seek is a single ray of light promising a dawn of new beginnings – a final chapter of my life that reads, *'Redeemed'.*

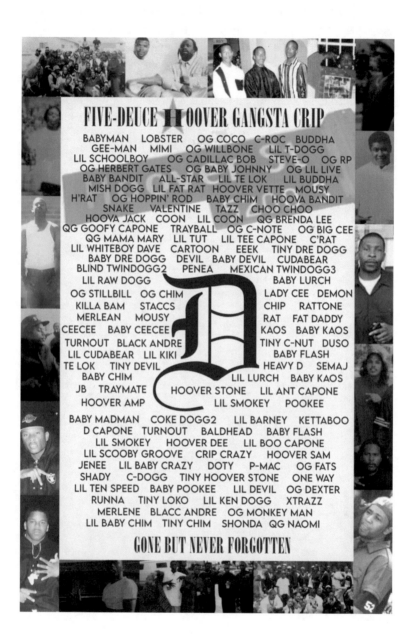

FIVE-DEUCE HOOVER GANGSTA CRIP

BABYMAN   LOBSTER   OG COCO   C-ROC   BUDDHA
GEE-MAN   MIMI   OG WILLBONE   LIL T-DOGG
LIL SCHOOLBOY   OG CADILLAC BOB   STEVE-O   OG RP
OG HERBERT GATES   OG BABY JOHNNY   OG LIL LIVE
BABY BANDIT   ALL-STAR   LIL TE LOK   LIL BUDDHA
MISH DOGG   LIL FAT RAT   HOOVER VETTE   MOUSY
H'RAT   OG HOPPIN' ROD   BABY CHIM   HOOVA BANDIT
SNAKE   VALENTINE   TAZZ   CHOO CHOO
HOOVA JACK   COON   LIL COON   QG BRENDA LEE
QG GOOFY CAPONE   TRAYBALL   OG C-NOTE   OG BIG CEE
QG MAMA MARY   LIL TUT   LIL TEE CAPONE   C'RAT
LIL WHITEBOY DAVE   CARTOON   EEEK   TINY DRE DOGG
BABY DRE DOGG   DEVIL   BABY DEVIL   CUDABEAR
BLIND TWINDOGG2   PENEA   MEXICAN TWINDOGG3
LIL RAW DOGG   BABY LURCH

OG STILLBILL   OG CHIM   LADY CEE   DEMON
KILLA BAM   STACCS   CHIP   RATTONE
MERLEAN   MOUSY   RAT   FAT DADDY
CEECEE   BABY CEECEE   KAOS   BABY KAOS
TURNOUT   BLACK ANDRE   TINY C-NUT   DUSO
LIL CUDABEAR   LIL KIKI   BABY FLASH
TE LOK   TINY DEVIL   HEAVY D   SEMAJ
BABY CHIM   LIL LURCH   BABY KAOS
JB   TRAYMATE   HOOVER STONE   LIL ANT CAPONE
HOOVER AMP   LIL SMOKEY   POOKEE

BABY MADMAN   COKE DOGG2   LIL BARNEY   KETTABOO
D CAPONE   TURNOUT   BALDHEAD   BABY FLASH
LIL SMOKEY   HOOVER DEE   LIL BOO CAPONE
LIL SCOOBY GROOVE   CRIP CRAZY   HOOVER SAM
JENEE   LIL BABY CRAZY   DOTY   P-MAC   OG FATS
SHADY   C-DOGG   TINY HOOVER STONE   ONE WAY
LIL TEN SPEED   BABY POOKEE   LIL DEVIL   OG DEXTER
RUNNA   TINY LOKO   LIL KEN DOGG   XTRAZZ
MERLENE   BLACC ANDRE   OG MONKEY MAN
LIL BABY CHIM   TINY CHIM   SHONDA   QG NAOMI

GONE BUT NEVER FORGOTTEN

Rest In Paradise

oG Judabean, Bay Loc (43 Hoover Crip) | Devil, Evil X-Ray, 8-Ball (59 Hoover Crip) | oG Huron, oG KW, Tim-Tim (74 Hoover Crip) | Lil Doc Rob (83 Hoover Crip) | Big Vamp (92 Hoover Crip) | Crazy Nell (94 Hoover Crip) | Andre " Devil" Ransom , Ben Nose, Fatbacc, oG Hogg (107 Hoover Crip) | Macc (112 Hoover Crip)

Hot Shot, Lil Q-Bone, oG John Hunt, Preschool, Captain Rainbow, Big Choo, Big Tee, Fat Dogg (52 Broadway Gangsta Crip) | oG Tookie Williams, oG Maynard (Westside Crip) | oG Big James Miller, Crazy Keith, Baby Brother, Big Phil, Warlock (Harlem Crip) | oG Pretty Boy (Rollin 60s) | Casper, Bub, Docthone (6-Pacc East Coast Crip) | Bertrain (43 Gangsta Crip) | oG Raymond Chatman (56 Syndicate Crip)

Sugar Bear (Untouchable Brims) Nana (Blood Stone Villains)
I also give my heartfelt condolences to any other loved ones that I may not have known passed away.

Made in the USA
Columbia, SC
02 August 2024

39894838R00320